WASHINGTON BABYLON

FROM GEORGE WASHINGTON TO DONALD TRUMP, SCANDALS THAT ROCKED THE NATION

MARK HYMAN

Post Hill
PRESS

A POST HILL PRESS BOOK
ISBN: 978-1-64293-152-5
ISBN (eBook): 978-1-64293-153-2

Washington Babylon:
From George Washington to Donald Trump, Scandals that Rocked the Nation
© 2019 by Mark Hyman
All Rights Reserved

Cover art by Cody Corcoran

Post Hill Press
New York • Nashville
posthillpress.com

Published in the United States of America

This book is dedicated to the men and women working in local newsrooms all across the nation. It is their tireless and dedicated work that has uncovered many of the biggest scandals—and other news stories. Their reporting is the bulwark of critical knowledge that has informed, empowered, and saved many lives. They and their work are truly appreciated.

TABLE OF CONTENTS

A NOTE TO THE READER

In recent years, the public has become more aware of incorrect, misleading, or false news and information. This phenomenon is not new. Promoting false information is as old as the Republic. Some eighteenth-century pamphleteers would knowingly publish rumor, innuendo, or false information as news.

The yellow journalism of William Randolph Hearst in the early twentieth century often influenced public opinion and even US policy. For years, the *New York Times* published one false dispatch after another from its Moscow bureau chief, Walter Duranty, glorifying life in the Soviet Union even in the face of contradictory information that millions of people were dying under brutal Soviet rule.

Today, national news outlets have been caught selectively editing or even doctoring videos, misstating or ignoring inconvenient facts, and citing non-credible, and perhaps even non-existent, anonymous sources in order to support their narratives. Some news outlets have been victimized by false reporting. Others have been complicit in it. The public has every right to be jaded about who or what to trust.

It should go without saying that little may dissuade those in the public who rely on social media platforms, entertainment websites, and late-night comedians as their sources of news and information. As a math professor once said to me, "Garbage in equals garbage out."

That brings me to this book. You may notice that I have used what some may call an excessive number of endnotes. An endnote (or footnote) is generally used to provide amplifying information or to attribute the use of another's material. I have used endnotes to do just that. In addition, I have added endnotes to aid the reader to easily find many of the facts and sources I have used in this book. I want the reader to be confident in the truthfulness and accuracy of what is written here.

You have every right to be skeptical. Recent history demands it. Skepticism is healthy and helps build a better, more accurate narrative of historical events, especially if the author is accountable. What you will find between the covers of this book is what I call *accountability jour-nalism*. That is why I have provided endnotes and why I ask you to do the following.

While I have strived to make this book completely accurate, I realize mistakes do occur. If you find a mistake, I ask you to bring it to my attention using the "Contact" page on my personal website: http://www.markhyman.tv. Please include a citation with the correct information.

FOREWORD

My wife, a former federal prosecutor, once told me that sex was involved in at least three-fourths of all crimes committed in America, to say nothing of all scandals erupting in America. I never asked about other countries. Amorous France springs to mind, and romantic Italy.

Though I am a member of the flower-child generation—the 1960s, that is—where idealists throughout the great Republic never tired of telling us that sex was a beautiful thing, my wife's revelation about sex underlying a lot of crimes and a lot of scandals struck me as somewhat deflating. I too thought of sex as a beautiful thing, at least until I saw Harvey Weinstein.

Now, having read Mark Hyman's *Washington Babylon: From George Washington to Donald Trump, Scandals that Rocked the Nation*, I have an answer for my wife. She forgot money, and politics, and simple stupidity as great contributors to crime and to scandal. Hyman makes this clear. An awful lot of scandals would never have taken place were it not for money, politics, and simple stupidity. Think of Anthony Weiner. He has a major role in chapter 11, though he could have also had a role in a dozen other chapters of this marvelous book.

There is an abundance of nullities in the pages that await you, made memorable solely for a grisly deed. For instance, Congressman Robert Potter from North Carolina, a figure of the early nineteenth century who became obsessed with his wife's passion for Louis Taylor, a fifty-five-year-old Methodist minister, and for Louis Wiley, a seventeen-year-old boy. One day something snapped in his cranium, and he went out and assaulted both men, leaving them castrated and near death. Needless to say, his career in the House of Representatives was over. Although he did not include it in the book, Hyman told me Potter's political fortunes did not end in the Tar Heel State. Potter later served in the cabinet of pre-statehood Texas, where he is now celebrated as the founder of the Texas Navy. Certainly sex was at the center of Congressman Potter's scandal, though it might have been something else altogether. For instance, he might have had a weird, idiosyncratic quirk about men named Louis, as both men were so named. Or he might have been set off by their disparity in age. At any rate, he made his contribution, if not to history, then at least to Hyman's book.

There are fourteen chapters in this book, with a multitude of scandalous men and women attracting Hyman's eye because of their "Bad Behavior," "Influence Peddling," "Bribes," and "Creepy Sexual Behavior," to name but a few of the chapter titles. Needless to say, I was attracted to every reference to the Clintons, a couple I thought I knew well. Hyman has uncovered wonders that I was unaware of, particularly as regards Hillary's infamous server. Then there is Mark Felt, late of the FBI, who was known as "Deep Throat" to the cognoscenti. I never knew that after his shadowy intercourse with Woodward and Bernstein he lived on to be convicted of authorizing illegal break-ins and searches against the Weather Underground that allowed Bill Ayers to go free. And there are revelations about FBI Director James Comey that are too delicious to reveal this early in the book. You will have to read it to believe it.

Hyman's research, I am saddened to say, shows neither end of the political spectrum weighted more heavily toward scandal than the other. Maybe it is because he is an objective reporter. All parties are represented. He holds all sides accountable: Republicans, Democrats, Socialists, Whigs, Democrat-Republicans, Federalists, Free Soil Party, and more. This, I must say, astonishes me. I had always thought the Federalists were pretty much straight arrows, and just from reading the headlines the last thirty years, I would have thought the Democrats were the most scandal-prone of the major parties. Hyman dissents, and he knows his history.

But let me return to the headlines of our day. Let me return to Bill and Hillary. Their names appear throughout this very fine book. I had my own personal experiences with them. During their impeachment interlude they tried to accuse me of scandal. If they had their way, I would have appeared in chapter 14 of Hyman's book, entitled "Media." The Clintons claimed that my colleagues at the *American Spectator* and I had obstructed justice, committed witness tampering, and even threatened a young man's life. Naturally, we were exonerated by the very same government that Bill presided over. So far as I know he has *never* been exonerated of his misbehavior.

That brings to mind once again my wife's observation about the cause of criminality and scandal. Sure, sex accounts for a lot of it. Yes, money and politics too are a motivation for misbehavior that leads to scandal. But simple stupidity and incompetence should not be overlooked. The Clintons tried and failed to put me in jail. Lyndon Baines Johnson would never have let me go free, and doubtless Hitler and Stalin would have been even more successful.

—R. Emmett Tyrrell, Jr.

INTRODUCTION

"According to Ms. Lewinsky, the President telephoned her at her desk and suggested that she come to the Oval Office on the pretext of delivering papers to him. She went to the Oval Office and was admitted by a plainclothes Secret Service agent. In her folder was a gift for the President, a Hugo Boss necktie.

"In the hallway by the study, the President and Ms. Lewinsky kissed. On this occasion, according to Ms. Lewinsky, 'he focused on me pretty exclusively,' kissing her bare breasts and fondling her genitals. At one point, the President inserted a cigar into Ms. Lewinsky's vagina, then put the cigar in his mouth and said: 'It tastes good.' After they were finished, Ms. Lewinsky left the Oval Office and walked through the Rose Garden."

> —*"Nature of President Clinton's Relationship with Monica Lewinsky"* Report by Special Counsel Kenneth Starr ("Starr Report")

For millions of Americans, the activities described above seemed to befit a Hollywood actor, rock musician, or professional athlete. Instead, the scintillating details belonged to the most powerful man on earth, who was attempting to insert his executive privilege into a most intimate encounter with an awestruck girl nearly thirty years his junior.

By default, the American public has high expectations for the nation's commander-in-chief and other federal officials. Yet, the reality is that the nation's capital has a long history of influential people behaving badly. They bounce personal checks, hire prostitutes, cheat on spouses, accept bribes, consort with criminals, brawl, and even commit murder.

Perhaps this underscores the adage about absolute power corrupting absolutely. Or it may be explained that trouble naturally results when there is a climate of heavy personal arrogance such as that found throughout the nation's capital. Whatever the reason, Washington, DC, has more than most cities' fair share of people behaving badly.

There may be no other place on the planet in which scandal shakes public confidence as it does in Washington, DC. This is true even when the scandal has nothing to do with the policy of state.

In France, the head of state is expected to have a mistress, and any revelation that he does is generally met by the French electorate with little more than a public yawn. Not so in the United States. There is an expectation that the president will remain true to his (or her) spouse, at least in deed. Still, no president has ever fallen from power for carrying on an extramarital affair.

Arkansas Governor Bill Clinton was elected President in 1992 in spite of his widespread reputation for womanizing. Before him, it was John Kennedy, Franklin Roosevelt, and Grover Cleveland. Cleveland was elected in 1884 while newspaper stories reported the details of the illegitimate child he allegedly fathered and for whom he admitted he was paying child support. Roosevelt carried on an extramarital affair with a former assistant to his wife for nearly three decades.

The story is different for those *seeking* the presidency. Former North Carolina Senator and 2004 vice-presidential nominee John Edwards self-destructed beginning in 2007 due, in part, to his extramarital affair with a ditzy, New Age-practicing groupie.

Edwards was the beneficiary of a slick narrative that portrayed his marriage as idyllic and him as a devoted husband and family man. Instead, Edwards was revealed to be a shallow womanizer who confided to his mistress, Rielle Hunter, that the pair would soon be together after Mrs. Edwards succumbed to cancer.

Adding to the Edwards scandal was that he fathered a baby with Hunter during the same period of time when his wife's breast cancer, once in remission, metastasized and became incurable. Unable to contain himself, Edwards secretly visited his mistress and their child in a Beverly Hills hotel room while he was furiously promoting himself to be picked as the vice-presidential nominee to Barack Obama. Edwards's hotel trip was documented by a supermarket tabloid.

Overall, public scandal may have ended more political careers than any other cause, aside from actual election defeat at the ballot box. Politicians and government officials have witnessed their sometimes meteoric rises to prominence and public adulation immediately come crashing down to earth, owing to a scandalous revelation.

The rule of thumb when it comes to scandal is that oftentimes it is not the actual scandal that most seriously sullies one's reputation, but rather the coverup that occurs in an attempt to obscure, obfuscate, or hide the original scandal.

The most famous example of this is the 1972 break-in at Democrat National Committee headquarters in the Watergate complex by campaign staffers loyal to President Richard Nixon. Nixon's political downfall and eventual resignation from office stemmed not from the break-in, of which he was originally ignorant, but from his coverup of the burglary after the fact.

The impact of Watergate as a political scandal cannot be overstated. It thrust the name "Watergate" into the American lexicon and led to the last half of the complex's name ("gate") to be used as a suffix to immediately identify an event as a scandal. Irangate, Nannygate, Pardongate, and Rathergate are but a few of the scores of events that have come to be recognized as scandals by the mere addition of "gate."

The Watergate scandal is fascinating because it not only damaged the reputations of so many individuals involved, but because it also launched the careers of several others. Nixon, Attorney General John N. Mitchell, White House staffers H. R. "Bob" Haldeman, John Ehrlichman, John Dean, and President Gerald Ford fell from grace owing to the Watergate scandal in one way or another.

Washington Post reporters Bob Woodward and Carl Bernstein, Watergate burglar G. Gordon Liddy, and then-congressional staffer Fred Thompson are among those who owe to the scandal their eventual rises to prominence.

W. Mark Felt, the *Washington Post* source known only as "Deep Throat" who provided Watergate details to reporters Woodward and Bernstein, was hailed for decades as a hero. Actually, Felt was a hero as long as he remained in anonymity. He was the associate director of the Federal Bureau of Investigation, the number-two position at the agency, when he fed secret law enforcement information to the *Washington Post* reporters.

Felt suffered his own fall from grace when it became known he was Woodward and Bernstein's secret source. Felt did not betray Nixon for any noble cause or altruistic reason, but instead because he was angered that Nixon passed him over for the position of director of the FBI when agency founder J. Edgar Hoover died. Felt was no longer revered as a hero, but instead was widely viewed as a petty, vindictive man.

It is ironic that many years after the Watergate break-in occurred, and long before his role in the scandal became known, Felt was pardoned by President Ronald Reagan for his own scandalous and criminal conduct. Felt had been convicted for ordering FBI agents to conduct illegal break-ins that were similar to the one committed by the Watergate burglars.

Perhaps the first event that comes to mind when one mentions a personal scandal is the hint of a possibility of an extramarital affair. Such affairs capture the attention and perhaps prurient interests of the American public, especially when elected officials are involved. The independent counsel's report that detailed the sexual activities between Bill Clinton and White House intern Monica Lewinsky was a hot item, passed from office to office, and was the topic of red-faced gossip for months in 1998.

There are sexual antics other than extramarital affairs that erupt into scandals when they become known. These have included strange and even bizarre sexual activities. The admission by a member of Congress that he and his wife engaged in sex one night while on the steps of the US Capitol building led a Washington, DC, comedy troupe to adopt the name Capitol Steps for its entertainment act.

Still, nighttime lovemaking in a public venue pales in comparison to some of the creepiest sexual acts, including sex with minor children, solicitation of prostitution, male castration, and rape. All of these events occurred featuring members of Congress.

Arguing, squabbling, and bickering are but a few approaches to airing grievances and disagreements with one another. Settling one's differences with spitting, fists, feet, cane beatings, or firearms—with deadly consequences—is quite another. Sometimes the differences were settled permanently. All of these became Washington, DC, scandals.

There are occasions when the proverbial skeleton in the closet is not a financial or sexual secret, but is one centered on politics. Business relationships, political ties, personal friendships, and campaign activities have sometimes raised more than just questions and eyebrows. They have become scandals and have sometimes damaged a political career or two.

Critics claim Washington is awash in the abuse of power and influence peddling. Neither of these is a recent phenomenon. They are as old as the Republic. Today, members of Congress are known for trading favorable legislation and earmarking appropriations in return for political support and contributions. More than a century ago, it was the trading of nominations to West Point and the Naval Academy in return for political favors.

There are times when simply following a legal process or a ruling on a court case becomes a scandal. Abrogating property rights in the infamous *Kelo v. City of New London* Supreme Court decision resonated with much of the public years after the 2005 decision was announced. The scandal was not the justices' deliberative process of the court case, but rather the actual decision rendered by the court.

American sovereignty and national security are very important to most of the American public. Scandals have erupted when foreign policy decisions are widely viewed as adversely affecting these two. The transfer of Panama Canal control may forever be known as the "Panama Canal Giveaway." The failed Bay of Pigs operation run by the CIA will likely continue to be the textbook example of what comprises a foreign policy disaster.

Even sports and entertainment scandals have impacted Washington, DC. Politicians have actually argued over what should constitute college football's post-season competition. The Bowl Championship Series gave way to a four-team playoff, but should it be expanded to eight teams? In past decades, Congress dove into the radio payola and TV quiz show scandals and debated allegations of athletes colluding with gamblers and throwing games in both the professional and amateur ranks.

This book is not an exhaustive compilation of all scandals that have rocked Washington. This volume could easily be three times as large, if it were. Nor is this the definitive list of the *most* scandalous stories. It is not. No doubt, scholars and observers could stay busy for years arguing over which scandals should make a top-ten list.

Not surprisingly, one party official would probably insist only scandals involving individuals of the other political party would most likely be worthy of a top-ten list. Because this is a historical look at scandals, political parties represented include Republican, Democrat, Whig, Federalist, Know-Nothing, Free Soil, and a few other political parties.

This book is merely a collection of scandalous stories that bounced around the echo chamber of Washington, DC, and sometimes the entire nation, and beyond. Some of these scandals remain infamous today, while others have faded into obscurity.

CHAPTER 1

FOREIGN POLICY AND THE MILITARY

"To underscore that these protests are rooted in an Internet video, and not a broader failure of policy."

> —White House talking points to prepare Susan Rice, ambassador to the UN, for appearances on Sunday news shows regarding September 2012 Benghazi attack.[1]

Conway Cabal

Thomas Conway was born in Ireland in 1735 and immigrated with his family to France. When he was a teenager, he joined the French Army and rose through the ranks. He was eventually promoted to the rank of colonel.

When the American Revolutionary War began, Conway volunteered his services to the Continental Congress. His offer was accepted, and he was given a commission in the Continental Army with the rank of brigadier general. In May 1777, Conway was given orders to report to General George Washington. Washington was the commanding general of the Continental Army.

For some observers, Conway distinguished himself at the Battle of Germantown on October 4, 1777. This was a major battle of the Philadelphia Campaign of the war. This campaign pitted the British Army, led by General Sir William Howe, against the Continental Army, led by General George Washington. It was the imposing threat from the British Army that forced the Continental Congress to abandon Philadelphia and relocate to York, Pennsylvania.

After capturing Philadelphia in late September, Howe left a small contingent of troops in the city and moved the bulk of his forces to nearby Germantown. Washington viewed this as an opportunity to deliver a crushing defeat to the British Army. In the previous several months, Washington suffered one military defeat after another. Washington hoped to capitalize on the element of surprise, but he was unable to achieve military success in his ambitious plan. The battle represented another defeat for Washington. Washington withdrew his forces and eventually encamped at Valley Forge for the 1777–1778 winter.

Conway thought his performance on the battlefield merited a promotion to major general. So, he asked for one. However, he did not request this promotion from his chain of command. Instead, he bypassed Washington and wrote directly to the Congress. Washington learned of this request and wrote his own letter stating that he thought there were more senior officers more deserving of promotion who were also American.

Conway did not like being rebuffed by Washington. While his promotion and reassignment were under consideration, he began lobbying for the replacement of Washington as general of the Continental Army. He had the perfect replacement in mind.

General Horatio Gates was hailed as a military genius. On October 17, 1777, only days after Washington's defeat at Germantown, Gates's numerically superior forces surrounded the troops of British Army General John Burgoyne at Saratoga in upstate New York.[2] Burgoyne was a key figure in the British strategy to split the New England states from the rest of the thirteen colonies. He was leading an invasion force from Quebec toward New York City with a plan to slice the colonies in half. The British believed this geographic separation would hasten the end of the war.

Gates's stunning victory not only caused Burgoyne to surrender his forces, but it also convinced the French to join the war on behalf of the Americans in early 1778. It was the Continental Army's greatest victory to date.[3] This was a key turning point in the Revolutionary War.

Gates's victory at Saratoga stood in contrast to the string of defeats Washington had suffered. Gates, Conway theorized, should replace Washington as general of the Continental Army. Conway wrote to Gates telling him so.[4] Conway was critical of Washington's military skills. In one letter he wrote, "Heaven has been determined to save your Country; or a weak General and bad Counselors would have ruined it."[5]

Conway and Gates were not alone in their criticism of Washington's military skills. Other senior military leaders and influential members of the revolutionary government formed a loose coalition of Washington critics that had been referred to as a "coterie of grumblers." Among this group were Brigadier General Thomas Mifflin, General Charles Lee, and leading independence figures Richard Henry Lee, Samuel Adams, Dr. Benjamin Rush, and John Adams.[6]

Mifflin served as Washington's aide before becoming the Continental Army's quartermaster general. Mifflin later became president of the Continental Congress and signed the Constitution. General Charles Lee was born in England and immigrated to the colonies in 1773. When the colonists declared independence, he volunteered to join the Continental Army with the hope that he would be appointed commanding general, a position that went to Washington. Richard Henry Lee was the author of the June 1776 resolution in the Second Continental Congress that urged the colonies to declare independence from England, as they did on July 4, 1776. Lee signed the Declaration of Independence.

Samuel Adams was a Massachusetts delegate to the Continental Congress and a signer of the Declaration of Independence. Rush was a well-respected surgeon and was also a signer of the Declaration of Independence. He was appointed surgeon general of the Continental Army, but was unhappy with the head of the Army Medical Service. He complained to Washington, who told him he should direct his complaints to the Continental Congress.

It was John Adams who nominated Washington to be general of the Continental Army. As the war progressed, Adams thought Washington was too cautious a general, and he soured over Washington's appointment. Adams would later serve two terms as Washington's vice president.

The contents of Conway's letter were leaked to Washington via the loose lips of Gates's twenty-year-old aide, James Wilkinson. Washington responded by writing to Gates and by sending a copy of his letter to Congress to put the entire episode out in the open and, hopefully, to rest. Gates denied his involvement and claimed there were forces attempting to discredit him.[7] Conway attempted a half-hearted defense of himself that included insulting Washington. Conway wrote to Washington, "An old sailor knows more of a ship than admirals who have never been at sea." Conway thought of himself as the veteran sailor and Washington as the rookie admiral.[8]

In response to the growing scandal, Conway sent his resignation to the Continental Congress, which rejected it. In December 1777, the Congress instead determined that Conway was worthy and promoted him to major general over the objections of Washington and ahead of nearly two-dozen more senior officers. Conway was then assigned as the inspector general of the Army. Gates was appointed the head of the new Board of War. Essentially, this placed Gates above Washington. These two promotions sickened Washington and caused morale among dozens of officers to plummet.

Eventually, Washington made public that he learned of the Conway and Gates correspondence from Gates's own aide, thereby confirming it was genuine. This prompted Gates to apologize and Conway to tender his resignation to the Continental Congress in April 1778. Washington thought these actions were not enough.[9] Washington encouraged his followers to challenge Conway and his allies to duels.

Wilkinson, the one-time aide to Gates, was shown letters from Gates that demeaned and criticized Wilkinson. Infuriated, Wilkinson challenged Gates to a duel. At the appointed time and place of the scheduled duel, Gates began sobbing and pleaded for Wilkinson to relent. He did.[10]

Brigadier General John Cadwalader was commander of Philadelphia troops under Washington, to whom he was intensely loyal. Cadwalader challenged Conway to a duel and Conway accepted. At their duel on July 4, 1778, Cadwalader shot Conway in the mouth, leaving a serious, but not fatal wound. Cadwalader reportedly stood over a profusely bleeding Conway and said, "I have stopped the damned rascal's lying tongue at any rate."

Assuming he would soon die from his wound, Conway wrote a letter of apology to Washington. He wrote, "My career will soon be over…Therefore, justice and truth prompt me to declare my last sentiments: You are in my eyes the great and good man. May you long enjoy the love, veneration, and esteem of these States whose liberties you have asserted by your virtues."[11]

Instead, Conway fully recovered and returned to France, where he rejoined the French Army as a major general.

Benghazi

Operation Iraqi Freedom was the war that toppled Saddam Hussein as the dictatorial leader of Iraq. The given reason for the Iraq war was that Hussein was believed to have a secret nuclear weapons program in violation of United Nations resolutions.

There was also an unintended, yet positive consequence of the war. In December 2003, Libyan leader Muammar Gaddafi surprised the world and announced he would discontinue his country's weapons of mass destruction program.[12] Clearly, the Iraq War had hastened his decision to abandon rogue nation status.

Libya had been a pariah nation in the eyes of the United States since Gaddafi's coup d'état in 1969. By the late 1990s, Gaddafi was slowly moving his nation in the right direction. In 1999, he agreed to meet US and British demands to assume responsibility and pay restitution to the families of victims killed in the 1988 bombing of Pan Am Flight 103 over Lockerbie, Scotland. Dismantling his nation's weapons of mass destruction program and inviting international inspectors into the country was a major step toward normalizing relations with the West, and most importantly, the United States.

Libyan authorities turned over weapons components and thousands of pages of documentation, which included correspondence with other nations. These papers revealed the name of A. Q. Khan, the Pakistani scientist who had been secretly transferring nuclear technology to Iran and North Korea, as well as Libya.

Relations between Libya and the United States were on the mend—until 2011.

By all accounts, President Barack Obama was reluctant to launch military action against Libya. Obama was a harsh critic of the Iraq War, and launching a war against Libya would show him to be hypocritical. The Arab Spring, an uprising by groups of citizens against their governments, had spread to several Arab nations. A rebellion was brewing in Libya, and a protest broke out on February 17, but it was one Gaddafi's security forces could probably manage.

It was Secretary of State Hillary Clinton who was the most forceful proponent of the United States initiating a war with Libya. Most of Obama's senior advisors urged the United States to sit this one out. However, Clinton "doubled down and pushed for military action" against Libya.[13] Clinton won over Obama. Ironically, the nation's top diplomat was the biggest advocate for war. The United States began attacks on March 19, 2011.

The decision by Obama to topple Gaddafi no doubt sent the wrong message to other rogue nations. Gaddafi gave up his nukes as the United States had demanded, only to be attacked by the United States. This turn of events may have convinced other rogue nation leaders to hold onto their nuclear, chemical, and biological weapons programs as an insurance policy.[14]

It is widely believed that the driving motivation for Clinton's push to attack Libya was to beef up her résumé in preparation for a 2016 run for the White House. It was Clinton's insistence that the Libya campaign was a resounding success that set in motion events leading to the biggest and most deadly debacle for US personnel in Libya.

Gaddafi was toppled from power by a US-led bombing campaign, joined by Britain and France. An Obama advisor called it "leading from behind."[15] Gaddafi was captured and gruesomely killed by rebel fighters on October 20, 2011. Cell phone video footage showed a long rod, or possibly a sword, was shoved up his rectum. The Libyan leadership vacuum created by Gaddafi's death was filled throughout much of Libya by Ansar al-Sharia and al Qaeda in the Islamic Maghreb. These were two powerful, radical Islamic terror groups.

J. Christopher Stevens was the US ambassador to Libya. Stevens's primary diplomatic post was in the Libyan capital city of Tripoli. However, he was frequently at the lightly defended facility in Benghazi, which was a hotbed of violence. Stevens was directed to spend more time in Benghazi because "Secretary Clinton wanted the post made permanent," according to Gregory Hicks. Hicks was the US deputy chief of mission, the de facto number-two diplomatic position in Libya. Hicks later testified before Congress that Clinton had intended to make a December 2012 announcement about the diplomatic upgrade in Benghazi.[16]

The reality was far different from the picture being painted by Clinton. The security situation in Benghazi was extremely dangerous and getting worse by the day. In April 2012, an improvised explosive device was thrown over the wall into the US consulate compound. Other attacks were made against the British ambassador, the Tunisian consulate, and against United Nations and International Red Cross officials. In June, a bomb blew a gaping hole in the security wall of the American Benghazi compound. The deteriorating security situation caused the British government to withdraw its diplomatic personnel and close its Benghazi offices in June.

The dramatic escalation in violence led State Department Regional Security Officer Eric Nordstrom, who was in Libya, to plead with State Department officials to increase security for US diplomats in Libya, especially in Benghazi. According to Nordstrom, State Department officials wanted to keep US security presence "artificially low."[17] In her 2013 testimony before Congress, Clinton assumed responsibility for the failed security of Benghazi.

Late in the evening of September 11, 2012, eleven years to the day after the 9/11 terrorist attacks, the Benghazi compound came under attack from a large group yelling, "Allahu Akbar!" The compound wall was quickly breached, and scores of attackers entered, firing automatic weapons and rocket-propelled grenades. Ambassador Stevens and consular officer Sean Smith were quickly killed.

Hours later, the annex housing CIA officials and CIA-contracted security personnel came under a mortar attack. Glen Doherty and Tyrone Woods were killed. Frantic calls were made to Washington, DC, during the attack requesting reinforcements. No reinforcements were sent.

Back in Washington, DC, emails were flying back and forth discussing the attack. Officials at the White House, State Department, and Central Intelligence Agency knew it was full-out assault by Islamic terrorists. In fact, Clinton emailed her daughter the evening of the attack, telling Chelsea that the perpetrators were Islamic terrorists. However, a narrative was crafted to tell the public a completely different story.

The day after the attack, the Obama administration falsely claimed that the attack had been spontaneous. The administration claimed the attack grew from the peaceful protest to a crudely made YouTube video named "Innocence of Muslims" that was considered demeaning to Muslims. That video was posted to YouTube months earlier and, at the time of the attack, had been viewed only a few dozen times. As a flurry of White House emails, memos, and messages confirmed, the Obama administration knew from the very beginning that the video was not the cause of the attacks. That public claim was quickly debunked.

The White House dispatched Susan Rice, the US ambassador to the United Nations, to make the rounds of Sunday news talk shows promoting the falsehood that the attack was a spontaneous event. Libyan officials and the suspected organizer of the attack, Ahmed Abu Khattala, said the video played no role in the attack. The attack, they said, was premeditated. Obama administration officials did not offer an explanation as to why peaceful protestors would be carrying rocket-propelled grenade launchers and automatic weapons.

At about 6 a.m. on September 12, an armed, fifty-vehicle Libyan convoy rescued the Americans from the annex and safely transported them to the Benghazi airport for evacuation. These Libyan rescuers were not from the transitional government aligned with the United States. In a bit of sad irony, these Libyans were former military officers loyal to Gaddafi. The individuals that the United States had ousted from power about a year earlier were the very ones that came to US assistance.[18]

It wasn't until September 20, nine days after the attack, that the Obama administration finally acknowledged the YouTube video explanation was untrue. White House Press Secretary Jay Carney grudgingly admitted the facility came under a premeditated attack from Islamic terrorists.

Six years after the YouTube video explanation was thoroughly discredited, and Carney's admission that the video claim was untrue, White House staffer Ben Rhodes, in his 2018 memoir, returned to falsely claiming the video was the cause of the attack.[19]

Retired Ambassador Thomas Pickering and retired Admiral Mike Mullen chaired the Accountability Review Board (ARB) that investigated the attack. The board found plenty of blame to go around, including US personnel in Libya who "did not demonstrate strong and sustained advocacy with Washington for increased security," and the "relatively inexperienced, American personnel" on that overseas assignment.

The board further found "certain senior State Department officials within two bureaus demonstrated a lack of proactive leadership and management ability in their responses to security concerns...[but] did not find reasonable cause to determine that any individual US government employee breached his or her duty." Interestingly, the board's claim that US personnel in Libya didn't push hard enough for increased security is contradicted by its subsequent claim that State Department officials didn't respond adequately to such requests.

The ARB report was dismissed as sloppy and incomplete.[20] The board didn't interview many key witnesses with deep knowledge of the attack. Some who were questioned by the panel said the probe was inadequate. The board demonstrated its lack of independence by consulting with Clinton's chief of staff on which witnesses should and should not testify. Shockingly, the board never even questioned Clinton. Perhaps this was because four of the five board members were appointed by her.

The Fall Guy

Edwin Wilson was born in 1928 in Nampa, Idaho, which is about a half-hour drive west of Boise. His family was dirt poor. He was bright, energetic, and entrepreneurial. He was always looking for ways to improve his position in life.

As a young adult, Wilson tried his hand at being a merchant seaman and then an Oregon lumberjack before attending the University of Portland. After graduation, he was commissioned through the Marine Corps Officer Candidates School and was sent to South Korea. While in South Korea, he suffered a serious injury requiring transfer back to the United States to be medically discharged.[21]

While on an airline flight, Wilson told the man sitting next to him of his injury and his desire to remain in the Marine Corps. That passenger recruited him to join the eight-year-old Central Intelligence Agency. In those days, CIA headquarters was located near the National Mall, adjacent to the State Department.[22]

In October 1955, like all other employees, Edwin Wilson joined the CIA as a covert employee. His first assignment was providing support and security to a U-2 spy plane based in southern Turkey. After several years, Wilson's request to join the clandestine service was approved. He was sent to college to get a graduate degree and then completed his training as a clandestine officer.

In 1964, Wilson was given a temporary assignment of providing advance services for vice-presidential candidate Hubert Humphrey. This gave Wilson the opportunity to rub elbows with powerful and influential Washingtonians. These connections would pay dividends for him throughout his professional life.

After the presidential election, Wilson was sent on a clandestine mission to Belgium, where he set up a CIA front company, Maritime Consulting. The shipping firm covertly transported everything from industrial products to weapons systems, to clients ranging from guerilla groups to established governments. [23]

Wilson founded a second CIA front company in 1969 named Consultants International. It performed the same services, but on a much grander scale.[24]

In 1971, Wilson left the CIA for a new clandestine service that was just starting. He was a perfect fit. The Office of Naval Intelligence was the first military intelligence service to launch its own clandestine organization. At Task Force 157, Wilson would be doing nearly the same thing he did for the CIA.

Task Force 157 started a pair of front companies named World Marine, Inc. and Maryland Maritime Company. Under Wilson's management, the two companies monitored commercial merchant activities and conducted intelligence collection in ports worldwide.[25] Wilson even purchased ships to be converted into spy platforms.

At both the CIA and Task Force 157 front companies, Wilson booked commercial shipping contracts when there was a lull in government assignments. It was thought to lend credibility to the cover stories that these were legitimate businesses. Wilson also pocketed the profits from the commercial contracts, with the apparent knowledge and approval of his supervisors.

The front companies' side business was very good, and Wilson quickly became a millionaire. He purchased a nearly 500-acre estate[26] near the scenic horse country of Middleburg, Virginia. In a matter of years, Wilson purchased three contiguous properties, creating an estate of nearly 2,500 acres, which he named Mount Airy. His neighbors included billionaire Paul Mellon, Senator John Warner and wife Elizabeth Taylor, and Washington Redskins owner Jack Kent Cooke.[27]

While Wilson was traveling for Task Force 157, his wife, Barbara, was entertaining guests at the Mount Airy estate. The guest list was a who's-who of Washington power players, including Vice President Hubert Humphrey, Republican Congressman Silvio Conte of Massachusetts, and Democratic Congressmen John Murphy of New York, Charles Wilson of Texas, and John Dingell of Michigan. Senators Strom Thurmond of South Carolina and John Stennis of Mississippi, a Republican and Democrat, respectively, were also frequent visitors.[28] This provided Wilson opportunities to lobby Congress on matters critical to the CIA and Task Force 157.

Also among Wilson's regular guests were countless CIA officials, including Theodore Shackley, the deputy director for clandestine operations. Even though he had left the CIA some years earlier, Wilson was often in the company of agency employees.

Task Force 157 was closed down in 1976, and this led to Wilson partnering with Frank Terpil, another former CIA employee. They launched Inter-Technology Transfer to ship electronics, weapons, and munitions to third-world nations. One customer with a big checkbook and a long shopping list was Libyan strongman Colonel Muammar Gaddafi. In addition to the arms export business, Wilson's company hired former Green Berets to run training camps for the Libyan army. Wilson told the former Green Berets they were CIA employees.

Business was going well for Wilson and Terpil until 1980. The partners and Jerome Brower, who owned a California-based explosives firm, were indicted on several federal charges over arms smuggling and supporting terrorist activities related to a 1976 shipment of explosives.[29] Wilson, who was visiting at the time, remained in Libya after he was indicted. After the indictments were announced, CIA officials denounced Wilson as a rogue former agent and claimed that any CIA employees who had been working with him had also gone rogue.

In June 1982, Wilson was lured to the Dominican Republic as part of an elaborate con. Wilson claimed an official US letter promised him immunity from arrest if he would agree to meet in a neutral location to discuss his case. Instead, Dominican officials immediately turned over Wilson to US Marshals for transport to New York.[30]

Five months later, in November, Wilson was convicted of arms smuggling charges in a lightning fast, two-day trial. In his defense,

Wilson claimed he was a contract employee for the CIA, and his activities were undertaken with the full knowledge of the agency. The CIA asked him to undertake military sales, Wilson maintained, in order to conduct intelligence collection against various countries.

A three-and-a-half page sworn affidavit from the third highest-ranking CIA official, Executive Director Charles Briggs, denied the agency had ever worked with Wilson after he left the agency in 1971.[31] Wilson's attorney claimed that he was denied court permission to introduce evidence showing that Wilson worked for the CIA.[32]

Wilson was sentenced to fifteen years in prison. The prosecutor labeled him a "merchant of death." He was convicted of arms smuggling in a second trial in January 1983 and sentenced to seventeen years in prison. In a third trial in March 1983, Wilson was acquitted of conspiracy to murder a Libyan dissident. At his fourth trial in October, he was convicted of soliciting the murders of at least six people, including federal prosecutors and prosecution witnesses.[33] He was sentenced to twenty-five years in prison. It was expected that Edwin Wilson would spend the rest of his life behind bars.

Wilson's partner, Frank Terpil, fled the United States after the indictments were handed down. In 1981, Terpil was tried in absentia for arms smuggling. He was convicted and sentenced to fifty-three years in prison. In 1995, it was learned he had sought refuge in Cuba.[34]

The first ten years of Wilson's incarceration were spent in solitary confinement. He passed his time by filing countless Freedom of Information Act requests for documents to bolster his claim that his gun running was done at the behest of the CIA. By late 1999, he cobbled together enough documents to definitively prove that what he was saying was true.[35]

In January 2000, the Justice Department admitted it knowingly introduced false testimony at Wilson's second trial. CIA Executive Director Charles Briggs's sworn affidavit was a lie.[36] Most of Wilson's shipping of arms and explosives was done at the request of the CIA. Documents showed that the CIA contacted Wilson at least eighty times after he left the agency.

The CIA contracted with Wilson to send weapons to Libya as a ploy to conduct intelligence collection. There were tense relations between the United States and Libya following the 1969 coup d'état by

Gaddafi. He shut down Wheelus Air Base in the capital city of Tripoli. At the time, it was the largest US military facility outside of the United States. In 1979, three years after Wilson began shipping arms to Libya, the United States declared Libya a state sponsor of terrorism. In 1980, when federal prosecutors stumbled upon Wilson's 1976 arms shipment, the CIA made Wilson the fall guy and claimed no knowledge of Libyan arms shipments.

It would not be until October 2003, nearly four years later, that Wilson's request to overturn his 1983 conviction was heard in federal court. US District Judge Lynn Hughes tossed the arms-smuggling conviction, scathingly noting "about two dozen government lawyers" were involved in the false testimony and that he questioned their "personal and institutional integrity." Hughes further rebuked the government by writing, "America will not defeat Libyan terrorism by double-crossing a part-time, informal government agent."[37]

Wilson was released in 2004 after serving twenty-two years in prison. His wife divorced him while he was locked up, and he was now penniless. He lost his property to a $24 million IRS lien.[38]

Not only had the CIA lied to the court, but Justice Department officials knew of the falsehood and consciously decided not to inform Wilson or the court, despite ethical and legal obligations to do so.[39] The seven federal prosecutors involved in Wilson's trials were implicated in the deceit, Wilson's lawyer claimed. At least one of the prosecutors had a hand in drafting the false CIA affidavit.

Wilson's attempt to fully clear his name was dealt a blow in 2007. He filed a lawsuit against eight people involved in the false affidavit and coverup. A federal judge dismissed the lawsuit, claiming that the former CIA executive director and the seven federal prosecutors had immunity in spite of any possible wrongdoing.

Edwin Wilson died in 2012 at the age of eighty-four.

Stolen Valor

Throughout his political career, John Kerry offered a rather heroic version of the events of February 28, 1969, that led to his being awarded the Silver Star. The Silver Star is the fourth-highest military award. Kerry spoke proudly of his Silver Star when he was campaigning for elected office. Yet, years earlier, he used the award as a prop when he claimed he threw away his medals while protesting the Vietnam War.

There had long been controversy over the circumstances of how Kerry earned his Silver Star. Lieutenant (junior grade) Kerry received the Silver Star when he was the officer-in-charge of Swift Boat PCF-94. A Swift Boat was a fifty-foot-long boat that was primarily operated along the coast and in larger inland waterways. A smaller, more agile patrol boat, referred to as a PBR, was used deeper inland on smaller, narrower waterways.

The question of Kerry's Silver Star erupted into a scandal when he launched his campaign for the presidency in 2004. Kerry offered one version of the events that led to his award. Eyewitnesses offered a far different account. The core of the dispute relates to the details surrounding the killing of a suspected Viet Cong guerilla by Kerry.

The heroic version of events offered by Kerry was presented in his 2004 campaign book, *Tour of Duty: John Kerry and the Vietnam War*. This version described a "guerilla holding a B-40 rocket launcher aimed right at them."[40] Kerry shot the enemy before he could fire on the Americans.

Kerry buttressed his version of events with a narrative of the events in the Silver Star certificate he publicly released. The problem with this certificate was that it was signed by Secretary of the Navy John Lehman. Lehman served as the Navy secretary under President Ronald Reagan, and the certificate promoted by Kerry on his presidential campaign website was generated sixteen years after he was awarded the Silver Star.

Shortly after he was elected to the Senate, Kerry contacted Lehman's office, alleged he lost his Silver Star certificate, and requested a new one. A staff member in Lehman's office, who wishes to remain anonymous, explained what happened. Kerry offered language for the replacement certificate. The staffer recognized the sensitive politics involved in the request: Kerry was a sitting US senator. The Navy Department, like every other federal agency, will go to great lengths to accommodate a sitting member of Congress, especially a senator.

The Navy Secretary's office treated the use of Kerry's proffered language as harmless, since Kerry had left military service more than a decade earlier. The language for the certificate offered by Kerry, even if it differed from the original, would have little impact. The expectation was that Kerry would likely hang the certificate in his Senate office.

The Navy quickly issued a replacement certificate utilizing Kerry's language. The problem with this turn of events was that a copy of Kerry's original Silver Star certificate existed and was readily available. Kerry merely had to request a copy of the original certificate from the US Navy archives. He chose not to go that route and instead requested a new certificate with the different language he suggested.

While the overall tone of the two certificates is similar, the 1986 version contained superlative language not found in the original certificate signed by Vice Admiral Elmo Zumwalt in 1969.

The now-declassified after-action report from PCF-94 that detailed the events of that day shed light on which certificate is more accurate. The after-action report is the personal responsibility of the Swift Boat's officer-in-charge, and it is the official account of the day's activities. Kerry was the officer-in-charge.

The events as described in the 1969 Silver Star certificate and the after-action report are nearly identical to the account reported in *Unfit for Command: Swift Boat Veterans Speak Out Against John Kerry*. Moreover, this account differed dramatically from Kerry's version of events as portrayed in *Tour of Duty*.

Most Swift Boat veterans believe Kerry's actions on February 28, 1969, were contrived as a way for Kerry to earn a medal for valor. According to eyewitnesses, Kerry concocted a plan ahead of time with his crewman Michael Medeiros "to turn the [Swift] Boat in and onto the beach if fired upon."[41] There was even "a prior discussion of probable medals for those participating [in the plan]."[42] It was the view of other Swift Boat veterans that "Kerry did follow normal military conduct and displayed ordinary courage, but the incident was nothing out of the ordinary and to most Swift and Vietnam veterans, Kerry's actions would hardly justify any kind of unusual award."[43]

Even the version offered in Kerry's campaign book suggested he shot a wounded man as he fled the battlefield. Using an M-60 machine gun, a crewman "managed to hit the fleeing foe in the leg."[44] The Swift boat was beached, and Kerry gave chase to the fleeing Vietnamese. According to the account given by Kerry's crewman years later, the "guerrilla got twenty or thirty meters down the path, just about in front of a lean-to, the [future] senator shot the guy."[45]

"Whether Kerry's dispatching of a fleeing, wounded, armed or unarmed teenage enemy was in accordance with customs of war, it is very clear that many Vietnam veterans and most Swiftees do not consider this action to be the stuff of which medals of any kind are awarded," according to the account in *Unfit for Command.*[46]

Kerry received the medal only two days after the event occurred and without the normal and proper review, which could typically take several months. This immediate approval of the award was done, Vietnam veterans pointed out, to boost morale.

In eyewitness accounts, "A young Viet Cong in a loincloth popped out of a hole, clutching a grenade launcher which may or may not have been loaded, depending on whose account one credits. Tom Belodeau, a forward gunner, shot the Viet Cong with an M-60 machine gun in the leg as he fled. At about this time, with the boat beached, the Viet Cong who had been wounded by Belodeau fled. Kerry and Medeiros (who had many troops in their boat) took off, perhaps with others, following the young Viet Cong as he fled, and shot him in the back, behind a lean-to."[47]

Kerry's original account written in his after-action report the very same day of the incident stated, "PCF 94 beached in center of ambush in front of small path when VC sprung up from bunker 10 feet from unit. Man ran with weapon towards hootch. Forward M-60 gunner wounded man in leg. OinC [officer-in-charge, Kerry] jumped ashore and gave pursuit while other units saturated area with fire and beached placing assault parties ashore. OinC of PCF 94 chased VC inland behind hootch and shot him while he fled capturing one B-40 rocket launcher with round in chamber."

The after-action report account closely resembled the version of events as described by several eyewitnesses and not the nerve-tingling version presented in *Tour of Duty.*

There was also controversy over the Purple Heart medals Kerry claimed he was awarded. A Purple Heart is given to someone wounded in combat. Kerry claimed he was wounded by the enemy on December 3, 1968, resulting in his first Purple Heart medal. Acting on a policy in place at the time that was available to those who were thrice wounded, Kerry requested an immediate transfer out of Vietnam only four months into his one-year assignment. He was not transferred because there were no Navy records documenting his having been wounded three times.

Kerry claimed to have been wounded the first time during a nighttime patrol in a Boston Whaler only days after he arrived in Vietnam. *Tour of Duty* provided an account of a wild firefight between Kerry and the Vietnamese enemy, during which a piece of enemy shrapnel "socked into my arm and just seemed to burn like hell."[48]

An eyewitness account offered a markedly different sequence of events. William Schachte, who later rose to the rank of rear admiral, was in the Boston Whaler alongside Kerry. According to Schachte's recollection, "Kerry picked up an M-79 grenade launcher and fired a grenade too close [to the Whaler], causing a tiny piece of shrapnel (one to two centimeters) to barely stick in his arm…There was no enemy fire."[49]

Lieutenant Commander Louis Letson was the Navy medical officer who treated Kerry's wound. "Dr. Letson used tweezers to remove the tiny fragment, which he identified as shrapnel like that from an M-79 (not from a rifle bullet, etc.), and put a small bandage on Kerry's arm."[50]

Two very critical documents were generated during the Vietnam War when someone was wounded by enemy fire. The first was a combat casualty card, a three-by-five inch, typewritten card. This card contained the main facts, such as the wounded serviceman's full name, military service number, rank, branch of service, the date and description of the wound, and the prognosis for recovery. Navy officials described combat casualty cards as "valuable as gold," and they were "protected like Fort Knox" because they were a key record often used to determine disability benefits after military service.

The second required document was a personnel casualty report. It was a mandatory report transmitted to Washington, DC, with the details of anyone wounded as a result of enemy action.

Combat casualty cards and personnel casualty reports exist for the wounds resulting in John Kerry's second and third Purple Hearts. However, Navy officials have never located a combat casualty card or a personnel casualty report for Kerry's injury for which he received his first Purple Heart. In fact, no Navy record has ever been unearthed documenting that there was any hostile action that occurred that specific night involving Kerry and the Boston Whaler. Officers in Kerry's chain of command recall turning down Kerry's request to be given a Purple Heart for his scratch.

The possibility certainly exists of Navy officials losing a combat casualty card or personnel casualty report. According to a Navy archivist, the possibility of losing both documents for the same individual and for the same event is "virtually impossible."

The lack of any definitive Navy documents, the absence of a combat casualty card and a personnel casualty report, and the failure by John Kerry to provide a full release of his medical records, are strong evidence that he was not wounded, as he had claimed.

Executive Order 9066

Ten weeks after the December 7, 1941, Japanese surprise attack on Pearl Harbor, Hawaii, President Franklin Roosevelt signed Executive Order 9066. The February 19, 1942, order directed the Secretary of War "to prescribe military areas in such places and of such extent as he or the appropriate Military Commander may determine, from which any or all persons may be excluded, and with respect to which, the right of any person to enter, remain in, or leave shall be subject to whatever restrictions the Secretary of War or the appropriate Military Commander may impose in his discretion."[51]

Roosevelt's order opened the door to what became the eviction and internment of tens of thousands of Japanese immigrants and American citizens of Japanese ancestry. There was no race or ethnicity identified in Roosevelt's order; however, it was understood that Japanese-Americans and resident aliens were the targets. There were three groups of Japanese who fell under suspicion of potentially being enemy spies and saboteurs. They were Issei (immigrants), Nisei (first-generation Americans born of Japanese ancestry), and Sansei (second-generation Americans of Japanese ancestry).

Japanese immigrants to the United States were relatively uncommon. Japanese immigration did not really begin until the latter half of the nineteenth century. For more than two centuries, Japanese law prohibited Japanese citizens from emigrating.[52] Complicating matters was the Japanese practice of assigning Japanese citizenship to a child born of a Japanese male, regardless of where the child was born.[53] Some Japanese believed they were subject to Japanese laws, regardless of where they lived.

There were other actions targeting the Japanese that were undertaken in the immediate aftermath of the December 7 attack. The Department of the Treasury froze the assets of thousands of US citizens of Japanese ancestry and Japanese immigrants. Other Japanese immigrants or Japanese-Americans who were deemed to pose potential threats to vital infrastructure or military installations were arrested and taken into custody.

US Army Lieutenant General John DeWitt was designated the military commander for the Western United States, which was comprised of Arizona, California, Idaho, Montana, Nevada, Oregon, Utah, Washington, and the Territory of Alaska.[54] On March 2, he issued Proclamation No. 1, stating that Japanese-Americans were ordered removed from the entire state of California and the western halves of Arizona, Oregon, and Washington.

Ten War Relocation Authority centers were established, where a total of about 120,000 Japanese-Americans were forcibly evacuated and were to spend the remainder of the war interned.[55] These included two centers each in Arizona, Arkansas, and California, and one center each in Colorado, Idaho, Utah, and Wyoming. The centers were often in remote locations. In many cases, the evacuees lived temporarily in harsh conditions, such as fairgrounds, cowsheds, or racetrack horse stalls, until more permanent facilities were constructed.[56]

Most Japanese-Americans left their homes only with whatever possessions they could carry. Many lost the possessions they left behind, including their homes and businesses.

Roosevelt's executive order and resulting evacuation and internment of Japanese-Americans occurred ten weeks after the attack, due to a change in public attitude. There was very little animosity toward Japanese-Americans immediately after the December 7 attack. The atmosphere of distrust grew in the weeks following the attack. This may have been hastened by comments in the Roberts Commission report.

Supreme Court Justice Owen Roberts led a five-man commission, appointed by Roosevelt on December 18, to investigate the circumstances leading up to the surprise attack. Over a period of five weeks, the commission interviewed 127 witnesses and reviewed more than

3,000 pages of documents, culminating in a twenty-one-page report on January 23, 1942.

According to the report, "There were, prior to December 7, 1941, Japanese spies on the island of Oahu. Some were Japanese consular agents and others were persons having no open relations with the Japanese [F]oreign [S]ervice. These spies collected and, through various channels transmitted, information to the Japanese Empire respecting the military and naval estawblishments and dispositions on the island."[57]

The report addressed the significant debate among various government entities as to whether mass arrests of *Issei*, *Nisei*, and *Sansei* Japanese in Hawaii should have been undertaken in the days following the attack. However, "the commanding general assert[ed] that their arrest would tend to thwart the efforts which the Army had made to create friendly sentiment toward the United States on the part of Japanese aliens resident in Hawaii and American citizens of Japanese descent resident in Hawaii and create unnecessary bad feeling."[58]

The brief excerpt from the Roberts Commission report that some spies "were Japanese consular agents and others were persons having no open relations with the Japanese [F]oreign [S]ervice," likely contributed to the change in public attitude toward the loyalty of Japanese-Americans.[59] Also, early reports were trickling into the American mainland of the atrocities perpetrated by the Imperial Japanese Army in the Pacific Theater, including in the Philippines, where there was a sizable American military presence. However, it was not just ethnic Japanese who were viewed with suspicion. About 16,000 Germans were arrested or interned and another 3,500 Italians faced the same fate.

There was no such harsh treatment of Japanese-Americans in the Hawaiian Islands, even though they also lived near strategic facilities and military installations. The nearly 160,000 Japanese-Americans and Japanese immigrants living in Hawaii represented more than one-third of the islands' population.[60] It is generally believed that a key reason they were also not incarcerated is because they were much too vital to the Hawaiian economy.

Additionally, the flood of sensational reports of ethnic Japanese aiding in the attack on Pearl Harbor were untrue. Reports of Japanese-Americans sabotaging aircraft and blocking roads were just that:

reports. In fact, the Honolulu chief of police stated that the various stories of Japanese-Americans engaged in sabotage were false.[61]

On January 2, 1945, interned Japanese-Americans were given permission to leave the War Relocation Authority centers and return to their homes. In 1988, as a result of the Civil Liberties Act signed into law by President Ronald Reagan, each surviving internee was given restitution of $20,000 and a US government apology for their evacuation, relocation, and internment.[62]

Draft Dodgers

The Vietnam War was the most unpopular American war in the twentieth century. Without a doubt, it was President Lyndon Johnson's war. He dramatically escalated US involvement in the war during his first full term of office. In 1964, there were a little more than twenty thousand American soldiers in South Vietnam. By 1968, that number had mushroomed to more than half a million servicemen and women.

Johnson's decision to increase US troop levels was made just days after his inauguration. According to Secretary of Defense Robert McNamara, Johnson's decision to dramatically increase the US troop presence in Vietnam was made "without adequate public disclosure."[63]

Between 1964 and 1973, nearly two million men were drafted into the military. Many of those who were drafted were ordered to a one-year tour of duty in South Vietnam.

US involvement in South Vietnam quickly became very unpopular among the American public, especially college students and other draft-age young men. The military draft was in force in the United States until January 1973. The anti-war movement included peaceful and violent protests against the military and other elements of the federal government.

Federal conscription was conducted by a lottery process. Each day of the year was drawn at random. The first date drawn became draft number one. The last date drawn became draft number 365 (or 366 in leap years when there was a February 29). Men with low draft numbers were almost certain to be drafted that year. High draft numbers were virtually certain not to be drafted.

Some men with low draft numbers who did not want to serve in the US military sought various ways to avoid military service, including exemptions, deferrals, and disqualifications. Still, others outright refused to report when called. Thousands fled the country, with most going to Canada, which offered safe harbor to draft resisters. According to some estimates, as many as forty-thousand people evaded military service by immigrating to Canada. About nine thousand had been convicted of various crimes of violating the Selective Service law.[64]

The resisters were viewed poorly and were called "draft dodgers" by most of American society, especially by US veterans, including retired military, and World War II and Korean War veterans.

On his first full day as president, Jimmy Carter made good on a campaign promise to unconditionally pardon every man who had refused to register for the draft, refused to report for induction when drafted, or fled the country. These were the civilians who had violated the Military Selective Service Act of 1967. In total, this is estimated to have been about two hundred thousand men. During the 1976 presidential race, Carter campaigned on the policy that "reconciliation calls for an act of mercy to bind the nation's wounds and to heal the scars of divisiveness."[65]

Carter issued Executive Order 11967 as his unconditional pardon of every man who avoided military service between August 4, 1964, and March 28, 1973.[66] However, Carter's amnesty excluded anyone who engaged in "acts of force or violence." Further, Carter's proclamation directed all investigations by the Justice Department to immediately cease, and anyone denied permission to reenter the United States was granted permission to return.

Not surprisingly, Carter's amnesty proclamation was met with widespread condemnation by countless public officials and millions of American servicemen, military retirees, and other veterans.

The Flip-Flop

The Panama Canal is one of the greatest engineering marvels of all time. The canal runs about fifty miles through Panama, connecting the Atlantic and Pacific Oceans. The fifteen- to twenty-five-hour journey to transit from one ocean to another was a dramatic improvement over the previous route. Prior to the Panama Canal, ships sailing from the United States' mid-Atlantic coast to the California coast would have to sail an additional eight thousand miles around Cape Horn, the southernmost point of the South American mainland. The American Society of Civil Engineers named the Panama Canal one of the seven man-made wonders of the world.[67]

The French were the first to seriously attempt to carve a canal through the Panama isthmus. In the 1880s, a French firm, employing thousands of workers in the region, began construction. After nearly a decade, the expenditure of about $250 million, and the deaths of more than twenty thousand workers, the firm went bankrupt.

A second French effort yielded little. This led to the US purchase of the French property and construction rights for $40 million in 1902.[68] A treaty was negotiated between the United States and Colombia because Panama was part of the South American nation at the time.

The Colombian legislature did not ratify the treaty, but new developments gave the United States hope that a deal could be reached. Panamanians were considering breaking away from Colombia. The United States signaled it would support the independence of Panama. When Panama declared independence on November 3, 1903, the United States stationed the gunboat USS *Nashville* (PG-7) off the coast to guard against Colombian troops attempting to retake control of the newly independent nation. The *Nashville*'s presence epitomized gunboat diplomacy.[69]

The Provisional Government Junta of the Republic of Panama, the name of the newly independent nation's government, appointed Philippe Bunau-Varilla as Envoy Extraordinary and Minister Plenipotentiary to the United States on November 6. Bunau-Varilla was the chief engineer of the French project. After France abandoned it, he actively lobbied the United States to purchase canal rights from the French.[70]

On November 18, 1903, the Hay-Bunau-Varilla Treaty was executed, giving rights and control of what would become the Panama Canal to the United States in perpetuity in return for $10 million and annual payments.[71] The United States also guaranteed the independence of Panama.[72] Both the US Senate and the new Panamanian government ratified the treaty.

The United States took control of French equipment and buildings that were in a serious state of disrepair after fifteen years of disuse. The United States began renovating whatever equipment and buildings it could, replaced others, and formulated a plan of action to build the canal.

Similar to the French approach, senior management and highly skilled positions were filled by Americans, while unskilled positions were filled by immigrants. Some immigrants were Western Europeans and others were from nations around the Caribbean Basin.

Just as critical to the success of the project were developments in sanitation, worker health, and living conditions. Chief among these was the implementation of precautionary measures arising from the discovery that yellow fever and malaria were mosquito-borne diseases.[73] Most of the more than twenty thousand French worker deaths were attributed to these two diseases and a few others, such as cholera. In fact, so many Europeans had fallen ill and died that Panama became known as "the white man's graveyard."[74]

The most difficult aspect of the construction was carving through the Continental Divide mountain range that ran through Panama. The project cut through the lowest point of the range, but still had to reduce the mountains from about three hundred feet above sea level to about forty feet. This had to be accomplished for a distance of about eight miles.

Canal construction included a pair of man-made lakes and six sets of locks that were used to raise and lower water levels as ships transited from one ocean to the other.[75] In mid-transit, a ship would be eighty-five feet above sea level to account for the differences in elevation of the middle of Panama as compared to the Atlantic and Pacific coastlines.[76]

After assuming control of the canal in 1904, the project took the United States about a decade to complete. It was opened and began operation in August 1914. Construction began midway through Theodore Roosevelt's presidency, encompassed the entire presidency of one-term William Howard Taft, and ended with the canal's opening during the first term of Woodrow Wilson.

For nearly seven decades, the ten-mile-wide and fifty-mile-long Panama Canal Zone was the territory of the United States. It was an American owned and operated canal. In spite of the 1904 treaty, this arrangement proved to be contentious, with many Panamanians objecting to what they viewed as a loss of sovereignty. Over the years, there were a few violent clashes between Panamanians and the US military forces providing security for the Canal Zone.

In response to accusations of imperialism and colonialism by satellite nations in the Soviet Union's orbit, the presidential administration of Richard Nixon began discussions in 1970 to change the arrangements between the United States and Panama.[77] In 1973, longtime diplomat Ellsworth Bunker was appointed to lead the US negotiations. Over the next several years, Bunker slowly drafted agreements that would shift control and ownership of the Panama Canal from the United States to Panama.

During the 1976 presidential race, President Gerald Ford advocated for a treaty to transfer canal control to Panama. His general election opponent did not. Jimmy Carter pledged the United States would continue its control of the Panama Canal.[78] During the October 6 debate on foreign policy issues held at San Francisco's Palace of Fine Arts, Carter said he would not give up "practical control of the Panama Canal Zone any time in the foreseeable future."[79]

After the election, and before he was inaugurated as the 39th president, Carter reversed himself on turning over control of the canal to Panama. In a January 3, 1977, interview with *Time* magazine, Carter was asked, "What do you hope to get done first?" Carter replied, "I think the Panama treaty ought to be resolved quite rapidly."[80]

The years of groundwork laid by Ellsworth Bunker helped US negotiators to finalize an agreement in principle. In order to increase the chances of Senate ratification, Carter and Panama leader General Omar Torrijos signed two treaties in September 1977.

The Treaty Concerning the Permanent Neutrality and Operation of the Panama Canal guaranteed the United States the right to intervene militarily if the neutrality of the Panama Canal Zone was at stake. The second treaty, The Panama Canal Treaty, called for the end of the US-controlled Panama Canal Zone in October 1979 and transition of control to Panama over the next twenty years. Panama would take complete control of the Panama Canal on January 1, 2000.[81]

The Senate narrowly ratified the two treaties by April 1978, each with a one-vote margin.

Bay of Pigs

Fidel Castro led the Cuban Revolution that overthrew President Fulgencio Batista on New Year's Eve 1958. After Castro assumed power, Cuban relations with the United States began to sour. Thousands of Cubans who worked for American interests or who were opposed to Castro's rule fled the island nation. Many Cuban expatriates settled in South Florida.

President Dwight Eisenhower grew increasingly concerned over the growing ties between Castro and the Soviet Union. It was the height of the Cold War between the United States and the Soviet Union. The Soviets gaining a military footprint about ninety miles from the United States posed a potentially serious threat.

In March 1960, Eisenhower gave approval to a CIA proposal titled, "A Program of Covert Action Against the Castro Regime," that laid out a plan to topple Castro.[82] By May, the CIA began assembling a group of anti-Castro Cuban dissidents that would later grow to nearly 1,400 members, who would train at a secret CIA facility in Guatemala. Named Brigade 2506, the paramilitary group of exiles received weapons and insurgency training from the CIA.

By August 1960, Castro had ordered the nationalization of US-owned businesses, including the Cuban Electric Company, the telephone company, hotels, banks, coffee and sugar plantations, and oil refineries.[83]

The CIA plan called for Brigade 2506 to transit by boat from Guatemala to Cuba and conduct an amphibious landing at Playa Girón, a beach in the Bay of Pigs on Cuba's southwest coast. Perhaps the biggest obstacle plaguing the operation was that it was not much of a secret in the United States—or anywhere else for that matter. By October, Cuba's foreign minister knew of Cuban exiles training in Guatemala for a possible invasion of the island.[84] The CIA station chief in Hamburg, West Germany, was told by a German businessman there were rumors of a US-trained military force in Guatemala that was preparing to invade Cuba.[85]

After he assumed the presidency in January 1961, John Kennedy gave final approval for the military operation. Unbeknownst to many involved in the planning at the time was the role carved out for the Mafia. It wasn't just legitimate owners who lost American businesses when Castro nationalized them. The Mafia had a sizable operation in

Havana, where it operated hotels, entertainment, and gambling interests. The Mafia was interested in ending Castro's rule so it could return
to Havana.

Santo Trafficante was the de facto head of the Mafia in Cuba. He
was also a close associate of Sam Giancana and John Rosselli. Kennedy
and Giancana already had a close relationship because Giancana helped
Kennedy capture the White House in the 1960 election (see chapter 3).[86]

Trafficante paired up Giancana and Rosselli with two Cubans who
were willing to assassinate Castro. The plan was to terminate Castro and
leave Cuba without senior government leadership just as Brigade 2506
was overwhelming Cuban forces.

Anyone not in the know regarding the existence of Brigade 2506
learned of its existence from a January 10, 1961, front-page article
published by the *New York Times*. The *Times* reported the United States
was training a group of exiles in Guatemala to take on the Castro regime.[87]

On April 15, 1961, eight CIA-owned World War II vintage B-26
Marauder bombers emblazoned with Cuban Air Force markings and
operated by Cuban exiles conducted air strikes against airfields and
naval facilities to neutralize a Cuban response to the amphibious landing
the following night.[88]

Kennedy's Mafia element of the plan never materialized. Neither
of the two Cubans contracted to kill Castro carried out their mission.
Castro survived and personally directed his military's response to the
Brigade 2506 invasion effort.[89]

The Cubans were anticipating the invasion force and were well
prepared to respond. The fourteen hundred members of Brigade 2506
were met by about fifteen thousand Cuban soldiers. Once the amphibious invasion force began to land, Kennedy had second thoughts and
decided to withhold the second wave of air support the morning
following the planned invasion. This decision doomed the mission as
the Cuban Air Force began attacking Brigade 2506, preventing them
from establishing a beachhead.[90]

By April 20, 1961, the Bay of Pigs invasion was over. Nearly twelve
hundred Cuban exiles were taken prisoner. At a press conference the
following day, Kennedy took blame for the debacle. He said, "There's an
old saying that victory has a hundred fathers and defeat is an orphan...I
am the responsible officer of the government."[91]

Wag the Dog

The full release of the Hollywood film *Wag the Dog* occurred on January 9, 1998, several days before the American public learned that President Bill Clinton had been carrying on a sexual affair with White House intern Monica Lewinsky. Starring Robert DeNiro and Dustin Hoffman, *Wag the Dog* was the story of a presidential sex scandal that was certain to derail the president's reelection. A White House dirty trickster, played by DeNiro, and a sympathetic Hollywood producer, Hoffman's character, concocted a story of a fake war in Albania. The plan was to distract public attention from the president's sex scandal by drawing interest to the war, in which American lives were at risk.

Furious with the White House at claiming a non-existent war existed, the CIA leaked that the war was over quickly. Fearful this would allow the president's sex scandal to return to front-page news, DeNiro's and Hoffman's characters let it be known that a US serviceman was trapped behind enemy lines and American forces needed to stage a rescue. Sadly, the trapped serviceman died in action and was given a hero's burial at Arlington National Cemetery. US patriotism was at a fever pitch and public approval of the president skyrocketed.

The plan worked. The public's attention was distracted from the sex scandal, and the president was safely reelected. Months later, that exact same scenario played out for real.

The investigation into Clinton's sexual affair with Lewinsky was getting worse by the day for the president. His emphatic denials were learned to be outright lies. It was learned he encouraged Lewinsky and others to lie. The final nail in Clinton's coffin occurred when Lewinsky turned over to federal investigators her semen-stained blue dress. Testing proved the DNA belonged to Clinton. The president could no longer lie his way out of his difficulties.

As the evidence mounted, Clinton faced a world of hurt. In trying to cover up his extramarital affair, the 42nd president committed perjury and obstructed justice. These were the same allegations Richard Nixon faced when House leaders made it clear in 1974 that they were likely to impeach him.

Desperate times call for desperate measures, and Clinton had his own wag-the-dog moment. On the same day Monica Lewinsky was to testify before the grand jury regarding Clinton's attempts to suborn perjury, Clinton ordered strikes against the Al-Shifa pharmaceutical factory in Khartoum, Sudan. Clinton claimed the medicine plant was producing chemical weapons for Osama bin Laden and there were financial ties between the plant and the al Qaeda leader. Neither Clinton claim was true.[92]

In fact, numerous Americans and Europeans who were working at or were familiar with the factory reported that it indeed produced medicines that were desperately needed in the region. Moreover, the plant did not have any of the easily observable characteristics of a chemical weapons factory, such as air-sealed doors, which are necessary when producing poisons. Nor were there Sudanese soldiers guarding the plant, as would be expected if it were engaged in the production of chemical weapons. The German ambassador to Sudan said the Clinton administration's claims of poisonous gas production at the medicine factory were a lie.[93]

Clinton's claimed reason for the strikes fell under further suspicion when it was learned that only he and a small handful of advisors made the decision. In a departure from protocol, most of the military Joint Chiefs of Staff were kept in the dark until just before the strikes began.[94]

After the strikes, the administration refused to offer any proof to buttress Clinton's claims that the factory was producing chemical weapons, as had become routine for presidents since the days of President Ronald Reagan. In addition, the Clinton administration refused the Sudanese government's request for international inspection of the destroyed plant to ascertain if it was producing poison gas, as Clinton had alleged.[95]

The Sudanese owner of the plant said his factory employed three hundred workers who manufactured mostly antibiotics. Al-Shifa supplied 60 percent of the pharmaceuticals that were critically needed in Sudan. The owner welcomed American officials to inspect the plant anytime they wanted, but they never asked.[96]

After the strikes, reporters interviewed factory workers and locals while aid workers were sifting through the rubble. American and foreign news reported that medicine vials were found strewn among the wreckage. There was absolutely no evidence of chemical weapons or chemical weapons production at the medicine factory.

There was worldwide condemnation of the United States over Clinton's missile strikes. "Bombing of Innocent Pharmaceuticals Plant Not US's Finest Hour," blared the headline of Canada's *Financial Post*.[97] London's *Daily Mail* front-page headline asked, "Clinton's Revenge: But Was His Real Target the Arab Terrorists or Lewinsky's Testimony?"[98] The *Scottish Daily Record* observed, "Convenient for Bill Clinton to Launch Raids on Terrorist Camps."[99]

The evidence undermining Clinton's claims forced the administration to finally come clean. Defense Secretary William Cohen admitted there were no direct ties to Osama bin Laden.[100] He also claimed defense officials were not aware the factory produced medicine, which is ironic, as that was what the Al-Shifa factory was known for in Sudan. As Sudanese officials suggested, the United States could have merely asked for an inspection of the plant to ascertain its purpose. It would have been impossible to hide any evidence of chemical weapons production, hide the munitions, and reconfigure the operation of the plant without being observed by US satellites. The Clinton administration never asked to inspect the plant.

As in the *Wag the Dog* movie, Clinton had his own act two. In fall 1998, the independent special counsel delivered his report on the Clinton investigation. It was damning. House Republicans felt they had no choice but to consider impeachment because Clinton had committed perjury and obstructed justice.

On December 16, 1998, the eve of the impeachment debate in the House, Clinton once again put servicemen and women in harm's way. Clinton ordered US airstrikes against Iraq. In a public announcement, Clinton stated, "Their mission is to attack Iraq's nuclear, chemical, and biological weapons programs and its military capacity to threaten its neighbors."[101]

Clinton claimed the timing of the strikes was appropriate because Iraqi President Saddam Hussein announced "six weeks" earlier that he would no longer cooperate with United Nations inspection missions. But Clinton's timeline was patently false. Saddam announced four-and-a-half months earlier, on August 5, that he would no longer cooperate in inspections.[102] Any doubt as to the motive behind the ordered strikes evaporated when Clinton called them off minutes after the impeachment vote was concluded.

Clinton's simultaneous bombing missions during the Lewinsky grand jury testimony and impeachment debate were widely viewed as wag-the-dog moments. In other words, Clinton's life imitated art.

Group Think

Operation Iraqi Freedom was launched on March 20, 2003. The purported reason for the US-led attack on Iraq was to stop Iraq's weapons of mass destruction program, including chemical, biological, and radiological programs. The evidence was irrefutable that Iraq had not abandoned earlier efforts to procure such offensive weapons, said Secretary of State Colin Powell in a February 5, 2003, address before the United Nations Security Council.

"[T]he facts and Iraq's behavior show that Saddam Hussein and his regime are concealing their efforts to produce more weapons of mass destruction," Powell told a rapt audience in a globally televised address. Powell continued, "My colleagues, every statement I make today is backed up by sources, solid sources. These are not assertions. What we're giving you are facts and conclusions based on solid intelligence."

Powell's confidence throughout his presentation was so persuasive that thirty-nine countries joined the United States in Operation Iraqi Freedom. It was the largest coalition of military forces ever assembled. One allied component of the coalition force was the Iraq Survey Group, a US-led international team of more than one thousand people whose primary task was to uncover Iraq's weapons of mass destruction program.

In late September 2004, eighteen months after Operation Iraqi Freedom began, the final report from the Iraq Survey Group was delivered to the director of the CIA.[103] The document confirmed earlier reporting that Iraq's military and foreign policy was exclusively developed by Saddam Hussein. Further, Hussein harbored intentions to restart his weapons of mass destruction programs when the opportunity presented itself. However, Iraq possessed relatively small amounts of chemical and biological weapons, which were not nearly enough to pose any serious military threat on a grand scale.

Only months after the war began, it was apparent that Operation Iraqi Freedom was based on faulty intelligence. On June 20, 2003, the

Senate Select Committee on Intelligence announced a bipartisan effort to conduct a "review of US intelligence on the existence of and the threat posed by Iraq's weapons of mass destruction (WMD) programs" and related issues.[104]

Even as US policymakers were taking steps to determine what, if anything, went wrong, there were still media reports that Iraq had a secret nuclear weapons program. CNN reported on June 25, 2003, the existence of "critical parts of a key piece of Iraqi nuclear technology, parts needed to develop a bomb program."[105]

In June 2004, the committee released the heavily redacted, 500-page report. All nine Republican and eight Democratic senators were unanimous in endorsing the report as representing a bipartisan consensus. The report noted that committee staffers were instructed "to disregard post-war discoveries" as the report was focusing on pre-war intelligence.

The Senate Intelligence Committee "focused its evaluation of the Intelligence Community's WMD analysis primarily on the October 2002 National Intelligence Estimate (NIE): *Iraq's Continuing Programs for Weapons of Mass Destruction.*"[106] It was the primary intelligence document laying out the case that Iraq had restarted its weapons of mass destruction program following its dismantling after the 1991 Gulf War.

The intelligence committee report included dozens of conclusions. The conclusions focusing on the nuclear weapons component of Iraq's WMD program were rather damning of the US intelligence community, and the CIA in particular.

In the first conclusion, the committee found, "Most of the major key judgments in...*Iraq's Continuing Programs for Weapons of Mass Destruction,* either overstated, or were not supported by, the underlying intelligence reporting. A series of failures, particularly in analytic trade craft, led to the mischaracterization of the intelligence."[107]

The intelligence community failed to "adequately explain to policymakers the uncertainties behind the judgments in the...National Intelligence Estimate."[108] Some of the failures may have been attributable to a key conclusion that the intelligence community suffered from "group think."[109]

Adding to intelligence community failure was the "'layering' effect, whereby assessments were built based on previous judgments without carrying forward the uncertainties of the underlying judgments."[110]

The Senate committee also found, "Intelligence Community managers throughout their leadership chains [failed] to adequately supervise the work of their analysts and collectors. They did not encourage analysts to challenge their assumptions, fully consider alternative arguments, accurately characterize the intelligence reporting, or counsel analysts who lost their objectivity."[111]

The intelligence community's human intelligence program (the use of spies) fell way short. This was due to "a broken corporate culture and poor management."[112] A human intelligence source, known by the code name Curveball, was relied upon heavily as a key source—in some cases the only source—"that Iraq had a mobile biological weapons program."[113] It turns out his information was deeply flawed, and warnings against relying on his reports were ignored.

Lastly, the Senate committee report was very critical of the CIA's failure to share intelligence with other intelligence agencies "to the detriment of the Intelligence Community's prewar analysis concerning Iraq's weapons of mass destruction programs."[114]

Following the release of the report, the committee vice chairman, Democratic Senator John Rockefeller of West Virginia said, "We in Congress would not have authorized that war, in 75 votes, if we knew what we know now."[115]

President George W. Bush addressed the intelligence failure in his memoir. He wrote, "Almost a decade later, it is hard to describe how widespread an assumption it was that Saddam had WMD. Supporters of the war believed it; opponents of the war believed it; even members of Saddam's own regime believed it. We all knew that intelligence is never 100 percent certain; that's the nature of the business."[116]

CHAPTER 2

BAD BEHAVIOR

"My intent was not to deceive anyone. For if it were, I would not have been so blatant...If I had intended to cheat, would I have been so stupid?"

—Joe Biden after being caught plagiarizing while attending Syracuse University College of Law.[1]

The Waiter

In spring 1856, in the nation's capital, Democratic Congressman Philemon Herbert of California fatally shot Thomas Keating, a waiter working in the Willard Hotel dining room. Herbert was twice tried and twice acquitted of murder.

The Dutch ambassador, Mr. Du Bois, was in the dining room and witnessed the murder. But he refused to be called as a witness, which proved damaging to the prosecution.[2]

The following is derived from witness testimony from the preliminary hearing before a pair of magistrates, held on May 8–9, 1856, as published in the *New York Daily Times*. The article appeared in the May 12th edition of the paper. US attorney for the District of Columbia, Philip Barton Key II, was the prosecutor.

According to eyewitness accounts, Herbert and a friend, William A. Gardiner, arrived in the Willard Hotel dining room after 11 a.m. and ordered breakfast. Waiter Jerry Riordan greeted the pair and returned with a partial breakfast order. The congressman demanded the rest of his breakfast order. Riordan told the pair that because breakfast service was over, the waiter would have to get permission from the office before any more breakfast meals could be prepared.

Herbert was not interested in waiting for a decision from the office. Instead, he ordered another waiter, Thomas Keating, to "get my breakfast, damned quick." He then called Keating "a damned Irish son of a bitch."

Keating's reply to Herbert was not clearly heard by the eyewitnesses. But whatever the response, it apparently set off Herbert. Herbert leaped from his chair and struck Keating on the back of his neck with a pistol. Keating grabbed a dish plate from a nearby table and prepared to throw it at Herbert but apparently thought better of it.

Herbert did not hesitate. He threw a chair at Keating. Keating threw the dish plate at Herbert. The two men then began to scuffle. Herbert's dining companion, Gardiner, grabbed a chair and broke it on Keating. The dining room steward and brother of the waiter, Patrick Keating, emerged from the kitchen and joined the melee. Gardiner struck Patrick Keating with a chair. Patrick Keating grabbed the barrel of Herbert's gun, which the congressman had been waving about.

The cook, a Frenchman named J. Devenois, emerged from the kitchen and attempted to break up the brawl. Patrick Keating lost his grip of Herbert's gun. With the gun now free, Herbert grabbed the collar of Thomas Keating with one hand and shot him. Keating collapsed to the floor, dead.

There were competing accounts on which party was winning the scuffle, which the *New York Daily Times* called "a thrill of horror in the community." Prosecution witnesses portrayed Herbert and Gardiner as the aggressors. Defense witnesses claimed Herbert was defending himself against several members of the dining room staff. Curiously, defense witnesses were unable to positively identify those they claimed to be perpetrators.

After the two-day preliminary hearing, magistrates Smith and Birch ruled there was ample evidence that a crime had been committed and referred the matter to the US District Court for the District of Columbia.

Herbert was acquitted of manslaughter charges in two separate trials. He declined to run for reelection later that year.

The Harlot Slavery

Charles Sumner was a US senator from Massachusetts. He was a member of the two-year-old Republican Party. Prior to becoming a Republican in 1855, he was a member of the Free Soil Party. He was a harsh critic of the institution of slavery in the years leading up to the Civil War.

In spring 1856, debate was taking place in Congress regarding the Kansas territory. Should the territory be admitted to the Union and under what preconditions? Would it be a slave state or a free state?

On May 19, 1856, Sumner rose to deliver a speech he titled "The Crime Against Kansas." He would speak for three hours before the Senate adjourned. He continued his remarks for another two hours the following day.[3] Regarding the movement to admit Kansas as a slave state, he said, "It is the rape of a virgin Territory, compelling it to the hateful embrace of Slavery; and it may be clearly traced to a depraved desire for a new Slave State, hideous offspring of such a crime, in the hope of adding to the power of Slavery in the National Government."[4]

Sumner's criticism of the institution of slavery was incendiary to those who supported the practice. Then he directed his attention to those he believed were responsible. "I derive well-founded assurances of commensurate effort by the aroused masses of the country, determined not only to vindicate Right from Wrong, but to redeem the Republic from the thralldom of that Oligarchy which prompts, directs, and concentrates the distant Wrong."[5]

Sumner singled out a pair of senators, who, he said, "have raised themselves to eminence on this floor in championship of human wrong: I mean the Senator of South Carolina [Mr. Butler] and the Senator from Illinois [Mr. Douglas] who, though unlike as Don Quixote and Sancho Panza, yet, like this couple, sally forth together in the same adventure."[6]

Then he turned his attention exclusively to Butler: "The Senator from the South Carolina has read many books on chivalry and believes himself a chivalrous knight with sentiments of honor and courage. Of course, he has chosen a mistress to whom has made his vows, and who, though ugly to others, is always lovely to him; though polluted in the sight of the world, is chaste in his sight: I mean the harlot, Slavery."[7]

Sumner wasn't finished. He blasted President Franklin Pierce for lying about the circumstances surrounding the admission of Missouri as a slave state. The slaveholding states had not "reluctantly acquiesced" in accepting the Missouri Compromise as Pierce had suggested. Sumner quoted from a letter by South Carolina's Charles Pinckney as claiming the Compromise "is considered here by the Slaveholding States as a great triumph."[8]

Sumner's remarks were considered so powerful among abolitionists that his speech was reprinted in newspapers in the United States and Europe. His speech was used as a campaign document in the 1856 presidential election.[9] As many as one million pamphlets memorializing his speech were distributed.[10]

Not all those present in the Senate chamber agreed with the tone and the message of Sumner's remarks. Illinois Senator Stephen Douglas wondered if it were all a trap. "Is it his object to provoke some of us to kick him as we would a dog in the street, that he may get sympathy upon the just chastisement?"[11]

Preston Brooks was a South Carolina Democratic congressman. He was also a cousin of Butler. Brooks was in the Senate gallery the first day of Sumner's speech. Brooks heard the Massachusetts senator liken his cousin to the Don Quixote of slavery. He waited until Sumner's complete speech was published the following day. He became incensed after reading all of Sumner's remarks and felt it was his duty to defend the honor of South Carolina and his cousin, whom he deemed was too elderly and frail to physically fight the Massachusetts senator.[12]

Brooks thought that, under the circumstances, Southern code prevented him from using a pistol or sword to exact revenge.[13] Some time earlier, Brooks had once joked that members of Congress should be required to check their firearms at the House cloakroom before entering the chamber.[14] There would be no firearms use when he defended the honor of his cousin and the Palmetto State.

Brooks walked with a noticeable limp from a bum hip that was injured in a duel.[15] He used a walking cane to compensate for the limp. He settled upon the cane as a weapon to use against Sumner.

After the Senate adjourned around midday on May 22, Brooks entered the Senate chamber in search of Sumner. Brooks sat in the back as senators and other hangers-on gradually exited the chamber. Sumner was at his desk with pen in hand, writing furiously. Brooks approached Sumner's desk.

"Mr. Sumner," Brooks said. "I have read your speech twice over very carefully. It is libel on South Carolina, and Mr. Butler, who is a relative of mine." As Sumner started to rise from his desk to face his accuser, Brooks began striking him repeatedly with his gold-headed cane. Brooks struck Sumner at least thirty times by his own count, shattering the cane in the process.[16] [17]

The attack was over in a matter of moments. Sumner lay covered in blood, unconscious, on the Senate floor. Others responding to the commotion had their own confrontation. Senator John Crittenden, a member of the Know-Nothing Party from Kentucky, approached Brooks as if to stop him. Democratic Representative Laurence Keitt of South Carolina implored Crittenden not to interfere and raised his own cane to emphasize his point.[18] Democratic Georgia Senator Robert Toombs, who was near the fracas, did nothing to stop it. "I approved of it," he later said of the assault.[19]

Brooks was later arrested for assault. But his reputation had been made. He was a hero of the pro-slavery movement. Abolitionists were shocked over the attack. The nation was divided, with Northerners generally viewing Brooks as the perpetrator and Southerners considering Sumner the instigator.

Anticipating a vote of expulsion, Brooks resigned his House seat. However, his constituency viewed him as a hero for his actions and immediately elected him back into Congress.[20]

Brooks was tried in court on a charge of assault. In a bench ruling, Brooks was fined a paltry $300. Among the reasons for such a light sentence was the reported ineffectiveness of the prosecutor, Philip Barton Key II. As the US attorney for Washington, DC, Key would find himself involved in more than one public scandal.[21]

Temporary Insanity

Teresa Bagioli was a stunningly beautiful woman who was preparing to be a wife in high society. Bagioli attended Manhattanville Convent of the Sacred Heart, where New York's Catholic elite sent their daughters in the mid-nineteenth century. She was in that class of young ladies that was described as "privileged American wholesomeness."[22]

Bagioli was taken with a charming and handsome young lawyer who was a friend of the family. Daniel Sickles proposed to the fifteen-year-old Teresa, and they quickly had a civil ceremony in the fall of 1852, followed by a church service in early 1853. By then, Sickles had been appointed to the influential office of corporate attorney for New York City, where some credit him with the initiative that created Central Park.[23]

In 1856, Sickles was elected to Congress, representing much of Manhattan. Dan, Teresa, and their infant daughter relocated to Washington, DC. Rather than live in a boarding house or hotel, which was the norm for many members of Congress, Sickles leased a stately home called Stockton Mansion on Lafayette Square. The White House could be seen from the top floor windows.[24] Sickles requested his newfound friend, Philip Barton Key II, take care of the paperwork for him. The pair met and became fast friends after an all-night card game.[25]

Philip Barton Key II was from a pedigreed family. One ancestor was John Key, who served as England's first poet laureate in the seventeenth century. His grandfather, John Ross Key, served with Maryland troops during the Revolutionary War, while his great-uncle and namesake, Philip Barton Key, served in the British Army. After the war, great-uncle Philip moved to England for a number of years, then returned to America and was eventually elected to Congress. A twentieth-century descendant was Francis Scott Fitzgerald, better known as writer F. Scott Fitzgerald.[26]

The most famous of Philip Barton Key's relatives was his father, Francis Scott Key. It was Francis Scott who composed the lyrics to "The Star-Spangled Banner" after witnessing the British bombardment of Fort McHenry in 1814.

Sickles had met Key on an earlier trip to Washington, DC. Key was the US attorney for Washington, DC, a prominent position that put him in the same social circles as the Sickles.

Teresa spent her days attending social engagements around Washington, DC. Key attended many of the same events. Some of the women noticed Key coincidentally attending many of the same functions as Teresa Sickles.[27]

Key was a widowed father of four children, the oldest being twelve. They lived under the care of a relative in one section of DC, while he lived alone in Georgetown. Key's bachelor lifestyle enabled him to serve as Mrs. Sickles's escort whenever her husband was unavailable.

By early 1858, there was an increasing number of Philip Barton Key and Teresa Sickles sightings on unexpected occasions. Apparently, Key wasn't just escorting Sickles to social receptions, but was spending considerable time with her when Daniel Sickles was away.

In February 1859, Daniel Sickles received an anonymous letter informing him that his young wife and Key had been secretly meeting. An outraged Sickles confronted his wife, who confessed to an affair that began in spring 1858. She confessed the pair had been engaging in intimate relations at various locations, including in their own home. Sickles became inconsolable. Compounding matters, Sickles was certain that all of fashionable Washington knew of the affair between his wife and Key.

Then an opportunity to exact revenge presented itself. On February 28, 1859, Key was wandering aimlessly around Lafayette Park waving a white handkerchief, easily in sight of Stockton Mansion. Signaling with a handkerchief was the manner in which Key communicated with Teresa regarding a rendezvous.[28] The Sickles's house servants saw him, as did a houseguest—as did Daniel Sickles. Sickles realized Key was waving the handkerchief to attract his wife's attention.

Sickles left his home and walked hurriedly toward Key. As he approached the federal prosecutor, he yelled, "Key, you scoundrel, you have dishonored my house—you must die!" With that, he pulled a pistol from his coat pocket and fired several times, striking Key twice.[29] Key swiftly died from his wounds.

Sickles was charged with murder. The shooting "had all of the scandalous elements expected to thrill the American reading public: adultery, politics, celebrity, and a handsome corpse." As such, it became front-page news in both large and small cities.[30]

A three-week trial took place in April 1859. The prosecution and defense teams called more than seventy witnesses. It was the defense strategy that was the most remarkable. Sickles employed eight high-powered attorneys. Their strategy was to portray Sickles's actions as the result of a temporary insanity caused by the pain, anguish, and humiliation of his wife's betrayal. It was the first-known instance of the temporary insanity defense in an American criminal trial.[31] It apparently worked. It took the jury about an hour to deliver a not-guilty verdict.

After the fatal altercation with Key, the notable accomplishments of Daniel Sickles began to accumulate. Sickles joined the Union Army in the run-up to the Civil War. He attained the rank of major general and commanded the Third Army (III) Corps (March 13, 1862–March 24, 1864) that fought at Antietam, Fredericksburg, and Chancellorsville. Of course, the most famous was the battle at Gettysburg. It was here that Sickles was struck by an artillery shell, causing him to lose his right leg. He survived the amputation and quickly became a hero to the public. His actions at the battle earned him a Medal of Honor. Years later, he served as an ambassador to Spain.

Joe's Plagiarism

Plagiarism, the use of the words of another without proper attribution, has been an unfortunate staple of Washington politics. Democratic Senator Joe Biden of Delaware had a long, sad history of passing off the words of others as his own. It started at least as early as his law school days.

During his first year at Syracuse Law School, Biden was called before the law school's disciplinary body to answer charges of plagiarism. After the board found him guilty, Biden "threw himself on the mercy of the board" and promised that he had learned his lesson, according to a school official. Biden's mea culpa was enough to convince the board not to expel him from the school.[32]

Years later, when it became known that Biden had been embroiled in a plagiarism scandal at Syracuse Law School, his Senate staff falsely told the press he had been exonerated by the disciplinary board.[33] Eventually, Biden came clean and admitted he had committed plagiarism. He confessed to lifting five entire pages from a law review article and including it as his own work in a paper he submitted. He argued that the public should disregard his "mistake" because it "was not in any way malevolent."[34]

The public became aware of Biden's tendency to plagiarize the words of others when he was running for the 1988 Democratic presidential nomination. Appearing before the California Democratic Party Convention on February 1, 1987, Biden told convention delegates that "each generation of Americans has been summoned" to test their devotion to democracy. This phrase was nearly identical to a phrase used by John Kennedy in his presidential inaugural address: "Each generation of Americans has been summoned to give testimony to its national loyalty."[35]

Biden also borrowed liberally from Kennedy's younger brother, Robert. Sometimes it was entire passages quoted nearly verbatim. The *Miami Herald* compiled several examples, including this one:

From the…Biden speech to the California Democratic Party:

"Few of us have the greatness to bend history itself. But each of us can act to affect a small portion of events and in the totality of these acts will be written the history of this generation."

From a speech Robert Kennedy gave at Fordham University in June 1967:

"Few will have the greatness to bend history itself. But each of us can work to change a small portion of events and in the total of all those acts will be written the history of this generation."[36]

According to *Time* magazine, Biden also lifted passages from Hubert Humphrey and others without attribution.[37]

Biden's tendency to use the work of others without attribution may reflect poorly on his character. But plagiarizing the life story of a British politician as his own raises serious questions about his overall judgment.

During an August 23, 1987, appearance before the Iowa State Fair, Biden told the audience about a thought that had occurred to him while he was on his way to the fair.[38] Biden said, "I was thinking to myself why was it that I was the first person, the first Biden in probably a thousand generations to go to university and to law school…Was it because our mothers and fathers were not as smart as we were?"

But Biden's thought was not nearly as spontaneous as he claimed. Biden's description of his family's struggles was nearly identical to one made by British Labour Party Leader Neil Kinnock on May 15, 1987, at the Welsh Labour Party Conference. Kinnock told party officials, "Why am I the first Kinnock in a thousand generations to be able to get to university?…Was it because our predecessors were so thick?"

Biden's line, "Those same people who read poetry and wrote poetry and taught me how to sing verse," was nearly identical to Kinnock's, "Those people who could sing and play and recite and write poetry."

Biden's address, "My ancestors, who worked in the coal mines of northeast Pennsylvania and would come up after twelve hours and play football," was not much different from Kinnock's, "Those people who could work eight hours underground and then come up and play football...." Except, as the *New York Times*' Maureen Dowd observed, Biden's relatives "seemed to stay underground longer."[39] And unlike Kinnock's father, who was actually a coal miner, Biden's dad was a used-car salesman.[40,41]

Biden's campaign staff explained away the failure to credit Kinnock in the Iowa State Fair speech as merely an oversight. But Biden used nearly the same campaign lines on several other occasions, and each time he failed to credit Neil Kinnock.

Biden ended his presidential bid on September 23, 1987.

"Racism is White"

"We have lost to the white racist press and to all the racist, reactionary Jewish misleaders," said Democratic Congressman Gus Savage of Illinois regarding his 1992 primary election defeat.[42] In spite of a long track record of racism and anti-Semitism, the six-term congressman managed to be reelected several times from a district located largely on Chicago's South Side.

The publisher of a chain of Chicago-based newspapers, Savage was first elected to Congress in 1980. In spite of the power of incumbency, Savage struggled to get reelected throughout his six terms, often receiving only about half of the primary vote, and never more than 52 percent.[43]

Shortly after assuming his seat in Congress, it became apparent that he was an ardent critic of Israel and US support of Israel. Savage was one of only three House members who opposed a measure that called for withholding US funds from the United Nations if it barred Israel from U.N. General Assembly proceedings. He warned, "The powerful Zionist lobby in this country must understand that it can no longer dictate to every member of Congress."[44]

Savage was not shy about his anti-Semitic leanings. He was a strong supporter of Nation of Islam leader Louis Farrakhan. He said Farrakhan's statements that "Hitler was a great man," and Judaism was a "gutter religion," were "historically, culturally and politically accurate."[45] "The press," Savage claimed, "is disproportionately represented by white liberals and Jews."[46]

In March 1989, Savage made an official visit to Kinshasa, Zaire. He was feted at a dinner hosted by US Ambassador William Harrop. In attendance were several staffers from the American embassy and officials with the Peace Corps. After the dinner, the group visited several nightspots around the capital city.

Savage specifically requested a female Peace Corps volunteer join him alone in his vehicle throughout the nightspot visits. "He tried to force me to have sex with him," the woman later complained.[47] Savage, she alleged, continually grabbed her during the two-hour period the three embassy cars hop scotched around nightspots. It wasn't until after the group returned to Savage's hotel that she stormed out after a "tense public encounter," according to an embassy staffer.[48]

The State Department later filed a complaint regarding Savage's behavior with the House Ethics Committee. But an investigation wasn't undertaken until after three Democratic members of the House requested the committee do so. The committee's investigation determined Savage made "sexual advances" toward the woman, but declined to issue any punishment because Savage sent a letter of apology to the woman.

Savage responded by claiming he was victimized by "white liberal" colleagues and "white media" over the incident.[49] Then he criticized the three Democrats who referred his case to the Ethics Committee.[50]

In 1990, Savage faced a stiff Democratic primary challenge from Mel Reynolds whom he had faced in the 1988 primary. During a campaign rally, Savage complained about what he called "pro-Israel" donations given to Reynolds's campaign. Savage read a list of Jewish-sounding names he claimed were contributors to Reynolds. Fellow Congressional Black Caucus members, House Majority Whip William Gray of Pennsylvania, and Representative Charles Rangel of New York, joined Savage at the rally, but said nothing of his bigoted remarks until several days after the primary and after relentless public criticism.[51]

The incumbent congressman beat his primary challenger in March 1990. In his victory remarks, Savage thanked Farrakhan for his support. Savage said his victory was a practice run for the following year, in which he predicted a black challenger would defeat incumbent Chicago Mayor Richard M. Daley. That challenger would "not [be] a crossover black, but a black who is proud of being black," he remarked. Crossover blacks, according to Savage, were those who campaigned with, for, or in support of white candidates. An example of a crossover black was Ron Brown, then-Chairman of the Democratic National Committee. Savage called Brown, "Ron Beige," because the black DNC chairman had endorsed white candidates for some offices.

Savage didn't let up on his bigoted tirades as he campaigned ahead of the general election. In April, he held a two-and-a-half-hour press conference. He continued his rant about "pro-Israeli" money pouring into his Republican opponent's coffers. He was warning black voters to avoid candidates who were backed by Jews. Moreover, he argued, he couldn't be accused of racism because "racism is white."[52]

The following summer, Savage had a blow up with a reporter. At first, Savage warmly greeted the man, but changed his attitude when the man introduced himself as a reporter. "I don't talk to you white [expletive]…in the white press," the reporter recalled.[53]

Some in Chicago approved of Savage's behavior. *Chicago Sun-Times* editorial board member Vernon Jarrett came to Savage's defense in a published endorsement, calling him "outspoken, scrappy," and a victim of a "big smear" over his remarks about his opponent's Jewish donors.

Reynolds again challenged Savage in the Democratic primary for a third time in 1992. Jarrett was not impressed with Reynolds. The newspaperman wrote that Reynolds's "biggest asset is the financial support of America's pro-Israel lobby."[54]

Reynolds defeated Savage in March 1992 and won the general election that November. Reynolds would then become embroiled in his own scandal.

Waitress Sandwich

Democratic Senators Edward "Ted" Kennedy of Massachusetts and Christopher Dodd of Connecticut were more than just close friends and drinking partners. The New England politicians became two-thirds of the infamous Kennedy-Dodd waitress sandwich. Alcohol-fueled high jinks involving the New England politicians were a frequent topic of conversation by many in Washington, DC. There were occasional reports of Kennedy and Dodd sightings at area restaurants, many of them unflattering. Alcohol was often involved.[55]

An Air Force crewman assigned to the 89th Airlift Wing told one story of Kennedy's drinking habits in the late 1980s. Based at Andrews Air Force Base, the 89th Airlift Wing is a special support unit of the US Air Force. Its mission is to provide flight services to the president, vice president, cabinet members, and other senior US officials.

According to the Air Force crewmember, Kennedy ordered "his morning orange juice" shortly after boarding an aircraft en route to a congressional junket. The crewmember brought the Senator a tall glass of orange juice. After taking a sip, the furious senator thrust the glass back at her, demanding *his* morning orange juice. A more experienced crewmember took the glass and showed his colleague how to prepare Senator Kennedy's morning orange juice. It was a tall glass filled with vodka and a splash of OJ.

In 1985, actress Carrie Fisher was working in the Washington, DC, area. A mutual friend set her up on a blind date with Chris Dodd. The pair ended up in a private dining room of a Georgetown restaurant, where they were joined by two other couples. One couple was Ted Kennedy and his date, Lacey Neuhaus. Alcohol flowed freely throughout the evening, but Fisher refrained from drinking, as she was on the wagon. At one point in the evening, Kennedy turned to Fisher and asked, "So, do you think you'll be having sex with Chris at the end of your date?" When she replied she wouldn't, Kennedy asked, "Why not? Are you too good for him?" Later in the evening, Kennedy asked Fisher about her masturbation habits.[56]

In December 1985, Kennedy and Dodd, then ages fifty-three and forty-one, were on a double date at a Capitol Hill restaurant named La Brasserie. Purchased by Lynne and Raymond Campet in 1978, the restaurant was known for its location, outdoor patio, and French-themed menu. It served many celebrities in the nearly three decades it was in business. Restaurant patrons included Vice President Al Gore,

Congressman Sonny Bono, and actors Paul Newman, Jimmy Stewart, and Jane Fonda.[57]

According to a profile of Ted Kennedy in *GQ* magazine, that night in December 1985, the two senators were accompanied by a pair of young blondes, and all four had gotten very drunk during a long evening at La Brasserie. Waitress Betty Loh said Kennedy consumed as many as four cocktails within the first thirty minutes, and that he also drank wine with dinner. The foursome was dining in a private room. Sometime after midnight the two women left the senators and headed to the ladies' room. The waitress, Betty Loh, also left the private room.[58]

Co-owner Raymond Campet then told waitress Carla Gaviglio the senators wanted to see her. Gaviglio entered the private room to check on the restaurant guests. *GQ* magazine describes what happened next:

As Gaviglio enters the room, the six-foot-two, 225-plus-pound Kennedy grabs the five-foot-three, 103-pound waitress and throws her on the table. She lands on her back, scattering crystal, plates and cutlery and the lit candles. Several glasses and a crystal candlestick are broken. Kennedy then picks her up from the table and throws her on Dodd, who is sprawled in a chair. With Gaviglio on Dodd's lap, Kennedy jumps on top and begins rubbing his genital area against hers, supporting his weight on the arms of the chair. As he is doing this, Loh enters the room. She and Gaviglio both scream, drawing one or two dishwashers. Startled, Kennedy leaps up. He laughs. Bruised, shaken and angry over what she considered a sexual assault, Gaviglio runs from the room. Kennedy, Dodd, and their dates leave shortly thereafter, following a friendly argument between the senators over the check.

According to the *GQ* profile, Kennedy had another incident at the same restaurant two years later. Kennedy had a lunchtime reservation for a private room at La Brasserie on September 25, 1987. Accompanied by a young woman, identified as a lobbyist, Kennedy and his lunch date allowed their sexual passions to dictate their behavior. The pair were interrupted in the private room by waitress Frauke Morgan when she walked in to offer the guests coffee. Morgan found Kennedy and his date on the floor with his trousers around his ankles, her dress pulled up, and the pair "screwing on the floor."[59]

The Kennedy-Dodd waitress sandwich was not the only time the two senators got carried away at a Washington, DC, restaurant. According to *GQ*:

> At [La Colline] in 1985, Kennedy and drinking buddy Senator Christopher Dodd of Connecticut did a "Mexican hat dance" on their own framed photographs. According to The Washingtonian magazine, which broke the story, "Kennedy spotted Dodd's framed photo [on the wall] and shouted, 'Who's this guy?' Laughing, he grabbed the photo from the wall and threw it on the ground, breaking the glass in the frame. Dodd, not to be outdone, located Kennedy's photo and returned the favor."

"Damned Poltroon"

Josiah Grinnell was something of a pacifist. Born in New Haven, Vermont, in 1821, he did not follow in his father's footsteps as a farmer. Instead, he attended the Oneida Institute in Whitestone, New York. There, students would study advanced theological or college classes while performing manual labor tasks to keep costs low. He eventually became a Presbyterian pastor and an abolitionist.

Grinnell befriended the president of Rock Island Railroad, who confided in Grinnell plans to build his railroad through Iowa. Using this insider information, Grinnell relocated to Iowa where he and several others purchased about five thousand acres in the path of the planned railroad. His goal was to start a Christian community named after himself along the railroad path. In 1859, Iowa College in nearby Davenport relocated to the village of Grinnell. The school was renamed Grinnell College in 1909.

Grinnell became involved in politics and was among the organizers of the Republican Party in Iowa. He first held state office and then won the 1862 election to Congress representing Iowa. He was reelected in 1864, but failed to secure his party's nomination in 1866.

Born in Kentucky in 1818, Lovell Rousseau initially became a lawyer in Indiana. He became a member of the Whig Party and briefly served in the Indiana legislature. He joined the army and served during the Mexican War.[60]

After the war, Rousseau returned to Indiana and was elected to the Indiana State Senate before moving to Kentucky. He left the Whig Party, joined the Republican Party, and was elected to the Kentucky State Senate in 1860. He worked feverishly to oppose Kentucky seceding from the Union and joining the Confederacy. When war broke out between the states, he resigned his Senate office and joined the Union Army, where he was promoted to major general.[61]

As the war was winding down, Rousseau resigned his commission and ran for a US House seat. In 1864, he was elected to the House, representing Kentucky. Less than a year after he took office, bitterness developed between Grinnell and Rousseau.

There was heated debate in Congress over proposed legislation to extend the controversial Bureau of Refugees, Freedmen and Abandoned Lands, typically known as the Freedmen's Bureau, which was due to expire. Some viewed the management of freed slaves as a state, and not a federal, matter. On the floor of the House on February 5, 1866, Grinnell denounced the "barbarous laws" of Kentucky because he felt they had not been amended in a timely fashion following the end of the Civil War. Grinnell felt this necessitated an extension of the Freedmen's Bureau.[62]

Regarding Rousseau, Grinnell said, "The honorable gentleman from Kentucky [Rousseau] declared on Saturday...that if he were arrested on the complaint of a negro and brought before one of the agents of [the Freedmen's Bureau], when he became free he would shoot him. Is that civilization? It is the spirit of barbarism, that has too long dwelt in our land—the spirit of infernal regions that brought on the rebellion and this war...I care not whether the gentleman was four years in the war on the Union side or four years on the other side, but, say that he degraded his State and uttered a sentiment I thought unworthy of an American officer."[63]

Reportedly, Rousseau did not let the insult pass. He responded to Grinnell's remarks at a speech he gave in New York City. Rousseau said, "A fling was made at my native State by a pitiable politician from Iowa...I believe it was one Grinnell."[64]

Grinnell did not leave well enough alone. On June 11, 1866, he launched a more ruthless attack on Rousseau, belittling his military career. "[I]f he is a defender of the President of the United States, all I have to say is, God save the President from such an incoherent, brainless defender, equal in valor in civil and military life…[W]hen there was a noise in camp the men said it was either a rabbit or General Rousseau… He has not led them in the battle, and it is all pretense; it is the merest mockery; it is the merest trickery, the merest blowing of his own horn, for him to say that he led our soldiers."[65]

For good measure, Grinnell questioned the loyalty to the Union by Kentuckians. "I am proud to say that I represent a district that sent thirteen thousand men into the army. Can the gentleman say as much? I did speak something about the men from Kentucky fighting on both sides."[66]

When the House adjourned that day, there was a physical confrontation between Rousseau and Grinnell just outside the Capitol Building. It would change the lives of both men.

The Speaker of the House appointed several members to the Select Committee on Breach of Privilege and charged them with investigating the incident and recommending what action be taken by the full House.

The Select Committee interviewed Grinnell, Rousseau, and witnesses to the altercation. Grinnell and Rousseau were permitted to ask questions of those who were testifying, as well as asking questions of one another.

According to Grinnell's testimony before the Select Committee on June 26, Grinnell had just left the Capitol through the east portico when Rousseau had touched his shoulder. "I have been waiting for an apology," Rousseau said to Grinnell. Grinnell replied, "You began the assault upon me in the House, and you should make the apology; I have none to make."[67]

Grinnell testified he first grabbed Rousseau by his coat collar. Rousseau responded by striking Grinnell with "five or six blows, until the cane broke." Rousseau used a rattan cane that did not cause any serious injuries.[68]

According to one eyewitness account, Grinnell said, "You have not hurt me." Rousseau replied, "I do not want to hurt you. I do not mean to hurt you. I want to degrade you." Then Rousseau called Grinnell a "damned coward" and a "damned poltroon" as he walked away.[69]

It was clear when Rousseau questioned Grinnell that the former wanted to establish he almost immediately began striking Grinnell to prove he was justified in order to protect his honor and that of Kentucky.

In his responses, Grinnell made it appear he provoked Rousseau to fight. "You should make the apology; I have none to make," Grinnell said to Rousseau, according to his testimony before the committee. Before Rousseau began the assault, Grinnell was the first to make physical contact, he told the committee: "I seized him by the coat collar."

In his cross-examination of Grinnell, Rousseau asked, "Did not I then instantly strike you with a cane and tell you I would teach you 'what of it'? Just as soon as the word came out of your mouth, whatever it was, declining an apology, did not I strike you instantly with the stick?" Grinnell answered, "I said I had no apology to make, and the blows came very soon." Rousseau persisted, "Did not the cane come instantly?" Grinnell responded, "I should say very soon."[70]

In his questioning of Colonel Charles Pennebaker, a Rousseau friend who witnessed the attack, Rousseau established that Grinnell did not initiate the physical confrontation by grasping Rousseau's coat collar, as Grinnell had testified. "Did Mr. Grinnell put his hand to my coat, and did you see me put my hand up as if to draw a weapon?" Rousseau asked. "No sir," Pennebaker answered.[71]

In his testimony, Rousseau said, "I am sure Mr. Grinnell did not touch me until I used my rattan on him until about the time it was broken…Mr. Grinnell did not allude to any apology from me…I struck him instantly as soon as from his manner I saw he declined to make an apology.[72]

In response to a question about his motive, Rousseau replied, "I denounced him. I told him he was very fierce in the House and said I, 'Now look at you, you damned cowardly puppy,' or something of that sort."

On July 2, 1866, the House of Representatives voted to expel Rousseau and voted disapproval of Grinnell's behavior.

The issue of defending one's honor was more important than establishing guilt over who started the physical altercation. Grinnell's unwillingness to defend himself hounded him for the rest of his life. After leaving the House, he failed to secure nominations when he pursued the governor's office, US Senate, and US House.[73]

In an autobiography published thirty-five years later, Grinnell was critical of Rousseau, who had died in early 1869. He implied Rousseau was drunk during the altercation and that Rousseau "was in my power."[74] In his retelling of the confrontation, Grinnell claimed he told Rousseau,

"I have you in my power, but I will not kill you." Rousseau, according to Grinnell, made a deathbed apology to Grinnell as repayment for Grinnell sparing his life.[75]

In contrast, Kentucky constituents picked Rousseau in a special election to fill the seat from which he had just been expelled. He left Congress in 1867 and rejoined the Army as a major general. That same year, Rousseau was sent to Alaska to officially receive the territory from Russia after it was purchased. He passed away in 1869 while supervising Reconstruction efforts in Louisiana.[76]

The Bad Temper

Cynthia McKinney was known for her divisive race- and religion-based politics as a six-term member of Congress representing Georgia. Yet, she managed to get reelected every two years in spite of her bigoted behavior. However, her political career in the Democratic Party came crashing down after she struck a Capitol Hill policeman.

In 1996, when McKinney was running in Georgia's newly formed 4th congressional district, she faced Comer Yates in the Democratic primary. Yates had lost a race two years earlier in the old 4th district. According to McKinney, Yates's supporters were "the holdovers from the Civil War days, the relics." She added, "You don't have to be a slave-holder to benefit from the wealth created by slavery."[77] They were "a ragtag group of neo-Confederates," she warned.[78]

McKinney's bigoted remarks targeted a man with solid Democratic credentials. His wife, Sally Yates, would later serve as the acting US attorney general in the Obama administration. Sally Yates would become enmeshed in her own controversy over her involvement in spying on the Trump presidential campaign.

The 1996 election year saw the dial turned up on anti-Semitic behavior. McKinney's father, Bill, who once served in the Georgia state-house with his daughter, was her campaign manager. While attending a campaign forum, Bill McKinney called his daughter's general election opponent a "racist Jew."[79] When asked why the challenger's religion was relevant, Bill McKinney replied, "Because he is running a race-based campaign trying to turn white people against Cynthia McKinney, a black woman."[80]

According to a profile in the *Atlanta Jewish Times*, McKinney seemingly engaged in damage control over her father's bigoted comment. Well-heeled donor Cookie Shapiro agreed to host a major fundraiser for McKinney in her home located in a tony area of the Atlanta suburbs. Flying in to headline the fundraiser was Tipper Gore, the wife of Vice President Al Gore. "I think [McKinney] was trying to keep me from canceling," said Shapiro. "She kept saying her father didn't speak for her."[81]

McKinney stopped communicating with Shapiro after the fundraiser. Years later, Shapiro recalled, McKinney neither accepted nor returned any of Shapiro's telephone calls. Shapiro believes McKinney was only using her.[82]

McKinney had no problem with the anti-Semitic hate speech of Nation of Islam officials. Unlike other members of the Georgia congressional delegation, McKinney voted against a 1994 congressional resolution condemning the hate speech of Nation of Islam senior representative Khalid Abdul Muhammad.[83]

According to McKinney, there was little difference between white Republicans and white Democrats. During the 2000 campaign, she said, "Gore's Negro tolerance level has never been too high. I've never known him to have more than one black person around him at any given time."[84] This comment was ironic considering Gore appointed as his campaign manager Donna Brazile. She was the first black woman to manage a major party presidential campaign.

In addition to her bigoted behavior, McKinney was a bona fide 9/11 "truther." She signed a petition called the "9/11 Truth Statement" that called for investigations into the September 11, 2001 terrorist attacks. According to McKinney, President George W. Bush had advanced knowledge of the attacks and let them proceed because his family and members of his administration had investments that would benefit from a war.

McKinney's tumultuous congressional career came crashing down after an altercation involving a Capitol Hill police officer. The 435 members of the House of Representatives are given a distinct lapel pin to wear. This device aids the Capitol Hill police force in identifying members of Congress and allows them to avoid routine security checks including magnetometers. McKinney had a habit of not wearing her pin.[85]

On March 29, 2006, McKinney entered a House office building while not wearing her congressional lapel pin. Complicating matters was that she had recently changed her hairstyle, abandoning the distinctive cornrows she had worn for years. Officers on duty did not recognize her as she skirted security procedures. According to several witnesses, McKinney ignored an officer who called for her to stop several times. Then an officer placed a hand on her. McKinney swung around and struck the officer with her cell phone.

The Capitol Hill police force deliberated for several days on whether to charge McKinney with assault. In return, she went on the offensive. In a draft statement, she said, "It is…a shame that, while I conduct the country's business, I have to stop and call the police to tell them that I've changed my hairstyle so that I'm not harassed at work."[86] She added, "The whole incident was instigated by the inappropriate touching and stopping of me—a female, black congresswoman."[87]

McKinney's lawyer was more aggressive in his response. James W. Myart, Jr., said, "Congresswoman Cynthia McKinney [was]…a victim of the excessive use of force by law enforcement officials because of how she looks and the color of her skin."[88]

McKinney backpedaled on her claims of who was to blame once it was learned that a grand jury was deliberating the matter, and members of the Congressional Black Caucus privately urged her to get the controversy under control.[89] Reversing course on her claims that the Capitol Hill police officer was a racist was not enough. McKinney lost the 2006 Democratic primary.

McKinney didn't immediately fade into obscurity. As her term was drawing to a close, she introduced articles of impeachment against President George W. Bush. The impeachment bill died in the House Judiciary Committee without any co-sponsors.

In 2008, McKinney accepted the Green Party nomination for president. She received about 162,000 votes, or about 0.12 percent of the votes cast.

In 2015, McKinney received a PhD from Antioch University in Los Angeles.[90] She wrote a glowing tribute to Venezuelan strongman Hugo Chavez as her dissertation.[91] Her description of Chavez as a "nation builder" obviously has not withstood the test of time.

"Bitch Set Me Up"

A few days before Christmas 1988, Washington, DC, metropolitan police were responding to a complaint that someone was selling drugs out of a downtown Ramada Inn hotel room. A hotel maid said she was approached by someone asking if she was interested in making a purchase.

The police arrived and approached the room belonging to Charles Lewis, who was suspected of making drug sales. Lewis had long been suspected as a drug dealer. Then the police retreated after they discovered that DC Mayor Marion Barry was in the room with Lewis. The sensitivity of this discovery required notification of the DC metropolitan police chain-of-command. This matter eventually landed on the desk of US Attorney General Richard Thornburgh, who approved a probe of Barry's alleged drug use.[92]

Reports of drug use had followed the three-term Democratic mayor over the previous decade. There were reports of him frequenting sketchy locations in the wee hours of the morning. Illegal drug use allegations were part of the rumors. Other legal difficulties plagued the mayor. Eleven city officials, including a top aide and his deputy mayor, had been convicted of financial crimes involving the city. Barry called those convictions an effort to "lynch black people another way."[93]

Hazel Diane "Rasheeda" Moore had been a girlfriend of Barry for a number of years. She had begun modeling as a teenager in Washington, DC, and then moved to New York. She appeared in several high-fashion magazines. After she returned to DC in 1986, she landed the first of two no-bid contracts with the city government. Sandwiched between the two contracts was some federal prison time.[94]

Moore left DC and moved out West. She was living in Los Angeles when she ran into legal difficulties. She worked out a deal to help federal prosecutors in a sting involving Barry in return for the dropping of charges against her.

After arriving back in Washington, DC, Moore called Barry and suggested the pair get together. Moore was staying at the Vista International Hotel, not far from the White House. Around 7:30 p.m. on January 19, 1990, the fifty-three-year-old Barry arrived at the Vista Hotel in his chauffeur-driven Lincoln Town Car. He was accompanied by an armed bodyguard. Moore called Barry on his car phone and invited him to her room. He left the bodyguard in the lobby and went to room 727. There was another woman in the room. Moore had a traveling companion with her.

Once in the room, Moore introduced the other woman. After some conversation, Barry asked the women if they had any drugs. The friend said she did, and Barry offered to buy some. The friend slipped into the hotel bathroom and returned with some crack cocaine.

Barry filled a pipe with some of the crack, lit it, and then inhaled twice. Three hidden cameras in the room recorded the activity. Moments later, FBI agents burst into the hotel room and handcuffed the mayor. Moore's friend was actually an undercover FBI agent. Reportedly, a hostage rescue team was standing by on the off chance that Barry's armed bodyguard attempted to intervene.[95]

Angry at his arrest, Barry blurted, "Bitch set me up. I shouldn't have come up here. Goddamn bitch." In order to protect him from embarrassment, the FBI quietly escorted Barry through the hotel basement disguised in a wig and sunglasses.

Barry was taken to FBI headquarters, where he underwent blood and urine tests, and agents took hair samples. Barry had cocaine in his system, according to the blood and urine tests. The hair samples would be used to determine long-term drug use.

The next morning, US Attorney Jay B. Stephens announced Barry had been charged with one misdemeanor count of cocaine possession. The charge carried a maximum of one year in jail and up to a $100,000 fine.

Barry had his first court appearance on January 20. He was released without having to post bail. US Magistrate Deborah Robinson ordered him to surrender his passport, take weekly drug tests, and phone the federal pretrial services office weekly. After he left the courthouse, he was heckled by critics and cheered by supporters. One man shouted, "You all right, Barry! You ain't done more damage than the white man do every day!"[96]

Ironically, at the time Barry was making his court appearance, his friend Charles Lewis was in another courtroom being sentenced. Lewis had pled guilty two months earlier to two counts of conspiracy to possess and distribute cocaine.

Two days after his arrest, Barry informed friends he would check himself into a clinic to combat his substance abuse problem. The following day, on January 22, Barry entered a South Florida facility for treatment of alcohol abuse.

When his trial began in June, Barry faced more than a dozen felony and misdemeanor charges, ranging from cocaine possession to lying to a federal grand jury. In the midst of his trial, Marion Barry and his wife, Effi, attended a rally led by Nation of Islam leader Louis Farrakhan. Barry and Farrakhan embraced on stage and Farrakhan urged him to run for reelection. "I want the mayor to run, Barry, run," he said.

After a two-month trial, a mixed-race jury delivered the verdicts. Barry was convicted of one charge and acquitted of a second charge. The jury deadlocked on the remaining twelve charges, leading the judge to declare a mistrial on those counts. After the trial was over, several jurors said they voted for acquittal because they believed some of the evidence against Barry had been fabricated by authorities.

In October 1990, Washington, DC, Mayor Marion Barry was sentenced to six months in jail and ordered to pay a $5,000 fine.

An Affair of Honor

There was bad blood between Aaron Burr and Alexander Hamilton, a pair of the nation's founders. There were several contributing factors that led to their toxic relationship.

The men were members of the two major political parties in the late eighteenth century. Burr was a Republican.* Hamilton was a Federalist. The political divide between the two parties was cavernous. Republicans believed Federalists were hell-bent on undoing the successes of the young nation's independence from Britain because they wanted to strengthen the power of the federal government at the expense of the states. The Federalists were convinced the Republicans would start an unholy alliance with France.

Farmers and tradesmen tended to vote Republican. Well-to-do landowners and merchants favored the Federalists. Among the Federalist voters were leftover Loyalists from the Revolutionary War.[97]

---

*   Although they were called Republicans, they were actually members of the Democratic-Republican Party. The party would later split into the Democratic Party and the Whig Party.

Aaron Burr was from a respected New Jersey family. His father was president of the college that became Princeton University. Hamilton was a bastard born in Saint Kitts in the British West Indies and immigrated to the American colonies as a teenager in 1772. Hamilton was a self-made man, who was likely embarrassed of his roots. In 1780, he married into the Schuyler family, one of the wealthiest families in New York.[98]

Burr and Hamilton were officers in the Revolutionary War. Burr rose to the rank of colonel. Hamilton became a major general. Hamilton was the key author of *The Federalist Papers* that helped convince the states to ratify the Constitution.

In 1789, President George Washington selected Hamilton to serve as the nation's first Secretary of the Treasury. In 1791, the New York legislature selected Burr over Philip Schuyler to be a US Senator. Schuyler was Hamilton's father-in-law.

In the 1790s, Burr and Hamilton were the two best lawyers in all of Manhattan. Prospective clients competed for their services.[99] When Hamilton was caught up in an extramarital relationship with Maria Reynolds (see chapter 3), it was Burr who represented Reynolds in her divorce.[100] In early 1800, the two lawyers teamed up as the successful defense counsel of a defendant charged in Manhattan's most notorious murder case of the day.[101]

As the eighteenth century drew to a close, the fortunes of Burr and Hamilton had changed from their early beginnings. Hamilton was married with seven, mostly young, children. He was established as a gentleman of wealth. Burr was a widower with one older daughter. And he was "dead broke."[102]

The nation's second president, John Adams, was a Federalist. In 1800, he was defeated in his quest for a second term by Thomas Jefferson, the candidate he beat four years earlier. Jefferson's running mate was Burr. At the time, the top two vote getters of the presidential electors became the president and vice president. Jefferson and Burr were tied with electoral votes in the 1800 election. This threw the election to the House of Representatives.

In the House, thirty-five straight ballots did not produce a result. Hamilton used his influence to help decide the election, which Jefferson won. Burr viewed Hamilton as the man who cost him the presidency.

As the 1804 election approached, it became obvious Jefferson was going to drop Burr as his running mate. Believing his political fortunes were in free fall, Burr decided to run for the governor's office in New York, which was an open seat, as the incumbent governor had been chosen by Jefferson to be his reelection campaign running-mate. Again, Hamilton influenced the election result. While publicly professing to stay neutral, Hamilton quietly lobbied for the eventual winner, Morgan Lewis. Twice, Burr thought, Hamilton had cost him the elected office he sought.

In March 1804, Hamilton attended a private dinner of several guests at the home of a backer of New York gubernatorial candidate Morgan Lewis. Not all the guests respected the privacy of the conversation at the dinner table that night. Dr. Charles Cooper transcribed several of Hamilton's critical remarks of Burr in a letter to a friend. Whether inadvertently or by design, excerpts of the letter were published in the *New York Evening Post*.[103]

Cooper alleged Hamilton referred to Burr "as a dangerous man." In a subsequent letter published in the *Albany Register* in April, Cooper added that Hamilton held even a "more despicable opinion" of Burr than previously revealed. These cutting remarks rubbed Burr the wrong way. The accumulation of Hamilton-originated insults and their fractious relationship had a profound effect on Burr.[104]

In mid-June, a letter from Burr demanding that Hamilton explain what was meant by the "despicable" comment was delivered to Hamilton. Rather than offering a vague reply that would have allowed both men to save face, Hamilton shrugged off Burr's demand, ensuring that animosity between the two would continue.[105]

It appeared both men were heading down the same path to defend their honor. Hamilton was a seasoned veteran of affairs of honor, or duels. On half a dozen occasions, Hamilton was in similar situations, but as with so many duels, negotiations between the two aggrieved parties defused the situation and satisfied each intended combatant's honor without their actually having to face one another with loaded pistols.[106]

In a subsequent letter to Burr, Hamilton appeared to welcome a duel when he wrote he would "abide by the consequences" of his remarks.[107] While the rhetoric between the two was heating up, their good friends and confidants were working feverishly to negotiate a peaceful settlement. In all, eleven letters were exchanged between Burr and Hamilton or their surrogates.[108] William Van Ness and Judge Nathaniel Pendleton, the seconds of Burr and Hamilton, respectively, met several times to deescalate the matter. A second is selected by a dueler to ensure the duel is carried out honorably.

Both Hamilton and Burr had become intransigent in spite of the best efforts of their seconds. On June 27, Van Ness served Pendleton with Burr's formal duel request. The agreed-upon date was two weeks later, July 11th. This date was settled on so that Hamilton could attend to the needs of his law firm clients through the final session of the New York State Supreme Court.[109]

Hamilton decided to observe duello, the traditional rules governing a duel, by discharging his pistol without actually firing at Burr. The tactic allows duelists to completely follow through on a duel, yet preserve their honor without actually harming one another. Hamilton may have thought that, once he fired his pistol into the ground, Burr would similarly discharge his.[110] Nevertheless, Hamilton was thorough enough in his preparations that he tidied up his personal affairs in the event he would be killed. He even drafted a new last will and testament on July 9, a mere two days before the scheduled duel.

In the days leading up to the duel, Hamilton and Burr continued to socialize with one another in public. They behaved civilly while together because, after all, they were still gentlemen. Observers could not have deduced what lay in store for the two. The duel was meant to be secret, since the practice was outlawed in New York, where both men lived, and New Jersey, where the duel was scheduled to take place.[111]

At five in the morning on July 11th, Burr and Hamilton departed from separate Manhattan piers in boats to cross the Hudson River en route to Weehawken, New Jersey, in order to avoid raising suspicions about their plans. Burr and Van Ness arrived first. They left their oarsmen with their boat. Hamilton and Pendleton arrived shortly thereafter. Hamilton's oarsmen also remained in their boat and were joined by medical doctor David Hosack. It was customary to have a doctor present at a duel.

The seconds measured off ten paces so that Hamilton and Burr could take their places. After they were given the command to commence, two shots were fired. The seconds disagreed on who fired first. Hamilton's shot missed Burr, whether by intention or by accident. Burr's shot found its mark. Hamilton was struck in the abdomen in a shot that would prove fatal the following day. He was given a hero's funeral.

Burr was mistaken if he thought a consummated duel with Hamilton would resurrect his political fortunes. Instead, he was indicted for murder, but, at the time, he was back in Washington, DC, to finish his final months as vice president. He then spent several years in the Louisiana Territory and Europe before finally returning to Manhattan, where his murder charge was long forgotten. He lived the remainder of his years as a practicing attorney.

CHAPTER 3

AFFAIRS

Perhaps nothing elicits greater interest from the public than the salacious details surrounding an extramarital affair. Such scandals have occurred in public life for centuries, yet they never fail to pique the interest of the public.

The Blue Dress

Reports of womanizing dogged the married Bill Clinton for years. While serving as the Arkansas governor, there were rumors he was frequently sneaking around Little Rock carrying on one illicit romance after another. It was later learned that, while he pursued the White House, he had Arkansas state troopers ferry women to secret rendezvous, help spirit him away from the governor's mansion undetected, and serve as lookouts in case Hillary Clinton arrived unexpectedly.

The rumors died down, but didn't dissipate after he was elected president. It was widely believed he carried on trysts with prominent women, including a politician's daughter and an actress. Yet, it was a two-year affair with an unpaid White House intern nearly thirty years his junior that most damaged his legacy.

Twenty-one-year-old Monica Lewinsky had graduated from Lewis & Clark College in 1995, and through family connections with Democratic mega-donor William Kaye, landed an unpaid internship in the office of White House Chief of Staff Leon Panetta.[1] Her work consisted of low-level administrative tasks. Her access to President Bill Clinton didn't occur until after there was a federal government shutdown later that fall. Unable to bridge an impasse over fiscal year 1996 appropriations, Clinton vetoed spending measures, which shut down the federal government. The shutdown forced the mandatory furlough of tens of thousands of federal workers deemed to be non-essential.[2] The unpaid interns were given greater responsibility in order to fill the shortfalls.

In mid-November 1995, Clinton joined a birthday celebration in Panetta's office. Lewinsky was there. She took advantage of the opportunity and flashed her thong underwear to Clinton. He invited her to visit him a little later in his private study just off the Oval Office.

While alone in the private study, Clinton and Lewinsky kissed for a bit. Lewinsky left, only to return later, where they become more intimate. Lewinsky performed oral sex on the president for the first time. It wouldn't be the last.

Over the next twenty-one months, Clinton and Lewinsky had dozens of in-person and telephone contacts. During that period, the pair engaged in sexual activity on ten occasions, usually in the windowless hallway just outside the president's private study. Most often, Clinton would remain standing and would lean against the doorway of the nearby bathroom. Lewinsky performed oral sex on him during nine of the sexual encounters. One time, the pair had genital-to-genital contact, but the two never engaged in sexual intercourse.

Occasionally, Clinton would fondle and kiss Lewinsky's breasts. On a few occasions, Clinton fondled her genitals. Sometimes he did it through her underwear and other times he had direct contact. One time, Clinton inserted a cigar into Lewinsky's vagina, placed it in his mouth and said, "It tastes good."[3]

Clinton didn't allow his extramarital affair to interfere with the affairs of state. On one occasion, he spoke on the phone with Republican Congressman Sonny Callahan of Alabama while Lewinsky performed oral sex on him. Another time, she serviced him while he was speaking on the phone with his political consultant, Dick Morris.

White House officials took notice of Lewinsky's frequent meetings alone with Clinton. In April 1996, with the general election a half-year away, they transferred Lewinsky from her unpaid internship at the White House to a $31,000 annual salary position at the Pentagon in the Public Affairs Office. Clinton promised her he would bring her back after the general election in November. It was at this time that Lewinsky began referring to Clinton as "the creep."[4]

Instead of plotting Lewinsky's return to the White House, Clinton was engineering a plan to move her further away. He received considerable help from a pair of Washington power players. Clinton pal and politically connected lawyer, Vernon Jordan, was pulling out all the stops and phoning major firms in Manhattan in an effort to land Lewinsky a lucrative job in the Big Apple.[5] About the same time, US Ambassador to the United Nations Bill Richardson offered the love-struck young woman a position on his staff at the UN.[6]

The scandal became public on January 17, 1998, when the *Drudge Report* broke the story. Matt Drudge's eponymous website reported that *Newsweek* had the scoop on the affair, but the weekly magazine "killed a story that was destined to shake official Washington to its foundation." The author of the *Newsweek* exclusive was reporter Michael Isikoff. Ironically, Isikoff joined the *Newsweek* staff some years earlier after his then-employer, the *Washington Post*, killed another exclusive story that detailed Clinton's sexual advances on a low-level Arkansas state employee when Clinton was the Arkansas governor.[7]

Paula Jones was the state employee who Clinton made sexual advances toward. A few years later, Jones filed a sexual harassment suit against Clinton. Hillary Clinton called the suit "a nuisance."[8] During the course of litigation, Bill Clinton gave a deposition, which he called "a farce," and he said he resented having to testify.[9] Clinton lied when asked if he had had a sexual encounter with Lewinsky. He instructed Lewinsky, if asked, to also lie about their relationship.

After news broke of the president's extramarital affair with a White House intern, Clinton delivered a blistering denial. "I want you to listen to me," said an angry-looking Clinton while he wagged his finger. "I'm going to say this again: I did not have sexual relations with that woman, Miss Lewinsky. I never told anybody to lie, not a single time, never. These allegations are false."

Clinton's denial was a lie. Lying to the American people in a public statement is one thing. Lying in sworn testimony is another. So is obstructing justice, which is what Clinton did when he encouraged Lewinsky to give false testimony.

Many in the media doubted the claims attributed to Monica Lewinsky. She said she had sexual contact with the president. He denied it. But Lewinsky had physical evidence that backed her claims. She had in her possession a blue dress she wore during one of their sexual encounters. Clinton ejaculated on her dress and she decided not to have it cleaned. DNA testing confirmed it was Clinton's biological matter on her dress. Her claims were believed.

Clinton reached an out-of-court settlement with Jones and paid her $850,000. Judge Susan Webber Wright found Clinton in contempt of court. In her ruling, she found: "The record demonstrates by clear and convincing evidence that the President responded to plaintiffs' questions by giving false, misleading, and evasive answers that were designed to obstruct the judicial process." She then imposed a financial penalty of $91,000 against Clinton.

The Professional Conduct Committee of Arkansas revoked Clinton's law license for a period of five years and fined him $25,000. After he left the presidency, the US Supreme Court permanently disbarred Clinton from practicing law before the high court.

No doubt, there were probably dark days in 1998 when Bill Clinton was pondering what fate held in store for him. His extramarital affair had become public knowledge, and he was being forced to deal with the consequences. His close friend, Jesse Jackson, had been visiting the family in the private quarters of the White House, offering spiritual guidance during this period. This was quite ironic as will be seen in the next section.

The Love Child

Never shy about seeking out the limelight, Jesse Jackson felt it was his duty to counsel President Bill Clinton over his extramarital dalliance with a White House intern. The married Jackson even brought along his pregnant mistress to one such White House meeting with Clinton.

The scandal was not broken by a cable news channel, television broadcast network, or broadsheet newspaper. It was the result of aggressive investigative reporting by a supermarket tabloid. The *National Enquirer* had the exclusive story of Jesse Jackson's affair with one of his employees that resulted in an out-of-wedlock birth. At the time the scandal broke, in January 2001, Jackson was hosting a program on CNN titled "Both Sides with Jesse Jackson."

In an apparent attempt to blunt the story before the *National Enquirer* hit newsstands, Jackson issued a statement admitting he had an extramarital affair. "I am father to a daughter who was born outside of my marriage," Jackson announced. "I love this child very much and have assumed responsibility for her emotional and financial support since she was born."[10]

Jackson was trying to get ahead of an *Enquirer* story headlined, "Jesse Jackson's Love Child." The tabloid had a photograph of Jackson and his mistress posing with Bill Clinton in the Oval Office in December 1998. The baby was born in May 1999, making it very likely Jackson's mistress was about four months pregnant when she and Jackson posed with the president.

Jackson hired Karin Stanford away from her job as an assistant professor of African American studies at the University of Georgia and put her charge of the Rainbow/PUSH Washington, DC, office. A four-year affair followed. Some years earlier, Stanford had made Jackson the subject of her dissertation when she was pursuing her doctorate at Howard University. In 1997, what began as a college dissertation was published as a book titled *Beyond the Boundaries: Reverend Jesse Jackson in International Affairs.*

By the time the affair had become public, Stanford was already living on the West Coast. A Rainbow/PUSH spokesman claimed Jackson had been paying $3,000 a month in child support and had paid $40,000 toward relocating Stanford from Washington, DC, to Los Angeles after her daughter, Ashley, was born.[11] However, it was later learned that the moving expenses actually came from the coffers of Jackson's non-profit Rainbow/PUSH coalition, raising questions as to whether payments were appropriate.[12] Jackson's lawyers demanded Stanford sign a non-disclosure agreement as a condition of the child support payments. She refused.[13]

What made Jackson's mistress and illegitimate child scandal so salacious was the role of counselor he played in the Clinton-Lewinsky scandal. According to *Chicago Tribune* columnist Clarence Page, "The White House held up Jackson as a model of moral authority to whom Clinton was turning."[14] "[Jackson] went to the White House and prayed with President Clinton. They got down on their knees...in the residence," said former Clinton staffer turned ABC News pundit George

Stephanopoulos.[15] The hypocrisy in all of this was Jackson was counseling the married Clinton for an extramarital affair with a woman who worked for him at the same time that the married Jackson was carrying on an extramarital affair with a woman who worked for him.

When he announced the affair, Jackson stated he would be "taking some time off to revive my spirit and reconnect with my family."[16] His son, Democratic Representative Jesse Jackson Jr., of Illinois said, "[F]or the Jackson family, this is an intensely personal and private matter, and that is how we intend to deal with it."[17] It wasn't clear how much fence-mending Jackson needed to undertake with his family, and more specifically, with his wife. Years earlier, she addressed the topic of other women and her husband. "My portion of Jesse Jackson is mine, and when I say that let me explain," she said. "I can't spend too much time worrying about other women."[18]

The fallout over the affair could not have been more different in terms of the way Jackson and Stanford were treated. Years later she wrote, "I was attacked by friends, strangers, and the black press without mercy, my only support coming from a few close friends and family." She continued, "Black religious leaders and congregations prayed for him and his 'family,' but not for our daughter and me."[19]

About a decade after the scandal broke, Jackson stopped making child-support payments, according to Stanford. Once again, the *National Enquirer* highlighted the matter at supermarket checkout stands with the headline: "Jesse Jackson is a Deadbeat Dad!" According to the article, Jackson was not making the legally required monthly $400 minimum payment and was in arrears by nearly $12,000.[20]

Monkey Business

Gary Hart was young, handsome, and telegenic. He was only thirty-eight years old when he was first elected in 1974 as a Democratic Senator representing Colorado. After he was reelected to his second term in 1980, he began considering national office.

In early 1983, Hart announced his intention to seek the Democratic nomination for president. He would be challenging the Democratic Party establishment candidate, Walter Mondale. Mondale had once served as a senator from Minnesota. However, it was Mondale's four-year stint as vice president to Jimmy Carter that qualified him as the nominee in the eyes of the party elders.

Hart had some innovative ideas about how to get the party's nomination, which drew on his earlier political career before he was elected to the Senate. Senator George McGovern of South Dakota, who sought the Democratic nomination for the 1972 election, appointed Hart his campaign chairman.

Hart implemented a strategy not attempted by any previous candidate. Hart wanted McGovern to focus on the relatively quiet Iowa caucuses. If McGovern could register a strong win in Iowa, then it would give him the momentum needed to carry him into the New Hampshire primary and into legitimate primary battle with Senator Edmund Muskie of Maine, who was an early primary favorite.

The strategy worked. McGovern won the Iowa caucuses and eventually the Democratic Party nomination. However, the primary success did not carry over to the general election. McGovern was soundly trounced by Richard Nixon.

When he decided to run for the Democratic nomination, Hart was relatively unknown nationally and was a decided long shot. In his own presidential run, he once again adopted an unusual strategy. He began campaigning in New Hampshire in September 1983, a full six months before the Granite State's first-in-the nation primary election.

The 1984 primary process became a real dogfight between Mondale and Hart before the Minnesotan finally pulled away in the delegate count. Mondale would eventually lose the general election to Ronald Reagan in record-setting fashion.

Hart's 1984 primary loss set him up as a favorite for the 1988 election. Reagan would be finishing his second term, so the race would be for an open seat.

In early 1987, as campaigns were being assembled, rumors began swirling that Hart was a womanizer. That spring, Hart's campaign had been debating on how to respond to the allegations he had been unfaithful to his wife.

After it was learned that Hart and his mistress Donna Rice joined another couple on a trip from Miami to Bimini on a boat named *Monkey Business*, Hart said, "Those who would test my character are in for a surprise. I may bend, but I do not break."[21]

On May 8, 1987, Hart declared he would no longer be seeking the presidential nomination.[22]

The Mobster's Girlfriend

"Kennedy's recklessness in the affair, once it was public knowledge, was a blow to his image and to the image of Camelot."[23]

President John Kennedy's affair with Judith Campbell did not receive widespread notoriety until a dozen years after he was assassinated. However, there were those who knew of the romance beforehand, including the FBI and Chicago mob bosses.

Judith was born into the well-to-do Immoor family in Pacific Palisades, California. The Immoors didn't associate with the hoi polloi. Instead, they rubbed elbows with the Hollywood elite. Entertainer Bob Hope was a family friend. The Immoors were so tied into the Hollywood scene that, in 1952, at the age of eighteen, Judith married actor Billy Campbell.[24] Six years later, they were another divorced Hollywood couple.

Judith Campbell was extremely attractive and very popular. As she explained in her autobiography, after she divorced Billy Campbell, she never again dined at home or alone. She was on a date every single night of the month. This was easy to accomplish because she wasn't encumbered with job responsibilities. In fact, late nights every night didn't pose a problem for her. She didn't need to rise early each morning for work because she had family money. She usually spent her days sleeping, followed by primping for the next night out on the town.

Campbell briefly dated Frank Sinatra. He was the superstar entertainer of the day. Sinatra sang, appeared in movies, and headlined a hit show in Las Vegas. The relationship ended because his wild lifestyle proved too much for Judith. She later wrote that Sinatra's inviting another woman into bed with the two of them was more than she could handle. The couple had an amicable breakup, and she stayed friends with Sinatra. Occasionally, Sinatra would invite Campbell to see his show with the other members of the Rat Pack at Las Vegas's famed Sands Hotel.

It was at the Sands in February 1960 that Campbell was introduced to then-Massachusetts Senator John "Jack" Kennedy by Sinatra after one of his shows. Kennedy was in the early stages of his presidential campaign, a race he would go on to win the following November. In a matter of weeks, Campbell and Kennedy began a torrid romance that lasted for more than two years. Kennedy would often telephone Campbell late at night when he was traveling to gossip about where she'd been and whom she had seen.[25]

About a month after her affair began with Kennedy, Campbell traveled to Miami Beach to watch Sinatra perform at the Fontainebleau Hotel. After the performance, Sinatra introduced Campbell to Salvatore "Sam" Giancana. The name didn't mean anything to Campbell. She didn't know Giancana was a mob kingpin. Giancana headed Chicago's organized crime venture, called "The Outfit." During one of her late-night phone calls with Kennedy, Campbell filled him in on who she met that day. Kennedy replied that he knew Giancana. Kennedy's father, Joseph Kennedy, and Giancana had worked out an arrangement regarding Jack's run for the White House.[26]

Campbell had a sexual encounter with Kennedy at his Georgetown townhouse one night when Jackie was away. Afterward, Kennedy asked her to deliver a satchel to Giancana. Inside the satchel was $250,000. Campbell understood the money was intended to help Kennedy win the presidency. Campbell would repeat the money-drop process later that summer. Campbell explained that she didn't realize Giancana was a mobster at the time, but only thought of him as an important member of Kennedy's campaign team.[27] By some measures, Giancana was both.

Campbell continued to act as a courier, passing written notes between Kennedy and Giancana even after Kennedy was elected President. At one point, Kennedy told her Giancana was going to help America eliminate Cuban dictator Fidel Castro. Sometimes participating in her meet-ups with Giancana was John Rosselli, another mobster. Rosselli was simultaneously working with a CIA case officer who claimed to be an American businessman willing to fund the assassination of Castro.[28]

About a year into her role as a courier, Campbell began a sexual relationship with Giancana, while she was still sleeping with Kennedy. The FBI had been surveilling Giancana and Rosselli and quickly reached the conclusion that Campbell was "a high-class whore" passed between the two organized-crime figures. It was during the Democratic National Convention in July 1960 that the FBI became aware

Kennedy and Campbell were "having a tryst." Some agents became physically ill when they realized the Democratic nominee for president was behaving this way.[29]

Kennedy was rather brazen in his affair with Campbell. Some of their assignations occurred in the White House. Still, the affair didn't become public until after the Church Committee issued its report on CIA assassinations in 1975. The public not only learned that Kennedy had been engaged in an extramarital affair, but that his paramour was the go-between of the president and a mob boss.

The Argentine Firecracker

Congressman Wilbur Mills was one of the most powerful people in America. The Arkansas Democrat was the longtime chairman of the House Ways and Means Committee. In other words, he ran the tax-writing committee that affected everyone and everything.

A Harvard Law School graduate, Mills was first elected to Congress in 1938. By 1958, he became chairman of the powerful tax committee. He held this position for nearly two decades. He is often identified as being a key architect of President Lyndon Johnson's Medicare program, launched in 1966.

Mills's power and influence were so pervasive that he flirted with seeking the Democratic nomination for president in 1972. Unfortunately, his performance in the early primaries was disappointing, causing him to drop out of the race.

In July 1973, Wilbur Mills went to the Silver Slipper nightclub located in northwest Washington, DC. Nestled between an adult cinema and an adult bookstore, the Silver Slipper was a strip club, and the featured performer the night Mills arrived was an Argentinean immigrant named Annabel Battistella, who went by the stage names Fanne Foxe, and the Argentine Firecracker.[30]

In her biography, Battistella said that on the night Mills was there, he greeted her after her performance and lavished praise on her dancing.[31] Mills then invited Battistella and another woman to his apartment for a nightcap. Shortly thereafter, Mills and Battistella began an affair.

Battistella stopped dancing once she and Mills began dating. Yet, the pair often frequented the Silver Slipper together. The pair also frequently quarreled. Occasionally, the couple attended the Silver Slipper with several other people including Mills's wife, Clarine "Polly" Mills. Wilbur Mills was sometimes generous at the strip club, buying expensive bottles of wine. According to a pair of strippers, Mills spent as much as $1,700 one night, paying his bill in cash.[32]

About a month after Mills began dating Battistella, Mills and his wife moved into the Crystal Towers Apartments in Arlington, Virginia. It was the same apartment building where Battistella lived.

At about 2:00 a.m. on October 7, 1974, US Park Police stopped a Lincoln Continental near the Jefferson Memorial driving at a high speed with its headlights turned off. Behind the wheel was Albert Gapacini. Also in the car were Gloria Sanchez, Liliane Kassar, Battistella, and Mills.[33] Police believed all of the vehicle's occupants had been drinking, and Mills and Battistella were intoxicated. They noticed Mills had scratches on his face, and his nose was bleeding. Battistella had black eyes.[34]

Without warning, Battistella ran from the car and dove into the nearby Tidal Basin. The Tidal Basin is a man-made reservoir built in the 1800s. Planted along the Tidal Basin are many of the cherry trees given to the city by the Japanese government. Surrounding the basin are several memorials, including the Thomas Jefferson, George Mason, Franklin Roosevelt, and Martin Luther King, Jr., memorials.

Dressed in an evening gown, Battistella dove into the Tidal Basin in what appeared to be a half-hearted suicide attempt. Park Police officers fished her out. The car's occupants were booked and then released.

It took a few days of media inquiries before Mills finally addressed the incident. Even then, his statement didn't appear to square with the facts and defied credulity. He claimed that Battistella fell ill during an evening out with friends and he was merely trying to get her home safely.[35] The scratches and bloody nose occurred when he attempted to restrain Battistella from leaving the car. "In the ensuing struggle her elbow hit my glasses and broke them resulting in a number of small cuts around my nose," he explained.[36] In her 1975 biography, Battistella wrote that she and Mills had "a lover's spat [that]…escalat[ed] stupidly into a knock-down-drag-out battle… Both of [their] eyes were black and blue."[37]

Then, Mills did what so many politicians do. He blamed his absent wife for his predicament. She was "blaming herself for not accompanying us that night even with her broken foot," Mills said.[38]

Mills was safely reelected in November 1974, in what was a very good election year for Democrats following the Watergate scandal. However, only weeks later, he appeared with Battistella at a burlesque club in Boston. He appeared to be drunk. Word of this second public incident with Battistella led Mills to relinquish the tax committee chairmanship. He retired from Congress at the end of his term following the 1976 elections.

The Thirty-Year Affair

Franklin D. Roosevelt was appointed Assistant Secretary of the Navy in the Woodrow Wilson administration in 1913. He and his wife, Eleanor, moved from New York to Washington, DC. Eleanor was eager to fill the role as the wife of a senior government official. Protocol at the time dictated she become an active member of the social circuit. She was to call on and be called upon by the wives of other government dignitaries. In order to accomplish this task, she believed she needed a social secretary.[39]

Twenty-two-year-old Lucy Mercer lived with her mother and sister. Both her mother and father came from distinguished and wealthy families. An ancestor on her father's side was a signer of the Declaration of Independence. However, Lucy's parents began squandering both family fortunes not long after they married. Before long, the fortunes were gone.[40]

The Mercer marriage fell apart, and her parents separated, but didn't divorce. With the family's finances gone, Lucy needed to work. A mutual acquaintance recommended Lucy to Eleanor as her social secretary. Eleanor hired Lucy to work three days a week. Mercer's tasks consisted of arranging Eleanor's calendar, answering correspondence, paying the family bills, and occasionally assisting with the children.[41]

The thirty-one-year-old Franklin would often meet Mercer as she arrived for work just as he was leaving for the Navy Department. He would greet her with, "Ah, the lovely Lucy." Within short order, Mercer's role with the Roosevelts expanded. She would often join them at the dinner table when the Roosevelts were entertaining guests. She was attractive and personable. She was a welcomed addition.[42]

Roosevelt viewed his assistant Navy secretary assignment as merely one rung of the ladder toward his eventual prize, the presidency. He was following the path of his cousin, Teddy Roosevelt. In 1914, Franklin Roosevelt made himself a candidate for the US Senate, a race he was confident he would easily win. Instead, he was trounced as New York's counties lined up behind another Democrat. He would continue in Washington for a while longer.

Roosevelt was paid by check every two weeks. In turn, he would pass his paycheck to Mercer to deposit at the bank. Initially, the relationship between Franklin Roosevelt and Lucy Mercer was strictly professional. However, by 1916, a romance had blossomed. This was made easier because Eleanor and the children left the nation's capital each summer to vacation at the family retreat on Campobello Island, one of Canada's Fundy Islands. In spite of Eleanor's absence, Mercer kept reporting for work at the Roosevelts' rented Washington, DC, home.[43]

By 1917, the Roosevelt marriage had become strained. Husband and wife were sleeping in separate bedrooms. After the United States entered World War I, Roosevelt traveled to Europe to observe the fighting. He stayed for more than two months, from July through September 1918. He caught a dose of the Spanish flu on his travel back to the United States. He was so sick, he was removed from the ship on a stretcher and spent a month in New York before he could return to the Navy Department in Washington, DC.[44]

While he was recovering, Eleanor unpacked his things and discovered love letters between Franklin and Mercer. The now twenty-seven-year-old Lucy had enlisted in the Navy as a yeoman and, not surprisingly, was assigned to the executive offices of the Navy Department, where Franklin worked. Eleanor offered to divorce her husband. Recognizing divorce as political suicide, Franklin wanted to remain married. He made a promise to end his relationship with Mercer.[45] That promise was a lie.

Franklin Roosevelt and Lucy Mercer continued their illicit love affair off-and-on over the years until he died in 1945. It was nearly a thirty-year romance that spanned his term as assistant secretary of the Navy, his failed run for the US Senate, his unsuccessful campaign as the vice presidential running mate of Ohio Governor James Cox, his term as New York governor, and his election as president in 1932. It lasted, in fact, until he died in office.

In the thirty-two years they knew one another, Lucy Mercer served as Eleanor's social secretary and, later, as an indispensable member of the Roosevelt household. After Franklin promised Eleanor he would break off the relationship, the pair continued to see one another. In 1920, twenty-nine-year-old Lucy married Winthrop Rutherfurd, a widower nearly thirty years her senior. The well-to-do Rutherfurd owned homes in Europe and America, including a thirty-three-bedroom mansion in New Jersey. She stayed married to him until he died in 1944.

Franklin Roosevelt and Lucy Mercer Rutherfurd were aided in their affair by family, friends, and acquaintances, who were ever so mindful of keeping it a secret from Eleanor. It appears they were successful in this endeavor for twenty-six years.

While the affair was the subject of gossip among people in the Roosevelt orbit for years, it did not become public knowledge until 1966, when it was revealed in *The Time Between the Wars*, by Jonathan Daniels.[46] Ironically, Jonathan Daniels was the son of Josephus Daniels, who was the secretary of the Navy when Franklin Roosevelt was his assistant secretary.[47]

Hiking the Appalachians

In December 1998, Representative Bob Livingston of Louisiana made a startling confession to his fellow House Republicans. He admitted to having been unfaithful to his wife of thirty-three years. Livingston was the Speaker of the House-designate. It was expected he would assume the Speaker's ceremonial gavel when a new Congress was convened in January 1999.

Livingston received support for his admission across party lines from other Congressmen. However, not everyone was so forgiving. One unsympathetic congressman was fellow Republican Mark Sanford of South Carolina. "The bottom line is, Livingston lied," Sanford told a cable news channel. "He lied to his wife." Sanford's comments would appear ironic a decade later.

In mid-June 2009, it had become obvious that Governor Mark Sanford was missing. A member of the GOP, Sanford was serving his second term as South Carolina's governor. Prior to being elected in 2002, Sanford had spent three terms in the US House of Representatives.

On Monday, June 22, 2009, it was apparent to several people that the Palmetto State governor was nowhere to be found. It was almost as if he had disappeared off the face of the earth. The lieutenant governor did not know where he was. Neither did any of his political allies—or his political opponents. First Lady Jenny Sanford indicated she had not spoken to him for several days. Even his state police security detail, which usually provided protection, did not know where he was.

It appeared the state's chief executive had completely vanished. Calls to his cell phone went straight to voice mail.

The governor's staff said they knew where he was, but only vaguely. The governor, a spokesman announced, was hiking the Appalachian Trail. Governor's office spokesman, Joel Sawyer, stated the state's chief executive was clearing his head after an exhaustive legislative session. "He's an avid outdoorsman," Sawyer explained. This was true. Sanford had a love of the great outdoors. He was a committed runner.

The last anyone had seen of Sanford was the previous Thursday. He climbed into a black Suburban sports-utility-vehicle belonging to his security detail and drove off without disclosing to anyone other than his immediate office where he was going or how long he would be away.

"I cannot take lightly that his staff has not had communication with him for more than four days, and that no one, including his own family, knows his whereabouts," complained Lieutenant Governor André Bauer.[48]

The problem with the governor being cut off and completely out of touch with state officials, noted Senator Jake Knotts, was "only one man [has] authority to act in case of emergency."[49]

Sanford called his chief of staff the morning of Tuesday, June 23, to check in. Following the phone call, Sawyer publicly explained that Sanford was stunned to learn of the brouhaha over his disappearance and promised to return from his hiking trip the following day.

Many interested observers probably expected Sanford to drive back to Columbia, South Carolina, from some location on the Appalachian Trail. However, after a receiving a tip, an enterprising journalist intercepted the South Carolina governor in the terminal of Atlanta's Hartsfield-Jackson International Airport on June 24.

The governor admitted he was not hiking the Appalachian Trail, as his staff claimed. Sanford said he left his staff with the impression that

that was his intention, but he claimed he changed his mind at the last moment and decided to do something "exotic." That something "exotic" was a spur of the moment decision to fly to Buenos Aires, Argentina, to spend a few days driving along the coastal highway to clear his head.

Sanford's lie quickly unraveled when it became obvious that driving the coastal highway near Buenos Aires was not as head clearing as one might think. Someone could literally *walk* Avenida Rafael Obligado Costanera in less than an hour, since it was about two miles long.[50]

Later that same day, Sanford stood alone at a press conference and announced he had been unfaithful to his wife and was in Argentina seeing a woman with whom he had been having an affair. "I've been unfaithful to my wife. I've let down a lot of people. That's the bottom line," he told assembled press. His wife, Jenny, issued a statement that day that she had requested her husband move out of their Sullivan Island home after several months of marriage counseling. She had learned of the affair in January 2009.

Sanford had met María Belén Chapur during a trip to Uruguay in 2001. The pair met again during the 2004 Republican National Convention in New York. The two began a sexual relationship when Sanford took an official trip to Brazil in June 2008. Later in 2008, they met two more times for trysts in New York and the Hamptons.[51]

Their intimate relationship was followed by passionate emails between the two that read like they were sent by love-struck teenagers. In one email, Chapur wrote she could have "stayed [embracing] and kissing you forever." In a later email, he wrote, "Do you really comprehend how beautiful your smile is? Have you been told lately how warm your eyes are and how they softly glow with the special nature of your soul?" Each professed their love for the other.

On June 30, Sanford indicated he was still hopeful of reconciliation with his wife. As for Chapur, "This was a whole lot more than a simple affair; this was a love story. A forbidden one, a tragic one, but a love story at the end of the day."[52]

By August, Jenny Sanford had moved out of the governor's mansion with their four sons. By the end of 2009, she had filed for divorce, which was finalized the following March. Sanford declared Chapur his soul mate, and the pair got engaged, but that engagement ended in 2014.

Articles of impeachment were considered by the South Carolina Legislature, but the legislative body ultimately decided to censure Sanford. He finished out his term as governor in January 2011.

Sally

Once upon a time, newspaper publisher James Thomson Callender was an admirer of President Thomas Jefferson. Callender was favorable to the Republican Party. It was his caustic writings on the opposition Federalist Party that landed Callender in prison for violating the Seditions Act. Jefferson thought the Seditions Act was unconstitutional, so he pardoned Callender and ordered the US marshal to return the fine Callender paid.

Because of his support of Jefferson, Callender thought it only fitting that Jefferson appoint Callender the postmaster of the Richmond post office. Jefferson demurred. This is what may have caused Callender to turn on Jefferson and become a critic and political enemy.

In 1802, Callender published at length in his *Richmond Recorder* newspaper allegations that Jefferson and a household slave, Sally Hemings, had five children together.[53] Callender wrote that Hemings served as Jefferson's "concubine" and that her oldest son's features "bear a striking resemblance to those of the president himself." In later writings, Callender personally attacked Sally, calling her a "slut as common as the pavement," and referring to her children as "a litter."[54]

Republican-aligned newspapers attacked the allegations as scurrilous, while papers favorable to the Federalist Party were too willing to keep the Jefferson-Hemings story alive. Rumors of a relationship between Jefferson and Hemings continued throughout his presidency until recent years, when it's been generally accepted that Hemings bore Jefferson's children.

Jefferson had over one hundred slaves that worked at his home, Monticello. They were employed as field hands and house servants. Jefferson kept track of all the details regarding his slaves in a document he called the "Farm Book." In this book, he annotated personal information such as names (first names only), birth dates, and dates of death. He also listed the food and supplies issued to each slave.[55] His Farm Book included the names and dates of the five children of Sally Hemings. They were born from 1795 to 1808. While Jefferson wrote down the names of the fathers of children born to his other female slaves, he didn't list a father for any of Hemings's children. [56]

One biographer had written that Jefferson was often drawn toward forbidden love. Targets of his affections included the wife of a good friend, a widowed mother, the wife of an Englishman, and the slave Hemings. At the time, critics of the rumors claimed the rumors were perpetuated by abolitionists who wanted to discredit slavery.

Sally Hemings's son, Madison Hemings, wrote that his grandmother was the child of an English ship captain named Hemings and a slave who belonged to a Welshman named John Wayles. Captain Hemings tried to buy the child, named Betty Hemings, but Wayles turned down a lucrative offer. Betty bore six children with a slave father, and then another six with Wayles, who took her as his mistress after his third wife passed away. One of those six mixed-race children was Sally, Madison's mother.[57] Because Sally's mother was half-white and her father was white, she was classified as a quadroon.[58]

Wayles's previous wife was the mother of Martha Wayles, whom Jefferson married. This made Sally the half-sister of Martha Wayles Jefferson. It had been said that Sally "bore a striking resemblance to her half-sister, Jefferson's deceased wife."[59]

Martha passed away in 1782 after ten years of marriage to Jefferson. In 1784, Jefferson was appointed US ambassador to France. His oldest daughter, fourteen-year-old Martha, accompanied him to Paris. His two younger daughters remained in Virginia. Then, in May 1787, Jefferson welcomed to Paris his eight-year-old daughter, Maria. Joining her was fourteen-year-old Sally Hemings, who was serving as Maria's caregiver.[60] Sally's older brother, James, was already in Paris. Jefferson brought him along when he first arrived in Paris in order to have James trained as a chef.

Because slavery was illegal in France, visitors with slaves would refer to them as servants. Jefferson did this in addition to paying both James and Sally salaries. To anyone outside of the family, James and Sally were salaried servants. It was in Paris that some speculate Thomas Jefferson and Sally Hemings may have begun their affair.[61]

In France, James and Sally could have petitioned the Admiralty Court and immediately been ordered freed. Both spoke French, and it was fashionable in Parisian society to hire African or mixed-race servants. Jefferson freed James after their return, but only after James taught his brother how to cook in the French style.[62]

At the time, law prohibited mixed-race marriage. It was widely known in the South that such relationships existed. Yet there was an expectation that the men involved in mixed-race relationships were to be discreet about it.[63]

Records point to Sally having five children. At least four were known to have grown to adulthood. There were two boys, named Madison and Eston, and a pair of girls named Beverly and Harriett. The boys were so light skinned that in the 1830 census both were listed as white.[64]

In his will, Jefferson freed Madison and Eston. By not pursuing them after they left Monticello without permission, Jefferson effectively freed Beverly and Harriett, as well. Jefferson did not free Sally in his will, but requested his daughter to do so after his death.[65]

DNA testing in 1998 proved that a Jefferson male was the father of Eston, but it could not be proved conclusively that the male was Thomas Jefferson. Still, there is widespread agreement that it was Thomas Jefferson who fathered Eston and perhaps all of Sally Hemings's children.[66]

The Intern

Robert Levy called the Metropolitan Police Department of the District of Columbia to report that neither he nor his wife, Susan, had heard from their daughter over the previous five days. The Levys' daughter, pretty twenty-four-year-old Chandra, had completed her paid internship with the Federal Bureau of Prisons and was due to head back to the University of Southern California.[67]

Levy was pursuing a graduate degree at USC when she took the Bureau of Prisons internship in Washington, DC, during her last semester of coursework in fall 2000. Levy was scheduled to graduate from USC in May 2001 with a degree in public administration.

The Levys apparently had not heard from Chandra since May 1. That was also the last time any of her known friends or acquaintances had reported seeing the girl with the head of dark hair.

DC police officers visited the college student's apartment. The apartment manager let them into the apartment, but they did not find any signs of foul play. The Levys also called area hospitals to see if their daughter had been admitted.[68]

There was intrigue with the disappearance. Family members reported to the police that Chandra had been having an affair with a married congressman.

Months earlier, in fall 2000, Levy and another USC student visited the Rayburn House Office Building. This building housed the office belonging to Democratic US Congressman Gary Condit, who represented California's 15th congressional district. He was Levy's hometown congressman.

The fifty-two-year-old Condit met with Levy and a friend in his congressional office, and then he personally gave the girls a guided tour of the US Capitol. Congressmen are helpful in tracking down a missed Social Security paycheck or in responding to a constituent's letter urging the member to vote a certain way on an issue. It's nearly unheard of for a congressman to take time out of his day to give a personal tour of the Capitol to a pair of twenty-something visitors.

In a matter of weeks, Condit and Levy were engaged in a full-blown affair. She would visit his Adams-Morgan geographic bachelor* apartment two to three times each week, often spending the night. Because he was married, the pair would generally remain inside his apartment, eating meals and watching television.

This wasn't Condit's first affair with a college-aged student. The eighteen-year-old daughter of a Modesto minister had carried on an affair with Condit seven years earlier. After he learned of the affair, the minister convinced his daughter to break it off.[69] Another college student engaged in a long affair with Condit in the mid-1990s. He even gave her a job in his DC congressional office. She eventually broke it off after experiencing pangs of guilt for dating the married congressman.[70]

There were more than just young women in their late teens and early twenties. Condit had a yearlong affair with a thirty-eight-year-old flight attendant that began in the months before his tryst with Levy.[71]

---

*   A "geographic bachelor" is a slang-term, commonly used by the military, to refer to the situation when the family lives in one location and the servicemember lives in another.

Levy's internship with the Bureau of Prisons should have ended when she completed the degree requirements for her master's degree in December. However, she was not ready to leave the nation's capital, as she wanted to continue her affair with Condit.

While Levy and Condit spent a considerable amount of time together, it was only under very strict rules laid down by the congressman. Condit had a system in place by which Levy would call a telephone number that had an answering machine that played soft music in the background. She was to leave a message, and he would get in touch with her. The pair concocted cover stories if they were ever recognized in public.[72]

Chandra Levy was among the lucky few that were going to attend the ball following the inauguration of George W. Bush as the 43rd US president on January 21, 2001. She was given a pair of tickets by Condit. He was unable to join her for obvious reasons. He was still a married man. So, Chandra invited an acquaintance who was a University of Southern California graduate living in DC. Robert Kurkjian was a few years her senior. The two were going as friends. Chandra had told him that she had a boyfriend, but that the boyfriend was not accompanying her to the ball.[73]

In the days before she disappeared, Levy unexpectedly joined Kurkjian at his apartment to eat pizza and pour out her heart over having to return to California and leave behind the unnamed married member of congress she was dating. Kurkjian attempted to convince her she was being played. Kurkjian doubted the sincerity of Condit's promise to Levy that he was going to leave Congress, become a lobbyist, divorce his wife, and marry Chandra. Levy was unconvinced by Kurkjian's arguments. In Kurkjian's view, Chandra Levy was "brainwashed."[74]

By mid-summer, Gary Condit's affair with Levy had become public knowledge. On August 23, 2001, Condit sat down and conducted a pair of back-to-back television interviews in an attempt to get his political career back on track. In March 2002, he was defeated in the Democratic primary. Condit left Congress as the end of his term in January 2003.

The missing person case, which had riveted the nation, quickly disappeared from public on the morning of September 11, 2001.

The Set Up

Alexander Hamilton was a bastard child born out of wedlock in the British West Indies. He was orphaned by the age of eleven. Due to his natural talents, he was sponsored to travel to the American colonies in order to continue his education. Hamilton attended King's College (today known as Columbia University) in New York City and earned his law degree.

Like many of his contemporaries, Hamilton participated in the American Revolutionary War. He began as an artillery officer and eventually became the aide-de-camp to General George Washington.[75]

After the war, Hamilton was appointed to represent the state of New York in the Congress of the Confederation. This was an early effort of the newly liberated colonies to begin self-governance.

Hamilton was an early leader of the Annapolis Convention, an attempt to improve upon the Articles of Confederation, which Hamilton and others saw as a meager effort to form a robust national government. Hamilton thought the Articles of Confederation did not allow for the proper instruments of government that he thought were necessary for the new nation.

It was at the subsequent Philadelphia Convention in which the Constitution was drafted. However, the colonies did not initially ratify the constitution. So, it fell upon Hamilton, James Madison, and John Jay to author the *Federalist Papers*. These were a series of essays published in installments that advocated for the adoption of the Constitution.

The trio kept their identities secret by publishing under the pseudonym "Publius." Seventy-seven essays were published in a ten-month period between October 1787 and August 1788. The essays appeared in the *New York Packet* and the *Independent Journal*. A two-volume publication included a total of eighty-five essays.

The *Federalist Papers* are credited with having made the difference in convincing the thirteen original colonies to ratify the Constitution.

After Washington was elected President, he appointed Hamilton as the Secretary of the Treasury. Hamilton served from 1789 to 1795. As secretary, Hamilton established the nation's founding economic policies, including the establishment of the government-owned Bank of the United States, and the ability of the federal government to fund state debt.

While serving as treasury secretary, the married, thirty-six-year-old Hamilton began an affair with twenty-three-year old Maria Reynolds, who was also married. One day, Maria went unannounced to Hamilton's Philadelphia home and claimed she had been abandoned by her husband, James Reynolds. Maria asked if Hamilton would give her enough money so that she and her infant daughter could travel to her family in New York.

Hamilton agreed to give her the money and visited her home later that evening in order to deliver it. The pair had a sexual encounter that night. Thus began an affair that lasted three years.[76]

James Reynolds, the husband of Maria Reynolds, discovered the affair, but rather than demand he defend his honor with Hamilton, as was customary at the time, Reynolds instead used this as an opportunity to blackmail Hamilton.[77]

Over the course of the three-year affair, Hamilton gave James Reynolds about $1,100 in hush money, a princely sum in those days.[78] Hamilton was never quite certain if Maria was "sincerely smitten with him," or if he was the victim of "a pair of lowlife tricksters."[79]

Reynolds became embroiled in a speculation scheme involving unpaid wages due to Revolutionary War veterans.[80] Reynolds attempted to weasel his way out of the mess by implicating Hamilton as an accomplice, claiming the hush money was actually an investment in the speculation.[81] Reynolds reasoned Hamilton would rather cover up for Reynolds than risk exposure of the affair with Maria Reynolds, and thereby tarnish his reputation.

Reynolds was wrong. Hamilton confessed to the affair and explained himself to Virginia Senator James Monroe and Representatives Frederick Muhlenberg of Pennsylvania and Abraham Venable of Virginia, who were serving as congressional investigators (Monroe would later be elected the 5th president of the United States). Hamilton even turned over the collection of love letters and other correspondence he had received from Maria and James Reynolds. The content of those letters was proof Hamilton had paid blackmail money to James Reynolds, and thus exonerated Hamilton of any wrongdoing regarding the speculation scheme.

Believing the affair had no impact on his official duties, the investigators agreed to keep the affair under wraps. However, the love letters

Hamilton turned over to Monroe and Muhlenberg would later come into play in publicly exposing the sex scandal.

Monroe was a friend and confidant of Thomas Jefferson. Hamilton and Jefferson were political and personal enemies. Monroe turned the letters over to Jefferson. The letters eventually made their way to the possession of a pamphleteer named James Thomas Callender. The letters were published, thereby exposing the affair. Hamilton responded by admitting the affair in a ninety-five-page document he titled, *Observations on Certain Documents*.

Hamilton died a few years later when he was mortally wounded during his duel with Aaron Burr. Interestingly, Burr was the attorney who represented Maria Reynolds when she divorced James after Hamilton ended the affair with her.[82]

CHAPTER 4

POLITICAL

"[Trump's opponents have] focussed [sic] on the possibility that Trump colluded with Russia, and that this, along with other crimes, might be exposed by the probe being conducted by the special counsel, Robert Mueller."

—Jane Mayer, *Vanity Fair*[1]

Petticoat Affair

On July 18, 1816, at seventeen years of age, Margaret "Peg" O'Neale married thirty-nine-year-old John Bowie Timberlake. After a series of failed business ventures and mounting debts, Timberlake returned to an earlier career as a merchant seaman. He was gone for months at a time. It was rumored that, while he was away, his wife was unfaithful to him. There was even speculation that others may have fathered the three children she bore.

That Peg Timberlake may not have been faithful to her absent husband was not surprising. As an adolescent, she had had a reputation of being flirtatious and on more than one occasion attempted to elope from her parents' home with someone she had recently met.

Her father, William O'Neale, owned the Franklin House in Washington, DC. It was a combination boarding house and tavern. Many of society's finest, including bachelor congressmen, members of Congress whose wives remained in their home states, and military officers, often boarded at the Franklin. The tavern was also a destination for visitors to the nation's capital. The owner's teenage daughter was known to engage in bawdry conversation with the lads and was rumored to have been sexually active with many.

John Timberlake took his own life while his ship was anchored in the Balearic Islands on April 2, 1828.[2] It was rumored he committed suicide over his wife's infidelity.[3] Because her husband was away for long periods of time, Peg Timberlake was used to life without him.[4] That may have accounted for why she broke society's norms during the expected period of bereavement.

Andrew Jackson was a boarder at the Franklin House when he was a US Senator. Like so many other Franklin House patrons, Jackson was taken with the twenty-four-year-old woman he called "Little Peg" when he first met her in 1823. Jackson's interest in Peg was more as father figure than as a suitor.[5] He may have become enamored of Peg because her exuberant personality and sullied reputation may have reminded Jackson of his wife.

A close friend of Jackson was Major John Henry Eaton. While serving as a senator in Washington, Eaton had been living at Franklin House. Eaton had become smitten with the recently widowed Mrs. Timberlake. After Jackson was elected president in 1828, Eaton asked and received the president-elect's encouragement to propose to the widow.[6]

Upon agreeing to marry, the two swiftly settled on a date. Unfortunately, to observers, the widow had not waited a sufficient amount of time following her late husband's death before remarrying. It had been less than a year since he died. Friends were concerned the marriage would damage the reputation of Eaton, and they tried to persuade him to delay. He did not.[7]

Mrs. Margaret Bayard Smith was a chronicler of polite society in Washington, DC, at the time.[8] She wrote that Peg was "a lady whose reputation, her previous connections with him [Eaton] before and after her husband's death, had totally destroyed…She has never been admitted into good society, is very handsome and of not an inspiring character and violent temper."[9] In sum, she was a bad and brazen woman.[10]

The couple were married on New Year's Day 1829. If Eaton thought the marriage would quell the rumors about the new bride, then he was sadly mistaken. There was already bad blood in Washington, DC, as Jackson had won a hard-fought political victory against an incumbent president, John Quincy Adams. Jackson's intention to appoint Eaton as his Secretary of War made matters worse. To have the husband of such a scandalous woman serve in the cabinet was unthinkable.

The role of political wives in the early nineteenth century was to join the entertainment circuit. Because of her reputation as a loose woman, the newly married Mrs. Eaton wasn't welcomed on the circuit by the other wives. Adding to the drama was that the recently widowed Jackson, whose wife Rachel had died a month after his election, had asked Peg Eaton to help oversee his inauguration festivities.

This was more than the other wives of Washington could tolerate. "Peg had become the most scandalous woman in Washington and a constant source of gossip among the city's newspapers, social crowd, and most important, the wives of Congress and Jackson's new cabinet."[11] The wives boycotted Jackson's inauguration and the attendant activities. This became known as the "Petticoat Affair."

The wives also refused to attend a formal dinner event with their husbands that would kick off the new administration. The boycott by the wives caused the husbands to decline to attend the cabinet dinner. Close friends and advisors tried to convince Jackson to defuse the entire situation by removing Eaton from his cabinet. But he refused.

It took considerable cajoling by Jackson before the cabinet dinner was finally held on November 1829—nine months after originally scheduled.

Jackson's administration limped along as a result of the Petticoat Affair, but also because he was surrounded by political enemies. Foremost among them was John C. Calhoun. Calhoun was Adams's vice president when Jackson defeated Adams in his reelection bid. As much as Calhoun and Jackson despised one another, Jackson was pressured to retain Calhoun as his vice president. Calhoun took advantage of every opportunity to slow Jackson's agenda.

Finally, in April 1831, Martin Van Buren offered to resign as Jackson's secretary of state. Eaton also resigned. This gave Jackson the pretext to completely reorganize his cabinet and replace political enemies with loyal supporters. Calhoun viewed Van Buren as his main competition for the presidency. He also thought the Petticoat Affair had so damaged Jackson's reputation that it would be in Calhoun's best interest to distance himself from Jackson. So, he resigned as vice president.

Instead of collapsing from the Petticoat Affair, Jackson persevered. He appointed Van Buren as his new vice president. Van Buren, with the endorsement of Jackson in the 1836 election, beat Calhoun as the next president.

Peg Eaton's scandalous reputation lasted into her later years. After her husband died, the now wealthy fifty-nine-year-old Peg hired a nineteen-year-old Italian dance instructor named Antonio Buchignani to teach dance lessons to her granddaughter. He apparently had a few dance moves to teach the young girl's grandmother. In spite of a forty-year age difference, Peg and Antonio married.[12]

The Hoax

On November 28, 1987, just two days after Thanksgiving, a fifteen-year-old girl was found by police wrapped in a trash bag in Wappingers Falls, New York, about a ninety-minute drive north of New York City. She was filthy. Her clothes were burned and torn. She was covered in feces and had racial slurs written on her. Tawana Brawley had been missing for four days when she was found. She told authorities she had been held in a wooded area for several days where she was repeatedly raped by a gang of white men including a police officer.

A sexual assault examination of Brawley was conducted, but medical authorities came up with startling results. There was no evidence a sexual assault had occurred. Nor was there any evidence Brawley had been exposed to the below-freezing elements that were present when she claimed to have been in the woods for several days. There was no missing-person report filed on the fifteen-year-old. She had recently brushed her teeth. Forensic evidence suggested she wrote the racial slurs on her body, as they were written upside down. There was even a report she was sighted at a party during the time she claimed to have been abducted. Her story appeared fabricated.

Because there were allegations of police involvement, Democratic New York Governor Mario Cuomo appointed State Attorney General Robert Abrams as a special prosecutor to investigate the matter. A grand jury was convened in February 1988 to look into the matter.

Al Sharpton immediately became Brawley's advisor. Sharpton would later gain a national reputation as a race-baiting hustler who would make outrageous claims of racist behavior. Joining him as advisor were controversial attorneys Alton Maddox, Jr. and C. Vernon Mason. The Tawana Brawley case quickly devolved into a circus-like atmosphere.

After early statements to police, both Brawley and her parents, on the advice of Sharpton and the attorneys, refused to participate further in an investigation.[13] Although Brawley and her family were not speaking, Sharpton and the two lawyers were doing plenty of talking.

According to the trio of Brawley advisors, groups conspiring with state and local officials to cover up the involvement of a white police officer and others were the Irish Republican Army, Ku Klux Klan, and the Mafia.[14] The episode got more bizarre by the day.

Nation of Islam leader Louis Farrakahn spoke to a group of one thousand protestors chanting, "Death to the KKK."[15] "When the courts won't find a white man guilty for a crime he committed, then *we* try *them*. Then we execute them," he exhorted.[16] Filmmaker Spike Lee included an image of a graffiti message reading, "Tawana told the truth," in one of his films.[17] Poet Amiri Baraka told a rally, "The police, prominent people, raped Tawana."[18]

Sharpton and the attorneys began soliciting contributions on behalf of the families. Reportedly, thousands of dollars were mailed to the advisors.[19] There was no public accounting of how much money was raised or how it was spent.

A couple of days after Brawley's discovery, part-time Fishkill, New York, police officer Harry Crist Jr., committed suicide. That officer, Sharpton and others suggested, was involved in the alleged abduction and rape. Fortunately, Crist had an alibi. Steven Pagones was the assistant district attorney for Dutchess County. Pagones explained that he and two other men were with Crist shopping in Danbury, Connecticut, during the time period in question. Additionally, Crist explained his own suicide by leaving a note that stated he was upset over the breakup with his girlfriend earlier in the day, and he was despondent over his failure to get hired as a state trooper.[20]

Sharpton, Maddox, and Mason countered that Pagones was lying. The three claimed Pagones was a racist and one of the alleged rapists.[21] In short order, people began stalking Pagones at work and at home. They screamed obscenities at him in public. He received threatening telephone calls. People following Sharpton's lead insisted Pagones was involved in the alleged sexual assault. However, a criminal investigation produced sixty witnesses who could vouch for Pagones's whereabouts during the four days of the alleged abduction.[22]

Perry McKinnon joined the team of Sharpton and the lawyers in January 1988 and quit a few months later. He was a former police officer who wanted to assist Brawley. He came forward in June and said Sharpton, Maddox, and Mason knew Brawley concocted her story from the very beginning. The allegations were a "pack of lies," McKinnon claimed. [23] The goal of Sharpton, Maddox, and Mason was an attempt to build their reputations, according to McKinnon. He quoted Sharpton as saying, "We beat this, we will be the biggest niggers in New York."[24]

After her initial interview, Brawley and her family refused to cooperate with investigators. Her mother, Glenda Brawley, was sentenced to thirty days in jail in June 1988 for refusing to testify at a grand jury hearing. Glenda Brawley evaded arrest for weeks before finally fleeing New York State with Tawana and the rest of their family.

The grand jury overruled State Attorney General Robert Abrams and voted to subpoena Tawana Brawley to appear before panel. Abrams had argued against it.[25] Brawley was subpoenaed but refused to appear.

A final report was issued by the grand jury in October 1988. The grand jury reached the conclusion that Brawley's allegations were fabricated because Brawley was fearful of getting into trouble for leaving home for several days. The four days she was away from home included a visit to her incarcerated boyfriend. She told a witness she was afraid of her mother's live-in boyfriend, Ralph King, who previously punished her for misbehaving, including staying out all night and skipping school. King once tried to beat Tawana at a police station after she was arrested for shoplifting. The temper-prone King had served seven years in prison for murdering his wife, Wanda Ann, by shooting her in the head four times in 1970.[26]

The grand jury took the rare step of also exonerating Pagones of any involvement in the Tawana Brawley incident. The attack on his reputation and the harassment he endured led Pagones to file a defamation lawsuit against Brawley, Sharpton, Maddox, and Mason in order to set the matter straight. Ten years would pass before he would get his day in court.[27]

In the months-long defamation trial, television pundit Geraldo Rivera arrived at the courthouse as a defense witness for Sharpton.

Rivera was barred from testimony because he did not have any information relevant to the defamation claims. He arrived because he wanted to defend Sharpton. "I believe history will ultimately regard him as one of the great civil-rights leaders in America," he told a media outlet.[28]

The jury found Sharpton liable for making seven defamatory statements about Pagones. Maddox made two, and Mason made one.[29] Brawley lost her defamation case by default in 1991 when she refused to participate in any of the legal proceedings. The jury awarded Pagones more than $500,000 in damages to be paid by Brawley, Sharpton, Maddox, and Mason.

Brawley fled to Virginia and dropped out of sight for several years. Maddox had his law license suspended over his role in the affair. Mason was later disbarred and became a Baptist minister.[30] Sharpton made a couple of failed runs for elected office and then was hired as television host by MSNBC.

Meddling

After World War II, the United States was promoting democracy and capitalism in the far reaches of the globe. The Soviet Union was imposing socialism everywhere it could, subjugating millions of people to misery. It was the first time in human history that the entire planet was the battleground for competing ideologies. The Cold War was begun.

Throughout the Cold War, the United States and the Soviet Union played a cat-and-mouse game, as each attempted to influence governments state by state. One tactic was influencing democratic elections in an attempt to achieve preferred outcomes. From funding candidates and parties to planting favorable news stories, both nations meddled in the democratic elections of other states. Russia continued this behavior after the breakup of the USSR.

According to a 2016 paper by postdoctoral fellow Dov Levin at UCLA, the Soviet Union (and later, Russia) and the United States meddled in democratic elections 117 times between 1946 and 2000. Both nations would "meddle in an election of another country in favor of a particular candidate or specific party."[31] The Soviet Union/Russia meddled thirty-six times, and the United States more than double that, at eighty-one times. Included were successful US-engineered coups d'état in Iran and Guatemala in 1953 and 1954, respectively.

Aside from the obvious coup results, meddling generally had little impact in other nations, or in the United States Levin wrote, "Electoral interventions by major powers in US presidential elections have historically been ineffective or counterproductive."[32]

The most recent American attempt to influence another country's democratic election was in 2015. A bipartisan Senate investigation reported that the Obama administration funneled money to a third-party group in Israel. The grant money was not permitted for election activity; however, "OneVoice used the campaign infrastructure and resources built, in part, with State Department grant funds to support V15." The V15 was a political group working to defeat Prime Minister Benjamin Netanyahu.[33]

A month before the 2016 US election, the Department of Homeland Security and the Director of National Intelligence issued a joint statement. The two agencies were "confident" that recent email hacks of the Democratic National Committee and Hillary Clinton campaign chairman John Podesta were directed by the Russian government. Nonetheless, the two agencies expressed confidence in state election systems, stating, "It would be extremely difficult for someone, including a nation-state actor, to alter actual ballot counts of election results."[34]

The November 8, 2016, presidential election results stunned most observers. Based on polling, former Secretary of State Hillary Clinton was the frontrunner throughout the entire campaign. She was the presumptive 45th president. How was career politician Clinton to explain her unexpected loss to political novice Donald Trump?

Liberal journalists Jonathan Allen of *Bloomberg News* and Amie Parnes of *The Hill* newspaper were granted extraordinary access to the Clinton campaign for a book they were co-authoring on the Democratic nominee's campaign.[35] Regarding post-election deliberations, they wrote, "Hillary declined to take responsibility for her own loss." Clinton's senior advisors "assembled her communications team at the Brooklyn headquarters to engineer the case that the election wasn't entirely on the up-and-up…[T]hey went over the script they would pitch to the press and the public. Already, Russian hacking was the centerpiece of the argument."[36]

Clinton blamed her election loss on the Russians. However, the Obama administration issued a statement: "We believe our elections were free and fair from a cybersecurity perspective."[37]

In a matter of weeks, the narrative shifted from a "free and fair" election to a stolen election. Outgoing officials from the Obama administration, including former National Intelligence Chief James Clapper, claimed without proof that Russia won the election for Trump.[38] Often implying he had classified intelligence backing his claims, former CIA Director John Brennan insisted that Trump colluded with Russia.[39]

Media outlets piled on, with news anchors and pundits repeating fantastical claims without evidence. The *Washington Post* and the *New York Times* shared the 2018 Pulitzer Prize for twenty stories alleging meetings and activities involving the Russians and Trump and others. Some of these stories have been proven false or lack corroboration.

CNN completely jettisoned its newsgathering and reporting roles and engaged in near continuous punditry with oddball guests. Disgraced anti-Trump lawyer Michael Avenatti appeared on CNN at least sixty-five times in a two-month period.[40] At press time, Avenatti was facing several allegations of criminal behavior and domestic abuse. In the twenty-two months between May 2017 and March 2019, there were 533,074 web articles published on the topic of Trump and Russian collusion. These generated 245 million interactions on Twitter and Facebook.[41]

In early January 2017, a declassified version of a US intelligence assessment was publicly released. It suggested Russian President Vladimir Putin authorized election meddling in retaliation for US attacks. "Putin publicly pointed to the [2016] Panama Papers disclosure and the [2010] Olympic doping scandal as US-directed efforts to defame Russia." Also, Putin blamed Clinton "for inciting mass protests against his regime in late 2011 and early 2012," coinciding with duma and presidential elections, respectively.[42]

According to the report, most of the election meddling consisted of news stories planted in Russia-based media outlets including RT (formerly Russia Today) and Sputnik.[43] RT and Sputnik are government-funded news outlets, much like Voice of America, BBC and Al Jazeera are government-funded. Neither Russian news organization is a news destination for most Americans. To suggest they were election influencers is a stretch.

Additionally, Moscow thought Trump could "achieve an international counterterrorism coalition against the Islamic State in Iraq."[44] Clinton was the secretary of state when President Barack Obama attempted to topple Syrian President Bashar al-Assad, leading to the rapid rise of the Islamic State in Iraq and Syria, which Obama arrogantly dismissed as the "jayvee team."[45]

Also in January 2017, adolescent-focused website BuzzFeed, infamous for memes and silly lists, published the Steele Dossier. The dossier was a thirty-five-page document authored by a British citizen purportedly using Russian sources. Paid for by the Clinton campaign and Democratic National Committee, the dossier made outlandish claims involving Trump and others connected to him. The demonstrably false dossier was widely debunked.*

Yet, in 2016, the Federal Bureau of Investigation had used the unverified dossier to obtain warrants from the Foreign Intelligence Surveillance Act (FISA) court to conduct surveillance on Trump and others, alleging there was collusion with Russia. FBI officials did not properly disclose to the FISA court the origin of the dossier, or the fact that it was funded by Trump's election opponent.

The FISA court's role is to approve investigations into a foreign power or the American agent of a foreign power. In this case, it was used to launch surveillance of an American citizen who happened to be the presidential nominee of the political party out of power.

In spring 2017, FBI Deputy Director Andrew McCabe secretly opened an investigation on Trump not based on any alleged crime, but because he feared he might be fired.[46]

Months-long investigations by the House Permanent Select Committee on Intelligence and the Senate Select Committee on Intelligence found no evidence of any coordination between the Trump campaign and Russia.

On May 17, 2017, Deputy Attorney General Rod Rosenstein appointed former FBI Director Robert Mueller as a special counsel.

---

* The author served in the US Intelligence Community for twenty-six years. No competent intelligence professional would give any credence to such a cartoonish, poorly written document that contained preposterous falsehoods.

Mueller was charged with investigating "any links and/or coordination between the Russian government and individuals associated with the campaign of President Donald Trump." He was also to investigate "any matters that arose or may arise directly from the investigation."[47]

Rosenstein's memo did not cite one crime Trump or others were suspected of committing. "Coordination" is not a criminal act, no matter how ominous or unsavory it may sound. Rosenstein's memo was a broad directive that gave Mueller wide latitude to investigate whatever he chose. Interestingly, coordination between individuals associated with the campaign of Hillary Clinton and Russians, which was intended to influence the election outcome, was studiously ignored by Mueller.

Mueller assembled a massive team of nineteen Washington, DC, lawyers, at least a dozen of whom were political donors to Clinton or other Democratic candidates,[48] about forty FBI agents, and dozens of support staff. For nearly two years, an investigation was conducted with well-orchestrated leaks to favored media outlets, including the *New York Times*, *Washington Post*, and CNN. More than 2,800 subpoenas were issued, dozens of wiretaps placed, 500 witnesses interviewed, and more than 500 search warrants executed.

Some of Mueller's team were embroiled in controversy. A senior FBI official was carrying on an extramarital affair with an FBI attorney. The pair had sent thousands of text messages back-and-forth discussing schemes to "stop" Trump from being elected president.[49] Mueller's lead prosecutor was found to have engaged in unethical conduct when he threatened witnesses in a previous investigation.[50]

According to the attorney general's summary of Mueller's March 2019 report, "The investigation did not establish that members of the Trump Campaign conspired or coordinated with the Russian government in its election interference activities." Nor did Mueller's report offer any evidence indicative of obstruction of justice although Mueller suggested he could not exonerate Trump. This is worth elaborating on because contemporaneous reporting grossly distorted the reality.

For over two hundred years, the American judicial system has been built upon a presumption of innocence. This includes during investigation, arrest, charging, and a courtroom trial. Only after an individual has been convicted does the presumption of innocence disappear. The claim Mueller did not "exonerate" Trump during his investigation is a political construct that has no meaning. No one ever has to be exonerated during a legal proceeding because they are forever presumed innocent until convicted.

Mueller's creative wordsmithing implying possible obstruction of justice ran counter to the plain language of the Constitution. According to Article II, all "executive Power shall be vested in a President." The only entities that are not an extension of the executive branch are the legislative and judicial branches (addressed in Articles I and III, respectively). As unpopular and as unseemly as it might be, Trump had the constitutional authority to hire, fire, and direct anyone and everyone in the executive branch as he saw fit, including Mueller. This is why the Constitution's framers gave Congress the authority to impeach.

In spite of Mueller's Herculean efforts to imply otherwise, an obstruction allegation would have been nearly impossible to prove since there was no underlying crime.[51]

The report did note there were several indictments and plea deals arising from the investigation, but not a single one involved anyone remotely associated with Trump or his campaign engaging in "collusion" with the Russian government. Potential violations of criminal law ranged from lying to investigators, failing to pay taxes, and failing to register under the Foreign Agent Registration Act (FARA). In years past, others previously found not to have registered under FARA were merely requested to comply with the law. This was the rare time anyone had ever been charged with a crime for failing to register.

Mueller's report also notes that a number of Russian military officers were indicted for allegedly hacking into computer systems with the intent of influencing the election. Mueller would know these allegations would never be proved or disproved because the Russian military officers would never travel to the United States to have their day in court. Mueller could have just as easily indicted ten thousand military officers. It was pure theater.

The only known attempt of a senior American politician to coordinate with the Soviet Union to affect a US election outcome occurred in 1983. Democratic Senator Edward Kennedy of Massachusetts sent a message to Yuri Andropov, the General Secretary of the Communist Party. Kennedy offered to work with the Soviets to develop a plan to defeat President Ronald Reagan in the 1984 election.[52]

Buddhist Temple

The political orbit of Bill Clinton and Al Gore shattered all records when it came to fundraising scandals. In fact, long after Clinton left the White House and Gore lost his 2000 presidential bid, Clinton-Gore associates were still getting indicted, tried, and convicted of breaking campaign finance laws.

By late 2002, the Federal Election Commission (FEC) handed down record-setting fines totaling more than $700,000 to several organizations, including the Clinton-Gore campaign, the Democratic National Committee, and several individuals who engineered illegal campaign donations. And this included only those the FEC caught. The campaign finance watchdog admitted it had to drop cases involving more than $3 million in illegal campaign contributions because many of the perpetrators were overseas foreigners, had fled the country, or were from organizations that disappeared.[53]

One case of a textbook example of illegal fundraising was an April 29, 1996, luncheon headlined by Al Gore. He attended a fundraising event at the Hsi Lai Buddhist temple in Hacienda Heights, near Los Angeles, California.

First and foremost, it is against federal law for tax-exempt entities such as religious organizations to participate in partisan political events. Politicians, especially veteran politicians like Gore, know this. Still, Gore attended a fundraising luncheon on the grounds of one of the largest Buddhist temples in the Western hemisphere.

The second obvious violation was that the temple monks and nuns who donated to the event were reimbursed by the Hsi Lai Buddhist temple. Using straw donors in this way evades contribution limits, violates campaign donation reporting rules, and is in direct violation of federal law.

The event was arranged by veteran Democratic fundraisers who were suspected or were known to have run afoul of election law. Born in China, John Huang was a top official with the Lippo Group, a company based in Indonesia that was suspected of Chinese government ties.[54] He left his lucrative job and joined the Democratic National Committee as a fundraiser. Huang had been involved in a number of sketchy or outright illegal contributions.

A $250,000 donation to the DNC, engineered by Huang, was returned because it was illegal money from a South Korean company.[55] Another donation of $425,000 from an Indonesian couple who were first-time donors was returned because the funds came from an overseas wire transfer of $500,000.[56] Foreign nationals who are legal permanent US residents are permitted to make political contributions, providing the contributions are from their personal funds earned in the United States.

More than $50,000 raised at the luncheon was given by the temples' monks and nuns, who had taken a vow of poverty. "Where would they get that kind of money?" asked Tzu Jung, the Buddhist organization's leader. Based in Taiwan and reached by telephone, Tzu Jung wasn't aware of the temple fundraiser.[57] It turns out the temple's religious workers were reimbursed for the contributions from temple funds, another violation of federal law.

Sioeng San Wong donated over $22,000 after attending the Gore luncheon. That donation and another for $250,000 to the Democratic National Committee came under suspicion by federal investigators who believed the money may have come from Chinese sources. The investigators were unable to question Wong, since he fled the United States. In addition, Wong's citizenship status was unknown.[58]

Another organizer of the Buddhist temple fundraiser was Taiwan-born immigrant Maria Hsia. She was the one who collected the $55,000 in straw donor contributions from the temple monks and nuns.

Foreign money being used as campaign contributions wasn't a surprise to federal officials. The FBI had sounded the alarm regarding the possibility of illegal Chinese money being funneled into California political campaigns. In 1996, the FBI warned four California politicians that they were vulnerable to Chinese money donations. They were Democratic Senators Barbara Boxer and Dianne Feinstein, Republican Representative Tom Campbell, and Democratic Representative Nancy Pelosi.[59]

When the scandal broke shortly before the November 1996 election, Gore claimed he didn't know the event was a political fundraiser. He insisted it was "a community outreach event."[60] But he changed his story after several White House and DNC documents dated before the temple luncheon materialized that listed the event as a fundraiser. One document turned over by the Vice President's office was a memo addressed to Gore from Huang that stated the event was a "fundraising lunch." A memo from Deputy White House Chief of Staff Harold Ickes addressed to Gore stated the event was expected to raise $250,000.[61]

The memos were damning enough, but it was also the presence of Huang and Hsia that should have made the event's mission obvious. The two were political fundraisers. Hsia had worked for Gore as a fundraiser since at least 1989. It's not credible to believe that Gore knew the two fundraisers were at the temple fundraiser, but that he didn't know they were collecting campaign contributions.

For nearly two years, US Attorney General Janet Reno had rejected repeated calls to appoint an investigator to examine the illegal campaign contributions and Gore's knowledge of them. FBI Director Louis Freeh urged her to seek an independent counsel. So did Charles LaBella, who had just stepped down as the head of Reno's Justice Department campaign task force.[62]

Finally, Reno took the baby step of announcing a ninety-day investigation to determine if a special counsel appointment was warranted. Some observers anticipated Reno would make a decision to appoint a special counsel. Other observers were not so certain, since Reno had been behaving as if she were the personal defense attorney for the Clinton White House.

In November 1998, Reno announced Justice Department investigators found no wrongdoing committed by Al Gore and Democratic Party entities and that she was closing the investigation.[63] However, the Justice Department would investigate those who arranged the Buddhist temple fundraiser. The Justice Department began with the premise that the Clinton-Gore campaign, the Democratic National Committee, and the campaign committee of Democratic Representative Patrick Kennedy of Rhode Island, who received some of the fundraiser proceeds, were victims of illegal activity.[64]

In March 2000, Hsia was convicted of funneling more than $165,000 in illegal contributions to the Clinton-Gore campaign and other Democratic candidates. John Huang, who pled guilty to conspiracy charges in 1999, testified against her.[65] US Judge Paul Friedman rejected prosecutors' calls for prison time and instead sentenced Hsia to ninety days of home detention, 250 hours of community service, and a $5,000 fine.

The Bigoted Pastor

In March 2008, momentum was building for what would become Senator Barack Obama's eventual nomination as the Democratic candidate for president. March was also the month a scandal erupted over his twenty-year relationship with Reverend Jeremiah Wright, the pastor of Chicago's Trinity Church.

ABC News showcased excerpts of controversial sermons delivered by Wright. For example, in a sermon delivered only days after the September 11th terrorist attacks in New York City, Washington, DC, and Shanksville, Pennsylvania, Wright declared America got what it deserved. "We bombed Hiroshima, we bombed Nagasaki, and we nuked far more than the thousands in New York and the Pentagon, and we never batted an eye," he sermonized. "And now we are indignant, because the stuff we have done overseas is now brought back into our own front yards. America's chickens are coming home to roost!"[66]

After the scandal broke, Obama attempted to distance himself from Wright, but only slightly. Obama wrote on March 14, 2008, "The statements that Rev. Wright made that are the cause of this controversy were not statements I personally heard him preach while I sat in the pews of Trinity or heard him utter in private conversation."[67]

In a speech four days later, Obama again addressed the Wright controversy. "As imperfect as he may be, he has been like family to me. He strengthened my faith, officiated my wedding, and baptized my children. Not once in my conversations with him have I heard him talk about any ethnic group in derogatory terms or treat whites with whom he interacted with anything but courtesy and respect...I can no more disown him than I can disown the black community."[68]

Obama claimed he never heard bigoted or racist remarks in any of Wright's sermons or conversations in spite of attending Trinity Church since 1985.[69] Unfortunately for Obama, his denials strained credulity. Obama said he routinely sought advice from Wright. The controversial minister was a key figure in so many critical moments in Obama's life. Obama even based his speech at the 2004 Democratic National Convention on Wright's sermon titled "Audacity to Hope."[70]

The reality is Jeremiah Wright had been making racist and bigoted remarks for years. He espoused a black separatist point of view. He also praised the deeply anti-Semitic Nation of Islam leader Louis Farrakhan.

For years, Wright would deliver "sermons laced with anti-American invective."[71] He opposed the great American melting pot. He denounced racial impurity, particularly when white men and black women have offspring. He called O.J. Simpson and Clarence Thomas "Negroes" for having married white women.[72] He was critical of Michael Jackson for marrying Lisa Marie Presley, and of Mike Tyson because white boxing manager Constantine "Cus" D'Amato adopted him.[73]

In a sermon titled "When You Forget Who You Are," Wright denounced assimilation. "It slowly kills you. You don't even realize what is happening to you, because when you assimilate, you forget who you are. As a matter of fact, sin and assimilation are just alike."[74] The consequences of assimilating, he sermonized, are "letting your behavior be determined by the enemy's expectations."[75] Do not behave in a manner acceptable to the enemy, he warned. Wright implied white people are the enemy.

"Negroes," whom he also called, "Uncle Toms,"[76] were those blacks who didn't support Louis Farrakhan's Million Man March.[77] He also referred to critics of the march as "colored," "Oreos," and "house niggras."[78] Anyone who practiced a white religion, such as Jehovah's Witnesses, were "darkies."[79]

Wright promoted the deeply anti-Semitic view that Jews control the media. He referred to the "Jerusalem Press," and the "Nazareth Broadcasting Company [NBC]."[80]

"Look around your church or neighborhood at the colors of African people today. America is the land of our trouble," he warned in his 1995 book, *Africans Who Shaped Our Faith.*

Wright lectured his parishioners, "When you forget who you are, you start letting your behavior be determined by the enemy's [white people's] expectations. How you act is based upon what they think. And that sickness is perpetuated, because through assimilation and acculturation, you now think just like they think."

Wright admonished his congregants, "If you are not European, stop pretending you are."

Wright's black separatist sermons have been notorious for racist comments about "white arrogance," "the United States of White America," and "the US of KKK." Wright accused the US government of conspiring against black people. "The government lied about inventing the HIV virus as a means of genocide against people of color. The government lied," he claimed in one sermon. Rather than asking for divine blessings for the United States, instead Wright urged, "God damn America!"

In August 2007, Wright delivered a eulogy at Morehouse College in Atlanta, Georgia. He referred to the nation's founding fathers as the "fondling fathers." He called Texas "the cradle of dehumanization," he made an ethnic slur about Italians and "their garlic noses," and he repeatedly mentioned "white enemies." Wright warned mourners of "white supremacist brainwashing, passing itself off as education."

After Obama was elected President, Wright was frustrated by what he thought were efforts to prevent him from meeting with Obama. "Them Jews ain't going to let him talk to me," Wright said.[81]

Wright and Obama helped organize Chicago-area participation in the 1995 march on Washington, DC, led by Farrakhan. Farrakhan's anti-Semitism was well known. Farrakhan once accused former President George H. W. Bush of "buck-dancing in a yarmulke for the Jews." Months before the 1995 march, Farrakhan was embroiled in an ugly, anti-Semitic episode. Khalid Abdul Muhammad, a senior Nation of Islam official, delivered three hours of remarks at New Jersey's Kean College that attacked whites, Jews, Catholics, homosexuals, and white South Africans.

Muhammad said, "[Jews] are a European strain of people who crawled around on all fours in the caves and hills of Europe, eatin' Juniper roots and eatin' each other…They're the blood suckers of the black nation and the black community."

Muhammad warned the audience of "Columbia Jew-niversity over in Jew York City." He called the U.N., the "Jew-nited Nations." He said Jews were named Rubenstein, Goldstein, and Silverstein because they "[have] been stealing rubies and gold and silver all over the earth. That's why we can't even wear a ring or a bracelet or a necklace without calling it Jewelry…but it's not jewelry, it's Jew-elry."

Muhammad argued Jews who perished in the Holocaust had it coming to them. He asked, "[D]on't nobody ever ask what did they do to Hitler?" Then he answered his own question, "They had undermined the very fabric of the society."

Prior to his Kean College address, Muhammad dismissed the "so-called Jew holocaust" at appearances in Dallas, Texas, and Washington, DC. He argued the film *Schindler's List* should be renamed "Swindler's List."

Countless public figures implored Farrakhan to repudiate Muhammad. Instead, Farrakhan stood by his friend both figuratively and literally. At a "Black Men Only" rally of 10,000, Farrakhan said, "We know that Jews are the most organized, rich and powerful people, not only in America, but in the world. They are plotting against us even as we speak." Then Farrakhan clasped Muhammad in an embrace on stage.

Even with Farrakhan's long history of racism, bigotry, and anti-Semitism, Wright remained a fervent supporter. In 2007, Wright praised Farrakhan as one who "will be remembered as one of the twenty- and twenty-first-century giants of the African-American religious experience." *Trumpet*, a magazine operated by Wright and Trinity Church, honored Farrakhan in November 2007 with the Rev. Jeremiah A. Wright, Jr. Lifetime Achievement Trumpeteer Award for his years of service.

It is understandable that when he began running for president Obama would not want his twenty-year relationship with the notorious pastor to trip him up. There was no way to explain away Wright's bigoted sermons and fraternization with Farrakhan. So, Obama did the next best thing. He pretended he didn't know about them.

It speaks volumes that one of Obama's biggest acolytes, White House staffer Ben Rhodes, could not bring himself to write one single sentence defending Obama's twenty-year close relationship with Wright in Rhodes's 2018 memoir regarding Obama.

High-Tech Lynching

Since the nation's founding, the process to add a new justice to the Supreme Court had been a gentlemanly affair. The president would nominate a candidate and the Senate would exercise its constitutional duty of "advice and consent." After reviewing judicial qualifications and temperament, nominees would often sail through the confirmation process.

There were exceptions in the modern era. There was firm opposition to the president's nominees when Franklin Roosevelt tried to pack the Supreme Court in an unprecedented attempt to add six justices to the nine-member court (see chapter 5). Lyndon Johnson's attempt to elevate Associate Justice Abe Fortas to chief justice was defeated because of justifiable concerns that Johnson's one-time personal lawyer was little more than his spy on the high court (see chapter 6).

A new practice regarding the confirmation process came into being when moderate Justice Lewis Powell announced his retirement in June 1987. Senate Democrats immediately planned to oppose virtually any nominee President Ronald Reagan would put forward.

Five years earlier, in 1982, Reagan had nominated to the Federal Appeals Court Robert Bork, who was confirmed unanimously. Literally minutes after Reagan nominated Bork, Democratic Senator Ted Kennedy of Massachusetts ignored addressing Bork's judicial temperament and qualifications, and instead launched "a major ideological attack."[82] Kennedy defamed Bork in a wild Senate speech. Even the steadfastly liberal *New York Times* wrote that Kennedy "stated his case in such vehement terms that he's scaring the Democrats more than the Republicans."[83]

In what is now widely viewed as a shameful episode in Senate history, Kennedy said the following:

Robert Bork's America is a land in which women would be forced into back-alley abortions, blacks would sit at segregated lunch counters, rogue police could break down citizens' doors in midnight raids, and schoolchildren could not be taught about evolution, writers and artists could be censored at the whim of the Government, and the doors of the Federal courts would be shut on the fingers of millions of citizens.

Bork's nomination was defeated in a near party-line vote. Again, the *New York Times* weighed in with an opinion writer likening Kennedy's anti-Bork speech to the worst excesses of disgraced Republican Senator Joseph McCarthy of Wisconsin.[84] Political attacks like Kennedy's became known as "Borking." Supreme Court nominations became political theater.

Associate Justice Thurgood Marshall announced his retirement at the end of the Supreme Court term in 1991. In July 1991, President George H. W. Bush nominated Federal Judge Clarence Thomas to fill the vacant Marshall seat. Because both Marshall and Thomas were black, this eliminated one potential line of political attack. Less than two years earlier, Thomas was confirmed to be a US Circuit Court Judge without any opposition by a simple voice vote in the Senate. Still, liberal activists vowed to defeat Thomas's nomination by any means possible. One activist announced, "We're going to Bork him. We're going to kill him politically."[85]

Rated "qualified" by the American Bar Association, Thomas sailed through the investigation and hearing process and appeared headed toward confirmation. Then the nation heard from a woman named Anita Hill.

The Senate Judiciary Committee reopened its investigation following a National Public Radio report that the FBI had derogatory information on Thomas that came from an interview with Hill. From 1981 to 1983, Hill worked for Thomas, first as an attorney advisor at the Department of Education, and then as his assistant when he was chair of the US Equal Employment Opportunity Commission.

Hill claimed Thomas began sexually harassing her when the pair worked at the Education Department. She claimed this behavior started after she turned down numerous date requests. She alleged Thomas's unwanted sexual comments continued while the pair worked at the Equal Employment Opportunity Commission (EEOC). Hill alleged Thomas talked about pornography, including man-on-beast sex. He referenced the size of his genitals and he talked about a porn star known by the name Long Dong Silver, she alleged. In one claim, Hill said Thomas examined a can of soda sitting on his desk and asked, "Who put pubic hair on my Coke?"

A pair of women who were at the Equal Employment Opportunity Commission claimed they could corroborate Hill's allegations. However, neither one was called to testify. Democrats, who held a 58–42 majority in the Senate, found neither woman credible. One was fired from the EEOC by Thomas for poor performance. This was one in a string of firings and resignations of this particular individual based on perfor-mance issues.[86] The other woman only cited hearsay and told Senate Judiciary Committee investigators incorrect information.[87]

On the other hand, a dozen women who served with Thomas at either the Education Department or the Equal Employment

Opportunity Commission came forward as witnesses in support of Thomas and vouched for his professionalism. Not one could imagine Thomas behaving in a manner as Hill had alleged.

Hill's allegations were viewed as not credible for several reasons. First, she followed Thomas from the Department of Education to the Equal Employment Opportunity Commission in spite of claiming he had made sexual advances and harassed her. Who would follow someone who made them extremely uncomfortable, observers asked? Second, telephone records showed Hill called Thomas repeatedly for seven years after she left the Commission.[88] Again, this is not the behavior of someone who felt threatened, as Hill had claimed. Third, it was recognized that Hill had an axe to grind. Thomas had promoted another woman to a position Hill believed should have gone to her.[89]

A bombshell was learned after the Senate hearing. FBI Special Agent Jolene Smith Jameson signed a sworn affidavit that Hill made comments in her public testimony "that were in contradiction with statements she made" to Jameson and the second FBI agent who interviewed her.

In his testimony in response to the Hill allegations, Thomas said:

This is not an opportunity to talk about difficult matters privately or in a closed environment. This is a circus. It's a national disgrace. And from my standpoint, as a black American, it is a high-tech lynching for uppity blacks who in any way deign to think for themselves, to do for themselves, to have different ideas, and it is a message that unless you kowtow to an old order, this is what will happen to you. You will be lynched, destroyed, caricatured by a committee of the US Senate rather than hung from a tree.

On the day of the full Senate vote on Thomas's nomination, the *Washington Post* urged confirmation in an editorial that stated, "The unproven word of a single accuser is not enough to establish guilt."[90]

Thomas was narrowly confirmed by a 52–48 vote. Forty-one Republican and eleven Democrats voted to confirm Thomas, while forty-six Democrats and two Republicans voted to reject his nomination. Thomas was sworn in as a Supreme Court justice on October 23, 1991.

Impeachment I

Andrew Johnson's rise to become the 17th president was very unusual. First-term Republican President Abraham Lincoln chose the Democrat Johnson to be his running mate for reelection in 1864 because Lincoln believed he needed the support of Union Democrats.[91] In some ways, Johnson was an easy and obvious choice.

Johnson was a US Senator representing Tennessee when the Volunteer State decided to secede from the Union. Johnson declared his loyalty to the Union and remained in Washington, DC. This curried favor with Lincoln, who chose Johnson to be his second-term running mate. Six weeks after Johnson was sworn in as vice president, Lincoln was assassinated.

The honeymoon period between Johnson and Congress was short-lived. By early 1866, Johnson had a fractious relationship with Congress. It was not just because Johnson was a Democrat and Congress was dominated by Republicans. The political chasm between Johnson and Congress was due to stark differences in their beliefs on post-Civil War America. Both were anxious to rebuild relations between the Union and what were the Confederate states; however, this is where the similarities ended.

Republicans wanted to readmit the Southern states to the Union, but only after they met certain preconditions. Chief among these was equal treatment of all people. Congressional Republicans also wanted swift emancipation for the nearly four million freed slaves and quick conferment of civil rights on all blacks.

Johnson was far less concerned with the Southern states making concessions beyond swearing loyalty to the United States, upholding the Thirteenth Amendment, and repaying war debt. Enacted after the end of the Civil War, the Thirteenth Amendment abolished slavery. In spite of this amendment, many of the Southern states had adopted "black codes" that placed restrictions on recently freed slaves, effectively ensuring they would be available as a source of cheap labor.

The black codes in some states limited blacks as to what kinds of jobs they could have. Other states allowed physical punishment and indentured servitude if blacks deviated from expected job employment, particularly in agriculture. Johnson favored a lenient approach in dealing with the Southern states and their black codes.

Johnson and the Democrats favored generous pardons of former Confederate leaders and thought it acceptable that these leaders take a significant role in rebuilding their states. Republicans wanted new leadership in the Southern states to effect a clean break with past slavery policies. These differences were manifested when Johnson and congressional Republicans clashed over significant legislation.

The Bureau of Refugees, Freedmen, and Abandoned Lands, often referred to as the Freedmen's Bureau, was an agency that helped freed slaves assimilate in society. The bureau provided provisions, clothing, and other assistance, as needed, to freed slaves. The Freedman's Bureau was established under President Abraham Lincoln in early 1865, shortly before he died, and was chartered to last one year. Its operation fell under the auspices of the War Department. Congress passed legislation to extend its charter beyond one year; however, Johnson vetoed the bill.

That was not the only legislation aimed at supporting freed slaves opposed by Johnson. Johnson vetoed the Civil Rights Act of 1865, which offered equal protection of all citizens, including blacks. In this instance, congressional Republicans gathered the necessary two-thirds majority to override Johnson's veto.

Republicans increased their numbers in both the House and Senate, resulting in veto-proof majorities in the 1866 mid-term elections. This allowed Congress to pass several Reconstruction Acts that levied certain requirements on the former Confederate states to meet before readmission to the Union. The most important among these was ratification of the Fourteenth Amendment to the Constitution. The Fourteenth Amendment has several clauses, including the Privileges and Immunities, and Due Process clauses. Arguably, the most important clauses relating to reunification were the Citizenship and Equal Protection clauses. Democrats bitterly opposed the Fourteenth Amendment. Reconstruction policies favored by Republicans also required the Southern states to give voting rights to black males.

It was widely believed that Johnson's use of executive powers did the most damage in stymieing the implementation of Reconstruction policies. Johnson's foot-dragging and his patronage system, in which he rewarded recalcitrant Southerners, only prolonged Reconstruction efforts.[92]

The War Department was critical to managing the Southern states, especially when it came to fulfilling requirements in order to be fully readmitted to the Union. Union troops were stationed throughout the South in order to supervise Reconstruction policies. The Secretary of War was Edwin Stanton, who was an Abraham Lincoln appointee. Stanton was a staunch Republican committed to carrying out Reconstruction policies.

Congress was concerned that Johnson would replace Stanton, who was the administration's most effective proponent of Reconstruction policies. In 1867, Congress passed the Tenure of Office Act that required the president to seek advice and consent of the Senate before removing any officeholder whose original appointment required Senate approval.

During the August 1867 congressional recess, Johnson suspended Stanton as war secretary and replaced him with General Ulysses Grant as interim secretary of war. Johnson believed Grant's philosophy would be closer to his. After returning from recess, the Senate issued a resolution of non-concurrence, causing Grant to resign. Johnson next appointed Major General Lorenzo Thomas in late February 1868 and sought the removal of Stanton from the office of secretary. Johnson ordered Thomas to personally deliver the letter of removal to Stanton.[93] Johnson reasoned that since Stanton was Lincoln's appointee, and not his, then Stanton was not covered by the Tenure of Office Act.[94]

The removal of Stanton was more than enough for Congress. Days later, on February 24, 1868, the House passed an impeachment resolution. On March 2 and 3, the House passed eleven articles of impeachment against Johnson. The impeachment trial began on March 5 with Supreme Court Chief Justice Salmon Chase, presiding. After several starts and stops due to procedural matters, the trial got underway and concluded on May 16. The Senate voted on the three charges against Johnson that were considered the easiest to garner enough votes to convict.[95] They fell one vote short of the necessary two-thirds majority to render a finding of guilty and to remove Johnson from office.

There were several reasons why some Republican senators voted for acquittal. It was generally believed the Tenure of Office Act would not withstand Constitutional scrutiny, and holding Johnson accountable for an unconstitutional law was unconscionable. Some were concerned impeachment could seriously damage the balance of power between the executive and legislative branches. Still, others were more worried about who would assume the presidency if Johnson were removed.

President pro tempore of the Senate, Benjamin Wade, voted to convict Johnson. Even though he was a Republican, it was widely viewed that Wade voted guilty for purely selfish reasons. The office of vice president was still vacant following Johnson's assumption of the presidency upon the assassination of Lincoln. That made the senate president pro tempore next in line for the presidency.[96] Even some Republicans thought he would be worse than the Democrat Johnson.

It became clear that a similar vote, falling short of a guilty verdict, was in store for the remaining eight impeachment articles. The Senate acquitted Johnson and adjourned the trial without voting on the remaining eight charges.

Impeachment II

In November 1995, President Bill Clinton began a twenty-one-month affair with a White House intern who was nearly thirty years younger. The first time they were alone in his private study just off the Oval Office, Monica Lewinsky performed oral sex on the president.

For nearly two years, Clinton and Lewinsky met in person dozens of times. On at least ten occasions when they were alone, they engaged in sexual activity, usually in the windowless hallway just outside the president's private study. The sexual activity mostly consisted of Lewinsky performing oral sex on the president. On other occasions when they were apart, they engaged in phone sex.

In December 1997, the Clinton-Lewinsky affair was swept up in a sexual harassment lawsuit that had been filed against Clinton. Paula Jones was an Arkansas state employee who claimed Clinton made sexual advances toward her when he was the Arkansas governor. Jones's lawyers learned of Clinton's affair with Lewinsky, and they added Lewinsky's name to their witness list. Jones's lawyers wanted to show a pattern of behavior whereby the president sexually harassed or demanded sexual favors from vulnerable women.

Judge Kenneth Starr had been appointed an independent counsel to investigate Clinton-related corruption in several matters, including the Whitewater real estate investment deal, an Arkansas investment scheme that had gone awry, and the "Filegate" and "Travelgate" scandals. US Attorney General Janet Reno authorized Starr to expand his investigation to include the Lewinsky scandal. Starr was investigating if Clinton had committed perjury, suborned perjury, or obstructed justice.

During the course of litigation in the Paula Jones lawsuit, Clinton gave a deposition, which he called "a farce," and said he resented having to testify.[97] Clinton lied when asked if he had a sexual encounter with Lewinsky. Clinton coached Lewinsky to swear a false affidavit denying their affair and their sexual encounters. He instructed her to hide the gifts he had given her. Clinton also coached presidential secretary Betty Currie to lie if questioned about whether he was ever alone with the intern. Additionally, Clinton enlisted the assistance of Washington, DC, super-lawyer Vernon Jordan to help find a job for Lewinsky—a job far away from the nation's capital.

The scandal became public on January 17, 1998, when the Drudge Report website broke the story. Upon hearing the news, Clinton delivered a blistering denial. "I want you to listen to me," said an angry-looking Clinton while he wagged his finger, "I'm going to say this again: I did not have sexual relations with that woman, Miss Lewinsky. I never told anybody to lie, not a single time, never. These allegations are false."

In August 1998, after ignoring several requests to voluntarily appear, Clinton was subpoenaed to appear before a grand jury. He mocked the grand jury process when he argued over the definition of "sexual relationship." As the Starr Report noted, "As to his denial in the Jones deposition that he and Ms. Lewinsky had had a 'sexual relationship,' the President maintained that there can be no sexual relationship without sexual intercourse, regardless of what other sexual activities may transpire."[98]

However, back in January when Clinton testified under oath during his deposition in the Jones lawsuit, he was told how "sexual activity" was defined in that legal proceeding. That definition was "[A] person engages in 'sexual relations' when the person knowingly engages in or causes—(1) contact with the genitalia, anus, groin, breast, inner thigh, or buttocks of any person with an intent to arouse or gratify the sexual desire of any person...'Contact' means intentional touching, either directly or through clothing."[99]

When Clinton appeared before the grand jury, he was asked about a previous denial during his deposition in the Jones lawsuit that he had engaged in sexual activity with Lewinsky. Clinton replied, "It depends on what the meaning of the word 'is' is. If the—if he—if 'is' means, is and never has been that is not—that is one thing. If it means there is none, that was a completely true statement."[100]

Clinton's lies in the Jones deposition and before grand jury became apparent in Lewinsky's testimony. She testified that the pair engaged in sexual activity on several occasions. Lewinsky testified she performed oral sex on Clinton at least ten times.[101]

Lewinsky's testimony could have been chalked up to a "he said, she said" case, where it was not easily discernable who was telling the truth and who was lying. However, Lewinsky had physical evidence to back her claims. She had in her possession a blue dress she wore during one of the times she performed oral sex on the president. Clinton ejaculated on her dress and Lewinsky decided not to have it dry-cleaned. DNA testing was conducted, comparing the biological matter on the dress with a reference sample from Clinton. DNA tests confirmed it was Clinton's semen on her dress.

At the heart of the House of Representatives impeachment proceedings was that Clinton had committed perjury, suborned perjury, and obstructed justice. However, Clinton and his supporters in the media attempted to portray the investigation and subsequent impeachment as the product of voyeuristic busybodies criminalizing a sexual relationship between two consenting adults. The *Washington Post* wrote, "Sex makes people do weird, stupid stuff."[102] The *Post* further explained the episode was merely "sexual hanky-panky."[103]

The House of Representatives began impeachment proceedings against Clinton following the November 1998 mid-term elections. Clinton faced four articles of impeachment. There were two counts of perjury, one count of obstruction of justice, and a single count of abuse of power.

On December 19, 1998, Clinton was impeached on two charges: perjury and obstruction of justice. On February 12, 1999, after nearly five weeks of motions, procedural maneuvers, closed-door sessions, and a trial, the Senate voted to acquit Clinton of both charges.

Nearly half of the Senators believed it was not proved Clinton had committed perjury or obstructed justice. However, the top jurists in Clinton's home state of Arkansas and in the United States thought otherwise. The Office of the Committee of Professional Conduct of the Arkansas Judiciary revoked Clinton's law license for a period of five years and fined him $25,000. After he left the presidency, the US Supreme Court permanently disbarred Clinton from practicing law before the high court.

The Radical

Simply put, William Charles "Bill" Ayers is one evil and despicable human being. Fortunately for him, he escaped judicial accountability for every criminal act he may have committed.

The halls of academia are oftentimes a place where social misfits, unrepentant radicals, and one-time dangers to society can feel at home. Ayers found his safe space at the University of Illinois at Chicago, where he eventually retired as a college professor. Teaching classes on the UIC campus was a far cry from Ayers's days as a 1960s radical, when he co-founded the Weathermen.

The Weathermen was a radical group with Communist sympathies that advocated the revolutionary overthrow of the US government and an end to capitalism. The Weathermen had its birth on college campuses, where like-minded students and non-students engaged in campus protests, often demonstrating against what the group claimed were American imperialism and institutional racism. The Weathermen organization was launched in June 1969 at the Students for a Democratic Society national convention.[104] Its members pledged militant action and violence to bring about changes to American society.

A manifesto titled "You Don't Need a Weatherman to Know Which Way the Wind Blows" was authored by Ayers and other would-be revolutionaries, including Bernardine Dohrn. Dated June 18, 1969, the manifesto stated, "The goal is the destruction of US imperialism and the achievement of a classless world: world communism." The enemy was the United States, what the manifesto called "a worldwide monster."

The manifesto contained the far left's usual revolutionary language. America is replete with "jail-like schools [where] kids are fed a mishmash of racist, male chauvinist, anti-working class, anti-communist lies." Police officers are deemed an obstacle for their "revolutionary struggle." "Pigs [police officers] are sweaty working-class barbarians who over-react and commit 'police brutality.'"

According to a top-secret report prepared by the Chicago Field Office of the Federal Bureau of Investigation, the Weathermen had "an unremitting commitment to armed struggle as the ultimate necessity to seize state power."[105]

The Weathermen idolized the worst examples of nations where endless human rights abuses and suffering were justified to further the causes of socialism and communism, such as Angola, Libya, Cuba, and China, just to name a few. Several Weathermen traveled to Cuba to meet with Cuban and North Vietnamese government officials. One Weatherman member, Linda Sue Evans, actually visited North Vietnam.

After her return from North Vietnam in August 1969, Evans spoke of her three-week trip and of being given the opportunity to hold an anti-aircraft gun. She said she wished an American aircraft had flown over at the moment she was holding the anti-aircraft gun.[106] She claimed that Americans held as prisoners of war by the North Vietnamese were receiving humane treatment.[107]

Among the earliest known violent events linked to the Weathermen was a September 1968 arson attack against the Navy ROTC building at the University of Washington that destroyed much of the edifice.[108]

An October 1969 rally of several hundred radicals in Chicago, promoted by the Weathermen and known as the "Days of Rage," became violent when attendees smashed storefront windows and damaged several cars. The instigators arrived prepared for violence by wearing motorcycle helmets and steel-toed boots for kicking, and carrying steel rebar for fighting.

The Weathermen were comfortable with violence. They claimed credit for the bombing of police cars in Chicago, and Berkeley, California, in late 1969 and early 1970. The group is suspected of a bombing that killed a San Francisco police officer in early 1970 and of responsibility for a police precinct bombing in Detroit.

Other bombings in 1970 that were tied to the Weathermen were at the National Guard Association building in Washington, DC, the New York City police headquarters, San Francisco's Presidio army base, the Marin, California, courthouse, a Queens, New York, traffic courthouse, and the campus of Harvard University.

During the next few years, the Weathermen were complicit in several more bombings, including at the US Capitol, the Pentagon, the

US State Department, the Massachusetts Institute of Technology in Cambridge, Massachusetts, several federal and state government buildings, and private business offices. In all, the group was believed to have been responsible for at least forty bombings during the period of 1969 to 1975.[109] These bombings resulted in millions of dollars of damage, serious injuries, and fatalities.

Ayers admitted complicity in the bombings of the New York City Police Department headquarters, the US Capitol, and the Pentagon, but claimed he had no role in bombings that killed and injured others. He later dismissed the "itsy-bitsy" Pentagon bombing as no big deal, since no one was killed.[110]

The Weathermen were not known to the public at large, but received unwanted notoriety in March 1970 when a bomb-making factory located in a Greenwich Village townhouse next door to actor Dustin Hoffman blew up.[111] Three Weathermen died in the explosion. One of those killed was Diana Oughton, who was the then-girlfriend of Ayers. Two women escaped with minor injuries. One was wearing clothes left in tattered shreds, and the other had her clothes completely blown off.[112] The group changed its name from the Weathermen to the Weather Underground as its members went underground in an effort to avoid detection and capture.[113]

As law enforcement began closing in on the Weather Underground, Ayers and his new girlfriend, Bernardine Dohrn, went on the run. Dohrn, who made the FBI's Ten Most Wanted Fugitives list,[114] was cut from the same cloth as Ayers. After Charles Manson's followers committed the grisly murders of actress Sharon Tate and four others, Dohrn remarked, "Dig it! Manson killed those pigs, then they ate dinner in the same room with them, then they shoved a forked into a victim's stomach."[115] Tate was eight-and-a-half months pregnant when she was repeatedly stabbed to death.

For several years, Ayers and Dohrn were among the FBI's most wanted criminals. They were underground trying to avoid capture and took odd jobs to get by before the pair emerged from hiding in 1980. Dohrn faced outstanding state criminal charges for assaulting a police officer and was convicted of aggravated battery and jumping bail. She was sentenced to a mere three years of probation.[116]

Ayers was much luckier. The law enforcement abuses of the FBI that were exposed during the Church Committee hearings tainted a number of federal criminal cases, including Ayers's and Dohrn's (see chapter 5). This led prosecutors to drop all federal charges against the pair. Ayers would not be held responsible for his past. He was free from threat of prison.

Dohrn had graduated from law school prior to joining the Weathermen. She harbored the idea of practicing law after she finished her sentence. However, her attempts to join the bars of New York and Illinois were rebuffed. The state bars would not admit her. They determined her unfit and, given her criminal past, questioned her support for the rule of law.[117]

Ayers reemerged in the American consciousness in the aftermath of the September 11th terror attacks. His biography, *Fugitive Days*, had been released only weeks earlier. In the acknowledgements, he mentioned his wife, children, and several hardened criminals and murderers, including eight domestic terrorists who were imprisoned for the killing of fourteen law enforcement officers, including Sundiata Acoli, Jamil Al-Amin, Herman Bell, and Mumia Abu Jamal.[118]

In *Fugitive Days*, Ayers admitted the Weathermen bombed numerous government and civilian targets including Bank of America, Chase Manhattan Bank, IBM, and General Motors.[119] He also told of spending a day in Baltimore department stores robbing wallets from unsuspecting customers and spending the stolen money on "fancy clothes."[120]

Included in a promotional campaign for the book was a photo of a defiant Ayers standing on the American flag.[121] Three decades after the violent activities of the Weather Underground, Ayers was still unrepentant. In a *New York Times* article that was published on the same morning when nearly three thousand people were killed in New York City in the September 11th attacks, Ayers said, "I don't regret setting bombs. I feel we didn't do enough."[122]

Ayers and Dohrn found acceptance in academia. Ayers was hired by the University of Illinois at Chicago and Dohrn got a job with Northwestern University. Their employers paid them handsomely enough that it allowed them to purchase a home in chichi Hyde Park, a neighborhood of Chicago that is so politically one-sided that 95 percent of its residents voted for John Kerry over George W. Bush in 2004.[123]

It was in Hyde Park in 1995, that Ayers met the up-and-coming Michelle and Barack Obama. The Obamas had also moved into Hyde Park. Ayers and Barack Obama were part of the same political and social circles.[124] Obama served for four years on the board of the Chicago Annenberg Challenge, alongside Ayers who authored the grant request with which he founded the organization.[125,126] The two were also among the nine board members of the Woods Fund of Chicago.[127]

Ayers and Obama appeared on an academic panel arranged by Michelle Obama. In 1997, Obama wrote glowing praise for Ayers's book, *A Kind and Just Parent: The Children of Juvenile Court,* in the *Chicago Tribune.*[128] Ayers and Dohrn hosted a campaign meet-and-greet for Obama in their home when Obama ran for the Illinois state senate in 1995. Ayers later became an Obama campaign donor.

The friendship of Obama and Ayers became a scandal when the relationship between the two was raised during a 2008 Democratic primary debate. Obama waved off his ties to Ayers, claiming he barely knew Ayers, who was just "a guy who lives in my neighborhood."

Some news outlets quickly came to Obama's defense. They dismissed Ayers's bomb-throwing past as of no consequence, arguing that Ayers and Dohrn were little more than your typical city neighbors.[129] A *Washington Post* columnist referred to questions regarding the Obama-Ayers relationship as "such tired tripe."[130] *Editor & Publisher* magazine called questioning their ties "perhaps the most embarrassing performance by the media in a major presidential debate in years."[131] *Time* magazine thought the Ayers debate question represented "extremely stupid politics."[132]

Other news outlets mounted a vociferous defense of the Obama-Ayers relationship[133,134,135,136] attempting to prove the pair did not really know one another, in spite of serving on the same boards, appearing together on a panel arranged by Michelle, Ayers's campaign support of Obama, and the recurring coincidence of the pair being at the same place at the same time.[137]

CHAPTER 5

ABUSE OF POWER

"The common ingredients of the Iran and Contra policies were secrecy, deception, and disdain for the law. A small group of senior officials believed that they alone knew what was right. They viewed knowledge of their action by others in the Government as a threat to their objectives... They testified that they even withheld key facts from the President."

—Report of the congressional Committees Investigating the Iran-Contra Affair.[1]

Arms-for-Hostages

There were two foreign events that occurred in 1979 that had a profound effect on the man who would be elected president the following year. Socialist revolutionaries toppled the democratic government of Nicaragua, and Islamic radicals stormed the US Embassy in Tehran, taking Americans hostage. These two events were at the heart of a foreign policy scandal that nearly sunk President Ronald Reagan during his second term.

To say the United States had strained relations with Iran was an understatement. President Jimmy Carter's disastrous policy regarding Iran paved the way for Islamic revolutionaries to topple Iran's US-friendly government and install a brutal and oppressive theocracy.[2] In spite of his drawbacks, Iranian leader Shah Mohammed Reza Pahlavi led a stable, secular, modern nation. Carter pressured the Shah to leave Iran in 1978. The following year, Iranians stormed the US Embassy in Tehran and seized fifty-two American diplomats and citizens. They were held hostage and not released until after Carter left the presidency in January 1981.

After the Sandinistas seized power in Nicaragua, the United States became concerned the Soviet Union could gain a toehold in Central America.[3] The Sandinistas were receiving aid from Cuba and the Soviet Union. In late 1981, the United States began providing military and economic support to the Contras, a Nicaraguan group fighting the Sandinistas. However, the US support was short-lived. Perhaps with the 1975 collapse of South Vietnam still fresh in their minds, Congress quickly soured on the Contras. By 1984, Congress had stipulated that the dwindling US financial aid could not be used to counter the Sandinistas.

The following year, Congress completely turned off the money spigot. The 1985 fiscal year appropriations cut off all aid to the Contras and passed a measure, known as the Boland Amendment, which made it illegal for the United States to provide any aid to the Contras.[4]

Faced with a lack of funding situation that would probably lead to the demise of the Contras, Reagan told his National Security Council to "keep the *Contras* together 'body and soul.'"[5] The National Security Council understood this to be a green light to do whatever was necessary. The National Security Council is strictly a presidential advisory body and has traditionally held no operational roles.[6]

The National Security Council believed it had a loophole that allowed it to engage in what were widely viewed as illegal activities. National Security Council staff claimed their organization was not an intelligence agency and therefore was not included in the "any other agency or entity of the United States involved in intelligence activities" that were prohibited from aiding the Contras, as stipulated in the Boland Amendment.

Starting in 1985, the Reagan administration secretly solicited other nations to provide financial support to the Contras. A few nations agreed to do so. This foreign aid was funneled to a secret group named the Enterprise, managed by Americans, which delivered support to the Contras.

On November 3, 1986, the Lebanese magazine *Al-Shiraa* broke the story of US officials conducting foreign policy seemingly at odds with US law and with Reagan's public statements. Robert McFarlane, the former National Security Advisor to Reagan, had secretly traveled to

Tehran the previous May to conduct negotiations with Iranian moderates about thawing relations between the United States and Iran. A deal was reached, the magazine alleged, in which Iran would cease financing terrorism in return for an end to US support to Iraq, and would include the sale to Iran of spare parts for US weapons systems.[7] Iran and Iraq had been engaged in war for most of the 1980s.

What the article left out was an attempt to further a deal between Washington, DC, and Tehran to release US hostages held in Lebanon. Several Americans had been kidnapped in the Middle Eastern nation in the previous few years. Iran had influence with the Islamic terror group Hezbollah, which was behind the abductions. The plan to swap hostages in return for weapons and spare parts was secretly proposed by Iranian officials in the summer of 1985.[8] Iran desperately needed spare parts for its inventory of US-made weapons systems.

The Iranians promised to arrange for the release of all seven Americans being held hostage in return for arms shipments. The United States requested Israel to act as the middleman, since there was an arms embargo in place that prohibited the sale of US weapons systems to Iran. Israel sent weapons and spare parts to Iran and the United States resupplied Israel. While the United States honored its end of the bargain, the Iranians did not keep their word. After several arms shipments over a period of months in late 1985, only one American was freed.

In his memoir, Reagan wrote, "Reestablishing a friendly relationship with this strategically located country—while preventing the Soviets from doing the same thing—was very attractive…We wanted to ensure that the next government in Tehran was moderate and friendly."[9]

In 1986, the Reagan administration decided to sell arms directly to Iran. It used the Enterprise, the private company used to support the Contras, to carry out the Iranian transactions and shipments. The Enterprise began to turn a profit from the Iranian arms sales. Marine Lieutenant Colonel Oliver North was the staffer overseeing the entire effort on behalf of the National Security Council. North directed the profits be spent to support the Contras. As a congressional investigation later determined, North managed this fund "without any of the accountability required of Government activities."[10]

After the *Al-Shiraa* story broke, media reports began to circulate that the Reagan administration had engaged in a secretive arms-for-hostages plan. On November 26, Reagan appointed former Senator John Tower of Texas, former National Security Advisor Brent Scowcroft, and former Secretary of State Edmund Muskie, two Republicans and a Democrat, respectively, to conduct an investigation into the scandal. It became known as the Tower Commission.

Reagan also sought the appointment of an independent counsel to conduct a thorough investigation. On December 19, at the request of Attorney General Edwin Meese, Lawrence Walsh was appointed as an independent counsel to investigate the scandal. Reagan was proactive in initiating two separate investigations to get to the bottom of the scheme with the understanding that they would, at the very least, be politically embarrassing, and, in the worst case, possibly yield criminal indictments.

This arms-for-hostages revelation was a shock to the public, as Reagan had taken a hard-line stand that the United States would never pay for the release of American hostages. Moreover, in 1984, the United States had designated Iran as a state sponsor of terrorism.[11] Reagan's hypocrisy caused his stratospheric poll ratings of 68 percent in May 1986 to plummet to 47 percent in December, only weeks after news broke of the arms-for-hostages scandal.[12]

Congress joined the Tower Commission and the special counsel in investigating the scandal. Democratic leaders in the House and Senate agreed to hold combined hearings instead of separate hearings in each chamber beginning in January 1987.

Congressional hearings did not go as planned. Attempts to portray some of the Reagan administration's principals of the secret dealings as unpatriotic freelancers became a public relations disaster. The American public was generally supportive of several of the participants. Most notable was the National Security Council staffer in charge of the effort, Lieutenant Colonel North. His public testimony before Congress was powerful. Democrats later regretted not stipulating that active-duty North not wear his Marine uniform. His medal-bedecked dress greens made him a sympathetic figure to the public.[13]

On February 27, 1987, the Tower Commission delivered a scathing indictment of the Iran-Contra affair. Muskie, a Democratic presidential candidate himself in 1972, delivered the summary in a news conference. Among the key points that led to the improper actions by the

National Security Council were the informality of the scheme, a lack of record keeping, failure to inform Reagan of the scope, the misuse of the National Security Council, and a lack of accountability.

The commission delivered a principal recommendation to strengthen the National Security Council. While the council went astray from its mission, the commission believed it still offered a valuable resource to each president it served.[14]

Independent Counsel Walsh concluded that several administration officials may have "violated laws and executive orders in the Iran/contra matter."[15] Arms sales to Iran and the provisioning of the Contras were among the violations of law, Walsh concluded.

Reagan distinguished himself from countless other presidents who shirked responsibility for their actions when caught up in a White House scandal. In a March 1987 televised address, Reagan came clean with the American people and assumed all blame for the Iran-Contra affair. He said:

> First, let me say I take full responsibility for my own actions and for those of my administration. As angry as I may be about activities undertaken without my knowledge, I am still accountable for those activities. As disappointed as I may be in some who served me, I'm still the one who must answer to the American people for this behavior.[16]

There was no evidence that Reagan knew the extent of the Iran-Contra dealings, according to the completed investigations. Administration officials intentionally withheld from Reagan key details.

Twelve individuals were indicted over their involvement in the Iran-Contra scandal. Five of them either had charges dismissed or had convictions overturned. In December 1992, shortly before he left office, President George H. W. Bush pardoned six of the remaining individuals embroiled in the Iran-Contra scandal. Among them were Robert McFarlane and Defense Secretary Caspar Weinberger.[17]

Forty years later, the Iranian people still live under inhumane and brutal conditions and suffer from economic stagnation. Additionally, the Iranian government continues to be a worldwide sponsor of terrorism.

Deep Throat

The Watergate complex consists of a half-dozen modern-architecture buildings that house a hotel, apartments, office suites, and retail businesses. The complex is nestled along the eastern bank of the Potomac River overlooking Roosevelt Island on one side and the start of official Washington, DC, on the other side, with the US State Department and the western end of the National Mall only steps away. Next-door is the John F. Kennedy Performing Arts Center. Construction was finalized on Watergate and the Kennedy Center in 1971.

The break-in that occurred at the Watergate office building in June 1972 established the use of "gate" as a suffix to add to any event to denote its status as a political scandal. A remarkable aspect of the burglary was how unnecessary it was. The break-in of the Democratic National Committee, which had its offices in a sixth-floor suite of the Watergate building, occurred in the months leading up to what was going to be a landslide reelection victory by Republican President Richard Nixon over Democratic challenger Senator George McGovern.

The seriousness of the break-in and the subsequent coverup was best summed up in the final report issued by the Senate committee investigating the scandal. "The Watergate affair reflects an alarming indifference displayed by some in the high public office or position to concepts of morality and public responsibility and trust. Indeed, the conduct of many Watergate participants seems grounded on the belief that the ends justified the means, that the laws could be flaunted to maintain the present administration in office."[18] The Watergate burglary also underscored the adage that often, it is not the act, but the cover-up, that is the real scandal.

The Democratic Party had been in disarray for a few years. Senator Edward "Ted" Kennedy of Massachusetts was considered by many in the party as the early front-runner for the 1972 Democratic nomination. He was the heir-apparent of Democratic royalty since his older brothers, John and Robert, had both been gunned down. However, Ted's reported drinking and womanizing, and the tragic drowning of a young woman in a car he drove off a bridge in 1969, delayed his entry into presidential politics.

McGovern championed liberal causes and issues that were far outside the mainstream of American political thought in the early

1970s. Nixon campaigned on achieving victory in Vietnam. McGovern preached immediate pullout. Democratic Senator Thomas Eagleton of Missouri famously remarked that McGovern would be unelectable once voters knew what he stood for. McGovern later selected Eagleton as his vice presidential running mate. Eagleton would be replaced on the ticket only three weeks after he was picked, when it was learned he underwent electroshock therapy during psychiatric analysis sessions.

There was little doubt that Nixon would easily be reelected. The question was how big the victory would be. In November, Nixon registered one of the biggest landslides in presidential election history. He captured more than 60 percent of the vote and won forty-nine states. McGovern won only Massachusetts and the District of Columbia. McGovern could not even carry his home state of South Dakota.

The heart of the Watergate scandal began nearly six months before Nixon was reelected. During the early hours of June 17, 1972, five men who worked for the Committee to Reelect the President, the Nixon reelection committee, were caught and arrested by Washington, DC, police officers. Bernard Barker, Virgilio Gonzalez, Eugenio Martínez, James McCord, and Frank Sturgis were apprehended in the offices of the Democratic National Committee. The five had broken into the party headquarters to make adjustments to listening devices installed on office telephones during an earlier break-in.

G. Gordon Liddy and E. Howard Hunt were officials with Nixon's reelection committee who were involved in the planning and overall supervision of the break-in. They were also part of an informal group known as the "White House plumbers," whose jobs were to prevent any leaks to the press of activities inside the Nixon reelection campaign. To some, the atmosphere of paranoia that appeared to engulf Nixon's campaign officials was merely a reflection of Nixon's personality.

The aftermath of the actual burglary was relatively quick and simple. A grand jury indicted Liddy, Hunt, and the five burglars in September 1972. By early 1973, Barker, Gonzalez, Hunt, Martínez, and Sturgis pled guilty. Liddy and McCord were convicted. However, the fallout from the burglary mushroomed into the biggest investigation of a political scandal since the Teapot Dome scandal fifty years earlier.

In the two-year period following the June 1972 Watergate break-in, simultaneous congressional and media investigations uncovered sweeping illegal activities tied to Nixon's reelection committee and key personnel in the office of the president. Over a period of several months, key aides and advisors to Nixon resigned, were fired, or were indicted.

One of the great mysteries of Watergate was the identity of Deep Throat, the nickname given to a key source who fed information to *Washington Post* reporters Bob Woodward and Carl Bernstein. Woodward and Bernstein reported much of the criminal activities involving Nixon and key staff.

When it became apparent that Richard Nixon would be impeached by the House and almost certainly be convicted by the Senate, he resigned from the presidency. Nixon tendered his resignation on August 8, 1974. One month later, in a national address from the Oval Office, President Gerald Ford declared, "Our long national nightmare is over," and issued Nixon a presidential pardon.

For years, it was presumed that Deep Throat was an individual acting in the best interest of the nation as he spoon-fed Woodward and Bernstein critical information. In 2005, W. Mark Felt, a former Deputy Director of the FBI, revealed that he was Deep Throat.[19] But rather than acting for altruistic reasons when he passed information to the *Washington Post* reporters, Felt was a bitter man who was seeking revenge against Nixon and the man who got the job he desperately wanted.[20] Felt was angry that Nixon passed him over as Director of the FBI when J. Edgar Hoover passed away in May 1972. Instead, Nixon picked an outsider, L. Patrick Gray, as the next director.[21]

Years later it was learned that Felt was the key figure ordering the FBI to violate civil rights and constitutional protections by engaging in illegal activities to pursue various groups and organizations at odds with US policies. Felt and an FBI assistant were convicted in 1980 of violating the civil rights of dozens of people. In hindsight, the most ironic moment was the courtroom appearance of Richard Nixon, who testified as a defense witness for Felt.

Richard Nixon came out of seclusion to testify as a defense witness to possibly save Mark Felt from being convicted of several felonies. Unbeknownst to Nixon, it was Felt who had ratted him out to Woodward and Bernstein. A bigger, self-respecting man would have never allowed Nixon to serve as a defense witness knowing he may have singlehandedly brought down Nixon. Apparently, Mark Felt had no reservations using the man he wanted to destroy.

Felt was convicted, and it was President Ronald Reagan who generously pardoned Felt to spare him from being incarcerated.[22]

Travelgate

"To the victor go the spoils" is a timeworn phrase first known to have been said by a US senator in 1832. It was a reference to the political patronage that benefits the winner of an election. To Hillary Clinton, it was an ironclad policy.

After the 1992 presidential election, but before Bill Clinton was sworn in as the 42nd president, Clinton's political supporters were exploring ways to cash in. One target was the White House Travel and Telegraph Office, commonly known as the White House Travel Office.

It was the responsibility of the White House Travel Office to schedule travel for the White House press corps that accompanied the president when traveling. The president and official members of his party are transported by the US Air Force 89th Airlift Wing located at Joint Base Andrews in Prince George's County, Maryland. Included in the 89th Airlift Wing is Air Force One.

The White House Travel Office contracts with commercial carriers to transport members of the White House press corps and then charges each traveling news organization a prorated amount of the cost. It is generally believed the White House began arranging travel for the press as early as the presidential administration of Andrew Johnson, who served from 1865 to 1869.[23]

On May 19, 1993, White House administrative chief David Watkins assembled five of the seven members of the White House Travel Office and told them they were fired effective June 5. He claimed poor management as the reason for their dismissal. As assistant to the president for management and administration, it was Watkins's responsibility to supervise the Travel Office.

The seven Travel Office employees had been working in the office between nine and thirty-two years. The director and deputy director, Billy Dale and Gary Wright, respectively, had been working in the office since 1961. The two employees who were not at the Watkins meeting were traveling abroad, one on an advance trip to Japan and the other on vacation in Ireland, when they heard press reports they had been fired and were accused of possible criminal wrongdoing.[24]

Catherine Cornelius assisted the Clinton campaign with travel during the 1992 race. In December 1992, a month before Clinton was inaugurated, Cornelius sent a memo to Watkins indicating her desire to be named the co-director of the Travel Office. The twenty-five-year-old Cornelius was a relative of Bill Clinton.[25] In all, Cornelius sent three memos to Watkins, replete with "significant errors" and "inaccurate" information, recommending changes to the Travel Office, including her appointment to head it.[26]

Two others behind the push to fire the Travel Office employees were Harry Thomason and Darnell Martens, who were longtime Clinton friends. Thomason was a Hollywood filmmaker who produced the campaign film *A Man from Hope*, which promoted Clinton's candidacy. He also produced events that were part of the Clinton inauguration. Thomason and Martens were partners with Dan Richland in an aviation consulting firm named Thomason, Richland & Martens, Inc. (TRM). It was their plan to have TRM take over White House Travel Office functions.

In its investigation, the Government Accountability Office (GAO) found that Cornelius, Thomason, and Martens "had potential personal or business interests in the Travel Office."[27] The GAO was also troubled by Thomason and Martens's "unrestricted access to the White House complex and their participation in discussions and activities leading up to the removal of the [Travel Office] employees." Thomason was even given an office in the East Wing. The GAO's concern arose over an obvious conflict of interest.

Thomason and Martens were not full-time government employees, nor were they special government employees. A special government employee is someone temporarily employed by the White House for no more than 130 days during any one-year period. Government employees and special government employees are bound by conflict-of-interest safeguards. In spite of having unrestricted access to the White House, the unpaid "volunteer" status was a loophole that meant neither Thomason nor Martens were required by rule or regulation to abide by conflict-of-interest restrictions.

Watkins admitted to GAO investigators that it was Thomason who had told him there was possible wrongdoing in the Travel Office. Reportedly, Martens told Thomason he had "heard a rumor" that there was "corruption" in the office, but no details were offered. According to the independent counsel's investigation, Thomason told more than one person there was a mysterious Georgetown bank used by the Travel Office, and that Travel Office employees were soliciting kickbacks.

No investigation ever substantiated Thomason's claims. One of the chief complaints Thomason made to Watkins about the Travel Office was that it had no intention of passing business to Thomason's firm, TRM. Dale's position was that the office was already dealing directly with the airlines. Adding a middleman would only raise costs.[28]

TRM was far from a heavyweight in the airline consulting business. Aside from the Clinton campaign, TRM had had only two other clients since its start-up in 1991. Additionally, Martens was the TRM president and its sole employee.[29]

Long before any concrete steps were taken to fire the Travel Office employees, Martens and Thomason were scheming on what was to occur next. The Travel Office was not the endgame. The real goal, according to a January 29, 1993, confidential memo from Martens to Thomason, was to have TRM appointed to oversee the federal government's entire fleet of non-military aircraft.

In the memo, Martens discussed "Washington opportunities." He proposed TRM "review all non-military government aircraft to determine financial and operational appropriateness."[30] To accomplish this, the pair needed first to prove TRM's bona fides as accomplished airline consultants and then be appointed by presidential executive order— hence, the takeover of the White House Travel Office.

On May 12th, Cornelius, Thomason, Martens, and Watkins met to discuss the Travel Office. Afterwards, Thomason met with First Lady Hillary Clinton. The First Lady then instructed Watkins to get "our people" into the Travel Office.[31] In a memo he sent to White House Chief of Staff Thomas McLarty, Watkins warned "there would be hell to pay" if they didn't replace the Travel Office employees "in conformity with the First Lady's wishes."[32]

On May 17, Travel Officer Director Billy Dale, unaware of the scheming that was underway, told Watkins he wanted to retire.

Watkins refused to accept the request. Two days later, Watkins fired Dale and the others.[33]

On May 18, Watkins received a report from audit firm KPMG regarding Travel Office operations. At the request of White House officials, KPMG began an audit just three business days before the firings. KPMG found the office had "significant financial management weaknesses…[and] poor accounting systems."[34] In its later review, the GAO found that, at least since the 1980s, and possibly earlier, "White House officials provided little guidance or oversight to Travel Office employees."[35] It was well into spring 1993 before Dale learned to whom to report in the Clinton administration.[36] Watkins later told GAO investigators that he did not provide any guidance to the Travel Office because he had higher priorities.[37]

The day of the firings, the White House requested World Wide Travel Service, Inc., and Air Advantage to immediately handle travel responsibilities. Both companies had connections to the Clintons, as they had provided air travel services to the Clinton campaign. The two companies were notified days in advance of the anticipated firings—in one case, before KPMG even commenced its audit.[38]

World Wide Travel Service quit two days after taking over as the scandal began dominating headlines. Air Advantage came under criticism when it pocketed a commission. Both World Wide Travel and Air Advantage were quickly replaced with American Express Travel, which was already an approved government contractor.

Six months earlier, World Wide Travel Service was confident it would get White House travel business under Clinton. World Wide President Betta Carney told Arkansas press outlets after Clinton was elected that she expected her firm to take over White House travel business. In December 1992, she wrote the Clinton transition team expressing a desire to provide travel services to the White House.[39] Betta Carney was a Clinton campaign donor.[40]

The firing of the Travel Office employees was a foregone conclusion. The White House press office prepared talking points on May 13th announcing the firings. This was one day before KPMG began its audit.[41] The KPMG audit was the official reason the Clinton White House gave for firing the employees. The same day, according to the independent counsel's investigation that was conducted later, the First Lady "was on the warpath" because "our people weren't there to serve the President."[42]

Looking back, another indicator the seven employees might soon be canned occurred when a long-stemmed rose, accompanied by a card from the president and First Lady, was delivered to each White House employee marking Clinton's one hundredth day in office. The Travel Office employees weren't among the recipients.[43]

As the build-up continued toward the eventual firings, White House officials were passing around fantastical stories of criminal activity. Included among these, Travel Office employees apparently owned "vacation home[s]," "racehorses," "a home in Switzerland," and were "soliciting kickbacks," "skimming funds," "crooks," reimbursed for personal travel, and played golf every Wednesday.[44] White House officials had demonized the seven Travel Office employees.

On May 19, White House Press Secretary Dee Dee Myers announced the firing of the Travel Office employees, then added that the FBI was conducting a criminal investigation. This revelation was a shock to the fired employees because no one at the White House had suggested they were suspected of criminal activity. Myers's announcement deeply annoyed the FBI, since the agency had not even begun a preliminary investigation.[45]

After several days of widespread criticism over the firings, which CNN pundits dubbed "Travelgate," the Clinton administration backtracked and informed five of the Travel Office employees that they were not fired. Instead, they were placed on administrative leave while the White House lined up jobs elsewhere in the federal government. The director and deputy director had already announced their retirements.

Six weeks after the firings, the White House issued a surprisingly critical report of how the Clinton administration bungled the matter. The report admitted the abrupt firings were "unnecessary and insensitive" and the employees should have been given specific reasons for their dismissal. Four White House officials were named for having acted improperly, but were merely given letters of reprimand.

On July 20, White House Deputy General Counsel Vince Foster committed suicide. Foster was consumed with depression and anxiety over his work in the Clinton transition team and, later, the White House.[46] He was virtually alone when he cautioned a White House hell-bent on firing the workers to instead take a more professional and balanced approach. It is widely believed that two major events contributed to the decision to kill himself: the Travelgate scandal and Hillary's humiliation of him only days earlier, in the presence of several others, by calling him "a little hick-town lawyer who was obviously not ready for the big time."[47]

The Department of Justice announced the indictment of former Travel Office Director Billy Dale on December 7, 1994. He faced charges of embezzlement. After a thirteen-day trial, jurors quickly rendered a not guilty verdict on November 16, 1995.

During the course of his investigation, the independent counsel confirmed that Hillary Clinton had at least eleven conversations with various individuals regarding the White House Travel Office. This directly contradicted the testimony she gave the Government Accountability Office, Congress, and the independent counsel, stating that she played no role in the firings. However, the independent counsel "concluded that the evidence was insufficient to prove to a jury beyond a reasonable doubt that…Mrs. Clinton committed perjury or obstruction of justice."[48]

Further, the independent counsel concluded Clinton was not truthful when she testified before the grand jury that she did not have a role in the firing of the White House Travel Office employees. Yet, the counsel wrote, "The available admissible evidence is insufficient to prove beyond a reasonable doubt that Mrs. Clinton knowingly made a false statement in her sworn denial of such a role or input."[49]

In her post-White House memoir, Hillary Clinton falsely wrote, "Before we moved into the White House, neither Bill nor I nor our immediate staff had known there was a White House Travel Office."[50] Contrary to Hillary's assertions, the Clinton staff was scheming on replacing the director with Bill's cousin several weeks before Bill Clinton's inauguration as the 42nd president.

COINTELPRO

COINTELPRO began in 1956 as a formal effort by the Federal Bureau of Investigation to disrupt domestic organizations the Bureau saw as a threat to national security. The name COINTELPRO was an acronym for counterintelligence program. However, the FBI went far beyond merely collecting intelligence on individuals and organizations it claimed posed a threat. It conducted covert actions that were clearly unlawful and unconstitutional.

The FBI ended the formal COINTELPRO program in 1971, when internal documents detailing the program's activities were about to be made public. The general public learned of COINTELPRO in 1976 when the Senate Select Committee to Study Governmental Operations with Respect to Intelligence Activities released its report. The committee, chaired by Democratic Senator Frank Church of Idaho, was often referred to as the Church Committee.

The Church Committee was formed to investigate abuses by the nation's intelligence agencies, including the Federal Bureau of Investigation, Central Intelligence Agency, and National Security Agency, as well as by the Internal Revenue Service. Many targets of abuse were thousands of Americans not guilty or even suspected of any crimes. One result of the Church Committee and its companion Pike Committee in the House of Representatives was the formation of House and Senate intelligence committees responsible for oversight of the nation's spy agencies.

The covert nature of COINTELPRO and other intelligence and law enforcement abuses meant a "victim may never suspect that his misfortunes are the intended result of activities undertaken by his government, and accordingly may have no opportunity to challenge the actions taken against him."[51]

Under COINTELPRO, the FBI targeted five categories of people and organizations. The FBI referred to these as the Communist Party USA, Socialist Workers Party, White Hate Group, Black Nationalist Hate Group, and the New Left.

The Communist Party USA, and the Socialist Workers Party were established organizations with formal membership that were often easy to identify. The Ku Klux Klan and similar organizations such as the American Nazi Party and the National States' Rights Party were slotted into the White Hate Group.[52]

Individuals or organizations placed in the Black Nationalist Hate Group didn't even have to espouse black nationalism. The supervisor in charge of the Black Nationalist Hate Group effort told Congress individuals or organizations were placed there because they were "primarily black."[53]

The category called the New Left was vaguely defined. In his deposition for Congress, the FBI supervisor of the New Left targeting effort said the defining criterion was "more or less an attitude." He further said the New Left was a "loosely-bound, free-wheeling, college-oriented movement."[54]

There were three goals of COINTELPRO activities. The first was to protect national security. This is where the classic counterintelligence model came into play. The FBI was monitoring the activities of the Communist Party USA to determine if it was acting in cooperation with Soviet intelligence in order to spread propaganda in the United States.

A second goal was to prevent violence. Rather than focusing on specific criminal acts, the FBI tried to limit membership in targeted groups. One FBI supervisor testified before Congress that the strategy was to deter membership to keep targeted groups as small as possible. However, by attacking a group's membership, freedom of assembly, and advocacy, the FBI was running afoul of the Constitution's First Amendment protections.

This strategy was further complicated because the FBI admitted that some of the groups or individuals it targeted had not been involved in violence. A 1968 FBI memorandum noted that the peaceful Reverend Doctor Martin Luther King, Jr., was targeted because he might "abandon his supposed 'obedience' to 'white, liberal doctrines' (non-violence) and embrace black nationalism."[55]

The third goal of COINTELPRO was to maintain the existing social and political order. The FBI presumed to have a responsibility to combat anyone who operated outside of what the bureau thought was the proper social and political order. For example, the FBI targeted a pair of students who publicly defended the use of a four-letter expletive.[56] According to an internal FBI memorandum, use of the expletive "shows obvious disregard for decency and established morality."[57]

Assistant to the FBI Director, William Sullivan, was in overall charge of COINTELPRO. In his 1975 testimony before Congress, he cautioned that the mission of COINTELPRO was "a rough, tough, dirty business and dangerous. It was dangerous at times. No holds were barred."

He further testified that the FBI "did not differentiate" between Soviet agents and US citizens. The FBI treated them the same.[58]

The FBI used numerous techniques honed during World War II in tracking wartime enemies in conducting its domestic surveillance and covert action missions. Some actions were intended to create disruption and havoc. These techniques included anonymously mailing magazine articles to targets to reinforce what the bureau thought was proper behavior. For example, a newspaper column that supported the US military presence in Vietnam was sent to organizations advocating withdrawal. A more aggressive tactic was mailing a letter to the spouse of a target accusing the target of infidelity.

The FBI would sometimes instigate violence among gangs. The bureau would also falsely identify targeted members in gangs or organizations as police informants. This could cause the expulsion of the target from the organization or could result in violence, even fatal violence, against the target by other members.

Another technique employed by the FBI was to work with cooperating media to plant questions to be asked of targets during news interviews. Or the FBI would pressure an employer to fire a target from his job. And it would also use the IRS to conduct audits on targets.[59]

Sullivan was right. COINTELPRO was "a rough, tough, dirty business."

In an internal review of COINTELPRO, the FBI acknowledged that some of its actions might have violated civil-rights laws, as well as mail, wire-fraud, and extortion laws. Despite this, the FBI reached the conclusion that it was necessary for the bureau to commit criminal acts and violate Constitutional protections afforded citizens because it was serving a greater good. The attitude among the bureau was that it was free to do whatever it wanted without regard to legal restrictions because, as one bureau witness testified before Congress, the FBI was hampered "because of something called the United States Constitution."[60]

When asked if there were concerns about law breaking or violating Constitutional rights during COINTELPRO operations, one FBI witness told Congress what was characterized as a "typical response" on this topic. He testified, "No, we never gave it a thought."[61]

There was also complacency about the questionable activities of COINTELPRO by higher-ups outside the FBI. Former Attorney General

Ramsey Clark, who served under President Lyndon Johnson from 1967 to 1969, testified he was far too busy to know about the FBI's activities. His predecessor, who served in the Johnson administration from 1965 to 1966, testified that regardless of what he thought, there was nothing he could have done to stop the FBI.[62]

COINTELPRO was officially terminated in April 1971. However, the Church Committee learned the FBI continued "COINTEL-PRO-type operations" after the formal program was shut down. The FBI merely continued similar operations as components of individual case operations. The only way for the Church Committee to determine the prevalence of COINTELPRO-like operations would have been to examine each of the FBI's more than half-million case files.[63] This appeared to be a nearly impossible task.

House Bank

On September 18, 1991, the Government Accounting Office[*] (GAO) delivered a bombshell report.[64] The US House of Representatives' "deposit fund," more commonly known as the House Bank, had been operating a check-kiting scheme that involved hundreds of current and past members of the House. Check-kiting is the process of writing a check with the knowledge that there are insufficient funds in the account to cover it, but anticipating that future deposits will become available.

The GAO had conducted a routine audit of the House of Representatives Office of the Sergeant at Arms. The GAO examined three appropriations funds and the House Bank. These four accounts are only some of the financial accounts under the supervision of the Sergeant at Arms.

After a previous audit, the GAO notified the Sergeant at Arms that there were a significant number of checks drawn on House Bank accounts that were returned due to insufficient funds. The GAO found "a lack of check-cashing procedures was a primary cause of the situation."[65]

The House Bank then adopted check-cashing procedures, but this did not eliminate or reduce the number of checks returned due to

---

[*]   The Government Accounting Office changed its name to Government Accountability Office in 2004.

insufficient funds. In fact, the number rose! In the new audit, the GAO found there were 4,006 checks returned due to insufficient funds in the six-month period prior to the implementation of check-cashing procedures. However, after the implementation of procedures, the number of returned checks in a six-month period grew to 4,325.

In a one-year period, House members bounced 8,331 checks. The GAO reported that in the most recent six-month period, 134 House Bank account holders wrote 581 bounced checks in the amount of $1,000 or more. Two-dozen account holders were averaging at least one bounced check a month.

After the blistering GAO report became public, the House voted 390–8 to close the House Bank and refer the scandal to the House Ethics Committee to investigate.[66]

On March 5, 1992, Democratic leaders announced a plan to identify only the top two-dozen worst offenders of the bank scandal. Republicans rebelled and demanded a full accounting of all members who bounced checks during the thirty-nine-month period identified in the GAO report. Bad publicity and Republican pressure caused the Democrats to abandon the plan to keep secret the identities of most offenders. This was a remarkable turnabout, since Republicans held only 166 of 435 House seats.

On March 12th, the House voted 426–0 to publicly release the names of everyone who bounced a check.[67] Full disclosure wouldn't occur until April in order to give House members time to perform damage control with their constituents. An early casualty of the scandal was Sergeant at Arms Jack Russ, who many Congressmen wanted to make the fall guy. He resigned on March 12, 1992.

The following month, the House Ethics Committee issued the explosive report. There were 325 former and current members of the House who had written 24,097 checks with insufficient funds to cover them: 205 Democrats had bounced 17,543 checks and 119 Republicans were responsible for 6,549 bad checks. The chamber's lone Democratic Socialist, Bernie Sanders, had written five checks that didn't have sufficient funds to cover them. Republican Tommy Robinson of Arkansas had written the largest number of bad checks: 996. Two-hundred-sixty-nine of the check bouncers were sitting members of Congress.

The scandal was far from over. US Attorney General William Barr appointed a retired federal judge as special counsel to determine if any laws were broken. Special counsel Malcolm Wilkey subpoenaed the House Bank records, but House Democrats responded that they would not comply with the subpoena. Again, public outcry and Republican pressure forced House leaders to back down. The House voted 347–64 to comply with the special counsel and turn over the subpoenaed records.[68]

By 1995, ten individuals associated with the banking scandal, including current and former members of Congress and other House officials, were convicted or pled guilty to various charges related to the banking scandal.

The public was appalled at the scandal. One poll registered 88 percent of voters calling it a "big deal."[69] There were others who saw it differently. University of California, Berkeley Professor Nelson Polsby said the scandal was much ado about nothing, it was "unscandalous," and the media's "willingness to puff it into a scandal was a disservice." He blamed the public's negative reaction to the scandal as the result of "opportunism by Republicans."[70]

Just as the House Bank scandal was starting to wind down, another House scandal was cranking up.

House Post Office

Robert Rota resigned as the US House Postmaster in March 1992. He had served in the House post office for twenty-five years, the last twenty as postmaster. His resignation occurred in the midst of a report that a US Capitol Police criminal investigation was underway, involving alleged drug dealing and embezzlement by House post-office employees.[71] Around the same time, a US Postal Service audit found a nearly $35,000 shortfall in the post office account.

In 1991, post-office employees told investigators with the US Attorney for DC that some employees were using post-office funds for personal expenses and were selling cocaine to others. Eventually, a half-dozen post-office employees were either charged with several counts of criminal charges or pled guilty to several criminal charges. Rota's resignation occurred after this and other improper behavior came to light. Post-office employees had been cashing official vouchers and campaign checks for House members. It is a violation of postal service rules to accept checks for anything other than postal products and services.

Democratic House Speaker Thomas Foley of Washington denied that Rota's resignation was related to the criminal investigations. Foley claimed Rota had been considering retirement for months. The Speaker said, "There is no spreading scandal here."[72]

Foley's denial of the scandal was answered with the revelation on May 14 that three House members had received grand jury subpoenas. Spending vouchers from January 1986 to April 1992 and related financial records were subpoenaed from Illinois Congressman and powerful Ways and Means Committee Chairman Don Rostenkowski, and Pennsylvania Congressmen Joe Kolter and Austin Murphy, all Democrats. House Sergeant at Arms Werner Brandt and House Clerk Donnald Anderson were also served with subpoenas demanding the two turn over financial documents under their control. All three congressmen professed their innocence and said they looked forward to the investigation exonerating them.

The subpoenas had been delivered more than a week earlier, on May 6. Foley and other senior Democratic leaders attempted to keep the existence of the subpoenas secret and didn't tell the Republican minority leadership, as is the protocol in such situations.[73] GOP leaders introduced a resolution that was passed with a bipartisan vote of 324–3 that directed Foley to produce the subpoenas in accordance with House rules and inform the entire chamber the reason for keeping the subpoenas secret. More than a hundred House members didn't vote.[74]

A House post-office employee told federal investigators that several members of Congress were cashing official House Bank checks under the guise that they were for stamp purchases. In reality, House members were pocketing the money. A related scam was to actually purchase stamps, but then trade them into the post office for cash. This was referred to as "cashing out." Both actions were prohibited under US Postal Service regulations and House rules. Moreover, failure to report the money as personal income would have been a violation of IRS tax law.

It wasn't a surprise to members that the House post office was being mismanaged. One of the earliest votes in the 1992 session was an order directing the Committee on House Administration to investigate the House post office.[75] A GOP resolution that would have created a separate committee composed of Democrat and Republican House members to investigate the post office was soundly defeated along a party-line vote.[76]

By July, the House Administration Committee completed its investigation. It was actually two investigations. The committee broke down along party lines, and each party conducted its own investigation. There was surprise when the full committee reconvened to exchange the two draft reports.

The Republican report found numerous shortcomings in House post office management and noted several unanswered questions that warranted further investigation. For example, there were "ghost employees" in the post office. These were friends or relatives of members who were on the post-office payroll but didn't perform any work.

The Democratic report found no serious wrongdoing and declared the matter closed. The Democrats, who enjoyed nearly forty-year control of the House of Representatives, ruled there would be no further scrutiny of the House post office.

Meanwhile, the ongoing federal investigation continued. Rostenkowski, Kolter, and Murphy had been under special scrutiny from federal investigators due to the high dollar amount of their post-office transactions. Rostenkowski had made nearly $55,000 in stamp purchases in the six years being scrutinized. Kolter bought more than $17,000 worth, and Murphy spent just over $9,000 on stamps.

Unlike a typical post office, the House post office did not report to the US Postal Service chain of command. Instead, the employees worked at the pleasure of the House Speaker. At this point, the Speaker was Tom Foley. Still, the employees were required to operate in accordance with postal service regulations and within the law. The reality, however, was that the post office had become ground zero in political patronage and nepotism. Several congressmen had family members working in the post office.

Federal law prohibits the solicitation of campaign donations from federal property. In addition, campaign contributions are not to be sent to members' congressional offices. Many members rented private post boxes near Capitol Hill for campaign correspondence. At least ten Congressmen had House post-office employees retrieve campaign-related mail, including political contributions, from their rented post boxes and deliver it to their official offices. This was a violation of federal law.

One Republican and nine Democratic congressmen were implicated in this campaign mail delivery scheme. They were Republican Jan Meyers of Kansas and the following Democrats: Dan Rostenkowski of Illinois, Dennis Hertel of Michigan, Nicholas Mavroules of Massachusetts, Mario Biaggi and Samuel Stratton of New York, Mary Rose Oakar and Edward Feighan of Ohio, Fernand St. Germain of Rhode Island, and Jim Moody of Wisconsin.

There were no developments in the House chamber regarding the post office for another year, when former Postmaster Robert Rota pleaded guilty to a number of criminal charges. He provided testimony to investigators that implicated Rostenkowski and Kolter in a money-laundering operation involving the post office. Rota said the House post office was "a convenient…and largely untraceable source of illegal cash for selected members of Congress."[77]

On July 22, 1993, just days after the damning revelations, the House voted 414–0 to refer the post-office scandal to the House Ethics Committee and turn over all relevant documents to the US Justice Department.[78]

Congressman Dan Rostenkowski was indicted on seventeen felony counts. Congressman Joseph Kolter was indicted on five counts. On April 10, 1996, Rostenkowski agreed to a plea deal. He pleaded guilty to two charges of mail fraud and was sentenced to seventeen months in federal prison. Kolter pleaded guilty to a single count of conspiring to embezzle from the federal government. On July 31, 1996, he was sentenced to six months in prison.

President Bill Clinton pardoned Rostenkowski in December 2000.

Court-Packing

When Democratic nominee Franklin Roosevelt was elected president in 1932, he was joined by a super-majority of Democrats in each chamber of Congress. Democrats (including Farm-Labor Party and Progressive Representatives who caucused with the Democratic Party) held a 60–36 advantage in the Senate and an even more stunning 318–117 majority in the House from 1933–1935. Two years later, Democratic majorities increased to 70–25 in the Senate and 332–103 in the House.

These super-majorities made it very easy to enact the many programs associated with Roosevelt's New Deal. Roosevelt's theory, endorsed by Democratic majorities in Congress, was that government should be managing the economy instead of the free market, and that there should be a centralization of power in the presidency. The executive branch made proposals, which the legislative branch passed without any hesitation. However, the third branch of government also had a say.

The US Supreme Court faced an astonishing number of court challenges to Roosevelt's New Deal programs. The high court ruled many of these programs unconstitutional. On May 27, 1935, the Supreme Court struck down Roosevelt's key construct, the National Industrial Recovery Act, on a day some referred to as "Black Monday." It was not even a squeaker of a case. The court unanimously declared unconstitutional "not just the program but its entire system of minimum wages, maximum hours, and workers' rights."[79]

The National Industrial Recovery Act was one of three significant court defeats that were announced on Black Monday. Roosevelt lost other cases both before and after Black Monday, in which Congress either ceded too much authority to the executive branch or allowed government to encroach on individual rights and economic freedoms.[80]

During Roosevelt's first term, the court also struck down as unconstitutional the Agricultural Adjustment, Guffey Coal, Railroad Retirement, and Bituminous Coal Conservation Acts. "No Supreme Court in history had ever struck down so many laws so quickly."[81] Even reliably liberal Supreme Court Justice Louis Brandeis voted against sacred Roosevelt programs. He privately told Roosevelt aides: "Go back and tell the president that we're not going to let this government centralize everything. It's come to an end."[82]

Roosevelt and Congress were enacting new programs at a phenomenal rate, matched only by the rate at which the judicial branch found them in violation of the Constitution. "Between 1933 and 1936, the court overturned acts of Congress at ten times the traditional rate."[83] By the end of 1935, Roosevelt was concerned that nearly all of his New Deal legislation would be found unconstitutional. His attacks on the Supreme Court became so unnerving that all nine justices, conservatives and liberals alike, boycotted his 1936 State of the Union address.[84]

Roosevelt breezed through his 1936 reelection with ease. Not only was he returned to the White House for a second presidential term, but he was also the beneficiary of increased Democratic majorities. The majorities were so lopsided that it was as if there was not a single Republican in all of Congress. Democrats held a 79–17 edge in the Senate and a 347–88 majority in the House.

In the lame duck period between election day and inauguration day, Roosevelt formalized a scheme that would effectively eliminate the judicial branch as an impediment to his plans. His closest political confidants were aghast when they learned of his plan. Author Jeff Shesol described the reaction of Roosevelt's senior staff when the 32nd president revealed his intentions to remake the Supreme Court.

> In January 1937, the president began to inform several top advisers about his plan. All were astounded; some were distraught. One senior counselor reacted with "extreme political fear and shock," confessing to a colleague he was "scared to death." What terrified him was precisely what delighted Roosevelt: the artfulness, the deviousness of making the case against the Court one of infirmity rather than ideology. When the cloak came off—as the president's men expected it would—Roosevelt's motives would stand exposed and integrity, they feared, would be in tatters.[85]

When Roosevelt's plan became public, his political opponents accused him of pursuing "dictatorial powers, and compared him to Machiavelli, Stalin, Hitler, [and] Mussolini…Even Vice President Garner held his nose and turned thumbs down" on Roosevelt's proposal. It was telling that the German and Italian press wrote that Roosevelt's intentions were similar to the actions of their autocratic leaders.[86] The Nazi and Fascist governments ruled Germany and Italy, respectively, when German and Italian newspapers were praising Roosevelt's intentions.

Roosevelt's scheme was to introduce legislation that would enable him to appoint one new justice up to six for every current justice who reached the age of seventy and had not retired. This would allow him to immediately appoint six. Roosevelt expected both chambers of Congress to rubber-stamp his bill as they had done with all of his other programs. Next, Roosevelt would nominate lackeys to the court who would support all of his programs.[87] Roosevelt was confident the seventy-nine Democrats in the Senate would confirm all of his nominees without question.

At least that was Roosevelt's plan.

The US Constitution never specified the number of justices on the Supreme Court. The number of justices on the high court had fluctuated since the nation's founding. There were six justices during the Supreme Court's very first term and ten justices in the midst of the Civil War.

In the nineteenth century, the Judiciary Act of 1869 was passed into law. Among other provisions regarding circuit courts, the law stipulated there to be a chief justice and eight associate justices. For nearly seventy years, this was the precedent.

Roosevelt wanted to have fifteen justices on the court. This, he thought, would ensure him a loyal panel of justices who would ignore Constitutional restrictions. Late in his first term, Roosevelt contemplated a constitutional amendment that would render the Supreme Court ineffective. However, he realized he did not have the public support to get such an amendment ratified.

Roosevelt announced his bill, the Judicial Procedures Reform Bill of 1937, in early February 1937. As is custom, he requested the House to first take up consideration of his proposal. Up until this point, Roosevelt had enjoyed an incurious Democratic majority that quickly approved one program after another. However, Roosevelt misjudged the House reaction this time.

The first error committed by Roosevelt was that he never consulted House leaders, as was customary when the executive branch wanted to introduce legislation. House leaders were as surprised as the public. The second error was that Roosevelt never considered House Democrats' fidelity to the Constitution. They were more loyal to the Constitutional construct of three separate but equal branches of government than they were to the titular head of the Democratic Party. Roosevelt's bill was not going to move in the House.

The Senate was approached next. In Senate hearings, administration witnesses testified that the current justices were too old to do their jobs, they were overworked, and, most critically, new justices were needed to rule favorably on New Deal programs. However, the Senate was not in favor of dramatically changing the court's makeup any more than the House. Even Democratic Senator Burton Wheeler of Montana, who was the first Senator to endorse Roosevelt's candidacy, called the court-packing scheme "sham reform."[88]

Roosevelt tried to rally public support for his proposal to change the Supreme Court by speaking directly to the public during one of his radio addresses known as fireside chats. In spite of his immense popularity, Roosevelt did not have any success. Polling showed the public was consistently opposed to his court-packing proposal. Ad hoc groups were springing up around the country opposed to remaking the Supreme Court. Even Vice President John Garner opposed Roosevelt's scheme.

In June 1937, the Senate Judiciary Committee voted down the bill and delivered sharp criticism of the proposal, calling it "a needless, futile, and utterly dangerous abandonment of constitutional principle." Still, the committee sent the bill to the full Senate for consideration.

Roosevelt was still confident he could get his bill passed in the Senate. Senate Majority Leader Joseph Robinson had blind loyalty to Roosevelt. It no doubt helped that Roosevelt promised to appoint Robinson to the Supreme Court upon the first vacancy. It was a promise Roosevelt had no intention of keeping.[89] Unfortunately for Roosevelt's plan, Robinson died before he could marshal enough votes to pass the bill. The legislation was soundly defeated on the Senate floor by a 70 to 20 vote.

Ironically, Roosevelt essentially got what he wanted before he died in 1944. Seven of the nine justices that were on the court when Roosevelt was first elected either retired or passed away. This allowed Roosevelt to appoint jurists who would unquestionably endorse his programs, regardless of Constitutional concerns.

Filegate

In December 1993, seven months after the Clinton administration fired the entire White House Travel Office, the administration requested the FBI file on Billy Dale, the former director of the Travel Office. Dale had retired from federal service more than half a year earlier. Dale had no reason to be at the White House, and there was no legal reason for White House officials to request his FBI background investigations. But they did. The FBI should not have forwarded Dale's file to White House staffers. But it did.

The request for Dale's FBI files was sent on a memorandum that included the name of the White House Counsel, Bernard Nussbaum, as the memorandum originator.[90] Nussbaum claimed he did not request the files. In fact, everyone at the White House denied sending the request in Nussbaum's name, but obviously someone sent it. The memorandum justified the request for Dale's confidential files by falsely claiming the White House wanted to grant him new security access. It was not until a congressional committee began investigating that the truth started coming out.

The complete FBI files on Billy Dale that went all the way back to the Kennedy administration, more than three decades earlier, were sent to the Clinton White House. Also sent to the White House were FBI reports on at least 338 Republican officials and officeholders.[91] Later reports peg this number closer to 900 FBI files. It was eventually learned that the total number of FBI files on GOP officials improperly requested by White House officials was nearly 1,300.

These files contained confidential information on the individuals and their immediate family members. There is confidential personal information and private financial information in a background investigation. White House officials claim they had no idea who requested the FBI records on their political opponents. Once the files arrived at the White House, Clinton administration officials claimed, the records were locked in a vault and no one looked at them.[92] Clinton administration officials never explained why they did not immediately return the records to the FBI if they were truly sent in error and they had no reason to examine them.

The House Committee on Government Reform and Oversight discovered the existence of Billy Dale's FBI file in the possession of White House officials only after the Clinton administration faced a contempt vote. The committee was at the tail end of its investigation into Travelgate. The committee learned the White House withheld more than three thousand pages of documents it claimed were "personnel" records and "deliberative material" from the White House Counsel's office. The White House cited executive privilege in withholding the records.[93]

The committee issued a subpoena on January 11, 1996, for all pertinent documents relating to Billy Dale. A vote for contempt of Congress was scheduled after the White House refused to comply with the subpoena. The White House delivered more than one thousand pages of documents the day the contempt vote was scheduled. None of the documents delivered to the committee met the criteria for executive privilege. They should have never been withheld. White House Counsel Jack Quinn told congressional investigators he had made a blanket claim of executive privilege at the direction of President Bill Clinton.[94]

Dale's FBI file was among those documents marked as having come from the White House Counsel's Office, where it should not have been kept.

Craig Livingstone and Anthony Marceca were in charge of the Office of Personnel Security in the Clinton White House. Their primary task was to keep tabs on who had White House access, remind staff when it was time to undergo a background investigation, and provide periodic security briefings. The actual background investigations were conducted by the Federal Bureau of Investigation, and the Secret Service was responsible for White House security, making the job assignments of Livingstone and Marceca merely administrative.

Livingstone was a Clinton campaign worker and a former bar bouncer.[95] He had no training and experience in security matters, but he did have a checkered employment history. Remarkably, Livingstone and White House officials denied knowing who recommended Livingstone for the job and who approved his hiring. Congressional investigators found FBI notes from an interview with Nussbaum who said Livingstone had come "highly recommended by Hillary Clinton."[96] She denied knowing Livingstone.

Marceca was a civilian employee for the Department of the Army who was detailed to the White House to work in the Office of Personnel Security at the request of Livingstone. The pair knew each other from work on past election activities. Reportedly, Marceca was an expert in investigation matters, although his performance at the White House suggested otherwise.

The answer to who requested the FBI background files kept changing. Livingstone initially explained the delivery of the FBI files detailing individuals from the previous two Republican administrations as an "innocent mistake." Later, a White House counsel to the president claimed records were mistakenly requested by unnamed "file clerks." Then White House officials claimed the records were requested by the Government Accounting Office, a claim denied by the GAO.[97] President Bill Clinton called it "a completely honest bureaucratic snafu."[98]

Livingstone's attorney later stated that an unnamed staff member accidentally used staff lists of the Reagan and Bush administrations when requesting FBI files. Left unexplained is how such staff lists would have been available to the Clinton administration when all documents, records, and files for each administration are collected and shipped to the National Archives for delivery to the respective presidential libraries.

The Clinton administration did not explain how no one on the staff questioned why FBI files were requested and delivered on such prominent and easily recognizable Republicans such as former Secretary of State James A. Baker, former National Security Advisor Brent Scowcroft and former spokesman Marlin Fitzwater.[99]

In a letter to the committee, a White House counsel later claimed the Republican files were requested in the "mistaken understanding" that officials from the previous two Republican administrations would "have access to the White House compound after the start of the Clinton administration." Further, the letter included a statement from Marceca that he examined the Republican files for "derogatory information," which he passed on to Livingstone.[100]

In congressional testimony, Clinton officials claim the Secret Service generated the list of names from the Reagan and Bush administrations, but they were unable to provide investigators with that list because they destroyed it after requesting the FBI files.[101] The Secret Service denied this claim, stating its database is incapable of generating an out-of-date list.[102]

In her memoir, Hillary Clinton offered her take on how the White House received hundreds of FBI files on prominent Republicans. She claimed the FBI sent records that were not requested, a claim contradicted by White House staff years earlier. "Livingstone and Marceca were trying to rebuild these OPS [Office of Personnel Security] records when they received from the FBI hundreds of files, including some from Reagan and Bush officials."[103]

It was learned during the course of the committee investigation that the Clinton administration abandoned safeguards that had been in place for decades. Only a small number of individuals with experience in security matters and with completed background investigations would have access to sensitive personnel files during previous administrations. The Clinton administration allowed virtually anyone, including college interns, to have unfettered access in many of the White House offices, including in the personnel security vault where the sensitive FBI files were stored.[104]

It is worth noting, this scandal may have never occurred if the FBI questioned why the Clinton administration requested sensitive background investigations on prominent Republicans who had not served in the White House for a decade or longer. C. Boyden Gray, the White House counsel to President George H. W. Bush, is convinced the FBI would not have honored a similar request if the Bush administration requested FBI background files on Carter administration officials.[105]

The FBI conducted an internal review of its practices. The general counsel stated the bureau "complied with all applicable law," but acknowledged it improperly provided 887 FBI files in response to the Clinton administration, whose request was "without justification and served no official purpose." The FBI further noted that improper Clinton administration requests for another 408 FBI records would not be honored.[106]

The House Committee on Government Reform and Oversight delivered an interim report of its investigation on September 28, 1996. It blasted the mishandling of sensitive FBI background files. There were many questions left unanswered, including who hired Craig Livingstone.[107]

The Office of Independent Counsel, Robert Ray, delivered his final report in March 2000, shortly before President Bill Clinton left office. Ray found no credible evidence that the Clintons or other senior White House personnel were personally involved in requesting and reviewing the FBI files.

IRS Targeting

The Internal Revenue Service (IRS) has access to the most private financial information an individual or organization possesses. One would expect IRS officials to act with integrity, treating sensitive information with the utmost care, and treating all individuals and organizations with fairness regardless of their political affiliations and viewpoints. Well, that's the expectation. The reality has been completely different.

The Treasury Inspector General for Tax Administration issued a report in May 2013. According to the report, the IRS "targeted specific groups applying for tax-exempt status."[108] This is critical, because without a final determination of its tax exemption status, an organization is prohibited from engaging in certain activities. Placing tax-exempt status in limbo also deters donors from contributing to an organization.

The inspector general began an investigation after it was learned that IRS officials were slow-rolling organizations' applications. In some cases, IRS officials were making inappropriate demands for organizational information or donor details that were not required for IRS determination.[109] Moreover, there were two types of organizations that were being targeted: conservative-leaning and Jewish groups. Both of these types of organizations were demonized by the Obama administration. Members of these groups were viewed as enemies of Barack Obama.

The Determination Unit of the IRS was responsible for reviewing organizations' tax-exempt applications. This unit used inappropriate criteria to flag organizations for further scrutiny. The inspector general determined that, in every case, each organization which used terms such as "Tea Party," "Patriot," or "9/12" in its name was singled out and forwarded to an ad hoc group of "specialists."[110] Applications that landed before these specialists often languished for months or even years.[111] Similar mistreatment was given to groups associated with Jewish causes. In addition to names such as "Tea Party," entities that espoused Constitutional principles, advocated for limited government, or called for government accountability were targeted.

Groups with liberal-sounding names received no such treatment. In fact, the inspector general found that several organizations that engaged in "significant political campaign intervention" that should have merited further scrutiny during the tax-exempt review process were not forwarded to the Determination Unit specialists. Not one of these organizations had a conservative-sounding name.[112]

It was obvious to IRS officials they were behaving improperly, if not illegally. Premeditation became obvious when it was learned IRS officials involved in the targeting violated the Federal Records Act by using a non-official instant messaging system that allowed the ringleaders and others to delete messages rather than archive them as required by federal law. Some IRS officials used multiple email accounts with fake names in an apparent attempt to evade scrutiny. Supervisor Lois Lerner operated a secret email account using the name of her dog, Toby Miles.[113]

The inspector-general report led to an investigation by the Department of Justice. One IRS official leaked confidential taxpayer information to an activist group closely aligned with the Obama administration.[114] Releasing confidential taxpayer information is a violation of federal law. An investigation conducted by a US House of Representatives Oversight and Government Reform Committee identified the leak by name. However, the James Comey-led Federal Bureau of Investigation declined to refer this individual or any of the targeting ringleaders for criminal charges.[115] The Department of Justice followed suit and astonishingly declared that it did not find any wrongdoing at the IRS.[116]

Inaction by the FBI and DOJ forced hundreds of targeted groups to seek redress in civil litigation against the Internal Revenue Service. There was a significant delay in forming the plaintiffs in a class action lawsuit because the IRS refused to turn over a list of organizations it targeted. This refusal led to a federal court ordering the IRS to turn over a list of all organizations targeted. When the IRS finally complied with the court order, the tax agency admitted it targeted more than 425 conservative and Jewish tax-exempt organizations.[117]

During this court proceeding over the group names, a unanimous panel of the Sixth Circuit Court of Appeals scolded the IRS lawyers for failing to uphold the law and behaving as if they were the legal defense team of the tax agency. A unanimous, three-judge panel wrote, "The lawyers in the Department of Justice have a long and storied tradition of defending the nation's interests and enforcing its laws—all of them, not just selective ones—in a manner worthy of the department's name. The conduct of the IRS's attorneys in the district court falls outside that tradition."[118]

In separate litigation, the IRS refused to answer if "anyone in the executive office of the president" made requests regarding confidential information.[119] A curious development occurred regarding the communication of one of the IRS supervisors at the center of scandal. IRS Commissioner John Koskinen testified before the House Oversight and Government Reform Committee that hundreds of man hours were spent attempting to comply with a committee's subpoena for Lerner's emails. Unfortunately, all of her emails were accidentally deleted. Koskinen also testified the email system's back-up tape drives had miraculously disappeared. Also, he said, Lerner's computer hard drive had been destroyed, as had her Blackberry.[120] As statistically impossible as it sounded, the IRS Commissioner claimed every possible avenue to recover Lerner's emails yielded negative results.

Before Koskinen, Doug Shulman was the IRS Commissioner during the first term of President Barack Obama. During the three-year period the IRS was targeting conservative and Jewish groups, Shulman visited the White House 118 times. He made more visits than the secretaries of State, Defense, and Homeland Security during the same time period—combined. This period of time also included the US-led war on Libya. In contrast, the last commissioner under President George Bush visited the White House just once in four years.

Stephanie Cutter admitted she met with Shulman several times in the White House. However, it was never explained why Cutter, who held a strictly political position as Obama's deputy campaign manager, was holding meetings with the IRS commissioner in the White House.

Sarah Hall Ingram headed the tax agency's tax-exempt organizations division, making her the most senior person in charge of the unit that was conducting the targeting. While serving in that position from 2009 to 2012, Ingram visited the White House a stunning 165 times.[121]

In October 2017, US Attorney General Jeff Sessions apologized on behalf of the United States to the more than 400 organizations targeted by the IRS. A financial settlement of $3.5 million was paid to these groups, as compensation.

None of the government officials complicit in the IRS targeting scheme were ever held accountable. No one was prosecuted, lost their job, or was even disciplined.

CHAPTER 6

FINANCIAL

"The choice we faced was between pursuing an informed response or panic. Unfortunately, we chose panic and are now about to spend $700 billion on something we have not examined closely."

—Republican Senator Richard Shelby of Alabama on federal government 2008 bank bailout legislation.[1]

Book Sales

World War II veteran Jim Wright was elected to Congress from the Fort Worth, Texas, area in 1954. He rose in prominence over the years until 1976 when he narrowly won the post of House majority leader, the second-ranking position in the Democratic majority-led House of Representatives. Wright became Speaker of the House after then-Speaker Thomas "Tip" O'Neill retired following the 1986 election.

In his second year as House Speaker, Wright came under scrutiny for several possible ethics violations. Allegations involved Wright's book, *Reflections of a Public Man*, and how it was published and sold. The watchdog organization Common Cause urged the House Committee on Standards of Official Conduct, often referred to as the Ethics Committee, to open an investigation.

The Ethics Committee did just that on June 9, 1988. There were six alleged violations of House rules the Ethics Committee was to investigate. Four of these dealt with business matters in which Wright's actions were deemed possibly improper, or in which he possibly had a business interest. The remaining two of the violations were regarding his book. Did Wright improperly use government resources in order to complete his book, and did he use campaign funds to pay for the book's publishing?

Democrats, who held a 258 to 177 seat majority in the House, were adamant that the charges were false and were upset Wright was being investigated. The public was concerned the investigation would be a whitewash. In order to gain credibility in the matter and to be viewed as "fair and objective," the Ethics Committee hired an outside special counsel to conduct the investigation. The committee hired Chicago attorney Richard Phelan, who was a hard-core Democrat. Phelan was a major fundraiser for Senator Paul Simon when the Illinois politician ran for the Democratic nomination for president in 1988, and Phelan was a delegate to the Democratic National Convention.[2]

Phelan quickly began his investigation with vigor and was uncovering facts Wright did not want made public, nor included in the Ethics Committee report. In an attempt to derail Phelan's investigation, Wright leaked a story to the *New York Times* that the special counsel had broadened his investigation beyond the original mandate.[3] The *Times* came through for Wright and published a story that included all of the clever clichés, including "witch hunt," "abuse of power," "wandering," and "politicized," that characterized the investigation as out of control.[4] The *New York Times* story had no public impact.

After interviewing more than seventy witnesses and reviewing thousands of pages of documents, Phelan delivered his completed investigation to the committee on February 21, 1989.

Regarding the costs associated with Wright's *Reflections of a Public Man,* the special counsel "concluded that there was no evidence on which to find that any campaign funds were used to produce and publish the book."[5] The special counsel also found there was no violation of using government resources to prepare the book. The counsel found that members of Wright's staff worked on the book "during the 'normal' 9 a.m. to 5 p.m. work day."[6] However, Wright's staff commingled official and book business during more than forty hours a week, so the counsel ruled there was no obvious violation.

It was during his investigation that the special counsel discovered there was a related book matter that did violate ethics rules. It dealt with the royalties Wright was receiving from book sales.

First, there was the relationship between Wright and the publisher, Madison Publishing of Fort Worth, Texas. Madison did not meet the expectation of what constituted an "established publisher."[7] For example, there was not a true royalty arrangement between Madison and Wright, as was typically found between a publisher and author. The counsel "concluded that a joint venture existed and not one of a true royalty arrangement."[8] Wright would receive 55 percent of the sale price for each book. Additionally, Madison Publishing did not market, distribute, or procure copyright protection of the book, as is typically done by an established publisher. In other words, Wright's book was self-published.

Second, it was apparent Wright was facilitating bulk purchases of his book at various speaking engagements to get around limits on honoraria. Federal law limited federal officials to $2,000 of honoraria for "any appearance, speech, or article" on an annual basis.[9] There was also a House rule that limited outside income to no more than 30 percent annually of a member's congressional salary. Book royalties were exempted, assuming the royalties resulted from book sales from an established publisher "under usual contract terms."[10]

The special counsel identified seventy-six bulk purchasers of Wright's book. Time constraints limited him to subpoenaing only nineteen of them. The special counsel found that eleven of the nineteen bulk book purchasers bought the books "in connection with speeches given by Representative Wright."[11]

There were other suspect bulk purchases. One bulk purchaser was a wealthy political supporter who bought one thousand copies.[12] Another large bulk purchase was made by the Teamsters' Union. Phelan issued the Teamsters a subpoena. The union refused to comply with the subpoena and Phelan backed down.[13]

The twelve-member Ethics Committee, evenly divided with six Democrats and six Republicans, unanimously found that Wright violated House rules at least sixty-nine times, according to its Statement of Alleged Violation.[14] This included business arrangement violations, as well as the bulk book purchase violations. The thirty-one-page document is the congressional equivalent of an indictment.

Eight of the charged violations included instances in which an organization, in lieu of paying Wright a typical $2,000 speaker's fee, would instead buy $2,000 worth of his book. In at least two cases, the organization did not receive all or even any of the books. In one case, Wright was paid $5,000 by a supporter in return for revised copies of the book. The book was never revised, and the supporter received only about half of the books he purchased.[15]

The ethics charges against Wright were only the latest in a string of ethics scandals that plagued the House of Representatives. When it became obvious Wright could not weather the scandal, he submitted his resignation on May 31, 1989, to take effect upon the election of a new Speaker. Wright vacated his congressional seat on June 30.

On May 4, after it had become apparent Wright was going to resign, the *Washington Post* published a story that it had been sitting on for two-and-a-half years.[16]

In 1973, nineteen-year-old John Mack attacked a girl without provocation. He crushed her skull with a hammer, stabbed her multiple times, slashed her throat, and left her for dead in an alley. Miraculously, she survived. She identified Mack as her attacker. He was arrested, charged, tried, and convicted. Mack was sentenced to fifteen years in the Virginia State Penitentiary. He never spent one day there. Instead, Mack served just two years in the cushier Fairfax County jail before being released to a job waiting for him on the staff of Jim Wright. John Mack was the brother of Wright's son-in-law.[17]

The Ultimate Insider

Attorney Clark Clifford was the ultimate Washington, DC, insider. He was an advisor to every Democratic president from the end of World War II until the end of the Cold War. He worked for Presidents Harry Truman, John Kennedy, Lyndon Johnson, and Jimmy Carter.

Clifford first arrived in Washington, DC, while serving as a young attorney in the Navy near the end of World War II. From 1944 to 1946, he served as the Assistant Naval Aide and then Naval Aide to Truman, and remained on Truman's staff as a special counsel until 1950.[18] Clifford has been credited with serving an integral role in developing Truman's 1948 election strategy.

After leaving the Truman administration, Clifford worked in Washington, DC, as an attorney in private practice. One of his clients was

Democratic Senator John Kennedy of Massachusetts. Clifford joined the administration after Kennedy was elected president. Kennedy appointed Clifford to the President's Foreign Intelligence Advisory Board in 1961. He became the chair in 1963.

Lyndon Johnson assumed the presidency upon Kennedy's death. Clifford served as an informal advisor to Johnson until 1968, when Johnson appointed him as the secretary of defense. It was during his tenure as defense secretary that the escalation of American troops in Vietnam reached its height of nearly 550,000.

Clifford joined the Carter administration as an informal advisor. Carter later appointed Clifford a special presidential emissary to India.[19] After he left the Carter administration, Clifford returned to his lucrative private practice where he became known as one of Washington, DC's, "super lawyers." He had an "insider's run of the halls of power."[20]

In 1991, Clifford was embroiled in one of the largest criminal bank frauds in world history. The Bank of Credit and Commerce International (BCCI) was a sophisticated global criminal enterprise. The privately held bank was founded with mostly Arab money in 1972 by Pakistani financier Agha Hasan Abedi, who counted Jimmy Carter among his many friends. BCCI had grown so large, with hundreds of branches in dozens of states, that by the 1980s it was among the ten largest private banks worldwide.

BCCI relied on the bank secrecy laws and weak regulatory regimes of Luxembourg and the Cayman Islands where it was registered. The weak laws and complex business structures allowed BCCI to hide its criminal activities of money laundering, illegal drug financing, arms trafficking, and other criminal enterprises. The bank made bribes, made payoffs, and gave sweetheart loans to government officials and influential figures in more than two-dozen countries. BCCI had a pair of outside audit firms, each of which was permitted to audit only half of its business operations. This prevented outsiders from having a complete picture of the activities of BCCI.

In 1982, several wealthy clients of BCCI purchased controlling shares of Financial General Bankshares, later renamed First American Bankshares. The Office of the Comptroller of the Currency (OCC), the federal regulator of US banks, had kept a wary eye on BCCI and was opposed to it owning or taking over the operations of a US bank.

Because the shares were purchased by BCCI's clients, the OCC was concerned the Bank of Credit and Commerce International would eventually be controlling First American.

Clark Clifford and his law firm partner, Robert Altman, were the US attorneys representing Bank of Credit and Commerce International. Outside of Washington, DC, legal and lobbying circles, Altman was best known as the husband of former *Wonder Woman* television actress, Lynda Carter.

Clifford gave his personal assurances to the US Federal Reserve that the Arab investors had purchased their shares in First American with personal funds or loans from banks other than BCCI. In order to instill further confidence in First American by the OCC, Clifford was named chairman and Altman was named president of First American. Over the next few years, First American became the biggest bank in Washington, DC.[21]

Clifford's representations to the Office of the Comptroller of the Currency were untrue.[22] It was in 1990 when US regulators learned that BCCI had gained a controlling interest in First American many years earlier. Most of the Arab investors purchased the First American shares using loans from BCCI and put up the First American shares as collateral. Most of them did not pay the loans, forfeiting the shares to BCCI. Bank of Credit and Commerce International achieved through subterfuge what it could not achieve legally.

When the story broke, "super lawyer" Clark Clifford and his law firm partner, Robert Altman, the two senior officers of First American Bankshares and lawyers representing Bank of Credit and Commerce International, claimed they did not know of the ownership situation. The defense of the man who was a counselor to four US presidents was that he did not know what was going on in the very bank he headed.

Adding further complications to Clifford's predicament, and casting doubt on his claimed ignorance, was the discovery by federal investigators that he had made about $6 million in profits from stock he purchased with an unsecured loan from BCCI.[23]

In 1992, the Senate Foreign Relations Committee began an investigation into the scandal.

Under testimony before the committee, one BCCI official took issue with Clifford's claim of ignorance. "It is very hard to believe, very, very hard to believe, almost impossible to believe…that Clifford and Altman did not know [about BCCI's ownership of First American]," he told the Senate committee investigating the scandal. His position that Clifford and Altman knew what was afoot was echoed by several other BCCI officials.[24]

In its final report, the Senate committee found that details of key meetings were often lacking. The most crucial meetings included only Clifford, Altman, Abedi, and Abedi's close assistant, Swaleh Naqvi, the latter of whom were BCCI's top two officials. Oftentimes, there were no notes from these meetings and other participants were excluded seemingly to eliminate any witnesses to what was discussed.

The committee also reported that the sworn testimony of Clifford and Altman was inconsistent with the testimony of others, as well as with contemporaneous documents. In sum, the committee found "both men [Clifford and Altman] participated in some of BCCI's deceptions in the United States."[25]

The Senate committee report detailed involvement by both Clifford and Altman as far back as 1978 in BCCI's plans to acquire First American Bankshares (formerly Financial General Bankshares). In addition, a newspaper quoted Altman in 1977 discussing his involvement in US bank acquisitions by foreign interests that turned out to be BCCI.[26] This contradicted his sworn testimony.

In 1992, Clark and Altman faced charges of fraud and lying to federal regulators. Altman was acquitted of fraud charges the following year. The Justice Department declined to try Clifford due to his health concerns. The last of the legal matters were settled when Clifford and Altman surrendered claims that First American owed the pair more than $18 million and the pair agreed to pay a $5 million fine to the Federal Reserve.[27]

Underscoring the weak defense of his actions, Clifford could only muster a single footnote addressing the BCCI scandal in his 709-page memoir, *Counsel to the President*.[28]

Spy on the High Court

Abraham "Abe" Fortas was born in Memphis, Tennessee. He attended undergraduate college at Southwestern Presbyterian University (present-day Rhodes College) and law school at Yale. Fortas taught at Yale after graduation and joined President Franklin Roosevelt's administration in a variety of capacities.

Fortas worked at the Securities and Exchange Commission, Department of Interior, and the Public Works Administration. He was an energetic supporter of Roosevelt's New Deal policies.

Fortas was a founding partner of Washington, DC, law firm, Arnold, Fortas & Porter, which became a powerhouse firm in the nation's capital. In 1948, Fortas successfully defended Lyndon Johnson over a dispute regarding the Democratic primary for US Senator in Texas, cementing his relationship with the rising Texas politician.

After Johnson assumed the presidency following Kennedy's assassination, he would turn to Fortas for advice on a number of issues, including the war in Vietnam, tax policy, and relations with Israel. Fortas's performance as a confidential advisor was so impressive to Johnson that he wanted to name Fortas the US attorney general. Fortas was disinterested.

Then Johnson realized he had a far greater need for the services of Fortas elsewhere. In 1965, Johnson engineered the resignation of Supreme Court Associate Justice Arthur Goldberg with the promise that he would be made US ambassador to the United Nations.[29] Johnson feared a replay of the Supreme Court versus the White House of Franklin Roosevelt. In the 1930s, the high court struck down as unconstitutional several of Roosevelt's New Deal programs. Johnson was concerned that some of his Great Society ventures were also unconstitutional and would face a similar fate. Johnson wanted a spy in the chambers of the Supreme Court, and he would have one if he nominated to the high court his longtime friend and confidant, Abe Fortas.

Fortas's nomination sailed through the confirmation process without any difficulty. In spite of expectations, Fortas was seemingly unconcerned with his responsibility to be a member of an independent judiciary. "Once on the bench, Fortas remained the President's lawyer."[30] Fortas and Johnson met and spoke regularly. "While the bulk of his advice to the president between 1963 and 1965 had concerned social policy, culture, and personnel, by 1966 he became involved in the tough domestic issues that were tearing the United States apart."[31]

In late 1965, Fortas struck up an unsettling relationship with troubled financier Louis Wolfson. At the time, Wolfson was under investigation by the Securities and Exchange Commission for illegal stock manipulation.[32] Wolfson offered to pay Fortas to serve as an advisor to the Wolfson Family Foundation to provide unspecified services. According to the agreement negotiated between the justice and the financier, Wolfson would pay "$20,000 per annum for your life, commencing January 1, 1966, with the understanding that the payments would be continued to Mrs. Fortas for her life should she survive you."[33] The only requirement Fortas had to meet in order to earn the generous salary was to attend the foundation's year-end meeting.[34]

The $20,000 annual salary was a considerable sum to pay Fortas to do nothing more than show up to a meeting only one day each year, especially since the Wolfson Family Foundation's annual revenue in 1966 was only $115,200.[35] Moreover, its annual monetary awards were less than $80,000.[36] Fortas was to be paid a quarter of the foundation's annual awards, ostensibly to do nothing.

Fortas may not have thought there was a problem with this arrangement, but his law clerk did. Law clerk Dan Levitt exploded upon learning of the deal. He knew this arrangement was fraught with ethical and legal landmines, especially since Wolfson's many legal challenges would be working their way through the judicial system.

Levitt convinced Fortas he had to resign from the foundation and Fortas did just that in June 1966. However, Fortas waited until December before he returned the $20,000 salary he was paid in the beginning of January for his role as an advisor for the year. He finally did so, but only after Wolfson was twice indicted.[37]

In June 1968, Supreme Court Chief Justice Earl Warren privately told Johnson he wanted to retire. On June 26, Johnson announced the nomination of Fortas to become chief justice and Appellate Judge Homer Thornberry to fill the vacancy created by Fortas's elevation from associate justice.

Fortas and Thornberry were not viewed favorably by many in the Republican Party. In fact, many Democrats were not pleased with the nominations of either one. Republicans and Democrats viewed both Fortas and Thornberry as Johnson cronies, and they worried how the unusually close relationship, especially with Fortas, could affect the court.

Some of the suspicions about the backdoor communications between Johnson and Fortas were proven true. It was learned during Fortas's chief-justice confirmation hearing that the associate justice had actually helped draft Johnson's 1966 State of the Union address.[38] This was viewed as crossing the boundary that separated the judicial and executive branches.

Next came the revelation that a seminar course Fortas was teaching at American University was not funded by the school. It was not unusual for a Supreme Court justice to teach a course or a seminar, with the understanding that the justice was being paid by the university. Fortas's American University salary actually came from a group of wealthy businessmen, which posed a tremendous potential conflict of interest.[39] Collectively, donors to Fortas's American University seminar salary "held forty seats as officers, directors, or partners in various business corporations that might one day have cases before the Supreme Court of the United States."[40]

In spite of the public uproar, both Johnson and Fortas were committed to moving forward with Fortas's nomination to be chief justice. Johnson, in particular, was convinced that the Senate, which held nearly a two-to-one Democratic advantage, with sixty-three seats to the Republicans' thirty-seven seats, would confirm Fortas. This did not happen. On September 26, the Fortas nomination failed on the Senate floor.

Fortas's problems did not end with his failed chief justice nomination. It was learned in 1969 that Wolfson, with whom Fortas struck up that unethical business relationship more than three years earlier, had requested help from Fortas. Wolfson had been convicted of criminal acts and was desperately seeking assistance. Johnson was retired from the presidency and Richard Nixon had been president for about ten weeks. In an April 11, 1969, letter to Fortas, Wolfson wrote, "Abe, I want you to do something for me. I cannot go to prison right now; if you could do anything to get me a Presidential pardon—have President Johnson call Mr. Nixon."[41]

Fortas claimed he never made that call. Nevertheless, the ethical and political baggage that Fortas had acquired in fewer than four years on the bench proved to be too much. On May 14, with a threat of impeachment growing by the day, Fortas resigned in disgrace from the Supreme Court.

Hush Money

In 1981, at the age of thirty-three, Henry Cisneros was elected mayor of San Antonio, Texas, making him the first Mexican-American to lead a major American city. A dozen years later, Bill Clinton nominated Cisneros be his first Secretary of Housing and Urban Development.

While he was mayor, Cisneros engaged in an extramarital affair with Linda Medlar, a two-time divorcée whose third husband was a local jewelry-store owner. Medlar had been a volunteer for Cisneros over the course of several campaigns. Their affair was the worst kept secret in the city. Everyone talked openly about it, but it was not until one local newspaper published an exposé that the rest of the media began reporting it.

Cisneros was already in proactive damage-control mode in anticipation of a run for statewide office when the exposé was published. Cisneros had been holding a series of one-on-one, off-the-record meetings with area reporters. He informed them of his extramarital affair in an elaborate plan to co-opt the media and gain their support if the affair was to become widely known by the public.

Legal difficulties ensued for Cisneros when he lied to FBI agents during the routine background check and interview that was conducted as part of his 1993 nomination to be HUD Secretary. He lied about the amount of money he paid to Medlar following their affair, claiming he gave her about $60,000 on humanitarian grounds because she had fallen on hard times after their tryst became public. In fact, Cisneros paid Medlar more than $250,000, a dizzying amount that smacked of hush money. The evidence against Cisneros was so overwhelming that in March 1995, US Attorney General Janet Reno was forced to appoint David Barrett as an independent counsel to investigate the wrongdoing.

Two years later, Cisneros was indicted on eighteen counts of conspiracy, giving false statements to federal investigators, and obstruction of justice. In September 1999, Cisneros worked out a plea deal with prosecutors and he pleaded guilty to lying to FBI agents. A deal was quickly negotiated when Cisneros learned that Medlar had taped dozens of telephone conversations in which Cisneros admitted he lied to the FBI. Cisneros was given neither jail time nor probation, but he was fined $10,000. Less than eighteen months later, Bill Clinton pardoned him, although Cisneros had not submitted a clemency request to the Justice Department.

Linda Medlar was the other woman in the married Cisneros's life. The two brazenly carried on a relatively open romance for years. When Cisneros began plotting a run for higher office, he ended the relationship. After the first press report made the affair completely public, Cisneros began paying Medlar hush money to impede investigations into the details of their affair.

While Cisneros was fighting his legal battles, Medlar had to contend with her own legal difficulties. Like Cisneros, Medlar lied to investigators about the money she received from Cisneros. She also lied on bank documents when she applied for a mortgage to purchase a home in Lubbock, Texas.

Medlar was indicted on twenty-eight counts, including bank fraud and money laundering. In September 1997, Medlar struck a plea deal with prosecutors, and she pled guilty to several charges. She was sentenced to three-and-a-half years in prison, but was released after eighteeen months for cooperating in the investigation against Cisneros. Linda Medlar, divorced for the third time following the revelation of her affair with Cisneros, was pardoned by Bill Clinton without her ever having filed a formal clemency petition.

S&L Bailout

There are two types of savings institutions that appear similar to most people: banks and savings-and-loans. Generally, they provide similar services, such as savings and checking accounts, consumer loans, and residential mortgages. Banks differ in that they often work with large commercial businesses, issue credit cards, and offer investment services. Savings and loans focus more on local services, particularly offering residential mortgages. Savings and loans are also referred to as "thrifts."

There is a third savings institution that differs markedly from the other two. Unlike banks and thrifts, credit unions are non-profit organizations. Any profits made by a credit union are returned to the members. Credit unions are locally focused and do not loan money to businesses.

There was high inflation in the late 1970s. In an attempt to counter this, the US Federal Reserve, which establishes US monetary policy, raised the discount rate it charged banks. This is the interest rate that savings institutions pay in order to borrow money from the Federal Reserve. The rate was increased from 9.5 to 12 percent. This had a devastating effect.

The discount-rate increase created a serious problem for all savings institutions, but most significantly for the nation's four thousand federal- and state-chartered savings and loans. Many had given long-term loans (such as residential mortgages) to borrowers at significantly lower interest rates. The sluggish economy made it difficult to attract new depositors, and the increased interest rates dramatically reduced the number of people qualifying for new mortgages, which had been a profit center for thrifts.

Because the depositor interest rates offered by thrifts were limited by federal regulators (by a rule called Regulation Q), some depositors withdrew their money and placed it elsewhere to get a higher rate of return.[42] In short, thrifts began losing money. In 1980, the net income for all thrifts was $781 million. In 1981 and 1982, it was *negative* $4.6 billion and $4.1 billion, respectively.[43]

The Federal Savings and Loan Insurance Corporation (FSLIC) was the federal insurer for thrifts. It had only a fraction of the financial reserves available to insure the nearly half-a-trillion dollars in outstanding mortgage loans held by thrifts. A big reason was because the FSLIC charged institutions the same insurance premium regardless of how risky the investments were, instead of rates commensurate with the likelihood of failure. About half of the nation's nearly $1 trillion in home mortgages were held by thrifts.[44] In fact, the thrifts' home-mortgage business was the "main engine of the housing industry."[45] It became apparent to Washington lawmakers that they faced a potentially catastrophic problem.

Congress decided the best resolution to the problem was to relax regulations and permit thrifts to invest in riskier ventures, such as land development deals, in order to grow out of their financial predicaments.

In order to accomplish this, in 1980, the Depository Institutions Deregulation and Monetary Control Act, which gave thrifts more flexibility, was passed by Congress and signed into law by President Jimmy Carter.[46] About the time of the bill's passage, the real estate market was starting to grow. Thrifts loaned increasing amounts of money to larger and riskier development deals.

There were some other missteps that occurred in Washington, DC. Congress approved some accounting gimmicks that allowed thrifts to mask their problems and allowed them to grow bigger while the underlying capitalization problems still existed. The federal regulator also abandoned some common sense limits on lending that increased the likelihood of failures.

Those failures finally began. Some of the riskiest real estate development deals began to collapse, which caused thrifts to fail. Losses grew worse by the day. In 1982, Washington enacted into law the Garn-St. Germain Depository Institutions Act that created a policy called "forbearance," among other provisions. Forbearance allowed failing thrifts to remain open with the hope that they might recover. It was almost like a Ponzi scheme. Insolvent thrifts were chasing potentially more lucrative but riskier investments in an attempt to recoup their mounting losses.

Unfortunately, savings-and-loans continued going out of business at an alarming rate. Among the more notable failures included Lincoln Savings and Loan, which led to the Keating Five scandal involving Senator John McCain and four other senators. There was the Silverado Savings and Loan, one of whose board members was Neil Bush, son of then Vice President George H. W. Bush. Another famous failure was the Madison Guaranty Savings and Loan Association that was integral to the Whitewater Development Corporation scandal involving Bill and Hillary Clinton.

The Federal Savings and Loan Insurance Corporation managed the closure of 296 thrifts from 1986 to 1989. However, the mounting number of failures exhausted all of FSLIC's money and cost taxpayers about $60 billion.[47] This forced Washington to step in and implement a bigger and more aggressive taxpayer-funded bailout.

In August 1989, Congress passed the Financial Institutions Reform, Recovery, and Enforcement Act of 1989 that created the Resolution

Trust Corporation (RTC). The RTC had the responsibility of resolving the remaining insolvent thrifts that held about $400 billion in assets. The RTC shuttered another 747 thrifts, in addition to the nearly three hundred closed by FSLIC. About one thousand of the nation's four thousand thrifts were shut down. The entire savings and loan bailout cost US taxpayers about $160 billion.[48]

Too Big to Fail

Troubles were brewing in the housing and housing finance markets for a number of years. It all came to a head in late 2008.

The housing finance markets could trace their problems back to the 1970s. There was a growing attitude in Washington, DC, that something should be done for those people who were turned down when applying for mortgage loans due to a lack of credit worthiness. In 1977, Congress passed, and President Jimmy Carter signed into law, the Community Reinvestment Act. The act created legislative and regulatory mechanisms that pressured banks into offering mortgages to those who wouldn't normally qualify for them.

These unqualified borrowers were often moderate- and low-income consumers who had poor credit ratings due to heavy debt, unemployment or underemployment, or a history of payment delinquencies. The types of loans this new category of borrowers qualified for were known as subprime loans. These loans were often charged much higher interest rates to compensate for the increased risk to the lender.

Banks found a creative way to package these riskier loans into a financial instrument called a mortgage-backed security. Mortgage-backed securities were bundled and traded among the banks and other financial institutions.

This was clearly a fiscal time bomb waiting to explode. Fortunately, a day of reckoning was postponed as long as home values continued to climb.

Home prices throughout the 1990s and into the 2000s were growing at a phenomenal rate. A homeowner would buy a house, flip it after a quick gain in price, and pour that money into another, more expensive home. In some cases, the homeowner would roll their consumer and other credit debt into a new loan when they would refinance their mortgage loan. This strategy would entice millions to assume larger amounts of consumer debt.

A housing bubble was created. The steady climb in housing prices came to an end when housing prices peaked in 2006 and began to fall dramatically. Millions of homes were "underwater." That is, the mortgage balances were greater than the value of the homes. Then the foreclosures began. The collapse in the home-mortgage market impacted other sectors of the economy, including real estate, homebuilders, retail, and investment communities.

Washington politicians began worrying about the impact of a housing market collapse on the banking industry. The banking industry was holding hundreds-of-billions of dollars of toxic loans. There was concern this could lead to the collapse of several financial institutions. The phrase, "Too big to fail," was coined. So, a plan was made to bail out the banks.

In October 2008, Congress passed the Emergency Economic Stabilization Act of 2008. President George W. Bush signed it into law. The act created the Troubled Assets Relief Program, which authorized the US Treasury to spend up to $700 billion to purchase distressed assets. It did so with US as well as foreign banks.

After the banks were bailed out, the question of consumer borrowers was raised. One revelation was that some banks had engaged in unscrupulous practices in lending money to borrowers. In February 2012, US Attorney General Eric Holder announced that the federal government and forty-nine states had reached a settlement with the five largest mortgage service providers. The National Mortgage Settlement would address mortgage servicing, foreclosure, and bankruptcy abuses by the industry.[49]

These are what some of the banks paid toward the settlement: Goldman Sachs, $5.1 billion; Deutsche Bank, $7.2 billion; JP Morgan Chase, $13 billion; Bank of America, $16.65 billion; Credit Suisse, $5.28 billion; Citigroup, $7 billion; Morgan Stanley, $2.6 billion; and Wells Fargo, $3.3 billion.

In an agreement approved by the US District Court for the District of Columbia in April 2012, the banks would pay about $110 billion to make borrowers whole. However, borrowers never saw most of this money. About $59 billion was paid to the US Treasury and other federal agencies. More than $5 billion was given to state governments. The remaining $45 billion was tabbed for consumer relief.

However, the banks didn't actually write checks for these amounts. In some cases, the banks received credit for taking certain actions. For example, Credit Suisse received credit for modifying the terms of mortgage loans—mortgage loans that were owned by other banks. JP Morgan Chase and Bank of America received credit for forgiving mortgages that had already been discharged in bankruptcies. Only $5 billion of the $110 billion was actual cash relief for homeowners, much of it for second mortgages. Moreover, the banks were permitted to write off much of the fines from their taxes.

US Housing and Urban Development Secretary Shaun Donovan of the Obama administration promised that one million homeowners would get mortgage write-downs. Less than 90,000 did. Other relief money was given to recipients that had little to do with consumer relief.[50] Holder's Justice Department funneled $1 billion to advocacy groups favored by the Obama administration.[51]

Some of the states spent money on programs unrelated to assisting financially distressed homeowners. The state of New York renovated horse stables as part of a $50-million upgrade at the state fairgrounds.[52] Illinois gave $100 million to community groups. New Jersey put $72 million and Virginia $60 million into their general funds.[53]

This is not what was promised.

Solyndra

The Great Recession hit the United States in 2008. Later that same year, freshman Senator Barack Obama was elected President. When he was inaugurated as the 44th president, Obama was joined by sizable Democratic majorities in the House and Senate. Democrats had a 257–178 bulge in the House and a 59–40 advantage in the Senate (including two independents who caucused with the Democrats).

Among the very first pieces of legislation passed and signed into law was the American Recovery and Reinvestment Act of 2009, known by the nicknames of the Recovery Act and the stimulus.

Aggressive legislation such as the stimulus had not been enacted since the days of Franklin Roosevelt. Nor would it have had a chance of passage if Obama did not enjoy an overwhelming Democratic majority in Congress. The theory behind the stimulus was that the government should step in and spend money on the economy to replace private investments. In theory, it would create jobs. Years later, it was obvious the act did not perform as envisioned.[54]

Four-decade records were set in the US unemployment rate,[55] the labor force participation rate,[56] and the time it took for the economy to finally recover.[57] Median household income at the end of 2015 was the same as at the end of 2007.[58] Obama was the first president in American history who did not have at least one quarter of economic growth of at least 3 percent.[59] Even the one-term Jimmy Carter registered 3 percent growth.

More than $800 billion was spent under the Recovery Act. There was virtually nothing to show for it years later. The spending followed the dictum offered by White House Chief of Staff Rahm Emanuel only days after Obama was elected president. Emanuel said, "You never want a serious crisis to go to waste. And what I mean by that is an opportunity to do things you think you could not do before."

Billions of dollars were misspent. According to the Congressional Budget Office, the federal government spent between $540,000 and $4.1 million on each job created by the stimulus.[60] In other cases, money went to pet causes[61] or to political supporters, donors, and cronies.

One lucky recipient of the largesse was Solyndra.

Solyndra was a Fremont, California, start-up that hit all the politically correct notes. It was located in the high-technology region of California that was home to Obama supporters and donors. It focused on green technology to battle man-made global warming and would reduce reliance on fossil fuel. And it claimed an innovative approach to energy development. Solyndra was the very first company to receive money from Obama's stimulus. "Solyndra quickly became the poster child for both the stimulus funding and the promise of green jobs."[62]

In March 2009, Solyndra announced it would receive $535 million from the US Treasury. The company announced it would "generate significantly more solar electricity" than competing technologies and the company would "employ approximately 3,000 people."[63] Solyndra promised its solar panel installation costs would be about half of its competitors' costs. However, Solyndra's business model was suspect[64] and its request for an Energy Department loan during the George Bush administration was turned down.[65]

Obama touted the company's promises during a May 2010 visit. During his visit, Obama said, "It is just a testament to American ingenuity and dynamism and the fact that we continue to have the best universities in the world, the best technology in the world, and most importantly the best workers in the world. And you guys all represent that."[66] Fifteen months after Obama's visit, Solyndra shut down its facility, laid off its approximately one thousand employees, and announced it would file for bankruptcy.

Although Solyndra was the first company to receive stimulus money, it was not the first to fail. Other green-energy companies in receipt of taxpayer-backed loans had already filed for bankruptcy.[67]

The collapse of Solyndra was not a surprise to everyone. In late 2010, Solyndra officials privately confided its precarious financial status to Energy Department officials. In February 2011, the Energy Department refinanced Solyndra's loan, allowing private investors who invested money into the venture after Solyndra had received US taxpayer-financed loans to get their money out first, long before the US taxpayers would get made whole.[68] It was a last-in, first-out policy.

Among the private investors benefitting from this scheme was billionaire George Kaiser, a prominent donor to Obama.[69] Accompanied by Solyndra officials, Kaiser visited the Obama White House sixteen times, including four times during the week the loan was announced.[70]

Solyndra represented a classic boondoggle. The company's factory cost nearly $250 million to build and included Disney tune-whistling robots and exotic "spa-like showers with liquid crystal displays of the water temperature."[71]

Solyndra was liquidated in 2012. Some of the firm's glass tubes made their way to the University of California Botanical Garden at Berkeley as part of a botanical artwork display.[72]

A four-year investigation by the Energy Department's Office of Inspector General (IG) was released in August 2015. Inspectors found that information provided to the Energy Department by Solyndra officials during the loan applications was at odds with information that Solyndra filed with the Securities and Exchange Commission. The inspector general further stated the Energy Department did not conduct a thorough and effective review of Solyndra's loan application.

The Department of Justice declined to prosecute any Solyndra officials for misleading private investors and Energy Department officials.

CHAPTER 7

SEX GONE WRONG

"Sex makes us do crazy things, and Official Washingtonians hate doing crazy things. They hate seeing people like them do crazy things."

—Marjorie Williams[1]

Capitol Steps

John Jenrette had a very bad 1980. On February 2, FBI agents knocked on the door of his Capitol Hill townhouse to inform him he had been caught in an FBI undercover sting called Abscam (see chapter 10). Jenrette was one of seven members of Congress, a senator and six congressmen, who were caught on audio or videotape accepting cash bribes. There was also a slew of local politicians and other wheelers and dealers nabbed in Abscam.

Jenrette was indicted on June 13, 1980 for taking a $50,000 bribe in return for promising to introduce legislation to benefit what Jenrette thought was a pair of Arab sheikhs. On June 24, he safely won the Democratic nomination to serve his fourth term in South Carolina's 6th congressional district, provided he won the general election. Jenrette lost the November general election. In between his primary victory and the general election, Jenrette was convicted of bribery after a five-week trial. His October 7 conviction didn't dissuade him from continuing his reelection effort.

No longer a member of Congress, fresh off a bribery conviction, and newly sober, Jenrette may have thought he could weather the storm with the love and support of his faithful wife. She had been his staunchest supporter immediately after he was arrested and throughout his trial.

In 1978, the *Washington Post Magazine* published a profile of four young women working on Capitol Hill. The article was titled "Gorgeous Blondes." One of the four was Rita Carpenter. Two years earlier, the Texas native married South Carolina Congressman John Jenrette.

Carpenter graduated with honors from the University of Texas in 1971. In a three-year span, she had a couple of jobs, served a stint in the Peace Corps, was a Clairol model, and was briefly married. She then became a researcher for the Texas Republican Party. The following year, she accepted the position as director of opposition research for the Republican National Committee.[2] It was August 1975, a month after she began working at the RNC, when she first met Jenrette.

The pair quickly became inseparable. It also caused a commotion. Carpenter was given an ultimatum at the RNC. Either give up her Democratic boyfriend or quit working for the national Republican Party. She chose Jenrette.

John Jenrette proposed to Rita Carpenter when the pair were attending the 1976 Democratic National Convention in New York's Madison Square Garden. They were married days later in a civil ceremony in Alexandria, Virginia. Jenrette's campaign consultant, Marvin Chernoff, served as best man.[3]

Rita would later tell of her husband's romantic and frisky side. During their courtship, he phoned her one evening during a late-night session in the House. "He called to say he missed me and had to see me," she wrote. She added, "I threw on a coat and walked up to the Capitol portico where John was waiting. He took my hand and led me into the shadows, and we made love on the marble steps that overlook the monuments and the city below."[4]

A Washington, DC, based comedy troupe later named itself the Capitol Steps, after the revelation of the Jenrettes' lovemaking on such prominent real estate.

While they were married, Rita entertained the idea of launching a country music singing career, but that never panned out. So, she played the role of congressional spouse, hating every moment of it, as she later revealed in a magazine column.

In December 1980, after Jenrette's criminal conviction and election loss, Rita penned a column for the *Washington Post* titled "Diary of a Mad Congresswife" that shared a number of intimate secrets. The final line was, "I've been through a lot with John Jenrette, and I'm not going to give up now."[5]

That column spared no one, including her husband, whom she accused of being a skirt-chasing drunk. She wrote that her husband's congressional staff thought of her "as a dumb blonde, a nagging problem best kept at arm's length." She opined, "Congress is a world of thirsts that can't be quenched. The drug habits, the drinking problems, the mistresses, the boyfriends, the broken homes attest to that."

There was considerable womanizing by married members of Congress, according to Jenrette. She wrote, "Every congressional wife learns there is something about a congressman that brings women out of the woodwork. He might be paunchy, middle-aged, balding and dressed in Robert Hal suits, but there will always be women willing to overlook such details."[6]

It wasn't much better for her husband's home state. Of South Carolina's 6th congressional district, she wrote, "If I never attend another Darlington, S.C., Moose Lodge meeting—during which grown men parade around a room with antlers on their heads—that will be fine."[7] To say Rita Jenrette was burning bridges was an understatement.

A month after the *Washington Post* column, in which she vowed she was "not going to give up," Rita Jenrette announced she would be divorcing her husband.

Days later, it was learned Rita had posed for a pictorial spread in *Playboy* magazine. Alongside the topless and seductive photos was an article she wrote about her congressional spouse experiences.

The Beauty Queen

If anybody was on the fast track to the White House, it was Charles Robb.

Chuck Robb was a Marine Corps officer who served as a White House military aide followed by a tour of duty in Vietnam, where he received the Bronze Star. He married Lynda Johnson, the daughter of President Lyndon Johnson. Robb was a moderate Democrat in Virginia, a state where Republican candidates had struggled in recent years to win statewide office. He was elected lieutenant governor when he was just thirty-eight years old. He subsequently served a term as Virginia governor and then was elected to the US Senate. On top of his political accomplishments, he was telegenic and was considered so squeaky clean that some referred to him as a "glass-of-milk governor."[8]

In 1991, after stating that he would not enter the 1992 race, Robb's name was being mentioned as a potential presidential candidate for 1996.[9] His political rise came to a screeching halt and began crashing down when an NBC News magazine show claimed Robb attended parties where recreational drugs were present, and that he had an affair with a beauty pageant winner.[10] By this point, Robb was already having a bad spring. A federal investigation of drug use in the Norfolk-Virginia Beach area of Virginia nabbed ten acquaintances of Robb's who were either indicted for drug use or were granted immunity.[11]

Robb's polished image was further damaged in early September 1991, when the October edition of *Playboy* magazine hit the newsstands.

Nineteen-year old Tai Collins won the pageant competition for Miss Virginia USA 1983. Eight years later, she posed nude for *Playboy* magazine, but it was the accompanying article that attracted much of the attention. In the article, entitled, "Tai Collins, The Woman Senator Charles Robb Couldn't Resist," Collins claimed to have carried on an eighteen-month affair with Robb while he was serving as governor and she was the reigning Miss Virginia.

Collins said she had no compelling interest in revealing her fling with the married governor some years earlier. However, she was being hounded by the press running down rumors of the affair, fending off demands to remain quiet from Robb's people, and being chased by a private detective investigating Robb's alleged extracurricular activities. Additionally, Collins claimed to have received threatening phone calls warning her to be quiet. In posing for *Playboy*, her plan was to get the affair out in the open in order to put an end to the intimidation and get on with her life.

As Collins told it, she met then-Governor Chuck Robb in June 1983 shortly after she won the pageant title. She and Robb participated in a ribbon-cutting ceremony. Shortly thereafter, he began pursuing her. After a couple of requests, she agreed to join him for dinner one evening. A pair of Virginia State Troopers picked her up. Before she left her apartment, she told her roommate, "I don't know what he wants. I don't know what to expect. I'm kind of scared. But on the other hand, there's excitement and the unknown and I want to go, so I'm going to go."[12]

For ten months, the relationship was strictly platonic—dinner and dancing at hotspots, and attending the occasional party. Robb would often have a young male staffer accompany the pair when they were in public in order to give the impression Collins was in the company of the young man and not the governor.

On February 7, 1984, Robb invited Collins to join him at the luxury Pierre Hotel overlooking Central Park in the heart of Manhattan. The pair were in Robb's suite drinking champagne when he asked her to give him a massage. When she agreed, Robb stripped nude for the massage. That was the night the pair first had a sexual encounter, she claimed. A sexual relationship continued for the next eight months.

Collins said she never harbored an illusion that Robb would leave his wife for her. As she recalled, Robb told her that he would never leave a president's daughter, who had access to money and power, for "some unknown," since his goal was to be president one day.[13]

After a while, the pair stopped seeing one other. The end of the affair was mutual, Collins claimed. She had no contact with him for several years, until he began running for the US Senate in 1988. That is when Collins began receiving phone calls and visits from Robb's longtime chief of staff, David McCloud, and his personal attorney, Robert Nussbaum. Collins claimed McCloud and Nussbaum were imploring her not to reveal the illicit relationship. Robb later acknowledged that McCloud and Nussbaum met with Collins, but insisted the meetings were to determine if there was any relevance to her claims.

Then Collins began receiving death threats from anonymous phone callers. She was convinced that someone broke into her home when she was out. She claimed her telephone lines were cut. She became deeply concerned for her own safety, she explained.

Collins said the *Playboy* story and pictorial spread was a fallback option. She approached the *Washington Post* a year earlier. She spoke several times with reporters Thomas Heath and Donald Baker. The reporters, she said, spent about half a year on the story verifying details. They were close to publishing an exposé, she claimed, but presidential widow Lady Bird Johnson requested her friend and *Washington Post* owner, Katharine Graham, kill the story.[14] The *Washington Post* admitted the two reporters worked on the story for five months, but chose not to publish because the story "did not rise to the level that we could print."[15]

Others in the news media chose not to believe Collins. CBS News morning show host Harry Smith told her that posing nude for *Playboy* didn't "exactly enhance [her] credibility."[16]

CNN's Larry King was more aggressive in supporting Robb's denials during her appearance on King's show. "You realize that Senator Robb is highly respected...Married to the daughter of a former president," he said to Collins. King continued, "He's bright. He's effective. He's well respected in the Senate. He's well respected as a Governor. He was popularly elected twice, right? A governor, popularly elected to the Senate, a powerful figure in the state of Virginia. I mean, what I mean by credibility being on his side."[17]

Robb admitted Collins was in his Pierre Hotel suite in 1984. He also admitted to receiving a naked massage, but he claimed nothing further happened. He also took issue with Collins's claim that the pair shared a bottle of champagne. It was a bottle of wine, not champagne, he insisted.

A statement from Robb's Senate office blasted Collins over the affair claim. The statement read: "Tai Collins, a professed devout Christian... sold nude photographs of herself to *Playboy* magazine...Her commercial motivation is obvious. Put simply, this is a case of fabrication for profit. Senator Robb has repeatedly explained that no affair ever took place—platonic, romantic, sexual or otherwise."

In response to a reporter's question, Robb's wife, Lynda said, "I know Chuck Robb. He has never had an affair with anybody. She has not had any sexual adventures with my husband. I am outraged that this woman would sell her body to *Playboy* and try to use some fantasy, some scurrilous fantasy, to do this."[18]

Playboy hosted a press conference featuring Tai Collins to address her article and photo layout and to answer questions. In a bit of irony, one of the reporters covering the event was a correspondent from the television tabloid show *A Current Affair*. That correspondent was Rita Jenrette.

For all the angst Collins's claims caused Chuck Robb, her moment of notoriety evaporated rather quickly. Before the end of September 1991, Tai Collins "disappeared from the news with stunning swiftness."[19]

The Dike Bridge

Women, alcohol, and tragedy were intrinsic to Democratic Senator Edward "Ted" Kennedy of Massachusetts. It was that way throughout his entire adult life. Ted Kennedy experienced several tragic events involving women and alcohol. The most notable of tragic events occurred on a mid-July night in 1969. It took place on Chappaquiddick Island, just off Martha's Vineyard, a tony vacation destination off the Massachusetts mainland.

Ted Kennedy was one of six men who were partying all day and into the night with six women who were considerably younger. Five of the six men were married. The only unmarried man was the full-time chauffeur, who drove Kennedy everywhere. All of the women were single. The previous year, the women had worked on the presidential campaign of Ted's older brother, Senator Robert Kennedy, and were known as the "Boiler Room Girls."

When Kennedy later explained that night's tragic events, he gave a pair of reasons for the gathering. He and his family were continuing a thirty-year tradition of participating in the Edgartown Yacht Club Annual Regatta. Kennedy had a room at the Shiretown Inn in Edgartown, and he also had a rented cottage, which was a mere mile-and-a-half away on Chappaquiddick Island.

Kennedy claimed that the gathering at the secluded island cottage also served as a cookout to reward some of the campaign workers of his brother, who was gunned down over a year earlier. It was only happenstance that none of the men's wives attended and the only campaign workers invited to the cookout were young, single women. It was also a coincidence that there was an equal number of men and women.

Kennedy had been drinking heavily all day.[20] All the partygoers got "a little bombed."[21] At approximately 11:15 pm, Kennedy and one of the women, Mary Jo Kopechne, left the cottage where the party was being held in order to drive back toward the ferry landing and return to Edgartown. It was during this drive that he took a wrong turn and he drove off the Dike Bridge. The car landed upside down in the Poucha Pond.

Kennedy claimed that, after he freed himself from his sedan, and despite suffering from a "cerebral concussion and shock," he spent the next fifteen to twenty minutes diving into the water "seven or eight times" in an attempt to rescue Kopechne, who was still inside the car. Unsuccessful in his rescue efforts, Kennedy claimed he rested for fifteen to twenty minutes on the water's edge and then walked back to the rented cottage where the party was still underway.

Outside of the cottage, Kennedy quietly conferred with two of the male guests and asked them to accompany him to the submerged vehicle. They climbed into the only remaining car at the cottage and drove to the Dike Bridge, arriving shortly after midnight.

According to Kennedy, his cousin, Joseph Gargan, and close friend Paul Markham, spent the next forty-five minutes diving into the water "at some risk to their own lives" in repeated attempts to rescue Kopechne. They, too, were unsuccessful. So, the three drove to the ferry crossing, where Kennedy swore them to secrecy. Gargan and Markham left Kennedy at the ferry crossing and returned to the cottage, according to Kennedy.

In spite of being exhausted over his repeated rescue attempts, Kennedy claimed he swam the five hundred feet from Chappaquiddick Island to Edgartown on the mainland. He nearly drowned due to the channel's strong currents and his "weakened condition," he later told an inquest.

After arriving on the mainland, Kennedy walked to his hotel, went to his room, and lay down, but was unable to sleep due to worrying about Kopechne, he later testified. From the time he left the submerged car, Kennedy passed several homes, pay phones, and the hotel office, and yet he never once attempted to summon the police or other emergency services, according to his own statements and later courtroom testimony. Kennedy would later blame his failure to call the police on being thoroughly exhausted.

According to inquest testimony, Kennedy left his room at about two-thirty in the morning to complain to hotel staff about noise, asked what time it was, and then returned to his room. It is widely speculated Kennedy was attempting to establish an alibi that he was in the hotel room all night and was not involved in the car accident.[22]

The following morning, after claiming not to have slept, Kennedy showered and changed into fresh clothes. He was freshly shaven.[23] About eight in the morning, he chatted with several other regatta racers for about half an hour. Then, according to his statements, Kennedy left the

Shiretown Inn and returned to Chappaquiddick Island. He arrived at the Dike Bridge shortly after a diver, called by police, removed Kopechne's body from the sedan. Earlier that morning, the police were alerted to the presence of a submerged car by a pair of fishermen.

Instead of speaking with police on the scene, Kennedy left Chappaquiddick Island, returned to Edgartown, and reported the accident at the police station at about ten in the morning. It had been nearly twelve hours since his last drink. A blood alcohol test performed on Kennedy would have been meaningless. Kennedy dictated a statement devoid of details for the police and left. He did not tell authorities there had been a party at the cottage.[24] He was not interviewed by the police. None of the other ten partygoers who were witnesses to the day's events were interviewed by the police. Kennedy and the ten witnesses immediately left the area and, in some cases, the state.

The local coroner made a determination that Mary Jo Kopechne died from drowning, finalized the death certificate, and did not request an autopsy. After lab analysis determined Kopechne's blouse was stained with blood, and she had a blood alcohol content of 0.09 percent, the district attorney requested the body be exhumed and an autopsy be performed. Local Judge Bernard Brominski denied the autopsy request, but only after he was reelected to a new ten-year term as judge.[25]

There were no serious charges levied against Kennedy. A week after the accident, Kennedy pleaded guilty to the minor charge of leaving the scene of an accident. He was sentenced to two months in jail, with all jail time suspended. He then went on television to explain himself.

In a July 25 televised speech, Kennedy made himself the victim, rhetorically asking, "Whether some awful curse did actually hang over all the Kennedys." He also attempted to draw sympathy to himself by asking, "Whether somehow the awful weight of this incredible incident might in some way pass from my shoulders."

The problem with the timeline offered by Kennedy in his public statements and courtroom inquest is that it conflicts with testimony given by a law enforcement officer. Deputy Sheriff Christopher Look finished work shortly before 12:30 a.m. and had taken a boat from Edgartown to Chappaquiddick Island, where he was going to drive to his home on the island. He reported seeing Kennedy's car pass him with a man and a woman inside.[26] Look got a glimpse of the license plate number, which corresponded with the plate on Kennedy's Oldsmobile. Kennedy's car was in another area of the island that Kennedy denied visiting that night.

An inquest into the circumstances surrounding the death of Mary Jo Kopechne took place on January 5, 1970. Kennedy testified to Judge James Boyle of the Edgartown District Court that he attempted to make only two phone calls following the accident. One, he claimed, was unsuccessful. This claim, too, differs dramatically from other available evidence.

According to telephone records, someone using Kennedy's credit cards made sixteen long-distance phone calls the night of the tragedy and into the next morning.[27] Those called included Theodore Sorensen, an attorney who had been special counsel to President John Kennedy, around midnight. This was immediately followed by two calls to a Kennedy home in Hyannis Port, Massachusetts. All three calls were made from Chappaquiddick Island.

Then, from the Shiretown Inn, two calls were made at around three and five in the morning to the law firm of Kennedy's personal attorney, Burke Marshall. Next, a call was made to Kennedy's brother-in-law, Stephen Smith, at about 5:30 a.m. Subsequently, between six and eight in the morning, two calls each were made to Marshall's law firm and to Sorensen. At about 9:00 a.m., another call was made to Smith.[28]

Some of the calls were brief, lasting only a few minutes. Others were considerably longer. The first call to Smith was twenty-seven minutes long, and the last call to Sorensen lasted forty-two minutes.[29]

On February 18, 1970, Judge Boyle delivered his findings from the inquest. He found there were numerous inconsistencies in the sworn testimony, including by Kennedy. Boyle highlighted several facts that did not support Kennedy's claim that he and Kopechne left the cottage with the intention of returning to Edgartown that night. These included the fact that Kennedy rarely drove and completely relied on his chauffeur. Kopechne did not tell any of the other women she was leaving, and she left behind her purse and her hotel room key. As well, the ten other partygoers did not plan to spend the night at the cottage and anticipated using the two vehicles to return to the ferry landing.

Boyle found Kennedy's decision not to seek emergency help deeply troubling. However, he wrote, "The failure of Kennedy to seek additional assistance in the searching for Kopechne…does not constitute criminal conduct."

Boyle concluded, "I, therefore, find there is probable cause to believe that Edward M. Kennedy operated his motor vehicle negligently on a way or in a place to which the public have a right of access, and that such operation appears to have contributed to the death of Mary Jo Kopechne." In spite of his findings, Boyle chose not to issue an arrest warrant for Kennedy.

The district attorney did not seek an indictment against Kennedy, and he declined to charge Kennedy with any crimes related to the death of Kopechne. The tragic events and Mary Jo Kopechne's death on July 18, 1969, carried little weight with Massachusetts voters. Kennedy was easily reelected to his second full term as a US Senator the following year with more than 62 percent of the vote.

In March 1970, just a month after Judge Boyle delivered his findings, the local grand jury wanted to investigate the case; however, the district attorney refused to execute subpoenas for key witnesses, including Kennedy and other witnesses from that night. The grand jury was also refused a transcript of the January inquest. The lack of witnesses and evidence doomed the grand jury's investigation.[30]

It is unlikely that the public will ever know what truly happened that night. Mary Jo Kopechne and Ted Kennedy are both dead. An autopsy was never performed on Kopechne. Any of the remaining partygoers who may have known what really transpired have not come forward in nearly half a century. Aside from a deathbed confession, whatever secret may potentially exist will likely die with the remaining witnesses.

The Kopechnes paid for Mary Jo's funeral with the money they had set aside for her wedding day.[31]

"She Shot Me!"

The state of Utah was admitted to the Union on January 4, 1896. Days later, Salt Lake City attorney Arthur Brown was elected as a Republican to represent the Beehive State in the US Senate for a shortened term. In keeping with Senate rules of alternating six-year terms, Brown served a little more than a year. He was not a candidate for another term. When his term ended on March 3, 1897, Brown returned to Salt Lake City and resumed practicing law.

In the early morning hours of September 28, 1902, Arthur Brown was arrested by the sheriff of Salt Lake City, along with Anne Maddison Bradley, who was nearly thirty years his junior. The pair were charged with adultery. Both were married to other people. Brown was married to Isabel Cameron Brown. Bradley was married to Clarence Bradley.

It was Brown's wife who filed the adultery complaint against her husband. She had learned of an apartment he kept, where Brown and Bradley would secretly meet, which led to a confrontation between husband and wife. Brown and Bradley were brazen about their affair, often appearing in public together and Brown even introducing Bradley as his wife. However, it was his filing for divorce the previous day that was the tipping point for his wife.[32] Isabel Brown immediately petitioned the court for a separation allowance of $150 a month, which was granted.

The Browns and Bradley agreed to a three-way separation. He proposed going to Los Angeles to put distance between himself, his wife, and his mistress. Instead, he went to the Pacific Hotel in Pocatello, Idaho, for a rendezvous with Anne Bradley. Isabel Brown learned of the tryst and traveled to Pocatello to confront the lovers. A physical brawl that erupted between Isabel and Anne was broken up by Arthur. Isabel Brown had sworn she would kill Bradley.[33]

In a bit of irony, Isabel Cameron was having an affair with Brown in the 1870s when he was married to his first wife. He had purchased a home for her while he was still married.[34] Brown and Cameron were living in Kalamazoo, Michigan, at the time. Local authorities charged Brown with having deserted his wife and young daughter.[35] In 1879, rather than face charges, Brown fled Michigan and sought refuge in Salt Lake City. Utah was not yet a member of the Union. Cameron followed and married him there after his divorce from his first wife was finalized.

Anne Maddison was a prominent woman in Utah, where she had served as the editor of the Utah State Federation of Women's Clubs newsletter and was active in Utah politics. In 1902, the now-married Anne Bradley was elected secretary of the Utah Republican Committee. Utah was among the few states before the women's suffrage movement that permitted women to vote and hold office. Bradley ran for city auditor and lost.

It was at the Republican Convention in St. Louis, Missouri, in June 1896 that Isabel Brown introduced her husband to Anne Bradley.

The women had met socially at the convention. The Browns and Mrs. Bradley became close friends and frequently socialized at the Browns' home.[36] A romance eventually blossomed between Arthur Brown and Anne Bradley. In 1898, Bradley separated from her husband, Clarence, and sought a divorce. In 1900, Bradley gave birth to a son she named "Arthur Brown Bradley." Arthur Brown acknowledged paternity.

The pair faced separate trials for their adultery arrests. Brown pleaded not guilty in his trial and was acquitted. She entered a plea of guilty as a strategy to prove that she and Arthur Brown were a couple. She was given a suspended sentence.[37]

Brown's separation and divorce proceedings were not going very well in the first few months. He was ordered jailed in February 1903 for failing to pay the court-ordered $150 monthly maintenance allowance to his wife.[38] Brown made good on the missing alimony payments and then attempted to reconcile with his wife. In the meantime, Brown and Bradley carried on a tumultuous affair. He would promise to marry her, but he continued to stay married to his wife. Then, in November 1903, another son was born to Bradley, to which Brown also admitted he was the father.

In August 1905, Isabel Brown passed away from cancer. Brown was now free to marry Bradley, he told her. Brown encouraged her to finalize her long-lingering divorce and they could finally wed. In anticipation of the marriage, Bradley began using "Brown" as her last name.

In March 1906, Bradley gave birth to a third child she claimed was also Brown's. It only lived a few days. Bradley's only consolation on the loss of her newborn was an agreed-upon June wedding date. After an eight-year affair, the pair would finally marry.

As the date approached, Brown put off the wedding. Wedding plans were on-again, off-again over the next several months. Then Bradley got pregnant again and told Brown in late October 1906. He promised they would soon marry, but he was vague on the details. The emotional stress led her to miscarry.

In late November, Brown left Salt Lake City for Washington, DC, without saying goodbye. He had a case to argue before the Supreme Court. Bradley learned Brown had left money with instructions for her to purchase a ticket anywhere. Bradley realized Brown was trying to get rid of her. Instead, she decided to travel to Washington, DC, to confront Brown and deliver an ultimatum.

Bradley arrived in Washington, DC, the morning of December 8, 1906, after four days of travel by train. She went straight to the Raleigh Hotel where Brown was staying. She registered herself for a room. Then Bradley went to room 268, which was Brown's room, and knocked on his door. Brown was stunned to see her.

"I asked him if he was going to do the right thing by me," she later said.[39] Instead of answering her question, Brown slipped on his over-coat with the intention of leaving the room. Bradley reacted to his slight by shooting Brown. The first shot passed through his hand. The second entered his abdomen.[40] "I abhor acts of this character," she said, "but in this case it was fully justified."[41]

Theodore Tally was the manager of the Raleigh Hotel. After being informed of the shooting, he rushed to Brown's apartment. Sprawled on the floor, Brown pointed a bloody hand in the direction of Bradley and exclaimed, "She shot me."[42] Bradley was standing nearby, fully dressed, wearing her hat, coat, and only one glove.[43] Presumably, she removed the other glove to hold the pistol that was fired. Tally poured a glass of brandy and encouraged Brown to drink it while the hotel maid summoned help.

Brown was rushed into surgery at nearby Emergency Hospital, while Bradley was arrested and taken to the local police precinct. Among her early concerns was that she had neglected to tip "that little boy who carried my bag" to her hotel room at the Raleigh.[44]

Bradley also asked several questions about the grave medical condition of Brown. "I loved the ground he walked on," she repeated several times.[45] Her comments became so repetitive that law enforcement summoned medical authorities to evaluate her mental state.

According to news accounts, this wasn't the first time Brown had stared down the barrel of a pistol held by a lover. Both of Brown's wives had tried shooting him over his marital infidelities. Only Bradley's shot struck him.[46]

Brown succumbed to his wound about midnight on December 12, 1906. His grief-stricken daughter and son were at his bedside when he passed away. Alice was his daughter from his first marriage, and Max was Brown's son with his second wife.

A letter was delivered to Brown shortly before he passed away. It was from Annie Adams, an actress from New York he had known for twenty years.[47] When she was arrested, Bradley had in her possession earlier correspondence between Brown and Adams that she had found in Brown's home.[48] Apparently, Brown and Adams had made plans to marry on New Year's Day in New York.[49] No doubt this contributed to the fatal confrontation between Bradley and Brown.

After Brown passed away, Anne Bradley was charged with murder. Former Chief Justice of the Utah Supreme Court, George Bartch, and former Attorney General of Idaho, John Bagley, were personal friends of Bradley. They hired local attorney A. L. L. Leckie to represent her.[50]

Anne Bradley's murder trial was the trial of the new century. It was "the most sensational at the Capital since the murder of President Garfield" in July 1881.[51] The trial began on November 13, 1907. In closing arguments, the prosecutor called Bradley a dangerous woman. The defense claimed she was temporarily insane and not responsible for her actions. The case went to the jury on December 1. It rendered a not guilty verdict on December 3.

Arthur Brown had never planned to marry Anne Bradley, according to remarks in his last will and testament, dated August 24, 1906. "I have never married Annie M. Bradley and never intend to," he wrote in his will. He also wrote, "I do not devise to give or bequeath anything to any of the children of Mrs. Annie M. Bradley. I do not think either or any child born to Mrs. Bradley is or are mine…I expressly provide that neither nor any of them shall receive any part of my estate."[52]

Brown bequeathed his entire estate to Alice Brown and Max Brown, the children from his first two marriages. The two children he specifically disinherited were seven-year-old Arthur and three-year-old Mark.[53]

Anne Bradley filed a lawsuit contesting the will. She had in her possession letters from Brown in which he admitted paternity. Before the case went to trial, both sides reached a settlement. The two boys who were offspring of Brown and Bradley would receive $12,000 of Brown's estimated $75,000 estate.[54]

Sexual Frankenstein

When the twenty-seven-year-old, green-eyed blonde first arrived in Washington, DC, in 1979 from Wichita, Kansas, she was in awe of political power and those who held it. Paula Clifton was a two-time divorcée who became the lover of Hank Parkinson, who was twenty years her senior. In the preceding years, Clifton was married to and divorced from her high school boyfriend and a Wichita doctor. The high school graduate's employment included jobs as a bartender and a Playboy bunny.

Clifton and Parkinson decided to leave Wichita with plans to launch a political consulting firm in Washington. Their newly formed company was named Parkinson & Associates. She registered with both the House and the Senate as the firm's lobbyist.[55]

Clifton's lobbying career got kick-started in late 1979 when she arranged for Republican Congressman Thomas Railsback of Illinois to speak at a seminar one of her clients was arranging. The married Railsback was a geographic bachelor. His wife and family were living in Illinois. While in Washington, Paula became his constant companion for drinks, dinner, and even a Pittsburgh Pirates–Baltimore Orioles World Series game.[56]

Railsback introduced Clifton to other congressmen. One of them was another Republican, Delaware's Tom Evans. At forty-eight years old, Evans was twenty years older than her, just like her boyfriend, Hank. Clifton claims she immediately became smitten with Evans. An affair quickly developed between the lobbyist and the Congressman.[57]

Shortly thereafter, Paula and Hank decided to live apart, and she moved from their Georgetown townhouse to an apartment near the Kennedy Center, much closer to Capitol Hill. It just so happened that Evans often stayed in the next-door apartment that belonged to a bachelor friend. According to Clifton, the pair held lovemaking sessions in her apartment, her neighbor's apartment, or on the sofa in Evans's congressional office.[58]

After several months, the romance ended. Clifton decided to make a dramatic change in her life and married Hank Parkinson on March 19, 1980, in a civil ceremony. While her affair with Evans had ended, her late-night trysts with members of Congress and other Washington power players did not. She claimed affairs with several congressmen, but said it was less than a dozen. Because Hank often traveled, these sexual encounters would oftentimes take place in her own home. She also had the occasional one-night stand, including one in which she claimed she and a congressman videotaped their lovemaking and enjoyed watching the playback on her television.[59]

It was the videotaped sex session that became the subject of rumors, with some claims that as many as twenty members of Congress had been recorded *in flagrante delicto* with the blonde bombshell lobbyist. This may have been fueled by an allegation made weeks earlier by congressional wife Rita Jenrette that a female lobbyist had compromising videos of several members of Congress.[60]

Parkinson & Associates collapsed in October 1980. That was when the latest edition of *Playboy* hit the newsstands. Inside the pictorial spread of the "Women of Washington" was a photo of Paula wearing only a garter belt. She told the magazine, "Washington is basically a very horny city. For one thing, there are more women here than men. And men can be jerks with women and get away with it." Immediately after the magazine appeared, meetings were canceled, appointments broken, and telephone calls went unreturned. Paula Parkinson, the lobbyist for Parkinson & Associates, was now considered toxic on Capitol Hill.

The following month, Parkinson realized she was pregnant. She definitely knew it wasn't Hank's child, since he had had a vasectomy. She was confident she knew which Congressman was the father. She requested money for an abortion, which he promptly handed over via an intermediary.[61]

In March 1981, the *Wilmington News Journal* broke the story that tobacco industry lobbyist Paula Parkinson spent a week in the same house with several men, including three members of Congress, during a golf trip. The group had stayed at a Palm Beach, Florida, house in January 1980. The paper further reported that, several months after the golf excursion, all three House members voted against the Federal Crop Insurance Act of 1980, which Parkinson lobbied against. Those three votes had no impact, as the bill was passed overwhelmingly in the House with over 60 percent of the vote.

Republican Representatives Thomas Evans of Delaware, Thomas Railsback of Illinois, and Dan Quayle of Indiana were the three Congressmen in that rental house. Making matters worse for the three elected officials was that Parkinson's nude photo in *Playboy* magazine five months earlier had already made her a pariah on Capitol Hill.

According to Parkinson, the house full of men on the golf excursion had divvied up the rooms, with two people assigned to each bedroom. Railsback shared a room with a Delaware doctor. Quayle bunked with tobacco industry lobbyist William Hecht. [62] Parkinson and Evans had the only room with a king-sized bed and private bathroom.[63]

There were other members of Congress who participated in the golf vacation. They stayed at other locations in the Palm Beach area.

Only Evans knew in advance that Parkinson was joining the group. Quayle, who was already at the home when Parkinson arrived, played golf that day and departed the following morning. Another golfer joined the group and took Quayle's spot. Quayle's quick exit and his wife's support probably saved him from serious political backlash. Her backhanded comment, "Anyone who knows Dan Quayle knows that he would rather play golf than have sex any day," saved his political career but subjected him to ridicule.

By the time the scandal broke, Quayle had already been elected as the junior senator representing Indiana. Seven years later, he would be elected vice president as the running mate of George H. W. Bush. Congressmen Tom Railsback and Tom Evans lost their reelection bids in 1982.

By the time the scandal broke, Paula Parkinson had a far different view of members of Congress than the awestruck wonder she had when she first arrived in Washington, DC, two years earlier. "They're users. They're cruel, and they're certainly no better than I am," she told a reporter. "Their whole bit on the soapboxes is, 'I'm good and I'm pure and constituents love me because I do so much good for them.' And then you get them alone…"[64]

Republican Congressman Phil Crane of Illinois requested Attorney General William French Smith direct the Justice Department to investigate the matter and determine if any congressmen traded votes for sexual favors. Democratic House Speaker Tip O'Neill of Massachusetts declined to ask the House Ethics Committee to launch its own inquiry.[65]

The FBI began the inquiry only weeks after the scandal broke. After extensive interviews, the Justice Department reached the conclusion that no laws were broken and closed the matter in August 1981.

Paula Parkinson's newlywed husband apologized for his wife's extracurricular activities. He said, "I unwittingly created a sexual Frankenstein on Capitol Hill."[66]

The Porn Publisher

In fall 1998, the US House of Representatives was marching toward a likely impeachment vote of President Bill Clinton. Sexual activity with a recent college graduate nearly thirty years his junior was the least of Clinton's worries. In trying to cover up his extramarital affair, the 42nd president committed perjury and obstructed justice. These were the same allegations Richard Nixon had faced in 1974, when House leaders made it clear that they were likely to impeach him.

Much of the media ignored Clinton's felonious behavior. Instead, they characterized Clinton as the victim of morally righteous members of Congress who were indignant that he received oral sex in the White House.

Pornographic magazine publisher Larry Flynt saw it the same way. The publisher of *Hustler* magazine wanted to turn the tables on House Republicans. So, he took out a full-page advertisement in the *Washington Post*. The ad stated Flynt would pay up to $1 million to anyone who would come forward alleging they had "an adulterous sexual encounter with a current member of the United States Congress or high-ranking government official." As Flynt later explained, he was only interested in damaging Republicans.

One of the people fingered as a result of Flynt's *Washington Post* ad was Republican Representative Bob Livingston of Louisiana. Livingston wasn't just any House member, or just any Republican. He was the presumptive Speaker of the House of Representatives as of January 6, 1999.

Newt Gingrich resigned as House Speaker immediately following the poor showing of Republicans in the 1998 mid-term elections and in the wake of the revelation that he had an extramarital affair with a congressional staffer nearly half his age. That left the office of Speaker up for grabs. There was a scramble to lock up support when the next two in line seniority-wise, House Majority Leader Dick Armey and House Majority Whip Tom DeLay, both Republicans of Texas, declined to seek the post. Rank-and-file members quickly coalesced around the affable Bob Livingston.

On December 17, Flynt announced he had news to share. He would publish a story around New Year's Day alleging four women had extramarital affairs with Livingston. One affair was relatively recent. "I just wanted to expose the hypocrisy," claimed Flynt.[67]

Flynt wasn't the first to point out that some politicians strayed from their marriages. Some news outlets reported that Republican members of Congress had engaged in adulterous relationships. Dan Burton of Indiana announced he had a teenaged son from an extramarital affair in the 1980s, before he was elected to Congress. He made the announcement when he learned the *Indianapolis Star* was preparing a story. Burton stated his wife was aware of the child, he had taken responsibility for his actions, and he had been paying child support to the mother.[68]

The *Idaho Statesman* revealed that Helen Chenoweth of Idaho had an affair with a married man that ended a decade before she was elected to Congress. She was single at the time. The newspaper editor admitted the paper knew of the affair for years and didn't consider it newsworthy, but apparently had second thoughts in the shadow of Clinton's impeachment discussions.

The website *Salon* stated, "Ugly times require ugly tactics," when it revealed Henry Hyde of Illinois had an affair back in the 1960s, more than thirty years earlier.[69] The website made it clear it was retaliating against "Clinton's enemies." Hyde warned his colleagues that Clinton allies had hired a pair of law firms to find derogatory information on Republicans. He also informed them that intimidating federal officials while in the performance of their duties was a federal crime.[70]

Regarding the Larry Flynt-fronted revelation, it was learned he hadn't paid anyone a million dollars. His ad promised *up to* one million. In fact, he admitted, he was haggling over what he was going to pay some of the women who came forward. Flynt held the upper hand in the negotiation. After someone revealed the "who, what, when, and where" of their allegation, they had no leverage to force Flynt to pay. He could have paid as much or as little as he chose—or nothing at all. Flynt stated he felt that information implicating "some junior congressman from a remote state" wasn't worth much money.[71]

Debate regarding impeachment proceedings began on December 18. Shortly before the debate, Livingston told House Republicans in a closed session, "I have on occasion strayed from my marriage" of thirty-three years. He noted the important distinction between his and Clinton's adulterous relationship. "These indiscretions were not with employees on my staff, and I have never been asked to testify under oath about them." In contrast, Clinton was engaged in a sexual relationship with a White House subordinate who he encouraged to lie.

Republican Representative Mary Bono of California remarked, "If the president had done what Livingston did, we wouldn't be going through any of this." Republican John Edward Porter of Illinois echoed the sentiment stating, "I think the contrast between Bob's admission and telling the truth about this…and the president's lying under oath and to the American people about his transgressions is profound."[72]

The following day, December 19, Livingston stunned every member of Congress when he announced he would resign from Congress. "I was prepared to lead our narrow majority as Speaker and I believe I had it in me to do a fine job. But I cannot do that job or be the kind of leader that I would like to be under current circumstances. So, I must set the example that I hope President Clinton will follow," he said.

Democratic House Minority Leader Dick Gephardt of Missouri gave an impassioned speech imploring Livingston to reconsider resigning. "His decision to retire is a terrible capitulation to the negative forces that are consuming our political system and country," Gephardt said.[73] He added, "The politics of smear and slash-and-burn must end."[74]

Clinton's dirty tricks were widely believed to have been involved in outing Livingston and the other Republicans. ABC News correspondent Cokie Roberts reported that a White House associate was promoting the rumor that Livingston had an extramarital affair.[75] Immediate suspicion focused on Sidney Blumenthal. It was widely believed that it was Blumenthal who was behind the outing of Hyde due to his close ties to *Salon*. Blumenthal was a former *Washington Post* reporter who later became the DC bureau chief for *Salon*. He joined the Clinton White House as an advisor to Bill.

Blumenthal was infamous as the Clinton hatchet man who orchestrated the politics of personal destruction.[76] He earned the unflattering nickname "Sid Vicious."[77] Blumenthal wasn't trusted by Republicans or Democrats. As a case in point, the Obama administration barred him from a position in the State Department when Hillary Clinton was the Secretary of State. Hillary confidant John Podesta characterized him as a conspiracy nut.[78]

Blumenthal would later rise to infamy over his role in sending Hillary Clinton secret emails. The secret emails became known during an investigation of the 2012 attack against the US diplomatic facility in Benghazi that left four Americans dead, including the ambassador.

The Convict Congressman

First elected in 1980, six-term Democratic Congressman Augustus "Gus" Savage was as disgusting an individual as one could imagine. He was a bona fide racist, stating, "Racism is white. There ain't no black racism."[79] He frequently made anti-Semitic remarks and he denounced campaign contributions made by Jews to his opponents.

Savage claimed his political opposition was coming from the "suburban Zionist lobby."[80] He called his critics "faggots," "Oreos," and "white racists."[81] In 1990, the House Ethics Committee found that Savage made unwanted sexual advances toward a Peace Corps volunteer during an overseas junket, but the committee virtually dismissed the matter and only issued Savage a mild rebuke.[82]

In 1992, during his third attempt to unseat Savage, Mel Reynolds defeated the incumbent in the Democratic primary for Illinois's 2nd congressional district. Reynolds was a welcome relief to his constituents after the wildness of Savage.

Then rumors emerged in August 1994 that Reynolds had sexual relations with an underage campaign volunteer. Reynolds called a press conference to angrily deny the allegations and claim he was a victim of racism. He denounced the investigation, saying, "The investigation proves beyond a doubt a very sad truth about racism and bigotry in our city, and the role racism and bigotry play in our law enforcement decision-making process."[83]

Only days after his press conference, Reynolds was indicted on state felony charges of having sexual relations with a sixteen-year-old and requesting she get pornographic photos of another teenager. The age of consent in Illinois was seventeen.

Reynolds had carried on a sexual relationship with a teenaged girl from June 1992 to November 1993. Reynolds faced nearly two-dozen felony counts, including criminal sexual assault, aggravated criminal sexual abuse, child pornography, solicitation of child pornography, obstruction of justice, and communicating with a witness.[84]

In spite of the seriousness of the charges filed against him only three months earlier, Reynolds was safely reelected to Congress in November 1994. He even ran unopposed.

During the August 1995 trial, Beverly Heard, the former underage girl testified she engaged in a fifteen-month sexual relationship with

Reynolds. The pair had sex several times a week. She agreed to Reynolds's request that she striptease for a campaign supporter, and she and Reynolds engaged in a sexual threesome with a female staffer, all while she was still sixteen years old.[85] She also testified that Reynolds offered her $10,000 not to cooperate with prosecutors.[86]

Another witness testified she also had sexual relations when she was only sixteen years old, and Reynolds attempted to bribe her to remain quiet.[87]

On August 22, the jury convicted Reynolds of multiple counts of criminal sexual assault, criminal sexual abuse, obstruction of justice, and child pornography. The prosecution asked for a fifteen-year sentence. The judged handed down only five years in a September 28, 1995, decision. Reynolds resigned his congressional seat three days later.

The situation for Reynolds only worsened after his conviction on a variety of sex offenses in Illinois State Court. While he was preoccupied with his legal difficulties in the Illinois criminal justice system, authorities uncovered numerous irregularities with his campaign finances. This time, Reynolds was indicted in federal court. In April 1997, Reynolds was convicted of fifteen counts, including bank fraud, wire fraud, conspiracy to defraud the Federal Election Commission, and making false statements to federal investigators.

Reynolds remained defiant throughout his Illinois state and federal court trials. He denied any wrongdoing. However, during his sentencing following his federal convictions, Reynolds became contrite and admitted he broke the law. He was sentenced to six-and-a-half years in prison and was to begin serving his federal sentence once he completed his Illinois prison sentence in January 1998.

In early 2001, with more than three years remaining in his prison term, and at the request of Jesse Jackson, Bill Clinton commuted Reynold's federal sentence for bank fraud, wire fraud, false statements, and conspiracy to defraud. Due to his state convictions for obstruction of justice, sexual misconduct, and solicitation of child pornography, Reynolds was required to register as a sex offender. Once freed from prison, Reynolds went to work for Jackson at Operation PUSH.

DC Madam

Federal agents raided the San Francisco Bay-area home of Deborah Jeane Palfrey in October 2006. Palfrey had been under investigation for a couple of years for operating a business named Pamela Martin and Associates. While Palfrey described Pamela Martin and Associates as a high-end escort service, federal authorities said it was nothing more than a prostitution ring.

Because most of her escorts operated in the greater Washington, DC, area, Palfrey was dubbed the "DC Madam." What made her prostitution operation stand out from so many others was the reported high-pedigree of the women and the clientele. By all accounts, Palfrey hired only college-educated, professional women over the age of twenty-five. According to one news outlet, the men were allegedly among some of the most prominent and powerful in Washington, DC, including White House officials, members of Congress, FBI agents, and high-powered lawyers.

According to federal prosecutors, Palfrey operated her business from 1993 to 2006 using a cell phone and email from the comfort of her California home. Most of the escorts operated in the Washington, DC, area.

The scheme required the women to meet in area homes and hotels with the clients, who booked the appointments through Palfrey. The escorts would often be paid as much as $300 for a ninety-minute appointment. Palfrey described these appointments as part of a "legal, high-end erotic fantasy service," and she claimed she had no idea the women were having sex with the clients.[88] The women would then send about half of the payment to Palfrey in the US Mail using money orders.

One of the escorts was Rebecca Dickinson, who lived and worked in the Annapolis, Maryland, area between 2004 and 2007. Dickinson was a Navy officer assigned to the US Naval Academy in the food services division, which fed the more than 4,200 midshipmen attending the Naval Academy. Dickinson said she had sex with nearly every client.[89]

Palfrey said she had thousands of client phone numbers, but did not know the identities of her clients. However, one of the names that emerged was Republican Senator David Vitter of Louisiana. Vitter's cell phone number was among those in Palfrey's thousands of phone records that were posted on the internet. Through a spokesman, Vitter released a statement. "This was a very serious sin in my past for which I am, of course, completely responsible," the statement read. Vitter stated he used Palfrey's service in 2004, before he was elected to the Senate. He also claimed he had earlier confessed this indiscretion to his wife and was in marriage counseling.

Another name made public was that of Deputy Secretary of State Randall Tobias. Tobias resigned from the State Department, but claimed he used the service only for massages and not for sex.

On April 15, 2008, Palfrey was convicted by a jury in the US District Court for DC of racketeering, money laundering, and two counts of using the mail for illegal purposes. According to prosecutors, Palfrey employed more than 130 women during her thirteen-year operation.[90] She was scheduled for sentencing three months later.

On May 1, 2008, Palfrey was found having hanged herself in a shed near her mother's home in Tarpon Springs, Florida. She left behind a suicide note addressed to her mother that read, in part, "I cannot live the next 6 to 8 years behind bars for what you and I have both come to regard as this 'modern-day lynching,' only to come out of prison in my late 50s a broken, penniless and very much alone woman."

In 2016, Montgomery Blair Sibley, Palfrey's lawyer from her criminal trial, released the names of some of the organizations from which telephone calls were made to Palfrey to arrange escort services. These included: Department of Health and Human Services, FBI, General Services Administration, Internal Revenue Service, National Drug Intelligence Center, Department of Commerce, Department of State, Archdiocese of Washington, Embassy of Japan, Johns Hopkins University, and several large law firms.[91]

Client #9

In another era, one could envision Eliot Spitzer as the fire-and-brimstone revival preacher under the big tent, crusading against immoral behavior such as prostitution and calling for its participants to be held accountable. Instead, Spitzer was the New York State Attorney General, operating under the press conference room's bright lights, crusading against prostitution and demanding its participants be held accountable.

In April 2004, Spitzer, an elected Democrat, had a little bit of fire-and-brimstone to share in a written statement after the mass arrests of eighteen people in a major prostitution ring bust. "This was a sophisticated and lucrative operation with a multitiered management structure," wrote Spitzer. "It was, however, nothing more than a prostitution ring, and now its owners and operators will be held accountable."[92] This was but one of several prostitution busts Spitzer made. There was little doubt the married father of three teenage girls was taking an ironclad stand against prostitution.

Two years later, the crusading attorney general was elected New York's crusading governor. He promoted himself as a no-nonsense public official. His family, friends, and, it seems, much of the voting public, thought of him as "Mr. Clean." He did have his critics. They found him to be pompous, self-righteous, and arrogant. However, there was another side to Eliot Spitzer that was not publicly known.

While Spitzer was portraying himself as the anti-prostitution crusader, he was, at the same time, a high-roller john, paying tens of thousands of dollars to engage in kinky sex. Spitzer was such a spend-thrift when it came to prostitution that he wired money, totaling thousands of dollars at a time, to the shell company operating the Emperors Club VIP where he was procuring his prostitutes. Fees for the Emperors Club call girls ranged between $1,000 and $5,500 an hour.

Spitzer was caught in a prostitution sting when the FBI was listening in on a series of telephone conversations he had with the principals at the Emperors Club. A forty-seven-page FBI affidavit of the calls referred to Spitzer as, "Client #9." Beginning on February 12, 2008, the telephone calls dealt with the deposit Spitzer had sent to the Emperors Club via the mail for an upcoming appointment.

A prostitute using the professional name "Kristen" was scheduled to meet Spitzer at the Mayflower Hotel in Washington, DC, the following night, Valentine's Day eve. Spitzer had agreed to pay for Kristen's round-trip train tickets between New York City and Washington, DC, cab fare, hotel room, room service, and any other incidentals, in addition to her payment for sex services. Spitzer was confident he had a $400 or $500 credit that should cover Kristen's visit until the deposit arrived, but his point-of-contact at the Emperors Club said that wasn't enough. They needed the deposit before they would let Kristen leave for the appointment.

The deposit arrived the following afternoon and Kristen was off to the nation's capital to hook up with the Empire State governor. After their tryst that night, Spitzer paid Kristen nearly $4,300, which included an additional $1,500 to have as a credit on his account for future appointments.

After her appointment, Kristen called her contact at the Emperors Club. She was asked what she thought of Spitzer, since other prostitutes apparently found him to be very difficult. According to the affidavit, the contact said, "He would ask you to do things that, like, you might not think were safe." "I have a way with dealing with that…I'd be like listen dude, you really want the sex?" Kristen replied.

On March 7, federal agents arrested four people who were accused of operating the Emperors Club. None of the prostitutes or customers was arrested. Three days later, news broke that Spitzer was the Client #9 listed in a federal affidavit. After that revelation, Spitzer spoke to the press at a hastily arranged press conference. With his wife at his side, he said, "I have acted in a way that violated the obligations to my family and that violate my, or any, sense of right and wrong."[93] However, Spitzer never specified the act or acts for which he was apologizing.

After three days of public outcry and bipartisan calls to step down, Spitzer resigned as governor on March 12, 2008.

It was not just blind luck that caught Spitzer. He was moving money in banking transactions that attracted the attention of the Internal Revenue Service. The amounts were significant, and the fact that they involved a sitting governor suggested a number of scenarios, such as blackmail or bribery. The FBI was called in to investigate the suspicious banking activity.[94] Upon further inspection, the FBI realized Spitzer was paying for high-end call girl services and was trying to disguise his payments.

Evidence indicated that Spitzer had been paying for the call girls to rendezvous with him all over the country. Spitzer had spent more than $100,000 on Emperors Club prostitutes in just a two-year period.[95]

Spitzer could have potentially faced a variety of federal criminal charges, including violation of the Mann Act, a century-old law prohibiting interstate prostitution. Fortunately for Spitzer, prosecutors declined to charge him.

Two years later, Spitzer's rehabilitation was complete, at least according to CNN. The cable news channel hired Spitzer in June 2010 to co-host a prime-time talk show. In spite of Spitzer's absence of tele-vision hosting experience, the Atlanta-based cable channel thought the disgraced Spitzer was an excellent choice to pair with *Washington Post* columnist Kathleen Parker on a program titled *Parker Spitzer*. From the very get-go, the show was "dreary TV and a dud in the ratings."[96]

Only four months after the fall 2010 launch, CNN sacked Parker and rebranded the program, *In the Arena*, with Spitzer as solo host. Four months later, *In the Arena* was canceled.

According to self-proclaimed Russian escort Svetlana Zakharova, Spitzer's affinity for high-priced prostitutes did not end with his resigning from office over the Emperors Club escapades. She claimed to have been Spitzer's regular prostitute between 2010 and 2016, because Spitzer's wife and girlfriend would not engage in the wild sexual activi-ties he desired.

Spitzer and Zakharova engaged in risky encounters in the Spitzers' apartment when his wife was not home. Spitzer would make his petite mistress climb into a large piece of luggage and wheel her past the building concierge in order to escape detection. The pair met regularly for trysts over a six-year period, until 2016, when she finally called the police claiming he assaulted her.[97]

The TV Tape

Heading into the end of September 2016, former Secretary of State Hillary Clinton held a slight but comfortable lead in nearly every single poll in a head-to-head match-up with entrepreneur Donald Trump for the 2016 presidential election. In nearly every poll, Clinton was up about five to six points and almost always outside the poll's margin of error. She was the apparent favorite.

Assuming there were no surprises or slip-ups over the next six weeks, Clinton was assured of being elected the 45th president of the United States.[98] However, there was a surprise in early October, and it was not one that would damage Clinton's front-runner status.

On Friday, October 7, only minutes apart, the *Washington Post* and NBC News published stories with an accompanying video that were deeply embarrassing to Trump.[99] About a five-and-a-half-minute video that was shot in September 2005 by a video photographer for the syndicated television program *Access Hollywood* caught Trump and *Access Hollywood* co-host Billy Bush engaged in a lewd conversation about women.

Trump was going to make a cameo appearance on the daytime soap opera, *Days of Our Lives*. *Access Hollywood* was recording a behind-the-scenes segment of Trump's arrival into the studio parking lot and then the soundstage to film his appearance. Both Trump and Bush were wearing live microphones that captured the pair's inappropriate conversation.

An October 8 *Washington Post* story transcribed much of the banter between Trump and Bush when they were accompanied by a small handful of staff of both Trump and *Access Hollywood*.[100] In reference to a woman the pair were discussing, Trump indicated he attempted to sexually pursue her. Trump said, "I did try and fuck her. She was married."

Then, as the bus pulled up toward the studio entrance, the pair apparently saw Arianne Zucker, the *Days of Our Lives* actress who was meeting Trump and would join him for his cameo appearance. "Your girl's hot as shit, in the purple," said Bush. Moments later, Trump said, "I've got to use some Tic Tacs, just in case I start kissing her. You know I'm automatically attracted to beautiful—I just start kissing them. It's like a magnet. Just kiss. I don't even wait." Then he continued, "And when you're a star, they let you do it. You can do anything. Grab them by the pussy. You can do anything."

Excerpts of the video dominated newscasts throughout the weekend and caused a national sensation. Countless Trump supporters backed away from the businessman's presidential campaign. Republican Speaker of the House Paul Ryan announced he would not join Trump for a previously scheduled campaign appearance the following day.

Critics weighed in and pointed out that, if Trump actually behaved in the manner he described, then he was guilty of committing sexual assault. Clinton tweeted, "This is horrific. We cannot allow this man to become president."

Bush, who had left *Access Hollywood* and was a member of the cast of NBC's *Today Show* when the tape aired, was the first casualty. He issued an apology saying, "Obviously, I'm embarrassed and ashamed. It's no excuse, but this happened eleven years ago. I was younger, less mature, and acted foolishly in playing along. I'm very sorry."

On Monday, October 10, NBC indefinitely suspended Bush from the *Today Show*, pending a full review. A week later, Bush resigned from the morning program.

Most of the reaction to the video was what would have been expected. Some was silly. The day following the tape's release, the company manufacturing the breath mint Tic Tac tweeted, "Tic Tac respects all women. We find the recent statements and behavior completely inappropriate and unacceptable." It is unlikely anyone would have held Tic Tac responsible for Trump's remarks.

Public opinion polling in the week following the tape's release showed that Trump suffered in his race with Clinton. In some polls, Clinton had a double-digit lead. However, in about two weeks' time, the race appeared to have tightened up.

Questions arose as to why an eleven-year-old tape was made public just one month prior to Election Day. NBC sources claimed the tape was discovered the previous Monday by *Access Hollywood* staffers.[101] However, celebrity news outlet TMZ learned from NBC sources that network executives had known about the tape since at least early August. Bush had openly discussed the existence of the tape two months earlier at the 2016 Olympics held in Rio de Janeiro.[102]

Rather than release the tape during the summer, NBC officials decided to wait until late in the campaign in order to inflict the most damage to Trump's presidential ambitions.[103] The plan was to delete segments of the video that included Bush in order to protect him and then run the tape in the October 7 edition of *Access Hollywood*.

As the weekend neared, there was concern that news coverage of the tape could get lost in breaking news of Hurricane Matthew. Days earlier, Hurricane Matthew was registering category-5 winds. It was the first category-5 Atlantic Ocean hurricane in a decade. Matthew would eventually make landfall on the US East Coast on October 8 as a category-1 hurricane.

An upset *Access Hollywood* staffer did not want to wait until Monday, and instead leaked the tape to the *Washington Post*,[104] which went to press in a matter of hours. This forced NBC News to hurry its story on the air.

The TMZ version of events is the most credible. The initial airing of the tape on *Access Hollywood* did not include embarrassing moments that included Bush. Moreover, according to their own claim, NBC executives knew of the tape for an entire workweek and they did not take any disciplinary action against Bush. Not until after Bush's role became public did NBC feign surprise, suspend Bush, and then negotiate his exit from the network.

The existence of the *Access Hollywood* tape appeared to have little public impact on Trump's candidacy. He was elected the 45th president of the United States on Tuesday, November 8, 2016.

CHAPTER 8

NATIONAL SECURITY

"History shows that espionage and security breaches are inevitable. Nonetheless, we can end our review on a guarded note of comfort: It is possible to react rationally to the inevitable by implementing steps to deter espionage, reduce the time between defection and its detection, and minimize the harm traitors can do."[1]

Julius and Ethel

For much of the early twentieth century, until World War II, it was fashionable for many on the political and cultural left to praise Marxism, communism, and socialism. Some openly preached abandoning capitalism and democracy in the US in favor of a Marxist form of government.

At the same time, there was also virulent opposition to Marxism in the lead-up to World War II and after. Cold War opposition to Marxism is obvious in this description of the Soviet Union-dominated Warsaw Pact nations: "Millions of helpless and innocent persons have perished behind the Iron Curtain through wholesale butchery, planned starvation, and the deliberate extermination of minorities."[2]

Julius Rosenberg and Ethel Greenglass met in 1936, while both were members of the Youth Communist League USA, the youth wing of the Communist Party in the United States, Julius and Ethel married three years later.

Shortly after they married, Julius started work as a civilian for the US Army. His electrical engineering degree landed him a position with the Army's Engineering Laboratories in Monmouth County, New Jersey.

Not long after he started, he also began spying for the Soviet Union. He gave his Soviet handlers thousands of pages of classified documents covering a range of US military weapons systems and electronics.

Rosenberg was fired from his position in March 1945, when it was discovered he was a Communist Party member. He began working for Emerson Radio, but was also let go from the company in late 1945 for the same reason.

Before he was fired from his Army engineering position, Julius had already recruited Ethel's brother, David Greenglass, to also spy for the Soviet Union. Greenglass had joined the Young Communist League USA years earlier when he was a teenager at the time Julius was dating his sister. The recruitment of Greenglass was a tremendous coup for Julius and the Soviets.

Greenglass was an Army enlisted soldier assigned to a machine shop, working on the highly secretive Manhattan Project at the Los Alamos National Laboratory in Los Alamos, New Mexico. Greenglass was unaware of the identity of the secret project he was working on until Julius Rosenberg informed him. His Soviet handler told Rosenberg of the Manhattan Project's top-secret mission.

The Manhattan Project developed the first nuclear weapons for the US. Scientists from Canada and the United Kingdom aided in the work. All three countries were allied with the Soviet Union against Germany during the war. However, the three Western countries knew better than to share nuclear weapons technology with the Soviets for fear of how it could be used against the free world after the war.

The finished product from the Manhattan Project that was used to end World War II was an atomic bomb named Little Boy. The Little Boy bomb was dropped on the Japanese city of Hiroshima on August 6, 1945. A similarly designed atom bomb named Fat Man was dropped on Nagasaki, Japan, three days later. These weapons hastened Japan to surrender, finally ending the war in the Pacific theater.

Julius scored another coup when he recruited Russell McNutt to also spy for the Soviet Union. McNutt worked at the Oak Ridge National Laboratory, which was another critical research facility engaged in the development of nuclear weapons. Oak Ridge is where weapons-grade uranium, which formed the explosive component of Little Boy and Fat Man, was created.

There were others Julius recruited to spy on behalf of the Soviet Union, but Greenglass and McNutt were the most valuable. This is why the Soviets were able to build their first nuclear weapon with such rapidity. They received stolen secrets from US spies.

The spy scandal was uncovered in 1949, when German-born British scientist Emil Julius Klaus Fuchs, who was working on the Manhattan Project, was discovered to have been passing top-secret documents to the Soviet Union. After he was arrested in February 1950, Fuchs admitted to passing highly classified documents to Harry Gold for transfer to a Soviet handler.

After Gold was arrested in May, he confessed his role and also named David Greenglass, to whom he was passing nuclear weapons secrets. The secrets Greenglass gave to the Soviets included weapons plans, the identities of many senior scientists, and the names of other workers who might possibly be recruited for espionage. The Soviet handler for this spy ring was identified as Anatoli Yakovlev, who was posing as a Soviet diplomat.

Greenglass was arrested in June 1950 and confessed his role in the spy operation. He and his wife gave information to the FBI that implicated both Julius and Ethel Rosenberg as the titular heads of the spy cell. By August 1950, both Rosenbergs had been arrested and charged with espionage. The same month, the Rosenbergs and Yakovlev were indicted on eleven counts of espionage.

In October, the Rosenbergs, Yakovlev, Greenglass, and accomplice Morton Sobell were indicted by a superseding indictment of espionage-related charges. Sobell, an engineer, was a college classmate of Julius Rosenberg, and Julius later recruited him as a Soviet spy.

Sobell was convicted of espionage and given a thirty-year sentence. He served eighteen years before being released in 1969. He fled to Cuba, where he lived for several years before returning to New York City. Over the decades, Sobell continued to protest his innocence. That all changed on September 11, 2008, when Sobell admitted he spied for the Soviet Union and implicated the Rosenbergs. He believed Ethel was not an active participant, but she was knowledgeable of the spy ring.[3] Even in his admission, he claimed he merely "helped an ally."[4]

A longtime expert on the Rosenberg spy case observed, "A pillar of the left-wing culture of grievance has finally shattered. The Rosenbergs were actual and dangerous Soviet spies. It is time the ranks of the left acknowledge that the United States had (and has) real enemies and that finding and prosecuting them is not evidence of repression."[5]

The Rosenbergs were tried for espionage in March 1951. They refused to testify and took the Fifth Amendment protection against self-incrimination. Based strongly on the testimony of David Greenglass, Ethel and Julius, his sister and brother-in-law, were convicted of espionage. The following month, the husband and wife were sentenced to death.

The Rosenbergs protested their innocence. Campaigns, often led by Communists, Socialists, and other Marxists, sprung up throughout the United States, claiming the Rosenbergs were framed. There were claims that anti-Semitism and anti-Communist hysteria led to unjustified prosecution, convictions, and death sentences. Prominent Marxists, especially those in academia and the arts industry, labeled the death sentences imposed on the Rosenbergs as crimes against humanity.

For the next two years, legal appeals were filed. Seven times, the appeals of Julius and Ethel Rosenberg were heard at the appellate court level. Each one was appealed to the US Supreme Court, and each time the court declined to take up the appeal. Presidents Harry Truman and Dwight Eisenhower turned down executive-clemency requests.

After the various avenues of appeals were finally exhausted, Julius and Ethel Rosenberg were executed by the electric chair at Sing Sing Correctional Facility in Ossining, New York, on June 19, 1953.

For more than four decades, the Rosenbergs were *causes célèbres* for the political and cultural left, who argued the Rosenbergs were guilty of nothing more than being victims of anti-Communist hysteria. However, in the mid-1990s, the declassification and release of intercepted Soviet communications from that time period proved the Rosenbergs were exactly as described. The pair were enthusiastic supporters of the Soviet Union and had engaged in espionage against the United States.

The Pumpkin Papers

Alger Hiss had a very impressive résumé. He graduated from Johns Hopkins University and Harvard Law School.[6] He was a law clerk to Supreme Court Justice Oliver Wendell Holmes, Jr., before practicing law in both Boston and New York City.[7] He was in the administration of President Franklin Roosevelt. He was a key member of the State Department. He was one of the few attendees joining Roosevelt at the Yalta Conference. He was the Secretary General of the United Nations Organizing Conference. And he was a Soviet spy who betrayed his nation.

Hiss had a rapid rise to power in the Roosevelt administration. After he left private law practice in New York City, he joined the Justice Department under Attorney General Homer Stille Cummings. He left Justice to become a Senate staffer for a couple of years. Hiss returned to the administration and took a position in the State Department as an aide to Assistant Secretary of State Francis Sayre.[8] In 1939, he assumed duties as an advisor in the State Department Office of Far Eastern Affairs.

In February 1945, Hiss was selected to be part of the very small contingent that accompanied Roosevelt when he met with British Prime Minister Winston Churchill and Soviet Premier Joseph Stalin at Yalta on the Crimean Peninsula in the Soviet Union. The goal of the three major allied nation leaders was to plan for post-war Europe.[9]

Two months after Yalta, Hiss was appointed the Secretary General of the United Nations Charter Conference, which laid the groundwork for the post-war organization. In 1946, Hiss left government service and became president of the Carnegie Endowment for International Peace.

Whittaker Chambers was a member of the Communist Party in the 1920s and 1930s.[10] He worked as a writer on several publications before being asked in 1931 to go underground in New York and work as a courier, receiving stolen documents from other American spies and passing them to Soviet agents.[11] In 1934, Chambers relocated to Washington, DC, and continued the same assignment.

In the mid-1930s, Chambers began to get disillusioned with the Soviet Union, particularly the purges. Chambers left the Communist Party in 1938 and denounced Communism. He took his family and went into hiding, fearful that he could be added to the list of other Soviet undesirables who were being purged on Stalin's orders.

Because he was a member of the Communist Party organization working in Washington, DC, Chambers knew many of the party members who occupied positions in the Roosevelt administration. In 1939, he gave a State Department official the names of eighteen Communist Party members and Communist sympathizers in the administration. When informed what Chambers had provided, Roosevelt dismissed the allegations. Also in 1939, Chambers resurfaced from hiding and joined the staff of *Time* magazine.[12]

Periodically, reports trickled in to the FBI that Hiss was a Soviet spy. However, Hiss had strong backers, including President Harry Truman, who denounced the suspicions surrounding Hiss. Then, in 1945, Soviet spy Elizabeth Bentley defected and named several Soviet spies in the administration, including Hiss.[13] This finally caused the FBI to undertake a thorough examination of all named suspects, including Hiss. Over a period of three years, the FBI investigated Hiss and others. The FBI also interviewed Chambers on multiple occasions between 1946 and 1947. Congress learned of the espionage allegations and decided to scrutinize the various claims.

In late July 1948, Bentley testified before the House Un-American Activities Committee. Days later, the committee subpoenaed Chambers to testify before the committee. He corroborated much of what Bentley had testified, including naming Hiss as a Communist Party member. Hiss denied the allegations. So, the committee subpoenaed both Chambers and Hiss to appear before the committee simultaneously.

Committee Chairman J. Parnell Thomas, a New Jersey Republican, started the hearing by announcing, "Certainly one of you will be tried for perjury."[14] During their appearance, Chambers accused Hiss of being a Communist, a charge Hiss denied. Hiss denied ever knowing Chambers, other than perhaps having briefly met him and knowing him by another name.[15] In his 1988 memoir, Hiss admitted to having known Chambers for a while and even renting an apartment to Chambers, but insisted he knew him by the name George Crosley.[16]

Weeks later, Hiss filed a libel lawsuit against Chambers for calling him a Communist. This caused Chambers to take a bold action. In November 1948, Chambers not only denounced Hiss as a Communist, but also labeled him a spy. In support of his charge, Chambers produced sixty-five pages of State Department documents Hiss gave to Chambers to pass on to Soviet agents. Included were four pages of notes in Hiss's handwriting.[17] Handwriting experts confirmed Hiss as the author of the notes.

Chambers not only revealed that Hiss was a spy, but that he, too, was one. Both men had previously testified under oath that they were not Soviet spies. Chambers had decided to hold onto this batch of papers after he decided to quit Communism. He hid the papers in the apartment of a relative with the belief that they could one day be handy. That day had arrived.

Two weeks later, Chambers led congressional investigators to the garden on his Maryland farm. At the garden's pumpkin patch, Chambers retrieved five rolls of 35-mm film from a hollowed-out pumpkin. The film was given to Chambers by Hiss in 1938. On the film were images of classified State Department documents. The film and the previously supplied State Department documents became known as the "Pumpkin Papers."[18]

The statute of limitations on espionage had expired, depriving federal prosecutors of the opportunity of charging Hiss with espionage. However, they were able to charge Hiss with perjury for denying under oath he committed espionage against the United States.

The first perjury trial of Hiss ended in mid-1949 with a hung jury. Character witnesses for Hiss at the trial included Ambassador John Davis, the 1924 Democratic presidential nominee; Democratic Governor of Illinois Adlai Stevenson II, who would be the Democratic presidential nominee in 1952 and 1956; and Supreme Court Justices Felix Frankfurter and Stanley Reed.

In addition to the testimony naming Hiss a Communist and a spy, there was forensic evidence that damaged Hiss's claims of innocence. The Woodstock-brand typewriter belonging to Hiss was examined. Typewritten specimens that copied the Pumpkin Papers were analyzed and were deemed an exact match.[19] Hiss's Woodstock typewriter typed the documents retrieved from the hollowed-out pumpkin. The second trial ended in early 1950 with convictions on two counts of perjury. Alger Hiss was sentenced to two concurrent, five-year prison sentences.

Hiss's case was twice appealed to the US Supreme Court, and in each appeal the high court declined to hear the case. Hiss began his prison sentence in March 1951.[20] President Harry Truman and Secretary of State Dean Acheson stated they continued to support Hiss.

A declassified intercept of Soviet KGB communications with a Russian spy who was present at the 1945 Yalta Conference with

Roosevelt was released by US intelligence in the 1990s. The description of the Russian spy appeared to fit Alger Hiss.[21]

Los Alamos

The first inkling the public had that there was a Chinese spy operation underway at the nation's nuclear weapons development program was a January 1999 *Wall Street Journal* article. The article reported that a pair of Taiwan-born American scientists had passed classified nuclear-weapons technology to Chinese agents.

In the late 1970s, one scientist working at the Lawrence Livermore National Laboratory in California leaked neutron-bomb technology to the Chinese. The lab is a Department of Energy nuclear security research facility. A second scientist at the Los Alamos National Laboratory in New Mexico gave laser technology to the Chinese in the mid-1980s. Los Alamos is a sister-research facility. The first scientist was fired, but never charged due to insufficient evidence. The second scientist spent one year in a halfway house as part of a plea bargain.[22]

The article mentioned that another scientist working at Los Alamos was suspected of providing the Chinese with classified information on the latest nuclear warhead technology in the 1980s, but the action was discovered only in recent years. That scientist was not identified, but later reporting indicated the suspect was another Taiwan-born American.

In March 1999, a 4,000-word *New York Times* article titled, "Breach at Los Alamos: A Special Report," claimed "China has made a leap in the development of nuclear weapons...[and] the miniaturization of its bombs."[23] China had lagged behind the United States in nuclear weapons technology, but made dramatic improvements after receiving classified weapons-information from an American scientist.

US intelligence obtained a Chinese document that described a new Chinese nuclear warhead that was eerily similar to the W88, which was the latest warhead in the US nuclear arsenal. US authorities were convinced the stolen information came from the Los Alamos lab, where the W88 warhead was designed.[24]

Just days after this revelation, a Taiwan-born American scientist was fired from Los Alamos. Although he was not charged with a crime, Wen Ho Lee was the chief suspect behind the stolen technology. This discovery brought a sharp rebuke from Congress. The Clinton administration had been heavily lobbying Congress to end a ban on the sale of nuclear technology to China. Congressional leaders were angry that the Clinton administration withheld information from Congress that China had stolen nuclear bomb technology.[25]

The Clinton administration's push for relaxed rules for China may have been influenced by outside factors. The Clinton-Gore 1996 reelection campaign and Democratic National Committee were the beneficiaries of nearly $3 million in illegal foreign campaign funds, with some it originating with the Chinese military. When discovered, the illegal campaign contributions were returned.[26]

There were growing concerns over the potential vulnerability of losing critical nuclear weapons secrets. US nuclear weapons laboratories had come under closer scrutiny as a result of the Clinton administration decisions to increase access to them by foreign delegations.

Even Democrats were critical of the Clinton administration's careless attitude toward the Chinese threat. Democratic Representative Norman Dicks of Washington took a swipe at the White House, calling the nuclear technology theft "a major technology failure."

This was not the first time Lee had come under suspicion of possibly passing critical nuclear-related secrets to the Chinese. Acting on information it had obtained, the FBI opened a foreign counterintelligence investigation of Lee on December 13, 1982. The FBI scrutinized his contacts, reviewed his telephone records, interviewed acquaintances, and administered a polygraph examination.

The FBI was concerned over several telephone calls Lee made from his office to the Coordination Council for North American Affairs. The council was the unofficial government representative of the Republic of China, located on the island of Taiwan. The Republic of China was the sworn enemy of Communist China. The United States ended formal diplomatic relations with Taiwan following formal recognition of the People's Republic of China.

The polygraph examiner determined Lee was non-deceptive in his answers regarding improper contact with foreign agents and the passing of nuclear secrets to a foreign power. Unable to develop considerable derogatory information on Lee, the FBI closed the investigation on March 12, 1984.

Although the FBI harbored concerns about Lee's loyalty, the Department of Energy denied investigation concerns were properly transmitted to the DOE in order to make determinations about continued access to highly classified information.

The FBI took a fresh look at a pair of trips Lee made to Communist China in 1986 and 1988. In both cases, Lee was given permission to attend Chinese government-sponsored science conferences.[27] US officials were now concerned he may have had contact with Chinese agents.

Questions also arose regarding a Chinese researcher Lee hired on a temporary basis in 1997, even though Lee had been under FBI investigation since 1996 for possibly passing nuclear weapons secrets to China. In spite of the ongoing investigation, Lee was granted access to a new sensitive position.[28] It was later learned that, on several occasions, Lee accessed certain facilities to which he was not permitted. He would often "tailgate," by quickly following behind other lab employees when they entered secure facilities.

In 1998, US intelligence officials sent a dire warning to senior Clinton administration officials, including the defense secretary, attorney general, national security advisor, energy secretary, and others. The report cited an "acute intelligence threat" posed by China and Russia.[29]

Several congressional committees had also investigated Chinese spying and lax security procedures regarding nuclear technology at the labs and elsewhere. The Clinton administration steadfastly ignored all the warnings in order to further relax policies with Communist China.

The *New York Times* published a harsh editorial criticizing calls to tighten access to the US nuclear technology labs. "Visits to United States labs help Russian scientists learn new technologies for dismantling Moscow's nuclear arsenal," the *Times* wrote.[30]

The FBI had its doubts as to whether Lee might have been spying for Communist China or Taiwan. In 1998, Lee spent nearly two months serving as an advisor to a Taiwan defense facility associated with nuclear weapons research. Los Alamos lab officials approved his trip.[31]

In spite of deep concerns and a three-year investigation, authorities never bothered to inspect Lee's Los Alamos computer. When they finally did in spring 1999, they found that, on dozens of occasions, Lee transferred classified data to his unclassified computer and then downloaded the data to removable computer tapes. When investigators began questioning him about his whereabouts, Lee attempted to delete evidence of the computer downloads. This led to his firing.

Several times over the course of the FBI investigation, the Justice Department denied FBI requests to issue a search warrant or to wiretap Lee's phones.

Finally, Lee was arrested in December 1999, after a federal grand jury indicted him on fifty-nine counts of illegally downloading highly classified nuclear technology secrets. Lee was accused of copying about fifty years' worth of nuclear weapons technology. Lee was accused of downloading the highly classified information to fifteen computer tapes, nine of which had gone missing. They were never found.

Yet after nine months of pretrial detention, and more than five years of investigation, federal authorities were unable to put together a credible case of espionage against Lee. In September 2000, the Justice Department negotiated a plea deal with Lee. The US government would drop all but one charge against Lee. In return, Lee would plead guilty to a single charge of improperly handling classified data and would be sentenced to time served.

Judge James Parker apologized to Lee for the government's case against him and for his pretrial incarceration for 278 days. President Bill Clinton also issued his own apology to Lee. In 2006, Lee was paid a total settlement of $1.6 million for violation of his privacy rights by the US government and five media organizations: ABC News, Associated Press, *Los Angeles Times*, *New York Times*, and *Washington Post*.

In his memoir, Lee wrote that supporters claimed he was a victim of racial profiling and that he was arrested merely because he was Taiwan-born. Fourteen Asian-American groups released a letter claiming Lee was a victim of "negative ethnic stereotypes and fueled by anti-Chinese hysteria."[32]

Lee argued in his memoir that it was racist "attitudes that tainted everything that happened to me."[33]

Loose Lips Sink Ships

The United States fought World War II in both the European and Pacific theaters. The naval battle was a big component of US military operations in the Pacific theater. Once the United States reconstituted its naval forces following the Pearl Harbor attack, its submarines began having tremendous success disrupting Japanese shipping. Operating out of Pearl Harbor, and Brisbane and Freemantle in Australia, US submarines were sinking as much as 100,000 tons of Japanese merchant shipping each month.

Andrew May was elected to the US House of Representatives in 1930 as a Democrat from Kentucky. He would go on to be elected for seven more terms. In 1939, he became chairman of the Committee on Military Affairs, a position he held throughout World War II.

In spring 1943, May went on a fact-finding trip to the Pacific theater. Upon his return, May gave a press conference on what he had learned in his travels. He discussed the success the US submarine force was having in attacking the Imperial Japanese Navy and Japanese merchant shipping. He also addressed the good fortune US submarines were experiencing in escaping serious damage from the Japanese Navy.

The reason why, May explained, was because the Japanese Navy was underestimating the depth to which US submarines could dive. This, he explained, resulted in the Japanese Navy setting its depth charge explosives to detonate at too shallow of a depth.

News accounts of May's press conference were published across the country, allowing them to come to the attention of Japanese intelligence. The Imperial Japanese Navy headquarters was informed, and it ordered its fleet to make the necessary adjustments. The Japanese Navy increased the amount of explosive in its depth charges by nearly 50 percent, from 242 to 357 pounds, and it increased the depth of detonation to occur at five hundred feet.[34] The Japanese Navy began having greater success in sinking US submarines.

Vice Admiral Charles Lockwood, Jr., who was Commander of Submarine Force, US Pacific Fleet, later wrote, "I hear…Congressman May…said the Jap depth charges…are not set deep enough…He would be pleased to know that Japs set 'em deeper now."[35]

The US Navy lost seven submarines to Japanese warships between the start of the war and mid-June 1943. It is generally thought that most of these losses were attributed to successful depth charge attacks. Following May's remarks, the US Navy's loss to Japanese warships more than doubled, to sixteen submarines.[36] According to Lockwood's estimates, May's leak "cost us ten submarines and 800 officers and men."[37]

In his post-war memoir, Lockwood stated the obvious, "The submarine's best defense against ships or aircraft was submergence."[38] The ability of a submarine to submerge to great depths to escape destruction was demonstrated during a March 1943 patrol of the USS *Kingfish* (SS-234). The *Kingfish* torpedoed and sank a Japanese troop transport in the East China Sea. It submerged and evaded detection.

Four days later, a Japanese destroyer sighted the *Kingfish* on the surface, forcing it to dive, but the water was only 350 feet deep in this particular area of the East China Sea. This severely limited the *Kingfish's* options. The crew rigged the ship for quiet, stopped maneuvering, and rested on the seabed hoping to avoid detection. For nearly eight hours, the Japanese destroyer continuously dropped depth charges, causing severe but not catastrophic damage.[39]

After the depth charge attack stopped, the *Kingfish* crew made emergency repairs to keep the submarine from taking on water. Several hours later, when it was dark, the *Kingfish* rose to the surface for a successful transit back to Pearl Harbor for repairs.[40]

Pentagon Papers

Robert McNamara commissioned a detailed history of US involvement in Vietnam from 1945 to 1967. McNamara was the secretary of defense for President Lyndon Johnson. It was Johnson who engineered the dramatic escalation of the number of US troops to Vietnam. The completed history project was titled, *Report of the Office of the Secretary of Defense Vietnam Task Force*. It later became known by the shorter, simpler name, the *Pentagon Papers*.

McNamara's motives for crafting the history are a bit cloudy because he did not inform Johnson, National Security Advisor Walt Rostow, or Secretary of State Dean Rusk of the report, which would have seemed natural. There was widespread speculation McNamara ordered the study at the request of Senator Robert Kennedy, who was expected to challenge Johnson for the 1968 Democratic presidential nomination, in the belief the report would be damaging to Johnson. "That was nonsense," McNamara would later write in his memoir. Yet, McNamara could not explain why he kept Johnson or his closest foreign policy advisors in the dark about the study.[41]

Adding more intrigue to McNamara's motives was that he bypassed the obvious process of using Defense Department historians to compile the report, instead creating an ad hoc group of military officers and civilians to secretly write it. They operated in such a way that they did not alert others to what they were doing.

Ho Chi Minh figured prominently throughout the report. Ho Chi Minh was a Vietnamese freedom fighter allied with the United States during World War II. The US military and Minh-led forces battled the Japanese army in the region of Southeast Asia that was known at the time as Indochina. The report also ended with Ho Chi Minh in 1967. In that year, the United States was approaching a troop strength in South Vietnam of nearly five hundred thousand. However, this time the US military was fighting North Vietnamese forces led by Ho Chi Minh.

The *Pentagon Papers* addressed several critical issues that were kept secret from the US public and would prove to be embarrassing if they had become known. Most of these issues focused on the size, scope, and mission of US involvement in South Vietnam at a time when Americans were not aware of any American presence in Southeast Asia. Under President Harry Truman in the late 1940s, the United States began providing covert aid to the French, who were fighting Communist forces. The French had colonized portions of Indochina in the late nineteenth century.

Clandestine efforts to undermine Communist leaders in North Vietnam continued under President Dwight Eisenhower in the 1950s. Then, in the 1960s, President John Kennedy approved a modest build-up of military advisors and authorized US assistance in overthrowing South Vietnam President Ngo Dinh Diem. This overthrow led to Diem's assassination.

The most dramatic changes regarding the US military posture in Southeast Asia occurred under Johnson after he assumed the presidency. In 1964, there were a little more than 20,000 American soldiers in South Vietnam. By 1968, that number had mushroomed to more than half a million servicemen and women.

In a bit of irony, Johnson scored a landslide reelection victory in 1964 by claiming his opponent, Republican Senator Barry Goldwater of Arizona, would increase US troop presence in Vietnam. Goldwater countered that he had no desire to send more US soldiers to Southeast

Asia. Johnson's election promises proved to be more persuasive to American voters. Johnson won reelection. Immediately thereafter, Johnson ordered an increased US troop presence from about 25,000 to about 185,000 servicemen in just one year's time.

McNamara later wrote that the decision to increase US troop levels was made just days after Johnson's inauguration. The decision was made "without adequate public disclosure."[42]

In 1969, Daniel Ellsberg was a civilian analyst at the Rand Corporation, a California-based think tank that analyzed military and international issues. Ellsberg was among the three-dozen individuals who compiled McNamara's report. Prior to working at Rand, Ellsberg spent two years in Vietnam witnessing both the successes and the failures of US operations. Ellsberg reached the conclusion that nearly all Vietnamese simply wanted the war to end regardless of who won.[43]

Ellsberg arrived in Vietnam a supporter of the war, and he left as a hardened opponent of US involvement in a war he considered unwinnable. He thought the McNamara report should be made public so that the American people would know the history and scope of US involvement in the region. In addition to the McNamara report, Ellsberg had a personal perspective he wanted to add. "I knew things about the situation in Vietnam worth passing on in my own voice," he wrote in his memoir.[44] In September 1969, he conspired with fellow Rand employee, Anthony Russo, to photocopy more than seven thousand pages of the top-secret report, with the intention of releasing them to the public.[45]

Over a period of months, Ellsberg was unsuccessful in his attempt to have several senators and National Security Advisor Henry Kissinger publicize the report.[46] After a series of disappointments, he decided to go to the press. By then, he had also taken a position as a research fellow at the Massachusetts Institute of Technology.[47]

Ellsberg approached the *New York Times* with his photocopy of the report. In June 1971, the newspaper began publishing portions of the report, which was dubbed the *Pentagon Papers*.* US Attorney General

---

* In his memoir, *Secrets* (pp. 206–207), Ellsberg claimed he began leaking secret and top-secret classified documents to the *New York Times* in March 1968, three years before he leaked the Pentagon Papers.

John Mitchell, under President Richard Nixon, sought and received a prior-restraint federal court injunction to stop the newspaper from publishing further excerpts. The *New York Times* appealed the injunction and the case quickly made its way to the US Supreme Court.

The *Washington Post*, having also been given portions of McNamara's report, began publishing excerpts only days after the *New York Times* started publishing the *Pentagon Papers*. Another federal court injunction was sought by the Justice Department to stop the *Washington Post*. However, this injunction request was denied. The US government appealed that decision and this case, too, found its way to the high court.

The floodgates had opened in June 1971. Assisted by a large group of like-minded volunteers dubbed the Lavender Hill Mob, Ellsberg distributed to nineteen newspapers portions or entire copies of the *Pentagon Papers*.[48]

The US Supreme Court combined both cases and agreed to hear *New York Times v. United States*. The court ruled 6–3 in favor of the newspapers. In his concurring opinion, Justice Hugo Black wrote:

> *Only a free and unrestrained press can effectively expose deception in government. And paramount among the responsibilities of a free press is the duty to prevent any part of the government from deceiving the people and sending them off to distant lands to die of foreign fevers and foreign shot and shell. In my view, far from deserving condemnation for their courageous reporting, the* New York Times, *the* Washington Post, *and other newspapers should be commended for serving the purpose that the Founding Fathers saw so clearly.*[49]

New York Times v. United States is a significant victory against prior-restraint (censoring articles pre-publication) and is viewed as a critical legal precedent that underscores the value and independence of a free press. The *New York Times* won a Pulitzer Prize for publishing the *Pentagon Papers*.

Ellsberg turned himself in for stealing and distributing the report. The newspapers may have had Constitutional protections, but he did not. He still committed a crime by stealing the papers. Ellsberg and Russo were indicted by a grand jury for stealing and possessing classified documents. The trial judge, however, declared a mistrial after he learned of the actions by Nixon's "plumbers."

The plumbers were political operatives working at the direction of Nixon in order to stop leaks damaging to the administration or the government. The plumbers broke into the office of Ellsberg's psychiatrist and attempted to steal records to use in discrediting him. Both Ellsberg and Russo were released from custody following the mistrial ruling. The federal government declined to retry them.

WikiLeaks

Bradley Manning had a troubled childhood. He appeared aimless until he acted on advice given to him by his father. In fall 2007, Bradley Manning enlisted in the Army shortly before his twentieth birthday. After basic training, Manning finished his requirements for the military occupational specialty of intelligence analyst. By 2008, he completed a special background investigation and was given a Sensitive Compartmented Information (SCI) clearance, which made him eligible to access top-secret SCI material.

Manning was assigned to his permanent unit, where he underwent additional training to prepare him for a combat environment. Then, in October 2009, Manning's unit was ordered to deploy to Iraq. In his assignment in Iraq, Manning was in an office where he had electronic access to thousands of classified intelligence documents. These documents provided a window into both the successes and the failures of US operations in Iraq. During this tour, Manning became a hardened opponent of the war in Iraq.

Overall, the military lifestyle proved too challenging for Manning. He was not a good fit when it came to the Army's discipline. This may have contributed to Manning's decision to break the law and steal classified information.

In early 2010, Manning began surreptitiously downloading thousands of intelligence messages and other classified documents to external media. He then transferred this classified material to his personal laptop. After just a few days, he copied nearly half-a-million classified documents.

Manning approached the *New York Times* and *Washington Post* with the stolen documents. Neither paper showed much interest, so in February 2010, Manning forwarded the classified information to

WikiLeaks, which was known for publishing classified information often provided by anonymous sources. Founded in late 2006, WikiLeaks claims it does not induce anyone to break the law, but merely publishes material that is offered to the organization. The online organization began publishing some of the reports Manning provided.

A month later, Manning downloaded a quarter-million State Department messages (referred to as "cables") and later forwarded them to WikiLeaks. Bradley Manning was behind the single largest leak of classified information in American history.[50]

Among some of the classified material Manning downloaded over a period of weeks were videos, including one referred to as "Collateral Murder." A pair of US Army Apache attack helicopters misidentified a group of Iraqi civilians as insurgents and misidentified camera equipment as weapons. The helicopters began an attack that killed several and wounded several more, including two children. Among the group were a pair of Reuters journalists. The online posting of this video and other material stolen by Manning elevated the profile of WikiLeaks and its founder, Julian Assange.

In May, Manning began an online conversation with a hacker and quickly confided he had stolen and leaked classified documents.[51] This information was reported to the Defense Department, resulting in Manning's arrest. In June 2010, the Defense Department filed several charges against Manning regarding the stolen and leaked classified information. On July 30, 2013, after a military trial, Manning was found guilty of espionage and theft, and was sentenced to thirty-five years in the military prison in Fort Leavenworth, Kansas.

In January 2017, President Barack Obama issued executive clemency and commuted Manning's remaining prison sentence.

After publication of the State Department messages, the Obama administration's Attorney General Eric Holder announced WikiLeaks was the subject of "active, ongoing criminal investigation." Holder suggested it was illegal to publish leaked classified information.[52]

The Obama administration argued WikiLeaks had an obligation to return any classified documents given to the organization instead of publishing them. Assange claimed the First Amendment protected the organization. Holder stated, "To the extent there are gaps in our laws, we will move to close those gaps, which is not to say that anybody at this point, because of their citizenship or their residence, is not a target or a subject of an investigation."[53]

In a 2010 interview, Assange stated that several US news organizations have aided WikiLeaks in legal matters related to press freedoms. These news organizations included the Associated Press, *Los Angeles Times,* and the National Newspaper Association.[54]

Fearful he would be extradited from the United Kingdom to the United States to face charges over publishing leaks, Assange sought and received asylum in the Ecuadorean Embassy in London in August 2012.

In April 2017, Director of the Central Intelligence Agency Mike Pompeo said, "WikiLeaks walks like a hostile intelligence service and talks like a hostile intelligence service…It's time to call our WikiLeaks for what it really is, a non-state hostile intelligence service."[55]

Pompeo continued, "Now, for those of you who read the editorial page of the *Washington Post,* and I have a feeling many of you do, yesterday you would've seen a piece of sophistry penned by Mr. Assange. You would've read a convoluted mass of words wherein Assange compares himself to Thomas Jefferson, Dwight Eisenhower, and the Pulitzer Prize-winning work of legitimate news organizations such as the *New York Times* and the *Washington Post.*"[56]

The Traitor

Jonathan Pollard was a traitor to the United States. I know this for a fact. I will explain later.

Jonathan Pollard was clearly a troubled man. In 1977, the twenty-three-year-old Stanford University graduate was turned down for employment with the Central Intelligence Agency because of past drug use and his inability to be truthful. He told tall tales about fictitious exploits of his father and himself.

That failure did not prevent Pollard from starting a career in the US intelligence community. In 1979, he gained employment with the Office of Naval Intelligence, working between two different buildings at the sprawling Suitland Federal Center in Suitland, Maryland. The fenced-in compound included buildings that were part of the US Census Bureau and a pair of buildings belonging to Naval Intelligence.

These two buildings were named NIC-I and NIC-II (Naval Intelligence Command-I and -II).

There were several organizations in these two buildings. Pollard bounced around a few organizations due to reassignments over performance and trust issues. In spite of behavioral and honesty concerns, Pollard managed to stay employed in Naval Intelligence and have access to top-secret Sensitive Compartmented Information for most of his brief career. Top-secret SCI clearance includes some of the nation's most closely guarded secrets.

At some point in 1984, Pollard made the decision he would spy against his country on behalf of Israel. He would later claim that, as a practicing Jew, he had an obligation to provide the Israeli government with intelligence he believed was critical to the security of the Middle East nation.

Pollard and his wife, Anne, were arrested by the FBI on November 21, 1985, while they were attempting to gain asylum at the Israeli Embassy in Washington, DC. Pollard was caught red-handed. He had stolen thousands of pages of classified documents. There were boxfuls of material he had spirited out of Naval Intelligence, taken home and handed over to his Israeli controller. Pollard's spying was a premeditated act.

There was no question about Pollard's guilt. So, he struck a deal with federal prosecutors. In early 1987, Pollard pleaded guilty to a charge that constituted espionage in the mind of most people and agreed to assist the United States in conducting a damage assessment of his spying in return for leniency for his wife. Pollard was sentenced to life imprisonment and his wife was given a five-year prison sentence.

It seemed almost from the day he was incarcerated that Pollard was the beneficiary of an organized campaign for his release by countless supporters in both the United States and Israel. They protested his conviction and incarceration. I heard all the arguments. "Pollard was spying for an ally." "He was providing critical intelligence needed by Israel." "He only gave intelligence on threat nations like Iraq and Iran." "None of his spying damaged the United States." I was lectured by Americans and Israelis alike that Pollard's imprisonment was a travesty.

All of those arguments were total balderdash.

I served in the US intelligence community in a variety of assignments, roles, and locations between 1985 and 2011. I was in intelligence as an active-duty military officer, in the reserve military, and as a civilian. I had assignments in the United States and abroad. I worked at various three-letter agencies (e.g. CIA, DIA, NSA). I even had an assignment with Naval Intelligence at the Suitland Federal Center. In fact, I started working at Suitland not long after Pollard began his prison sentence.

Even today, I honor the commitment I made to safeguard the classified intelligence to which I had access. Accordingly, I will address this topic in broad terms.

Once Pollard began cooperating with US officials, I was tasked with making a damage assessment of just a small portion of the classified material Pollard stole. It was material originated by my organization.

After Pollard was sentenced, I read the final classified damage assessment of his spying. It was a massive document that went into great detail.

I can state unequivocally that Pollard gave to Israel more than just intelligence related to Iran and Iraq. Pollard gave more than intelligence related to regional threats. Pollard gave intelligence that had absolutely nothing to do with Israel or the Middle East. He gave away intelligence that had no value to Israel's security. What Israel did with that intelligence is anybody's guess.

Most critically, Pollard exposed what we referred to in the intelligence community as "sources and methods." Pollard exposed not just the fruit of our nation's spying apparatus, but he also compromised the process, sources, and methods the United States used to gain valuable intelligence. Pollard did not just give away secrets. He gave away the inside scoop as to how we got our secrets.

Anyone who claims Pollard's spying did not damage the United States is either misinformed or dishonest.

Pollard was released from federal prison in 2015 and is now a free man. He will likely spend the reminder of his days in Israel. For the record, I am a strong supporter of Israel, the only free democracy in the Middle East. Yet, I still hold them responsible for running a spy operation against their greatest nation of support.

How the United States dealt with Israel over this inexcusable breach is best left to the statecraft of US officials at the highest level.

As far as Jonathan Pollard is concerned, I believe he deserved to breathe his last breath on this earth in an American prison. This is the only punishment befitting such a traitor.

Ramon Garcia

It was about money and personality. These were the prime motivations for Robert Hanssen when he chose to spy on his own nation. He violated his oath of office and betrayed his country in order to earn a few illicit dollars and to think of himself as an espionage mastermind.

The story begins not long after thirty-two-year-old Robert Hanssen joined the Federal Bureau of Investigation in 1976. The FBI's internal review of Hanssen's spying over a two-decade period for the Soviet Union (and later, the Russian Federation) portrayed him as an unlikely special agent. "He had poor interpersonal skills and a dour demeanor, and was an awkward and uncommunicative loner who conveyed a sense of intellectual superiority that alienated many of his co-workers," according to the inspector general's report.[57]

Hanssen began his spy career in 1979, a mere three years after he became an FBI special agent. This was after Hanssen had transferred from his first posting in Gary, Indiana, to his second assignment in the New York City field office. In New York, he was a member of the counterintelligence unit. Hanssen quickly volunteered his services to a *Glavnoye Razvedyvatel'noye Upravleniye* (GRU) officer. The GRU is the intelligence arm of the Soviet military. The FBI concluded Hanssen was attempting to overcome his "low self-esteem" and other personality flaws in his offer to sell his services to the Soviet Union.[58]

Hanssen was very discreet regarding his identity. He gave very little information to his GRU handler that could identify him or the US agency for which he worked.

This period of Hanssen's espionage lasted two years, ending in 1981. Hanssen didn't resume spying for the Soviets until late 1985. In his second phase of spying, Hanssen offered his services to the *Komitet Gosudarstvennoy Bezopasnosti* (KGB), the Soviet Union's foreign intelligence organization. He kept his identity secret and did not divulge that he had spied for the GRU some years earlier. Hanssen referred to himself as Ramon Garcia. This espionage period lasted six years, covering Hanssen's assignment in New York and subsequent transfer to FBI headquarters in Washington, DC.

According to the FBI, this six-year period was the most damaging to the United States in terms of what Hanssen revealed. Hanssen divulged the names of valuable Soviets who were sources working in cooperation with the FBI. Two of those who Hanssen compromised were Sergey Motorin and Valeriy Martynov, who were KGB officers assigned to the Soviet Embassy. These men were recalled to Moscow from their assignments in Washington, DC. Once back in the Soviet Union, both men were interrogated and then executed.[59]

A third man Hanssen compromised was Boris Nikolayevich, a KGB officer posing as a Russian news correspondent. Nikolayevich was also recalled to the Soviet Union, where he was sentenced to fifteen years in prison.[60]

It is believed that throughout his two decades of spying, Hanssen may have compromised as many as fifty agents and sources working on behalf of the United States. Many were executed.[61]

The KGB paid Hanssen at least $500,000 during this period. Hanssen spent much of the money on his home and family. The rest went to a stripper named Priscilla Sue Galey, whom he befriended. Hanssen gave her a Mercedes Benz automobile, showered her with cash and gifts, and even took her on trips to France and Hong Kong.[62]

In late 1990, Hanssen's brother-in-law, also an FBI special agent, reported Hanssen to an FBI supervisor. Hanssen's brother-in-law was troubled over a $5,000 wad of cash that was lying out in the open in Hanssen's home. There was no follow-up investigation.

Hanssen broke off his contact with the Soviets in December 1991, the same time the Soviet Union collapsed. The FBI believe Hanssen was concerned there was too much havoc and uncertainty, and that this made him vulnerable to detection while the Soviet Union was breaking up into separate states.

In 1999, Hanssen got back into the espionage business. He approached the *Sluzhba Vneshnei Razvedki* (SVR), the successor to the KGB as Russia's foreign intelligence service. Hanssen offered to spy on behalf of the Russian Federation. They accepted.

It was during Hanssen's third stint as a Soviet and Russian spy that he learned of an intense effort by the CIA and FBI to discover the identity of a very damaging Russian spy, known as a mole, working within the US intelligence community. The mole everyone was looking for, Hanssen realized, was him.

According to the FBI's arrest affidavit, Hanssen compromised the identities of numerous Soviet/Russian agents working on behalf of the United States. He also passed more than six thousand pages of documents to the GRU/KGB/SVR, some of which were classified top-secret SCI. In addition to the approximately $600,000 and diamonds he was given as payment, Soviet/Russian authorities also placed funds in escrow in a Moscow bank that totaled nearly $800,000 by the time Hanssen was arrested.[63]

The ineptitude of the FBI resulted in the Bureau filing documents regarding the mole-hunting efforts in a computer database to which Hanssen had access. Hanssen was able to monitor the Bureau's progress as it looked for the mole. Fortunately for Hanssen, the CIA and the FBI focused their suspicions on a CIA employee who was innocent.[64]

Hanssen did not manage to go undetected for a twenty-year period because he was some "master spy," the FBI later concluded. He escaped detection "because of longstanding systemic problems in the FBI's counterintelligence program and a deeply flawed FBI internal security program."[65] Hanssen was also fortunate that the 1993 discovery that CIA officer Aldrich Ames had been a Soviet double agent explained away several critical intelligence losses. Ames was the most damaging spy in CIA history. He was also the most damaging spy in US history until Hanssen.

Over a period of years, the FBI steadfastly refused to consider that the mole working inside the US intelligence community could be an FBI agent. Instead, the FBI was convinced the mole was a CIA employee.[66] The FBI mindset was enough to help Hanssen avoid detection for many years.

It was mostly happenstance, and not dogged investigation, that led to the discovery of Hanssen. A Russian spy handed over the SVR file on "B," which was how Hanssen was identified by his Russian handlers. Buried inside was an audiotape of a telephone conversation between Hanssen and his chief handler. An FBI special agent recognized Hanssen's voice on the audiotape.

After he was placed under surveillance, Hanssen was arrested in February 2001, immediately after delivering classified material to a dead-drop location in a Virginia park.

On July 6, 2001, Robert Hanssen pled guilty to fifteen counts of conspiracy, espionage, and attempted espionage, with each charge carrying a life sentence. Hanssen agreed to a plea deal in exchange for his wife keeping half of his FBI retirement annuity and the family home.

Mind Control

It was the stuff of science fiction movies. Imagine the ability to conduct mind control by forcing people to perform involuntary actions, and for them to later have no recollection of the events. Or how about wiping clean an individual's entire memory? Perhaps the ultimate truth serum could be developed, ensuring everything a suspect says is absolutely truthful. These were not the plots of a science fiction film. Instead, these attempts at behavioral modification and many similar programs were part of Project MKULTRA.

Created by the Central Intelligence Agency in 1953, MKULTRA was the umbrella program for a wide array of projects, experiments, and investigations that would presumably give the United States a competitive advantage over the Soviet Union and Communist China in order to help the West win the Cold War. There was also a defensive component to the project. The CIA wanted to understand if either, or both, the Soviets and Chinese were employing similar techniques against Americans. If so, the CIA wanted to develop countermeasures. Project MKULTRA used biological, chemical, radiological, and psychological tools to further its experimentation.

Project MKULTRA was a highly classified program to which very few had access. The CIA expected there would be a massive public outcry if MKULTRA became publicly known. There was also the matter of the subjects of the experiments. Some were volunteers from the ranks of the CIA. Others were unwitting participants, including federal employees, the military, prisoners, hospital patients, the mentally ill, prostitutes, and even total strangers found in social settings.

Much of the program was discontinued in 1963. In 1973, about the time the Watergate scandal had reached a peak, CIA Director Richard

Helms directed that all paperwork, documents, and any other written
evidence of MKULTRA be destroyed. Most of it was.

When the Church Committee hearings were conducted in 1975,
there was the public revelation that MKULTRA existed, but little about
the program was learned. Most of the CIA personnel who had worked
in the program had retired, and documents related to the program were
no longer in existence.

Two years later, in 1977, seven boxes of documents related to
MKULTRA were discovered. These records had been mislabeled and
were mistakenly placed in records storage unrelated to MKULTRA. The
discovery of these documents led to a new hearing in the US Senate.

According to a Supreme Court opinion in an MKULTRA-related
case, MKULTRA "consisted of some 149 subprojects which the [Central
Intelligence] Agency contracted out to various universities, research
foundations, and similar institutions. At least 80 institutions and 185
private researchers participated. Because the Agency funded MKULTRA
indirectly, many of the participating individuals were unaware that they
were dealing with the agency."[67]

On August 3, 1977, CIA Director Admiral Stansfield Turner testified
before the Senate Select Committee on Intelligence regarding MKUL-
TRA.[68] This was after the discovery of the seven boxes of documents.
Turner testified there were fifteen broad categories of programs that
incorporated the 149 subprojects. Some of these included: research into
the effects of behavioral drugs and/or alcohol, research on hypnosis,
acquisition of chemicals or drugs, aspects of magicians' art useful in
covert operations, studies of human behavior, sleep research and behavioral changes during psychotherapy, and the effects of electro-shock.

Turner testified the CIA used "'cut-out' (i.e. intermediary) funding
mechanisms…to conceal CIA's sponsorship of various research projects."
The CIA did this because it worked with "80 institutions…includ[ing]
44 colleges or universities, 15 research foundations or chemical or
pharmaceutical companies…12 hospitals…and 3 penal institutions."
The CIA did not want its partner institutions to know of the agency's
involvement.

The most light shone on MKULTRA came from a declassified (with
redactions) 1963 inspection report from the CIA's inspector general. The
IG noted there were few written records for the MKULTRA program,

owing to its sensitivity and the realization that the public would find the operation distasteful if it became known. The IG observed, "Research in the manipulation of human behavior is considered by many authorities in medicine and related fields to be professionally unethical."[69] In addition, the "testing of MKULTRA products places the rights and interests of US citizens in jeopardy."[70]

The IG report noted that only two CIA individuals knew the full scope of the MKULTRA program, and most of that knowledge was "unrecorded." The IG believed that, if discovered, key agency employees would disavow any knowledge of the program.

The most controversial aspect of Project MKULTRA was the "covert testing of materials on unwitting US citizens [that began] in 1955." This was the primary reason why the inspector general observed multiple times throughout the report the damage that could result if the Agency's MKULTRA operations were discovered.

The inspector general believed the agency's biggest vulnerability arose from the testing on unwitting subjects. The IG was concerned the program could be compromised if an unwitting test subject suffered an adverse reaction necessitating medical attention, which could lead to the discovery that a drug had been administered. In such a case, the CIA would "request…cooperation from local authorities in suppressing information."[71]

In the inspection report, the IG recommended discontinuing testing on US citizens, but noted testing could continue by "deep cover agents overseas" on foreigners.[72] The overseas testing was an element of a subprogram named MKDELTA. This subprogram also involved the use of drugs for conducting interrogation of foreign agents. However, the IG noted that, "Some case officers have basic moral objections to the concept of MKDELTA and therefore refuse to use the materials."[73]

One of the most scandalous developments of Project MKULTRA was the death of one of the unwitting test subjects from a drink spiked with the hallucinogenic drug, lysergic acid diethylamide (LSD), often referred to as "acid." This is how his death was described in the 1977 Senate investigation report:[74]

The most tragic result of the testing of LSD by the CIA was the death of Dr. Frank Olson, a civilian employee of the Army, who died on November 27, 1953. His death followed his participation in a CIA experiment with LSD. As part of this experiment, Olson unwittingly received approximately 70 micrograms of LSD in a glass of Cointreau he drank on November 19, 1953. The drug had been placed in the bottle by a CIA officer, Dr. Robert Lashbrook, as part of an experiment he and Dr. Sidney Gottlieb performed at a meeting of Army and CIA scientists.

Shortly after this experiment, Olson exhibited symptoms of paranoia and schizophrenia. Accompanied by Dr. Lashbrook, Olson sought psychiatric assistance in New York from a physician, Dr. Harold Abramson, whose research on LSD had been funded directly by the CIA. While in New York for treatment, Olson fell to his death from a tenth story window in the Statler Hotel.

Nearly all the records associated with MKULTRA were destroyed on the January 31, 1973, order of CIA Director Richard Helms. Years later, Helms told journalist David Frost the reason why he ordered the destruction. Helms said, "Since this was a time when both I and the fellow who had been in charge of the program were going to retire there was no reason to have the stuff around anymore."[75]

One of the documents that survived Helms's destruction order was the April 3, 1953, memorandum to CIA Director Allen Dulles, requesting permission to launch the program that would later become MKULTRA. The CIA's acting deputy director of plans who signed that original request was Richard Helms. Perhaps the more likely reason why Helms gave the destruction order was to protect himself.

Mishandling Emails I

John Deutch served as the director of central intelligence for President Bill Clinton between May 1995 and December 1996. He began his tenure by launching a massive political correctness campaign aimed at fast-tracking the hiring and promotion of women and minorities as part of a strategic diversity plan.

However, the action he undertook to handcuff the ability of case officers—CIA employees that work clandestinely—to meet with bad actors on the world stage seriously undermined human intelligence collection efforts and had widespread repercussions, especially regarding the growing threat of terrorism. CIA case officers and agents—foreigners in the employ of, or working with, US intelligence officers—must some-times associate with undesirable elements if they are to gather valuable intelligence. However, Deutch thought they shouldn't associate with unsavory people.

After Deutch left the CIA, classified information was discovered on the government-owned laptop he was using at home. He stored large amounts of sensitive intelligence on the laptop designated for the storage of only unclassified information. Moreover, the laptop was connected to a modem, which made all of the information vulnerable to exploita-tion by hostile governments. Mishandling of classified information is a serious breach of security for persons working with such information. Of all people, the CIA director should have known better.

CIA security specialists immediately commenced an investigation of Deutch's mishandling of the classified material. Upon conclusion of the eighteen-month investigation, the CIA's Office of General Counsel declined to refer the matter to the Department of Justice, as was stan-dard protocol in such matters. The CIA also decided not to disclose the matter to the Intelligence Oversight Committees of the Congress or the Intelligence Oversight Board of the President's Foreign Intelligence Advisory Board.[76]

The CIA's inspector general picked up the matter where the agen-cy's general counsel office left off, by opening a formal investigation in March 1998. Shortly thereafter, the inspector general's office referred the matter to the DOJ.

A Justice Department investigation confirmed that Deutch know-ingly mishandled classified information. Yet in April 1999, Attorney General Janet Reno declined to pursue criminal charges against him. Instead, she directed an investigation to determine the fitness of Deutch to retain his security clearances.

Simultaneously, the Defense Department launched its own inves-tigation regarding Deutch's handling of classified information while he served as under secretary of defense for acquisition and technology from April 1993 to March 1994, and as deputy secretary of defense from March 1994 to May 1995.

Forensic analysis of the information technology equipment Deutch used revealed he had 675 pages of text stored on unclassified computers and related media that "contain[ed] many entries that include[d] collaterally classified material and should, therefore, have been marked and treated as classified when written."[77] A further review found that an additional fourteen entries contained references to special access programs—information that is classified at the absolute highest levels. A fifteenth entry also referred to a special access program when Deutch entered the information, but the entry was no longer classified when the review was conducted.

Nearly another two years elapsed before Deutch finally admitted his guilt in improperly safeguarding classified material. He was negotiating a plea agreement with Justice Department officials when Clinton preempted the entire matter by pardoning Deutch on January 20, 2001.

Mishandling Emails II

Hillary Clinton served as the secretary of state for President Barack Obama between January 2009 and January 2013. She began and ended her tenure by violating federal law and concealing her email communications from the State Department, Congress, the national archivist, and the public.

The steps she took to conduct government business on a privately owned computer server and email system was unprecedented. No other secretary of state or any other Cabinet official is known to have utilized a private server in their home to shield emails from congressional oversight and public accountability.[78] Federal law requires every agency to retain records in any and all forms involved in the conduct of the business of government. Records under consideration for disposal must first be submitted to the national archivist for review and a determination before they may be destroyed.[79]

In spite of federal law, Hillary Clinton had a private email server located in her Chappaqua, New York, home, which was used to conduct personal business, political business, campaign business, and government business. The unsecured server did not have necessary security protections to safeguard the system from penetration by hostile state and non-state actors. Officials of the National Archives and Records Administration called it a serious breach.[80]

There was no formal request of the State Department nor notification of the State Department that Clinton would be using the server and a private email system to conduct the nation's business. In fact, Clinton operated the server for the entire four years she served as secretary of state and neither notified the State Department, nor properly archived emails, as required by law.

The existence of Clinton's private emails were only discovered when a hacker penetrated the private emails of longtime Clinton hatchet man Sidney Blumenthal.[81] Clinton wanted to appoint Blumenthal to a State Department position; however, the Obama White House banned Blumenthal from having a role in the administration.[82] Blumenthal was among those orchestrating the "birtherism" attacks against Barack Obama during the 2008 presidential race going so far as visiting the McClatchy News DC Bureau to encourage a reporter be dispatched to Kenya to investigate Obama's alleged birthplace.[83]

Clinton's aides claim she used a private email server only because the State Department had fuzzy guidelines on this matter.[84] The State Department inspector general issued a report after an investigation into Clinton's email practices and found nothing further from the truth. In fact, the State Department had very specific and detailed guidelines.

The inspector general found: "The Department's current policy, implemented in 2005, is that normal day-to-day operations should be conducted on an authorized Automated Information System (AIS), which 'has the proper level of security control to…ensure confidentiality, integrity, and availability of the resident information.'"[85] Further, the IG found federal law enacted in 2002 "requires Federal agencies to ensure information security for the systems" used to perform government business.[86]

Clinton insisted former Secretary of State Colin Powell encouraged her to use a private email system. That claim was not true, according to Powell. He had explained he had used his personal AOL email account to address unclassified matters. This was only because the State Department did not have an unclassified email system when he assumed the office of Secretary of State. That would come years later. The State Department had only a classified system at the time.[87]

Powell was displeased Clinton tried to use him as a defense in her use of an unsecured email server. He wrote a colleague, "I warned her (Clinton) staff three times over the past two years not to try to connect it to me."[88]

In late 2014, before the existence of Clinton's secret email server became public knowledge, Clinton's chief of staff decided which emails would be forwarded to the State Department for archiving. After this was completed, Clinton directed the destruction of at least thirty thousand emails that had not been properly reviewed or archived. According to federal law, the national archivist determines which emails may be destroyed.

Only days after the existence of Clinton's private server became public in March 2015, the House Select Committee on Benghazi subpoenaed the emails on the server. Platte River Networks, the firm managing the server, had not destroyed the thirty thousand emails as Clinton had ordered months earlier. In spite of the existence of a subpoena for the emails, Platte River Networks manually destroyed tens of thousands of emails using a process named BleachBit that is designed to prevent document recovery.[89]

A large amount of sensitive intelligence was stored on Clinton's server, which was not approved for the storage of classified information. Moreover, the server was connected to unsecured public communications systems, which made all of the information vulnerable for exploitation by hostile governments. Mishandling of classified information is a serious breach of security. Of all people, the secretary of state should have known better.

An investigation confirmed that Clinton mishandled classified information. The FBI was aware of more than two thousand emails that contained classified information. Some had the classification markings and others had that information removed. By August 2015, it was learned that at least two emails were classified top-secret Sensitive Compartmented Information (SCI) with the Talent Keyhole abbreviation TK.[90] This is a much more restrictive classification than top secret.

A more thorough examination conducted by the intelligence community inspector general found there were several emails that were classified at categories above top secret.[91] Some of the classifications were so sensitive that the intelligence community inspector general had to be read into the program before he could be informed of the sensitive nature of the information.[92]

In spring 2016, it became public knowledge that the FBI was conducting a criminal investigation of Clinton's mishandling of classified information. There were two significant non-public developments surrounding the investigation. In early May, FBI Director James Comey circulated a draft statement among FBI personnel that exonerated Hillary Clinton from any legal consequences for the private email server and for mishandling classified information. The main problem with this was that more than one dozen key witnesses had yet to be interviewed, including the subject of the investigation, Hillary Clinton.

The May 2 draft named Clinton guilty of "gross negligence" in mishandling classified material. According to federal law, anyone who "through gross negligence permits [classified material] to be removed from its proper place of custody or delivered to anyone in violation of his trust, or to be lost, stolen, abstracted, or destroyed…Shall be fined under this title or imprisoned not more than ten years, or both."[93] Obviously, labeling Clinton guilty of "gross negligence" would warrant referral for criminal prosecution. Subsequent drafts replaced that term with "extremely careless," which was an innocuous term not included in federal statute.[94]

The other non-public development was a secret June meeting between Bill Clinton and Attorney General Loretta Lynch on a government plane on the tarmac of Phoenix Airport. Clinton and Lynch claimed the meeting was impromptu, and that the two merely engaged in idle chitchat. Neither one brought up potential criminal charges facing Hillary, they claimed.

In the end, the Clinton-Lynch meeting had no bearing on the matter. On July 1, Comey announced the FBI investigation into Clinton's mishandling of classified material was complete. "Although we did not find clear evidence that Secretary Clinton or her colleagues intended to violate laws governing the handling of classified information," Comey said, "there is evidence that they were extremely careless in their handling of very sensitive, highly classified information." Therefore, Comey was not making a criminal referral. However, it was wrong for Comey to imply that intent was key to whether there should be a criminal referral. The statute makes no mention of intent when addressing the criminal act.

CHAPTER 9

INFLUENCE PEDDLING

"One question, among many raised in recent weeks, had to do with whether my financial support in any way influenced several political figures to take up my cause. I want to say in the most forceful way I can: I certainly hope so."

—Charles H. Keating, Jr. of Financial Lincoln & Savings regarding campaign contributions to five US Senators

Crédit Mobilier

The steam locomotive made its debut in England in 1804. It quickly began to overtake horse-drawn carts on rail as a more effective method to move goods. Steam locomotives were being used to connect English cities, first with goods and then with people. By the 1820s, the steam locomotive had become the most efficient way to transport passengers.

The earliest steam locomotives in the United States were imported from England. Chartered in 1827, the Baltimore and Ohio Railroad became the first locomotive company in the US. B&O was an attempt to compete with the use of canals and inland waterways to navigate trade routes to the West. By May 1830, the B&O was up and running with its first section of rail open for business. Other railroads began to appear and, over the next two decades, track was being laid and steam locomotive-driven trains were being added throughout the East Coast.

Westward expansion in America was occurring throughout the middle of the nineteenth century. However, travel to the West Coast was time-consuming. Many travelers would take the months-long trip by ship around the southern tip of South America. Crossing the western mountain ranges and the great prairies was deemed impractical and dangerous.

Congress wanted to shorten the time needed to travel from coast to coast. It enacted the Pacific Railroad Act of 1862, which was intended to incentivize private construction of a nearly 1,800-mile, transcontinental railroad and a companion telegraph line. The 32nd parallel was designated as the route and there would be generous land grants for rights-of-way. The Central Pacific and the Union Pacific were the two companies selected to complete the construction. The Union Pacific was capitalized with $100 million from the federal government. In addition, the Railroad Act created financial incentives for each mile of track laid by each company.

In 1863, the Central Pacific began building from Sacramento eastward and the Union Pacific started building westward from Omaha. The two railroad companies would eventually meet at Promontory, Utah, in May 1869 when the ceremonial final spike was driven into the track to commemorate linking the two rail lines.

In May 1864, the directors and major shareholders who chartered the Union Pacific also chartered a duplicate company named Crédit Mobilier of America, but the participation of the same people in the two different companies was kept secret. Union Pacific officials claimed Crédit Mobilier was a separate entity hired by Union Pacific as the general contractor to build the rail line. In reality, the business relationship was an elaborate scheme for shareholders of Union Pacific to shield themselves from the financial risks of the Union Pacific and to guarantee themselves profits from Crédit Mobilier.

Crédit Mobilier would charge Union Pacific exorbitant costs and fees to build the railroad. Union Pacific would add a modest profit to these invoices and pass them on to the federal government for reimbursement. Because the officers and directors of Crédit Mobilier and Union Pacific were the same, Union Pacific would attest that the Crédit Mobilier charges were legitimate.

The remaining challenge was to ensure Congress kept appropriating funds to continue funding Union Pacific. This was accomplished in November 1866, when Union Pacific replaced president Thomas Durant with Oliver Ames.[1] Oliver Ames's younger brother was Massachusetts Republican Congressman Oakes Ames, who was an influential member of the Committee on Railroads in the US House and was the point man in Congress supervising the railroad construction effort. It was a responsibility President Abraham Lincoln personally assigned.[2]

Shortly after Oliver Ames became the head of Union Pacific, his brother Oakes began selling stock in the highly successful Crédit Mobilier to other Congressmen below the actual trading value in return for promises to vote for legislation and appropriations favorable to Union Pacific. Ames sold stock to nine House members and two senators.[3] He was selling to those members of Congress "where it would do the most good."[4] These Congressmen could immediately sell the Crédit Mobilier stock at the prevailing rate and make a handsome profit. This vote-rigging scheme continued for the next few years, until construction was completed.

Meanwhile, Crédit Mobilier shareholders were making a ridiculous amount of money, due to the dividends that were being paid. The dividends were paid in a combination of Union Pacific bonds, Union Pacific stock, and cash. In 1868, the annual dividend was 280 percent.[5] In contrast, the government-issued bonds for Union Pacific were paying only 6 percent.[6]

Although the transcontinental railroad was completed in 1869, there were simmering conflicts among the various participants for the next few years. This came to a head on September 4, 1872, when the *New York Sun* published an explosive story under the headline, "The King of Frauds: How the Credit Mobilier Bought Its Way Through Congress."[7]

The *Sun* published an exposé that named members of the House and Senate who were allegedly involved in the scheme. The public outcry led the House to form a special committee to investigate the allegations.

A dozen members of Congress—eleven Republicans and one Democrat—were accused of having taken part in the scheme, including Congressmen William B. Allison (R-IA), Oakes Ames (R-MA), George S. Boutwell (R-MA), James Brooks (R-NY), Roscoe Conkling (R-NY), James Garfield (R-OH), and Speaker of the House James Blaine (R-ME). Senators suspected in the scandal were James A. Bayard, Jr. (D-DE), James Harlan (R-IA), John Logan (R-IL), James W. Patterson (R-NH), and Henry Wilson (R-MA). Vice President and former Speaker of the House Schuyler Colfax (R-IN) was also implicated.

Nearly all of them escaped any serious repercussions. However, on February 27, 1873, the House of Representatives censured Oakes Ames and James Brooks.

Selling the White House

"This has become an urban myth, like the alligators in the sewers of New York. It is just not true," said Amy Weiss Tobe, the press secretary for the Democratic National Committee. Tobe was responding to reports in 1996 that the Democratic National Committee had partnered with President Bill Clinton to sell access to the White House and federal officials in return for steep campaign contributions to the party.[8]

It turns out that Tobe's denial was not true. In fact, party officials, at the behest of Clinton and his staff, were engaged in a fire sale for access to all things presidential. *Forbes* magazine broke the news with the brief report that party donors of $100,000 or more could join official government trade missions. Anyone writing a check of at least $130,000 would get to spend the night in the Lincoln Bedroom at the White House.[9]

The Center for Public Integrity examined records and disclosed that at least seventy-five Democratic donors had stayed in the Lincoln Bedroom or Queen's Bedroom during the first three years of the Clinton administration. The list the center compiled was a who's-who of heavy hitters in Democratic fundraising circles. Sprinkled in were Hollywood celebrities who were vocal Clinton supporters, such as Barbra Streisand, Jane Fonda, and Chevy Chase.[10]

When the scandal was raised with Clinton, he dismissed that he was selling access to the White House. He claimed he merely invited friends and supporters for a White House stay. However, the facts established that Clinton had turned the White House into a fundraising factory. Terry McAuliffe, who was the national finance chair for the Democratic Party, sent a memo to Clinton before he was inaugurated, outlining a plan to reward major donors. These included inviting big donors to join Clinton "for breakfast, lunch or coffee." McAuliffe's memo listed the names of the top ten Clinton fundraisers. McAuliffe also suggested having donors join Clinton for "golf games, morning jogs, etc." Clinton responded by writing, "Yes, pursue all 3 and promptly—and get other names of the 100,000 or more. Ready to start overnight right away. Give me the top 10 list back, along w/ the 100, 50,000."

In a sworn statement, a Clinton staffer admitted she wrote the word "overnights" in capital letters alongside the names of the top ten fundraisers McAuliffe listed, but she said she could not recall the details of why she wrote it. It was Clinton's handwriting on the back of the memo that urged overnight stays start immediately. The problem was that exchanging a night in the White House in return for a campaign contribution was just like collecting checks from donors to attend White House coffees. Both acts were violations of federal campaign-finance laws.[11]

The Lincoln bedroom sleepover controversy got an added boost when a photograph became public that showed Clinton chum Linda Bloodworth-Thomason and actress Markie Post hopping on the bed in the Lincoln bedroom. Bloodworth-Thomason and her husband were embroiled in the White House Travel Office scandal in the early days of the Clinton administration.

Nearly one thousand guests visited the White House overnight, with most sleeping in the Lincoln Bedroom, during the first three years of the Clinton presidency. The Clintons were not the only First Family to have overnight guests, but the sheer number of Clinton guests was impressive. There were 938 White House guests between 1993 and 1996, which was nearly four times the 284 that spent the night all four years of the George H. W. Bush presidency.[12]

According to one media report, two-dozen White House overnight guests gave $100,000 or more to the Democratic National Committee. The Clintons ran the Democratic Party as an offshoot of the Clinton-Gore reelection campaign, so they pulled the strings on how the Democratic National Committee spent its money. This group of Lincoln-Bedroom guests gave nearly $5.5 million to the Democratic National Committee.[13]

Once it became indisputable that the Clinton administration was selling access to the White House in return for campaign contributions, pressure began to build for the Justice Department to launch an investigation. US Attorney General Janet Reno declined.

Illegal Contributions

Chang Joon Kim was born in Seoul, Korea in 1939. The translation of his name means "Golden Splendid Law." He legally changed his first name to Jay. The Korean War split the nation in two, eventually forcing Kim and his family to flee further south to avoid North Korean soldiers. Kim spent some time in South Korean universities, then he served a one-year stint in the South Korean army. After he was discharged, he immigrated to the United States on a student visa. Kim returned to school, where he earned a bachelor and master's degree in engineering and, some years later, he founded the firm, JayKim Engineering, Inc.

Kim's first run for elected office was successful when he won a seat on the city council of Diamond Bar, California, in 1990. Diamond Bar is a suburban community located midway between Los Angeles and San Bernardino. The following year, he was voted mayor by the other city-council members. Then, in 1992, Kim ran for Congress as a Republican in California's newly formed 41st congressional district. That newly formed seat had arisen from the reapportionment following the 1990 census. In November 1992, Jay Kim was the first Korea-born American to be elected to Congress.

Only six months after he was sworn in as a member of Congress, the *Los Angeles Times* broke a major story regarding Kim. Someone had leaked to the *Times* hundreds of pages of financial records from JayKim Engineering. According to the paper, the company provided free rent, office equipment, staffing, and other services to Kim's campaign committee, in violation of the Federal Election Campaign Act.[14]

In addition, JayKim continued to pay Kim his full salary, even though he was campaigning full-time and was rarely at the company, according to Sung Woo Min, who purchased the company from Kim shortly after the 1992 election.[15] In total, JayKim paid more than $400,000 of Kim's campaign-related expenses. According to the *Times*, costs included $30,000 for office stationery, photocopying, printing, mailing, and travel expenses, about $17,000 for office space, and $78,000 in salaries.[16]

When asked about the seemingly illegal payments, Kim insisted that they were the result of sloppy bookkeeping measures, and he had every intention of reimbursing the company with campaign funds. He also claimed the expenses he needed to reimburse amounted to no more than $1,000.[17] He also asked rhetorically, if he owned the company and the building, then why would it be necessary for him to pay rent to himself?[18]

Fred Schultz, the firm's former chief financial officer, and Kim disagreed on the failure by the firm to bill the campaign. Kim claimed that Schultz failed to send an invoice to the campaign after repeated requests he do so. Schultz claimed Kim ordered him not to bill the campaign since it had no money to pay the expenses.[19]

In August 1993, about a month after the newspaper exposé, Kim's campaign returned nearly $21,000 in campaign donations that may have violated federal campaign-finance law. About $11,000 was returned to Korean churches, which are barred from making political contributions. About $10,000 was returned to donors that appeared to be corporations, also a violation of law.[20]

The FBI subpoenaed Kim's campaign records in March 1994. His 1992 campaign manager claimed Kim knowingly broke campaign finance laws, a charge the Republican Congressman denied. In spite of the controversy, Kim announced his intention to run for reelection. Kim beat six challengers to win the June primary and he won the November general election en route to a second term in Congress, in spite of political baggage from the 1992 campaign. The fact that no criminal charges had been filed against him obviously helped his reelection efforts.

Kim's second term was relatively uneventful, until December 1995, when Korean Air Lines admitted to federal investigators that the airline made illegal contributions to Kim's 1992 campaign. The airline funneled a pair of $2,000 contributions through two employees who were foreign nationals.[21]

Weeks later, Korean auto manufacturer Hyundai made a similar admission of making illegal campaign contributions to Kim. Korean Air Lines was slapped with a $250,000 fine and Hyundai Motor America was hit with a record fine of $600,000.[22]

Two months later, in February 1996, Korean electronics manufacturer Samsung pleaded guilty to making an illegal campaign contribution to Kim's campaign and agreed to pay a $150,000 fine.

In spite of these developments, Kim handily won reelection to his third term in November 1996. However, the following month his campaign treasurer, Seo Kuk Ma, was indicted for allegedly accepting illegal campaign contributions.

Then, in July 1997, Jay Kim and his wife reached an agreement with the US Attorney's Office to plead guilty to accepting more than $230,000 in illegal campaign contributions during his 1992 campaign.[23] In March, Kim was sentenced to two months of house detention, placed on one year of probation, and fined $5,000.

Kim broke his 1992 campaign pledge to seek only three terms and announced he was running for reelection to a fourth term. He lost the June 1998 Republican primary.

The Torch

One might consider Robert Torricelli the typical New Jersey Democratic politician. He was born in New Jersey and attended the state university, Rutgers University, where he received his undergraduate degree in 1974. He then graduated from Rutgers Law School in 1977. He quickly got involved in Democratic politics and worked for New Jersey Governor Brendan Byrne, Vice President Walter Mondale, and the 1980 Democratic National Convention.

In 1982, Torricelli successfully ran for the House of Representatives, where he served for seven terms before turning his attention to the US Senate. Former NBA great Bill Bradley was retiring from the Senate, and Torricelli defeated his Republican opponent for the seat in November 1996. Known as a combative partisan, Torricelli was often referred to by his nickname, the Torch. Even fellow Democrats were critical of his "abusive manner and questionable ethics."[24]

Early in Torricelli's first year in the Senate, it was learned he was the recipient of troubling and, in some cases, illegal campaign contributions. By March 1997, he returned $1,000 to John Huang, who was a key figure involved in a multimillion-dollar fundraising scandal involving President Bill Clinton and numerous Democrats.[25] In October 1998, it was learned Torricelli was the recipient of illegal campaign contributions from a Miami resident.[26]

Then came more revelations of illegal campaign contributions in January 1999,[27] and again in May 1999.[28] The May discovery implicated China-born businessman David Chang, who had already been embroiled in a fundraising scandal in 1997. In that case, Chang cooperated with prosecutors, who pursued charges against Republican Congressman Jay Kim of California for accepting illegal campaign contributions. Federal prosecutors declined to charge Chang in that case.

Chang was well known in Democratic Party circles. He raised a lot of money for Democratic candidates and organizations. Among his recipients was Bill Clinton. In fact, Chang had been a frequent visitor to the Clinton White House.

Only two years after the Kim scandal, Chang was at the center of a money laundering scandal in which illegal contributions he earmarked for Torricelli were passed through straw donors who pretended they had given the contributions.[29] According to federal authorities, Chang gave more in campaign donations to a slew of Democratic candidates in one year than he declared to the Internal Revenue Service as his income. Torricelli responded to the scandal by stating, "I am a victim, the campaign is a victim."[30]

By early 2000, a federal investigation revolving around illegal contributions to Torricelli was well underway. Federal agents delivered subpoenas to several people who were suspected of making illegal campaign contributions to Torricelli.[31] As many as fifteen donors were subjects of the Torricelli fundraising probe.[32] By mid-2000, six of the people under federal investigation pleaded guilty to making the illegal contributions to Torricelli's Senate campaign.[33] Torricelli and his staff denied any knowledge of the illegal funds.

In September 2000, it was revealed that after Chang was initially arrested in December 1999 in connection with the fundraising scandal, he spent the weekend in New Jersey's Hudson County Correctional Center. Chang told the FBI several men he did not know visited him in the jail, intimidated him, and told him to stay silent during the Torricelli fundraising probe. According to visitor logs, one of Chang's visitors had links to Torricelli. That visitor was a prison official who normally worked weekdays, but stopped by that weekend, he claimed, to check on the welfare of Chang.[34]

By February 2001, Torricelli became the focus of federal investigators who wanted to determine if he possibly directed efforts to make the illegal campaign contributions. Chang told investigators he lavished Torricelli with campaign cash and gifts, including Italian suits and Rolex watches, in return for a promise by Torricelli that he would help Chang in a trade deal with the North Korean government that had gone awry.[35,36] According to Chang, he had a quid pro quo with Torricelli, which the Senator never honored.

Another donor, who gave illegal donations that he falsely claimed came from others, told federal investigators that he was pressured by Torricelli and his staff to raise $20,000 for Torricelli's 1996 campaign.[37]

In the midst of the probe, the Justice Department, led by Republican Attorney General John Ashcroft, subpoenaed the home telephone records of an Associated Press reporter who had been covering the Torricelli investigation in an effort to learn the identities of his sources.[38]

In January 2002, observers were shocked when the Justice Department abruptly announced it had ended its investigation into Torricelli's fundraising scandal, and it declined to pursue any charges against Torricelli or any of his staff. At this point, Torricelli had spent about $2 million on legal fees.

Seemingly cleared of breaking any laws, Torricelli turned his attention to his reelection, which was only eleven months away. Democrats cleared the field for him. Torricelli expected to raise and spend more than $15 million on his 2002 campaign. There was a crowded field of challengers vying for the Republican Party nomination. First-time candidate Douglas Forrester won the Republican nomination by hammering Torricelli over the fundraising scandal.

As the general-election campaign progressed, Torricelli began falling further behind in the polls to his Republican challenger. In late September, Torricelli trailed the relatively unknown Forrester by thirteen points in one poll. Torricelli then made the abrupt decision to drop his bid for reelection.[39]

Although the deadline for registering as a candidate had passed, and many ballots had already been printed, the New Jersey Supreme Court ordered Torricelli's name on the ballot to be replaced by Frank Lautenberg, who had retired as one of New Jersey's US Senators two years earlier. Lautenberg won the general election a month later.

Eyebrows were raised in 2008 when Torricelli decided to give $1.5 million to his own Rosemont Foundation.[40] The money was left over from Torricelli's 2002 election campaign. While it is permissible to give left over campaign funds to other political campaigns or to a charity, the expectation is the charity would not be so closely connected to the donor.

Keating Five

Charles Keating Jr. and the Lincoln Savings and Loan Association became the faces of the savings-and-loan crisis. Swept up in the Lincoln Savings and Loan failure and the subsequent criminal and ethics investigation were five US Senators who attempted to influence federal regulators investigating irregularities at the thrift prior to its collapse.

Keating was chairman of the Phoenix, Arizona, based real estate and home construction firm, American Continental Corporation. In 1984, American Continental purchased Irvine, California, based Lincoln Savings and Loan Association. Under Keating's tutelage, Lincoln dramatically built up its assets by expanding beyond home loans to investments in real-estate deals, high-yield "junk" bonds, and other, riskier investments.[41]

By 1985, leadership at the Federal Home Loan Bank Board, the federal regulator for savings-and-loans, had become alarmed at the large amount of savings-and-loan money being invested in risky ventures. Bank Board Chairman Edwin J. Gray implemented a rule that no more than 10 percent of a savings and loan's assets could be held in a direct investment. Gray was worried at the massive financial exposure to the federal government's insurance funds if savings and loans were to collapse.

Keating pushed back against the Bank Board's direct investment limits. He hired private economist Alan Greenspan, who would later be appointed chairman of the US Federal Reserve in 1987 by President Ronald Reagan, to craft a paper advocating how safe direct investments were for Lincoln and other savings-and-loans.[42]

By early 1987, Keating turned to a handful of powerful Senators to aid him in his battle with Gray and the Bank Board. Arizona Senators Dennis DeConcini (D) and John McCain (R), and Democrats Alan Cranston of California, Don Riegle Jr. of Michigan, and John Glenn of Ohio pressured Gray to back off of Lincoln Savings and Loan.

These senators were no strangers to Keating. DeConcini received $48,000 in campaign contributions from Keating and his associates; McCain got $112,000 and free trips on Keating's private aircraft; Cranston took in nearly $1 million for various groups he controlled, including $39,000 for his reelection effort. Riegle received more than $76,000 in campaign contributions and nearly $250,000 went to Glenn for his political action and reelection committees.[43]

On April 2, 1987, DeConcini hosted a meeting with Gray in his Capitol Hill office. Joining them were Cranston, Glenn, and McCain. In a striking departure from the way meetings are typically conducted on Capitol Hill, the senators requested no staffers attend.[44] DeConcini kicked off the meeting with a reference to "our friend at Lincoln."[45] Gray told the senators he had little knowledge of the specifics of Lincoln and the regional Bank Board office would be better situated to address their concerns.

A follow-up meeting took place in DeConcini's office on April 9 with all five senators and James Cirona, president of the Bank Board's San Francisco regional office, and William Black and Michael Patriarca of the Federal Savings and Loan Insurance Corporation. The regulators later said the five senators pressured them regarding their oversight of Lincoln.[46] DeConcini and Glenn were forceful in requesting the regulators ease up on Lincoln. However, it was McCain who made the regulators most nervous, Black later explained.

William Black was the deputy director of the Federal Savings and Loan Insurance Corporation, the federal agency insuring customers' savings-and-loan deposits. According to Black's notes of the meeting, McCain said, "One of our jobs as elected officials is to help constituents in a proper fashion. ACC [American Continental Corporation] is a big employer and important to the local economy. I wouldn't want any special favors for them." However, Black and the other regulators said McCain's comments had the opposite effect. It made them "nervous" about what was really going on with McCain and the other senators.[47]

The following month, the San Francisco Bank Board completed a yearlong audit of Lincoln and offered its recommendation: the troubled savings and loan should be seized. For nearly a year, the audit and recommendation were not acted upon. Then, in March 1988, the Federal Home Loan Bank Board in Washington, DC, took over the Lincoln investigation and launched a new audit.

In 1989, news broke about the meetings in DeConcini's office and the pressure applied to the regulators on behalf of Keating by the five senators. McCain attempted to distance himself from the other four senators by claiming he was merely an elected official ensuring a constituent was being treated fairly. However, McCain's relationship with Keating was not as innocuous as he claimed. His ties with Keating went much deeper than the other four senators.

It was revealed that McCain and his family had flown at least nine times on Keating's company jet or on chartered jets to vacation destinations without having disclosed them, as required by House and Senate rules. McCain was first a member of the House, and later the Senate, when he took those trips. The McCain family vacationed at Keating's lavish vacation home on the private island Cat Cay in the Bahamas. The McCains even brought along their daughter's babysitter.[48] McCain did not disclose these vacation gifts in financial or ethics filings.

McCain reimbursed Keating for the flights and vacation expenses after Keating's office contacted the senator and told him the Internal Revenue Service had questions about the expenditures.

The Keating-McCain entanglements did not end there. McCain's wife, Cindy, and her father invested nearly $360,000 in a partnership with Keating in Phoenix's Fountain Square shopping center in 1986, a year before McCain came to Keating's aid. McCain claimed he had no knowledge of his wife's investment, and therefore it did not pose a conflict of interest in his acting on behalf of Keating with federal regulators.[49]

The House and Senate Ethics Committees announced that McCain's reimbursement to Keating satisfied any ethics concerns the committees might have had regarding McCain's unreported jet and vacation travel.

By the time the public learned of the role of McCain and the other senators on behalf of Keating, American Continental Corporation had become insolvent. The huge debt of the failed Lincoln investments caused American Continental to collapse. In April 1989, federal regulators seized Lincoln Savings and Loan Association. Lincoln was nearly worthless. More than twenty thousand depositors lost their life savings.

Lincoln Savings and Loan became the costliest of the savings-and-loan failures. It cost the federal government nearly $3.5 billion to cover depositors' losses.

In November 1990, the Senate Ethics Committee began a fourteen-month-long probe of the scandal. It later launched another pair of investigations largely focused on John McCain. Throughout the Ethics Committee probe of Keating and the senators, there was a series of orchestrated leaks of committee documents and internal discussions to the press. These documents were closely held by the committee, but were also provided to each of the five senators to protect their due process rights.[50]

The documents and deliberations that were leaked were always favorable to McCain and damaging to the other four senators, hence why investigations were launched into McCain's possible role in orchestrating the leaks. Under Senate rules, a senator leaking privileged information was subject to censure and possibly expulsion from the chamber. McCain refused to cooperate in the investigations. The results of the two parallel investigations into the leaks were inconclusive, although investigators strongly believed McCain was behind them.[51]

Upon the conclusion of the Senate Ethics Committee investigation, Alan Cranston was reprimanded. Dennis DeConcini and Don Riegle were criticized for their conduct, which while deemed not illegal, "gave the appearance of being improper." John Glenn and John McCain were criticized for using "poor judgment" in their work on behalf of Keating.

Conveniently for everyone involved, the Senate Ethics Committee publicly released its findings in February 1991, in the midst of Operation Desert Storm, when public attention was focused on American forces fighting in Kuwait and Iraq.[52]

It would be another decade before the legal case involving Charles Keating drew to a close. Keating was convicted of dozens of charges in both California state and federal trials that were later overturned. On the eve of a federal retrial, Keating negotiated a plea deal to the four-and-a-half years he had already served in prison.

Charles Keating died in 2014 at the age of ninety.

Vicuña Coat

Sherman Adams may have been destined to serve in the White House, since he was a descendant of the second and sixth presidents, John Adams and John Quincy Adams. Born in Vermont, Adams lived most of his life in Vermont and New Hampshire. In the first forty years of his life, he was lumberman. He was very successful in the timber industry, until his co-workers encouraged him to run for political office.

He ran as a Republican and won a seat in the New Hampshire General Assembly in 1940. After he was reelected in 1942, he was elected Speaker of the House. Two years later, he won a seat in the US House of Representatives. In 1946, Adams challenged incumbent New Hampshire Governor Charles Dale and lost by a whisker in the Republican primary. Two years later, Adams won the primary and general elections.

Adams set the example as a loyal and dedicated public servant. He encouraged others to follow his lead. He received widespread praise when he took control of state spending and implemented an austerity program in the famously low-tax state. After having conquered New Hampshire state politics, Adams looked toward national politics.[53]

Adams was not a supporter of Republican Senator Robert Taft of Ohio who was considered an early front-runner for the 1952 nomination for President. Taft was in the isolationist wing of the Republican Party. Adams preferred a candidate who was more likely to engage in foreign affairs.

There was a small but growing movement of Republicans who were encouraging General Dwight Eisenhower to run for president. At the time, Eisenhower was the Commander of Supreme Headquarters of Allied Forces in Europe. Adams organized a draft-Eisenhower movement for New Hampshire's first-in-the-nation presidential primary. Eisenhower scored an impressive victory in the March 1952 New Hampshire primary, which led to a winning general election campaign.

After he was elected president, Eisenhower rewarded Adams by appointing him to a position referred to as "presidential assistant." In its functioning, the assignment was modeled after a position prevalent throughout the military: chief of staff.

In his new role, Adams was the gatekeeper to the president. Some called him the "second most powerful figure in the executive branch."[54] He reviewed and filtered the minutiae that previous presidents faced. Adams set the agenda, approved presidential meeting requests, synthesized policy papers, and made administrative decisions on behalf of the president. Adams turned down so many requests to see Eisenhower he was dubbed the "Abominable No Man." Adams created the role of presidential chief of staff.

Adams quickly developed a reputation as a straitlaced, no-nonsense, "frugal public servant, eating ham and cheese sandwiches at his desk, rather than accepting pricey meals."[55]

In early 1958, the House Special Subcommittee on Legislative Oversight was conducting hearings on the functioning of federal regulatory agencies. In the course of its investigation, the committee learned New England textile manufacturer Bernard Goldfine sent lavish gifts to several government officials in an attempt to gain assistance in battles he was having with a pair of regulatory agencies. The committee learned

Adams was one of the recipients. Adams insisted he personally testify before the committee in order to clear his name.

In a June 17 appearance, Adams told the committee he accepted from Goldfine a vicuña coat and an Oriental rug, which he maintained was merely loaned for his Washington, DC, home. Adams also admitted Goldfine paid about $2,000 in hotel expenses, including a stay at the Waldorf Astoria in New York City.[56] In return, Adams called the Securities and Exchange Commission and the Federal Trade Commission to inquire about the status of two different investigations involving Goldfine's East Boston Company.[57]

No evidence was uncovered of any wrongdoing by Adams. Still, the appearance of impropriety was devastating to Adams's reputation. More significantly, the Republican Party saw the scandal as scuttling the party's opportunity to retake control of Congress in the 1958 mid-term elections. Twelve of the fourteen Republicans running for reelection in the Senate demanded Adams's resignation.[58]

On September 22, 1958, Adams resigned from his White House role in the most public way possible. He did so in a live, eight-minute television appearance. In his national broadcast, Adams delivered fiery remarks in which he charged the Democratic Congress with engineering a smear campaign intended to damage Eisenhower.

"These efforts, it is now clear, have been intended to destroy me, and, in so doing, to embarrass the administration and the President of the United States," he told a television audience. While his actions were clearly imprudent, Adams confessed, he insisted he did nothing wrong. "I had never influenced nor attempted to influence any agency, or any officer or employee of any agency in any case, decision or matter whatsoever," he told viewers. Then he charged the committee with accepting "completely irresponsible testimony and, without conscience, gave ear to rumor, innuendo and even unsubstantiated gossip."

Upon his resignation, Adams ended eighteen years of public service and began retirement. In what can be viewed as a metaphor, after he left the television studio at the conclusion of his resignation remarks, Adams climbed behind the wheel of his station wagon. In the back was a set of golf clubs.[59]

The Fundraiser

Norman Hsu was a bundler. He organized and collected political donations from several political donors, then bundled them together and gave them to a single election candidate. He was well known in Democratic Party circles for his ability to corral a lot of campaign cash. In 2007, he was such a prolific fundraiser for Hillary Clinton's 2008 presidential campaign that he was recognized as one of her elite fundraisers and was designated a "HillRaiser."

Hsu was born in Hong Kong and immigrated to the United States as a young man. He received college degrees from the University of California at Berkeley and the Wharton School of the University of Pennsylvania. By 1982, Hsu started several business ventures, only to have each of them fail.[60] However, Hsu's business ventures were not exactly what they seemed. He was operating a classic pyramid scheme, according to the California Attorney General's office.[61]

After nearly a decade, and a series of business failures, Hsu accumulated a mountain of debt, forcing him to declare bankruptcy. In 1990, Hsu was accused by California authorities of forgery and fraud. Two years later, after discussions and negotiations, Hsu reached a plea agreement with prosecutors to serve three years in prison and pay a $1 million fine. Hsu never appeared for the formal court sentencing in 1992. Instead, he fled to Hong Kong.[62] While living in Hong Kong, Hsu launched a number of businesses only to watch them fail.

Years later, Hsu returned to the United States and passed through immigration control without incident, in spite of having an outstanding warrant for his arrest. Once again, Hsu began launching businesses, including in the apparel industry. Unfortunately, Hsu was no more successful in operating businesses in the United States in the 1990s than he was in the 1980s.

It was during the late 1990s that Hsu turned his attention to political contributions and fundraising. He relocated from California to New York. He began donating money to federal candidates during the 1998–2000 federal election cycle. Initially, Hsu contributed modest amounts of campaign donations to Democratic Representative Grace Napolitano, who represented parts of Los Angeles County, California. These were "hard money" campaign donations that were regulated by the Federal Election Commission and had strict limits of $2,000 to a candidate for each election (primary and general), and no more than $5,000 to each political action committee.

Hsu became much more involved in the 2003–2004 cycle, donating about $75,000 to several federal candidates, including Democrats Hillary Clinton, Ted Kennedy, Barack Obama, and John Kerry.[63]

Hsu gave about $120,000 the following 2005–2006 election cycle. In addition to Clinton and Kennedy, Hsu gave money to several other prominent Democratic senators including Maria Cantwell of Washington, Dianne Feinstein of California, Bill Nelson of Florida, and Debbie Stabenow of Michigan.[64] About the same time, Hsu began writing checks in large amounts of money that were unregulated by the Federal Election Commission. These were "soft money" donations.

Hsu became very active in the high-dollar Democratic Party circles in New York. One night, he rented a New York nightclub to celebrate Democratic election victories and ordered anyone who was not a supporter of Hillary Clinton's 2008 presidential ambitions to immediately vacate the premises.[65]

Hsu became a dues-paying member of the Clinton Global Initiative, and he was asked to join the board of trustees of the very chichi New School in Manhattan. Three years earlier, Hsu was virtually anonymous. Now, he was the political fundraising king of Manhattan.

In the first several months of 2007, Hsu gave more than $100,000 to Democratic candidates and causes in hard money donations. Most were candidates for the US Senate, including Byron Dorgan of North Dakota, Al Franken of Minnesota, Kirsten Gillibrand of New York, Mary Landrieu of Louisiana, Frank Lautenberg of New Jersey, Mark Pryor of Arkansas, John Rockefeller of West Virginia, and presumptive presidential candidate Hillary Clinton.[66]

Norman Hsu's world came crashing down when the *Wall Street Journal* published an August 2007 article raising questions about his political donations and donations to the Hillary Clinton campaign from others who had curious ties to Hsu. A Clinton campaign spokesman came to Hsu's defense saying, "[T]here has been no question about his integrity or his commitment to playing by the rules."[67] By this time, Hsu had contributed about $850,000 in hard- and soft-money donations to Clinton's various presidential campaign organizations.[68]

After the *Journal* article appeared, Hsu complained that Barack Obama, who was badly trailing Clinton in the polls, had the negative stories about Hsu planted in the press.[69] Hsu's claim was backed up by another journalist, who reported that the Obama campaign was actively dishing as much dirt on Clinton as was humanly possible.[70]

Days after the *Wall Street Journal* article appeared, Hsu returned to California and surrendered to authorities. The warrant issued for his arrest in 1992 was still valid. He was scheduled to return to the court-house a week after his initial court appearance to surrender his passport and to attend a hearing to reduce his $2 million bail. Hsu did not show. He fled, again.

Hsu was captured days later in Colorado. In 2008, a California court sentenced Hsu to three years in prison as punishment for his original California fraud charge. In 2009, he was sentenced to twenty-four years in federal prison following his convictions for mail fraud, wire fraud, and violations of federal campaign finance laws.

The Canadians

"We are committed to the strategy of developing Uranium One as a platform for the global growth of ARMZ's business," said Vadim Jivov, Chairman of JSC AtomRedMetZoloto (ARMZ) Uranium Holding. Jivov was celebrating the January 2013 agreement to purchase the remaining stock it did not already own of Uranium One, a Canadian firm that had extensive mine holdings in the United States, for a price of $1.3 billion. JSC ARMZ is a subsidiary of Rosatom,[71] the $70 billion Russian govern-ment-owned nuclear energy company.

In June 2010, Rosatom (Russian State Atomic Nuclear Agency) announced its purchase of 51 percent of Uranium One. Some of the holdings of Uranium One were US uranium mines, a strategic asset that required US government scrutiny. The Atomic Energy Act of 1954 mandated that the US Nuclear Regulatory Commission make a determination if a license transfer was in the security interest of the United States.[72]

Three months earlier, in March 2010, Secretary of State Hillary Clinton met privately with then-Russian Prime Minister Vladimir Putin and President Dmitri Medvedev to discuss several issues, including nuclear matters. Those private talks may have included discussions of Rosatom's intention to purchase Uranium One.

US government scrutiny included more than just the Nuclear Regulatory Commission. The heads of several major US government agencies were members of the Committee for Foreign Investment in the United States. This committee had responsibility to review all sales involving a strategic US asset.

Several cabinet secretaries and other agency heads were members of the committee, including: Hillary Clinton (State), Tim Geithner (Treasury), Gary Locke (Commerce), Robert Gates (Defense), Steven Chu (Energy), Janet Napolitano (Homeland Security), Eric Holder (Attorney General), Ron Kirk (US Trade Representative), and John Holdren (Office of Science and Technology Policy).[73]

As is typical in similar committees, the principal members could appoint a subordinate as a proxy to carry out their wishes. Clinton instructed Jose Fernandez to act on her behalf as her committee representative. Suggestions made later that committee principals were not knowledgeable on the topic and had no idea how their subordinates would vote are patently absurd.

In October 2010, the nine-member Committee for Foreign Investment unanimously approved the first-ever sale of US uranium mines to the Russian government. After the purchase of the remaining 49 percent of the stock was announced in January 2013, Rosatom chief executive officer Sergei Kiriyenko told Russian President Vladimir Putin, "Few could have imagined in the past that we would own 20 percent of US [uranium] reserves."[74]

Republican Senator John Barrasso of Wyoming was among those in Congress most concerned regarding the sale. Six uranium mines in Wyoming were sold to the Russians, as well as mines in Arizona, Colorado, Nevada, New Mexico, Oregon, South Dakota, Texas, Utah, and a uranium processing facility in Texas. "Russia has a disturbing record of supporting nuclear programs in countries that are openly hostile to the United States," Barrasso wrote in a December 21, 2010, letter to President Barack Obama. Barrasso continued, "Russia has directly aided Iran's nuclear development and agreed on October 15, 2010, to help Venezuela's nuclear program. This record is at great odds with our own national security."[75]

Other members of Congress were concerned that uranium from US mines could make its way to Iran. The Russian government helped build Iran's Bushehr nuclear plant and it would need uranium to keep operating.[76]

US uranium assets have been a target of Russian statecraft for decades. In 1992, Russia used its considerable uranium assets to economically damage the US uranium mining industry. The Commerce Department found Russia, Kazakhstan, Kyrgyzstan, Tajikistan, Uzbekistan, and the Ukraine had been dumping uranium on the worldwide market at less than half the price of its actual value.[77] The dumping at prices below what it cost to actually mine uranium caused severe financial hardships, resulting in the closure of several US mining operations.

The 2010 sale of one-fifth of US uranium mines to Russia had its origin several years earlier. In 2004, a pair of Canadians, Frank Giustra and Ian Telfer, partnered to create Canadian uranium mining company UrAsia Energy Limited. Giustra was the founder and chief executive of movie studio Lions Gate Entertainment before he made the switch to running an investment firm and then becoming a mining tycoon. Telfer had partnered with Giustra on several other investment deals.

UrAsia was a very rare uranium mining company in that it did not own any uranium mines, nor did it have any experience in uranium mining. However, what UrAsia founder Giustra did have was a former US president as a loyal and valuable benefactor. In September 2005, Bill Clinton flew to the Kazakhstan capital of Almaty with Giustra aboard the would-be mining executive's private MD-87 jet, an airline jetliner that typically hauls more than 135 passengers.[78]

Upon arrival, the pair had a banquet with Kazakhstan president Nursultan Nazarbayev. At the event, Clinton offered high praise and endorsed Nazarbayev's bid to head an international democracy organization. Days later, Giustra was given the right to purchase three government-owned uranium mines.[79]

It is well established that big business deals occur in Kazakhstan only with government approval. Moreover, a strategic asset, such as uranium, would not land in the hands of a start-up shell company over bigger, established mining companies with impeccable reputations of success unless Nazarbayev personally approved the deal.

Nazarbayev, who has held office since 1990 and is routinely reelected with nearly 100 percent of the vote, is an iron-fisted despot. Even his opponents claim they voted for him. He was a Socialist Party official before the break-up of the Soviet Union. He has reportedly stashed away billions of dollars he plundered from his nation. His regime is guilty of rampant human rights abuses. Regime critics are often jailed.

That a former US president would publicly praise Nazarbayev was shocking. Clinton's glowing remarks contradicted the official US narrative of the Kazakhstan despot. The United States has maintained cool-at-best relations with Kazakhstan since it became apparent the country was democratic in name only.

Reportedly, before Clinton and Giustra flew to Almaty to close the deal with the Kazakh dictator, there was some backroom dealing going on. Senator Hillary Clinton had lobbied Kazakh Prime Minister Karim Massimov to approve UrAsia's mine purchase or risk the consequences.[80]

After Clinton and Giustra returned to the United States, Giustra made one of the biggest donations ever to the Clinton Foundation of more than $31 million.[81] Several months later, Giustra pledged an additional $100 million to a Clinton Foundation offshoot named the Clinton-Giustra Partnership. In December 2008, as a condition of becoming US Secretary of State, Hillary Clinton signed an agreement to report all donations given to the Clinton Foundation. Giustra's more than $130 million in donations to the foundation were kept secret.

In February 2007, South African mining company SXR Uranium One and UrAsia Energy Limited struck a deal to merge and become $5 billion company.[82] The merged company would become the world's second-largest publicly traded uranium mining company. Two months later, the deal was completed, with UrAsia owning 60 percent of the new company. In less than three years, Giustra and Telfer's UrAsia went from a shell company to a global uranium-mining conglomerate.

Telfer was named chairman of the new company. Giustra stepped down from the new company's board due to a conflict of interest. In addition to his leadership position in UrAsia, Giustra also headed Endeavour Financial, which scored a $12 million payday as financial advisor for the merger.[83] Telfer served as Uranium One chairman of the board until 2015.[84] Both Giustra and Telfer owned millions of shares of stock and millions of dollars more in stock options in the new Uranium One.[85]

Uranium One experienced a bumpy road in the early going. In 2009, only two years after the merger, Uranium One found itself in a precarious situation with the Kazakhstan government. There was concern the mining company might be taken over by the former Soviet republic as fallout from a corruption investigation of Giustra business associate, Moukhtar Dzhakishev. Clinton, Giustra, and Dzhakishev had been wheeling and dealing together for at least a couple of years.

Dzhakishev was a Kazakhstan official who was there when Clinton and Giustra flew into Almaty in 2005. It was Dzhakishev who coordinated the UrAsia purchase of the three Kazakh mines. In early 2007, Dzhakishev flew to the United States and met with Giustra and Clinton at the former president's Chappaqua, New York, home to discuss business issues in which the Kazakhstan government needed US government support.

By 2009, Dzhakishev had fallen out of favor with the Kazakhstan government amid corruption allegations. Concerned over the possibility of a Kazakh government takeover, Uranium One officials met with US Embassy staff in the Kazakhstan capital city and requested US officials intercede on behalf of the Canadian company. Amazingly, they did just that.[86] At this time, Hillary Clinton was the US Secretary of State. The State Department acted on behalf of a Canadian company in the midst of a conflict with the Kazakh government. About the same time, Uranium One chairman Ian Telfer made a $1 million contribution to the Clinton Foundation.

In June 2010, Rosatom proposed purchasing a majority share in Uranium One, thereby triggering a review by the Committee for Foreign Investment in the United States. The very same month, Bill Clinton was offered a $500,000 speaking fee by Renaissance Capital, an investment bank with Kremlin ties that was selling Uranium One stock.[87]

Clinton's previous Moscow speech was five years earlier for less than $200,000. In 2005, when Bill Clinton last gave a speech in Moscow, Hillary Clinton was only one of a hundred US Senators. In 2010, she was the sole US Secretary of State. The Uranium One-Rosatom deal received the Committee for Foreign Investment approval and the purchase was completed in December 2010.

Telfer's first contribution to the Clinton Foundation was $1 million. By 2013, when the rest of Uranium One was sold to the Russians, Telfer and entities directly tied to him had given the Clinton Foundation about $2.35 million.[88]

All totaled, Giustra, Telfer, and several other individuals who profited from the various UrAsia, Uranium One, and Rosatom deals gave about $145 million to the Clinton Foundation.[89] None of these donations were disclosed by the Clinton Foundation as Hillary had promised in the 2008 memorandum of understanding she had signed.

After the initial Uranium One sale to Rosatom was approved, Congress became deeply concerned that the Russian government now controlled one-fifth of all US uranium assets. The Nuclear Regulatory Commission (NRC) assuaged their concerns by repeatedly claiming neither Rosatom nor its subsidiary, ARMZ, would be given a license to export uranium from the US mines to a foreign country. The NRC promise allayed concerns that the Russians would drain the United States of valuable uranium assets.

However, there was some regulatory sleight-of-hand taking place. The Nuclear Regulatory Commission secretly modified an existing license by a third party to transport abroad US uranium on behalf of Rosatom.[90]

While the Rosatom takeover of Uranium One was playing out, the Federal Bureau of Investigation was quietly investigating Vadim Mikerin. He was the chief representative of Rosatom in the United States. In 2009, the FBI learned Mikerin was engaged in extensive racketeering including bribery, extortion, and kickbacks. Either the FBI did not inform the Committee for Foreign Investment of this information, or it did, and the committee dismissed it as irrelevant when considering Rosatom's purchase of Uranium One. The Justice Department did not negotiate a plea deal with Mikerin until August 2015, long after the Rosatom-Uranium One deal was finalized.[91]

CHAPTER 10

BRIBES

"There were many parts, aspects, facets, to the complicated puzzle of the Abramoff scandal. It took on the drama of Congressional players, Indian tribes, junkets, foreign sweat shops, overseas intrigue, and many more rumors and fact that leapt onto the front pages of the newspapers and dominated the nightly news."

—Former Republican Congressman Robert W. Ney of Ohio[1]

Teapot Dome

The availability of oil had national security implications in the early twentieth century. The United States Navy fleet was converting from coal-fired to oil-fired propulsion plants on its ships. Navy leaders wanted to ensure there was a reliable supply of oil, especially for their warships in the event that there was a national emergency.

In 1915, the federal government set aside three areas of federal land believed to be rich in oil. Elk Hills and Buena Vista Hills, several miles to the west of Bakersfield, California, were designated Naval Oil Reserve numbers one and two, respectively. Number three was located in Teapot Rock on the outskirts of Casper, Wyoming. A nearby rock formation bore a resemblance to a teapot with a dome lid, giving rise to the area's nickname of Teapot Dome.

By the end of the First World War, the nation's thirst for oil was dramatically increasing. The proliferation of affordable Ford and General Motors cars was driving the demand for gasoline. So much oil was being consumed, there were warnings the US oil supply was nearly exhausted and the nation would soon run out.[2]

In the 1920 presidential election, first-term Republican Senator Warren Harding of Ohio was the long-shot candidate who was elected in a landslide. He was the first senator to have won the White House. After he was sworn in, Harding immediately went from his inauguration straight to the US Senate floor to personally read aloud the names of his cabinet nominees. The Senate voted unanimously to confirm all of them in about ten minutes' time. Fellow Republican Albert Fall, senator from New Mexico, was his choice to be Secretary of the Interior.[3]

One month after he became interior secretary, Fall met with Secretary of the Navy Edwin Denby. Fall thought that all mineral rights, to include oil, should fall under the jurisdiction of the Interior Department. The pair agreed all three Naval oil reserves should be transferred from the jurisdiction of the Navy Department to Interior. They approached Harding with their plan, which he approved on May 31 via an executive order.[4] On July 12th, without any public notice, Fall signed a lease with the Pan American Petroleum and Transport Company, owned by Edward Doheny, to drill offset wells near the two California oil fields.[5]

In late 1921, Doheny sent his son, Ned, with a friend to Fall's Washington, DC, apartment with a black bag filled with $100,000 in cash. The money, both Doheny and Fall would later argue, was merely an interest-free loan and not a bribe for the oil field leases.[6]

The money was a welcomed relief to Fall. He was nearly broke, and one year earlier he had contemplated resigning from the Senate in order to enter a more lucrative career. He even sold his share in the *Albuquerque Morning Journal* newspaper to an Oklahoma Democratic senator he despised as too liberal. Fall was forced to execute the newspaper sale because he did not have enough money to pay the taxes on his ranch.[7]

In December 1921, Fall entertained Mammoth Oil Company President Harry Sinclair, among others, at his Three Rivers, New Mexico, ranch. Mammoth was a subsidiary of the oil giant Sinclair Consolidated Oil Corporation. Fall and Sinclair did some horse-trading that night. Literally. Sinclair sent to Fall's ranch six heifers, a bull, two boars, four sows, and a thoroughbred racehorse. In return, Fall agreed to lease the Teapot Dome oil fields to Mammoth.[8]

On April 7, 1922, Fall, Denby, and Sinclair executed a secret lease for Teapot Dome, which Fall promptly filed away in his locked desk.[9] The next month, Sinclair gave Fall $269,000 in cash and bonds.

In a matter of days, competing oil companies began asking questions of their senators and congressmen. Why were lease agreements secretly negotiated and signed without a competitive bidding process, many of them asked, even though competitive bids were not required under the Mineral Leasing Act of 1920? This led to a Senate resolution demanding answers from the Navy and Interior Departments.[10]

In less than a year, Fall secretly leased three of the federal government's most lucrative oil fields to a pair of giants in the oil industry. Fall was handsomely rewarded in return. However, he did not do a very good job of keeping his windfall secret. Fall began buying additional property and making improvements at a conspicuous rate that became noticeable to others who questioned how he came into his newfound riches.[11]

In response to the Senate's demands, the Navy and Interior Departments sent copies of both leases. Harding offered strong support for his cabinet secretaries by telling the Senate the oil field activities "had my entire approval."[12] Fall told the Senate that every action he took was proper and was in keeping with Harding's executive order. He also argued that his action to lease drilling rights was beneficial to the Navy since nearby private wells were siphoning oil from the Navy fields.[13] It was better to drill for oil before it all dissipated, he argued. In spite of the secretive nature of the leases, those in the Senate asking questions of the transactions could not find anything illegal.

Questions about the leases did not subside, however. Even the public was taking an interest in the scandal. Under pressure, Fall decided to resign as interior secretary in January 1923. Although there were plenty of suspicions, it was never proved that Harding received bribes from Sinclair. Then on August 2, 1923, Harding unexpectedly died. Vice President Calvin Coolidge assumed the presidency. Coolidge announced he was committed to rooting out all corruption.

The Senate Committee on Public Lands and Surveys began its formal investigation after Harding's death. The committee called before it countless witnesses between October 23, 1923 and May 14, 1924. The investigation had gone so poorly, yielding no incriminating information, that several members suggested shutting it down.[14]

It was Doheny's testimony on January 24, 1924, that opened up an entirely new line of inquiry. Doheny testified that he lent Fall $100,000. Upon questioning, Sinclair admitted he gave Fall some cattle. These revelations caused the Senate to call for a special counsel to be appointed.

There had been a tremendous amount of partisan bickering taking place in Washington, DC, at this time. The Teapot Dome scandal only worsened it. Harding, Coolidge, and Fall were Republicans. Their loudest critics were Democrats.

The Democrats were already planning to campaign on the theme of Republican corruption in the 1924 elections. However, Coolidge undercut their strategy by demonstrating professionalism and integrity.[15] Coolidge responded to the calls for a special counsel in King Solomon fashion. In an action that silenced claims of partisan favoritism, Coolidge appointed two special counsels, one Republican and one Democrat.

The Republican corruption election strategy backfired on the Democrats. Denby and Attorney General Daugherty would soon resign their cabinet posts. Fall had resigned months earlier. The three cabinet members closely identified with the growing scandal would soon be gone. However, it was Doheny who most blunted the Democratic election strategy.

Although Doheny was embroiled in the scandal with the Republican Fall, he was first and foremost a Democrat. Doheny was a generous donor to Democratic candidates and causes. He had four cabinet members from the Woodrow Wilson administration on his payroll. Most damning was he also had on his payroll William Gibbs McAdoo. Until this discovery, McAdoo was the leading contender for the 1924 Democratic presidential nomination.[16]

Coolidge's special counsel appointments paired Owen Roberts with Atlee Pomerene. A Republican, Roberts was an accomplished and well-respected Philadelphia attorney. Pomerene was a retired Democratic senator from Ohio. Despite some misgivings about their qualifications and experience, both men were overwhelmingly confirmed by the Senate on February 18, 1924. Navy Secretary Edwin Denby immediately resigned after the Senate confirmations.

Coolidge had his doubts about Attorney General Harry Daugherty and Daugherty's willingness to provide the necessary resources to Roberts and Pomerene in order to conduct a thorough investigation. Instead, Coolidge assigned Secret Service agents to serve as special counsel investigators. Facing an obvious lack of confidence by Coolidge and mounting criticism from not having acted sooner on behalf of the Justice Department, Daugherty resigned as Attorney General on March 28.

Roberts and Pomerene immediately went to work. They were thorough and exhaustive. They sent investigators all over the country and interviewed potential witnesses by the dozens. They scoured financial records. By March, the special counsels pursued criminal indictments against Fall, Doheny, and Sinclair. Roberts and Pomerene also sought civil lawsuits to have the oil leases canceled.

The special counsels pursued civil litigation against Doheny's Pan American Petroleum. A civil trial began on October 21, 1924. Federal prosecutors argued that the leases for Naval oil reserve numbers one and two in Elk Hills and Buena Vista Hills were obtained fraudulently and should be declared null and void. On May 28, 1925, a federal judge agreed.

A similar suit was filed against Mammoth Oil, but proved to be more problematic. The trial opened in March 1925. Some witnesses refused to testify, others had faulty memories, and still others fled the country. In June, a federal judge ruled against the US government and dismissed the case. The special counsels appealed the ruling and the US Court of Appeals for the Eighth Circuit reversed the decision. The Teapot Dome contract was canceled.

Then the criminal prosecutions began. However, the criminal trials did not go as well for the US government.

Fall and Doheny faced charges of conspiracy to defraud the United States over the Elk Hills and Buena Vista Hills oil leases. Their trial began in November 1926. A jury found both men not guilty.

The October 1927 trial against Fall and Sinclair on charges of defrauding the government was declared a mistrial when it was learned that Sinclair hired a team of private detectives to follow the jury. Sinclair faced trial on a separate charge of criminal jury tampering for hiring the detectives. He was found guilty and sentenced to six months in prison.

A new trial began on April 2, 1928, on the fraud charges, but Sinclair was the only defendant this time. Fall was in ill health, and the special counsels declined to pursue criminal charges against him in this matter. The jury found Sinclair not guilty.

While he was spared from the fraud trial, Fall still faced bribery charges. In spite of his deteriorating health, his bribery trial began on

October 7, 1928. Fall was convicted and sentenced to one year in prison and was fined $100,000. He was the first cabinet member to have been convicted of a felony.

Fall's appeal of the conviction fell short at the appellate court. In July 1930, both Republican and Democratic leaders from New Mexico petitioned President Herbert Hoover to pardon Fall. Hoover, who succeeded Coolidge as President, was the secretary of commerce under both Harding and Coolidge. The president denied the executive clemency request.[17]

Fall finally headed off to serve his prison sentence. To make matters worse, Fall's 700,000-acre ranch was sold in a sheriff's sale because he was unable to repay the $100,000 loan to Doheny.[18] The sad irony for Fall was that he was convicted for bribery, in part because the $100,000 was treated as a bribe, and he lost his home due to his failure to repay the $100,000, which was considered a loan. Fall left prison bankrupt. He died in 1944.

Doheny faced a separate trial for offering the bribe to Fall. The prosecutors presented the same evidence that got Fall convicted. It was not enough. The jury acquitted Doheny. However, tragedy befell Doheny. His son, Ned, who delivered the $100,000 to Fall, was killed by his friend, Hugh Plunkett, in a murder-suicide. Apparently, Plunkett was fearful the pair would be charged as accomplices for delivering the cash to Fall.

Sinclair's bribery trial ended the same way as that of Doheny. Sinclair was acquitted of the charge.

Coolidge considered Roberts's work as special counsel to be exemplary. In fact, Roberts received widespread praise by many observers for his performance. For his reward, Coolidge appointed Roberts to the US Supreme Court.

There were a pair of significant legal decisions that arose from the Teapot Dome scandal. In a related matter, the brother of Attorney General Harry Daugherty refused to appear before a Senate committee. In a 1927 decision, the Supreme Court ruled that Congress had the authority to subpoena private citizens to appear before it to carry out an investigation as part of its duty to craft legislation.[19] In a similar case, the high court held in 1929 that Congress had the investigatory power to question private citizens.[20]

Abscam

In March 1978, the Long Island, New York, office of the FBI devised an undercover plan that would eventually ensnare hoodlums and government officials engaged in corrupt practices.[21] Abscam was the FBI's first-ever major public-corruption investigation of elected officials. It was the brainchild of FBI supervisor John Good. At the heart of the operation was Mel Weinberg, a career hustler and con artist who had worked as an informant for the FBI in the past. Weinberg agreed to work for the FBI as part of a plea deal in a fraud conviction.

The plan was to portray Weinberg as the American agent of Kambir Abdul Rahman and Yassir Habib, a fictional pair of wealthy emirs of the United Arab Emirates. The emirs were anxious to surreptitiously transfer money from their own country to investments in the United States. The undercover operation's name, Abscam, was a contraction of "Abdul" and "scam." Abdul Enterprises, Ltd., was the name of Rahman's fictitious business operation.[22]

The original focus of the sting was stolen artwork and forged securities. After the operation was up and running, it nabbed several smalltime criminals. The political element began in late 1978, when Angelo Errichetti, the mayor of Camden, New Jersey, got involved. He was not only a city mayor but was simultaneously a New Jersey state senator. Errichetti was the most powerful Democrat in southern New Jersey.[23]

The list of criminal enterprises Errichetti delivered on was lengthy, ranging from stolen property, to illegal guns, to government contracts, to the names of other government officials open to being bribed. In a year, Errichetti was at the heart of one illegal deal after another.[24]

Errichetti made good on his promise to deliver other government officials who were willing to accept a bribe. All the public officials indicted were captured on videotape or audiotape willingly accepting cash bribes of $50,000. By the time Abscam ended its operation, one US Senator and a half-dozen members of Congress were indicted for bribery and related charges.[25]

Not every member of Congress who held a meeting with the undercover operation took the bribe money. Senator Larry Pressler of South Dakota, who was running an underfunded Republican presidential primary campaign, was asked if he would introduce legislation on behalf of the sheikhs in return for $50,000. Pressler replied, "[I]t would not be proper for me to promise to do anything in return for a campaign contribution."[26]

Democratic Senator Harrison Williams Jr. of New Jersey was indicted along with Democratic Congressmen John Jenrette of South Carolina, Raymond Lederer of Pennsylvania, Michael Myers of Pennsylvania, John Murphy of New York, and Frank Thompson Jr. of New Jersey. The lone Republican was Congressman Richard Kelly of Florida. Joining them were a New Jersey state senator, a pair of Philadelphia councilmen, and two well-connected Philadelphia lawyers.

A little-reported fact from the Abscam operation was the sheer number of government officials implicated in activities that ranged from highly questionable to possibly illegal who were never charged. A racketeer caught on tape bragged that US Attorney General Griffin Bell, at the request of President Carter, killed a tax evasion charge against Carter supporter and Newark Mayor Kenneth Gibson.[27] Robert Del Tufo, head of the US Attorney's Office in Newark, was appointed by Bell to be the Justice Department official who would kill the tax charge.

The Newark US Attorney's Office was seemingly never on the same page as the rest of the Justice Department regarding Abscam. After the sting operation came to an end, the Justice Department divvied up the more than thirty targets among four US Attorney's offices. Months later, three of the offices had gotten indictments, while the Newark office hadn't even empanelled a grand jury. The Justice Department reassigned those targets to another office. [28] Del Tufo resigned shortly after the Abscam indictments were handed down.

Georgia politicians, and staunch Carter supporters, Senator Herman Talmadge and Congressman Wyche Fowler Jr. were in the midst of an apparent bribery sting when both "lost interest in the deal rather abruptly," almost as if they were informed it was an FBI undercover operation.[29] It shouldn't be overlooked that after Bell stepped down as attorney general in late 1979, he went on to manage the reelection campaign of Talmadge.[30] Then again, maybe Talmadge and Fowler were just lucky.

Other politicians whose names were embarrassingly mentioned in recorded conversations by unscrupulous characters were Democratic House Speaker Tip O'Neill of Massachusetts, Majority Leader

James Wright Jr. of Texas, Majority Whip John Brademas of Indiana, House Judiciary Committee Chairman Peter Rodino of New Jersey, and Congressman John Murtha of Pennsylvania. Republicans mentioned included Senators Strom Thurmond of South Carolina and Jacob Javits of New York, and Representative Norman Lent of New York.[31]

Senator Williams's involvement focused on a titanium mine. In return for a secret 18 percent share in the mine, Williams promised to use his office to deliver multimillion-dollar government contracts. At one point during the sting, he bragged that he could personally approach President Jimmy Carter to land the contracts.[32]

The Congressmen were caught up in a proposal to introduce bills to obtain citizenship or some other legal status for the two emirs who thought they might need to flee their country. In return for their proposed legislation, each Congressman was promised $50,000 in cash. Nearly every Congressman who attended the Abscam meeting agreed to be bribed. Each time, they were videotaped.

A particularly embarrassing comment caught on tape was made by Congressman John Jenrette of South Carolina. When asked if he was willing to accept the bribe, he responded, "I got larceny in my blood; I'd take it in a goddamned minute."[33] It turned out that Jenrette's remark might not have been his most embarrassing moment in Washington, DC, (see chapter 7).

Early in the morning of Saturday, February 2, 1980, scores of FBI agents fanned out up and down the East Coast and knocked on the doors of Abscam targets.[34] Arrests were made. Eventually, a dozen people were convicted.

"Gimme Five"

If the typical American described a Washington, DC, lobbyist as a smarmy, self-dealing, bribe-paying scoundrel, then Jack Abramoff might have fit that description.

Like many who leave a job in Congress or have great political connections on Capitol Hill, Jack Abramoff got into the lobbying business. He parlayed his strong ties to Capitol Hill Republicans, who captured a majority in the House of Representatives for the first time in forty years, into his first job as a lobbyist.

In late 1994, Abramoff signed on with the lobbying shop of Seattle-based law firm, Preston Gates Ellis and Rouvelas Meeds, LLP. Many lobbyists have an area of expertise. For Abramoff, it became representing Native American tribes.

Among Abramoff's first clients was the Mississippi Band of Choctaw Indians. Abramoff focused on tribal casinos and gambling issues. He scored early lobbying successes in both Washington, DC and some state capitals, which attracted the interest of other Indian tribes.

In just a few years, Abramoff signed on to lobby for six Indian tribes. These were the Mississippi Band of Choctaw Indians; the Coushatta Tribe of Louisiana; the Saginaw Chippewa Indian Tribe; the Agua Caliente Band of Cahuilla Indians; the Ysleta del Sur Pueblo of Texas (or the Tigua Tribe); and the Pueblo of Sandia, New Mexico.

Abramoff left Preston Gates in December 2000, and the following month joined the lobbying arm of Miami-headquartered law firm, Greenberg Traurig, LLP, where he hired former DC staffers. Some ex-staffers worked for powerful politicians such as Republican House Majority Leader Tom DeLay of Texas and Democratic Senator Harry Reid of Nevada. Abramoff was a great catch for Greenberg Traurig. His $6 million in annual revenue vaulted Greenberg Traurig into the top ten of DC lobbying firms.[35]

Like any good lobbyist, Abramoff also had a network of contacts at various federal agencies, executive departments, and in House and Senate offices that would be receptive audiences to his lobbying issues. He was quickly gaining a reputation as a successful, high-powered lobbyist.

Just as important as his government employee ties, Abramoff had a close relationship with *Roll Call* reporter John Bresnahan, which gave Abramoff the vehicle to spin a favorable narrative of Capitol Hill politics. Bresnahan was so tight with Abramoff and his staff that he was involved in "gambling, friendships, weddings, newspaper acquisitions, or [in] John's attacking Jack's foes."[36] Bresnahan would later move on to *Politico*. Clearly, Jack Abramoff was poised to enjoy tremendous success.

It was in 2001 that Abramoff began building his stable of clients consisting of Native American tribes. He also formed a partnership of sorts with Michael Scanlon. It was a partnership the pair kept secret from anyone else. Scanlon had previously worked as a communications staffer for DeLay before Scanlon launched a public affairs consulting firm named Campaign Capitol Strategies.

The initial plan was for Abramoff to help Scanlon build Campaign Capitol Strategies into a $3 million a year consulting practice and then sell it for a three-times-multiple of revenue, with Abramoff and Scanlon splitting the proceeds. This is not illegal and is not unlike countless business proposals across America. However, this plan differed from so many others as to how it was executed.

In their business scheme, Abramoff would recommend his Indian tribe clients hire Campaign Capitol Strategies for public affairs and grassroots lobbying services. Scanlon would overcharge the tribes for CCS services and would give Abramoff half of the profits.

In one example, the Saginaw Chippewa Tribe of Michigan paid CCS $1.9 million for grassroots activities. The actual cost of the activities was about $300,000, leaving Abramoff and Scanlon to split the remaining $1.6 million as pure profit.

In another example, Scanlon charged the Coushatta Tribe of Louisiana nearly $1.4 million for a database that actually cost Scanlon about $100,000 to establish through a third-party vendor.[37] Scanlon wasn't just placing a markup on CCS services; he was grossly overcharging clients. Oftentimes, the overbilling was to the tune of millions of dollars.

This secret Abramoff-Scanlon partnership arrangement was never disclosed to Abramoff's clients. From 2001 to 2003, Scanlon received about $66 million in fees from Abramoff's clients, of which he gave Abramoff about $21 million, representing half of Scanlon's actual profits.[38] Abramoff and Scanlon referred to this secret arrangement as, "Gimme five."[39]

Some of the millions of dollars Abramoff and Scanlon received from the tribes were spent on activities or purchases that offered little or even no benefit to the tribes. Abramoff used some of the tribes' money to support a private foundation called the Capital Athletic Fund that was purportedly founded to help finance Eshkol Academy, an Orthodox Jewish boys day-school located in a Washington, DC, suburb. He also used tribal funds to finance his restaurants, Signatures, Archives, and Stacks Delicatessen. Scanlon invested his money in real estate.[40]

The pair engaged in double-dealing when it came to the Tigua tribe in El Paso, Texas. Abramoff and Scanlon secretly supported the successful efforts by Texas officials to shut down the Tigua Tribe's Speaking Rock Casino in El Paso. They didn't even do it with their own money. Abramoff convinced the Louisiana Coushatta to fund efforts to shut down the Tigua casino using the argument that the El Paso casino posed a threat to the Coushatta casino, even though nearly a thousand miles separated the two gambling locations.

The closure of the Tigua tribe's casino set up an opportunity for Abramoff to pitch his lobbying services to the Tigua. Abramoff suggested he had a plan and the clout to get the casino reopened. He offered to work for the tribe pro bono, on the condition that the tribe hire Scanlon for his firm's grassroots services. Abramoff did not inform the tribe that he would receive half of Scanlon's profits.

Throughout this period of aggressive lobbying, Abramoff also encouraged his clients to make political contributions to key Democratic and Republican members of Congress. About two-thirds of the contributions went to Republicans, who were in the majority for the first time in forty years after the 1996 elections and held key committee chairmanships.

The end for Abramoff started in January 2003. A couple of the tribes held deep concerns over the millions of dollars they were spending on Abramoff and Scanlon. Questions of expenditure amounts led to quarrelling between the tribes and their lobbyist. So, they approached Tom Rodgers, a member of the Blackfeet Nation and also a lobbyist, to ask for help. Rodgers quietly collected invoices and documents and released them to a couple of sympathetic members of the press. A critical article of Abramoff and his lobbying affairs appeared in the *Washington Post* on February 22, 2004.[41] Rodgers also sent a packet of material to the Justice Department.[42]

Greenberg Traurig fired Abramoff on March 2. Abramoff recognized what he did wrong. "I had broken laws. I had violated the gift ban and caused scores of representatives and staff to do the same," he later wrote. "I hadn't revealed to my clients that I shared in the profits with Scanlon. I used non-profit organizations to conceal our political activities on behalf of the clients. I failed to register representations when trying to deceive our opponents."[43]

After federal investigators compiled enough evidence against him, Abramoff reached a plea deal. On January 3, 2006, he pleaded guilty to conspiracy to bribe public officials, mail fraud, and tax evasion. The mail fraud charges were related to a casino-boat operation he owned. Abramoff was sentenced to nearly six years in federal prison.

After the scandal broke, some members of Congress filed amended reports with the Federal Election Commission regarding political contributions given by or at the direction of Abramoff. Others thought it necessary to reimburse the tribes for some of their contributions.

There were plenty of politicians who wanted to undo their ties to Abramoff. Democratic Senator Tom Harkin of Iowa did not properly report a pair of fundraisers held in Abramoff's skybox at the MCI Center in downtown Washington, DC. Republican Representative J. D. Hayworth of Arizona reimbursed the tribes for some expenses from several fundraising events. Senator Byron Dorgan of North Dakota was the senior Democrat on the committee investigating Abramoff, which prompted him to return $67,000 contributed by Indian tribes represented by Abramoff.[44]

About a dozen Washington, DC, staffers were convicted of crimes related to the Abramoff scandal. Republican Congressman Robert Ney of Ohio was the most prominent of those on Capitol Hill caught up in federal crimes.

After Abramoff was indicted, he reached a plea agreement in which he fingered Ney as having received bribes from Abramoff. Ney was the beneficiary of expensive tickets to sporting events, political contributions, and trips to Lake George, New Orleans, and Scotland in return for supporting specific legislation, according to Abramoff associates.[45] In one instance, Scanlon contributed to a GOP party fundraiser immediately after Ney agreed to place a favorable statement in the *Congressional Record*.[46]

Ney admitted his failings in his autobiography. "In dealing with Jack Abramoff, I crossed the line. It was not direct bribery and we could not be charged with that, but it surely was not good, nor was it legal. I ate and drank free at his expense, traveled with him to Scotland, and threw the ethics laws to the wind."[47]

On October 13, 2006, Friday the 13th, Ney pleaded guilty to conspiracy to defraud the United States and to filing false financial disclosures. He was sentenced to thirty months in prison.

Prisoner #94405-198

Earning an annual congressional paycheck of just over $160,000 is more than most Americans ever dream about. On top of that, pulling down a yearly Navy commander retirement of about $40,000 translates into a very comfortable salary. But there is no way even a $200,000 annual income could finance the purchase of a $2.5 million southern California home, a Washington, DC, condominium, a yacht, a Rolls-Royce, and many other expensive toys. However, Republican Congressman Randall "Duke" Cunningham of California did just that.

Duke Cunningham was a hero in Navy circles in the early 1970s. He was a Navy fighter pilot who flew combat missions over North Vietnam. Piloting the F-4 Phantom II, Cunningham and his radar intercept officer shot down five North Vietnamese tactical aircraft.[48] The radar intercept officer (RIO) sits behind the pilot in the cockpit of the F-4 and operates the radar and other electronic systems.

His Vietnam tour experience made Cunningham a Navy legend. On May 10, 1972, Cunningham shot down three Soviet-made MiG tactical aircraft, for a total of five shoot-downs, giving him "ace" status. While en route to the carrier USS *Constellation*, a surface-to-air missile struck Cunningham's Phantom, causing both him and his RIO to eject. A Marine Corps helicopter rescued both men.[49]

Cunningham followed his Vietnam deployment with an assignment at the Navy Fighter Weapons School at Naval Air Station Miramar, a short distance from San Diego. Known as "Top Gun," the school teaches junior officers the skills to improve their airmanship as pilots and RIOs. Some may be familiar with the fictionalized account of the school portrayed in the film *Top Gun*.

Cunningham retired from the Navy in 1987 and settled in the San Diego area. In 1990, he challenged an incumbent congressman and narrowly won. He would go on to be reelected to Congress for another seven terms.

As with most people with prior military service, Cunningham was considered a natural fit for military and intelligence committee assignments. Occasionally, he was brash and overbearing in dealing with other members of Congress, but he probably received a pass for his attitude because he was considered a war hero.

There was a curious development involving Cunningham in 2003. The Californian congressman sold his home in the San Diego suburb of Del Mar to a buyer for $1.675 million. Interestingly, the home was sold without having been included on the realty multiple listing service and without a realtor executing the sale.[50] A month later, the new owner placed the home back on the market at the steeply discounted price of $975,000. This new owner happened to be the founder of defense contractor, MZM Inc., and he was no stranger to Cunningham.

The home sat on the market for nearly a year before it was sold at the dramatically lower price. After Cunningham sold his Del Mar home, he purchased another home for $2.55 million in Rancho Santa Fe, a tony community in northern San Diego County.

Mitchell Wade founded the defense firm, MZM, in 1993. According to local news reports, the firm struggled to land government business for the first decade it was in business. However, around the timeframe of the Cunningham home purchase, MZM began receiving multimillion-dollar defense contracts. The year Cunningham sold his house, MZM landed $41 million in defense contracts.[51] According to one news report, MZM received more than $160 million in government contracts in just a few years' time after the Cunningham home sale.[52]

When news broke in 2005 regarding the seemingly odd home purchase, immediate relisting, and eventual resale, a company representative explained MZM bought the single-family home in an effort at "expanding our company presence in San Diego."[53] The company placed the residence back on the market, the representative said, after company officials realized the home did not fit the company's business needs. To be sure, it seemed strange that a defense firm would purchase a home in a residential neighborhood about twenty miles north of downtown San Diego as an ideal location to conduct business or to increase the company profile.

A few weeks after the home-sale story broke, teams of federal agents from the Federal Bureau of Investigation, the Internal Revenue Service, and Defense Criminal Investigative Service raided Cunningham's new home, MZM's Washington, DC, offices, and other property belonging to Wade. One of the Wade properties searched was a forty-two-foot yacht in Washington, DC. Cunningham had been living on the yacht when

Congress was in session and was paying dock and maintenance fees in lieu of rent.[54]

The investigation revealed at least three other individuals were embroiled in Cunningham's scandal. These included a San Diego-area defense contractor, a New York developer, and a mortgage company president. Government documents allege Cunningham accepted more than $2 million in bribes consisting of cash and gifts, including a used Rolls-Royce automobile.[55]

By mid-July, Cunningham decided not to seek a ninth term in Congress. In a press conference, with his wife by his side, Cunningham addressed the investigation into his finances. "I want to assure my constituents that I have acted honorably in the performance of my duties in Congress. This truth will be evident in time," he said.[56]

Faced with overwhelming evidence, on November 28, 2005, Cunningham released a statement admitting he behaved illegally, and he intended to plead guilty to charges of conspiracy and tax evasion. "The truth is—I broke the law, concealed my conduct, and disgraced my high office. I know that I will forfeit my freedom, my reputation, my worldly possessions, and most importantly, the trust of my friends and family."

On March 3, 2006, Randall "Duke" Cunningham was sentenced to eight years and four months in federal prison. Cunningham became prisoner #94405-198 at the United States Penitentiary in Tucson, Arizona.

Cold Hard Cash

Investor Lori Mody told the FBI in March 2005 that Democratic Congressman William Jefferson of Louisiana was soliciting bribes from her in order to support her business deal in Nigeria. Louisville, Kentucky-based iGate was a technology company that wanted to provide broadband services for internet and television in the west African nation. Mody had invested $3.5 million in the tech firm. Jefferson's involvement with iGate began years earlier.

Vernon Jackson was the owner of iGate, which delivered high-speed internet and other broadband services over existing telephone lines. Jackson thought iGate's technology would be the perfect vehicle to bring the internet to developing nations with poor infrastructure.

Jefferson was a vocal advocate for American investment in Africa. Jackson thought Jefferson would wholeheartedly support his efforts to bring iGate technology to the continent. Jefferson agreed.

In 2000, Jefferson began using his contacts in Africa and his bully pulpit to promote adoption of iGate technology in Nigeria. Jefferson had a relationship with Nigerian Vice President Atiku Abubakar, who owned a home in the Washington, DC, suburb of Potomac, Maryland. However, the following year, Jefferson informed Jackson the congressman's services would no longer be free. They would come at a cost.

Jefferson told Jackson the financial terms of his support going forward included a monthly consulting fee, a cut of iGate's sales, and a million iGate shares. Jefferson directed the monthly consulting fee to be paid to a firm he set up that was managed by his wife and employed his five children. Over the course of five years, Jackson transferred nearly $500,000 to the ANJ Group.

Brett Pfeffer was on Jefferson's congressional staff in the late 1990s. In 2003, he was hired by Lori Mody, who was seeking advice on business investments. Pfeffer introduced Mody to Jefferson.

Jefferson sold Mody on a proposal to invest as much as $45 million in iGate. It was a sure hit, he told her. Jefferson would create a company, owned by Mody, that would partner with a Nigerian telecommunications firm to use iGate technology to deliver broadband services to Nigerians. Mody would only have to make a $3.5 million investment up front to get started.

After Mody's investment was made, Jefferson then informed her there were financial considerations she must meet in order to move forward to ensure Jefferson could win Nigerian government approval for Mody's venture. Jefferson offered to lobby the Export-Import Bank of the United States to provide low-interest loans to help finance the venture. Jefferson demanded part ownership of the newly formed company owned by Mody in return for his efforts. Jefferson was so bold as to make a bribe request of Mody in the House members' private dining room.[57]

Uncomfortable with Jefferson's demands and worried about her multimillion-dollar investment, Mody approached the FBI in spring 2005. Beginning in March, the FBI placed a hidden wire on Mody, as she conducted a series of meetings with Jefferson. Their telephone calls were wiretapped.[58]

Over the next couple of months, Jefferson insisted his family's stake in Mody's Nigerian telecommunications venture be increased to nearly one-third. Jefferson's family would also have to take partial ownership in Mody's other Nigerian-related business ventures.

In a taped conversation, Jefferson told Mody that he needed $100,000 in cash in order to bribe Nigerian officials regarding Mody's Nigerian investments. On July 30, 2005, Mody met with Jefferson at the Ritz-Carlton Hotel in Arlington, Virginia's, Pentagon City to hand over a briefcase filled with the bribe money. The FBI provided the cash and had recorded the serial numbers for all the bills. The FBI recorded the money exchange on videotape.[59]

Two days after Mody gave the money to Jefferson, she called him. Jefferson told Mody he had already passed the money to his Nigerian contact, who "was very pleased."

Four days later, the FBI raided Jefferson's New Orleans home and found $90,000 of the bribe money stashed in containers in his refrigerator's freezer. The recovered bills' serial numbers matched those that the FBI had recorded.

In January 2006, Pfeffer pled guilty to bribery and confirmed to federal investigators that Jefferson was demanding bribes and kickbacks from iGate to conduct business in Nigeria.[60] Pfeffer was sentenced to eight years in prison "on charges of conspiracy to commit bribery and aiding and abetting the solicitation of bribes by a member of Congress," according to the Justice Department.

On May 3, Vernon Jackson pled guilty to paying bribes to Jefferson. In September 2006, he was sentenced to eighty-seven months in prison after pleading guilty to charges of "conspiracy to commit bribery and the payment of bribes to a public official."

On May 20, 2006, armed with an eighty-three-page affidavit, more than a dozen FBI agents raided Jefferson's congressional office.[61] The agents were in the Rayburn House Office Building for about eighteen hours. This was the first known incidence of the FBI raiding the official office of an active member of Congress. House Speaker Dennis Hastert, a Republican, gave a spirited defense of the separation of the executive and legislative branches. He personally addressed his concerns with President George W. Bush. Hastert demanded the immediate return of papers removed from the Democratic Congressman's office.

Citing a possible violation of "the constitutional principle of separation of the powers and the speech or debate clause," Bush ordered the Justice Department to seal all records seized from Jefferson's congressional office for a period of forty-five days. This would give congressional leaders and the Justice Department time to work out an agreement, Bush said.

The dispute landed in court, where US District Court Judge Thomas Hogan ruled the FBI search was legal. Hogan was not persuaded by the arguments put forth by Hastert and Democratic Minority Leader Nancy Pelosi of California that the independence of the legislative branch was violated by the search. "The Speech or Debate Clause does not make Members of Congress super-citizens, immune from criminal responsibility," Hogan wrote in his opinion.

Voters of Louisiana's 2nd congressional district didn't seem too concerned that Jefferson was a subject of a very public corruption investigation. The voters reelected him in the 2006 election.

The *New York Times* refused to be persuaded by the overwhelming facts of the case, including a pair of guilty pleas and a conviction. The paper labeled the criminal investigation of Jefferson an "obvious partisan political target."[62]

In June 2007, Jefferson was hit with sixteen criminal charges including bribery, conspiracy, and money laundering, among other charges that were detailed in a nearly one-hundred-page indictment. After a 2009 trial, Jefferson was convicted on eleven corruption charges. The jury recommended Jefferson forfeit $470,000 as ill-gotten gains and surrender millions of shares of company stock he acquired as part of his bribery scheme.

Jefferson was sentenced to thirteen years in prison. His appeal of his conviction was unsuccessful. However, Jefferson was released from prison in late 2017 after sixty-five months in prison on the joint recommendation of prosecutors and defense attorneys.

In May 2018, former Congressman William Jefferson filed for Chapter 7 bankruptcy.

The Last Laugh

Alcee Hastings began practicing law in 1963. Fourteen years later he became a Broward County, Florida, circuit-court judge. On August 28, 1979, President Jimmy Carter nominated Hastings to the US District Court for the Southern District of Florida. On October 31, he was confirmed by the US Senate and received his commission on November 2.

Hastings had been on the federal bench for less than two years when the Federal Bureau of Investigation heard rumors that Hastings was involved in a bribery scheme. Hastings's longtime friend William Borders Jr. was a Washington, DC, lawyer and the former president of the National Bar Association, an association of about eight thousand black lawyers.[63] According to the scuttlebutt, Borders claimed Hastings would hand down favorable sentences in return for bribes. The FBI decided to test this lead to see if there was any truth to it.

Frank and Thomas Romano were brothers who had been convicted of racketeering in a 1980 trial before Judge Hastings. The FBI had a retired special agent pose as one of the Romano brothers. Borders had not met either brother. The undercover agent approached Borders to discuss how to get the brothers' three-year prison sentence reduced to probation and to have a majority of their seized financial assets returned.

The proposal to reduce the sentence to probation and to have $845,000 returned to the Romanos would cost a $150,000 bribe, according to Borders. Hastings, Borders claimed, would get most of that money. The undercover agent gave Borders $25,000 as a down payment.

On October 5, Borders told the undercover agent in a phone call that Hastings would return most of the forfeiture. The very next day, Hastings issued a court order that $845,000 be returned to the Romanos, and he reduced the sentence of the two convicts.[64]

Borders met with the undercover agent for the rest of the bribe. When the balance of $125,000 changed hands, Borders was immediately arrested. Hastings, who was in Washington, DC, when the pay off occurred in nearby Arlington, Virginia, immediately fled back to Florida. Borders was tried and convicted in early 1982 and was sentenced to five years in federal prison.

Federal prosecutors had a more difficult time proving their bribery case against Hastings. FBI agents immediately arrested Borders after he accepted the bribe, instead of following him until he paid Hastings his share. Borders's premature arrest would place a higher burden on federal prosecutors to prove their case. Borders complicated matters by refusing to testify against Hastings, forcing prosecutors to mount a case based solely on circumstantial evidence.

During his criminal trial, Hastings mounted a defense that included more than four-dozen witnesses who testified about the now-disgraced judge's integrity. Hastings also had an answer for the amazing coincidence of how Borders negotiated a bribe to have $845,000 returned to the Romanos, and Hastings immediately thereafter ordered the exact same amount returned. It was "rain-making," Hastings explained.

According to Hastings testimony, Borders, who was in Washington, DC, at the time, somehow knew that Hastings, operating out of a South Florida courtroom, was going to order a return of $845,000. Armed with that information, Borders lied to the undercover agent that Borders would orchestrate what was already going to occur. For this, Borders would make a quick $150,000 and he would keep all the money.

On February 4, 1983, after deliberating over three days, the jury reached the conclusion that Hastings's explanation made sense to them. They delivered a not-guilty verdict. Hastings was exonerated, but only briefly.

Judges in the Eleventh Circuit filed a formal complaint with the Judicial Council in March 1983. The Eleventh Circuit was home to Judge Hastings's court. One of the responsibilities of the Judicial Council is to investigate judicial misconduct. After a three-year investigation, the Council concluded that Hastings committed perjury, tampered with evidence, and conspired to gain financially by accepting bribes.[65] "Judge Hastings attempted to corruptly use his office for personal gain," the council concluded. "Such conduct cannot be excused or condoned even after Judge Hastings has been acquitted of the criminal charges."[66] The US Circuit Court of Appeals voted on September 2, 1986, to recommend Hastings be impeached. The Judicial Conference was the next level up. A twenty-seven-judge panel reached the same conclusion and found Hastings broke federal law.

On March 17, 1987, the Judicial Conference informed the US House of Representatives that Hastings should be impeached and removed from office. Beginning in May 1988, a special committee of the US House examined the case forwarded by the Judicial Conference. On August 3, 1988, the House voted in favor of seventeen articles of impeachment of Hastings by a vote of 413 to three. These impeachment articles included conspiracy, bribery, perjury, falsifying documents, thwarting a criminal investigation, and undermining public confidence "in the integrity and impartiality of the judiciary."[67] Hastings supporters protested he was a victim of racism.[68] In March 1989, the US Senate voted to proceed with the articles of impeachment.

On October 19, 1989, the US Senate convicted Hastings on eight of the seventeen articles of impeachment. He was ordered to be immediately removed from office. However, the Senate committed a major blunder. US Constitution Article I, Section 3 states that impeachment may include "disqualification to hold and enjoy any Office of honor, Trust or Profit under the United States." The Senate failed to vote on including this provision in Hastings's impeachment trial.

After Hastings was removed from the federal bench, he began private practice. One client he represented was the racist and anti-Semitic Yahweh ben Yahweh, the leader of a black supremacist cult called the Brotherhood. Yahweh went to prison, convicted of several charges, including conspiracy to commit murder, as he exhorted his followers to kill "white devils."[69] Fifteen "white devils," who were mostly homeless, and "black blasphemers" were slain. Yahweh ordered one victim decapitated.[70]

In 1992, three years after he was impeached, tried, and convicted, former Federal Judge Alcee Hastings ran for the US House in Florida's heavily Democratic 23rd congressional district. Hastings was trailing in the race. Then on September 19, 1992, US Judge Stanley Sporkin overturned Hastings's impeachment, ruling the Senate acted improperly in how it conducted the impeachment trial.[71] This ruling bolstered Hastings's candidacy. The Senate ignored the ruling, since the Constitution gives the Senate sole authority to impeach federal officials.

On November 3, 1992, Alcee Hastings was elected to the very same legislative chamber that impeached him. He still serves today.

Controversy continued to follow Hastings. In 2014, the US Treasury paid $220,000 to settle a claim that Hastings had sexually harassed a female staffer. It was also learned that Patricia Williams, who was Hastings's longtime girlfriend, was being paid the maximum salary for a congressional staffer of nearly $170,000 a year. Williams had been a member of Hastings's congressional staff since he began serving.

"Beam Me Up"

There may not have been a more colorful and quirky character in Congress, and perhaps in all of Washington, DC, in the last several generations than Democrat Jim Traficant. One could not help but notice his head of hair. Some wondered if he was wearing a really bad toupee. Others thought perhaps he was having a bad hair day. Every day. For nine congressional terms.

Traficant's fashion sense was either incredibly awful, or he wore awful clothes because of the attention they drew to him. He would sometimes wear two-piece suits of denim, polyester, or wild plaid, with skinny neckties and bell-bottom trousers, reminiscent of the 1970s. Often, his catchphrase when he would finish remarks on the floor of the US House of Representatives was to look skyward and say, "Beam me up!"

Yes, Jim Traficant was quite the colorful character.

James Traficant was a native Ohioan. He was a high school and college jock. He quarterbacked the University of Pittsburgh football team and briefly pursued a professional career with the Pittsburgh Steelers and the Oakland Raiders. Both teams cut him from their squads.

In 1980, Traficant was elected sheriff of Mahoning County, Ohio, which included the city of Youngstown. He made national headlines in early 1982 when he took out a personal loan of $50,000 to use in an undercover drug operation because there was too much bureaucratic red tape to get it from the county coffers.[72]

In August 1982, he was indicted by a federal grand jury for racketeering and making false statements, for allegedly accepting $163,000 from organized-crime figures, and for not taking action against certain illegal activities once he became sheriff. Traficant called the charges "low-down, dog-faced lies."[73]

While awaiting trial on his Racketeer Influenced and Corrupt Organizations (RICO) charges, Traficant again made national news when he refused to carry out court-ordered foreclosure notices on ten area homeowners. Traficant vowed not to enforce removing people who were victims of a struggling economy from their homes.[74] Ruling Traficant was in contempt of court, the judge sentenced him to one hundred days in jail, ten days for each foreclosure notice he refused to execute.

Traficant's actions endeared him to the constituents of the mostly blue-collar Mahoning County. In a show of support, citizens lined the path between the courthouse and police station when he was escorted to carry out his jail sentence.[75] Traficant was released after three days in jail, when he agreed to execute foreclosures in compliance with the law.

In April 1983, Traficant entered a federal courtroom prepared to represent himself in his federal trial, even though he was not a lawyer. Yet, he was no stranger to courtrooms. In his two years as sheriff, he pursued dereliction of duty charges against the Youngstown mayor and other city officials, battled with judges over their home foreclosure notices, and attempted to arrest ten FBI agents for bungling a robbery case. Reporters called his flamboyant courtroom style "The Traficant Show."[76]

After an eight-week trial, the jury deliberated for four days before rendering a not guilty verdict. Traficant's explanation that he was not accepting a bribe, but rather was conducting his own undercover sting operation, apparently gave jurors reasonable doubt.[77]

Running as a Democrat, Traficant rode his popularity into Congress after upsetting a three-term Republican in the 1984 election. He would be reelected eight times without ever facing serious opposition.

Traficant never quite fit in with the Democratic caucus. He was bipartisan in his approach to politics, which sometimes angered Democratic Party officials. On the other hand, Republicans apparently viewed him as too much of a wild card to embrace him, even after Democrats stripped him of committee assignments.

In May 2001, Traficant was indicted by a federal grand jury for allegedly taking bribes. It was alleged that business contractors performed work at his Ohio farm in return for advancing their interests in Congress. It was also claimed he had members of his congressional staff do unpaid chores on his farm, such as bailing hay.[78]

Traficant's February 2002 trial started with some fireworks. As he did nearly two decades earlier, Traficant chose to represent himself. Judge Lesley Wells of the US District Court in Cleveland warned that his oratory style on the House floor would not be tolerated in her courtroom. Aware of Traficant's immense popularity in his congressional district, Wells ordered no jurors could come from Mahoning County.[79]

In a two-month trial filled with theatrics, vulgarity, insults, and rebukes from the judge, Traficant hoped to replicate his courtroom success from 1983. The jury thought otherwise, convicting him on all ten racketeering charges he faced.

As required by House rules, the Committee on Standards of Official Conduct, commonly known as the House Ethics Committee, quickly launched an ethics investigation of Traficant. On July 19, 2002, the committee unanimously recommended his expulsion from the House.[80] On July 24, 2002, the US House of Representatives voted 420–1 to expel Traficant from the chamber.

The following month, Traficant entered federal prison to serve an eight-year sentence. He was released in 2009 and died in 2014, following a farm accident.

CHAPTER 11

CREEPY SEXUAL BEHAVIOR

"[He] couldn't spot a whorehouse in his own basement."

> —Columnist Patrick Buchanan commenting on Massachusetts Representative Barney Frank's claim he did not know his live-in boyfriend was operating a homosexual prostitution ring from Frank's apartment.[1]

Potterizing

Robert Potter was first elected to Congress in the 1828 election. He assumed office in March 1829. His first term was relatively unremarkable, but he accomplished enough to earn reelection in 1830.

Potter was married to Isabella Taylor. For reasons that are unclear today, Potter had an intense jealous streak, and he presumed his wife was being unfaithful to him. This came to a head in August 1831.

Isabella had a pair of cousins who frequently visited the Potter home. One was fifty-five-year-old Louis Taylor, who was a local Methodist minister. The other was seventeen-year-old Louis Wiley. Potter was convinced his wife was having affairs with both men.

On Sunday, August 28, Minister Taylor stopped by the Potter residence. Potter's pent-up suspicion exploded. He accused Taylor of carrying on an adulterous relationship with his wife. Taylor denied these charges. After a heated argument, Potter "pounced on him like a wild beast, beating him senseless."[2]

With Taylor beaten and subdued, Potter used a sharp knife and castrated the minister. "I have been very merciful and kind to you," Potter said to Taylor. "I have spared your life."[3] Potter then took Taylor to his own home, put him to bed, and cautioned him not to breathe a word of what occurred, or else Taylor would be a disgraced man.

Potter wasn't finished with exacting revenge on those he viewed as competition for the affections of his wife. He then went looking for the teenaged Louis Wiley. He found Wiley at his home and "sprang upon him like a tiger, treating him as he had Taylor."[4]

According to an unconfirmed account, Potter surprised each man by throwing a rope around the neck and tightening it until near unconsciousness. Then he lashed together the hands and feet of each man. Only then did Potter castrate each one. After the second attack, Potter called for the local doctor to inspect both victims.[5] Potter's act of castration became known in North Carolina as "Potterizing."

Potter was arrested the very next morning and was jailed without bail. Authorities were concerned either or both victims might die. This would elevate the charge from assault to murder. Both men survived.

A trial to face charges stemming from the attack on Wiley was held on Monday, September 5, 1831, eight days after the attacks. Potter represented himself. His defense strategy was simple. Potter pleaded not guilty under the theory that he was defending the "sanctity of the marriage bed."[6] His defense, while novel, did not rescue him from a guilty verdict for assault. Potter was sentenced to six months in jail and fined $1,000.

The trial for his attack on Minister Taylor was deferred until such time it was apparent that Taylor was to survive. That trial took place in March 1832. Potter was again convicted for assault with a deadly weapon and was sentenced to two years in prison.

Once Potter entered jail following his conviction in the Wiley attack, he resigned his House seat. In a letter to friends, he explained it was necessary he resign his seat in Congress if he had lost the confidence of the voters, even though he thought he was unfairly convicted. Potter was convinced he was the victim of political opponents, not the guilty party of a violent attack. In announcing his decision to resign his seat, he wrote, "I cheerfully return to my constituents the appointment to which they advanced me in the public service."[7]

Potter wrote an open letter to the public while still in jail in 1832. He argued he should not be jailed, but instead "should be applauded" for attacking an adulterer.[8]

After he finished his prison sentence, Potter immediately announced his candidacy for the North Carolina legislature's lower chamber. In spite of his notorious behavior, Potter was a dynamic speaker and campaigner. He was elected to the North Carolina House of Commons after a bruising campaign that was called "Potter's War."

In spite of his election win, 1834 yielded tragedy for Potter. His wife filed for and was granted divorce and was also granted custody of both children. Isabella Taylor Potter changed her last name, and the last names of their two children, to Pelham, which was her mother's maiden name. Unfortunately, Isabella died later that year. Their daughter, Susan, contracted pneumonia and also died. Their son, Robert Jr., was considered "mentally incompetent."[9] Potter lost everything personal in his life.

Potter's election to the North Carolina House of Commons did not escape controversy. His bombastic style and habit of verbally attacking those with whom he disagreed made him an enemy of most representatives in the chamber. The other representatives were desperate to find a way to prematurely end his term in the House. Potter gave them one. He was playing cards, when he accused his opponent of cheating. A scuffle ensued. Potter drew a pistol and a knife on his opponent. Such behavior was in violation of House rules.

Potter was charged with "Public reports that were 'highly injurious' to member's reputation and 'derogatory to the dignity of this House,' touching on his conduct since he took his seat as a member."[10] The House of Commons debated the charge facing Potter on January 1, 1835,[11] and voted to expel him from the chamber the following day.[12]

The Sex Ring

Most Americans have no appetite for creepy sexual behavior, especially if it involves public officials. Yet, some voters ignore the worst behavior in people. This was the case when voters reelected Democrat Barney Frank to Massachusetts' 4th congressional district. They did this in spite of knowing that Frank hired a prostitute, invited him to move in, and then used his special status as a member of Congress to intercede on his boyfriend's behalf by having parking tickets canceled and lying to his paramour's probation officer.[13]

Steven Gobie was a drug felon and homosexual prostitute when Frank purchased his services through a personal advertisement. The relationship between the two moved very quickly, and Frank invited Gobie to move into his Capitol Hill apartment. It was here that Gobie set up shop and began running a homosexual prostitution ring. What the unmarried Frank never publicly explained was why he would engage in the risky behavior of starting a relationship with a prostitute, rather than simply joining the singles scene like most other people. It was this period of Frank's life that he later referred to as the "hustler incident."[14]

It was widely known throughout the homosexual community that Frank was one of them. In fact, it was hardly a well-kept secret in Washington. Even though he was in the closet, to many it was hardly a surprise. Frank was active in gay and lesbian affairs and had marched in several editions of the national gay pride parade.

Occasionally, members of the print media would ask him to confirm or deny rumors he was homosexual. He would typically respond that his sexual orientation was no business of the public.

Hiring homosexual prostitutes was not a new activity to Frank.[15] In March 1985, he thumbed through the personal ads in the *Washington Blade*, the oldest newspaper serving the Washington, DC, homosexual community. Frank settled on one classified that read, "Exceptionally good-looking, personable, muscular athlete is available. Hot bottom plus large endowment equals a good time. Greg."[16] Greg was the professional name Steven Gobie used.

Frank hired the homosexual prostitute for an hour of sex that began as a business relationship and then blossomed into a very personal relationship. Still, Frank wanted to keep his relationship with Gobie a secret. As Frank later admitted, he had "taken great pains to conceal the relationship [with Gobie] from the people in [Frank's congressional] office." His attempts at concealment were unsuccessful.[17]

Gobie already had an extensive crime rap-sheet by the time he and Frank became a couple. Gobie had been convicted of cocaine possession, oral sodomy, and child pornography.[18] Gobie's felony past did not appear to matter to Frank. At forty-five years of age, he may have fallen in love with the twenty-eight-year-old prostitute.

In a matter of weeks, Gobie was living with Frank in the Massachusetts congressman's Capitol Hill apartment. Frank told those who asked that Gobie was his housekeeper and personal assistant. In spite of Frank's attempts to conceal the affair, staffers in Frank's congressional office knew better.[19]

Most people were probably indifferent to how Frank spent his personal life. However, Frank crossed the line when he abused his position as a member of Congress and pulled strings to benefit Gobie. Frank allowed Gobie to use his personal car with congressional license plates, which includes congressional perks regarding traffic and parking violations.

During their relationship, Gobie drove Frank's car all over DC and managed to rack up a stunning thirty-three parking tickets. This proved to be no problem as far as Barney Frank was concerned. All of Gobie's parking tickets were dismissed.[20] There was no escaping the truth. Frank sheepishly admitted he used his congressional privileges to have Gobie's parking tickets canceled.[21]

Frank's irresponsible behavior did not end there. Frank wrote letters[22] on congressional stationery to Gobie's Virginia parole officer stating that Gobie was employed by the Congressman, although Frank had never withheld federal income or Social Security taxes, as required by law.[23] Simply put, Frank lied.[24] Frank's later attempt to reduce Gobie's probation was not met with success.

The pair had become such constant companions that Gobie joined Frank at a White House bill-signing ceremony.[25] The relationship continued for more than two years, until Frank's landlady complained about the homosexual prostitution ring that was being run out of Frank's apartment.[26] By then, the telephone number for an escort service was being forwarded to Frank's apartment.[27]

After news broke in August 1989 regarding the homosexual prostitution ring, Frank held a press conference in his congressional district. Barney Frank, whose arrogance, sarcasm,[28] and condescension were boundless, who wanted everyone to believe he was always the smartest man in the room, fell back on the defense that he was a victim and was duped by Gobie.[29] Thirty years later, Frank continued to portray himself as the victim in the scandal.[30]

Frank's defense of his role in the scandal was that he had no idea Gobie was operating a prostitution ring from his own apartment.[31] Frank insisted the House of Representatives needed not begin a formal ethics investigation.[32] Years later, Frank's recollection of his protests may have dimmed, because in his 2015 autobiography he claimed he welcomed a House Ethics Committee investigation as a vehicle to clear him of some allegations.[33]

A nearly yearlong investigation was conducted by the House Ethics Committee. It delivered a unanimous recommendation by all twelve members that Frank be reprimanded for his behavior. The House followed the Ethics Committee recommendation and voted 408–18 to reprimand Frank. Immediately after members left the House floor, Frank spoke to reporters. Displaying his usual combative personality, Frank appeared to shake off any semblance of humility and instead charged he was a victim of a gay-bashing agenda.[34] Frank did not appear to have learned his lesson.

Sexting

Anthony Weiner and Huma Abedin were an up-and-coming power couple in Democratic politics. Weiner was elected to Congress in 1998 from New York's Ninth District, which encompassed much of Brooklyn and Queens. Abedin had been a confidante of Hillary Clinton since she was a twenty-one-year-old intern. The pair were favorites of Bill and Hillary Clinton and were sometimes likened to the Clintons. Abedin and Weiner got engaged in 2009 and married the following year, with Bill Clinton officiating the service.

The two were opposites in some respects. Abedin was known for being quiet and secretive, often avoiding the public limelight. Weiner was loud, obnoxious, glib, and insulting, and he appeared to crave public attention.

In late May 2011, Weiner sent a photo of himself from the waist down dressed only in boxer shorts, covering what appeared to be an erection. Weiner sent the image to a female college student in Seattle he had never met. The image and an accompanying story were posted on the Big Government website on May 28.

Two days later, Weiner denied sending the photo, claimed his social media account was hacked, and suggesting the photo may have been of him, but was digitally altered.[35] A Weiner spokesman followed up the denunciation with a claim that an attorney had been hired to explore legal options.[36] Curiously, Weiner did not request an investigation by either the Federal Bureau of Investigation or the New York Police Department.

While the brouhaha, dubbed "Weinergate," became the fodder of comedians, various online outlets, and cable news channels, Democratic consultants dismissed the episode as not particularly damaging for Weiner's expected run for New York City mayor in 2013.[37]

On June 6, a series of photos that were definitively images of Weiner were published by Big Government. Included were a photo of a bare-chested Weiner and a photo of him sitting on a sofa wearing a t-shirt. Weiner had exchanged these and other intimate photos with a second woman.[38] Later that day, a tearful Weiner admitted that he had sent the photos and lied about them, but had no intention of resigning.[39]

There was more bad news for Weiner. In early June, it was reported that Weiner had sent unsolicited photos of himself, some sexually explicit, to several more women using social media.[40] Some of the women were shocked at how quickly Weiner engaged in racy or sexually explicit chatter. Another female with whom Weiner was privately communicating was a young teen still in high school.[41]

The Congressional Research Service, a division of the Library of Congress, issued a May 2011 report on text messaging that also warned against "sexting." According to the report, sexting is "youth writing sexually explicit messages, taking sexually explicit photos of themselves or others in their peer group, and transmitting those photos and/or messages to their peers."[42] It was as if the report was written with Weiner in mind.

The chorus of Weiner's critics got bigger and louder, with several prominent Democratic members of the House of Representatives asking him to leave his congressional seat. Yet, the *New York Times* criticized calls for him to resign. It takes "brazenness for a man to send lewd pictures of himself" to women he has never met, the paper opined. "But it takes 200-proof gall" to ask that he step down, the paper said.[43]

In a case of attacking the messenger, the *New York Times* claimed the worst part of the Weiner fiasco was the involvement of the BigGovernment website that exposed Weiner's behavior.[44] The man behind BigGovernment was Andrew Breitbart. In 2009, Breitbart helped bring down the activist group Acorn, which was heavily funded with federal money, for engaging in seemingly illegal activity. Abedin dismissed Breitbart as a "not entirely reputable right-wing blogger."[45]

The *Times* did not offer such spirited defense for another New York Congressman, Republican Christopher Lee, who resigned his seat. Lee sent a shirtless photo of himself to a woman he met online. He resigned less than four hours after the episode was made public.

While public interest in Weinergate was escalating, White House spokesman Jay Carney emphasized the administration's disinterest. Carney called the Weiner affair "a distraction."

Weiner resigned on June 16, 2011.

In early 2013, Weiner declared himself rehabilitated and reentered politics.[46] He became a candidate for New York City mayor and rocketed to the head of the pack of Democratic candidates. Weiner was aided by a very nicely timed *New York Times Magazine* puff-piece that was published shortly before he jumped into the mayoral race.[47]

A year earlier, in the summer of 2012, *People* magazine published a sympathetic profile of him as rumors circulated that he was considering running for mayor.[48] Then, in July 2013, more lewd photos of Weiner emerged. Calling himself "Carlos Danger," Weiner had been sexting with another woman as recently as a few months earlier.

During the primary campaign, Weiner admitted he had been sexting with several women, but he refused to drop out of the mayoral race. In September 2013, Weiner finished the primary election with less than 5 percent of the vote.[49]

Three years later, Weiner was again in hot water over his sexting with women. A pair of media outlets reported stories accompanied by photos of Weiner he had sent to more women he claimed he had never met. In September 2016, the *Daily Mail* reported Weiner had knowingly been sexting with a fifteen-year-old schoolgirl. He reportedly encouraged her to engage in rape fantasies, and the pair exchanged nude photos and videos.[50]

Based on the *Daily Mail* report, the FBI and the New York Police Department opened investigations. Electronic devices belonging to Weiner and Abedin were seized. Thousands of emails, some classified, belonging to former Secretary of State Hillary Clinton, were found on Weiner's laptop. Included were countless emails Clinton and the State Department withheld from federal investigators during an investigation into Clinton's improper use of a private email server for State Department business (see chapter 8).

In May 2017, federal authorities declined to prosecute Weiner for child pornography charges and allowed him to plea to a single charge of transmitting obscene material to a minor. In September, Weiner was sentenced to twenty-one months in federal prison and was ordered to register as a sex offender. He reported to prison in November 2017.

While Weiner was formalizing his plea agreement in May 2017, Abedin filed for divorce. In early 2018, Abedin quietly withdrew her divorce petition. It was speculated the couple may have opted to remain married in order to take advantage of spousal immunity in the event that either one became a target of further investigations.[51]

Boy-Whore Capital

Robert Bauman was a reliable, conservative Republican politician. He was elected to Congress in 1973 representing the rural congressional district on Maryland's Eastern Shore. He prevailed in a special election to fill the seat of a congressman who had committed suicide. This would not be the first time Bauman spent time in the US House of Representatives. He was a House page when he was a teen.

Bauman had the best conservative bona fides. He was considered the unofficial leader of House conservatives, he was a personal friend of former California Governor and presidential aspirant Ronald Reagan, and he was president of the 200,000-member American Conservative Union.

Bauman was such a supporter of a US military victory in Vietnam that he reportedly named a daughter Victoria. Bauman was considering challenging fellow Republican and US Senator Charles Mathias for the GOP nomination. Bauman did not think Mathias was conservative enough.

Bob Bauman was also gay, which he kept secret from nearly everyone.

On October 3, 1980, Bauman appeared in District of Columbia Superior Court in Washington, DC, and entered a plea of innocent. He had been charged with soliciting sex from a minor earlier that spring. Reportedly, Bauman paid a sixteen-year-old boy fifty dollars for the opportunity to perform oral sex on the youth.[52]

A friend of the boy witnessed the encounter and took notice of the congressional license plate on Bauman's car. He reported the incident to DC police, which ultimately launched an investigation. Normally, the DC police do not investigate homosexual activity between consenting adults. The age of consent in Washington, DC, was sixteen. In this case, a DC police officer made an offhand remark about Bauman soliciting gay sex to an FBI agent, who launched the investigation of Bauman.[53]

The US prosecutor told the judge the US Attorney's Office would not pursue charges against first-time offender Bauman if he agreed to enter a court-supervised treatment program. Bauman agreed to do so.

Bauman announced the day before the court hearing that, having realized he was an alcoholic, he had given up drinking on May 1. To aid in his recovery, Bauman entered Alcoholics Anonymous the previous spring and had sought counseling. He claimed the realization that he had a drinking problem occurred when he got drunk that March, which led to the sex allegations. Dr. Albert Dawkins told a local newspaper he was Bauman's doctor and lifelong friend, and it was his medical opinion that Bauman was "in no way, shape or form an alcoholic."[54]

Bauman issued a statement after his court appearance. Included was his intention to continue running for reelection, with the general election only a month away. In part, the statement said, "I strongly emphasize that this allegation involves only my personal conduct and has nothing to do with my office or duties. My drinking occurred away from my official duties and did not impair my work."[55]

The chairmen of the Republican National Committee and the Maryland Republican Party, Bill Brock and Allan Levey, respectively, both announced continued support for Bauman in his reelection campaign. However, leaders of three conservative organizations, the Committee for the Survival of a Free Congress, the Religious Roundtable, and the American Association of Christian Schools, requested Bauman step down from Congress. The largest newspaper in the congressional district, the *Salisbury Daily Times*, demanded Bauman resign from Congress.[56]

The *Washington Post* called into question Bauman's fitness to represent the residents of Maryland's Eastern Shore. "Bauman," the paper wrote, "was not elected by the residents of San Francisco."[57] Years later, the *Washington Post* wrote that "much of Washington smiled" when the personal tragedy struck Bauman.[58] The *Economist* magazine labeled Bauman a "bad apple."[59] However, the *Easton Star-Democrat*, a Maryland Eastern Shore newspaper, endorsed Bauman's reelection over the election of his Democratic challenger, writing Bauman's "proven record in the House of Representatives, is the better choice."[60]

On November 4, 1980, Robert Bauman lost his reelection attempt by about 5 percent of the vote.

The arrest of Bauman thrust into the public eye male prostitution in Washington, DC. According to one newspaper account, the mostly teen prostitutes appealed to older men known as "chicken-hawks." Many of these chicken-hawks, according to the paper, were professional men including doctors, lawyers, lobbyists, and congressional staffers. The thriving teen male-prostitution trade had made Washington, DC, known "in a lot of gay circles as the boy-whore capital."[61]

"Hi, Honey"

Allan Howe was elected to Congress in 1974 as part of the anti-Richard Nixon sentiment that swept the nation following the Watergate scandal. He had quite the impressive résumé heading into the election. From 1954 to 1960, Howe was a delegate to the Utah Democratic Convention. He was tabbed as an alternate to the 1960 Democratic National Convention that nominated John Kennedy.

As a young man, Howe served as the president of the Young Democrats of America.[62] He worked as a staffer and then later as the administrative assistant for Senator Frank Moss from 1959 to 1964. Howe went on to serve as Utah assistant attorney general from 1965 to 1966 and then as administrative assistant to Governor Calvin Rampton from 1966 to 1968.

Howe began his congressional career in January 1975. He had an unremarkable record, as was the case with most freshmen members of Congress. He was near the tail end of his first term in Congress when he skyrocketed from anonymous to notorious. Howe was arrested by the vice unit of the Salt Lake City Police Department on June 12, 1976, for allegedly soliciting sex from a pair of police decoys posing as prostitutes.

It was a deeply embarrassing and humiliating experience for several reasons. Howe was a Mormon, married, and a member of Congress.

However, when he held a press conference on June 18, Howe claimed that the police version of events was completely false. Accompanied by his wife and five children, Howe told a group of cheering supporters that he was the target of a political attack and he had no intention of withdrawing from his reelection race. He demanded a speedy trial so he could clear his name.

According to the police, late one evening, Howe was on West Second Street, which was an area known for prostitution. He approached two women sitting in a parked car and allegedly offered twenty dollars for undefined sex acts. The women were police officers Margaret Hamblin and Kathleen Taylor, posing as prostitutes. According to the officers, Howe began the conversation with "Hi, honey. What are you up to?" before spelling out what he hoped twenty dollars would buy him.[63]

Major Democratic politicians, including Moss, for whom Howe had once worked, and Utah's major newspapers, the *Deseret News* and the *Salt Lake Tribune*, urged Howe to withdraw from the race.[64]

On July 23, Howe was found guilty by a jury in a Salt Lake City Court trial of a misdemeanor charge of soliciting sex. He was fined $150 and given a suspended thirty-day jail sentence. Declaring his innocence and claiming he was entrapped, Howe vowed to appeal his conviction. He also vowed to stay in the race.[65]

Howe did not heed pleas from the Utah Democratic establishment to withdraw from the race in favor of another Democratic candidate. On September 19, the Utah Democratic Party formally withdrew its endorsement of Howe. The party then endorsed the candidacy of Daryl McCarty as a write-in candidate for the November 2 general election.

Republican David Daniel Marriott defeated Allan Howe for Utah's 2nd congressional district race on November 2, 1976, by a vote of 53–40 percent. Write-in candidate McCarty captured 7 percent of the vote.

In March 1977, a federal judge dismissed Howe's petition to overturn his July 1976 conviction of soliciting sex. Howe claimed the two police officers lied in their accounts of the conversation he had with the two women. Howe also claimed he did not get a fair trial due to pretrial publicity.[66]

After his election defeat, Howe and his family moved permanently to the Washington, DC, suburb of Arlington, Virginia. He began a lucrative two-decade lobbying career on Capitol Hill. Howe died in December 2000 at the age of seventy-three.

"One Man Crime Wave"

Fred Richmond was a workhorse in New York City Democratic politics. Starting in the late 1950s, he served as an official in the Democratic National Committee, attended the 1964 Democratic National Convention as a delegate, and served on the New York City Council. In 1974, Richmond was elected to the US House of Representatives from the 14th congressional district representing Brooklyn.

It was 1977, early in Richmond's second term in Congress, when he solicited sex from a sixteen-year-old boy he brought home. The boy's parents learned of the encounter and immediately notified authorities. In February 1978, Richmond brought another young man home and offered him money in exchange for sex. That second person was an undercover police officer.[67]

Richmond's attorney reached a plea deal with prosecutors. They would drop the charges if Richmond, the divorced father of one son, attended a first-time-offender rehabilitation program.

Richmond faced a Democratic primary challenge in September 1978. Bernard Gifford, a doctor of biophysics and former deputy chancellor of New York City schools, campaigned hard against Richmond. Gifford, who was black, made Richmond's solicitation of sex from a sixteen-year-old black male a cornerstone of his campaign by calling Richmond a "sick man" in desperate need of psychiatric care.[68]

Richmond enjoyed support among the 14th congressional district's affluent liberals and Hasidic Jews, while Gifford was backed by the district's black and Hispanic communities. Richmond was the wealthiest member of the US House. The vastly outspent Gifford campaign fell short as Richmond cruised to victory in the Democratic primary.

In late 1981, a takeover battle of a St. Louis, Missouri, steel manufacturer by a New York-based manufacturer of steel and plastics revealed that Richmond was earning an outside salary in violation of House rules. The House limited earning outside income to no more than 15 percent of congressional salaries. There were exceptions such as book royalties and retirement pay.

Richmond had announced his retirement from Walco National Corporation in 1978 in order to avoid running afoul of the then newly implemented House ethics rules limiting outside income. The hostile acquisition involving Walco National landed in federal court, where it was learned Richmond faked his retirement in order to continue running Walco. The $100,000 Richmond was receiving annually was not retirement pay, but was instead his employment salary.[69]

The arrangement also gave Richmond access to company resources and a company-subsidized apartment to further his political ambitions. Additionally, the courtroom judge criticized Richmond's use of money from a charitable foundation for political purposes.

The judge learned that Walco National filed false documents with the Securities and Exchange Commission that concealed the true relationship between the firm and Richmond.[70] The judge also reported that Richmond had secretly arranged a personal loan to an editor of the *New York Daily News* and then paid off the loan when the editor defaulted. The newspaper suspended the editor, pending an investigation.[71]

There was even more bad news for Richmond. Walco National employees were planning campaign activities and managing fundraising events for Richmond while on company time. This was an apparent violation of campaign laws. Richmond's campaign officials countered that only volunteers were assisting the campaign and only on their own time, but admitted they were using Walco National offices. However, Richmond's financial disclosures did not show any payments to Walco National for the use of offices, as required by election law.[72]

It was further learned that Richmond had full use of a company-owned, chauffeur-driven automobile, and Walco National paid nearly $350,000 over a four-year period for the maintenance and upkeep of a multimillion-dollar apartment owned by Richmond. None of this was disclosed in Richmond's ethics disclosures or campaign filings.[73]

Thousands of dollars in contributions to Richmond's reelection campaign had come from straw donors, it was reported. Several people were given cash in exchange for writing personal checks, oftentimes with the payee name left blank. Those checks were later cashed by the Richmond campaign. Most of the checks came from employees or subcontractors of a Brooklyn shipyard operator who received millions of dollars in government contracts, often with the assistance of Richmond.[74]

By the spring, a federal grand jury was hearing from prosecutors and witnesses regarding Richmond and his activities. Among the new allegations was that, in 1981, Richmond helped get a job for an escaped prison convict in the House of Representatives. The fugitive was arrested in Manhattan after offering to perform a sex act on an undercover police officer in exchange for money. He was driving Richmond's personal car at the time of his arrest.[75]

Richmond faced an avalanche of criminal, ethics, and misbehavior charges. Among these was the allegation that as many as nine current and former congressional staffers had purchased marijuana and cocaine on Richmond's behalf.[76]

Richmond was facing so many criminal allegations that one newspaper writer called him a "one man crime wave."[77] On August 25, 1982, Richmond resigned from Congress and pled guilty to three criminal charges, including tax evasion and possession of marijuana. Eight other charges, including possession of cocaine and aiding an escaped felon, were dropped in return for Richmond's promise to never again run for political office.[78]

In 2009, a letter to the judge who sentenced Richmond was made public for the first time. Richmond's congressional chief of staff, Bill Thompson, pleaded with the judge not to impose a prison sentence on Richmond. The humiliation Richmond suffered from getting caught was punishment enough, wrote Thompson.

The letter became public just as Thompson was challenging Michael Bloomberg, who was running for reelection as New York City mayor. Demonstrating no loyalty in return, Richmond dismissed Thompson's candidacy and endorsed Bloomberg for reelection.[79]

The Rape Trial

It was boys' night out on Good Friday, March 29, 1991, in Palm Beach, Florida, for the Kennedys. Thirty-year-old William Kennedy Smith was out drinking, carousing, and meeting women with his twenty-four-year-old cousin, Patrick Kennedy, a Rhode Island state legislator, and his fifty-nine-year-old uncle, US Senator Edward "Ted" Kennedy.

The three were at a local nightclub drinking and chatting up the girls. Smith met twenty-nine-year-old Patricia Bowman, and the two talked and danced until the nightclub closed. Smith asked Bowman if she would drive him home, as his uncle and cousin had left without him. Once they arrived at the guarded Kennedy compound, Smith offered to give her a tour of the mansion. After the tour, the pair talked and walked along the beach. On these points, Smith and Bowman were in agreement. Where they differ is in what happened next.

Smith claimed that in the early hours of Saturday, March 30, the pair engaged in consensual sex. Bowman claims she was attacked and savagely raped. She reported the sexual assault to the Palm Beach Police hours later.

Initially, the Palm Beach Police were tight-lipped about the alleged sexual assault. Local reporters noted that the police routinely informed the press of rape reports, but the police were withholding all information regarding this incident because the Kennedys were involved. Public notification of the alleged assault did not occur until the following Monday, after the Easter weekend and after the three Kennedys had left Florida.

After about a week, Palm Beach Police confirmed that Ted Kennedy's nephew had been accused of rape. The police also admitted they had not yet interviewed any of the Kennedy family regarding the allegations.

William Kennedy Smith released a statement denying he was involved in any incident. When Bowman reported to the police that she had been raped, she also turned over to them an antique urn she took from the Kennedy mansion after the alleged attack. Fearing the Kennedy family would deny she was on the property, Bowman allegedly took the urn to prove she was at the home if the police doubted her rape allegations.

Once the Kennedy name had been released, this created a media frenzy not previously seen. The incident became the subject of tabloid newspapers and tabloid TV shows. The alleged rape was a staple of CNN programming, the only twenty-four-hour national news channel at the time. It would be another five years before MSNBC and Fox News Channel would launch.

Overwhelmed by the resulting media circus that brought 300 journalists to the Palm Beach area, Bowman's family hired local attorney David Roth to protect her interests and to navigate her way through the investigation. Roth confirmed that his client had declined several lucrative financial offers to tell her story because she was only interested in seeking justice.

Roth was invited to make media appearances on behalf of his client. Among the first programs he visited was CNN's *Larry King Live* on April 9, 1991. Roth found himself in the crosshairs of a hostile interview.

"Why does the victim of a crime need a lawyer?" was the first question King asked. He continued, "Victims usually testify and either the accused is found guilty or not guilty."

King then explained to the viewers that the Kennedy family had experienced so much tragedy over the years, and that Ted "has carried the heavy mantle his brothers left behind." King then welcomed to his program a Democratic consultant and a Palm Beach socialite to balance the rape accusations. It was clear that CNN, as with many of the major media outlets, had sided with the Kennedy clan. It was going to be a rough ride for Bowman.

Reputable media organizations typically observe the industry protocol of shielding the identity of an alleged victim of a sexual assault until after the criminal proceedings have ended. However, such media restraint didn't last very long when it came to the Kennedy accuser. Two weeks after the alleged attack, the checkout stand tabloid *The Globe* published Bowman's name and photograph. NBC News quickly followed suit and identified Bowman on April 16.[80]

The following day, the *New York Times* not only named Patricia Bowman, but it also published a nearly 1,800-word, extremely critical profile of her that no doubt made Smith's criminal defense team smile. The *Times* informed readers that Bowman was a poor student and an unwed mother who "had a little wild streak," that she frequented nightspots where the rich would hang out, and that she had racked up seventeen traffic tickets. The article also implied Bowman's mother was a gold digger.[81] It was as if the *New York Times* was making the case on behalf of William Kennedy Smith that Patricia Bowman was not to be believed.

The same day as the critical article profiling Bowman, the *New York Times* published a 1,000-word article that portrayed Ted Kennedy as the victim in the affair. The *Times* reported Kennedy was not going to be distracted from his senatorial duties by the rape case. It quoted one unnamed Democratic Senator as saying, "The guy just can't seem to get out from under a black cloud."[82]

Bowman claimed that after they walked along the beach, Smith stripped off his clothes to go swimming. This made her uncomfortable. When she attempted to leave the premises, Smith tackled her, threw her to the ground, and raped her. Afterwards, she claimed to have been too distraught to have driven her own car and had run into the Kennedy mansion. There she called a friend, announced she had been raped, and pleaded with her friend to pick her up. Bowman's friend confirmed this account to the police and said she picked up a hysterical Bowman at the Kennedy mansion.

The police report identified bruises near Bowman's ankle where she claimed Kennedy grabbed her. According to a medical report made available about a week after the incident, Bowman suffered bruises, abrasions, and a possible broken rib. These injuries appeared consistent with Bowman's version of events. DNA evidence confirmed the presence of Smith's semen inside Bowman.

Bowman's attorney, Roth, told the press that investigators hired by the Kennedys were attempting to intimidate witnesses. According to Roth, the woman who picked up Bowman from the Kennedy mansion was warned that unflattering information about her would be leaked if she testified on behalf of Bowman.

It took nearly six weeks before State Attorney David Bludworth filed second-degree sexual assault charges against William Kennedy Smith. Seven years earlier, Bludworth was criticized for improperly withholding investigative reports in the drug overdose death of another Kennedy. David Kennedy, the son of the late Robert Kennedy, suffered the fatal drug overdose. A local judge questioned if Bludworth was working for the Kennedys rather than the public. [83]

According to details included in the criminal charges, Smith allegedly said, "Stop it, bitch," when Bowman was attempting to fight off his attack. The Palm Beach Police reported Bowman showed no signs of deception on polygraph and computer voice-stress analysis tests.[84] Bowman's admission during her polygraph examination that she had been sexually intimate with seven men over the previous five years was released to the public.[85]

There appeared to be a smear campaign orchestrated against Bowman. A reporter for the tabloid TV program *A Current Affair* told police in a sworn statement that he was pursuing damaging information about Bowman's past sexual history that was hinted to him by a Kennedy lawyer.[86]

The criminal trial that one news outlet dubbed "The Trial of the Century" began on December 2, 1991. Much of it was broadcast on CNN with the face of Patricia Bowman obscured by a large blue dot. The prosecution had experienced a major setback before the trial got underway. Judge Mary Lupo denied the introduction of testimony from three women who had come forward alleging William Kennedy Smith had raped them between 1983 and 1988. Prosecutor Moira Lasch had requested Lupo recuse herself for her propensity of making "negative facial expressions" during jury selection.[87] Lupo refused.

In describing the upcoming trial, *Newsweek* explained that Bowman would possibly have to answer questions about "what she was wearing, what she was doing at the bar, [and] how she spoke to Smith."[88]

During the cross-examination of Bowman, Smith's defense lawyer, Roy Black, admonished her for memory lapses of that night. Bowman testified, "The only thing I can remember about that week is Mr. Smith raped me." Black shot back, "I know you've been prepared to say that."

In his testimony, Smith described Bowman as mentally unstable, a woman who twice engaged in consensual sex and then devolved into kind of a *Fatal Attraction*-obsessed woman. He testified that after the second sexual encounter, he swam several laps in the swimming pool while she watched.

During Lasch's cross-examination of Smith, she asked him about contradictory testimony from other witnesses. Lupo ordered the jury from the courtroom, then admonished Lasch, "If you ask one more question along these lines, you will not get away with it."

On December 11, the jury deliberated for a mere hour and nineteen minutes before delivering a verdict of not guilty. At a Kennedy victory party that night at a local bar, a juror joined in the hugging and kissing.[89]

Years later, Dr. William Kennedy Smith was working for the Center for International Rehabilitation. The Chicago-based organization provided assistance to landmine victims. In 2004, Smith's office assistant, Audra Soulias, filed a lawsuit against the doctor, alleging he engaged in a pattern of workplace sexual harassment. She also claimed that in January 1999, Smith sexually assaulted her but stopped short of rape. An Illinois judge dismissed her lawsuit.

Another work colleague, Laura Hamilton, reportedly reached a six-figure settlement with Smith after she was prepared to file a lawsuit alleging that she was the victim of several years of unwanted physical touching and sexual advances by Smith. This culminated, Hamilton claimed, with Smith raping her during a business trip to Croatia in 2002.

House Pages I

The news broke in July 1982 that House pages and members of Congress had engaged in sexual activities and drug parties. In 1982, there were about one hundred teens, most between fourteen and seventeen years old, who served as pages in the House and Senate. About two-thirds of the pages served in the House. Their responsibilities had varied over the decades. In the early 1980s, they would attend classes during the morning and run errands in the afternoon into the evening for members of the House and Senate.

According to early news reports, a page had come forward alleging members of Congress were "preying on pages." The teen claimed some staff members were recruiting pages for the Congressmen. A former page appeared on a television news program and alleged he had sex on several occasions with a Congressman, including in the representative's Capitol Hill office.[90] Another former page came forward and claimed it was not unheard for a member of Congress and staff members to ply underage pages with alcohol, with the intention of engaging in sexual relations.[91]

Democratic Representative Louis Stokes of Ohio, who chaired the House Ethics Committee, announced his committee would launch an immediate investigation into the predator claims, but the committee would not investigate the drug allegations. The House hired Joseph A. Califano Jr. to serve as the special counsel to investigate the allegations. Califano was the Secretary of Health, Education, and Welfare under President Jimmy Carter.

While the investigation was underway, the House of Representatives revamped the House page system, particularly with respect to living arrangements. An office building was converted into a dormitory where pages would be required to reside. Professional staff was hired to supervise the pages and nightly curfews were established.

After a nearly one-year investigation by Califano, the House Ethics Committee released its findings. Califano could not find evidence corroborating allegations made by the two former pages the previous summer. However, he did uncover misconduct involving two House members and a House employee.

Republican Representative Daniel Crane of Illinois had engaged in a sexual relationship with a seventeen-year-old female page in 1980. Crane and the page gave sworn testimony the pair had engaged in sexual relations on about five occasions in the Congressman's apartment. The page testified she did not drink any alcohol and that the sex was consensual.

Democratic Representative Gerry Studds of Massachusetts had started an affair with a male page in 1973. Evidence suggested the boy was sixteen years old when the affair began. Studds served alcohol to the boy and got him drunk before engaging in sex with him, according to the report. Studds later took the teen with him on a two-week congressional junket to Europe.[92] The age of consent in Washington, DC, was sixteen, so Studds did not break any laws regarding sexual misconduct. According to his own deposition, Studds had made sexual advances toward two other male pages.

The third adult implicated in the scandal was a House employee. According to Califano, James Howarth, who worked for the House Doorkeeper, engaged in a sexual relationship with a seventeen-year-old female page in 1980.

Califano recommended the House act on his findings. He urged the firing of Howarth; however, "neither expulsion nor censure is warranted" in the cases of Crane and Studds, he suggested. According to Califano, the pages engaged in consensual sexual relations with the two Congressmen, therefore only light punishment should be considered.

By an 11–1 vote, the House Ethics Committee recommended to the full House that Howarth be fired and the two Congressmen be reprimanded. A reprimand is the most lenient form of punishment for a House member. It is a rebuke of the actions by an offending member that is registered by a vote of the full House. Reprimand could include the mere adoption of a report detailing misconduct.

There was a groundswell of support in the House to reprimand Crane and Studds and to put the entire episode behind the elected body. However, a small number of Congressmen urged consideration of stiffer penalties, including expulsion. Republican Congressmen Newt Gingrich of Georgia and Chalmers Wylie of Ohio spoke for the need of tougher sanctions against the two Congressmen. Both men would have been fired from their jobs if they were police officers or teachers, Gingrich observed.

Some Representatives argued the humiliation of having been caught was more than enough punishment. Republican Floyd Spence of South Carolina said, "The public disclosure of the facts of these cases has already placed an indelible stain on the reputations of these members." Democrat Parren Mitchell of Maryland argued against censure. He said the two offending Congressmen had "[a]lready [been] embarrassed, already humiliated, already stripped" of committee assignments, and to censure them only degraded the integrity of the House of Representatives.[93]

The House had settled on a compromise offered by Republican Minority Leader Robert Michel of Illinois. Michel introduced a measure for both men to be censured rather than merely reprimanded. Censure is considered a stiffer penalty than reprimand, but it falls far short of expulsion. The full House must record a majority vote censuring the member. Additionally, the member being censured must stand in the well of the House floor and listen while the resolution of censure is read aloud.

On July 20, 1983, the first to be censured was Crane. He was visibly upset as he stood in the well of the House floor, facing the other House members. Crane addressed the House. He announced he had apologized to his wife, family, and friends, and then he apologized to the full House "for the shame I have brought down on this institution."[94] The resolution was read aloud and a vote in favor of the censure resolution was passed 421–3. Even Crane voted for his own censure.

Studds was the next to face his colleagues. Unlike Crane, Studds struck a defiant tone. A week earlier, Studds declared there was nothing improper about his conduct. "It is not a simple task for any of us to meet adequately the obligations of either public office or private life, let alone both," he said.[95] Studds stood in the House well, as required by House rules, but instead of facing his colleagues, he turned his back toward them while the censure resolution was being read. After the 420–3 vote, Studds returned to his seat where several members of the Massachusetts delegation went over to shake his hand.[96]

Crane was defeated the following year in the Republican primary. Studds was easily reelected in his Massachusetts district in 1984 and would go on to be reelected five more times before retiring.

House Pages II

Mark Foley was a member of the so-called Republican Revolution. They were the large group of Republican challengers who won a net gain of fifty-four House seats in the 1994 mid-term elections. Those victories helped the Republicans capture the majority in the US House of Representatives for the first time in forty years.

Foley won his freshman race with about 58 percent of the vote. He would go on to win reelection five times, often receiving about two-thirds of the vote each time. He was an immensely popular and successful member of Congress.

In early 2003, Foley was readying himself to run for the US Senate. His plan was to challenge incumbent Democrat Bob Graham. Graham would later announce his retirement and would not seek a fourth term. In the spring, Democratic activists began circulating rumors that Foley was gay. In a conference call news conference, Foley denounced those promoting rumors about his sexuality. "People can draw whatever conclusions they want to. There are certain things we shouldn't discuss in public. Some people may think that's old fashioned, but I firmly believe it's a good rule to live by," Foley said.[97]

The *Sun-Sentinel*, a south Florida newspaper owned by the Tribune Company, outed Foley by hinting he was gay.[98] The *Broward New Times*, a sister publication of the *Village Voice*, picked up the story and addressed Foley's sexuality. Mainstream newspapers began pressing Foley to either confirm or deny he was a homosexual. Foley responded those were inappropriate questions and had no bearing on his congressional performance. After Foley's telephone press conference, a *Sun-Sentinel* editor acknowledged the newspaper was contemplating publishing a follow-up article on the subject of Foley's sexual orientation.[99]

At the time gay rumors surfaced in Florida newspapers, Foley had amassed nearly $3 million in campaign donations and was considered a formidable challenger to Graham. By year's end, he anticipated having about $5 million in campaign funds, with nearly a year to go in fundraising before the 2004 election.[100]

Foley dropped out of the Senate race in September 2003, after his father was diagnosed with cancer. Foley said it was an inappropriate time to be running a statewide campaign, while his father was battling for his life. Three years later, Foley found himself battling for his political life.

On September 24, 2006, copies of emails Foley sent to a former House page were published on a blog named Stop Sex Predators. Four days later, ABC News published a story on the emails. After seeing the ABC News report, another former page forwarded to the news organization dozens of pages of sexually explicit instant-messages exchanged between Foley and a former page.

On the morning of September 29, ABC News contacted Foley's office to get a response to the batch of instant messages it had. Representative Mark Foley resigned from Congress that day.

Immediately following his resignation, the House Ethics Committee launched an investigation of Foley's behavior with House pages. The investigation found Foley was known to be a little too chummy with many of the pages, which was probably why he was so popular among them. In 2002, he was voted by the pages to be their graduation speaker when they finished their program.[101]

A former page told House investigators he maintained regular contact with Foley. When he was in college in the fall of 2001, Foley sent him a message discussing his penis size. The former page reported this email to a member of Congress, who conveyed concerns to Foley, who apologized. The former page said the two remained in contact and Foley never again behaved inappropriately.[102]

In the late summer of 2005, another former page exchanging emails with Foley became uncomfortable with the frequency and the tone of the emails he received from the congressman. The emails were relatively innocuous, but overly friendly, including one time when Foley asked for a picture of the former page.

The former page forwarded the emails to a House staffer, telling her they made him uncomfortable and asked for some feedback. She shared the emails with others. Matt Miller of the Democratic Caucus received the forwarded emails. In late 2005, rather than forward the emails to the Ethics Committee, Miller instead faxed them to some media outlets and gave them to the Democratic Congressional Campaign Committee, a campaign arm of the Democratic National Committee chaired by Democratic Congressman Rahm Emanuel of Illinois.[103]

The *Miami Herald*, *St. Petersburg Times*, and *Harper's* magazine received copies of the emails, but did not publish stories because they did not find anything significantly wrong with them, other than sounding a bit creepy.

In spite of behavior that pushed the boundaries of what was acceptable, no evidence ever emerged that Foley had engaged in any physical contact with pages until after they left the program and were no longer minors.[104] Two former pages claimed they had sexual relations with Foley, but only after they became legal adults.[105]

The Federal Bureau of Investigation and the Florida Department of Law Enforcement launched separate investigations of Foley's contact with current and former House pages. Both law enforcement organizations closed their investigations without referring any criminal charges.

Four years later, *Newsweek* magazine addressed the scandal, suggesting Foley was a hypocrite because he was an anti-gay congressman caught in a gay scandal. Except *Newsweek*'s article was completely wrong. Foley was not anti-gay. In fact, the *Sun-Sentinel* said Foley "has a terrific record on gay rights, better than many Democrats," and in 2000 Foley had a 100 percent rating from the Human Rights Council.[106]

The YMCA

Lyndon Johnson was only a month away from the 1964 presidential election, a race he would go on to win by a landslide, when one of his closest confidants was arrested. Walter Jenkins, aged forty-six, had been arrested after reportedly having sex with a sixty-year-old man in a shower of a Washington, DC, YMCA, only two blocks from the White House.

Jenkins had been one of Johnson's most loyal and longest-serving assistants. Jenkins joined freshman Congressman Johnson in 1939 when the Texas politician was first elected to the US House of Representatives. Aside from his military service during World War II, Jenkins had worked for Johnson when he was in the House, Senate, the vice presidency, and the White House.

Jenkins was a married father of six children when he was arrested. He blamed his engaging in a sex act with another man on "fatigue, alcohol, physical illness and lack of food."[107] After he was arrested, Jenkins admitted he had been arrested in the same YMCA bathroom in 1959 for similar behavior.

Jenkins paid a fine, left the police station, and did not initially inform White House staff of what happened to him. When the *Washington Post* began asking questions about his arrest, then Jenkins consulted with White House advisor Abe Fortas, who Johnson would later appoint to the Supreme Court (see chapter 6). Fortas briefed Johnson on the arrest, and the president directed Fortas to have Jenkins resign.

After learning of the arrest, the *Chicago Tribune* agreed to not publish the story.[108] Fortas and presidential advisor Clark Clifford visited all three Washington newspapers, the *Washington Post*, *Washington Star*, and *Daily News*, and requested they keep the story under wraps. The DC papers agreed to do so, but eventually published stories after the United Press International (UPI) broke the news.[109]

White House officials directed Jenkins to check himself into a hospital, alleging he was suffering from exhaustion. This was an attempt to build an alibi that he was suffering from medical ailments in the event the arrest began damaging Johnson's election campaign. Jenkins spent several weeks in George Washington University Hospital after he resigned.

Lady Bird Johnson told her husband she wanted to help out Jenkins by giving him a high-level job at the Johnsons' family-owned television station in Austin. Johnson discouraged the First Lady from doing so, as he wanted to maintain as much distance as possible from Jenkins.[110]

The First Lady instead called *Washington Post* editor Russell Wiggins and requested the paper aid the White House in the matter. The newspaper did just that. Several newspapers published editorials sympathizing with the plight of Jenkins while not explicitly acknowledging his behavior.[111]

Johnson contacted FBI Director J. Edgar Hoover and requested an investigation of Jenkins. Reportedly, Johnson wanted to ensure Jenkins had not been compromised by foreign agents or blackmailed, possibly posing a security risk. Privately, Johnson directed a specific conclusion be reached. He wanted the FBI to report the event was a setup by

Republican operatives intent on embarrassing the Johnson administration. The FBI did not reach that conclusion, because it was untrue.[112]

The FBI investigation concluded that Jenkins's behavior did not result in any security risk. After interviewing more than 560 individuals and reviewing countless records, there was no indication any foreign government had compromised Jenkins.[113]

Johnson's general election opponent, Republican Senator Barry Goldwater of Arizona, decided not to campaign on the Jenkins scandal. In spite of the political value of the episode, Goldwater did not want to capitalize on the misfortune of Jenkins.

Johnson was elected president over Goldwater in November 1964 by one of the biggest landslide victories in history.

CHAPTER 12

THE LAW

"[T]he sleaziness and recklessness of the pardons reeks of Clinton's worst excesses: grandiosity, self-indulgence, sentimentality; and...a sense that he was beyond rebuke, somehow beyond punishment, and the normal rules just didn't apply to him."[1]

—Joan Walsh, *Salon*

The Fries Rebellion

Waging war was an expensive proposition; the colonies learned this when they were fighting for their independence from Britain. The colonies incurred significant debt during the American Revolution. After the war, the Continental Congress passed the Land Ordinance of 1785, which allowed the new government to sell land in the Western Territory (later known as the Northwest Territory) to settlers and speculators as a mechanism to raise money.

A few years later, the US Congress passed, and President George Washington signed into law, the Tariff Act of 1789. This July 1789 law was the first major piece of legislation enacted by the new government. The intent was to generate additional revenues to pay off war debts and to protect domestic manufacturers by levying a high tariff on imported products, especially those arriving on non-US flagged ships.

The tariffs on imports and excise taxes levied on valuable commodities such as alcohol, tobacco, and refined sugar were the sole sources of revenue for the United States.

John Adams succeeded Washington as president in 1797. Relations between the United States and France had gotten chilly precisely because relations between the United States and Britain had thawed.

America had ratified the John Jay Treaty with Britain, which the French government found threatening. France retaliated by attacking American merchant ships. Anticipating a war with France convinced federal lawmakers they needed to raise money in order to rebuild the Army, Navy, and Marine Corps. They estimated about $2 million was needed. This led lawmakers to levy the first-ever direct tax on US property in July 1798.

Taxes had been very unpopular with the colonies several years earlier. "No taxation without representation" was a familiar rallying cry for those colonists who sought independence from the British crown. The new government's decision to impose its own tax on the people was not warmly welcomed in many quarters. This direct tax was imposed on land, dwellings, and slaves.

Each state was assigned an amount it was responsible to raise. The state of Pennsylvania's share of the $2 million was more than $237,000. The other fifteen states had to raise the balance of about $1,750,000.

There were very few slaves in Pennsylvania that could be taxed, so the bulk of the tax would be levied primarily on dwellings and land. Tax assessors would take measurements of each dwelling and count the number of windows in order to assess taxes for each home. The predominately German-descent farmers in southeastern Pennsylvania were not enthusiastic about paying the tax. In addition, they were suspicious of the tax assessors who were gathering information on private homes.

John Fries was a popular local auctioneer who was known to many of the farmers in the region. In February 1799, he took it upon himself to organize a resistance to the tax by holding a series of meetings to strategize on a response. In March, Fries assembled a group of several hundred men who chased tax assessors from the area. The group then freed a handful of tax resisters from the Bethlehem, Pennsylvania, jail.

Fries and his followers were labeled as being guilty of sedition and treason. The Pennsylvania militia was called upon to put down the resisters. The militia never found the band of rebels because they had dispersed, but it did apprehend Fries and two other leaders. All three were charged with treason, tried, and convicted. They were then sentenced to death.

Learning of the sentence, President John Adams elected to show compassion toward Fries and the other two. In April 1800, Adams pardoned all three. He followed up their pardons on May 21, 1800, with a "full, free and absolute pardon" to the rest of the tax resisters. Adams's pardon was opposed by most of his cabinet and is deemed to have contributed to his reelection defeat by Thomas Jefferson.

The Pardon

President Gerald Ford announced on live television on September 8, 1974, that he was pardoning Richard Nixon for "all offenses against the United States which he, Richard Nixon, has committed or may have committed."

Ford felt it was time to move the nation forward and to put an end to the scandal that had plagued the country for two years. He later commented, "I thought perhaps the public would consider the resignation of a President as sufficient punishment, shame and disgrace. I thought there would be greater understanding and perhaps forgiveness."[2] In prepared remarks following his oath of office as the new president a month earlier, Ford said of Nixon's resignation, "[M]y fellow Americans, our long national nightmare is over. Our Constitution works; our great Republic is a government of laws and not of men."

Unfortunately for Ford, the resignation of the nation's 37th president didn't satisfy those who wanted Nixon's head on a platter. The White House telephone switchboard lit up with an overwhelming percentage of callers opposed to the executive clemency. While supportive of a pardon, Nixon's enemies in Congress first wanted the former president indicted, tried, and convicted before Ford pardoned him. In other words, they were no longer satisfied with Nixon having been driven from the White House. They wanted to humiliate him.

Impeachment was no longer an option since Nixon had already resigned from office. Instead, Watergate Special Prosecutor Leon Jaworski researched if he was able to undo the pardon in order to prosecute Nixon as a private citizen. Ultimately, Jaworski "came to the conclusion that a President had a Constitutional right to grant a pardon, regardless of his motives."[3]

The press, which had lost interest in merely reporting news developments, now went on the offensive. The *Washington Post* referred to the pardon as "a cover-up." The *New York Times* said it was an attack on the "integrity of the Government."

About a week after the pardon was issued, Nixon called Ford late one night. According to Ford's notes of the call, Nixon offered to reject the pardon if that would help matters and stem the flood of criticism Ford was receiving. Ford rejected the generous offer outright.[4]

The public and political outcry continued for weeks. They were cries of a deal, with speculation that Ford promised Nixon a pardon in return for Ford's ascension to the presidency. It reached a point that Ford thought the only way to resolve the matter and finally put it to rest would be to appear before Congress and testify on the matter. His horrified aides tried to talk him out of it. But Ford was resolute. He offered to testify.[5]

On October 17, 1974, President Ford appeared before the House Judiciary Subcommittee on Criminal Justice. According to Subcommittee chairman, Democratic Representative William Hungate of Missouri, it was the first time a president had testified before a congressional committee.[6] Ford's willingness to set the precedent might have been made easier by the fact that only ten months earlier, Ford was a sitting member of the US House of Representatives. He only became vice president in December 1973, following the resignation of Spiro Agnew.

Ford made it clear that he volunteered to appear before the committee in order to set the record straight on the circumstances and his reason for issuing Nixon a pardon. "I wanted to do all I could to shift our attentions from the pursuit of a fallen President to the pursuit of the urgent needs of a rising nation," he testified before the committee.[7]

Ford also testified that in early August 1974, when White House Chief of Staff General Alexander Haig told him that Nixon might possibly resign from office, the pair discussed a variety of scenarios. The half-dozen options ranged from Nixon remaining in office and daring the Congress to impeach him, to resigning. At no time, Ford insisted, was there ever a deal to pardon Nixon in return for his resignation.[8]

Ford was nominated by Nixon and confirmed by the Senate to fill the office of the vice president after Spiro Agnew resigned. Ford then became president when Nixon resigned. Ford was the first and only person to serve as both the vice president and president without having been elected to either office. His only race for the White House ended in November 1976 when Jimmy Carter defeated him.

Years later, Ford acknowledged that he anticipated his pardon of Nixon might possibly cost him the White House. "But if I hadn't pardoned Nixon," he later told his biographer, "we would have had a Nixon problem for two and a half years."⁹

Pardongate

There have been controversial presidential pardons since George Washington granted the very first one in 1795. However, there has never been such scandal over executive clemency as there was when 177 pardons and commutations were doled out by President Bill Clinton, literally in the dead of night, only hours before George W. Bush was sworn in as the 43rd president.

There are established Justice Department guidelines to be followed for every executive clemency application to ensure a basic level of qualification before an individual receives serious consideration. There are five major issues to be considered by the Justice Department's pardon attorney before forwarding a favorable recommendation to the president.

These issues include the applicant's post-conviction conduct, character, and reputation. First, has the applicant "demonstrated [an] ability to lead a responsible and productive life?" Second, the seriousness and recentness of the offense are to be considered to "avoid denigrating the seriousness of the offense or undermining the deterrent effect of the conviction." Third, the applicant should accept "responsibility, remorse and atonement" for committing the offense. Clemency is "[official] forgiveness rather than vindication." Fourth, does the applicant have a demonstrated need for relief? Pardon attorney guidelines note that a compelling need to restore employment licenses or bonding may make the difference in an otherwise marginal case. Lastly, input from "concerned and knowledgeable officials" is required. This is to allow prosecutors, trial judges, prison officials, parole officers, and victims to comment and/or make recommendations, either favorable or unfavorable.

The Department of Justice review also includes a rigorous criminal background check. This is to ensure an intended recipient has been forthright and honest in the clemency application and has led a law-abiding life since the commission of earlier crimes.

The Clinton family, staff, and Friends of Bill skipped due diligence and circumvented established DOJ procedures by appealing directly to Bill to issue clemency without any legal and criminal review. In dozens of cases, Clinton awarded pardons and commutations to individuals who did not even seek them and had therefore never submitted an application that would have undergone scrutiny to ascertain the facts. Others refused to accept responsibility for their crimes, a key component before gaining consideration.

Clinton handed out 177 executive clemency decisions during his last few hours as president. Forty-six recipients, or nearly one in three, did not have a current application on file with the Department of Justice when Clinton pardoned them or issued commutations. Thirty recipients had not submitted a clemency application at all. Another fourteen had previously filed applications, but Clinton had denied clemency. Two more lucky recipients had filed applications with the Justice Department, but they were deemed ineligible because they did not meet the bare minimum requirement of having waited five years since their release from imprisonment. Inexplicably, they all received executive clemency from Clinton.

The process became so absurd during the late hours of Clinton's final night as president that the pardon attorney had to resort to conducting internet searches looking for news stories of criminal involvement to determine an applicant's fitness for clemency. Dozens of the last-minute pardons and commutations were clearly undeserving. Some of those inappropriate clemency decisions were more scandalous than others.

Clinton executed a sharp break from the Justice Department standards and historical precedent and began issuing pardons and commutations to individuals who were defiant rather than contrite and remorseful. Several refused to acknowledge, let alone accept, responsibility for their crimes, a key component of DOJ guidelines to be considered for pardons or commutations.

Bill Clinton reviewed more than three thousand petitions for clemency from the day he took office until early August 1999. Compared to other recent presidents, Clinton was stingy in approving executive clemency requests. Of the 3,229 clemency requests that reached his desk during his first eighty months in office, he turned down every single one except for three. Clinton's disapproval rating was a stunning 99.9 percent. That is, until Hillary Rodham Clinton decided to run for the seat of New York's retiring US senator, Daniel Patrick Moynihan. Then everything changed.

When it was clear Hillary would run for the Senate, Bill dished out clemency to a dozen Puerto Rican terrorists who were guilty of a decade's worth of murder and domestic terrorism. Clinton even gave them the luxury of a month to decide to accept his offer of freedom in return for the simple agreement of not returning to a life of committing terrorism. The terrorists were conflicted and took the entire month before electing to accept the proffered clemency.

The pardon Clinton issued his last day in office that received the most press went to fugitive billionaire Marc Rich. His ex-wife Denise Rich was a close friend and mega-donor to the Clintons. She was a frequent guest at the White House,[10] having visited the White House on nineteen occasions, including sleepovers in the Lincoln Bedroom,[11] and Bill Clinton had visited the attractive, multimillionaire divorcée in her Manhattan penthouse.[12] Denise Rich gave $450,000 to the Clinton library,[13] $120,000 to Hillary Clinton's Senate campaign,[14] $40,000 to underwrite the entertainment at Hillary's October 2000 birthday bash,[15] $10,000 to the Clintons' legal defense fund,[16] and nearly $7,400 in gifts to Hillary.[17]

Marc Rich and his business partner, Pincus Green, fled the United States ahead of a fifty-one count federal indictment for tax evasion and other crimes, including trading with the enemy, which could have led to a sentence of 325 years in prison. The pair even renounced their US citizenship.[18] Yet, Clinton pardoned both.

Five days after Clinton pardoned him, Rich was at it again. Rich's company was buying oil from worldwide pariah Saddam Hussein as part of the UN's corrupt Oil-for-Food Programme.[19]

To be fair, critics can easily understand Clinton's pardon of his own half-brother, Roger Clinton, for a 1980s conviction for cocaine dealing. "If you can't give your brother a pardon," wrote Steve Dunleavy of the *New York Post*, "who can you pardon?" However, at the time, Roger was under active investigation by the Federal Bureau of Investigation and that fact alone should have immediately disqualified him from any consideration of giving him a pardon for drug dealing. Nevertheless, Bill Clinton pardoned him.

Clinton's many pardons and commutations were so indefensible that long-time Clinton apologist and former advisor Lanny Davis could not bring himself to write even a single paragraph of spirited defense of the clemency decisions in his book. Davis's *Scandal: How "Gotcha" Politics is Destroying America* was a noble effort to excuse and explain away Clinton scandals, but when it came to the pardons, Davis took a pass. For that matter, Hillary also skipped the topic entirely in her *Living History*.

For his part, Bill Clinton made a meager effort to explain away his scandalous pardons. He devoted barely three pages out of his nearly 1,000-page autobiography, *My Life*, to the matter. Not surprisingly, his comments were replete with one lie after another.

Among the many legitimate criticisms of the pardons was the fact that Hillary's brothers, Hugh and Tony Rodham, and Clinton's half-brother, Roger, profited from them.

Hugh Rodham was paid more than $200,000 to lobby President Clinton on a clemency request for Carlos Vignali, a drug dealer convicted of his role in conspiring to ship 800 pounds of cocaine into Minnesota.[20] Vignali's sentence was commuted to time served.

Rodham was also paid nearly $250,000 to prod his brother-in-law into issuing a pardon for Almon Glenn Braswell for his convictions for perjury and mail fraud. The US Attorney for Los Angeles had been investigating Braswell for a year and a half over allegations of money laundering and tax evasion—a fact which, taken alone, should have immediately disqualified Braswell from pardon consideration—when he was pardoned.[21] Two years later, Braswell was indicted, arrested, and pled guilty to the new federal charges.

Hillary's youngest brother, Tony Rodham, received nearly $250,000 in "consulting fees" around the time he was lobbying Clinton to pardon Edgar and Vonna Jo Gregory. The Gregorys were convicted of several federal bank-fraud charges and wire fraud. Rodham told CNN's *Larry King Live* in March 2001 that he asked Bill Clinton to pardon the couple.[22]

Roger Clinton and George Locke, who Roger served alongside in prison over his cocaine distribution conviction, partnered with

Dickey Morton to form CLM LLC. The company was most notorious for hustling pardons in 2000 to potential clients without delivering on their promises.[23] The trio made hundreds of thousands of dollars off gullible, pardon-seeking victims. Roger submitted to his brother a list comprising fewer than ten names of individuals Roger wanted his brother to pardon.

One of those promised a pardon was Garland Lincecum. He was sentenced to seven years in prison for fraud. Lincecum claimed he met with Morton and Locke, with Roger Clinton looking on, and finalized a deal to get a presidential pardon in return for $305,000. Lincecum was told his name would be among a list of six names that Roger was going to have pardoned before Bill Clinton left office.[24] Lincecum never received the pardon.

In contrast to the dozens of applications that received special consideration or head-of-the-line privileges due to Clinton family connections, there were another 7,032 clemency petitioners who had properly filed their applications months or years in advance. These applicants did not receive pardons or commutations.

When Clinton left office on July 20, 2001, he had not bothered reviewing 1,512 pardon and commutation applications that met all the guidelines, were properly investigated, and were forwarded to him by the Justice Department.

The Sedition Act

The United States was involved in an undeclared maritime war with France between 1798 and 1800 that was called the Quasi War. The war was the result of post-Revolutionary War differences with France and the thawing of frosty relations between the United States and Britain, which annoyed France.

Fearing a possible invasion by France, in 1798 the Congress passed, and President John Adams signed into law, the Alien and Sedition Acts. These were four separate laws, three of which dealt with alien issues, including naturalization and deportation matters. The fourth law was the Sedition Act. All four laws had a sunset clause, whereby they would expire on March 3, 1801, the day prior to the end of Adams's presidency.

These laws were overwhelmingly favored by the Federalist Party and were passed with very little opposition. The Federalists controlled most of the federal government, including nearly every important elected office, with the exception of the office of vice president. That office was occupied by Republican Thomas Jefferson. It was intentional and not an oversight that the vice president was not included among the protected institutions covered by the Sedition Act. Federalist officeholders were protected, but the Republican officeholder was not.

Enacted on July 14, 1798, the Sedition Act made statements that were critical of certain federal government institutions and officeholders a crime. According to the act, it was illegal for a person to "write, print, utter or publish...any false, scandalous and malicious writing [against Congress or the President]...or to excite against them...or to stir up sedition within the United States." Federalists did not hide their desire to use this law as a tool to silence Republican critics, especially Republican-leaning newspapers. There is no question this act was a direct violation of the First Amendment's speech protections.

Matthew Lyon was born in Ireland in 1749. When he was fifteen years old, Lyon traveled to Connecticut as an indentured servant.[25] By the time he was nineteen years old, he earned his freedom and resettled in the territory between New Hampshire and New York, which he later helped found as the state of Vermont. By age twenty-five, he joined the Green Mountain Boys regiment and later fought with the Continental Army in the Revolutionary War.

After the new American government was formed, Lyon ran unsuccessfully for the second Congress of the US House of Representatives in 1790. He was also unsuccessful in his candidacies for the third and fourth Congresses. In Lyon's case, the fourth time was the charm. He was elected to the fifth Congress as a Democratic-Republican for the term beginning in March 1797. Democratic-Republicans were generally referred to as Republicans.

In the early nineteenth century, the Democratic-Republican Party split up into two factions, with the Democratic Party arising from one group and the National Republican Party, and later the Whig Party, from the other. This faction was not the same as the modern-day Republican Party, which formed in 1854.

The Federalists had near-total control over the federal government. Aside from Jefferson in the vice president's office, the Republicans controlled very little. The Federalists and Republicans were on opposite sides of the major issues. Federalists wanted a stronger central government, desired closer ties with Britain, and generally favored the interests of the wealthy and educated class of landowners. The Republicans favored limited federal power, more power in the hands of the states, an alliance with France, and popular participation in government. The two parties were fierce political competitors. Lyon typified this fierce competitiveness.

Lyon was a staunch critic of President John Adams. Lyon wrote a letter that was critical of the president. It was sent to the *Vermont Journal* on June 20, but was not published until July 31, nearly three weeks after the Sedition Act was passed. In his letter, Lyon wrote that Adams was "swallowed up in a continual grasp for power, in an unbounded thirst for ridiculous pomp, foolish adulations and selfish avarice." Lyon further claimed Adam was responsible for "the sacred name of religion employed as a state engine, to make mankind hate and persecute one another." In other words, Lyon accused Adams of perverting Christianity to justify America's Quasi War with France.

Lyon's letter was written and sent about a month prior to the passage of the Sedition Act. This critical detail did not matter to the US Attorney for Vermont, Charles Marsh, because he was only concerned with the publication date.[26] On October 5, Lyon was indicted by a grand jury in the US Circuit Court for the District of Vermont.

The indictment referred to Lyon as a "malicious and seditious person and of a depraved mind and wicked and diabolical disposition and deceitfully wickedly and maliciously contriving to defame the government of the United States and…John Adams the President."

Lyon faced additional counts of violating the Sedition Act for having read aloud the poetry of Joel Barlow, who was an ardent critic of US foreign policy toward France.[27]

The US Marshal arrested Lyon on October 6 and brought him before a federal judge the following day to enter his plea. His trial began on October 9. Marsh was the federal prosecutor. Marsh argued that Lyon violated the law because of his published letter and for having read aloud Barlow's poetry in a manner that was "highly disrespectful to the administration."[28] Because there was no attorney available to represent him, Lyon represented himself in his two-hour defense.[29] Lyon's primary defense was twofold. First, he alleged he was a victim of *ex post facto*; he was being held liable for action taken before the proposed legislation became law.

US Supreme Court Justice William Paterson, who signed the Constitution, was presiding as the trial judge. He would not allow Lyon's *ex post facto* defense. Nor would he allow Lyon's second point, which was that the Sedition Act was in conflict with the First Amendment, making it an unconstitutional law.

The jury was composed entirely of Federalist Party members, as the marshal only solicited jurors from towns and villages that were known Federalist strongholds. At the end of the trial, the jury deliberated and found Lyon guilty of violating the Sedition Act for his published letter, as well as critical writings that were published in his pamphlet *The Scourge of Aristocracy, and Repository of Important Political Truth.*

Justice Paterson sentenced Lyon to four months in jail and fined him $1,000, plus court costs of $60.96. Lyon was immediately taken to jail to begin his sentence.

Complicating matters was that Lyon was in the midst of his reelection campaign for a second term in Congress. His prosecution, conviction, and imprisonment made him a martyr. He campaigned by writing letters and columns for his newspaper from his communal jail cell.[30] In spite of being incarcerated, Lyon won reelection in a landslide with 65 percent of the vote.

When Lyon was released from jail on February 9, 1799, he said, "I am on my way to Philadelphia." This was the seat of the US government at the time. On February 22, the House took up a resolution to expel Lyon from the House, but the measure failed. Lyon did not run for reelection from Vermont in 1800, but instead moved to Kentucky, where he was elected to four terms in Congress, beginning with the 1802 election.

On July 4, 1840, Congress passed legislation to refund Lyon's heirs his fine and court costs with interest.[31]

Kefauver Hearings

After World War II, there was concern in many cities that Prohibition-era gangsters were growing in size and influence in the post-war years. It was widely believed some politicians and bureaucrats were partnering with powerful criminal elements.

In 1950, the federal government was lobbied by the American Municipal Association, representing the nation's cities, to take action to stem the rise of organized crime. A number of local commissions found corrupt local government officials had been aiding and abetting organized-crime syndicates. In May 1950, the US Senate formed the Special Committee on Organized Crime in Interstate Commerce. The committee was chaired by Democratic Senator Estes Kefauver of Tennessee and became known as the Kefauver Committee.

The five committee members, Kefauver, Democrats Lester Hunt of Wyoming and Herbert O'Conor of Maryland, and Republicans Charles Tobey of New Hampshire and Alexander Wiley of Wisconsin, met in fourteen major cities around the nation over a fifteen-month period.

It was understood that investigating organized crime would take the committee to cities tightly controlled by Democrats. A Democrat, Kefauver realized this could be politically damaging to his own party. He was undeterred. Kefauver vowed to lead a "no stones unturned, no holds barred, right down the middle of the road, let the chips fall where they may" inquiry.[32]

More than six hundred witnesses were interviewed and testified, including governors, mayors, sheriffs, police officers, and organized-crime figures. Some contempt-of-Congress and local indictments resulted from the hearings.[33]

What made the Kefauver hearings unique was the subject matter, and that they were among the very first congressional committee hearings to be televised. When the committee arrived in New Orleans in January 1951, a local television station was granted permission to televise some of the hearings. In Los Angeles, a handcuffed mobster was brought before the committee to testify on television.[34] A pair of Detroit television stations followed suit in covering the Motor City hearing. By the time the hearings moved to New York City, a phenomenon had already developed. Five of the city's seven television stations broadcast a week's worth of hearings. People were glued to their television sets. It became theater to watch committee members grill members of organized crime.

The original plan was for the special committee to conclude its hearings by the end of February 1951. The public interest was so high that the Senate extended the committee by six months to conclude on September 1, 1951.

Committee investigators and lawyers would arrive ahead of the full committee to conduct interviews and issue subpoenas. The hearings were impactful in many ways, including revelations of how many federal, state, and local elected officials had ties to organized crime. Democratic Florida Governor Fuller Warren narrowly survived an impeachment attempt by the Florida legislature for refusing to cooperate with the committee.

Public interest in the Kefauver hearings reached a fever pitch in March 1951. One hearing included the testimony from mob boss Frank Costello, who headed the Luciano crime syndicate, one of the five organized-crime families that ruled New York. Unlike other members of organized crime subpoenaed to appear before the committee, Costello refused to invoke his Fifth Amendment protections against self-incrimination and instead chose to testify.

A condition of Costello's testimony was that the television cameras were not to show his face. Instead, the cameras focused on his hands. Costello's hands were fidgety and made for compelling television viewing. It is estimated that there were approximately six million television sets in American homes in early 1951. Yet, an estimated thirty million people watched some of the most dramatic hearings. It seemed every set in America was tuned to the Kefauver hearings.

The televised hearings were so influential, they catapulted freshman Senator Kefauver to political stardom. He ran for president in 1952 and beat incumbent President Harry Truman in the New Hampshire primary. Truman reevaluated his candidacy for reelection and withdrew. Kefauver won the most Democratic primaries but lost his party's nomination to Adlai Stevenson, who lost the 1952 general election to Dwight Eisenhower. In the 1956 general election, with Kefauver as his vice-presidential running mate, Stevenson would again lose to Eisenhower.[35]

One legislative development credited to the Kefauver hearings was the Racketeer Influenced and Corrupt Organizations (RICO) Act, passed in 1970.

Kelo

US Naval Submarine Base New London is actually located opposite of New London on the other side of the Thames River in Groton,
Connecticut. However, located in New London was the Navy Undersea
Warfare Center, an underwater-sound research facility that traced its
origins to World War II. In 1996, the center's activities were consolidated with a facility in Rhode Island and the Undersea Warfare Center
was closed.

The closure of the Warfare Center represented a loss of about 1,500
jobs that hurt a small city already faced with high unemployment. So,
the city turned to its dormant New London Development Corporation
to help turn things around. The NLDC was a private, nonprofit organization that was chartered to aid development within the city of New
London. The NLDC crafted a plan to redevelop the Fort Trumbull area
of New London.

The plan called for a major development, anchored by a research
facility of pharmaceutical giant Pfizer Inc., and joined by other office
buildings and limited housing. The plan would "create in excess of
1,000 jobs...[and] increase tax and other revenues."[36] The city approved
the NLDC plan in January 2000 and conferred authority on the NLDC
to either purchase property or seize it in order to make way for the
planned development.

The theory behind the plan was that the businesses and residents
of the revitalized Fort Trumbull would pay more in tax revenues
than the existing 115 properties. The existing properties comprised
mostly single-family dwellings and rental properties, forming a
quaint New England neighborhood. Among those homeowners was
eighty-two-year-old Wilhemina Dery, who had lived in the same
home since her birth in 1918. Her husband, Charles, had lived in the
home since the 1940s.

The NLDC began offering to buy out the current property owners
to make way for the development. Many voluntarily sold their homes,
although the term "voluntary" was subject to interpretation. It was
widely understood that anyone who would not sell their property
could expect to have it condemned and then seized by local authorities.
Reportedly, owners who were initially reluctant to sell were subjected to

harassment, including "late night phone calls…[and] dumping of waste on their property."[37]

Eventually, all of the existing property owners sold out, with the exception of nine owners of fifteen properties. Ten of the properties were owner-occupied, and the other five were rental properties. The owners were led by Susette Kelo.

Acting on behalf of the City of New London, the NLDC began condemnation proceedings against the holdouts. The city wanted to condemn the properties and then seize them using eminent domain. An important point was that neither the city nor its development arm, the NLDC, ever declared the community or the properties blighted. Such a declaration is common before a jurisdiction would attempt to seize property using eminent domain. The City of New London relied on the fact that collecting more tax revenues fulfilled the "public use" criteria within the meaning of the Takings Clause of the Constitution's Fifth Amendment.

Kelo and her fellow homeowners sued the City of New London in Connecticut court. They were represented pro bono by a public-interest law firm, Institute for Justice. After a lower court split-decision of sorts, both parties appealed to the Connecticut Supreme Court. In 2004, Connecticut's high court ruled 4–3 that the takings were constitutional. In fact, all seven justices believed the takings were constitutional, but the three dissenting justices "would have imposed a 'heightened' standard of judicial review for takings…because the City failed to adduce 'clear and convincing evidence' that the economic benefits of the plan would in fact come to pass."[38]

The petitioners appealed to the US Supreme Court, which agreed to hear the case. In an opinion authored by Justice John Paul Stevens, the Supreme Court ruled 5–4 in favor of the takings. In the majority opinion, Stevens acknowledged "it has long been accepted that the sovereign may not take the property of A for the sole purpose of transferring it to another private party B." He also acknowledged that the condemned property would not be made available for "use by the general public. Nor will the private lessees of the land in any sense be required to operate like common carriers, making their services available to all comers."[39]

Stevens also wrote that there was precedent to condemning property that had been ruled "blighted." Yet, the Fort Trumbull properties had not been deemed blighted. Notwithstanding valid arguments to rule against the city, the high court majority decided the seized properties did, indeed, serve a "public benefit." Moreover, the Supreme Court majority "decline[d] to second-guess the City's considered judgments about the efficacy of its development plan."[40]

Not content with the Supreme Court victory, the City of New London hit the *Kelo* plaintiffs with bills for property taxes and $33,000 in overdue rent. City officials took the position that ever since the condemnation in November 2000, the petitioners were squatters living on property that did not belong to them and therefore owed the city $600 monthly rent payments for the nearly five years the litigation took place.[41]

Republican Governor Jodi Rendell successfully negotiated a settlement among the homeowners and city officials. The city dropped its claim of back rent and increased the amount of money it would pay the owners for the seized property. The NLDC took control of the properties and the homeowners were forced to vacate their homes and move elsewhere. But the redevelopment of the Fort Trumbull area never occurred as promised.

In early 2019, the neighborhood where Charles and Wilhemina Dery and their neighbors once lived sits vacant. The homes were long ago bulldozed to make way for the planned development and envisioned tax riches for the New London city elders. The Boston-based development firm that was given exclusive rights to develop more than ninety acres of Fort Trumbull couldn't arrange financing. Pfizer lost interest in the property after its 2009 merger with another pharmaceutical giant, Wyeth, and elected to move its research facilities elsewhere. The New London Development Corporation was disestablished and replaced by a similar development group, the Renaissance City Development Association. The RCDA has been unsuccessful in several attempts to fully develop Fort Trumbull.

The large swath of Fort Trumbull where a proud neighborhood of 115 homes once stood was designated in 2011 a public-waste site by city officials for area residents to dump storm debris.

Going for the Win

Shortly after the September 11, 2001, terror attacks, seventeen people became ill from the effects of the deadly bacteria, anthrax. Another five died. Three letters containing anthrax spores were mailed to public figures in Washington, DC, and New York City. Two of the fatalities were postal workers at a Washington, DC, mail facility. It is presumed they were exposed to anthrax contained in one or perhaps both of the two letters mailed to Democratic Senators Tom Daschle of South Dakota and Patrick Leahy of Vermont.

It is believed three other deaths were tied to whoever was behind the first two letters, but that has only been conjecture. An employee of the *National Enquirer* parent company was fatally stricken in Florida, a ninety-four-year-old woman in Connecticut died, and a Manhattan clerk perished from anthrax infection. No letters or other devices that carried anthrax spores were ever recovered in those deaths. About the same time, three hoax letters containing harmless powder were mailed from Florida to various recipients.

The nation was uneasy. The September 11th attacks were fresh on everyone's mind. It was immediately presumed foreign agents from either al Qaeda or Iraq were responsible. There was intense pressure on federal investigators to apprehend a suspect or suspects.

Robert Mueller was the newly appointed director of the Federal Bureau of Investigation, the lead agency in the anthrax investigation. Mueller took over an FBI reeling from a very bad decade in the 1990s. The agency bungled several high-profile operations, sometimes at the cost of millions of dollars in settlements, and at other times resulting in the tragic loss of human life.

An FBI sniper executed an improper shoot-to-kill order and fatally shot a woman holding a baby during the 1992 standoff at Ruby Ridge, Idaho.[42] FBI Special Agent Van Harp was embroiled in the illegal shoot-to-kill order coverup. A Justice Department investigator recommended Harp be disciplined.[43] Instead, he was promoted.[44] The U.S. government paid a multimillion-dollar settlement over the tragedy.

The FBI took over from the Bureau of Alcohol, Tobacco and Firearms as the lead law enforcement agency in the 1993 siege of the Branch Davidians complex in Waco, Texas. The FBI operation ended disastrously, causing the fiery deaths of seventy-six worshippers, including twenty children.[45]

The FBI was caught completely unaware when immigrant Islamic jihadists, encouraged by a prominent US-based radical sheikh, carried out the 1993 World Trade Center bombing. Only good fortune prevented the North Tower from toppling into the South Tower. Still, six people died and more than one thousand were injured.

The FBI fingered security guard Richard Jewell as the 1996 Olympic Park bomber. Jewell was initially hailed as a hero for discovering a pipe bomb before it exploded. The bomb detonated before everyone at the park could be safely evacuated. One person was killed and more than one hundred were injured. In spite of his heroics, the FBI insisted Jewell was the bomber. Acting on FBI leaks, several news organizations defamed Jewell. Months later, the FBI cleared Jewell, and the real perpetrator was eventually caught. Jewell received financial settlements from several news outlets for defaming him.

In 1999, the FBI accused US scientist Wen Ho Lee of stealing nuclear secrets and passing them to China. He was jailed in solitary confinement for nearly a year while the FBI attempted to build a case against him. No criminal case could be made against Lee and he was released from imprisonment with an apology. The US government paid him a seven-figure settlement.

For two decades, the FBI allowed informant Whitey Bulger to continue his crime spree. His criminal activity included countless murders. The agency let the Irish mobster and his crime family do as they please in return for tips on the Italian mafia. Bulger only passed on worthless information. FBI Special Agents John Connolly and John Morris were accomplices to Bulger's criminal activity, including murder. The FBI complicity with Bulger became public in 1997.

The FBI involvement with Bulger was so corrupt that the agency permitted the murder conviction of four innocent men, Peter Limone, Joe Salvati, Henry Tameleo, and Louis Greco, by allowing a witness to lie, and by withholding exculpatory evidence in order to protect another informant and Bulger criminal accomplice. Three of the four men were given death sentences. Their sentences were later changed to life imprisonment.[46]

In the 1980s, the acting US Attorney for the Massachusetts District pressured the Massachusetts Parole Board to keep the framed men imprisoned. That federal prosecutor was Robert Mueller, who would become the FBI Director two decades later. The four innocent men were eventually exonerated after serving more than three decades in prison, after secret FBI files revealed the bureau's corruption. The men were paid a settlement of nearly $102 million, although only two received the money directly, since Tameleo and Greco died in prison. Mueller's knowledge of the FBI and Whitey Bulger scheme has never been fully explained.[47]

Then there was the granddaddy of them all. The FBI and the rest of the intelligence community were asleep at the switch as twenty Muslim immigrants took flight lessons in order to fly jumbo jets into buildings during the 2001 terror attacks.

All of this tremendous baggage meant the FBI desperately needed a big win in order to restore public trust in the agency. It was now faced with that opportunity as long as it could solve who was behind the fall 2001 anthrax attacks. FBI Special Agent Van Harp, of Ruby Ridge coverup infamy, was placed in charge of the investigation.

Progress was slow going, even though more than one thousand agents combed leads. The agency was under tremendous pressure from Senators Daschle and Leahy. Then, scientist Barbara Rosenberg began piecing together a profile of the type of individual she thought might be responsible, hinting it was a government employee who worked in biomedical research. Rosenberg began posting her analysis on the internet and some in the media weighed in, bringing attention to her theory.

Three months after the anthrax letters appeared, *New York Times* columnist Nicholas Kristof penned a column titled, "Profile of a Killer." Kristof described the perpetrator as an American working in one of the military's biological weapons program.[48]

In a few months' time, Kristof began taunting the FBI in column after column for its failure to find the anthrax killer. The "anthrax killer remain[s] at large" and could wreak panic by "send[ing] out 100 anthrax letters," Kristof wrote.[49] The "failure to capture the anthrax killer [is] suggesting to Iraq and other potential perpetrators that they might get away with an attack" and it was time "to light a fire under the FBI."[50]

Kristof began making references to an unnamed American who worked at the US Army Medical Research Institute of Infectious Diseases at Fort Detrick, Maryland, as the likely culprit. Kristof later admitted that numerous FBI agents were feeding him information on the investigation.

While the FBI was feeding Kristof information, Kristof was using this inside knowledge to bash the agency for "bumbling," "lackadaisical ineptitude," "lethargy," and "plodding in slow motion." Kristof identified an individual who federal investigators would later call a "person of interest." Kristof merely referred to him as "Mr. Z."[51] Kristof would continue to mock the FBI for being "unbelievably lethargic in its investigation," while suggesting his Mr. Z was also involved in anthrax hoaxes in the 1990s.[52]

The constant criticism by the *New York Times* may have spurred the FBI to take public action. FBI agent Harp did not like coming under outside pressure. The FBI asked and received permission in June 2002 to search the Fort Detrick-area apartment of Steven Hatfill, a medical doctor who once worked at the Army medical research facility. Nothing was found. After a month of weathering heavy criticism, the FBI returned for another search. This time agents were armed with a search warrant and had live-television-news crews in tow.

The FBI had previously been quietly talking to Hatfill. However, that discreet investigation came to an end and the renewed investigation of Hatfill was a full-fledged media circus. There were as many as two- to three-dozen persons of interest, but the FBI decided to make Hatfill's investigation a public relations spectacle. Somebody, presumably inside the FBI, tipped off the media.

The FBI employed a scorched-earth policy toward Hatfill. He was fired by his government contractor. The teaching position he lined up at Louisiana State University ended the day it was to begin, after the FBI pressured the university to cancel his employment.

Agents began openly questioning family, friends, acquaintances, and coworkers. Hatfill's picture was flashed to the locals in Princeton, New Jersey, where it was believed the two known anthrax letters were mailed.[53] He was brazenly tailed by FBI agents like paparazzi chasing a celebrity. On one occasion, an FBI agent drove over Hatfill's foot with a sports utility vehicle. The driver was not charged, but a local police officer issued Hatfill a jaywalking ticket.

Hatfill escaped to his girlfriend's condominium in northern Virginia in order to get some peace. In response, the FBI installed a camera on a post aimed at the condo. Agents were stationed out front.

The harassment did not stop. One day, Hatfill was twice stopped for lane-change violations by two different police officers only minutes apart. It seemed every cop had his number. News organizations pondered when the killer was going to be jailed.

Hatfill was working on a novel about a bioterrorism attack. The only copy of the novel was on the computer the FBI confiscated from his home. Excerpts from the novel appeared in the press.[54] There were media reports that Hatfill took Cipro before the anthrax attacks. Cipro is an antibiotic often used to treat anthrax exposure, as well as other bacterial infections. The media reports did not include the fact that Hatfill was prescribed Cipro by his doctor to treat an infection after sinus surgery. Someone inside the FBI was leaking to the media.

Media reports claimed Hatfill had access to anthrax at Fort Detrick. To the contrary, Hatfill did not have access to the highly secure facility where contagious bacteria such as anthrax were stored. Hatfill was a virologist and worked in a completely different section of biomedical research.

Hatfill had previously visited a friend at his rural home in northern Virginia. The *New York Times* called it a "safe house." The *Times* implied he was involved in a massive genocidal anthrax attack on thousands in Rhodesia, where he attended medical school.[55] Actually, the Rhodesia anthrax was natural-borne from a diseased cattle herd.

An FBI consultant analyzed the two brief notes in the anthrax letters. One was fifteen words long, the other twenty-four words. He also looked at the hoax letters. Then he penned a 9,600-word article in *Vanity Fair*, in which he named Hatfill as the "suspect" behind the anthrax letters.[56]

The FBI leaked to the press that it flew in from California three dog-handlers and three bloodhounds when agents first searched Hatfill's apartment. The dogs supposedly "hit" on Hatfill. What was not reported in the press was the two major bloodhound organizations, the Law Enforcement Bloodhound Association and the National Police Bloodhound Association, reported those handlers and their hounds as being unreliable for criminal investigations.[57]

There was not one scintilla of physical evidence tying Hatfill to the anthrax attacks. He had ironclad alibis for the times the letters were mailed. He voluntarily took and passed a polygraph test. The FBI could not produce one plausible motive for Hatfill to carry out the attacks. Yet, the law-enforcement agency persisted in pointing the finger at the scientist as the likely culprit.

The FBI's orchestrated leaks of half-truths and misinformation may have been intended to force Hatfill to crack. FBI agent Harp admitted he had personally leaked information to at least a dozen journalists. Hatfill had become so hated by the public that he stopped leaving his girlfriend's condo. He remained indoors for weeks at a time, became depressed, and began drinking heavily. He later said suicide was never an option because it would have allowed the FBI to posthumously declare him guilty.

It was highly unprofessional and possibly legally suspect that the FBI was leaking so much information to so many media outlets. That this was occurring with regularity in such a high-profile investigation suggests it was being done with the approval of FBI Director Mueller.

In late 2003, Hatfill finally sued the Justice Department, the FBI, and several news outlets. Hatfill's ironclad alibis and the complete lack of evidence tying Hatfill to the anthrax letters forced the FBI to tacitly admit it had been harassing an innocent man. The federal government took the rare step of formally exonerating Hatfill of involvement in the anthrax attacks and paid him a nearly $5-million settlement. Several news organizations also reached settlements with Hatfill.

Hatfill's lawsuit against the *New York Times* was eventually dismissed. The courts ruled Hatfill had a higher burden to prove the newspaper acted maliciously because he was a "public figure." The irony is Hatfill was completely anonymous and only became a public figure after the FBI, the *New York Times*, and others falsely accused him of mailing the anthrax letters.

The FBI then turned its attention to another Fort Detrick biomedical researcher, Bruce Ivins. The agency's treatment of Ivins was eerily similar to its harassment of Hatfill. Ivins was searched, investigated, his wife and daughters were questioned, and he was publicly followed wherever he went. The FBI portrayed him as an imperfect man with character flaws. This meant Ivins was just like millions of other people. Damning circumstantial evidence offered by the FBI included the fact that Ivins owned handguns. Yet, like the Hatfill case, the FBI did not uncover one credible piece of physical evidence tying Ivins to the letters.

Ivins descended into depression after a year of around-the-clock surveillance and harassment. On July 29, 2008, Bruce Ivins took his own life. A week later, the FBI declared Ivins the sole source of the anthrax letters and the agency closed the case. The FBI finally got a win.

Several scientific experts claim the FBI lacked the evidence to reach the conclusion Ivins was the source of the anthrax letters.[58] Ivins's colleagues insist the FBI got the wrong man.[59]

Waterboarding

At a press conference marking his one-hundredth day as president, Barack Obama denounced as torture the techniques US officials used sparingly during what was referred to as an "increased pressure phase" when interrogating the September 11th mastermind and two other senior al Qaeda operatives. Obama announced his administration would not prosecute CIA officers who used the tactics, but he left open the possibility of punishing others, including senior Bush administration officials.

Obama referred to the techniques described in a Justice Department memorandum as "a dark and painful chapter in our history." However, it was striking that Obama refused to concede that the interrogation of three major al Qaeda figures by using such techniques kept the United States safe by thwarting at least one major terrorist attack following September 11, 2001. More than half of what the CIA knew about al Qaeda came from the three senior figures who were waterboarded.[60]

The interrogation procedures are identified in an August 1, 2002, memo from the Justice Department's Office of Legal Counsel (OLC).[61] The memo detailed ten different techniques permitted to be used under strict control and under the direct supervision of medical professionals to protect the physical and mental health of the al Qaeda leaders. Some of these techniques were used on about a dozen high-value prisoners.

None of these techniques involved the breaking of arms and legs, gang-raping of women while male family members were forced to watch, or hanging from ceiling shackles while a tormentor applied electricity, as was performed by the Saddam Hussein government.

Any reasonable reading of the OLC memo would reach a different conclusion than Obama's torture characterization of the techniques. The following are examples of what Obama labeled torture.

One technique is the "facial hold." According to the memo, "The facial hold is used to hold the head immobile. One open palm is placed on either side of the individual's face. The fingertips are kept well away from the individual's eyes."

There is "walling," where "the interrogator pulls the individual forward and then quickly and firmly pushes the individual into [a flexible, false] wall...[T]he head and neck are supported with a rolled hood or towel that provides a c-collar effect to help prevent whiplash. To further reduce the probability of injury, the individual is allowed to rebound from the flexible wall...[T]he idea is to create a sound that will make the impact seem far worse than it is."

"Cramped confinement" consists of an individual being placed in a confined space. The individual is able to stand or sit down in the larger confined space and may only sit in the smaller space. The individual may be confined in the larger space for up to eighteen hours and only two hours in the smaller space.

This differs markedly from the cramped confinement technique used in US military interrogation training. The US Navy version of the confinement box was much more confining than the version approved for use on the al Qaeda terrorists. In the Navy version, the subject cannot stand, fully sit, or completely lay down, forcing the individual to assume a contorted position. A Navy trainee may be locked in the box overnight, while al Qaeda terrorists are limited to only two hours.

Then there is the dreaded insect technique. Interrogators would tell the individual they "intend to place a stinging insect into the [confinement] box with him. [Interrogators] would, however, place a harmless insect in the box...such as a caterpillar." This technique was used against one prisoner who had a fear of insects.

Another enhanced interrogation technique is "wall standing," in which "the individual stands about four to five feet from a wall, and his feet spread approximately shoulder width. His arms are stretched out in front of him, with his fingers resting on the wall. His fingers support all of his body weight."

It was waterboarding that garnered the most attention, because this is the technique CIA personnel used when interrogating three senior al Qaeda officials. Obama stated, "I do believe that [waterboarding] is torture." The *New York Times* labeled it "gruesome," "shocking," and "near-drowning."[62] In fact, it is none of the three.

In waterboarding, the "individual is bound securely to an inclined bench...A cloth is placed over the forehead and eyes. Water is then applied to the cloth in a controlled manner...[as] the cloth is lowered until it covers both the nose and mouth." While performing this technique "air flow is slightly restricted for 20 to 40 seconds...[creating] the perception of drowning." Most importantly "the individual *does not breathe any water into his lungs* [italics added]." A medical professional observed waterboarding to ensure no prisoner was harmed.

Waterboarding was performed on three senior al Qaeda figures: Abu Zubaydah, Ramzi bin al-Shibh, and Khalid Shaikh Mohammed. Zubaydah was captured in March 2002, but was uncooperative and refused to answer many questions, prompting the CIA to request a legal determination to see if enhanced interrogation techniques were permitted. This request resulted in the OLC memorandum.

Zubaydah gave valuable information that led to the capture of bin al-Shibh, whose information led authorities to Mohammed, the confessed mastermind behind the September 11 attacks and the man who personally decapitated *Wall Street Journal* reporter Daniel Pearl. Mohammed was also involved in the planning of the bombings of the World Trade Center in 1993 and Indonesia's Bali nightclub in 2002 that killed more than 200.

The chain of events that led to the capture of Shaikh Mohammed in March 2003 began when Zubaydah broke down after a mere thirty-five seconds of waterboarding in summer 2002. After his subjection to waterboarding, Mohammed revealed intelligence that allowed US officials to disrupt a post-9/11 follow-up terrorist attack planned for Los Angeles and other West Coast targets.

Waterboarding was used in interrogation only in 2002 and 2003.[63] The *New York Times* falsely reported that Mohammed and Zubaydah were waterboarded an astonishing 266 times.[64] Other news organizations echoed the claim. Yet, that number was not true, according to both men. The pair told Red Cross officials they were collectively waterboarded less than fifteen times.[65]

Yet, waterboarding "darken[ed] the country's reputation [and] blur[red] the moral distinction between terrorists and the Americans who hunted them," editorialized the *New York Times* in a news article that ignored the intelligence value of the information gleaned from using the technique. Such denunciation is ironic coming from a newspaper located in the same city where nearly three thousand were killed in a terror attack masterminded by one of the three men being waterboarded.

In fact, the four military services have used waterboarding for years in their search, evasion, resistance, and escape training for aircrew and special-forces personnel. The Navy has subjected personnel to waterboarding as an interrogation technique since the 1970s. The Air Force administered waterboarding to more than 25,000 personnel in the ten-year period prior to the 9/11 attacks. Overall, tens of thousands of US servicemen and women have been waterboarded since the early 1990s.

Over a thirty-year career as a Navy pilot, Captain Ken Kropkowski attended survival, evasion, resistance, and escape training more than once at the US Navy's Remote Training Site in Warner Springs, California. He was thrown against a wall, spent a night in a confinement box with a hood on his head while his interrogators banged on the box to deprive him of sleep, was forced to undergo wall standing until his arms gave out, and endured waterboarding. Twice. Waterboarding is not torture, according to Kropkowski. "There's no pain actually. I don't see how you can equate that with torture," he said. "There's no trauma. There's no lasting effect."

Media criticism of waterboarding only began in 2005, after it was learned that the Bush administration approved use of the techniques with high-value prisoners from the war in Afghanistan. There was media disinterest in the technique in the previous three decades when it involved US military personnel.

Obama's opposition to a non-lethal, non-injurious form of interrogation used on known terrorists is in stark contrast to his position that he possessed the authority to order deadly drone strikes against Americans.

Obama ordered more drone strikes in his first year in office than George Bush ordered during his entire presidency. During his eight-year presidency, Obama is known to have ordered nearly 550 drone strikes that killed nearly 3,800, including 324 civilians. In 2011, he quipped to his aides, "Turns out I'm really good at killing people. Didn't know that was gonna be a strong suit of mine."[66] In 2018, a former staffer wrote Obama "saw the necessity of drones."[67]

On September 30, 2011, a drone strike killed Anwar al-Awlaki, a US citizen born in New Mexico, who became a Muslim cleric and was associated with al Qaeda on the Arabian Peninsula. This first US drone strike in Yemen in nearly a decade also killed another American citizen, Samir Khan, from North Carolina. The Obama administration had added al-Awlaki to its "kill list" in 2010.

Two weeks later, on October 14, a drone strike killed Abdulrahman al-Awlaki, the sixteen-year-old son of the American cleric. The Obama administration claimed he was an al Qaeda militant in his twenties. The family produced a birth certificate showing the boy was born in Denver in 1995. The family said the boy was killed with several other teenagers who were having an evening barbecue.[68] There was no known information tying the teen to any terror activity.

In 2009, Obama left open the possibility of prosecuting attorneys in the Justice Department's Office of Legal Counsel for writing a memo stating non-lethal enhanced interrogation techniques were legal. In 2011, Obama relied on another memo from the Office of Legal Counsel, now staffed with his appointees, which stated that he had the authority to order fatal drone strikes against American citizens.[69]

In a speech before Northwestern University School of Law, US Attorney General Eric Holder elaborated on the Obama administration's opinion that there existed presidential authority to order drone strikes targeting Americans. Holder emphasized the relevance of "the Fifth Amendment's Due Process Clause, which says that the government may not deprive a citizen of his or her life without due process of law." However, this due process is met, Holder argued, not by any judicial approval, but merely by the president making a decision that an American posed a potential threat and therefore was deemed a legitimate target.[70]

Wrongful Conviction

It was during the lead-up to Operation Iraqi Freedom that President George W. Bush delivered his 2003 State of the Union address. Bush's January 28 speech was widely viewed as outlining the evidence and rationale for a US-led war against Iraq. In his speech, Bush relayed intelligence passed on to the United States by British Intelligence. Bush said,

"The British government has learned that Saddam Hussein recently sought significant quantities of uranium from Africa." This line later became known as the "sixteen words" by Bush's political opponents.

In an address to the United Nations Security Council in March 2003, the head of the International Atomic Energy Agency testified on the topic of an alleged sales agreement between Iraq and Niger, a major source of yellowcake uranium often used in nuclear weapons production. According to the director, a senior Iraq official visited Niger in February 1999. Nonetheless, the atomic energy agency reached the conclusion the yellowcake uranium sales agreement between Iraq and Niger was "not authentic."[71]

On July 6, 2003, the *New York Times* published an op-ed titled "What I Didn't Find in Africa," by Joseph Wilson, a retired diplomat. Wilson, a fierce critic of Bush, reported he traveled to Niger in 2002 to confirm the British intelligence claim. Wilson, who undertook a similar trip to Niger in 1999, was recommended for this assignment by his wife, Valerie Plame.[72] At the time, Plame was working as an analyst at the Central Intelligence Agency.[73]

Wilson wrote that he spent "eight days drinking sweet mint tea" and asking Nigerien officials if the African nation sold yellowcake uranium to Iraq. They told him they did not. Satisfied there was no uranium sale, Wilson returned to the United States to report what he learned. His *Times* column suggested the US intelligence community should have accepted his findings over that of British Intelligence counterparts, and therefore, he argued, the United States "went to war under false pretenses."[74]

About a week later, newspaper columnist Robert Novak wrote that CIA officials dismissed Wilson's findings as "less than definitive" and his report probably never reached the desk of CIA Director George Tenet. This is likely why Tenet never questioned the "sixteen words" when he reviewed the draft of Bush's prepared remarks. In his column, Novak also wrote that Wilson's wife was "an agency [CIA] operative on weapons of mass destruction."[75]

It was that revelation that led Bush's critics to claim the Bush administration was retaliating against Wilson for his pointed criticism of the Iraq war's rationale. Years earlier, Plame worked undercover in Europe as a CIA case officer; however, she no longer met the criteria of the

Intelligence Identities Protection Act of 1982. That act made it a criminal offense to knowingly disclose a CIA employee's identity.

Nonetheless, a firestorm raged over who leaked the identity of Valerie Plame. The White House announced its full and complete cooperation in any probe.

On December 30, 2003, US Attorney General John Ashcroft recused himself from supervising the investigation into the Plame affair in order to avoid even an appearance of a conflict of interest, since critics insisted the White House was engaging in dirty tricks. Deputy Attorney General James Comey, in his capacity as the acting Attorney General in this matter, named his close friend US Attorney Patrick Fitzgerald a special counsel to determine if any laws were broken by revealing Plame's employment.

Deputy Secretary of State Richard Armitage immediately notified Fitzgerald that he had revealed Plame's identity to Novak during a casual conversation earlier that summer. Armitage claimed he did not realize Plame had previously worked undercover. Fitzgerald asked Armitage to keep this admission a secret. Armitage agreed.[76]

At this point, it was obvious that no one at the White House had leaked Plame's name, as critics suggested. Fitzgerald chose not to prosecute Armitage. Instead, he focused his attention on White House officials. Even without any evidence, the popular narrative in the press was that the White House had orchestrated an attack on Wilson. "It is appalling...the president should allow anyone on his staff to reveal the identity of a covert CIA agent," opined the *Arizona Daily Star*.[77]

According to the *Washington Post*, Wilson was certain White House advisor Karl Rove was behind the alleged attack. Wilson said he wanted to see "Karl Rove frog-marched out of the White House in handcuffs."[78] Democrats insisted it was either Rove or Vice President Dick Cheney's chief of staff, Lewis "Scooter" Libby, who was behind the leak.[79]

The *Post* went even further than most news outlets and claimed, "two top White House officials called at least six Washington journalists and disclosed the identity and occupation of Wilson's wife."[80] Further, the *Post* quoted an unnamed administration officially allegedly saying, "Clearly, it was meant purely and simply for revenge."[81]

As the special counsel investigation revealed, no one in the administration leaked Plame's name or her employer, underscoring that the sensational *Washington Post* report was demonstrably false.

In his investigation, Fitzgerald subpoenaed *New York Times* reporter Judith Miller to appear before a grand jury and reveal the sources of her 2003 reporting on Iraq. It was believed Miller and Libby might have spoken in July 2003, even though Miller did not write a story regarding Wilson or Plame.

Miller refused to reveal her sources, instead vowing to protect their confidentiality. Fitzgerald sought and received a contempt of court ruling and had Miller jailed. One of the sources Miller spoke with was Libby. Confident he didn't reveal Plame's name, Libby sent a letter to Miller reaffirming his earlier waiver to confidentiality and telling her, "Your reporting, and you, are missed." Libby implored Miller to feel free to reveal the conversations she had with him and he ended his letter with the lines: "Out West, where you vacation, the aspens will already be turning. They turn in clusters, because their roots connect them. Come back to work—and life."

Ironically, it was Miller's testimony that proved critical in convicting Libby. The other nine journalists who testified at Libby's trial testified he never mentioned Plame's name.[82]

In her reporter's notebook, Miller had written the four-word phrase in parentheses, "(wife works in Bureau?)." After her release from jail, Miller couldn't recall with whom she had spoken or the context of the phrase she had written more than two years earlier. Fitzgerald helped her out. As he prepared Miller for her grand jury testimony, Fitzgerald convinced her that the four-word phrase was a reference to Libby having told Miller that Joe Wilson's wife, Valerie Plame, worked at the CIA. That is exactly what Miller testified to the grand jury and later testified at Libby's trial.

Miller's testimony contradicted Libby. He testified he never revealed Plame's name. Based on Miller's testimony, Libby was convicted of perjury, obstruction of justice, and making false statements. He was sentenced to thirty months in prison and fined $250,000.

In 2010, Judith Miller was reading Valerie Plame's memoir *Fair Game*, which had been published three years earlier. Plame wrote that in 1989, she began an assignment at the US Embassy in Athens, Greece, where she assumed the cover of working for the State Department.[83] When Miller read that passage, the light went off. Plame's memoir finally put into context the four-word phrase Miller wrote in her notebook.

Miller realized the State Department is organized in *bureaus*. The CIA is organized in *divisions*. Libby knew Plame worked at the CIA, where they have divisions. He did not know of Plame's brief cover as a State Department employee, where they had bureaus.

Miller was able to put it all together. If Libby had mentioned Plame and her employment, he would never have mentioned "bureau," because they do not have bureaus at the CIA. And if Libby had mentioned Plame and "bureau," then he did not leak her CIA employment. No matter which way it went, it was obvious Libby never committed a crime.

Miller recalled that, at about the same time she had spoken with Libby, she had also interviewed several people from the State Department. Miller then realized her four-word phrase likely referred to a conversation with a State Department employee who may have thought Plame worked there. Miller was overcome by guilt. "Had I helped convict an innocent man?" she wrote in her memoir.[84]

Miller realized Fitzgerald had manipulated her by steering her toward the narrative that Libby had told her Plame was a CIA employee. Making this obvious was the fact that Fitzgerald had Plame's classified employment record and probably knew that Miller's "bureau" reference in her four-word note referred to Plame's time at the State Department and not any employment with the CIA.

Fitzgerald refused to turn over to Libby's attorneys Plame's classified employment records, as they had requested. If Fitzgerald had, Libby's attorneys might have immediately cleared up Miller's recollection regarding the meaning of the four-word phrase. However, it wasn't really necessary for the Libby defense team to request Plame's employment records. Fitzgerald had a legal and ethical duty to turn over to the defense any exculpatory evidence. He had such evidence, but he did not turn it over or even disclose it.

So, if Fitzgerald knew Libby never committed a crime, then why was he so hell-bent on charging him with one? The real goal of Fitzgerald's investigation became obvious. Miller began digging after she read Plame's memoir and realized an innocent man had been convicted. Miller spoke with Libby's lawyer, Joseph Tate. Tate relayed a conversation he had with Fitzgerald, when he asked the special prosecutor why he was pursuing an innocent man. According to Tate, Fitzgerald told him, "Unless you can deliver someone higher up—the vice president—I'm going forth with the indictment."[85]

Fitzgerald already knew there was no orchestrated leak of Plame's name. In fact, no one was ever charged with leaking her name, although that was the sole reason James Comey appointed Fitzgerald as special counsel. Fitzgerald was charged with the "investigation into the alleged unauthorized disclosure of a CIA employee's identity."

Fitzgerald's efforts were not about uncovering who leaked Plame's identity. He learned that Armitage leaked her identity only days after his appointment as special counsel. Fitzgerald's goal was to get Libby to "flip" and offer Cheney's head on a platter. No person was more hated by the political left than Dick Cheney. An innocent man was convicted of a crime he did not commit in an attempt to "get" Cheney.

Apparently believing at the time that the conviction was just, President George Bush commuted Libby's prison term on July 2, 2007, but left in place the $250,000 fine Libby was ordered to pay.

On April 13, 2018, more than a decade after the conviction, President Donald Trump pardoned Scooter Libby.

CHAPTER 13

ENTERTAINMENT

"The narrative was properly about race, sex and class...We went a beat too fast in assuming that a rape took place...We just got the facts wrong. The narrative was right, but the facts were wrong."[1]

—Evan Thomas, Managing Editor, *Newsweek*, commenting on the alleged Duke lacrosse team gang rape

Fatty

Roscoe Conkling Arbuckle was the one of the first mega stars of Hollywood. He was a child prodigy who could sing, dance, and make the audience laugh with his antics. He was one of the breakout stars of the silent-movie era. By the time he was thirty years old, Arbuckle signed an unheard of $1-million-a-year contract with Paramount Pictures.

Born in 1887, Arbuckle was a sixteen-pound baby at birth and was chubby as a child. Because both his parents were slender, his father presumed the child was not his, so he named the baby after Roscoe Conkling, a disgraced New York politician caught up in the Crédit Mobilier scandal (see chapter 9). Roscoe was extremely heavy as an adult and was known by the nickname Fatty, which he absolutely hated. He began show business when he was just a youngster in the late-nineteenth century, and by the time he was in his teens, he was touring with vaudeville troupes.

After he married petite actress Minta Durfee in 1908, the pair occasionally performed together. In 1910, the Arbuckles joined a tour that traveled to Hawaii, China, Hong Kong, and the Philippines. Upon their return, Arbuckle transitioned from vaudeville to movies.[2]

Starting in the 1910s, Arbuckle began appearing in so-called "one-reelers." These were the short black-and-white shows that were only one movie reel, or about ten minutes in length. Fatty Arbuckle was a bona fide star. Only Charlie Chaplin was more famous.

On September 3, 1921, Arbuckle and a couple of friends, Fred Fishback and Lowell Sherman, who were perhaps Hollywood's first-ever entourage, set off on a road trip from Los Angeles to San Francisco. They were driving Arbuckle's $34,000 Pierce-Arrow Model 66 convertible touring car. It cost nearly one hundred times more than a new Ford Model T, which was sold for just under $400.[3] The three were going to let down their hair and have some fun over the Labor Day weekend.

The trio rented three rooms on the top floor of the St. Francis Hotel. One suite was designated the party room, to which several women were invited on Labor Day Monday. On September 5, after a day and night of heavy-duty carousing among fifteen to twenty guests, one partygoer became extremely ill. Aspiring actress Virginia Rappe became inconsolable, claiming she was in extreme pain in her abdominal area. The hotel doctor diagnosed her as extremely intoxicated and gave her morphine to ease the pain and calm her down.

Prohibition had gone into effect eight months earlier, so the hotel revelers were drinking illegal, and in some cases bootleg, alcohol. This may have figured into the physical distress of Rappe. Apparently, she suffered chronic cystitis, and the condition was exacerbated by alcohol. Observers thought poorly made bootleg booze was to blame.[4] The three different doctors who examined her over two days diagnosed her as the victim of alcohol poisoning.[5]

Rappe's condition had not improved, so she was taken to a sanitarium on September 7. Wakefield Sanitarium had a reputation for performing abortions. The following day, she died of peritonitis from a ruptured bladder. Suspicion immediately fell on Arbuckle as the cause of the ruptured bladder. He was so heavy, it was presumed his large size and heavy weight may have caused her bladder to rupture when he was raping her, as one of Rappe's companions had alleged. There were uncorroborated claims that Arbuckle raped Rappe with objects ranging from a soda bottle to a chunk of ice.

The prosecutor initially charged Fatty Arbuckle with murder and then reduced the charged to manslaughter in the death of Virginia Rappe.

Arbuckle went to trial on November 14, 1921, a little more than two months after Rappe's death. This was yet another "Trial of the Century."

Public interest in the trial was fueled by the Hearst newspaper empire. William Randolph Hearst was the king of yellow journalism, and the Arbuckle trial represented a great business opportunity. The Hearst papers flogged the trial and spun up readers with salacious stories and unconfirmed rumors. That Arbuckle spent that Labor Day partying while still dressed in his pajamas and bathrobe only fueled the image of a partying playboy. Arbuckle became a hated man.

On December 4, a mistrial was declared after the jury was reported to be deadlocked after five days of deliberation. This led to a second trial that began on January 11, 1922. That trial, too, resulted in a deadlocked jury and a mistrial declaration.

A third trial began on March 13, 1922. Four weeks later, the jury was sent to the jury room for deliberation. Six minutes later, the jury was ready to return to the courtroom to render its verdict. Not only did the jury find Fatty Arbuckle not guilty, but it also wrote a letter of apology to Arbuckle. The jury believed Arbuckle suffered a miscarriage of justice to have to undergo three trials when "there was not the slightest proof adduced to connect him in any way with the commission of a crime."

Relieved at finally being exonerated, Arbuckle issued a statement that signaled his intentions. "[A]fter the quick vindication I received I am sure the American people will be fair and just. I believe I am due for a comeback."[6] Although Arbuckle had finally been exonerated, the damage had been done. His Hollywood career was over. The Motion Pictures Producers and Distributors of America banned Arbuckle from ever again working in the motion-picture industry.[7]

Arbuckle was forced to sell his home and many of his possessions in order to pay the nearly $750,000 in legal bills he accumulated in defending himself in court.

Black Sox

Long before baseball players had a players' union, before collective bargaining agreements, and before free agency, players were limited on where to play big-time baseball. Decades ago, Major League Baseball had the reserve clause, which required a player to get the team owner's release before playing for another team.

This was also a time when players were sometimes on teams with stingy owners. Baseball was America's pastime and big games were big business. Yet some players had to scrape by financially.

Heading into the 1919 World Series, several players on the dominant Chicago White Sox were willing to accept a bribe to throw the series and allow the underdog Cincinnati Reds to win.[8] At least one gambler agreed to pay $100,000, to be split among the cooperating players.

First baseman Charles "Chick" Gandil was the ringleader among the players. He conspired with a pair of gamblers, Joseph "Sport" Sullivan and Bill "Sleepy" Burns, to craft the plan. Gandil held the initial meeting among the players in on the fix in his New York hotel room during a late-season road trip. These players included Eddie Cicotte, Claude "Lefty" Williams, Oscar "Happy" Felsch, Charles "Swede" Risberg, George "Buck" Weaver, and Fred McMullin.[9]

An eighth player implicated in the scandal was "Shoeless" Joe Jackson. Jackson did not attend the two player meetings where the fix was discussed,[10] yet he still received a $5,000 payment from the gamblers. It was the height of irony that Jackson led all batters during the series, suggesting he may have never tried to throw the game.

It's generally agreed, but not definitively proven, that mob boss Arnold Rothstein was funding the $100,000 bribe.[11] The signal that the players agreed on to start the fix was that pitcher Cicotte was to strike the game's first batter with the second pitch of game one, on October 1, 1919. Cicotte hit the batter and the fix was on.[12]

The World Series fix happened to be one of the worst kept secrets. It appeared many gamblers knew, or at least speculated, that there was a plan to throw the series. Betting on the underdog Reds dramatically boosted the odds, making the series nearly even money. Eventually, the Reds won the best-of-nine series, 5–3.

Sport scholars today are not exactly certain which gamblers and which players were involved. There were so many confessions, recanting of confessions, grand jury testimonies, and incidents of finger-pointing that it's understandable if there is skepticism over who was involved, who paid a bribe, and who received a bribe.

It is widely agreed that the game's best hitter, "Shoeless" Joe Jackson, never attended any of the player meetings, but he still got a piece of the action.

The performance of some of the players during the World Series was so uncharacteristic that sports reporter Hugh Fullerton of the *Chicago Herald-Examiner* actually took notes.[13] This would come into play later.

Rumors of the fix swirled around the White Sox the following season. However, it was not until late in the 1920 season that a grand jury was empaneled to look into the allegations. Pitcher Eddie Cicotte confessed his role to the grand jury, telling them, "I don't know why I did it...I needed the money. I had the wife and kids."[14] In short order, eight players came under suspicion.

White Sox club owner Charles Comiskey wasted no time in suspending the players still on his team's roster, even though the Sox were in a neck-and-neck race with the Cleveland Indians to win the American League pennant. Seven of the eight players involved in the scheme still played for the White Sox. The eighth player, Chick Gandil, did not return to the Sox for the 1920 season. Instead, he was playing for a semi-professional team.

In late October 1920, the grand jury indicted the eight ball players and five gamblers, Abe Attell, Bill "Sleepy" Burns, Billy Maharg, Arnold Rothstein, and Joseph "Sport" Sullivan.[15] A trial began in June 1921. Some of the evidence that was going to be presented at the trial was mysteriously missing. This included the signed confessions of Cicotte and Jackson, who coincidentally recanted their earlier confessions.

After three hours of deliberations, the jury returned not-guilty verdicts for all defendants. They could return to playing baseball, or so they thought.

Major League Baseball was attempting to clean up its image. The league's governing body, the National Commission, was viewed as ineffective. So, the club owners persuaded retired federal judge Kenesaw Mountain Landis to take over management. Landis's requirement was that he not chair the National Commission, but instead assume the role of sole Baseball Commissioner. In addition, he insisted on unbridled authority to make binding decisions that were in the best interest of baseball.

Days after the eight players were exonerated, Landis issued his own order:

Regardless of the verdict of juries, no player who throws a game, no player who undertakes or promises to throw a game, no player who sits in confidence with a bunch of crooked ballplayers and gamblers, where the ways and means of throwing a game are discussed and does not promptly tell his club about it, will ever play professional baseball.

Buck Weaver had attended the two meetings where a fix was discussed, but he declined to be a participant. However, Landis's proclamation stipulated that those with knowledge of throwing a game who failed to come forward were also banned, including Weaver.[16]

Fred McMullin was a utility infielder, who saw very little playing time in the 1919 World Series and was invited to join the other players involved in the fix. He was only included because he overheard the players scheming and insisted that he be cut in for the bribe or he would turn in the players.

Some have assumed the moniker Black Sox resulted from the eight ballplayers who cheated in the World Series. However, it's been reported the nickname arose long before the scandal. White Sox club owner Comiskey was notoriously stingy. One way he cut costs was to reduce the frequency with which club officials washed team uniforms. According to legend, the players' uniforms got so filthy, they began to look black, hence the nickname, Black Sox.

Wardrobe Malfunction

There was an incredible buildup to Super Bowl XXXVIII. The game was played on February 1, 2004, at Reliant Stadium in Houston, Texas. The Carolina Panthers were something of the Cinderella team. The Panthers were an expansion team that began in 1995. During the 2001 season, the Panthers finished with only a single win, versus fifteen losses.

The New England Patriots were coming off a 14–2 record and featured a young quarterback who had captured Super Bowl MVP honor only two years earlier, after the Patriots registered their own improbable run and upset a heavily favored opponent.

The game lived up to the hype. The two teams set a Super Bowl record by scoring a combined thirty-seven points in the fourth quarter. The game was tied at twenty points each, with just over one minute to play, when Patriots quarterback Tom Brady marched New England down the field. The game ended in exciting fashion, as New England place-kicker Adam Vinatieri kicked a forty-one-yard field goal in the final seconds to win the game.

While the Super Bowl is typically among the most-watched US television events each year, Super Bowl XXXVIII set the record as the most-watched Super Bowl of all time. Nearly 144 million viewers watched some or all of the game.[17]

Super Bowl XXXVIII is considered by many sports enthusiasts as among the greatest Super Bowls of all time. Super Bowl XXXVIII is also known for the halftime entertainment, which became a scandal.

Singing the national anthem prior to the start of the game and performing at halftime are coveted opportunities for musicians. Paul McCartney, the Rolling Stones, the Who, U2, Bruce Springsteen, Michael Jackson, Lady Gaga, Beyoncé, and Madonna are just a few of some of contemporary music's greatest performers who were the featured halftime entertainment at Super Bowls over the years.

The halftime entertainment for Super Bowl XXXVIII featured Janet Jackson, Justin Timberlake, Jessica Simpson, Kid Rock, Nelly, and P. Diddy. The nearly twelve-minute performance consisted of extravagant stage visuals, dozens of dancers, strobe lights, and smoke. This has become the standard formula for nearly every Super Bowl halftime performance.

This performance set itself apart from the others by what occurred in the closing moments. Jackson performed her chart-topping, Grammy-nominated song "Rhythm Nation" and was then joined by Justin Timberlake for a duet performance of his gold-record song "Rock Your Body." The two pop stars engaged in several suggestive dance moves throughout their duet. As the performance drew to a close, Timberlake pulled Jackson's bustier, uncovering her right breast as he sang the final line, "Bet I'm gonna have you naked by the end of this song."

There were many conflicting accounts of what happened, versus what was supposed to happen, versus who was in the know and who engineered the act. The official account from nearly everyone involved was that the baring of Jackson's breast was a wardrobe malfunction.

No matter the cause, the Federal Communications Commission did not find the incident amusing. It fined the CBS television network $550,000 for airing Jackson's naked breast.[18] CBS paid the fine and then challenged it in federal court. After an eight-year legal battle that included a pair of appeals to the US Supreme Court, a Third Circuit Court of Appeals decision vacating the fine stood as the final word on the legal matter.[19]

Presumed Guilty

The Duke University men's lacrosse team threw a party on the night of March 13, 2006. The party was held just off campus at a house that was the residence for the senior players. Alcohol was in abundance. One of the players called an escort service to hire a pair of exotic dancers to entertain the team. He was told two girls would arrive at 11:00 p.m. for a two-hour performance.

Single mother of two Crystal Mangum was a student at North Carolina Central University, a predominately black college, located only a few miles from the Duke campus. Mangum had been working off-and-on as a stripper since at least 2002.[20] She arrived at the players' residence at 11:40 p.m., about a half-hour after Kim Roberts, the other dancer. Mangum had difficulty standing. Each dancer was given $400.

After about a fifteen-minute performance, there were crude and vulgar taunts traded between the players and strippers regarding sex toys and penis sizes. The women stopped dancing, causing some of the players to leave the house. After about forty minutes of back-and-forth discussion, the dancers left the premises. Immediately thereafter, house residents asked all the partygoers to leave before the neighbors registered noise complaints.

Both women got into Roberts's car. A player assisted Mangum because she was obviously impaired. Mangum later admitted she had mixed alcohol and prescription narcotics before arriving at the party. After the women left, Roberts called 911 and reported she was called a racial slur by one of the players. The police arrived to investigate, but the house was vacant. Everyone had already left.

The women got into a heated exchange after they left. Roberts stopped at a supermarket and requested the store security guard assist her in removing Mangum from her car. The security guard called the police, who arrived and removed Mangum.

Officers found Mangum to be impaired and not in complete control of her faculties. The officers took Mangum to Durham Center Access, a mental-health crisis and detoxification treatment facility, for evaluation. It was at the center that Mangum claimed she had been violently gang-raped. According to Mangum, several players separated her from Roberts and forcibly dragged her into a bathroom where she was choked, beaten, and gang-raped over a period of about a half-hour. Mangum was immediately transferred to Duke University Medical Center for a thorough medical examination.

The sexual assault examination did not show any of the physical injuries typically associated with the attack Mangum claims she suffered. Medical authorities did observe some swelling in her genitals. Mangum said this was caused by using a vibrator while performing at an earlier engagement elsewhere that evening.

On March 14, Durham police launched an investigation that violated standard law enforcement investigation protocols.[21] On multiple occasions, police showed Mangum photo lineups, asking her to identify her attackers. The lineups consisted only of photos of the lacrosse-team players.

Test results from Mangum's sexual assault examination revealed DNA from several males was found on her underwear and inside her, including from her boyfriend. However, DNA results excluded all of the players as potential assailants in the alleged sexual assault. Mangum gave as many as a dozen different versions of her alleged attack. She identified lacrosse players from lineups she claimed were at the party, but were proven to be elsewhere. Kim Roberts, the other stripper, told investigators she was with Mangum the entire evening except for a few minutes and that Mangum's numerous claims were lies.

Roberts later changed her story and suggested there may have been an attack. She also contacted a New York public-relations firm asking for advice on "how to spin this to my advantage."[22]

Nonetheless, Durham County District Attorney Michael Nifong gave dozens of media interviews claiming with certainty that a rape had occurred and some of the players were guilty of the attack. In spite of the abundance of contradictory evidence, Nifong's insistence a crime was committed may have been bolstered by questionable police behavior.

Durham police were accused of intimidating a witness in an attempt to get him to recant the alibi he had given on behalf of one player who was not present.[23] In his thirty-three-page investigative summary, police investigator Sergeant Mark Gottlieb made statements that often differed from all other available evidence.[24] According to a published report, Gottlieb had a history of targeting Duke University students, often arresting them for misdemeanors that warranted the equivalent of a parking ticket.[25]

In July 2006, the conduct of some Durham police officers came under scrutiny when two of them, including Gottlieb, were involved in an off-duty brawl outside a sports bar.[26]

By the middle of May, three players had been arrested on charges of kidnapping, first-degree sex offense, and first-degree forcible rape. David Evans, Collin Finnerty, and Reade Seligmann, if convicted, were facing decades-long prison sentences.

Nifong was intent on pursuing criminal charges against the three players in spite of significant amounts of exculpatory evidence. Seligmann was not present at the house during the time of the alleged assault and had ample evidence proving he was elsewhere. As was later revealed, the testing lab Nifong hired to perform a second round of DNA tests was instructed by Nifong to withhold certain exculpatory evidence that cleared the three players.

Because there was no evidence a rape had taken place, on December 22, 2006, Nifong was forced to drop the first-degree forcible rape charges against Evans, Finnerty, and Seligmann, yet he continued with the kidnapping and sexual offense charges.

A week later, the North Carolina State Bar filed a seventeen-page complaint of ethics charges against Nifong for professional misconduct. In January 2007, the State Bar filed more serious charges against Nifong of withholding evidence and lying to the court. By then, North Carolina Attorney General Roy Cooper had taken over the case.

In April 2007, Cooper announced that all charges against Evans, Finnerty, and Seligmann were dropped, and he declared the players to be innocent. Cooper declined to file charges against Mangum for making false claims.

While the criminal investigation was underway, Duke University officials made a rush to judgement. In a public letter titled "What Does a Social Disaster Sound Like?" eighty-eight Duke faculty members abandoned due process and presumed the players guilty. The Duke lacrosse team head coach, Mike Pressler, was forced to resign. Duke University President Richard Brodhead canceled the team's season. Heading into the season, the team was favored to win the national championship after finishing as runner-up the previous year.

The New Black Panthers arrived in Durham offering to provide security and then protested outside the Duke University Campus. Jesse Jackson promised his Rainbow/PUSH Coalition would pay for Mangum's college tuition even if she were lying so she wouldn't "have to stoop that low to survive."[27]

The players never stood a chance in the court of public opinion. National media outlets published stories that flogged the scandal's narrative of quintessential political correctness. Privileged white boys who attended elite prep schools were playing a sport not found on the inner-city playgrounds. They assaulted a minority female, a single mother of two, who was doing whatever was necessary just to make ends meet.[28]

The *New York Times* denigrated the athletes by describing them as "a clubby, hard-partying outfit with roots in the elite prep schools of the Northeast."[29] The paper's former public editor called the *Times'* coverage "everything that's wrong with American journalism."[30] The biggest sin, according to a *Newsweek* article, may have been that most of the Duke student body was "white and privileged."[31] That May 1, 2006, edition of *Newsweek* had a cover photo of a lacrosse player emblazoned with the title "Sex, Lies & Duke."

A CBS News report cherry-picked details that presented an impression of events that did not occur.[32] The *Washington Post* editorialized the accused were "[a] bunch of jocks at an elite university in the once-segregated South—privileged white kids who play lacrosse, a sport that conjures images of impossibly green suburban playing fields surrounded by the Range Rovers of doting parents."[33] The paper criticized the "cone of silence that has descended on the lacrosse team" because none of the players confessed that a rape occurred.[34]

Even a news columnist in the local newspaper, the Raleigh *News & Observer*, got into the act, stating matter-of-factly that the athletes "were just a little too drunk, a little too 'worked up.'" The paper added, "Every member of the men's lacrosse team knows who was involved, whether it was gang rape or not." "Shut down the team," the paper blasted.[35]

The false rape allegation scarred the lives of so many. The falsely accused players were victims of confrontations, threats, public criticism, and damaged reputations. Some players were given failing grades as retaliation by activist faculty.[36] The house that was the residence of some of the players was torn down.

Crystal Mangum, who had an extensive criminal record including car theft, saw her life spiral further downward. In November 2013, she was convicted of murder in the stabbing death of her boyfriend and was sentenced to prison for thirteen to eighteen years.

In 2007, disgraced Durham County District Attorney Michael Nifong was unanimously disbarred from practicing law by the North Carolina State Bar over several ethical and legal concerns. It was widely speculated Nifong pursued the case because he was locked in a tight election race for the Democratic nomination for district attorney and was appealing for black votes. Nifong was appointed to the position following a vacancy, and polling had him substantially trailing his opponent.[37] Nifong was later jailed for making false statements to the court.

In 2014, Mark Gottlieb, the Durham police sergeant in charge of the Duke lacrosse investigation, who built a reputation of unfairly targeting Duke students, took his own life.

Duke University settled lawsuits with lacrosse players David Evans, Collin Finnerty, and Reade Seligmann, and lacrosse coach Mike Pressler, for the rush to judgement that defamed all four. According to various reports, Duke paid the players as much as $20 million each. Duke also settled a lawsuit by thirty-eight other lacrosse players. Terms were not disclosed. According to one estimate, Duke spent as much as $100 million to undo the damage school officials created by ignoring due process and treating the athletes as violent gang rapists.

Even today, some activists refuse to acknowledge the incontrovertible facts years after they became widely known. A 2016 *Vanity Fair* article claims the North Carolina State Bar "was used to subvert justice" by calling out Nifong's unethical behavior. Implying a gang rape may have still occurred, *Vanity Fair* stated, "We'll never know what really happened in that bathroom."[38]

"He Misremembered"

Dominant is a word often used to describe Major League Baseball pitcher Roger Clemens. He played for nearly a quarter-century on four different teams: the Boston Red Sox, Toronto Blue Jays, New York Yankees, and Houston Astros. He had 354 wins, 4,672 strikeouts, and an earned-run average of 3.12. He won an amazing seven Cy Young Awards and he was an eleven-time all-star and two-time World Series champion. Without a doubt, Roger Clemens is among the greatest baseball pitchers of all time.

But was some of his longevity and achievements due to cheating?

By the 1990s, Major League Baseball had a growing problem with baseball players using illegal performance-enhancing drugs, including human growth hormones and anabolic steroids. Team owners wanted a comprehensive testing program for substance abuse. The players' union opposed mandatory random drug testing. Finally, an agreement was reached in 2002.

In March 2006, baseball Commissioner Allan "Bud" Selig hired George J. Mitchell to lead an independent investigation into the use of illegal performance-enhancing drugs by major-league players. Mitchell had previously served as US Senate Majority Leader and was the US Special Envoy to Northern Ireland under President Bill Clinton.

More than seven hundred interviews were conducted with baseball players, staff, and others associated with Major League Baseball.[39] The final report was delivered to the commissioner of baseball in December 2007. Among those named in the report as having used performance-enhancing drugs was Roger Clemens. A major source for the allegations of Clemens's use was Brian McNamee.

McNamee was hired as the strength-and-conditioning coach for the Toronto Blue Jays in 1998. This was just after Clemens joined the club. Also new to the club was Jose Canseco.[40] According to the Mitchell report, Clemens approached McNamee in June 2008 and asked McNamee to inject him with the anabolic steroid Winstrol. McNamee injected Clemens with Winstrol several times over a period of time.[41]

Clemens was traded to the New York Yankees in 1999, and McNamee was hired by the club the following year. According to McNamee, he was employed by the Yankees as the assistant strength-and-conditioning coach and was simultaneously working for Clemens as his personal trainer. McNamee claimed he injected Clemens with testosterone and human growth hormone in 2000 and testosterone in 2001.[42]

Jose Canseco wrote a book about his Major League Baseball career. In his kiss-and-tell memoir, he wrote he'd "never seen Roger Clemens do steroids." However, he claimed Clemens often talked about the benefits of steroids. Canseco also claimed Clemens used the phrase "B12 shot," which Canseco said was code for a steroid injection.[43]

The Committee on Oversight and Government Reform in the US House of Representatives decided it should investigate the baseball steroid scandal. The days leading up to the hearing took on a bit of a circus-like atmosphere, observed one member. Clemens was posing for photographs and signing autographs with House members and staffers during office visits.[44]

On February 13, 2008, the committee convened a hearing that included three witnesses. Joining Roger Clemens and Brian McNamee at the witness table was Charlie Scheeler, who served as an investigator for the Mitchell team.

There appeared to be a partisan divide among the committee members during the four-and-a-half hour hearing. Republicans appeared to believe Roger Clemens, while Democrats were in the Brian McNamee camp. The tone of some committee members was evident. Democratic Congressman Elijah Cummings of Maryland immediately began hectoring Clemens as he kicked off the questioning.

Cummings: I first want to make sure that you're very clear. You understand that you're under oath, is that correct?

Clemens: That's correct, Mr. Cummings.

Cummings: And you know what that means. Is that correct?

Clements: That's correct.

Cummings: Very well.

McNamee stunned the committee when he stated that he saved a used needle and bloody gauze pads he said he used when injecting Clemens. The pitcher's DNA, McNamee claimed, would be found on these items. He turned them over to the Justice Department for DNA testing. Officials later reported the needle contained traces of Clemens's DNA and steroids.[45]

Later, as Republican Representative Dan Burton of Indiana was wrapping up his questioning, he shared the following remarks with McNamee.

Burton: You're here as a sworn witness. You're here to tell the truth. You're here under oath. And yet we have lie, after lie, after lie, after lie, where you've told this committee and the people of this country that Roger Clemens did things that—I don't know what to believe. I know the one thing I don't believe, and that's you.

Adding to the drama of the hearing was the revelation that a sworn statement was given to the committee by Andy Pettitte. Pettitte was a then-retired major-league pitcher who was a Yankees teammate of Clemens and remained his friend after both retired from the professional sport. In his February 4 statement, Pettitte claimed Clemens told him that Clemens had used human growth hormone.

When Cummings challenged Clemens with Pettitte's statement, Clemens responded, "I believe Andy has *misheard*." Clemens further offered, "My problem with what Andy says, and why I think he *misremembers* is that if Andy Pettitte knew that I had used HGH…he would have come to me and asked me about it."

On several other occasions during his testimony, Clemens accused Pettitte of *misremembering* what occurred.

According to news reports, there were at least a half-dozen FBI agents sitting in the committee hearing room.[46] With so many G-Men in attendance, one can only wonder if some of them were present only to ask for an autograph.

Although Democrats and Republicans lined up behind their respective men during the hearing, there was bipartisan agreement after the hearing that Roger Clemens had not been truthful. On February 27, 2008, the committee sent a referral to the Justice Department suggesting an investigation be opened regarding Clemens's testimony.

In January 2009, a grand jury was convened to hear evidence regarding Clemens's committee testimony. Clemens was indicted in August 2010 on perjury and obstruction charges.

Clemens's first trial began the following year, but ended quickly after the judge declared a mistrial. Clemens's second trial began the following summer and lasted nine weeks with a slew of witnesses called to testify.

In June 2012, Roger Clemens was acquitted of all charges.

The Movie Executive

There is no shortage of men and women in Hollywood who will advocate for nearly any cause. Protecting an endangered species. Safeguarding an obscure religion. Standing vigilant for the environment. But for decades, the one thing they did not stand up for was the safety of women in the clutches of a serial sexual predator.

Harvey Weinstein was an incredibly successful Hollywood film executive. He and his brother, Bob, founded independent film distributor Miramax. They ran it for twenty-five years before leaving and launching the Weinstein Company in 2005. Harvey was known as a brash, mercurial producer, prone to fits of rage, but apparently beloved by countless actors and actresses. He racked up industry recognition and awards by the armload.

Weinstein was known for supporting numerous social causes. In discussing his motivation for promoting a 2012 documentary on bullying, Weinstein said, "I have four daughters, and this is a movie about making the world better for them."[47]

Weinstein had powerful friends in powerful positions. He was chummy with Barack and Michelle Obama and Bill and Hillary Clinton. Weinstein was a major political fundraiser for Obama.[48] In 2017, he gave an internship to the Obamas' oldest daughter.[49] He threw a $33,000-a-head presidential fundraiser for Hillary Clinton in 2016.[50] He was a major fundraiser for Democratic politicians and liberal causes.

Weinstein was given a neverending list of awards and recognition by advocacy groups and others. He was made an honorary Commander of the Order of the British Empire, which is just below Knighthood and two positions above the Member of the Order of the British Empire title awarded to Beatle John Lennon. There were likely few people Weinstein could not immediately get on the telephone.

In fall 2017, former MSNBC host Ronan Farrow was in the final weeks of a ten-month-long investigation regarding Weinstein. Several women had gone on the record with Farrow alleging Weinstein had sexually harassed, sexually assaulted, or raped them. Days before his blockbuster 7,500-word story was to run in *New Yorker* magazine,[51] the *New York Times* scooped Farrow on the exclusive.[52]

Weinstein's behavior may have been news to the general public, but reporting since the scandal first broke indicates it had been an open secret in the entertainment industry for decades.

Weinstein had a years-long modus operandi. He would identify a young, attractive, aspiring actress and offer to meet with her in a public location, such as a hotel restaurant, in order to discuss an acting role. Oftentimes, a female assistant to Weinstein would meet the wannabe actress, only to inform her the meeting was moved to Weinstein's suite.

The actress would enter Weinstein's hotel room to find chilled champagne and fresh strawberries waiting. Shortly after arriving, Weinstein would excuse himself, only to return moments later dressed in only a bathrobe and holding a container of oil. He would ask the actress to give him a massage that would quickly turn into a sexual assault or coercion to perform oral sex on Weinstein, with the understanding that a Hollywood career hinged on compliance.

Little can match the sheer depravity of Weinstein's reported bad behavior. However, the fact that so many in the entertainment industry knew of it, but chose to do nothing, is equally disturbing. For many actors, actresses, and film executives, Hollywood fame and fortune were more important than anything else. Of the many employees in Weinstein's own companies who witnessed or knew of Weinstein's predatory behavior, very few reported it or quit their jobs.[53]

Some of Weinstein's employees called it "a culture of complicity."[54] In 2015, one Weinstein Company employee who alleged to have been the victim of sexual misconduct by Weinstein wrote a letter to company executives claiming, "There is a toxic environment for women at this company."[55] The company executives apparently did nothing.

The *Times* story claimed that Weinstein reached settlements with eight women over sexual misconduct. Even with a trail of allegations and settlements, Weinstein still kept his job.

Weinstein's attorney was Lisa Bloom, who earned a reputation representing women who were the victims of sexual assaults and unwanted sexual contact. In the early days of the scandal, Bloom defended Weinstein as "an old dinosaur learning new ways."[56] It is doubtful Bloom would have accepted such an excuse if her client was one of Weinstein's alleged victims.

Weinstein's defense was the belief that the many sexual encounters were consensual. According to Weinstein, he was just too gosh-darned nice to people. He said, "In the past I used to compliment people, and some took it as me being sexual, I won't do that again."[57]

Collectively, there were about a dozen women in the *New York Times* and *New Yorker* articles who claimed to have been victims of Weinstein. In a matter of months, that number grew to fifty,[58] sixty-three,[59] eighty-two,[60] or eighty-three,[61] depending on who was counting.

The battle of which media outlet would be the first to report the Weinstein sex scandal was between the *New York Times* and the *New Yorker*. Yet, NBC News had the story months earlier. However, news executives ordered Ronan Farrow to shut down his investigation. This led to Farrow leaving NBC News and taking the story to the *New Yorker*.[62]

CHAPTER 14

MEDIA

"When considered over all, Mr. Blair's correction rate at The Times *was within acceptable limits."*[1]

> —*New York Times* May 11, 2003 article describing the early performance of Jayson Blair before he began churning out plagiarized works, fabricated quotes, factual errors, and falsified datelines in dozens of articles.

The Anti-Semite

Helen Thomas was the doyenne of the Washington, DC, press corps. She had a long and storied career and spent nearly every day of it covering events in the nation's capital. She became a White House correspondent for United Press International covering presidents, starting with John Kennedy and ending with Barack Obama. She had covered the White House for so long that she had a chair reserved for her in the front row of the White House Briefing Room.

Thomas registered a lot of firsts. She was the first woman to join the White House Correspondents Association, the first woman to join the Gridiron Club, and the first woman to be an officer of the National Press Club.

Although Thomas was employed as a news correspondent, she did little to conceal the fact she was politically liberal. Her questions often began with a left-of-center point-of-view. A colleague once wrote Thomas's questions "left little doubt where she stood on an issue."[2] By the 1980s, Thomas abandoned what little pretense she had about being a news journalist and engaged in sideshow theater, asking questions of the

"Have you stopped beating your wife?" variety. One liberal publication wrote that Thomas asks "eccentric, combative, accusatory, and unreasonably phrased questions."[3]

To the delight of liberal supporters, Thomas was particularly harsh in her confrontations with Republican presidents and their press secretaries. In her writing, she routinely condemned Republicans and praised Democrats. A liberal columnist wrote that Thomas "never masked her crush on Democrats."[4] It became clear she was a liberal icon when media outlets denounced President George W. Bush for not calling on her during a March 6, 2003, presidential press conference.[5] It was the first time in years Thomas was not called upon.

Occasionally, Thomas's reporting betrayed her hatred of Israel. In the last few decades, anti-Semites have disguised their anti-Semitism by not criticizing Jews directly, but by criticizing their spiritual home, Israel. Efforts at delegitimizing the state of Israel and branding its Jewish citizens as "Zionists" are attempts to attack Jews while avoiding being labeled anti-Semitic.

At least as far back as President George H. W. Bush, Thomas would refer to Israel as an occupying force. In her reporting, she would omit the context of Arab-Israeli military conflicts, such as the 1967, 1973, and 1982 wars, leaving the impression they were unprovoked Israeli military attacks.[6]

Thomas's anti-Semitism was not a well-kept secret. *The Guardian* newspaper referred to Thomas as "a garden variety anti-Semite" whose anti-Semitic views had been known for years.[7] Reportedly, the Anti-Defamation League had been monitoring her anti-Semitic statements.[8]

In 2000, Thomas left United Press International and joined the Hearst Newspapers as a commentator. At Hearst, her anti-Semitic leanings flourished.

Thomas did not play party favorites when it came to the topic of Israel. Presidents, Republicans and Democrats alike, were beholden to Israeli interests, Thomas would write. Thomas wrote Lyndon Johnson made the mistake of not internationalizing Jerusalem, Ronald Reagan "gave the Israelis pretty much what they asked for,"[9] and George W. Bush gave "unrelenting favoritism toward Israel."[10]

Even presidential candidates were too chummy with the Jewish state, Thomas believed. John Kerry permitted "Israel's illegal land grab."[11] Kerry's

2004 general-election opponent, incumbent President George W. Bush, made "a bid for the Jewish vote" with his Middle East peace policies.[12]

Thomas did not spare Senator Hillary Clinton from criticism. Clinton had supported Palestinian statehood, but as senator, Clinton "had to cater to a new constituency...[and] make the ritual trip to Israel."[13] This wasn't the only time Thomas made veiled references to the so-called Jewish lobby, a favorite target of anti-Semites.

When it came to matters of Islam, the United States, according to Thomas, was always wrong. Weeks after *Newsweek* magazine apologized for a false May 2005 story that claimed American servicemen flushed a Quran down the toilet at the Guantanamo Bay Detention Facility, Thomas continued to report the falsehood as if it were true.[14]

Thomas often wrote that Palestinians "have lived in misery"[15] in Gaza due to Israeli and US policies. Not once did she consider that the policies of Hamas and Fatah, the two groups running Gaza, might have anything to do with their situation.

Thomas criticized George W. Bush for the United States not recognizing Hamas as the legitimate government of Gaza and for not providing foreign aid to the region.[16] Thomas omitted that, at the same time, the United Nations, European Union, and Russia also refused to provide aid to Gaza until Hamas renounced violence and recognized Israel's right to exist. Instead, Hamas rained rockets down on Israeli civilians, armed suicide bombers, and pledged the destruction of the Jewish state. Thomas dismissed US support for the Palestine Liberation Organization because it was more aligned with Israeli interests.[17]

Barack Obama demonstrated himself to be the most hostile US president to Israeli officials and causes. Yet, Thomas warned, "Palestinians hoping for a change in US policy shouldn't be looking to Sen. Barack Obama" because he was also beholden to Israeli interests.[18]

On June 3, 2010, a video went viral of Thomas telling Jews they should leave Palestine. She made the comments days earlier when attending a White House ceremony on Jewish heritage. Thomas said, "Tell them to get the Hell out of Palestine. Remember, these people [Palestinians] are occupied. And it's their land. It's not Germany, it's not Poland." She continued, "They [Jews] should go home." When asked, "Where is their home?" she replied, "Poland, Germany, and America, and everywhere else."[19]

Many observers including other journalists immediately denounced Thomas's remarks, calling them "indefensible." Several observed that her notion of ethnic cleansing in Israel was no different from someone demanding all the blacks in America should go back to Africa.

Thomas tried to save her job by apologizing and claiming those remarks did not reflect her real views. Under pressure, Thomas resigned from Hearst days later. Reaction was swift. Her reserved front row seat in the White House Briefing Room was removed. Her name was stricken from various awards, including one from her alma mater and another bestowed upon recipients for tolerance. How ironic. Her agent dropped representation of her. Her book co-author parted ways, and she was dropped from a speakers' bureau.

In spite of her anti-Semitic views and tirade, Thomas still had fervent supporters. A journalist who accompanied Thomas when she made the video-recorded remarks criticized the citizen-journalist for having the temerity to post the remarks online.[20] Another journalist called the man who captured the remarks a "provocateur,"[21] although he was merely a rabbi, part-time blogger, and proud father accompanying his son to a White House event.

Nearly a year later, Thomas gave an interview to *Playboy* magazine. She repudiated her apology, told the interviewer her comments on Israel reflected her actual feelings, and then launched into an anti-Semitic tear of denouncing Jews. "[The Jews are] using their power, and they have power in every direction…Power over the White House, power over Congress…Everybody is in the pocket of the Israeli lobbies," she said. "Same thing with the financial markets. There's total control…It isn't the two percent," she added.[22]

Two years after her anti-Semitic remarks, Thomas was bestowed with a journalism award from the Palestinian Authority.

The Pulitzer Prize

"Jimmy's is a world of hard drugs, fast money and the good life he believes both can bring… Every day, Ron or someone else fires up Jimmy, plunging a needle into his bony arm, sending the fourth grader into a hypnotic nod."[23]

Janet Cooke of the *Washington Post* wrote a powerful story about an eight-year-old heroin addict in Washington, DC. The article described a heartbreaking situation of a child living in horrible conditions and getting injected with heroin in an urban neighborhood notorious for drug dealing.

The *Washington Post* followed Cooke's article with an editorial addressing "Jimmy's World" and its "starkly revolting and heart-rending detail." The editorial added, "So repugnant, depressing and foreign to most people is this morally corrupt 'world' of one child in the city."[24] The *Post* wanted its readers to know it had published one very special story.

In fact, the *Post* could not get enough of "Jimmy's World." The newspaper's ombudsman wrote, "The writer did her job extraordinarily well...The reporter made the city face what it knew." The paper emphasized Cooke had promised to protect the identity of Jimmy and others in her story as a trade-off in order to tell such a powerful and compelling story. According to the ombudsman, Cooke offered Jimmy the only promise that was kept. Everyone else—teachers, cops, and society—had failed to keep their promises.[25]

The newspaper was so proud of Cooke's work that assistant managing editor Bob Woodward of Watergate fame submitted it for consideration for a Pulitzer Prize. On April 13, 1981, Cooke's story won the award. Enthusiastic about awarding the prize to the first black female journalist winner, the Pulitzer committee shifted Cooke's entry to another category to make that happen.[26]

After reading the story, Washington, DC, Mayor Marion Barry was deeply concerned about the plight of the eight year old. Barry said, "We're going to try to find that 8-year-old heroin addict...An 8-year-old boy on heroin and his mother says it's okay. Isn't that incredible? I couldn't believe it. We're going to try to help the boy if we can find him." Citing the promise to maintain confidentiality, the *Post* declined repeated requests by city officials to provide any helpful information to locate the child.

Undeterred, Barry directed DC Police Chief Burtell Jefferson to take all necessary steps to locate the boy. Several city agencies and officials were involved in the effort to locate the child. It became a virtual manhunt.[27]

A psychiatrist quoted in the original story told city officials she knew the family and had been in touch with the mother. Yet, she turned down a request by city officials to assist in locating the boy in order to render aid.

Nearly three weeks after the story first appeared, Barry announced city officials were abandoning their search for the family. Not only were they unsuccessful in finding any clues regarding the child's identity or location, but they were starting to believe that at least some of the story had been fabricated. The mayor said, "I've been told the story was part myth and part reality." The *Washington Post* launched a spirited defense of the article.[28]

Officials at the *Toledo Blade* newspaper took keen interest in the story after the Pulitzer awards were announced. Cooke had worked at the paper before she was hired at the *Washington Post*. However, they noticed discrepancies between Cooke's biography contained in the newspaper's personnel files and the one accompanying the Pulitzer Prize announcement. According to the press announcement, Cooke graduated *magna cum laude* from Vassar College and earned a master's degree from the University of Toledo. The folks at the *Toledo Blade* knew this to be untrue.

Telephone calls were made to the *Post*. A day later, the truth was known. Not only had Cooke embellished her résumé, but she had fabricated the story about Jimmy. There was no boy. No family. No child heroin addict. It was all untrue.

The *Washington Post* notified the Pulitzer committee of the deception and returned the prize. Cooke was asked to resign from the newspaper.

The fraud perpetrated by Cooke was exacerbated by the *Washington Post*. In spite of its reputation for fact checking, the *Post* failed in even the most basic task of confirming the résumé of its prospective hire. The paper also failed to fact-check such an explosive story, even when other reporters at the paper suspected there were serious flaws with Cooke's work.[29]

Affirmative Action

The apparent lack of supervision and editorial oversight and the failure to conduct meaningful fact checking led to a major embarrassment at the *New York Times*. This became evident when it was learned that the paper's rising star had fabricated, falsely reported, or plagiarized one story after another.

Jayson Blair was on the uber-fast track at the *New York Times*. He conducted a summer internship at the paper in summer 1998. Some at the paper were so infatuated with Blair, he was invited to continue at the paper as an intern, a likely path to a full-time job. Blair returned to the *Times* in June 1999. He was hired as an intermediate reporter only five months later. By early 2001, Jayson Blair was a full-time staff reporter.

Blair was offered a staff reporter promotion by senior *Times* officials without even consulting his supervisor.[30] In late 2002, Jayson Blair was promoted to a position as a national reporter that allowed him to travel the country and report on major news stories. The failure to even speak to Blair's supervisor, who had "misgivings"[31] about Blair, is strong evidence that *Times* officials were concerned about issues other than newsroom performance. Jayson Blair was black. His supervisor believed race played a role in his meteoric rise at the paper.[32]

Jayson Blair's questionable behavior and suspect journalistic practices began before he worked at the *New York Times*. Blair transferred to the University of Maryland in 1995. He quickly became a favorite son of sorts of the faculty at the university's Philip Merrill College of Journalism. His opinion of himself knew no bounds. He referred to himself as "a journalistic boy wonder," who possessed "unmatched...reporting" because he was so "talented,"[33] making him "a campus star."[34] On the other hand, he was unpopular with most of the students working at the school newspaper the *Diamondback*.[35]

School officials viewed Blair as extremely talented and possessing great initiative. In recommending him for a coveted scholarship, one journalism school administrator wrote, "Mr. Blair is the most promising journalist at his age that I have encountered in my career in journalism and journalism education."[36]

Blair's fellow students generally viewed his work as slipshod and questioned his journalistic ethics. One student remarked, "With Jayson, he lied most of the time."[37]

In spite of concerns registered by several students, journalism school officials aggressively promoted Blair for one prestigious opportunity after another. There were internships at the *Washington Post, Boston Globe*, and *New York Times*. School officials were firmly behind his selection as editor-in-chief of the *Diamondback*, to the disappointment of many students on the staff. When Blair left the university paper, the staff threw a celebratory party—without him present.[38]

The *New York Times* apparently never asked Blair if he had finished his college education and graduated from the University of Maryland when he returned for his second internship. In fact, he had not graduated, despite attending the university for several years. It was astonishing that the newspaper did not conduct even the most cursory check of whatever employment documents Blair completed.

The end for Blair began in late April 2003, when a Texas newspaper contacted a *Times* editor to discuss shocking similarities between a Blair story and one that the Texas paper had previously published. Blair resigned from the *New York Times* on May 1.

On May 11, 2003, the *New York Times* published more than 13,000 words in a pair of stories that addressed problems with dozens of Blair's stories. Most amazingly, the *Times* admitted it had only thoroughly scrutinized the previous six months' worth of articles, even though Blair had been working at the paper for nearly four years and had a hand in nearly seven hundred published stories.[39]

The paper admitted that at least eighty-five stories contained plagiarized works, fabricated quotes, factual errors, or falsified datelines (reporting from actual locations) to which Blair had not traveled. In his 2004 memoir, *Burning Down My Masters' House*, Blair claimed a "toe-touch was a popular and sanctioned way at the newspaper to get a dateline on a story by reporting and writing it in one location, and then flying in simply so you could put the name of the city where the news was happening at the top of the story."[40]

The practice of misrepresenting one's work was not unusual, according to a pair of freelance journalists who worked for the *New York Times* for several years. Lisa Suhay, a freelancer for the paper for four years, said that while it was "common practice" for interns and newsroom assistants to actually conduct much of the first-hand reporting, they were "paid to be invisible, a nonentity," and they were to receive "no credit."[41]

Freelancer Milton Allimadi said that in the two years he worked for the *Times*, he wrote stories where the byline was given to a full-time *Times* reporter in spite of the *Times* reporter "barely" adding anything to the article.[42]

The same month Blair left the *Times*, another reporter exited the paper under similar circumstances. Pulitzer prize-winning reporter Rick Bragg resigned after the paper suspended him for putting his name on the byline of a story largely written by a freelancer.[43] Bragg said he was merely the victim of post-Blair hysteria at the *Times*.

Like the *Times* freelancers, Bragg claimed it was commonplace for the paper's reporters to rely on the work of "stringers and researchers and interns and clerks and news assistants." Bragg also echoed Blair in claiming *New York Times* editors were "fully aware" of the "toe-touch" practice of claiming a dateline for a location barely visited.[44]

While probably not intended, the *Times'* review of Blair's work was also a stunning indictment of the paper's deeply flawed newsroom practices, and the lack of effective management and editorial oversight that allowed rampant journalistic malpractice to exist for so long.

Not everybody at the *Times* was wearing rose-colored glasses when it came to Jayson Blair. His newsroom deceit attracted the attention of at least one editor, who warned others at the *Times* a year before Blair was finally caught, but apparently that warning had little effect. That editor emailed a two-sentence warning, "We have to stop Jayson from writing for the Times. Right now."[45] Blair was given a written reprimand after that email, but he was then given a prestigious promotion a mere six months after that prescient warning.

Blair could not hide his disgust for that supervisor, who he believed "was working overtime to undermine me in the background."[46] Blair recounted that the supervisor was just one of several *Times* newsroom personnel with whom Blair had experienced conflict and confrontation.

After his assignment to the national desk, complaints were registered by people who were purportedly quoted or were the subjects of Blair's stories. Yet, these complaints were not acted upon by *Times'* management.[47]

When Blair was assigned to report on the Washington, DC, sniper case, no one at the *Times* was curious enough to ask about the unnamed sources that figured prominently in one explosive front-page story. Apparently, they did not exist.[48]

Critics have claimed that Blair's deception was allowed to continue for so long because of the paper's affirmative-action policies. *New York Times* officials dispute this, but at the same time, the paper admitted

Blair's presence "help[ed] the paper diversify its newsroom."[49] Blair's supervisor midway through his *Times* employment said, "I think race was the decisive fact in his promotion."[50]

The debate over whether the *New York Times* ignored obvious warning signs in favor of an affirmative-action hire have little bearing on the deception to which the newspaper was a party. Bad journalism is bad journalism. The fact of the matter is, Blair's news stories reported falsely on many people and events and misled tens of thousands of readers who did not realize they were the victims of one lie after another.

The University of Maryland journalism school did not escape sharp criticism. A group of thirty former *Diamondback* staffers sent a letter to journalism officials after the Blair scandal broke. Their chief complaint was that their warnings went unheeded in the one year Blair was the paper's editor-in-chief.

Some warnings were made to the school. Other warnings were not made because students were "fearful of a culture inside of the College of Journalism that fostered the belief that speaking out could hurt internship possibilities and career hopes," according to the letter.[51]

The *New York Times* offloaded to the University of Maryland some of its culpability. According to the *Baltimore Sun*, the *Times* conducted an internal review in addition to its public mea culpa. The *Sun* wrote that Blair's shortfalls were not handled properly at the school. "Thus, the first CHOKE POINT passed, a lost opportunity when a more successful inquiry or different input from the university could have set the newspaper on a different path."[52]

The failure of the *New York Times* to provide proper supervision and editorial oversight and its failure to conduct meaningful fact checking were somehow the fault of the University of Maryland, according to the internal review.

He Lied, People Died

Twelve million. That was the number of people who likely perished during the Ukrainian Holodomor. Loosely translated, *holodomor* means, "murder by starvation." This genocide has also been referred to as the Great Famine of 1932. Some estimates peg the number of deaths at fourteen million people.

The Holodomor was a man-made famine engineered by Soviet leader Josef Stalin to target the people of the Ukraine. Even after the Ukraine came under czarist rule in the eighteenth century, Ukrainians continued to be a very proud people who celebrated their heritage. Ukrainian national pride continued after the socialist Bolsheviks seized power.

Ukrainian national pride was viewed with suspicion by Soviet officials, who thought it might pose a threat to total Soviet rule. After Stalin succeeded Lenin as leader, he implemented a plan to exterminate millions of Ukrainians, especially those who resisted brutal Soviet policies.

The Ukraine had long been known as the breadbasket of Europe because of the fertile land and the success of its farmers. The Ukraine could easily feed its own people and export grain abroad. Implemented in 1928, the Soviet Five-Year Plan called for the abolition of private property. This led to the confiscation of all farms, livestock, and equipment from peasant farmers in order to create agricultural collectives. The socialist philosophy was that private ownership was wrong, and society would benefit if the peasants collectively farmed crops for the state to control.

Ukrainians who did not willingly surrender their farms and join the collectives were arrested, executed, or exiled to the gulags in Siberia. Exiled Ukrainians were carried in cattle trains by the millions to the relatively few Siberian villages. Once the villages were populated beyond capacity, the rest of the exiles were dumped in the wilderness to fend for themselves. As many as seven-million Ukrainians perished.[53]

By 1932, most Ukrainian farmland had been absorbed into the collectives. Stalin decreed that grain production in the collective farms was to be increased by nearly 50 percent. Some of the grain went to the cities to feed factory workers. The rapid growth in factory workers was part of the Five-Year Plan to increase industrialization. Factories were also busy building weapon systems to outfit the growing Soviet Army. The rest of the grain was sold to the West to help fund the industrialization efforts.

Plaguing Stalin's agriculture plan was that he had eliminated many of the most productive farmers. Those who remained working on the collectives had little incentive to produce. They were paid very little for their efforts. When farm quotas fell short, Stalin looked for and found a scapegoat, the *kulaks*.

The term *kulak* was actually a Soviet construct. Any Ukrainian peasant who owned a small plot of farmland or possessed any livestock was deemed a *kulak*. Stalin insisted the *kulaks* were responsible for the failure of the agricultural aspect of his Five-Year Plan. Soviet officials began calling the *kulaks* parasites and bloodsuckers and charged them with preying on the Soviet people. Stalin declared the *kulaks* enemies of the state and he sought to have them exterminated.

Stalin's larger strategy was to destroy Ukrainian nationalism and break the spirit of the Ukrainian people so they could not oppose Soviet policies. He accomplished this in several ways. Ukrainian leaders were imprisoned or murdered. Orthodox churches were demolished or taken for other uses. Priests were killed. Even the Ukrainians' distinctive, embroidered clothing was confiscated and destroyed. Successive gun registration policies led to gun confiscations in order to disarm the people.

However, Stalin's most effective method of liquidating the Ukrainians was to starve them. He took all of the grain and livestock. Everything edible was confiscated, and troops would inspect every property in search of hidden food. Family cats and dogs disappeared as the people ate them to survive. The people were forced to subsist by eating forest animals, grass, weeds, tree bark, and whatever scraps they could scrounge. Ukrainians were issued internal passports as a mechanism to limit their movements and to keep them confined to the Ukraine. The only Ukrainians who did not lose everything were those who worked on the collectives. Not surprisingly, Holodomor stopped at the Russian border.

By the winter of 1932, Ukrainians were dying of starvation at a rate of 25,000 a day, sometimes in the shadow of full granaries waiting for sale to the West and guarded by the military. Grain that could not be shipped was often dumped into the sea or left to rot in order to prevent the Ukrainians from having it. Stalin's starvation policy was absolute. He turned all 235,000 square miles of the Ukraine into a giant death camp.

While the people starved, Soviet party leaders feasted on meat, fruits, vegetables, and delicacies in party dining halls. Sometimes these dining halls were in the very same villages where the people were literally dying of starvation in the streets.

Informing the West of the Holodomor by western correspondents was difficult, but not impossible. Soviet censors scrutinized every news dispatch before it was transmitted. Enterprising journalists found other ways to smuggle their dispatches abroad.

Walter Duranty arrived in Moscow as the *New York Times* bureau chief in 1921. Duranty was one of the American intelligentsia and progressives who idealized and idolized the Soviet Union and socialism as preferable to capitalism and democratic rule. Fawning over the Soviet model was all the rage with the political Left. A Soviet propaganda book titled *New Russia's Primer* was translated into English and became an American bestseller among progressives. The book claimed the collectivization of the farms was better than private ownership.[54]

Honesty and truthfulness were strangers to Duranty. In 1928, Duranty co-wrote a short story with H. R. Knickerbocker, a reporter for the International News Service. Knickerbocker did most of the writing. Duranty submitted the work, titled "The Parrot," for consideration in the O. Henry book of short stories. It was both accepted and picked as the best short story for 1929, worthy of a cash prize. Unfortunately, Duranty claimed he alone wrote the story and did not credit Knickerbocker.[55]

Duranty was nothing short of being a Soviet propagandist. Years later, columnist Joseph Alsop summed up Duranty this way: "Duranty... covered up the horrors and deluded an entire generation by prettifying Soviet realities...He was given a Pulitzer Prize. He lived comfortably in Moscow, too, by courtesy of the K.G.B."[56] Alsop also said of Duranty that, "Lying was his stock in trade."

One of Duranty's contemporaries was Malcolm Muggeridge, who was the Moscow correspondent for the *Manchester Guardian*. Muggeridge arrived in Moscow as a fan of socialism. He had every intention of becoming a Soviet citizen, where he would live out his days in the socialist paradise. His view of the Soviet way of life quickly soured when he witnessed first-hand the brutality and suffering under Soviet rule.[57] The disparity between the horrors he witnessed and what Duranty sent to the *New York Times* led Muggeridge to call Duranty "the greatest liar I ever knew in 50 years of journalism."

The British Embassy concluded that Duranty was nothing more than a propagandist of the Soviet Union. One British diplomatic assessment described Duranty as "being in the pay of the Soviet Union."[58]

Duranty sent dispatches to the *New York Times* that were outright Soviet propaganda. Duranty told a US diplomat at the American Embassy in Berlin that "in agreement with the *New York Times* and the Soviet authorities" his reports from Moscow "always reflect the official position of the Soviet regime."[59]

Duranty wrote positive stories from Moscow that oftentimes had little relationship to the truth of what was taking place. Duranty was awarded the 1932 Pulitzer Prize in Correspondence for "his series of dispatches on Russia especially the working out of the Five-Year Plan." The award made him the most celebrated journalist in Moscow and one whose writing was accepted as more authoritative than that of others.

Early in his first term as president, Franklin Roosevelt decided to recognize the USSR. Duranty's dispatches, which portrayed a positive but wildly inaccurate view of life in the Soviet Union, have been widely viewed as critical in convincing Roosevelt to recognize the Soviet Union. Duranty even accompanied the Soviet foreign minister to the White House for the formal announcement of American recognition of the Soviet state. Upon his return to Moscow, Duranty was rewarded with an exclusive one-on-one interview with Stalin, whom he called "a great statesman."

Undeterred by the Soviet censors, some journalists found ways to get their dispatches to the West, oftentimes under pseudonyms so they would not be expelled. Muggeridge sent dispatches via the British Embassy's diplomatic pouches. His columns described the horrific famine in the Ukraine where the people "had for weeks next to nothing to eat."[60]

Another journalist was Gareth Jones. He spent several weeks in the famine-stricken Ukraine and then returned west to relay what he had seen in a series of public talks and first-hand accounts published in the *Manchester Guardian*. He relayed an estimate from Kazakhstan that one million of its five million people had starved to death.

In March 1933, Duranty and the *New York Times* took the lead in labeling Muggeridge and Jones liars. Duranty first met with Constantine Oumansky, the head of the Soviet Press Office, to craft the language Duranty would use to discredit Jones.[61]

Denying there was a famine, Duranty wrote the "village markets [were] flowing with eggs, fruit, poultry, vegetables, milk and butter...A child can see this is not a famine but abundance." Duranty declared the work of Muggeridge and Jones "an exaggeration of malignant propaganda."[62] Based on the wildly different accounts, the *Guardian* fired Muggeridge. Muggeridge had been publicly defamed in the pages of the *New York Times* and now found himself unemployed as a result. Jones's reputation as a journalist was in tatters.

In late 1933, when other reports trickled out of the Soviet Union indicating the situation was much worse than Duranty reported, he changed his approach to writing columns and simply downplayed the seriousness of the situation. Duranty wrote, "There is no actual starvation or deaths from starvation but there is widespread mortality from diseases due to malnutrition, especially in the Ukraine, North Caucasus and Lower Volga."[63]

Duranty coined the phrase, "You can't make an omelet without breaking eggs." In other words, the end justifies the means. Duranty believed the socialist system was the best, and it was acceptable for there to be some loss of life and suffering along the way.

Duranty insisted the only people dying from hunger in the Ukraine were those who refused to work.[64] Duranty even wrote a detailed account of the conditions in Odessa in spite of never having visited the Black Sea city.[65] Duranty was spouting Soviet propaganda and the *New York Times* willingly published it.

Duranty was not blind to what was happening. He privately estimated that as many as ten million Ukrainians died from famine, but the Soviet apologist that he was, he continued to write accounts for the *New York Times* that dramatically downplayed the death toll.[66]

The truth of Holodomor in the Ukraine became widely known after the end of World War II. Twice, campaigns were mounted to convince the Pulitzer Prize committee to revoke Duranty's award. It refused both requests.

It would be a half-century after it was known Duranty had filed false and deceptive reports before the *New York Times* seriously addressed the matter. Columbia University historian Mark von Hagen reviewed Duranty's worked and declared Duranty "frequently writes in the enthusiastically propagandistic language of his sources," and that "there is a serious lack of balance in his writing." Von Hagen recommended the Pulitzer Prize committee "should take the prize away."[67] The *New York Times* did not publicly call for the Pulitzer committee to rescind the award.

Korangate

"[S]ources tell Newsweek: interrogators, in an attempt to rattle suspects, flushed a Qur'an down a toilet and led a detainee around with a collar and dog leash."[68]

That explosive sentence in the May 9 issue of *Newsweek* magazine alleging bad behavior by US military personnel at the detention facility in Guantanamo Bay, Cuba, led to fatal violence in several Muslim countries. There was more to *Newsweek*'s 325-word article. It claimed ten military interrogators had already been disciplined for misbehavior. Among the claims was that one woman removed her top and sat on a detainee's lap. Another woman allegedly wiped a detainee's face with what she said was menstrual blood.[69]

On May 10, a Pakistani activist blasted the United States over the *Newsweek* report. Several Pakistani politicians joined the denunciation of the United States.[70] This was one of many chain protests in Pakistan, Afghanistan, and other Muslim countries. Four people died and more than seventy were injured when students in the Afghan city of Jalalabad rioted, including burning an effigy of President Bush and chanting, "Death to America."[71]

Another three were killed and more than seventy-five injured in violent demonstrations near the Afghanistan capital of Kabul.[72] After three days, there were violent protests in nearly one-third of Afghanistan's thirty-four provinces. US aid organizations were attacked. In an effort to calm protestors, Secretary of State Condoleezza Rice announced a full investigation would be conducted, as the United States does not tolerate any disrespect of the Muslim holy book.[73]

In about five days' time, fourteen protestors had died and well over one hundred were injured from violent demonstrations in which protestors clashed with police officers and Afghan security forces.[74]

Muslim clerics in neighboring Pakistan led largely peaceful demonstrations against the United States. Thousands of students in Yemen's capital of Sanaa took to the streets chanting, "Death to America." Anti-American protests erupted in Gaza and Indonesia.

A Defense Department investigation did not find evidence that any US personnel had mistreated the Koran. Authorities had investigated earlier claims by detainees of Koran mistreatment, but found them not to be credible. However, Defense investigators found one Muslim detainee had torn pages from a Koran and flushed them down a toilet with the intention of clogging it.[75]

On May 15, *Newsweek* editor Mark Whitaker acknowledged that the magazine's original story contained errors. He posted the following note to readers: "We regret that we got any part of our story wrong, and extend our sympathies to victims of the violence and to the US soldiers caught in its midst."[76]

The following day, on May 16, *Newsweek* issued the following press release: "Based on what we know now, we are retracting our original story that an internal military investigation had uncovered Qur'an abuse at Guantanamo Bay."

At least nineteen people died in violent clashes as thousands protested over the false *Newsweek* story.[77]

"In His Pajamas"

Dan Rather had a long and storied career with CBS News. He started working in journalism at several local news outlets in Texas before moving on to CBS News assignments at the White House, London, and Vietnam.

By 1970, Rather became a contributor to the Sunday evening news-magazine *60 Minutes*, and he occasionally anchored weekend editions of the CBS *Evening News*. In 1981, Rather succeeded Walter Cronkite as the main anchor for CBS *Evening News*. He would later join the new mid-week news magazine *60 Minutes II*, something of a clone of the weekend edition.

Rather was not shy about exposing his political leanings. He often peppered his newscast with editorial comments that made it was obvious to the viewers what he thought of some public figures. Viewers responded by making CBS *Evening News* the last-place weeknight network news program.

Rather inserted himself into the hard-fought 2004 presidential election in an ignominious way. Senator John Kerry of Massachusetts was the Democratic nominee challenging Republican incumbent George

W. Bush of Texas, who was running for a second term. Kerry made his one-year tour of duty in Vietnam the foundation of his presidential run. Even Kerry's campaign book, *Tour of Duty*, was a memoir of his Vietnam service. Critics attempted to portray Bush as a draft-dodger who avoided a possible Vietnam assignment by receiving politically connected treatment to join the Texas Air National Guard.

In a *60 Minutes II* segment titled "For the Record," broadcasted on September 8, 2004, Rather presented several pages of memos dated 1972 and 1973 that purportedly came from the personal files of Bush's Air National Guard commander, Lieutenant Colonel Jerry Killian. The memos were critical of Bush's military service, claimed Bush failed to meet his military obligations and was insubordinate, and revealed that Killian was pressured to write favorable performance reviews of Bush.

The memos seemingly supported the claims of Bush critics that Bush dodged the military draft and benefitted from the connections of his influential father, George H. W. Bush. During this period of time, the elder Bush was a former Congressman, had served as US ambassador to the United Nations, and was at the time serving as chairman of the Republican National Committee.

In "For the Record," Rather insisted the memos, which he claimed came from the personal files of the deceased Killian, had been authenticated by experts retained by CBS News. The Bush-whacking story immediately dominated the news landscape.[78] Seemingly every news outlet was running with stories that Bush skipped out on his military obligations while avoiding Vietnam service.[79] The *Washington Post* alone published five articles the following day totaling nearly fifteen-thousand words, flogging the Rather story.

However, there was another response that emerged only hours after the *60 Minutes II* broadcast. Astute bloggers examined the images of the purported Killian memos and noticed some physical anomalies.

Among the most prominent anomalies was the use of proportional spacing in the memos. The manual typewriters, and nearly every single electric typewriter in widespread use at the time, gave each character the same amount of space regardless of the width of the letter. An "i" and an "l" received the same amount of space as a "g" or a "k." This is because the typewriter carriage advanced the same distance each time any key was struck.

It wasn't until the introduction of word processors, and later, personal computers, that these smarter devices could advance the cursor the appropriate amount of space for the selected key. This is proportional spacing.

The other prominent anomaly was the type font in the Killian memos. The memos were produced using a font known as Times New Roman. The Times New Roman font was created in the 1930s by the *London Times* newspaper for use in its broadsheet printing, but it was not used in typewriters in the 1970s. It was not until the 1980s that software giant Microsoft began adding Times New Roman to its Word program.

There were other questionable elements of the memos. For example, the superscript "th" was used in the purported memos, whereas that was rarely the norm at the time unless someone manually adjusted the carriage a half-line to type "th" as a superscript. The experts Rather and his crew consulted were shown only portions of the memos; most had misgivings about some or all of the memos' authenticity.

One observer noted the documents appeared to have been photocopied several times to give them the appearance they were old, which also made it very difficult to compare the memos' signatures with a known Killian signature. Rather dismissed the criticism as the work of "partisan political operatives."[80]

The "For the Record" story fell apart under fact checking led by bloggers. This led to a famous boast by Jonathan Klein, the former executive vice-president of CBS News who claimed the news organization's news-gathering and analysis skills were far superior to the work of some guy at home sitting behind his computer dressed "in his pajamas."[81] Clearly, Klein was dead wrong.

For nearly two weeks, Rather and CBS News steadfastly defended the "For the Record" segment as accurate. As evidence mounted that the memos were forgeries and the "For the Record" story was journalistically flawed, the network began expert shopping by posting notices on liberal conspiracy websites asking for help. Eventually, CBS News publicly admitted the documents had not been authenticated as legitimate, as Rather had claimed on-air.[82]

There was more bad news for the "For the Record" segment. It was learned that an anti-Bush activist who had a history of promoting conspiracy theories was the actual source of the memos.[83] The CBS source once likened Bush to Hitler.[84] Rather's claim that the memos came from the personal files of Killian was not supported by the available facts. In fact, Killian's son came forward stating his father had the highest opinion of Bush's performance and the son disputed the authenticity of the memos.

There was more bad news when it was learned Rather's executive producer introduced the source of the memos to a Kerry campaign official and continued to pass messages between the two. This was a major breach of journalism ethics.[85]

Dates and individuals cited in the Rather segment did not match documented events. A man described as a corroborating witness transferred from the Air National Guard unit before the purported memos were written. Further damaging *60 Minutes II*'s credibility was the discovery that Rather's team had contacted the Kerry election campaign regarding the progress of the story.

CBS News hired former US Attorney General Dick Thornburgh, and Louis Boccardi, the former president of the Associated Press, to investigate facts surrounding the story. The January 2005 Thornburgh-Boccardi report was damning.[86] Much of the process in producing the "For the Record" segment was journalistically flawed. In response, nearly everyone associated with the story was fired, asked to resign, or quietly ushered out of CBS News. In March 2005, Rather stepped down from the CBS *Evening News* anchor chair and left the network. *60 Minutes II* was canceled later that year.

In spite of the facts, Dan Rather continues to insist his "For the Record" story was accurate. Even Hollywood joined Rather's conspiracy bandwagon. A 2015 film starring Robert Redford as Dan Rather was a sympathetic portrayal that left many viewers believing the forged memos were authentic.

Half-Empty

He was the biggest star at one of the most popular progressive publications in America. Stephen Glass was a rock star at the *New Republic* magazine. Just barely out of college, the twenty-three-year old Glass was elevated to writing feature stories for the *New Republic* not long after he started as an intern. In between, he was briefly an editorial assistant with the periodical. By age twenty-five, the magazine's wunderkind was named an associate editor.

The feature stories Glass was turning out were funny, quirky, and were getting a lot of attention. He was the *New Republic*'s equivalent of a shock jock. No high-profile subject was too big for him to take on. Whether it was colleges, trade associations, advocacy groups, or public service organizations, Glass was the David to their Goliath.

Glass was getting so much attention in the progressive literary community that other liberal outlets began throwing money and writing assignments his way, including *George*,[87] *Harper's*,[88] *New York Times Magazine*,[89] *Rolling Stone*,[90] and *Slate*.[91] *Mother Jones* was awaiting an article from Glass when the scandal broke.[92] Glass also had articles published in *USA Today*[93] and the *Washington Post*.[94] Fortunately for Glass's deception, most of those outlets willingly suspend disbelief in the face of contradictory facts in favor of promoting a progressive narrative. Glass also worked for about a year at the Heritage Foundation's *Policy Review*[95] before he landed at the *New Republic*.

While Glass's star at the *New Republic* was ascending, targets of his articles were registering complaints one after another. The people and organizations he attacked claimed his articles contained untrue statements, fictitious details, and even total fabrications. The *New Republic* unquestionably backed Glass, even as the criticism and complaints mounted. Editor Michael Kelly demanded the Center for Science in the Public Interest apologize to Glass for its pointed criticism of a Glass article attacking CSPI.[96]

Kelly's full-throttle defense of Glass in spite of very detailed criticism pointing out factual errors was an embarrassment for the magazine. Kelly referred to a critique by *Extra!* magazine as "dishonest, wrongheaded and clearly motivated by devotion to ideology, rather than by any concern for truth or accuracy."[97]

Kelly further blasted *Extra!*, writing, "I take criticism of TNR seriously, when it comes from a credible source. That doesn't include you…[D]on't expect me to accept you as the arbitrer [sic] of what constitutes shoddy."[98]

As the facts demonstrated, the *New Republic*'s insistence that Glass's work was buttoned up underscored the magazine's blind devotion to promoting a progressive narrative over reality. In short, the *New Republic*'s steadfast endorsement of shoddy work made it clear it was the magazine that was the non-credible source.

When the staff at the *New Republic* were faced with the undeniable truth that Glass was fabricating articles, editor Charles Lane fired him. Lane was hired after Kelly left months earlier. Much of the staff began a review of everything Glass wrote for the magazine. They reached the conclusion that at least twenty-seven of the forty-one articles he had authored were partly or completely fabricated. Amazingly, this occurred despite the magazine's rigorous fact-checking process that was modeled after the *New Yorker*'s fact checking.[99]

Glass would "present...elaborate orchestrations of made-up scenes and characters...passing them off as journalism," observed a *Vanity Fair* review of the scandal. That review noted Glass succeeded in his deception by creating "fake notes, a fake Web site, a fake business card, and [fake] memos."[100]

After the scandal broke, Kelly, who left the *New Republic* to work at *National Journal*, was still defending Glass. Kelly said, "[I]n fairness to him, you have to say there is a great deal to it that is manifestly true and that does reflect exceptional talent."[101]

Glass's skirting the truth may have begun long before he began working at the *New Republic*. While attending the University of Pennsylvania, Glass joined the staff of the student-run newspaper, the *Daily Pennsylvanian*. He wrote an attention-grabbing story of hanging out with a group of crack-smoking, whore-chasing homeless men that, in retrospect, may have also been fabricated.[102]

In an eerie coincidence, a college classmate and fellow *Daily Pennsylvanian* staffer, Sabrina Rubin Erdely, later became notorious for authoring a *Rolling Stone* article that was discredited, costing the magazine millions of dollars to settle multiple claims of defamation. Erdely wrote an article accusing innocent fraternity members of engaging in a gang rape. Ironically, Erdely wrote a column after the *New Republic* scandal broke calling Glass a "weenie" and a "con man," and trashing his proclivity for fabricating articles.[103]

Perhaps Erdely was merely seeking revenge on Glass. Reportedly, Glass reprimanded Erdely for fabricating an article for the *Daily Pennsylvanian* when she was a staff writer and he was the editor.[104]

In a 2014 reflection of the scandal, the *New Republic* acknowledged Glass "had been making up characters, scenes, events, whole stories from first word to last."[105] It is worth mentioning that throughout the 6,100-word article, it addressed the conflict between Chuck Lane, the editor who replaced Michael Kelly, and Stephen Glass.

That confrontation and other comments in the article leave readers with the impression that it was dogged investigation by the *New Republic* staff that uncovered the fraud. Yet, nothing could be further from the truth. The magazine was busy defending Glass when countless parties addressed the fraudulent nature of his articles. The *New Republic* failed to mention it was Forbes Digital Tool (present-day Forbes.com) that broke the story on the entire fraud.[106] It's as if the *New Republic* was channeling Stephen Glass.

Serial Plagiarism I

"I made a terrible mistake. It is a serious lapse and one that is entirely my fault. I apologize unreservedly to [Jill Lepore], to my editors at Time, and to my readers."[107] That was the apology offered by Fareed Zakaria on August 10, 2012, after he was caught plagiarizing a 7,700-word *New Yorker* article by Lepore for an article that he published in *Time* magazine.

Zakaria regularly wrote columns for *Time* and the *Washington Post*, and he hosted a program on CNN. *Time* and CNN suspended Zakaria for a week, a relatively light punishment for someone who had been dogged in the past for using the work of others without attribution. In a matter of days, all three outlets claimed they reviewed Zakaria's other work in their respective news organizations and pronounced him free of scandal.

Three years earlier, in 2009, Jeffrey Goldberg of *The Atlantic* noticed that Zakaria used some of Goldberg's work without proper attribution. Goldberg cited a May 2009 Zakaria column in *Newsweek* magazine.[108] Zakaria was the magazine's editor at the time. In a column titled "What You Know About Iran is Wrong," Zakaria had the following sentence: "In an interview last week, Israeli Prime Minister Benjamin Netanyahu described the Iranian regime as 'a messianic, apocalyptic cult.'" Goldberg observed that the sentence was worded to leave the reader with the impression that Zakaria interviewed Netanyahu. However, Goldberg pointed out, it was he who interviewed Netanyahu when the Israeli prime minister offered that description of the Iranian regime, and Goldberg reported it in the March 2009 issue of *The Atlantic*.[109]

Goldberg further noted the interview was conducted in March and not "last week" (in May), as Zakaria claimed. This was probably not a case of Zakaria carelessly forgetting to properly attribute the interview to Goldberg. If that were so, then Zakaria would have at least mentioned the interview took place in March and not two months later, which he implied when he wrote "last week." The wording suggests conscious deception on the part of Zakaria.

Goldberg then reported Zakaria had another sentence in the same *Newsweek* column that appeared to have been copied from Goldberg's work, yet again. This time the material came from a *New York Times* op-ed Goldberg authored.[110]

One failure to properly attribute work might be a mistake. But two failures appear to indicate a pattern of intentionally appropriating the work of others without attribution. As one *Washington Post* columnist wrote, "It didn't come as a huge surprise" to learn Zakaria was "embroiled in a plagiarism scandal."[111] That observation probably should have set off alarms at the *Post*, but it apparently did not.

Then came the revelation that Zakaria had lifted the work of another author to add to his 2008 book *The Post-American World*. Zakaria used a quote from a technology official that first appeared in a book published in 2005. Clyde Prestowitz, the author of the 2005 book, claimed he contacted Zakaria, and Zakaria's editor and publisher, about his work being used without attribution, but none of the three responded to him.[112]

Zakaria defended his failure to attribute because it would "interrupt the flow for the reader," as if footnotes in his written work would present some kind of obstacle not found in other footnoted works. However, the updated version of *The Post-American World* properly cited Prestowitz's work.[113]

There was more. Back in 1998, Zakaria wrote a story for *Slate* about the martini cocktail. Yep, he generously appropriated the work of another. In this case, Zakaria copied from an article authored by Max Rudin in *American Heritage*.[114]

Zakaria's record of appropriating the work of others did not end with those four cases.

In August 2014, exactly two years after Zakaria apologized for plagiarizing Lepore, a pair of citizen watchdogs published a detailed takedown of Zakaria engaging in the same bad journalistic behavior. The anonymous watchdogs, blogging under a website named Our Bad Media, gave a dozen examples of Zakaria again using the work of others without giving proper credit.[115]

The *Washington Post* and CNN both dismissed the watchdog report, with CNN going so far as stating the news organization had "the highest confidence in the excellence and integrity" in Zakaria's work.[116] Zakaria denied he plagiarized.

Undeterred, the media watchdog bloggers followed up the following month, September 2014. This time, Our Bad Media detailed two dozen times Zakaria used the work of others without proper attribution in his CNN show. This time, the *Washington Post* and CNN did not publicly comment, but the two media outlets and others including *Slate* and *Newsweek* began posting editor's notes to Zakaria's work addressing his failure to properly attribute the work he appropriated from other authors.[117]

Zakaria, who holds a PhD from Harvard University, appears to be challenged when it comes to properly citing the work he borrows from others. However, it does appear CNN and the *Washington Post* are finished with disciplining him when he violates commonly accepted rules of journalism.

Serial Plagiarism II

BuzzFeed is an entertainment website known for sandwiching adolescent-focused memes and silly lists in an ocean of advertisements. It's been compared to Gawker, a gossip website that declared bankruptcy and shut down in 2016.[118] On its website, BuzzFeed claims it is an "international news organization" that focuses on "breaking news quickly and accurately." Its editor claims it is "one of the largest news and entertainment sites on the web."[119] Apparently, the public does not think so highly of the gossip platform.

A 2014 Pew Research Center survey of several media outlets had bleak news for BuzzFeed. Not including talk radio and cable-TV pundit programs, BuzzFeed was the least trusted media outlet in America, with only 6 percent of respondents reporting they trusted the site.[120] When radio and cable talk-shows were included, BuzzFeed was the only media outlet more "distrusted" than "trusted" by every single ideological group, from consistently liberal to consistently conservative.[121]

One of BuzzFeed's preoccupations when not accusing others of plagiarism is defending itself against allegations of plagiarism. Unfortunately for BuzzFeed, its plagiarism record is a dismal one.

In April 2017, BuzzFeed alleged Supreme Court justice nominee Neil Gorsuch had plagiarized the work of another in his 2006 book, *The Future of Assisted Suicide and Euthanasia*. The article alleged two paragraphs that included seven endnotes in a 320-page book were plagiarized.[122]

BuzzFeed claimed the work that was plagiarized was a 1984 *Indiana Law Journal* article titled "The Legislative Response to Infant Doe," by Abigail Lawlis Kuzma. The alleged plagiarized author, Kuzma, disagreed with BuzzFeed, noting, "Given that these passages both describe the basic facts of the case, it would have been awkward and difficult for Judge Gorsuch to have used different language."

Professor Emeritus John Finnis of Oxford University called the BuzzFeed claims nonsense. "In all the instances mentioned, Neil Gorsuch's writing and citing was easily and well within the proper and accepted standards of scholarly research and writing in the field of study in which he and I work," said Finnis, who supervised Gorsuch when he was a student at Oxford.[123]

In 2016, BuzzFeed accused reality show personality Khloé Kardashian of plagiarism by "stealing her tweets." Kardashian tweeted silly questions that had been tweeted by Yahoo! and other websites. One example was, "Do Siamese twins pay for one ticket or two tickets when they go to movies and concerts?"[124] Such juvenile humor has been in circulation for decades. BuzzFeed even called its gossip article an "investigation."

Cosmopolitan magazine ridiculed the BuzzFeed article and pointed out that BuzzFeed routinely engaged in identical behavior. For example, BuzzFeed published an article titled "28 Times Yahoo Had Answers To All Your 'Sexy' Questions."[125]

Less than two years after BuzzFeed's Kardashian article, *Fast Company* magazine pointed out that BuzzFeed appeared to have plagiarized an original joke that appeared online only days earlier.[126]

The big scandal for BuzzFeed erupted in 2014, when it was learned that, in dozens of instances, BuzzFeed had published content plagiarized from other sources. BuzzFeed issued a mea culpa of sorts, claiming that after it launched its "writers didn't have journalistic backgrounds and weren't held to traditional journalistic standards," but it promised to do better.[127]

That 2014 plagiarism admission was not an isolated incident. More than a half-dozen individuals and entities have come forward alleging BuzzFeed has used content created by others without attribution and, in some cases, compensation. In 2016 website Tech.Co listed six times BuzzFeed improperly used the content of others, including using copyrighted photos, plagiarizing a student's short film, lifting articles from other websites, and copying YouTube videos.[128]

A 2016 Change.org petition asked advertisers to stop advertising with BuzzFeed. The petition listed several examples of online content on BuzzFeed that appeared to be copied from others.[129] Also in 2016, a *Washington Post* article listed several others who have claimed BuzzFeed stole their ideas, lifted their material, or copied their content without attribution or compensation.[130] In 2018, a pair of Australian sisters who operate a YouTube channel alleged BuzzFeed was stealing their content.[131]

"A Journalistic Failure"

The 2014 magazine story was the type that would infuriate nearly every reader. "Jackie" was a freshman student who was invited on a date by an upperclassman. The pair went to his fraternity's party, where Jackie was brutally raped just weeks after starting her college career. In fact, she was gang-raped by seven men with another two men egging them on. It turned out the rape was part of a pledge ritual. One of the men, unable to sexually perform, "shoved [a beer] bottle into her."[132]

The three-hour attack occurred in a darkened upstairs bedroom of her date's fraternity house while a raucous party raged downstairs. When the victim later regained consciousness, she fled to the first floor, where the late-night festivities were still underway, but no one reacted to the disheveled, barefoot teen with a blood-splattered dress and beaten face.[133]

The gang rape took place at Phi Kappa Psi chapter house at the University of Virginia in Charlottesville, according to *Rolling Stone* magazine, which published the tragic story. Sabrina Rubin Erdely was the author of the explosive piece.

Reaction to the story was swift. The day after the story appeared, the Phi Kappa Psi chapter voluntarily surrendered its fraternity agreement with the school and ceased all chapter activities, pending an investigation.[134] University President Teresa Sullivan went a step further, immediately suspending all fraternity and sorority activities and requesting the Charlottesville Police Department launch a criminal investigation.[135]

A group of protestors vandalized the Phi Kappa Psi chapter house by spray-painting graffiti on the building and smashing windows with rocks and cinder blocks. Fraternity members were bullied, called names, received threats, and had hateful comments posted on their social media accounts. Most fled the chapter house and went into hiding.

The *Washington Post* led a journalism crusade against the university in publishing nearly twenty stories in about a ten-day period after the *Rolling Stone* article appeared, attacking the alleged perpetrators, the fraternity, the university, the campus atmosphere and just about anything else related to the University of Virginia. The *Post* demanded a "sea change in the college's culture,"[136] charged that the University's "frat boys...are not men,"[137] and editorialized that the alleged perpetrators "belong in prison."[138]

A couple of independent writers began probing the *Rolling Stone* article shortly after it was published. The writers questioned the fantastical account and reached the conclusion that the Erdely story may not have been on the up-and-up.[139]

Once other journalists started asking questions, the *Rolling Stone* story quickly fell apart. The fact that there is a Phi Kappa Psi fraternity at the University of Virginia in the city of Charlottesville was among the few details that could easily be proved. But many more details in Erdely's story could not be. In fact, many of the details Erdely included in her story were proven to be untrue. Yet, even as the *Rolling Stone* story was quickly unraveling, the magazine issued a strong statement of support for the article. "Through our extensive reporting and fact-checking, we found Jackie to be entirely credible and courageous and we are proud to have given her disturbing story the attention it deserves," said the statement.[140]

Key details in the story were just not true. There was no party at Phi Kappa Psi fraternity house the night of the alleged attack. There was no fraternity member by the name or description that Jackie reported. Jackie's description of the fraternity house layout did not match the actual layout. Further, the pledging of freshmen to the Phi Kappa Psi fraternity occurs in the spring and not the fall, when the alleged attack occurred.[141]

The *Rolling Stone* article addressed three friends of Jackie who arrived to pick her up after the alleged assault. The article implied Erdely spoke with them. She did not. Their version of events differed dramatically from Jackie's. For example, when the trio met Jackie after the alleged incident, she told them a far different story then Erdely reported. They also said she was not battered and bloodied, as was reported in the *Rolling Stone* article.[142]

In fact, Jackie's friends had their suspicions about Jackie's fraternity-member date long before the alleged date-turned-rape occurred. Jackie told them his name and gave them a photo of him and his telephone number. However, no one by the name was enrolled as a student at the school, the photo was taken from the social media account of a high school classmate of Jackie's, and the telephone number belonged to a burner phone.[143]

Erdely never made an attempt to speak with any of the alleged perpetrators—the very people she was maligning in her article.[144] When Erdely conducted a nearly forty-five-minute interview of University President Teresa Sullivan, she did not once mention the alleged gang rape.[145]

On December 5, more than two weeks after the *Rolling Stone* story first appeared, the magazine published an online note stating, "There now appear to be discrepancies in Jackie's account."[146]

In January, the Charlottesville Police Department reported they could not find any credible evidence that supported the *Rolling Stone* account.[147]

On April 5, 2015, a 12,000-word scathing analysis of the *Rolling Stone* magazine article by the Columbia University Graduate School of Journalism was published.[148] The magazine requested the school look into how the magazine got such an explosive story so wrong. The report underscored that the magazine did not follow the most basic rules of journalism, resulting in perhaps the biggest media debacle of 2014.

It is easy to see how *Rolling Stone* managed to write such an agenda-driven, nonfactual story about the University of Virginia. The school represented so many traits that many progressives find offensive. As pointed out in the magazine article, the school has a student body of "overwhelmingly blond students," "a reputation for wealth," and "old-money privilege," it was steeped in "patriarchy," and it "[wa]sn't an edgy or progressive campus by any stretch." The University of Virginia was just the sort of entity progressives love to hate.

Yet, *Rolling Stone* apparently did not learn the lesson of another rush-to-judgement false claim made against an elite university. Merely a three-hour drive away is Duke University, where another false gang rape claim was championed by news outlets only nine years earlier.

Curiously, not a single *Rolling Stone* employee involved in the "A Rape on Campus" article was fired over the scandal.

In November 2016, *Rolling Stone* magazine and Sabrina Rubin Erdely were ordered by a jury to pay $3 million to a University of Virginia administrator, who was defamed in the magazine's fake gang rape story.

In June 2017, the magazine agreed to pay nearly $1.7 million to the Phi Kappa Psi fraternity in order to settle a defamation lawsuit.

As of this writing, another defamation lawsuit stemming from the false gang-rape article was pending against *Rolling Stone* magazine.

In what some observers may consider an incredible case of irony, back in 2004, Sabrina Rubin Erdely wrote an article about the *New Republic* writer Stephen Glass.[149] Glass was the reporter who famously cut corners, fabricated conversations, and failed to follow even the most basic tenets of journalism in order to crank out one sensational yarn after another. Erdely claimed to have been a friend of Glass when the two attended the University of Pennsylvania. It is not known if anyone fact-checked that claim.

The Master of His Domain

Bill O'Reilly was the undisputed king of primetime cable-news network programming. The brash and abrasive talk show host ruled the ratings of cable news networks for more than sixteen straight years. No doubt this is why the host of *The O'Reilly Factor* was reportedly a powerful and influential personality on the Fox News Channel.

O'Reilly weathered some miscues during his reign as cable television's number-one talking head without it seriously affecting his viewer ratings. For example, on three occasions in 1999 and 2000, he left viewers with the impression he won at least two George Foster Peabody Awards when he was anchoring the magazine format entertainment show *Inside Edition*.[150] A Peabody is generally considered the most prestigious award in television news. In fact, *Inside Edition* won a single George Polk Award, a similarly prestigious journalism award, but after O'Reilly had left the show.[151]

Long before the Me Too movement began, O'Reilly was at the center of a sexual harassment claim that did little to scare away his loyal viewers. In October 2004, O'Reilly reportedly paid about $9 million to settle a sexual harassment claim involving a producer for his show.[152] Andrea Mackris had filed a sexual harassment lawsuit that included lurid claims of O'Reilly pressuring Mackris to engage in telephone sex with him. According to her complaint, O'Reilly called her at her home in August 2004 and suggested she purchase a vibrator. "It became apparent that Defendant was masturbating as he spoke," the complaint alleged.

Then, in January 2017, a story broke alleging O'Reilly had sexually harassed Fox News colleague Juliet Huddy in 2011. According to a 2016 letter from Huddy's lawyers addressed to Fox News, O'Reilly repeatedly called Huddy and pressured her to engage in a sexual relationship with him. Occasionally, it sounded as if O'Reilly was masturbating when he called her, according to the letter. Both Fox News and O'Reilly dismissed the allegations, according to spokesmen.[153]

A *New York Times* investigation published on April 2, 2017, alleged that as many as five women received payments totaling $13 million to settle claims related to inappropriate behavior by O'Reilly. According to the investigation, inappropriate behavior included "verbal abuse, lewd comments, unwanted advances and phone calls in which it sounded as if Mr. O'Reilly was masturbating."[154]

Among the women making allegations was Wendy Walsh, a regular guest on *The O'Reilly Factor*. Walsh claimed O'Reilly led her to believe he would help her land a lucrative employment position with the cable outlet, but reneged when she rebuffed his advances.[155]

Other women who lodged allegations and who received settlement payments over a nearly fifteen-year period included Rachel Witlieb Bernstein, Laurie Dhue, and Rebecca Gomez Diamond. Former Fox News personality Andrea Tantaros also alleged she was sexually harassed by O'Reilly, according to a lawsuit she filed. Tantaros claimed Fox News conducted surveillance against her, including using hidden cameras, in retaliation for registering harassment complaints against O'Reilly. Tantaros's suit was dismissed by a judge in May 2018.[156]

Bernstein alleged O'Reilly behaved poorly and mistreated her by yelling at her in front of other employees. The other women alleged O'Reilly sexually harassed them while working for Fox News Channel.

O'Reilly responded to the *New York Times* investigation with a written statement. "Just like other prominent and controversial people I'm vulnerable to lawsuits from individuals who want me to pay them to avoid negative publicity," read the statement. It continued, "But most importantly, I'm a father who cares deeply for my children and who would do anything to avoid hurting them in any way. And so I have put to rest any controversies to spare my children."

The irony of O'Reilly's for-the-children statement is that he lost custody of his minor-aged children in 2015, following a messy divorce and custody battle amid allegations of domestic abuse.[157] According to 2014 court records, O'Reilly's teen daughter witnessed him "choking her mom" before "drag[ging] her down some stairs."[158]

Immediately after the April 2 *New York Times* investigation appeared, advertisers began pulling their commercials from *The O'Reilly Factor*. Using phrases such as. "We don't feel this is a good environment," and, "The recent and disturbing allegations…" Mercedes-Benz and Hyundai stopped buying commercials on O'Reilly's show.[159]

In less than one week, dozens of advertisers withdrew their commercials from *The O'Reilly Factor*. Among the companies that stopped paying for advertisements during O'Reilly's program were Bayer, BMW, GlaxoSmithKline, Lexus, Mercedes-Benz, and T. Rowe Price.[160]

On April 19, it was announced that Bill O'Reilly would not be returning to his program or the Fox News Channel. Over the next several months, O'Reilly professed his innocence and dismissed allegations of misconduct against him as unfounded.

On a September 19, 2017, appearance on the *Today Show*, O'Reilly portrayed himself as the victim of a "political hit job." Under tense grilling from *Today Show* anchor Matt Lauer, O'Reilly alleged there was a conspiracy against him.[161] Two months after the O'Reilly interview, Lauer would be fired after several women came forward alleging inappropriate sexual behavior by the *Today Show* anchor.

Then more bad news came for the former *Factor* host. A story broke that O'Reilly paid a $32 million settlement to a former contributor of *The O'Reilly Factor* in January 2017. Lis Wiehl had been a regular for Fox News for fifteen years. She alleged she was subjected to sexual harassment and a nonconsensual sexual relationship, and was the recipient of unsolicited pornographic material.[162]

O'Reilly did not remain silent after Wiehl, the seventh woman to come forward alleging inappropriate behavior and sexual harassment by O'Reilly. The reported total payout by both Fox News and O'Reilly to women who lodged allegations was $45 million. None of the allegations were true, insisted O'Reilly. "It's politically and financially motivated," he claimed. He also signaled he would not engage in litigation to prove his innocence. He said, "I'm not going to sit here in a courtroom for a year and half and let my kids get beaten up every single day of their lives by a tabloid press."[163]

It is the rare occurrence when a public figure assumes all responsibility for their misbehavior or bad judgement. O'Reilly is among the majority who shirk responsibility and instead parcel out blame to others. What may set O'Reilly apart from that group was whom he blamed for his difficulties: the Almighty.

"You know, am I mad at God? Yeah, I'm mad at him," he said in column on his website. He added, "I wish I had more protection. I wish this stuff didn't happen. I can't explain it to you. Yeah, I'm mad at him."[164]

ENDNOTES

CHAPTER 1

1   Email from Benjamin Rhodes, Subj: RE: PREP CALL with Susan: Saturday at 4:00 p.m. ET, September 14, 2012.
2   Paul David Nelson, *General Horatio Gates: A Biography*, (Baton Rouge: Louisiana State University Press, 1976), 141.
3   Preston Russell, "The Conway Cabal," *American Heritage* 46, no. 1 (February/March 1995).
4   Nelson, *General Horatio Gates*, 157.
5   Ron Martin, "Dissent in the Ranks," National History Education Clearinghouse, undated, accessed October 19, 2018, https://teachinghistory.org/history-content/ask-a-historian/24484.
6   Ibid, "Dissent in the Ranks."
7   Russell, "The Conway Cabal."
8   Ibid, "The Conway Cabal."
9   Nelson, *General Horatio Gates*, 42
10   Russell, "The Conway Cabal."
11   Ibid, "The Conway Cabal."
12   Carla Anne Robbins, "In Giving Up Arms Libya Hopes to Gain New Economic Life," *Wall Street Journal*, February 12, 2004.
13   Jo Becker and Scott Shane, "Hillary Clinton, 'Smart Power' and a Dictator's Fall," *New York Times*, February 27, 2016.
14   Reza Sanati, "A Troubling Lesson From Libya: Don't Give Up Nukes," *Christian Science Monitor*, August 30, 2011.
15   Ryan Lizza, "The Consequentialist," *The New Yorker*, April 25, 2011, accessed June 8, 2019, https://www.newyorker.com/magazine/2011/05/02/the-consequentialist.
16   Julian Pecquet, "Benghazi Witness Points Finger at Clinton on Lapses in Consulate Security," *The Hill*, May 21, 2013.
17   Susan Cornwall and Mark Hosenball, "US Officer Got No Reply to Requests for More Security in Benghazi," *Reuters*, October 9, 2012.
18   Final Report of the Select Committee on the Events Surrounding the 2012 Terrorist Attack in Benghazi, H.R. Rep. No. 114-848, at I-144 (2016), accessed September 27, 2018, https://www.congress.gov/congressional-report/114th-congress/house-report/848/1
19   Ben Rhodes, *The World As It Is: A Memoir of the Obama White House*, (New York: Random House, 2018), 177-179, 279-280, 362-364.

20   Tennille Tracy, "Pickering Defends Benghazi Review Board Report," *Wall Street Journal*, May 12, 2013.

21   Peter Maas, *Manhunt*, (New York: Random House, 1986), 15-18.

22   Ibid, 18.

23   Ibid, 23.

24   Ibid, 32.

25   Ibid, 49.

26   Ibid, 37.

27   Ibid, xiv-xv.

28   Ibid, 52.

29   Laura A. Kiernan, "3 Indicted in Terrorist Aid Scheme," *Washington Post*, April 26, 1980.

30   Al Kamen and Patrick E. Tyler, "Edwin Wilson Said Enticed Back to US by 'Deal' Offer," *Washington Post*, June 23, 1982.

31   Deborah Tedford, "Justice Dept. Admits False Testimony," *Houston Chronicle*, January 19, 2000.

32   Daniel F. Gilmore, "Edwin Wilson called 'Merchant of Death,'" *United Press International*, December 20, 1982.

33   Arnold Lubasch, "Ex-CIA Agent Convicted of Attempted Murder," *New York Times*, October 21, 1983.

34   Stephen Engelberg, "Cuba Holds Ex-CIA Man US Sought for 15 Years," *New York Times*, September 19, 1995.

35   Cathy Burke, "Jailed Spy: Files Prove That Feds Lied," *New York Post*, November 9, 1999.

36   Tedford, "Justice Dept. Admits False Testimony."

37   Kim Cobb and Rosanna Ruiz, "Ex-CIA Agent's Conviction Tossed," *Houston Chronicle*, October 29, 2003.

38   Lee Hockstader, "Jailed Ex-Spy Blocks Auction On Va. Estate," *Washington Post*, October 3, 1984.

39   Vernon Loeb, "Fallout From a CIA Affidavit; Rogue Ex-Agent Seeks to Overturn '83 Conviction," *Washington Post*, April 24, 2000.

40   Douglas Brinkley, *Tour of Duty: John Kerry and the Vietnam War*, (New York: William Morrow, 2004), 290.

41   John E. O'Neill and Jerome R. Corsi PhD., *Unfit for Command: Swift Boat Veterans Speak Out Against John Kerry*, (Washington, DC: Regnery, 2004), 82.

42   O'Neill and Corsi, *Unfit for Command*, 82.

43   Ibid, *Unfit for Command*, 81.

44   Brinkley, *Tour of Duty*, 291.

45   Brinkley, *Tour of Duty*, 291.

46   O'Neill and Corsi, *Unfit for Command*, 83.

47   Ibid, *Unfit for Command*, 83.

48   Brinkley, *Tour of Duty*, 147.

49   O'Neill and Corsi, *Unfit for Command*, 36.
50   Ibid, *Unfit for Command*, 37.
51   Exec. Order No. 9066, 7 Fed. Reg. 93 (Jan. 6, 1942).
52   Wendy Ng, *Japanese American Internment During World War II*, (Connecticut: Greenwood, 2002), 1-2.
53   Ibid, 5.
54   Ibid, xix.
55   "Semiannual Report of the War Relocation Authority, for the Period January 1 to June 30, 1946," Harry S. Truman Presidential Library and Museum, not dated, accessed March 11, 2019, https://www.trumanlibrary.org/whistlestop/study_collections/japanese_internment/documents/index.php?pagenumber=4&documentid=62&documentdate=1946-00-00&collectionid=JI&nav=ok.
56   "Japanese Relocation During World War II," National Archives, undated. Accessed March 11, 2019, https://www.archives.gov/education/lessons/japanese-relocation
57   S. Doc. No. 79-244, at 12 (1946).
58   Ibid.
59   Audrie Girdner and Anne Loftis, *The Great Betrayal: The Evacuation of the Japanese Americans during World War II*, (London: MacMillan, 1969), 100
60   Ng, *Japanese American Internment…*, 23.
61   Morton Grodzins, *Americans Betrayed: Politics and the Japanese Evacuation*, (Chicago: University of Chicago Press, 1949), 130.
62   Commission on Wartime Relocation and Internment of Civilians Act of 1988, Pub. L. No. 100-383, 102 Stat. 903 (1990).
63   Robert S. McNamara, *In Retrospect: The Tragedy and Lessons of Vietnam*, (New York: Times Books, 1995), 169.
64   Susan Fraker, Jon Lowell, Eleanor Clift, and Mary Lord, "After the Pardon," *Newsweek*, January 31, 1977.
65   Allen Pusey, "Carter Pardons Vietnam-Era Draft Dodgers," *ABA Journal*, October 2014.
66   Exec. Order No. 11,967, 42 Fed. Reg. 4331 (1977).
67   "Seven Wonders," American Society of Civil Engineers, accessed March 16, 2019, https://web.archive.org/web/20100802060056/http://www.asce.org/Content.aspx?id=2147487305.
68   Donald Barr Chidsey, *The Panama Canal: An Informal History*, (New York: Crown, 1970), 103.
69   Chidsey, *The Panama Canal*, 117.
70   Philippe Bunau-Varilla, *From Panama to Verdun: My Fight for France*, (Philadelphia: Dorrance, 1940), 150.

71   Office of the Historian, "The Panama Canal and the Torrijos-Carter Treaties." Accessed January 31, 2019, https://history.state.gov/milestones/1977-1980/panama-canal.

72   Paul J. Scheips, *The Panama Canal: Readings on its History*, (Delaware: Michael Glazier, 1979), 125.

73   Sylvia Engdahl, *Perspectives on Modern World History: Building the Panama Canal*, (Detroit: Greenhaven Press, 2012), 25-27.

74   David McCullough, *The Path Between the Seas: The Creation of the Panama Canal 1870-1914*, (New York: Simon and Schuster, 1977), 140

75   Thomas J. Cutler, *The US Naval Institute on the Panama Canal*, (Annapolis: Naval Institute Press, 2016), 24.

76   Engdahl, *Perspectives on Modern World History*, 39.

77   Jimmy Carter, *Keeping Faith: Memoirs of a President*, (Toronto: Bantam, 1982), 154.

78   James Wooten, Untitled, *New York Times*, June 24, 1976.

79   Office of the Historian, "The Panama Canal and the Torrijos-Carter Treaties," State.gov, accessed January 31, 2019, https://history.state.gov/milestones/1977-1980/panama-canal.

80   Don Richardson, *Conversations with Carter*, (Boulder: Lynne Rienner Publishers, 1998), 68.

81   Office of the Historian, "The Panama Canal and the Torrijos-Carter Treaties," State.gov. Accessed January 31, 2019, https://history.state.gov/milestones/1977-1980/panama-canal.

82   "The Bay of Pigs Invasion/Playa Girón: A Chronology of Events," National Security Archives, George Washington University, accessed September 21, 2019, https://nsarchive2.gwu.edu/bayofpigs/chron.html.

83   Ibid.

84   Ibid.

85   Seymour M. Hersh, *The Dark Side of Camelot*, (Boston: Little, Brown, 1997), 207.

86   Ibid, 204-205.

87   "The Bay of Pigs Invasion/Playa Girón," National Security Archives, George Washington University, accessed September 21, 2019, https://nsarchive2.gwu.edu/bayofpigs/chron.html.

88   Ibid.

89   Hersh, *The Dark Side of Camelot*, 213.

90   Michael Voss, "Bay of Pigs: The 'Perfect Failure' of Cuba invasion," *BBC*, April 14, 2011.

91   "The Bay of Pigs Invasion/Playa Girón," National Security Archives, George Washington University, accessed September 21, 2019, https://nsarchive2.gwu.edu/bayofpigs/chron.html

92   Christopher Hitchens, "Close But No Cigar," *The Nation*, October 5, 1998.

93   Ibid.

94   John Diamond, "Most JCS Members Not Consulted Before Afghanistan, Sudan bombings," *Associated Press*, October 6, 1998.

95   Tim Weiner and Steven Lee Myers, "After the Attacks: The Overview," *New York Times*, August 29, 1998.

96   "Plant's Owner 'Never Met Bin Laden,'" *Birmingham (UK) Post*, August 24, 1998.

97   John Bierman, "Bombing of Innocent Pharmaceuticals Plant Not US's Finest Hour," *Financial Post*, September 11, 1998.

98   Ian Cobain, "Clinton's Revenge," *Daily Mail*, August 21, 1998.

99   "Convenient for Bill Clinton to Launch Raids on Terrorist Camps," *(Scottish) Daily Record*, August 21, 1998.

100   Terry Atlas and Ray Moseley, "'Smoking Gun' for Sudan Raid Now in Doubt," *Chicago Tribune*, August 28, 1998.

101   "Attack on Iraq," *New York Times*, December 17, 1998.

102   Youseff M. Ibrahim, "U.N. Tries to Cajole Iraq into Cooperating on Arms Inspections," *New York Times*, October 14, 1998

103   "Comprehensive Report of the Special Advisor to the DCI on Iraq's WMD," CIA.gov, accessed January 4, 2019, https://www.cia.gov/library/reports/general-reports-1/iraq_wmd_2004.

104   Press Release, United States Senate Select Committee on Intelligence, June 20, 2003, accessed March 17, 2019, https://web.archive.org/web/20030627215056/http://intelligence.senate.gov/030620.htm.

105   "CNN Obtains Evidence Iraq Had Secret Nuclear Weapons Program," *Lou Dobbs Tonight*, June 25, 2003.

106   Sen. Rep. No. 108-301, at 8 (2004).

107   Ibid, at 14.

108   Ibid,16.

109   Ibid,18.

110   Ibid, 22.

111   Ibid, 23.

112   Ibid, 24.

113   Ibid, 26.

114   Ibid, 27.

115   Dana Priest and Dafna Linzer, "Panel Condemns Iraq Prewar Intelligence," *Washington Post*, July 10, 2004.

116   George W. Bush, *Decision Points*, (New York: Crown, 2010), 268-269.

CHAPTER 2

1   E. J. Dionne, Jr., "Biden Admits Plagiarism in School but Says it Was Not 'Malevolent,'" *New York Times*, September 18, 1987.

2 Thomas Keneally, *American Scoundrel: The Life of the Notorious Civil War General Dan Sickles*, (New York: Doubleday, 2002), 67.

3 Edward L. Pierce, *Memoirs and Letters of Charles Sumner*, (Boston: Roberts Brothers, 1893), 448-449.

4 *The Works of Charles Sumner, Vol IV*, (Boston: Lee and Shepard, 1875), 140.

5 Ibid, 143.

6 Ibid,144.

7 Ibid,144.

8 Ibid,153.

9 Ibid, 127.

10 David Donald, *Charles Sumner and the Coming Civil War*, (New York: Alfred A. Knopf, 1961), 302.

11 Ibid, 286-287.

12 Ibid, 290-291

13 Ibid, 291.

14 Ibid, 289.

15 Williamjames Hull Hoffer, *The Caning of Charles Sumner: Honor, Idealism, and the Origins of the Civil War*, (Baltimore: The Johns Hopkins University Press, 2010), 7.

16 David Donald, *Charles Sumner and the Coming Civil War*, (New York: Alfred A. Knopf, 1961), 294-295.

17 Hoffer, *The Caning of Charles Sumner*, 9.

18 Ibid, 9.

19 Donald, *Charles Sumner and the Coming Civil War*, 296.

20 Archibald H. Grimke, *Charles Sumner: The Scholar in Politics*, (New York: Funk & Wagnalls, 1892), 284-285.

21 Williamjames Hull Hoffer, *The Caning of Charles Sumner: Honor, Idealism, and the Origins of the Civil War*, (Baltimore: Johns Hopkins University Press, 2010), 80-81.

22 Thomas Keneally, *American Scoundrel: The Life of the Notorious Civil War General Dan Sickles*, (New York: Doubleday, 2002), 18.

23 Ibid, 23-24.

24 Ibid, 75.

25 Nat Brandt, *The Congressman Who Got Away with Murder*, (Syracuse: Syracuse University Press, 1991), 11.

26 Ibid, 12-13.

27 Keneally, *American Scoundrel*, 82.

28 James A. Hessler, *Sickles at Gettysburg*, (New York: Savas Beatie, 2015), 9.

29 Keneally, *American Scoundrel*, 124-129.

30 James A. Hessler, *Sickles at Gettysburg*, (New York: Savas Beatie, 2015), 12.

31   Ibid, 13-16.

32   E. J. Dionne Jr., "Biden Was Accused of Plagiarism in Law School," *New York Times*, September 17, 1987.

33   Ibid.

34   Lee May, "Biden Admits Plagiarism in Writing Law School Brief," *Los Angeles Times*, September 18, 1987.

35   Maureen Dowd, "Biden Is Facing Growing Debate On His Speeches," *New York Times*, September 16, 1987.

36   "The Similarity in Biden Speeches," *Miami Herald*, September 18, 1987.

37   Lily Rothman, "This Is What Happened the First Time Joe Biden Ran for President," *Time*, October 21, 2015.

38   Maureen Dowd, "Biden's Debate Finale: An Echo From Abroad," *New York Times*, September 12, 1987.

39   Ibid.

40   David Wilsford, *Political leaders of Contemporary Western Europe: A Biographical Dictionary*, (Westport: Greenwood Publishing Group, 1995), 236.

41   John M. Broder, "Father's Tough Life an Inspiration for Biden," *New York Times*, October 23, 2008.

42   Steve Neal, "Williamson Embraces Savage's Game," *Chicago Sun-Times*, September 16, 1992.

43   *Politics in America, 1992* (Washington, DC: Congressional Quarterly, 1991), 360–361.

44   Mike Robinson, "Savage Condemns 'Zionist Lobby,'" *Associated Press*, 12 May 1982.

45   George F. Will, "The Worst Congressman," *Washington Post*, March 5, 1992.

46   Neal, "Williamson Embraces Savage's Game."

47   Michael Oreskes, "Lawmaker is Accused of Sexual Impropriety," *New York Times*, July 29, 1989.

48   Ibid.

49   "Topics of the Times: Racism to Gus Savage," *New York Times*, April 4, 1990.

50   Steven A. Holmes, "Panel is Critical of Representative," *New York Times*, February 3, 1990.

51   "Topics of the Times: Racism to Gus Savage," *New York Times*, April 4, 1990.

52   Ibid.

53   Howard Kurtz, "How Not to Say 'No Comment:' Reporter Recounts Rep. Savage's 'Tirade,'" *Washington Post*, June 26, 1991.

54   Vernon Jarrett, "Incumbents Deserve Re-election in Two South Side Districts," *Chicago Sun-Times*, March 10, 1992.

55   Francis Storrs, "Ted Kennedy's Living History," *Boston Magazine*, November 30, 2009, accessed September 3, 2017, https://www.bostonmagazine.com/2009/11/30/living-history-ted-kennedy-remembered/.

56   Carrie Fisher, *Shockaholic*, (New York: Simon & Schuster, 2011), 39–46.

57   "Capitol Hill Bids Adieu to La Brasserie Restaurant," *Washington Times*, August 2, 2005.

58   Michael Kelly, "Ted Kennedy on the Rocks," *GQ Magazine*, February 1990, accessed September 5, 2017, https://www.gq.com/story/kennedy-ted-senator-profile.

59   Ibid.

60   Leonard Schlup, *Lovell Harrison Rousseau, American National Biography Online*, Oxford University Press, 1999. Accessed November 24, 2017, http://www.anb.org/articles/04/04-00870.html

61   Leonard Schlup, "Lovell Harrison Rousseau," AmericanNationalBiography.org, accessed November 24, 2017, http://www.anb.org/articles/04/04-00870.html.

62   H.R. Rep. No. 39-90, at 40 (1866).

63   Ibid, 41.

64   Ibid, 42.

65   Ibid, 42.

66   Ibid, 43.

67   Ibid, 16.

68   Ibid, 16.

69   Ibid, 16.

70   Ibid, 10.

71   Ibid, 21.

72   Ibid, 25.

73   Philip M. Lucas, *Josiah Bushnell Grinnell, American National Biography,* (Oxford University Press, 1999), https://doi.org/10.1093/anb/9780198606697.article.0400440.

74   Josiah Grinnell, *Men and Events of Forty Years: Autobiographical Reminiscences of an Active Career from 1850 to 1890*, (Boston: D. Lothrop Company, 1891), 163.

75   Ibid, 170.

76   Leonard Schlup, "Lovell Harrison Rousseau."

77   Jim Wooten, "4th Congressional District: Rep. McKinney, an Insider Running as an Out," *The Atlanta Journal-Constitution*, June 26, 1996.

78   Chris Suellentrop, "Cynthia McKinney," *Slate*, April 19, 2002.

79   Bill Nigut, "Deconstructing Cynthia McKinney," *Atlanta Jewish Times*, November 5, 1999.

80   Kevin Sack, "Tensions Over Racism and Anti-Semitism Have Surfaced in Georgia House Campaign," *New York Times*, October 16, 1996.

81   Nigut, "Deconstructing Cynthia McKinney."

82   Ibid.

83   Wooten, "4ᵗʰ Congressional District…".

84   Suellentrop, "Cynthia McKinney."

85   Ibid.

86   Laurie Kellman, "Lawyer Says McKinney a Victim of 'Being in Congress While Black,'" *Associated Press*, March 31, 2006.

87   Bob Kemper, "McKinney Accuses Capitol Hill Cop of Racism," *The Atlanta Journal-Constitution*, April 1, 2006.

88   Kellman, "Lawyer says McKinney a Victim…".

89   "Rep. McKinney Apologizes for Altercation with Capitol Cop," *Grand Rapid Press*, April 7,2006.

90   Cynthia Ann McKinney, "'El No Murio, El Se Multiplico!' Hugo Chávez: The Leadership and the Legacy on Race," (PhD thesis, Antioch University, 2015), https://aura.antioch.edu/etds/208/.

91   Ibid.

92   Neil A. Lewis, "Mayor of Washington is Yielding Duties After Cocaine Arrest," *New York Times,* January 20, 1990.

93   Ronald J. Ostrow, "Barry Charged with Crack Cocaine Possession," *Los Angeles Times*, January 20, 1990.

94   "Ex-Model Connected with Barry Arrest Was Awarded Contract," *United Press International*, January 27, 1990.

95   John Cassidy, "Drug-bust Mayor May Escape His Honey Trap," *Sunday (London) Times*, January 21, 1990.

96   Tracy Thompson and Michael York, "Barry Turns Over Government Power," *Washington Post*, January 20, 1990.

97   Paul Collins, *Duel with the Devil: The True Story of How Alexander Hamilton & Aaron Burr Teamed Up to Take on America's First Sensational Murder Mystery*, (New York: Crown Publishers, 2013), 36.

98   John Sedgwick, *War of Two: Alexander Hamilton, Aaron Burr, and the Duel that Stunned the Nation*, (New York: Berkley, 2015), 110.

99   Collins, *Duel with the Devil*, 92.

100   Ibid, 94.

101   Ibid, 114.

102   Ron Chernow, *Alexander Hamilton*, (New York: The Penguin Press, 2004), 697.

103   Ibid, 680.

104   Sedgwick, *War of Two*, 325.

105   Chernow, *Alexander Hamilton*, 685.

106   Ibid, 683.

107   Ibid, 686.

108   Sedgwick, *War of Two*, xvii.

109   Chernow, *Alexander Hamilton*, 689.

110   Ibid, 690.
111   Ibid, 692.

CHAPTER 3

1   Jeff Leen, "Lewinsky: Two Coasts, Two Lives, Many Images,"
       Washington Post, January 24, 1998.
2   Clinton T. Brass, "Shut-down of the Federal Government: Causes,
       Processes and Effects," *Congressional Research Service*, February 18,
       2011.
3   Kenneth Starr, "Nature of President Clinton's Relationship with Monica
       Lewinsky," accessed September 18, 2018, https://www.washingtonpost.
       com/wp-srv/politics/special/clinton/icreport/icreport.htm.
4   Jeff Leen, "Lewinsky: Two Coasts, Two Lives, Many Images,"
       Washington Post, January 24, 1998.
5   "Clinton Accused: Time Line," *Washington Post*, September 13, 1998.
6   Byron York, "Slick Billy," *American Spectator*, December 1998.
7   Charles McGrath, "Reporter on Retracted Newsweek Article Put
       Monica on the Map," *New York Times*, May 17, 2005.
8   Hillary Rodham Clinton, *Living History*, (New York: Simon & Schuster:
       2003), 440.
9   Ibid, 440.
10   Jamal Eric Watson, "Political Scientist Karin Stanford Reborn as a Hip
       Hop Scholar," *Diverse Issues in Higher Education*, March 3, 2011.
11   Peter Slevin and William Claiborne, "Jackson Apologizes, to Take Time
       Off," *Washington Post*, January 19, 2001.
12   "Operation PUSH Documents Financial Ties with Jackson Lover,"
       CNN.com, February 1, 2001, accessed September 18, 2018, http://
       edition.cnn.com/2001/US/02/01/jackson.money/index.html.
13   "Mother Wants Jesse Jackson to 'Be a Father' to Illegitimate Child,"
       CNN.com, August 16, 2001, accessed September 18, 2018, http://www.
       cnn.com/2001/US/08/16/jackson.mistress/index.html?_s=PM:US.
14   Howard Kurtz, "Tabloid News Again Floods Mainstream; Jesse
       Jackson's Affair 'Legitimate' Story," *Washington Post*, January 19, 2001.
15   "Jesse Jackson Admits Affair, Illegitimate Child," *ABC News*, January 18,
       2001.
16   Pam Belluck, "Jackson Says He Fathered Child in Affair With Aide,"
       New York Times, January 19, 2001.
17   Slevin and Claiborne, "Jackson Apologizes, to Take Time Off."
18   "Jesse Jackson Admits Affair…," *ABC News*.
19   Marc Morano, "Jesse Jackson's Mistress Claims Blacks
       'Scapegoated' Her," *CNS News*, July 7, 2008, accessed

September 18, 2018, https://www.cnsnews.com/news/article/ jesse-jacksons-mistress-claims-blacks-scapegoated-her.

20   Patricia Shipp, "Jesse Jackson is a Deadbeat Dad!" *The National Enquirer*, January 19, 2012, accessed September 18, 2018, https://www. nationalenquirer.com/celebrity/jesse-jackson-deadbeat-dad/.

21   Paul Taylor, "Hart to Withdraw From Presidential Campaign," Washington Post, May 8, 1987.

22   "Faced with More Revelations, Hart Withdrawing from Race," *St. Petersburg Times*, May 8, 1987.

23   Hersh, *The Dark Side of Camelot*, 295.

24   Ibid, 296–297.

25   Ibid, 300.

26   Ibid, 299-300.

27   Ibid, 303-306.

28   Glenn Kessler, "Trying to Kill Fidel Castro," *Washington Post*, June 27, 2007.

29   Hersh, *The Dark Side of Camelot*, 311.

30   Stephen Green and Margot Hornblower, "Mills Admits Being Present During Tidal Basin Scuffle," *Washington Post*, October 11, 1974.

31   Annabel Battistella, *Fanne Foxe*, (New York: Pinnacle, 1975), 112.

32   Green and Hornblower, "Mills Admits Being Present…."

33   "Man in Car Incident Mills, DC Police Say," *Pittsburgh Post-Gazette*, October 10, 1974.

34   Green and Hornblower, "Mills Admits Being Present…."

35   "Mills Keeping off Hill as Speculation Swirls," *Pittsburgh Post-Gazette*, October 12, 1974.

36   Green and Hornblower, "Mills Admits Being Present…."

37   Battistella, *Fanne Foxe*, 154.

38   Green and Hornblower, "Mills Admits Being Present…."

39   Joseph E. Perisco, *Franklin & Lucy*, (New York: Random House, 2008), 79.

40   Ibid, 28–31.

41   Ibid, 81–82.

42   Ibid, 83–84.

43   Ibid, 86–94.

44   Roger Daniels, *Franklin D. Roosevelt: Road to the New Deal, 1882-1939*, (Urbana, Illinois: University of Illinois Press, 2015), 37-38.

45   Ibid, 38–39.

46   Ibid, 17

47   Ibid, 161.

48   Jim Davenport, "SC Governor to return to work after mystery trip," *San Diego Union-Tribune*, June 23, 2009.

49   John O'Connor & Clif LeBlanc, "Sanford Back Wednesday, His Office Says," *The State*, June 23, 2009.

50   Gina Smith, "Sanford Met in Atlanta After Returning from South America," *The State*, June 24, 2009.

51   "Governor Says He 'Crossed Lines' with Women," *Brownsville Herald*, June 30, 2009.

52   Ibid.

53   Francis D. Cogliano, *Thomas Jefferson: Reputation and Legacy*, (Charlottesville, VA: University of Virginia Press, 2006), 170.

54   Annette Thomas Gordon-Reed, *Jefferson and Sally Hemings: An American Controversy*, (Charlottesville, VA: University Press of Virginia, 1997), 61.

55   Fawn M. Brodie, *Thomas Jefferson: An Intimate History*, (New York: W.W. Norton & Company, 1974), 23.

56   Joyce Appleby, *Thomas Jefferson*, (New York: Times Books, 2003), 74.

57   Brodie, *Thomas Jefferson*, 82–83.

58   Gordon-Reed, *Jefferson and Sally Hemings*, 160.

59   John B. Boles, *Jefferson: Architect of American Liberty*, (New York: Basic Books, 2017), 469.

60   R. B. Bernstein, *Thomas Jefferson*, (New York: Oxford University Press, 2003), 66.

61   Boles, *Jefferson: Architect of American Liberty*, 151-152.

62   Ibid, 202.

63   Ibid, 265.

64   Gordon-Reed, *Jefferson and Sally Hemings*, 2.

65   Boles, *Jefferson: Architect of American Liberty*, 469-470.

66   Appleby, *Thomas Jefferson*, 75.

67   Scott Higham and Sari Horwitz, *Finding Chandra: A True Washington Murder Mystery*. (New York City: Scribner, 2010), 25-26.

68   Ibid, 55.

69   Ibid, 28.

70   Ibid, 72-75.

71   Ibid, 94-97

72   Ibid, 124.

73   Ibid, 132-133.

74   Ibid, 134-135.

75   Chernow, *Alexander Hamilton*, 85.

76   Ibid, 362.

77   Joanne B. Freeman, *Affairs of Honor: National Politics in the New Republic*. (New Haven: Yale University Press, 2002).

78   Chernow, *Alexander Hamilton*, 409.

79   Chernow, *Alexander Hamilton*, 365.

80   Freeman, *Affairs of Honor*, 72.

81   Chernow, *Alexander Hamilton*, 409–410.

82   Ibid, 418.

CHAPTER 4

1   Jane Mayer, "How Russia Helped Swing the Election for
        Trump," *The New Yorker*, October 1, 2018, accessed March
        27, 2019, https://www.newyorker.com/magazine/2018/10/01/
        how-russia-helped-to-swing-the-election-for-trump.

2   Jonathan Daniels, *The Randolphs of Virginia*, (New York: Doubleday,
        1972), 257.

3   Richard E. Ellis, *Andrew Jackson*, (Washington, DC: CQ Press, 2003),
        276.

4   John F. Marszalek, *The Petticoat Affair: Manners, Mutiny, and Sex in
        Andrew Jackson's White House*, (New York: Free Press, 1997), 46.

5   Robert P. Watson, *Affairs of State: The Untold History of Presidential
        Love, Sex, and Scandal, 1789-1900*, (Lanham, Maryland: Rowman &
        Littlefield, 2012), 191.

6   Robert V. Remini, *The Life of Andrew Jackson*, (New York: Harper &
        Row, 1977), 174.

7   Marszalek, *The Petticoat Affair*, 47.

8   Daniels, *The Randolphs of Virginia*, 248–249.

9   Ibid, 253.

10   Ibid, 254.

11   Watson, *Affairs of State*, 194.

12   Ibid, 199.

13   "Evidence Points to Deceit by Brawley," *New York Times*, September 27,
        1988.

14   Ralph Blumenthal, "Abrams Considers a Possible Hoax in Brawley
        Case," *New York Times*, June 16, 1988.

15   "1,000 March to Protest Racial Violence," *Associated Press*, December
        12, 1987.

16   Robert D. McFadden, *Outrage: The Story Behind the Tawana Brawley
        Hoax*, (New York: Bantam Books, 1990), 137.

17   Michael Gartland, "Pay-up Time for Brawley," *New York Post*, August 4,
        2013.

18   McFadden, *Outrage*, 334.

19   Blumenthal, "Abrams Considers a Possible Hoax...."

20   Frank Bruni, "Mourning a Son Tied to the Brawley Case," *New York
        Times*, April 5, 1998.

21   Frank Bruni, "Finally, His Day in Court: Man Wrongly Accused in
        Brawley Case Will Be Heard," *New York Times*, March 15, 1998.

22   "Evidence Points to Deceit by Brawley," *New York Times*, September 27, 1988.

23   "Former Aide Says 'Too Many Lies' Surround Teen's Rape Story," *Associated Press*, June 15, 1988.

24   Ford Fessenden, "Ex-Sharpton Aide is Subpoenaed; Advisers Labeled 'Frauds,'" *New York Newsday*, June 16, 1988.

25   "Grand Jury Decides to Subpoena Brawley," *Chicago Tribune*, August 16, 1988.

26   McFadden, *Outrage*, 93-95.

27   Frank Bruni, "Finally, His Day in Court...."

28   Gersh Kuntzman, "'Tawana Brawl' Judge KOs Geraldo," *New York Post*, June 18, 1998.

29   "Winner in Brawley Suit Says Victory is Bittersweet," CNN.com, July 14, 1998, accessed December 2, 2017, https://archive.li/ksYLE.

30   Michael Gartland, "Pay-up Time for Brawley...."

31   Dov H. Levin, "When the Great Power Gets a Vote: The Effects of Great Power Electoral Interventions on Election Results," *International Studies Quarterly*, 2016.

32   Dov H. Levin, "Sure, the US and Russia often meddle in foreign elections. Does it matter?" *Washington Post*, September 7, 2016.

33   Permanent Subcommittee on Investigations, *Review of US State Department Grants to OneVoice*, (Washington, DC: US Senate, July 12, 2016), 19.

34   Joint Statement from the Department of Homeland Security and the Office of the Director of National Intelligence on Election Security, October 7, 2016.

35   Jim Geraghty, "Shattered Illusions," *National Review*, April 19, 2017, accessed March 27, 2019, https://www.nationalreview.com/2017/04/shattered-jonathan-allen-amie-parnes-clinton-campaign-dysfunction-revealed/.

36   Jonathan Allen and Amie Parnes, *Shattered: Inside Hillary Clinton's Doomed Campaign*, (New York: Crown, 2017), 395.

37   "US Statement on Reliability of Election Results," *New York Times*, November 26, 2016.

38   Mayer, "How Russia Helped Swing the Election for Trump."

39   David Jackson, "John Brennan: Donald Trump's Denial of Russian Collusion is 'Hogwash,'" *USA Today*, August 16, 2018, accessed March 27, 2019, https://www.usatoday.com/story/news/politics/2018/08/16/john-brennan-donald-trump-denial-russian-collusion-hogwash/1006293002/.

40   David Rutz, "CNN, MSNBC Have Given Stormy Daniels Lawyer Michael Avenatti $175 Million in Earned Media," *Washington Free Beacon*, May 11, 2018.

41   Neil Rothschild, "The Social Media spread of Trump/Mueller," Axios,
       March 25, 2019, accessed March 27, 2019, https://www.axios.com/
       robert-mueller-donald-trump-social-media-reach-0586790d-711f-42fe-
       b3e1-21acc54cdfa6.html.

42   "Background to 'Assessing Russian Activities and Intentions in Recent
       US Elections:' The Analytic Process and Cyber Incident Attribution
       (ICA 2017-01D)," January 6, 2017.

43   Ibid.

44   Ibid.

45   David Remnick, "Going the Distance," *The New Yorker*, January
       27, 2014, accessed March 27, 2019, https://www.newyorker.com/
       magazine/2014/01/27/going-the-distance-david-remnick.

46   Matt Zapotosky and John Wagner, "McCabe Says He Quickly Opened
       FBI Investigation of Trump for Fear of Being Fired," *Washington Post*,
       February 2019.

47   "Appointment of Special Counsel to Investigate Russian Interference
       with the 2016 Presidential Election and Related Matters," Order No.
       3915-2017, (May 17, 2017).

48   Deroy Murdock, "The Mueller Probe: A Year-Old Hyperpartisand
       Circus," *National Review*, May 18, 2018, accessed March
       28, 2019, https://www.nationalreview.com/2018/05/
       robert-mueller-russia-probe-democrats-dominate-staff/.

49   Adam Goldman and Michael S. Schmidt, "F.B.I. Agent Peter Strzok,
       Who Criticized Trump in Texts, Is Fired," *New York Times*, August 13,
       2018.

50   Margot Cleveland, "Missing: Key Documents About Alleged
       Misconduct By Robert Mueller's Lead Prosecutor," *The Federalist*,
       January 14, 2019, accessed March 27, 2019, https://thefederalist.
       com/2019/01/14/missing-key-documents-alleged-misconduct-robert-
       muellers-lead-prosecutor/.

51   William P. Barr, "Letter to Chairs and Ranking Members of House and
       Senate Judiciary Committees," March 24, 2019.

52   "Letter regarding Senator Kennedy's request to the General Secretary
       of the Communist Party Comrade Y.V. Andropov, Committee on State
       Security of the USSR," May 14, 1983.

53   Thomas B. Edsall and Edward Walsh, "FEC Issues Record Fines in
       Democrats' Scandals," *Washington Post*, September 21, 2002.

54   Thomas Farragher, "Road to Fundraising Scandal Led Straight Through
       California," *San Jose Mercury News*, July 6, 1997.

55   Ruth Marcus and Ira Chinoy, "A Fund-Raising 'Mistake:' DNC Event in
       Buddhist Temple," *Washington Post*, October 17, 1996.

56   Nathan Abse, "Campaign Finance Probe: 94 Who Aren't Talking,"
       Washington Post, June 9, 1998.

57   Marcus and Chinoy, "A Fund-Raising 'Mistake.'"

58   John Howard, "Campaign Fund-Raising Controversy Hits California Politics," *Associated Press*, April 22, 1997.

59   Farragher, "Road to Fundraising Scandal...."

60   "Al Gore and the Temple of Cash," *New York Times,* February 22, 1998.

61   Ibid.

62   Roberto Suro and Michael Grunwald, "Reno Orders 90-Day Investigation of Gore," *Washington Post*, August 27, 1998.

63   Ronald Ostrow, Robert Jackson, and Ronald Brownstein, "Reno Won't Pursue Gore Investigation," *Los Angeles Times*, November 25, 1998.

64   Neil A. Lewis, "Veteran Gore Fund-Raiser Goes on Trial," *New York Times*, February 8, 2000.

65   Bill Miller, "Hsia is Convicted of Illegal Donations," *Washington Post*, March 3, 2000.

66   Jeremiah Wright, "The Day of Jerusalem's Fall," Sermon, September 16, 2001.

67   Barack Obama, "On My Faith and My Church," *Huffington Post*, March 14, 2008, accessed November 9, 2017, https://www.huffingtonpost.com/barack-obama/on-my-faith-and-my-church_b_91623.html.

68   Barack Obama, "A More Perfect Union," *Constitution Center*, March 18, 2008, accessed November 3, 2017, https://constitutioncenter.org/amoreperfectunion/.

69   Manya A. Brachear, "Rev. Jeremiah A. Wright, Jr.: Pastor Inspires Obama's 'Audacity,'" *Chicago Tribune*, January 21, 2007.

70   Ibid.

71   Ken Dilanian, "Defenders say Wright has Love, Righteous Anger for USA," *USA Today*, March 19, 2008.

72   Frank Madison Reid III, Jeremiah A. Wright Jr., and Colleen Birchett, *When Black Men Stand Up for God,* (Chicago: African American Images, 1996), 68.

73   Ibid, 79.

74   Jeremiah A. Wright Jr., *What Makes You So Strong? Sermons of Joy and Strength*, (Valley Forge, PA: Judson Press, 1993), 66.

75   Ibid, 72.

76   Reid, Wright, and Birchett, *When Black Men Stand Up for God*, 45.

77   Ibid, 34-35, 37, 99.

78   Ibid, 80.

79   Ibid, 81.

80   Ibid, 31.

81   David Squires, "Rev. Jeremiah Wright says 'Jews' Are Keeping Him from President Obama," *Daily Press*, June 10, 2009.

82   James Reston, "Washington; Kennedy and Bork," *New York Times*, July 5, 1987.

83 Ibid.

84 Tobin Harshaw, "Kennedy, Bork, and the Politics of Judicial Destruction," *New York Times*, August 28, 2009.

85 John Fund, "The Borking Begins," *Wall Street Journal*, January 8, 2001.

86 Mark Paoletta, "Anita Hill and the Smokeless Gun," *Washington Examiner*, March 21, 2016.

87 Transcript of Proceedings, Telephonic Interview of Susan Jane Hoerchner, United States Senate Committee on the Judiciary, October 10, 1991.

88 Michael Wines, "The Thomas Nomination: Phone Logs Leave a Trail of Questions," *New York Times*, October 11, 1991.

89 Clarence Thomas, *My Grandfather's Son: A Memoir*, (New York: Harper, 2007), 243.

90 Editorial, "The Thomas Nomination," *Washington Post*, October 15, 1989.

91 *The Impeachment of Andrew Johnson (1868) President of the United States*, US Senate. Accessed January 19, 2019, https://www.senate.gov/artandhistory/history/common/briefing/Impeachment_Johnson.htm

92 Michael Les Benedict, *The Impeachment and Trial of Andrew Johnson*, (New York: W. W. Norton, 1973), 49.

93 Hans L. Trefousee, *Andrew Johnson: A Biography*, (New York: W.W. Norton, 1989), 312-313.

94 Benedict, *The Impeachment and Trial of Andrew Johnson*, 95.

95 *The Impeachment of Andrew Johnson (1868) President of the United States*, US Senate, accessed January 19, 2019, https://www.senate.gov/artandhistory/history/common/briefing/Impeachment_Johnson.htm.

96 Trefousee, *Andrew Johnson*, 287.

97 Clinton, *Living History*, 440.

98 *Nature of President Clinton's Relationship with Monica Lewinsky*, (Washington, DC: US Government Printing Office), accessed March 5, 2019, https://web.archive.org/web/20001203073600/http://icreport.access.gpo.gov/report/6narrit.htm#N_1091_

99 Ibid.

100 "The President's Grand Jury Testimony (cont.)," *Washington Post*, September 22, 1998.

101 *Nature of President Clinton's Relationship....*

102 Donna Britt, "Appalled, but Not Shocked," *Washington Post*, August 21, 1998.

103 William Raspberry, "In the Beginning, Monica Was 5," *Washington Post*, September 14, 1998.

104 Ron Jacobs, *The Way the Wind Blew: A History of the Weather Underground*, (New York: Verso, 1997), 13.

105   Federal Bureau of Investigation (Chicago Field Office), Foreign Influence–Weather Underground Organization (WUO) CG 100-40903, classified Top Secret, August 20, 1976, 3.

106   Terrorism: Review of 1988 and the Prospects for 1989 (Transcript), press briefing at George Washington University, The Elliott School of International Affairs, December 19, 1988.

107   Federal Bureau of Investigation, Foreign Influence–Weather Underground Organization....

108   Sarah Anderson, "Blast from the Past: The UW in the rRotous 1960s and '70s," *The Daily*, January 18, 2007.

109   Editorial, "And Now for the Rest of the Story," *Washington Post*, March 17, 1990.

110   Bill Ayers, *Fugitive Days*, (Boston: Beacon Press, 2001), 261.

111   Douglas Robinson, "Townhouse Razed by Blast and Fire: Man's Body Found," *New York Times*, March 7, 1970.

112   Ibid.

113   "Return of the Weatherman," *Newsweek*, November 2, 1981.

114   Ayers, *Fugitive Days*, 194.

115   Dinitia Smith, "No Regrets for a Love of Explosives," *New York Times*, September 11, 2001.

116   Susan Chira, "At Home With: Bernadine Dohrn: Same Passion, New Tactics," *New York Times*, November 18, 1993.

117   Ibid.

118   Ayers, *Fugitive Days*, 295.

119   Ibid, 228.

120   Ibid, 199.

121   Marcia Froelke Coburn, "No Regrets," *Chicago Magazine*, August 1, 2001.

122   Dinitia Smith, "No Regrets for a Love of Explosives: In a Memoir of Sorts, a War Protester Talks of Life With the Weathermen," *New York Times*, September 11, 2001.

123   Peter Slevin, "Uncommon Ground," *Washington Post*, October 16, 2008.

124   Trevor Jensen, Robert Mitchum, and Mary Owen, "Turbulent Past Contrasts with Quiet Academic Life: Friends, Daley Defend Ex-Radical, Obama neighbor," *Chicago Tribune*, April 18, 2008.

125   Linda Lenz, "Annenberg Challenge a Radical Enclave? Gimme a Break!" *Chicago Sun-Times*, August 30, 2008.

126   Stanley Kurtz, "Obama and Ayers Pushed Radicalism on Schools," *Wall Street Journal*, September 23, 2008, accessed June 9, 2019, https://www.wsj.com/articles/SB122212856075765367.

127   Larry Rohter and Michael Luo, "'60s Radicals Become Issue in Campaign of 2008," *New York Times*, April 17, 2008.

128 Jo Becker and Christopher Drew, "Pragmatic Politics, Forged on the South Side," *New York Times*, May 11, 2008.

129 Jensen, Mitchum, and Owen, "Turbulent Past Contrasts...."

130 Tom Shale, "In the Pa. Debate, the Clear Loser is ABC," *Washington Post*, April 17, 2008.

131 Jim VanDeHei and John F. Harris, "Obama's Secret Weapon: the Media," *Politico*, April 18, 2008.

132 Jeff Jacoby, "Obama's 'Mainstream' Friends," *Boston Globe*, April 27, 2008.

133 Sam Dillon, "Obama Looks to Lessons From Chicago in His National Education Plan," *New York Times*, September 10, 2008.

134 Scott Shane, "Obama and '60s Bomber: A Look Into Crossed Paths," *New York Times*, October 4, 2008.

135 Peter Slevin, "Former '60s Radical Is Now Considered Mainstream in Chicago," *Washington Post*, April 18, 2008.

136 "Guilt by Association," *Chicago Tribune*, April 18, 2008.

137 Bernie Quigley, "Obama and Bill Ayers: Together from the Beginning," *The Hill*, September 24, 2008.

CHAPTER 5

1 S. Rep. No. 100-216, at 11 (1987).

2 Peter L. Hahn, "How Jimmy Carter Lost Iran," *Washington Post*, October 22, 2017.

3 S. Rep. No. 100-216, at 3 (1987).

4 Public Law 98-473, 98 Stat. 1935–1937.

5 Alfonso Chardy, "Report Blasts Reagan 'Zealots:' President Ordered Covert Aid, Panel Finds," *Miami Herald*, November 19, 1987.

6 National Security Act of 1947, 50 U.S.C. 3001 (1947).

7 *Al-Shiraa*, Beirut, November 3, 1986.

8 S. Rep. No. 100-216, at 6 (1987).

9 Ronald Reagan, *An American Life*, (New York: Simon and Schuster, 1990), 504.

10 S. Rep. No. 100-216, at 4 (1987).

11 State Sponsors of Terrorism, US Department of State, January 19, 1984.

12 Frank Newport, Jeffery M. Jones, and Lydia Saad, "Ronald Reagan From the People's Perspective: a Gallup Poll Review", *Gallup*, June 7, 2004.

13 Sean Wilentz, *The Age of Reagan: A History, 1974-2008*, (New York: Harper, 2008), 235-237.

14 *Tower Commission Report*, (Washington, DC, 1987), V-4 - V-7.

15 Lawrence E. Walsh, *Iran-Contra: the Final Report*, (Washington, DC, 1993), xiii.

16   "Text of the President's Speech on his Role in Arms-for-Hostages Swap," *Chicago Tribune*, March 5, 1987.

17   Pardons Granted by President George H. W. Bush (1989-1993), Department of Justice.

18   S. Rep. No. 93-981, at xxiv (1974).

19   Hank Stuever, "The Illuminating Experience of Being Kept in the Dark," *Washington Post*, June 1, 2005.

20   Michael Dobbs, "Revenge Was Felt's Motive, Former Acting FBI Chief Says," *Washington Post*, June 27, 2005.

21   Dan Balz and R. Jeffrey Smith, "Conflicted and Mum For Decades," *Washington Post*, June 1, 2005.

22   David Von Drehle, "BI's No. 2 Was 'Deep Throat:' Mark Felt Ends 30-Year Mystery of The Post's Watergate Source," *Washington Post*, June 1, 2005.

23   *White House Travel Office Operations (GAO/GGD-94-132)*, United States Government Accountability Office, May 1994, 14.

24   Ibid, 46.

25   Ibid, 50.

26   Ibid, 50.

27   Ibid, 45.

28   Toni Locy, "For White House Travel Office, a Two-Year Trip of Trouble," *Washington Post*, February 27, 1995.

29   Final Report of Independent Counsel Robert W. Ray in re: William David Watkins and in re: Hillary Rodham Clinton, October 18, 2000.

30   Ibid, 62.

31   *White House Travel Office Operations (GAO/GGD-94-132)*, United States Government Accountability Office, May 1994, 53.

32   Final Report of Independent Counsel Robert W. Ray...., 222.

33   *White House Travel Office Operations*, 48.

34   Ibid, 3.

35   Ibid, 7.

36   Ibid, 51.

37   Ibid, 24.

38   Ibid, 67-68.

39   Final Report of Independent Counsel Robert W. Ray...., 52.

40   Locy, "For White House Travel Office, a Two-Year Trip of Trouble."

41   Final Report of the Independent Counsel in Re Madison Guaranty Savings and Loan Association, January 5, 2001, 103.

42   Ibid, 122.

43   Locy, "For White House Travel Office, a Two-Year Trip of Trouble."

44   Final Report of the Independent Counsel in Re Madison Guaranty...., 125-128.

45   Richard L. Berke, "Travel Outfit Tied to Clinton Halts Work for White House," *New York Times*, May 22, 1993.

46   David Von Drehle & Howard Schneider, "Foster's Death a Suicide: Report Ascribes Fatality to Personal Collapse," *Washington Post*, July 1, 1994.

47   Ronald Kessler, The Secrets of the FBI, (New York: Crown Publishers, 2011), 108-109.

48   Final Report of the Independent Counsel in Re Madison Guaranty...., 15-17.

49   Final Report of the Independent Counsel in Re Madison Guaranty...., 17.

50   Clinton, *Living History*, 172.

51   Select Committee to Study Governmental Operations with respect to Intelligence Activities, *Intelligence Activities and the Rights of Americans Book II*, US Senate, April 26, 1976.

52   Select Committee to Study Governmental Operations with respect to Intelligence Activities, *Supplementary Detailed Staff Reports on the Intelligence Activities and the Rights of Americans Book III*, US Senate, April 23, 1976, 19.

53   Ibid, 4.

54   Ibid, 4.

55   Ibid, 6.

56   Ibid, 7.

57   Ibid, 7.

58   Ibid, 7.

59   Ibid, 8.

60   Ibid, 10-11.

61   Ibid, 11.

62   Ibid, 12.

63   Ibid, 13.

64   Financial Audit: House Office of the Sergeant at Arms–Periods Ended 6-3-90 and 12-31-89 GAO/AFMD-91-11, September 18, 1991.

65   Ibid, 8.

66   Roll Call Vote 294, House Resolution 236, 102nd Congress, October 3, 1991.

67   Roll Call Vote 44, House Resolution 393, 102nd Congress, March 12, 1992.

68   Roll Call Vote 91, House Resolution 440, 102nd Congress, April 29, 1992.

69   Stephen Chapman, "The House Bank Scandal: Hype, Not Substance," *Chicago Tribune*, March 19, 1992.

70   Basil Talbott, "Bank Scandal Coverage Stirs Heated Debate," *Chicago Sun-Times*, April 17, 1992.

71   Michael Ross and Sara Fritz, "House Postmaster Quits Amid Growing Scandal," *Los Angeles Times*, March 20, 1992.

72   Jack Sirica, "House Postmaster Quits Under Fire," *New York Newsday*, March 20, 1992.

73   Larry Margasak, "Grand Jury Subpoenas Lawmakers' Expense Records in Post Office Probe," *Associated Press*, May 14, 1992.

74   Roll Call Vote 126, House Resolution 456, 102nd Congress, May 14, 1992.

75   Roll Call Vote 6, House Resolution 340, 102nd Congress, February 5, 1992.

76   Roll Call Vote 7, House Resolution 340, 102nd Congress, February 5, 1992.

77   Douglas Frantz, "Rostenkowski Implicated in Postal Scam," *Los Angeles Times*, July 20, 1993.

78   Roll Call Vote 357, House Resolution 222, 103rd Congress, July 22, 1993.

79   Jeff Shesol, *Supreme Power: Franklin Roosevelt vs the Supreme Court*, (New York: W.W. Norton, 2010), 2.

80   Robert Dallek, *Franklin D. Roosevelt: A Political Life*, (New York: Viking, 2017), 217.

81   Shesol, *Supreme Power*, 2.

82   Dallek, *Franklin D. Roosevelt: A Political Life*, 218.

83   Shesol, *Supreme Power*, 2.

84   Dallek, *Franklin D. Roosevelt: A Political Life*, 270.

85   Shesol, *Supreme Power*, 4.

86   Dallek, *Franklin D. Roosevelt: A Political Life*, 272.

87   Ibid, 272.

88   Burton K. Wheeler, "First Member of the Senate to Back the President in '32-," *Chicago Forum*, March 10, 1937, accessed November 7, 2018, http://academic.brooklyn.cuny.edu/history/johnson/wheeler.htm.

89   Dallek, *Franklin D. Roosevelt: A Political Life*, 276.

90   Stephen Labaton, "Data on Travel Office Head Sought After His Ouster, Letter Shows," *New York Times*, June 6, 1996.

91   H. Rep.104-862 (1996).

92   Labaton, "Data on Travel Office Head Sought...."

93   H. Rep. 104-862 (1996).

94   Ibid.

95   Christopher Lee, "Flops Are No Fluke in the Annals of Political Payback," *Washington Post*, September 19, 2005.

96   H. Rep. 104-862 (1996).

97   Ibid.

98   George Lardner and John F. Harris, "Panetta Offers Apology Over Files 'Mistake,'" *Washington Post*, June 10, 1996.

99   "FBI Files Fiasco," CNN.com, accessed January 3, 2019, http://www.cnn.com/ALLPOLITICS/1997/gen/resources/fbi.files/.

100   H. Rep. 104-862 (1996).

101   George Lardner Jr. and Susan Schmidt, "Livingstone Resigns, Denying Ill Intent," *Washington Post*, June 27, 1996.

102   George Lardner, "Secret Service Says Databank Couldn't Have Produced Outdate Pass-Holder List," *Washington Post*, June 16, 1996.

103   Clinton, *Living History*, 371-372.

104   H. Rep. 104-862 (1996).

105   George Lardner, "Ex-White House Counsels Puzzled by Pass-Holder List," *Washington Post*, June 12, 1996.

106   "Excerpts of F.B.I. Report on Files," *New York Times*, June 15, 1996.

107   H. Rep. 104-862 (1996).

108   *Inappropriate Criteria Were Used to Identify Tax-Exempt Applications for Review (Reference Number: 2013-10-053)*, Treasury Inspector General for Tax Administration, May 14, 2013.

109   Ibid, 5.

110   Ibid, 8.

111   Ibid, 5.

112   Ibid, 9.

113   Robert W. Wood, "IRS Reveals Lois Lerner's Secret Email Account Named For Her Dog," *Forbes*, August 25, 2015.

114   Eliana Johnson, "Investigation IDs IRS Leaker," *National Review*, October 30, 2013.

115   Sari Horwitz, "No Criminal Charges Will be Filed Against Ex-IRS Official Lois Lerner," *Washington Post*, October 23, 2015.

116   Evan Perez, "First on CNN: DOJ closes IRS investigation with no charges," CNN, October 23, 2015.

117   NorCal Tea Party Patriots, et al., v. Internal Revenue Service, Case No. 1:13-cv-341.

118   Stephan Dinan, "Court rebukes IRS for Tea Party Targeting, Orders Release of Secret List," *Washington Times*, March 22, 2016.

119   Cause of Action v. Internal Revenue Service Civil Action No. 13-0920 (ABJ)

120   "IRS Emails," *Behind the Headlines*, March 5, 2015, accessed November 17, 2018, https://behindtheheadlines.net/3515-irs-emails/.

121   "IRS Scandal," *Behind the Headlines*, July 1, 2014, accessed November 17, 2018, https://behindtheheadlines.net/7114-irs-scandal/.

CHAPTER 6

1   David M. Herszenhorn, "A Curious Coalition Opposed Bailout Bill," *New York Times*, October 3, 2008.

2 John M. Barry, *The Ambition and the Power*, (New York: Viking Press, 1989), 679.
3 Ibid, 665.
4 Irvin Molotsky, "Wright Inquiry Examining Events Occurring Long Ago," *New York Times*, November 13, 1988.
5 Statement of the Committee on Standards of Official Conduct, In the Matter of Representative James C. Wright, Jr., US House of Representatives, April 13, 1989, 19.
6 Ibid, 43.
7 Ibid, 32.
8 Ibid, 20.
9 2 USC. §441i.
10 Statement of the Committee on Standards of Official Conduct, In the Matter of Representative James C. Wright, Jr., US House of Representatives, April 13, 1989, p. 30.
11 Ibid, 21.
12 Barry, *The Ambition and the Power*, 713.
13 Ibid, 665.
14 Statement of Alleged Violation, In the Matter of Representative James C. Wright, Jr., US House of Representatives, April 13, 1989.
15 Ibid, 5-11.
16 Barry, *The Ambition and the Power*, 734.
17 Ken Ringle, "Memory and Anger: A Victim's Story," *Washington Post*, May 4, 1989.
18 "Clark M. Clifford," website for the historical office of the secretary of defense, accessed January 8, 2019, https://history.defense.gov/Multimedia/Biographies/Article-View/Article/571292/clark-m-clifford/.
19 Bart Barnes, "Washington Insider Clark M. Clifford Dies," *Washington Post*, October 11, 1998.
20 Marilyn Berger, "Clark Clifford, a Major Adviser To Four Presidents, Is Dead at 91," *New York Times*, October 11, 1998.
21 Ibid.
22 Sen. Rep. No. 102-140, at 6 (1992).
23 Berger, "Clark Clifford, a Major Adviser To Four Presidents...."
24 Sen. Rep. No. 102-140, at 6 (1992).
25 Ibid.
26 Art Harris and John F. Berry, "Arab Investors Want Lance to Manage Funds: Arabs Want Lance to Direct Investments," *Washington Post*, December 18, 1977.
27 Sharon Walsh, "BCCI Saga Ends with Settlement," *Washington Post*, September 24, 1998.
28 Clark Clifford, *Counsel to the President: A Memoir*, (New York: Random House, 1991), 268.

29   David A. Kaplan, "The Reagan Court—Child of Lyndon Johnson?" *New York Times*, September 4, 1989.

30   Laura Kalman, *Abe Fortas: A Biography*, (New Haven: Yale University Press, 1990), 294.

31   Ibid, 306.

32   Ibid, 322.

33   Ibid, 324.

34   Bruce Allen Murphy, *Fortas: The Rise and Ruin of a Supreme Court Justice*, (New York: William Morrow, 1988), 199.

35   Kalman, *Abe Fortas: A Biography*, 364

36   Murphy, *Fortas: The Rise and Ruin...*, 197.

37   Kalman, *Abe Fortas: A Biography*, 362

38   Ibid, 351.

39   Ibid, 326

40   Murphy, *Fortas: The Rise and Ruin...*, 499-500.

41   Ibid, 552.

42   Kenneth J. Robinson, "Savings and Loan Crisis: 1980-1989," *Federal Reserve Bank of Dallas*, November 22, 2013.

43   *An Examination of the Banking Crises of the 1980s and Early 1990s*, vol. 1, Federal Deposit Insurance Corporation, December 1997, p. 168.

44   Robinson, "Savings and Loan Crisis."

45   L. William Seidman, *Full Faith and Credit: The Great S&L Debacle and Other Washington Sagas*, (New York: Times Books, 1993), 175.

46   Robinson, "Savings and Loan Crisis."

47   Seidman, *Full Faith and Credit*, 209.

48   *An Examination of the Banking Crises...*, 169.

49   "National Mortgage Settlement," the website for the United States Department of Justice, February 9, 2012, accessed May 19, 2019, https://www.justice.gov/ust/national-mortgage-settlement.

50   "National Mortgage Settlement Summary," the website of the National Conference of State Legislatures, September 4, 2013, accessed January 13, 2019, http://www.ncsl.org/research/financial-services-and-commerce/national-mortgage-settlement-summary.aspx.

51   Tom Schoenberg, "US Ends Bank Penalty Practice Called 'Slush Fund' by GOP," *Bloomberg*, June 7, 2017.

52   Lucinda Shen, "Here's Where the $110 Billion in Wall Street Fines Went," *Fortune*, March 20, 2016.

53   "National Mortgage Settlement Summary."

54   Josh Zumbrun, "Grading the Economic Stewardship of the Obama Era," *Wall Street Journal*, January 18, 2017.

55   "The Employment Situation—October 2009," website for the Bureau of Labor Statistics, November 6, 2009, accessed December 19, 2018, https://www.bls.gov/news.release/archives/empsit_11062009.pdf.

56   Susan Jones, "Record 95,102,000 Americans Not in Labor Force: Number Grew 18% Since Obama Took Office in 2009," CNS News, January 6, 2017, accessed December 19, 2018, https://www.cnsnews.com/news/article/susan-jones/record-95102000-americans-not-labor-force-number-grew-18-obama-took-office.

57   Editorial, "Sorry, This Is Still The Worst Economic Recovery Ever," *Investor's Business Daily*, December 31, 2015.

58   Ibid.

59   Tyler Durden, "Barack Obama Is Now The Only President In History To Never Have A Year Of 3% GDP Growth," Zero Hedge, January 27, 2017. Accessed December 19, 2018, https://www.zerohedge.com/news/2017-01-27/barack-obama-now-only-president-history-never-have-year-3-gdp-growth.

60   "Estimated Impact of the American Recovery and Reinvestment Act on Employment and Economic Output from January 2012 Through March 2012," website of the Congressional Budget Office, May 2012, accessed December 19, 2018, https://www.cbo.gov/publication/43274.

61   Mark Hyman, "Ecotality," Behind the Headlines with Mark Hyman, November 14, 2013, accessed December 19, 2018, https://behindtheheadlines.net/111413-ecotality/.

62   Dana Hull and Steve Johnson, "The Man Behind Solyndra's Rise and Fall: Chris Gronet," *San Jose Mercury News*, November 27, 2011.

63   Press Release, Solyndra Offered $535 Million Loan Guarantee by the US Department of Energy, website for the DOE, March 20, 2009, accessed December 19, 2018, https://www.energy.gov/articles/obama-administrationadministration-offers-535-million-loan-guarantee-solyndra-inc.

64   Martin Lamonica, "Solyndra Bankruptcy Was Disaster Waiting to Happen," CNET, September 6, 2011, accessed December 19, 2018, https://www.cnet.com/news/solyndra-bankruptcy-was-disaster-waiting-to-happen/.

65   Matthew Mosk, Brian Ross, and Ronnie Greene, "Emails: Obama White House Monitored Huge Loan to 'Connected' Firm," *ABC News*, September 13, 2011.

66   Scott McGrew, "Solyndra to Declare Bankruptcy," NBC *Bay Area News*, August 31, 2011, accessed December 19, 2018, https://www.nbcbayarea.com/news/local/Solyndra-Shutting-Down-128802718.html.

67   Ronald D. White, "Solar Panel Firm Solyndra to Cease Operations," *Los Angeles Times*, September 1, 2011.

68   Carol D. Leonnig and Joe Stephens, "FBI Searches Offices of Solyndra: Lawmakers Say They Were Misled About Firm's Finances," *Washington Post*, September 8, 2011.

69 Editorial, "Solyndra and the Stimulus," *Los Angeles Times*, September 2, 2011.

70 Mark Hyman, "Solar Bailout," Behind the Headlines with Mark Hyman, September 22, 2011, accessed December 19, 2018, https://behindtheheadlines.net/092211-solar-bailout/.

71 Alison Vekshin and Mark Chediak, "Solyndra's $733 Million Plant Had Whistling Robots, Spa Showers," *Bloomberg News*, September 28, 2011.

72 Mark Dufrene, "Solyndra Solar Tubes Reborn as Botanical Garden Sculpture," *Mercury News*, August 22, 2012.

CHAPTER 7

1 Marjorie Williams, "No Sex, Please! We're in Washington," *Washington Post*, September 22, 1991.

2 Lynn Darling, "The Blond Ambition of Rita Jenrette," *Washington Post*, September 16, 1980.

3 Rita Jenrette and Kathleen Maxa, "Diary of a Mad Congresswife," *Washington Post*, December 7, 1980.

4 "More Disclosures by Mrs. Jenrette in Playboy Magazine," *Associated Press*, February 20, 1981.

5 Jenrette and Maxa, "Diary of a Mad Congresswife."

6 Ibid.

7 Ibid.

8 Kent Jenkins, Jr., "The Impolitic Robb: Besieged Senator's Future Viewed Darkly," *Washington Post*, September 18, 1991.

9 David S. Broder, "All Eyes on '96," *Washington Post*, April 17, 1991.

10 Jean McNair, "Senator Denies Report of Extramarital Sexual Encounter," *Associated Press*, April 26, 1991.

11 Donald P. Baker & Robert F. Howe, "Outraged Robb Denounces Prosecutor," *Washington Post*, April 27, 1991.

12 Interview on *Larry King Live*, CNN, September 4, 1991.

13 Ibid.

14 Ibid.

15 Howard Kurtz, "The Robb Story Snowball," *Washington Post*, April 30, 1991.

16 "'Tai Collins Discusses Alleged Affair with Chuck Robb," CBS *This Morning*, September 3, 1991.

17 Interview on Larry King Live, CNN, September 4, 1991.

18 Eric Brace, "Personalities," *Washington Post*, September 3, 1991.

19 Marjorie Williams, "No Sex, Please! We're in Washington," *Washington Post*, September 22, 1991.

20 Edward Klein, *Ted Kennedy: The Dream That Never Died*, (New York: Crown Publishers, 2009), 85-86.

21   Leo Damore, *Senatorial Privilege: The Chappaquiddick Cover-up*, (Washington, DC: Regnery Gateway, 1988), 76.
22   Klein, *Ted Kennedy: The Dream That Never Died*, 91.
23   Leo Damore, *Chappaquiddick: Power, Privilege, and the Ted Kennedy Cover-up*, (Washington, DC: Regnery Publishing, 1988), 118.
24   Ibid, 78.
25   Ibid, 339.
26   Ibid, 136.
27   Ibid, Appendix 4.
28   Federal Bureau of Investigation, Subj: Chappaquiddick (Mary Jo Kopechne), Freedom of Information, undated.
29   Federal Bureau of Investigation, Subj: Chappaquiddick (Mary Jo Kopechne), Freedom of Information, undated.
30   Klein, *Ted Kennedy: The Dream That Never Died*, 101.
31   Damore, *Senatorial Privilege*, 109
32   "Wife Complains: Ex-US Senator Arthur Brown and Mrs. Bradley Arrested in Salt Lake City on Criminal Charge," *Boston Daily Globe*, September 29, 1902.
33   "Woman's Bullet Proves Fatal: Former Senator Arthur Brown Dies," *Courier Journal*, December 13, 1906.
34   Ibid.
35   "Ex-Senator Shot by Wronged Girl: Tragedy in Washington Hotel Sequel to Scandal That Shocked Utah Years Ago," *Chicago Daily Tribune*, December 9, 1906.
36   "Brilliant Career Twice Marred by Private Life," *Courier Journal*, December 13, 1906.
37   "Ex-Senator Shot by Wronged Girl…"
38   "Pays No Alimony; Sent to Jail," *Chicago Daily Tribune*, February 6, 1903.
39   "Former Senator of Utah is Shot by Woman: Arthur Brown Badly Wounded by Mrs. Anna M Bradley," *San Francisco Chronicle*, December 9, 1906.
40   "Ex-Senator Shot by Wronged Girl…"
41   "Former Senator of Utah is Shot by Woman…"
42   Ibid.
43   "Shoots an Ex-Senator; Woman Wants Marriage," *New York Tribune*, December 9, 1906.
44   "Ex-Senator Shot by Wronged Girl…"
45   Ibid.
46   Ibid.
47   "Senator Brown Dead: Mrs. Bradley Not Told; Woman Who Shot Him Must Now Face a Murder Charge," *New York Times*, December 13, 1906.

48   "Ex-Senator Near Death: Little Hope for Arthur Brown, Who Was Shot by Mrs. Bradley," *New York Tribune*, December 11, 1906.

49   "Mrs. Adams Had Planned to Wed Senator Brown: Actress' Mother Says Ceremony Was to Have Been in New York on Jan. 1," *St. Louis Post-Dispatch*, December 14, 1906.

50   "Ex-Senator Near Death…"

51   "Mrs. Bradley's Plea is Insanity: Slayer of Senator Arthur Brown Declares No Jury Will Convict Her of Crime," *Indianapolis Star*, October 21, 1907.

52   "Woman Acquits Mrs. Bradley for Slaying Arthur Brown," *St. Louis Post-Dispatch*, November 13, 1907.

53   "Post Mortem Revenge of Senator Brown: He Disinherits the Children of His Slayer Mrs. Bradley," *The Arizonan Republican*, December 22, 1906.

54   "Sons of Utah Woman Who Shot Utah Senator Get $12,000," *St. Louis Post-Dispatch*, September 20, 1910.

55   Rudy Maxa, "The Paula Parkinson Story," *Washington Post*, March 29, 1981.

56   Ibid.

57   Ibid.

58   Ibid.

59   Ibid.

60   "Congressman Says Sharing Vacation House With 'Blond Bombshell' Was Mistake," *Associated Press*, March 9, 1981.

61   Maxa, "The Paula Parkinson Story."

62   Tom Raum and Janet Staihar, "Blonde Lobbyist Writing Book: Congressmen Nervous," *Associated Press*, March 7, 1981.

63   Maxa, "The Paula Parkinson Story."

64   Ibid.

65   Tom Raum, "Crane Seeks Probe on Influence of 'Sexual or Other Favors,'" *Associated Press*, March 10, 1981.

66   Thomas Ferrar, "Washington News," *United Press International*, March 26, 1981.

67   Howard Kurtz, "Larry Flynt, Investigative Pornographer," *Washington Post*, December 19, 1998.

68   "Burton Admits to Fathering a Child During an Extramarital Relationship," *Associated Press*, September 4, 1998.

69   Howard Kurtz, "Larry Flynt and the Barers of Bad News," *Washington Post*, December 20, 1998.

70   Larry Margasak, "Hyde Acknowledges Extramarital Affair in '60s," *Associated Press*, September 16, 1998.

71   Kurtz, "Larry Flynt, Investigative Pornographer."

72   Eric Pianin, "Livingston Rejected GOP Advice: Party Officials Urged Him to Hold Off on Disclosure of Affairs," *Washington Post*, December 19, 1998.

73   William M. Welch, "Illinois Congressman Likely Next Speaker," *USA Today*, December 21, 1998.

74   Pianin, "Livingston Rejected GOP Advice…"

75   Howard Kurtz, "White House Angry About GOP Charge," *Washington Post*, December 18, 1998.

76   Eli Lake, "Sid Blumenthal is Hillary Clinton's Worst Friend," *Miami Herald*, October 16, 2016.

77   Rich Lowry, "The Return of Sid Vicious," *Politico*, May 20, 2015.

78   Lake, "Sid Blumenthal is Hillary Clinton's Worst Friend."

79   Clarence Page, "Racism, Prejudice, and the Underuse of Economic Power," *Chicago Tribune*, May 16, 1990.

80   William E. Schmidt, "In Chicago, Renewed Uproar on Bigotry," *New York Times*, March 24, 1990.

81   John Camper, "Everything Falls in Place for Savage," *Chicago Tribune*, March 22, 1990.

82   John Camper and Andrew Fegelman, "Savage Overcomes Tough Challenge," *Chicago Tribune*, March 21, 1990.

83   F.N. D'Alessio, "Illinois Congressman Denies Having Sex with Minor," *Associated Press*, August 12, 1994.

84   Michael Sneed and Maureen O'Donnell, "Reynolds Indicted: 19 Counts Include Sex Abuse, Child Porn," *Chicago Sun-Times*, August 19, 1994.

85   Lee Bey and Maureen O'Donnell, "Beverly Heard Testifies: 'We Had Sex;' Affair Lasted 15 Mos., She Says," *Chicago Sun-Times*, August 7, 1995.

86   James Webb, "Woman Says Congressman Paid For Silence in Sex Case," *Associated Press*, August 9, 1995.

87   Lee Bey and Maureen O'Donnell, "2nd Woman Tells of Sex with Reynolds as Minor," *Chicago Sun-Times*, August 9, 1995.

88   Jason Leopold, "New Details on the Infamous DC Madam Scandal Emerge," Vice, April 5, 2017, accessed October 23, 2018, https://www.vice.com/en_us/article/8qje7b/inside-the-us-postal-services-investigation-into-the-dc-madam-v24n3.

89   Chris Amos, "Navy Officer Testifies in DC Madam Case," *Navy Times*, April 12, 2008.

90   Justin Rood, "DC Madam: Guilty," *ABC News*, April 15, 2008.

91   Neal Augenstein, "Ex-Lawyer Starts Disclosing Who Called 'DC Madam,'" WTOP, April 11, 2016, accessed October 23, 2018, https://wtop.com/presidential-election/2016/04/ex-lawyer-starts-disclosing-who-called-d-c-madam/.

92   William K. Rashbaum, "18 Arrested in Lucrative Prostitution Ring Out of Staten Island," *New York Times*, April 8, 2004.

93   Keith B. Richburg, "Spitzer Linked to Prostitution Ring by Wiretap," *Washington Post*, March 11, 2008.

94   William K. Rashbaum, "Revelations About Governor Began in Routine Tax Inquiry," *New York Times*, March 11, 2008.

95   Peter Elkind, "Eliot Spitzer's Flameout," *Fortune*, April 13, 2010.

96   Nick Summers, "How Eliot Spitzer Said Goodbye to Kathleen Parker at CNN," *Daily Beast*, February 28, 2011, accessed January 6, 2019, https://www.thedailybeast.com/how-eliot-spitzer-said-goodbye-to-kathleen-parker-at-cnn

97   Larry Celona, "Eliot Spitzer Snuck Me into His Apartment in a Suitcase: Ex-Mistress," *New York Post*, December 20, 2018.

98   Hope Yen, "Early votes: High Interest Buoys Clinton in Key States," *Associated Press*, September 28, 2016.

99   "Here's the Audio: Trump Lewd Comments About Women Caught on Tape, @KatyTurNBC reports," NBC News, accessed January 15, 2016, https://twitter.com/BraddJaffy/status/784488175792041984.

100   David A. Farenthold, "Trump Recorded Having Extremely Lewd Conversation About Women in 2005," *Washington Post*, October 8, 2016.

101   Sharon Waxman, "How 'Access Hollywood' Found the Trump Tape— And Why NBC News Probably Leaked it (Exclusive)," The Wrap, October 7, 2016, accessed January 15, 2019, https://www.thewrap.com/how-access-hollywood-found-the-trump-tape-and-why-nbc-news-probably-leaked-it-exclusive/

102   "NBC Staff & 'Access' Brass Knew About Outtakes Months Ago," TMZ, October 11, 2016, accessed January 15, 2019, http://m.tmz.com/#!article/2016/10/11/donald-trump-tape-billy-bush-nbc-access-staff-knew/

103   "NBC Planned to Use Trump Audio to Influence Debate, Election," TMZ, October 12, 2016, accessed January 15, 2016, http://m.tmz.com/#article/2016/10/12/nbc-trump-tape-billy-bush-plan-election-debate/.

104   "'Access' Staffer Wanted Tape Out Before Debate," TMZ, October 11, 2016, accessed January 15, 2019, http://m.tmz.com/#!article/2016/10/11/donald-trump-hurricane-matthew-access-hollywood-leak/.

CHAPTER 8

1   Commission for the Review of FBI Security Programs, *A Review of FBI Security Programs*, (Washington, DC: Department of Justice, March 31, 2002), 107.

2   *Trial by Treason: The National Committee to Secure Justice for the Rosenbergs and Morton Sobell*, (Washington, DC: United States Government Printing Office, August 25, 1956), 1.

3   Sam Roberts, "57 Years Later, Figure in Rosenberg Case Says He Spied for Soviets," *New York Times*, September 12, 2008.

4   Morton Sobell, "Letter: The Rosenberg Case," *New York Times*, September 19, 2008.

5   Ronald Radosh, "Case Closed on the Rosenbergs," *Los Angeles Times*, September 17, 2008.

6   John Chabot Smith, *Alger Hiss: The True Story*, (New York: Holt, Rinehart and Winston, 1976), 2

7   Ibid, 58.

8   Ibid, 100.

9   Allen Weinstein, *Perjury: The Hiss Chambers Case*, (Stanford, California: Hoover Institution Press, 2013), 372-373.

10   Sam Tanenhaus, *Whittaker Chambers: A Biography*, (New York: Random House, 1997), 45.

11   John Earl Haynes and Havey Klehr, *Early Cold War Spies: The Espionage Trials That Shaped American Politics*, (Cambridge, Massachusetts: Cambridge University Press, 2006), 93-94.

12   Tanenhaus, *Whittaker Chambers*, 154.

13   "Alger Hiss," FBI.gov, accessed February 19, 2019, https://www.fbi.gov/history/famous-cases/alger-hiss.

14   "The 1948 Alger Hiss-Whittaker Chambers Hearing Before HUAC," History, Art & Archives, August 25, 1948, accessed February 19, 2019, https://history.house.gov/Historical-Highlights/1901-1950/The-1948-Alger-Hiss–Whittaker-Chambers-hearing-before-HUAC/.

15   "Alger Hiss Convicted of Perjury," History.com, accessed February 19, 2019, https://www.history.com/this-day-in-history/alger-hiss-convicted-of-perjury.

16   Alger Hiss, *Recollections of a Life*, (New York: Seaver Books, 1988), 207

17   Weinstein, *Perjury*, 187-188.

18   Ibid, 203.

19   Ibid, 275.

20   Hiss, *Recollections of a Life*, 215.

21   Haynes and Klehr, *Early Cold War Spies*, 135.

22   Carla Anne Robbins, "China Received Secret Data On Advanced US Warhead," *Wall Street Journal*, January 7, 1999.

23   James Risen and Jeff Gerth, "Breach at Los Alamos: A Special Report; China Stole Nuclear Secrets for Bombs, US Aides Say," *New York Times*, March 6, 1999.

24   Ibid.
25   James Risen, "US Fires Suspected of Giving China Bomb Data," *New York Times*, March 9, 1999.
26   John Fund, "Not All Foreign-Influence Scandals Are Created Equal," *National Review*, July 17, 2017, accessed February 5, 2019, https://www.nationalreview.com/2017/07/chinese-illegally-donated-bill-clinton-reelection-campaign-media-downplayed/.
27   Erik Eckholm, "China Says Los Alamos Scientist Gave It No Secrets on Warheads," *New York Times*, March 23, 1999.
28   James Risen, "FBI Interviews Chinese Man in Spy Case," *New York Times*, March 27, 1999.
29   James Risen and Jeff Gerth, "1998 Report Told of Lab Breaches and China Threat," *New York Times*, May 2, 1999.
30   Editorial, "Safeguarding Nuclear Secrets," *New York Times*, March 30, 1999.
31   Matthew Purdy and James Sterngold, "The Prosecution Unravels: The Case of Wen Ho Lee," *New York Times*, February 5, 2001.
32   Wen Ho Lee, *My Country Versus Me*, (New York: Hyperion, 2001), 224.
33   Ibid, 330.
34   Flint Whitlock and Ron Smith, *The Depths of Courage: American Submariners at War with Japan, 1941-1945*, (New York: Berkley Caliber, 2007), 193-194.
35   Clay Blair Jr., *Silent Victory: The US Submarine War Against Japan*, (Philadelphia: J.B. Lippincott, 1975), 424.
36   Naval History Division, *United States Submarine Losses: World War II*, (Washington, DC: Office of the Chief of Naval Operations, 1963), 8
37   Blair Jr., *Silent Victory*, 424.
38   Charles A. Lockwood, *Sink 'Em All*, (New York: E. P. Dutton & Co., Inc. 1951), 116.
39   Larry Kimmett and Margaret Regis, *US Submarines in World War II: An Illustrated History*, (Seattle: Navigator Publishing, 1996) 68.
40   Ibid, 68.
41   Robert S. McNamara, *In Retrospect: The Tragedy and Lessons of Vietnam*, (New York: Times Books, 1995), 282.
42   Ibid, 169.
43   Steve Sheinkin, *Most Dangerous: Daniel Ellsberg and the Secret History of the Vietnam War*, (New York: Roaring Book Press, 2015), 155-156.
44   Daniel Ellsberg, *Secrets: A Memoir of Vietnam and the Pentagon Papers*, (New York: Viking, 2002), 181.

45   Daniel Ellsberg, "Remembering Anthony Russo," Antiwar.com, August 7, 2008, accessed November 4, 2018, https://www.antiwar.com/blog/2008/08/07/ellsberg-remembering-anthony-russo/.

46   Dana Priest, "Did the Pentagon Papers Matter?" *Columbia Journalism Review*, Spring 2016.

47   Ellsberg, *Secrets*, 333-334.

48   Eric Lichtblau, "The Untold Story of the Pentagon Papers Co-conspirators," *The New Yorker*, January 29, 2018.

49   *New York Times* Co. v. United States, 403 US 713 (1971).

50   Matthew Shaer, "The Long, Lonely Road of Chelsea Manning," *New York Times*, June 12, 2017.

51   Evan Hansen, "Manning-Lamo Chat Logs Revealed," *Wired*, July 13, 2011.

52   Pete Yost, "Holder says WikiLeaks Under Criminal Investigation," *Seattle Times*, November 30, 2010, accessed December 20, 2018, https://www.seattletimes.com/seattle-news/politics/holder-says-wikileaks-under-criminal-investigation/.

53   Charlie Savage, "US Weighs Prosecution of WikiLeaks Founder, but Legal Scholars Warn of Steep Hurdles," *New York Times*, December 2, 2010.

54   Stefan Mey, "Leak-o-nomy: The Economy of Wikileaks (Interview with Julian Assange)," Medien-Ökonomie-Blog, January 4, 2010, accessed October 13, 2018, https://stefanmey.wordpress.com/2010/01/04/leak-o-nomy-the-economy-of-wikileaks/.

55   Transcript, A Discussion on National Security with CIA Director Mike Pompeo, Center for Strategic & International Studies, April 13, 2017, accessed May 16, 2019, https://www.csis.org/analysis/discussion-national-security-cia-director-mike-pompeo.

56   Ibid.

57   Office of the Inspector General, *A Review of the FBI's Performance in Deterring, Detecting, and Investigating the Espionage Activities or Robert Philip Hanssen; Unclassified Executive Summary*, (Washington, DC: Department of Justice, April 14, 2003), 4.

58   Ibid, 8.

59   Ibid, 9.

60   "Affidavit in Support of Criminal Complaint," Arrest Warrant and Search Warrants, United States v. Robert Philp Hanssen, February 2001.

61   Jeff Stein, "Riddle Resolved: Who Dimed Out American Traitor and Super-Spy, Robert Hanssen?" *Newsweek*, November 1, 2018, accessed February 16, 2019, https://www.newsweek.com/who-dimed-out-american-traitor-super-spy-robert-hanssen-1196080.

62   "Ex-Stripper Describes Her time with Accused Spy," CNN, May 22, 2001, accessed February 16, 2019, https://web.archive.org/

web/20041114093843/http://archives.cnn.com/2001/US/05/22/hanssen.
stripper/.

63   "Affidavit in Support of Criminal Complaint," Arrest Warrant and
       Search Warrants, United States v. Robert Philp Hanssen, February 2001.

64   Ronald Kessler, *The Secrets of the FBI*, (New York: Crown Publishers,
       2011), 123-124.

65   Office of the Inspector General, *A Review of the FBI's Performance in
       Deterring, Detecting, and Investigating the Espionage Activities or Robert
       Philip Hanssen; Unclassified Executive Summary*, (Washington, DC:
       Department of Justice, April 14, 2003), 12.

66   Ibid, 13.

67   CIA v. Sims, 471 U.S. 159 (1985).

68   *Joint Hearing before the Select Committee on Intelligence and the
       Committee on Human Resources, Project MKUltra, the CIA's Program of
       Research in Behavioral Modification*, 59th Cong. 6 (1977).

69   J.S. Earman, *Memorandum for: Director of Central Intelligence, Subject:
       Report of Inspection of MKULTRA*, July 26, 1963, 1-2.

70   Ibid, 2.

71   Ibid, 15.

72   Ibid, 15.

73   Ibid, 19–20.

74   *Joint Hearing before the Select Committee on Intelligence and the
       Committee on Human Resources, Project MKUltra, the CIA's Program of
       Research in Behavioral Modification*, 59th Cong. 74 (1977).

75   "An Interview with Richard Helms," website of the CIA, accessed
       February 5, 2019, https://www.cia.gov/library/center-for-the-study-of-
       intelligence/kent-csi/vol44no4/html/v44i4a07p_0021.htm.

76   Improper Handling of Classified Information by John M. Deutch
       (1998-0028-IG), Report of Investigation, Central Intelligence Agency,
       February 18, 2000.

77   *Memorandum for the Secretary of Defense, Subj: Review of Allegations
       Regarding Dr. John Deutch*, January 19, 2001.

78   Michael S. Schmidt, "Clinton Used Personal Email at State Dept.," *New
       York Times*, March 3, 2015.

79   Records Management by Federal Agencies, 44 USC 31 §3101

80   Michael S. Schmidt, "Clinton Used Personal Email at State Dept.," *New
       York Times*, March 3, 2015.

81   "'Guccifer' Hacks AOL Account Of Sidney Blumenthal, Ex-Clinton
       Adviser, Following Bush Family Email Breaches," *International Business
       Times*, March 15, 2013.

82   Peter Baker and Jeff Zeleny, "Staff Chief Wields Power Freely, But
       Influence Comes With Risk," *New York Times*, August 16, 2009.

83   David Goldstein, "Two Clinton Supporters Reportedly Shared Obama 'Birther' Story in 2008," *The Enterprise*, September 17, 2016.

84   Josh Gerstein, "Clinton Private Email Violated 'Clear-cut' State Dept. Rules," *Politico*, March 5, 2015.

85   Office of Inspector General, *Office of the Secretary: Evaluation of Email Records Management and Cybersecurity Requirements*, (Washington, DC: State Department, May 2016), 27.

86   Ibid, 27.

87   Deirdre Walsh, "Hillary Clinton's Emails with Colin Powell Released," CNN, September 8, 2016.

88   "Newly Leaked Emails Show Former US Secretary of State Powell Unloads on Trump, Clinton," *Shanghai Daily*, September 15, 2016.

89   Matt Zapotosky, "Republican Seeks New Clinton Inquiry," *Washington Post*, September 7, 2016.

90   Bradley Klapper and Ken Dilanian, "AP Exclusive: Top Secret Clinton Emails Include Drone Talk," *Associated Press*, August 15, 2015.

91   Rosalind S. Helderman and Tom Hamburger, "Intelligence Community Watchdog Reconfirms That Dozens of Clinton Emails Were Classified," *Washington Post*, January 19, 2016.

92   Ken Dilanian, "Hillary Clinton Emails Held Info Beyond Top Secret: IG," NBC News, January 19, 2016, accessed March 10, 2019, https://www.nbcnews.com/news/us-news/hillary-clinton-emails-contained-info-above-top-secret-ig-n499886.

93   Gathering, Transmitting, or Losing Defense Information, 18 USC § 793.

94   Erin Kelly, "Grassley Seeks More Info About Comey's Decision on Clinton," *USA Today*, November 7, 2017.

CHAPTER 9

1   Stephen E. Ambrose, *The Men Who Built the Transcontinental Railroad 1863-1869*, (New York: Simon & Schuster, 2000), 191.

2   Ibid, 132.

3   Ibid, 227.

4   Ibid, 374.

5   Ibid, 270.

6   Ibid, 190.

7   Ibid, 373.

8   Margaret Ebrahim, "Fat Cat Hotel," *The Public I*, August 1996, accessed October 15, 2018, https://iw-files.s3.amazonaws.com/documents/pdfs/fat_cat_hotel_1996_08.pdf.

9   Kate Bohner, "Tuna with Tipper," *Forbes*, June 17, 1996.

10   Ebrahim, "Fat Cat Hotel."

11   "Strange Bedfellows," *Newsweek*, March 9, 1997.

12   Liz Essley Whyte, "Clinton White House Sleepover Guests Still Writing Checks," *Center for Public Integrity*, October 26, 2015.

13   "Lincoln Bedroom Guests Gave $5.4 Million," CNN, February 25, 1997.

14   Claire Spiegel, "Firm's Funds Misused in Campaign by Rep. Kim," *Los Angeles Times*, July 14, 1993.

15   Claire Spiegel, "Rep. Kim Withdrew Funds as Firm Foundered," *Los Angeles Times*, July 15, 1993

16   Spiegel, "Firm's Funds Misused...."
"

17   Claire Spiegel, "Kim Hires GOP Advisers to Audit Campaign," *Los Angeles Times*, July 16, 1993.

18   Elaine S. Povich, "Finance Probe Stains Reformer's Image," *Chicago Tribune*, October 10, 1993.

19   Claire Spiegel, "Ex-Finance Chief Says Kim Knew Firm Paid Expenses," *Los Angeles Times*, July 18, 1993.

20   Claire Spiegel, "Kim Reports Returning $21,000 to Donors," *Los Angeles Times*, August 6, 1993.

21   Elyssa Getreu, "Korean Airlines Admits Making Illegal Contributions to Congressman," *City News Service*, December 6, 1995.

22   Elyssa Getreu, "KAL, Hyundai Fined $850,000 for Illegal Contributions to Rep. Jay Kim," *City News Service*, December 18, 1995.

23   "Lawmaker to Plead Guilty in Campaign Case," *Associated Press*, August 1, 1997.

24   Art Levine, "The Man Who Would Be King," *New Jersey Star-Ledger*, August 13, 2000.

25   Leslie Wayne, "Fund-Raiser Helped Members of Congress," *New York Times*, March 2, 1997.

26   David Johnston, "Miami Businessman Is Indicted in 1996 Campaign Finance Case," *New York Times*, October 1, 1998.

27   Karen DeMasters, "State Democrats Fined on Campaign Finances," *New York Times*, January 3, 1999.

28   "Ex-Party Chief Admits Aiding Illegal Gift," *New York Times*, May 28, 1999.

29   Robert D. McFadden, "F.B.I. Raids the Office of a Big Donor to Politicians," *New York Times*, October 3, 1999.

30   Donald Wald, "Torricelli Insists: 'I am a victim,'" *New Jersey Star-Ledger*, March 7, 2000.

31   David M. Halbfinger and David Kocieniewski, "Fund-Raisers Are Summoned in Torricelli Campaign Inquiry," *New York Times*, March 6, 2000.

32   "Illegal Donations Charged In '96 Torricelli Campaign," *New York Times*, April 1, 2000.

33   "A $5,000 Fine for a Donation to Torricelli," *New York Times*, October 13, 2000.

34   David Kocieniewski and Tim Golden, "US Investigates Jail Visits to Torricelli Donor," *New York Times*, September 20, 2000.

35   Ana M. Alaya and Robert Cohen, "Donor: Torricelli Went Back on Word," *New Jersey Star-Ledger*, August 9, 2001.

36   Tim Golden and David Kocieniewski, "US Said to Focus Campaign Inquiry on Torricelli Role," *New York Times*, February 7, 2000.

37   Jeff Whelan, "Torricelli Pressured Me, Says Contributor," *New Jersey Star-Ledger*, May 25, 2001.

38   "Torricelli Investigators Check Reporter's Calls," *New Jersey Star-Ledger*, August 28, 2001.

39   Evan Osnos and Jeff Zeleny, "Embattled Torricelli Quits N.J. Senate Bid," *Chicago Tribune*, October 1, 2002.

40   "New 'Torch' Questions," *Tribune-Review*, May 3, 2008.

41   Nathaniel C. Nash, "Showdown Time for Danny Wall," *New York Times*, July 9, 1989.

42   Ibid.

43   "The Lincoln Savings and Loan Investigation: Who Is Involved," *New York Times*, November 22, 1989.

44   William L. Seidman, *Full Faith and Credit: The Great S&L Debacle and other Washington Sagas*, (New York: Random House, 1993), 233-235.

45   Dan Nowicki and Bill Muller, "McCain Profile: The Keating Five," *The Arizona Republic*, March 1, 2007.

46   Ibid.

47   Bill Muller, "The Life Story of Arizona's Maverick Senator McCain," *The Arizona Republic*, April 3, 1999.

48   Charles R. Babcock, "McCain Repays Keating Firm for Trips," *Washington Post*, October 12, 1989.

49   Ibid.

50   Mahtani Sahil, "McCain First, Second, and Always," *The New Republic*, November 1, 2008.

51   Ibid.

52   Richard L. Berke, "Ethics Unit Singles Out Cranston, Chides 4 Others in S.& L. Inquiry," *New York Times*, February 28, 1991.

53   Birkner, Michael J., Sherman Llewelyn Adams, "American National Biography," 1999.

54   "Sherman Adams Dies; Ike Aide Quit Over Vicuna Coat," *Los Angeles Times*, October 27, 1986.

55   Arnold Sawislak, "The Vicuna Coat Scandal," *United Press International*, October 28, 1986

56   "Sherman Adams Dies; Ike Aide Quit Over Vicuna Coat."

57   James Brooke, "Sherman Adams is Dead at 87: Eisenhower Aide Left Under Fire," *New York Times*, October 28, 1986.

58   Robert Healy, "Sherman Adams Out: Quits Under Fire, but Says: 'I Have Done No Wrong,'" *Daily Boston Globe*, September 23, 1958.

59   Ibid.

60   "Life and Times of Norman Hsu," *The Mercury News*, September 18, 2007.

61   Ianthe Jeanne Dugan, "What Made Norman Run?" *Wall Street Journal*, September 8, 2007.

62   "Life and Times of Norman Hsu."

63   Federal Election Commission, accessed January 28, 2019, https://www.fec.gov/data/receipts/individual-contributions/?two_year_transaction_period=2004&contributor_name=norman+hsu&min_date=01%2F01%2F2003&max_date=12%2F31%2F2004.

64   Ibid.

65   Dugan, "What Made Norman Run?"

66   Federal Election Commission, accessed January 28, 2019.

67   Brody Mullins, "Big Source of Clinton's Cash Is an Unlikely Address," *Wall Street Journal*, August 28, 2007.

68   Ianthe Jeanne Dugan, "Hsu is Accused of Ponzi Scheme" *Wall Street Journal*, September 21, 2007.

69   Dan Morain, "The Nation: Hsu's Letter Seemed to Be a Suicide Note, Some Recipients Say," *Los Angeles Times*, September 13, 2007.

70   Marc Ambinder, "Teacher and Apprentice," *The Atlantic*, December 1, 2007.

71   "ARMZ Uranium Holding Acquires 100 Prc of Uranium One Inc Shares," *ITAR-TASS*, January 16, 2013.

72   Claire-Louise Isted, "ARMZ Plans to Buy Outstanding Shares of Uranium One for About $1.3 Billion," *Platts Nuclear Fuel*, January 21, 2013.

73   James K. Jackson, *The Committee on Foreign Investment in the United States (CFIUS)*, (Washington, DC: Congressional Research Service, July 3, 2018), 14.

74   Jo Becker and Mike McIntire, "The Clintons, the Russians and Uranium," *New York Times*, April 24, 2015.

75   Senator John Barrasso, "Letter to President Barack Obama," December 21, 2010.

76   David Stellfox, "Completion of Uranium One-ARMZ Deal Stalls on Concerns About US Subsidiaries," *Platts Nuclear Fuel*, October 18, 2010.

77   Thomas W. Lippman, "Commerce Dept. Rules Ex-Soviets Guilty of Uranium 'Dumping,'" *Washington Post*, May 30, 1992.

78   Jo Becker and Don Van Natta Jr., "Ex-President, Mining Deal and a Donor," *New York Times*, January 31, 2008.

79   Ibid.

80   Peter Schweizer, *Clinton Cash: The Untold Story of How and Why Foreign Governments and Businesses Helped Make Bill and Hillary Rich*, (New York: Harper, 2015), 29.

81   Becker and Van Natta Jr., "Ex-President, Mining Deal and a Donor."

82   Laura King, "SXR to Buy UrAsia Energy," *Daily Deal*, February 13, 2007.

83   Andy Hoffman, "A Rich Deal for Directors of UrAsia," *The Globe and Mail*, March 16, 2007.

84   *Uranium One, Audited Annual Consolidated Financial Statements for the years ended December 31, 2014 and 2013.*

85   Andy Hoffman, "How a Tiny Miner's Bet Went Nuclear," *The Globe and Mail*, February 13, 2007.

86   Jo Becker and Mike McIntire, "The Clinton Connection to Russia's Mining Empire," *New York Times (International)*, April 24, 2015.

87   Becker and McIntire, "The Clintons, The Russians and Uranium."

88   Peter Koven, "'There Was No Lobbying:' Miners Giustra, Telfer Deny Allegations About Clintons," *National Post's Financial Post & FP Investing*, April 25, 2015.

89   Schweizer, *Clinton Cash*, 34-36.

90   John Solomon and Alison Spann, "Uranium One Deal Led to Some Exports to Europe, Memos Show," *The Hill*, November 2, 2017, accessed March 1, 2019, https://thehill.com/policy/national-security/358339-uranium-one-deal-led-to-some-exports-to-europe-memos-show.

91   United States v. Vadim Mikerin, Docket No: 8:14-CR-00529-TDC (2015).

CHAPTER 10

1   Robert W. Ney, *Sideswiped: Lessons Learned Courtesy of the Hit Men of Capitol Hill*, (Cleveland: Changing Lives Press, 2013), 127.

2   Laton McCartney, *The Teapot Dome Scandal: How Big Oil Bought the Harding White House and Tried to Steal the Country*, (New York: Random House, 2008), 28.

3   Ibid, 60-61.

4   Executive Order No. 3474 (1920).

5   McCartney, *The Teapot Dome Scandal*, 88.

6   M. R. Werner and John Starr, *Teapot Dome*, (New York: The Viking Press, 1959), 55.

7   Ibid, 3-4.

8   McCartney, *The Teapot Dome Scandal*,106.

9   Werner and Starr, *Teapot Dome*, 63.

10   S. Res. 282

11   Werner and Starr, *Teapot Dome*, 64.

12   McCartney, *The Teapot Dome Scandal*, 115.

13   Robert W. Cherny, "Graft and Oil: How Teapot Dome Became the Greatest Political Scandal of Its Time," *History Now*, June 2009, accessed November 1, 2018, https://historynewsnetwork.org/article/92780.

14   McCartney, *The Teapot Dome Scandal*,175.

15   Cherny, "Graft and Oil."

16   Ibid.

17   McCartney, *The Teapot Dome Scandal*, 313.

18   Werner and Starr, *Teapot Dome*, 280.

19   McGrain v. Daugherty, 273 US 135 (1927)

20   Sinclair v. United States, 279 US 263 (1929).

21   Michael J. Sniffen, "FBI Undercover Operation Implicates Public Officials," *Associated Press*, February 2, 1980.

22   Leslie Maitland, Untitled, *New York Times*, February 3, 1980.

23   Robert W. Greene, *The Sting Man: Inside Abscam*, (New York: Penguin Books, 1981), 149-155.

24   Ibid, 156.

25   Charles R. Babcock, "FBI 'Sting' Snares Several in Congress," *Washington Post*, February 3, 1980.

26   Greene, *The Sting Man*, 293.

27   Ibid, 10.

28   Ibid, 315

29   Ibid, 10.

30   Ibid, 245.

31   Ibid, 11.

32   Leslie Maitland, "Williams is Indicted With 3 for Bribery in New ABSCAM Case," *New York Times*, October 31, 1980.

[957] Greene, *The Sting Man*, 213.

33   [958] Ibid, 290.

34   [959] Sniffen, "FBI Undercover Operation Implicates Public Officials."

35   [960] S. Rep. 109-325, at 3 (2006), accessed October 9, 2018, https://www.govinfo.gov/content/pkg/CRPT-109srpt325/pdf/CRPT-109srpt325.pdf.

36   [961] Ney, *Sideswiped*, 189.

37   [962] S. Rep. 109-325, at 9 (2006).

38   [963] Ibid, 7.

39   Ibid, 9.

40   Ibid, 10.

41   Susan Schmidt, "A Jackpot From Indian Gaming Tribes: Lobbying, PR Firms Paid $45 Million Over 3 Years," *Washington Post*, February 22, 2004.

42   Susan Crabtree, "The Man Who Blew the Whistle on Jack Abramoff Tells the Story of How He Did It," *The Hill*, January 26, 2010.

43   Jack Abramoff, *Capitol Punishment: The Hard Truth About Washington Corruption from America's Most Notorious Lobbyist*, (Washington, DC: WND Books, 2011), 234.

44   Jonathan Weisman and Derek Willis, "Democrat on Panel Probing Abramoff to Return Tribal Donations," *Washington Post*, December 14, 2005.

45   Pete Yost, "Former Aide to Rep. Ney Pleads Guilty," *Associated Press*, May 8, 2006.

46   Ney, *Sideswiped*, 165.

47   Ibid, 171.

48   Seth Hettena, *Feasting on the Spoils: The Life and Times of Randy "Duke" Cunningham, History's Most Corrupt Congressman*, (New York: St. Martin's Press, 2007), 15.

49   Ibid, 29–33.

50   Marcus Stern, "Cunningham Defends Deal with Defense Firm's Owner," *San Diego Union-Tribune*, June 12, 2005.

51   Ibid.

52   Mark Walker, "Feds Raid Cunningham Home, MZM Offices and Boat," *San Diego Union-Tribune*, July 2, 2005.

53   Marcus Stern, "Cunningham Defends Deal…."

54   Mark Walker, "Feds Raid Cunningham Home…."

55   Onell R. Soto, "'Overwhelming Case' Forced Cunningham to Accept Deal," *San Diego Union-Tribune*, November 30, 2005.

56   William Finn Bennett, "Cunningham Says He Will Step Down At the End of Term," *North County Times*, July 15, 2005.

57   David Johnston and Jeff Zeleny, "Congressman Sought Bribes, Indictment Says," *New York Times*, June 5, 2007.

58   Allan Lengel, "Va. Woman Wore a Wire in Rep. Jefferson Inquiry," *Washington Post*, May 9, 2006.

59   Matthew Barakat, "Filing: Tape Shows Lawmaker Taking Money," *Associated Press*, May 21, 2007.

60   Ana Radelat, "Former Congressional Aide Pleads Guilty to Bribery," *USA Today*, January 11, 2006.

61   Allan Lengel, "FBI Says Jefferson Was Filmed Taking Cash," *Washington Post*, May 22, 2006.

62   Carl Hulse, "FBI Raid Divides G.O.P Lawmakers and White House," *New York Times*, May 22, 2006.

63   Steven Komarow, Untitled, *Associated Press*, October 9, 1991.

64   "The Impeachment Trial of Alcee L. Hastings (1989) US District Judge, Florida," Senate.gov, accessed September 5, 2018, https://www.senate.gov/artandhistory/history/common/briefing/Impeachment_Hastings.htm.

65   Ibid.

66 Donald Scarinci, *Constitutional Law Reporter*, June 13, 2017.

67 "The Impeachment Trial of Alcee L. Hastings...."

68 Ruth Marcus, "Senate Removes Hastings," *Washington Post*, October 21, 1989.

69 Michael Warren, "Attorney: Threats to Kill 'White Devils' Weren't Literal," *Associated Press*, January 3, 1992.

70 Michael Warren, "Black Sect Leader, Six Followers Convicted of Conspiracy," *Associated Press*, May 27, 1992.

71 "Impeached Judge Feels Vindicated," *New York Times*, September 19, 1992.

72 "Sheriff's Department Borrows Money for Bust," *Associated Press*, January 18, 1982.

73 "National News Brief," *United Press International*, August 12, 1982.

74 "Sheriff Refuses to Comply with Order," *Associated Press*, February 10, 1982.

75 Rosemary Armao, "Sheriff Taken to Jail," United Press International, February 16, 1983.

76 "Domestic News," *United Press International*, April 25, 1983.

77 Brian Tucker, "Sheriff Acquitted of Federal Charges," *Associated Press*, June 16, 1983.

78 David Johnston, "US Charges Traficant, Colorful Ohio Congressman, With Taking Bribes," *New York Times*, May 5, 2001.

79 Francis X. Clines, "Lawmaker Is Cautioned on Trial Behavior," *New York Times*, February 6, 2002.

80 H.R. Rep. 107-594 (2002), accessed December 8, 2019, https://www.govinfo.gov/content/pkg/CRPT-107hrpt594/html/CRPT-107hrpt594-vol1.htm.

CHAPTER 11

1 Stuart E. Weisberg, *Barney Frank: The Story of America's Only Left-Handed, Gay, Jewish Congressman*, (Amherst, Massachusetts: University of Massachusetts Press, 2009), 376.

2 Ernest G. Fischer, *Robert Potter: Founder of the Texas Navy*, (Gretna, Louisiana: Pelican Publishing Company, 1976), 23.

3 Ibid, 23.

4 Ibid, 23.

5 Ibid, 24.

6 Ibid, 24.

7 Ibid, 25.

8 Ibid, 25.

9 Ibid, 26.

10   "Disciplinary Actions by the General Assembly Against Members of
       the House or Senate," wesbiste of the North Carolina General Assembly,
       accessed November 15, 2018,
       http://www.ncleg.net/library/Documents/
       DisciplinaryActionsAgainstMembers.pdf.

11   *Journals of the Senate and House of Commons of the General Assembly
       of North Carolina at the Session 1834–1835*, p. 231, accessed November
       15, 2018, http://digital.ncdcr.gov/cdm/ref/collection/p249901coll22/
       id/490191/.

12   Ibid.

13   Barney Frank, *Frank: A Life in Politics From the Great Society to
       Same-Sex Marriage*, (New York: Farrar, Straus and Giroux, 2015), 142.

14   Ibid, 177.

15   Weisberg *Barney Frank*, 334.

16   Ibid, 334.

17   Ibid, 335.

18   Ibid, 334.

19   Ibid, 335.

20   Ibid, 383.

21   Ibid, 142

22   Ibid, 383.

23   Ibid, 362-363.

24   Ibid, 142

25   Ibid, 335.

26   Ibid, 335.

27   Ibid, 380.

28   Ibid, 388.

29   Ibid, 364, 374.

30   Frank, *Frank: A Life in Politics…*, 141-144.

31   Ibid, 376.

32   Ibid, 363.

33   Ibid, 142.

34   Weisberg *Barney Frank*, 392.

35   Maria Newman, "Congressman Says Hacker Sent Lewd Photo Using
       His Name," *New York Times*, May 30, 2011.

36   Ashley Parker, "Congressman, Sharp Voice on Twitter, Finds It Can Cut
       2 Ways," *New York Times*, May 31, 2011.

37   David W. Chen, "Analysts Weigh In on Weiner's Future," *New York
       Times*, June 2, 2011.

38   Michael Barbaro and Jeremy W. Peters, "Web Site Posts Image Said to
       Be of Bare-Chested Weiner," *New York Times*, June 6, 2011.

39   Andy Newman, David Chen, and Michael Barbaro, "Weiner Says He
       Sent Photos and Lied, But Won't Resign," *New York Times*, June 6, 2011.

40   Michael Paulson, "Online Flirtation With Weiner Started With One Word," *New York Times*, June 7, 2011.

41   Jennifer Preston, "Weiner Says He Sent Private Messages to Girl," *New York Times*, June 11, 2011.

42   Patricia Moloney Figliola and Gina Stevens, *Text and Multimedia Messaging: Emerging Issues for Congress*, (Washington, DC: Congressional Research Service, May 18, 2011), 9.

43   Jim Dwyer, "It's a Scandal, Sure, but Hardly a Reason to Undermine the Will of Voters," *New York Times*, June 10, 2011.

44   Ross Douthat, "Privacy and the Weiner Scandal," *New York Times*, June 14, 2011

45   Jonathan Van Meter, "Anthony Weiner and Huma Abedin's Post-Scandal Playbook," *New York Times Magazine*, April 10, 2013.

46   Kevin Robillard, "Weiner announces N.Y.C. Mayoral Run," *Politico*, May 22, 2013.

47   Jonathan Van Meter, "Anthony Weiner and Huma Abedin's Post-Scandal Playbook," *New York Times Magazine*, April 10, 2013.

48   Sandra Sobieraj Westfall, "Anthony Weiner 'I Feel Like a Different Person,'" *People*, July 30, 2012.

49   Max Ehrenfreund, "Bill de Blasio leads in New York City mayoral primary: Voters Reject Anthony Weiner," *Washington Post*, September 11, 2013.

50   Alana Goodman, "Exclusive: Anthony Weiner Carried on a Months-Long Online Sexual Relationship With a Troubled 15-Year-Old Girl Telling Her She Made Him 'Hard,' Asking Her to Dress Up in 'School-Girl' Outfits and Pressing Her to Engage in 'Rape Fantasies,' *Daily Mail*, September 21, 2016, accessed December 11, 2018, https://www.dailymail.co.uk/news/article-3790824/Anthony-Weiner-carried-months-long-online-sexual-relationship-troubled-15-year-old-girl-telling-hard-asking-dress-school-girl-outfits-pressing-engage-rape-fantasies.html.

51   Julia Marsh, "Huma Abedin and Anthony Weiner Withdraw Their Divorce," *New York Post*, January 10, 2018.

52   Jim Adams, "Bauman Pleads Innocent to Morals Charge," *Associated Press*, October 3, 1980.

53   Ron Shaffer, "Offhand Remark by DC Officer Tripped Bauman," *Washington Post*, October 10, 1980.

54   "Dateline: Washington," *United Press International*, October 3, 1980.

55   Benjamin Weiser and Jackson Diehl, "Rep. Bauman in Court: Bauman, Facing Solicitation Charge, Reveals Alcoholism; Faces Solicitation Charge," *Washington Post*, October 3, 1980.

56   "GOP Backs Bauman, but Newspapers Call for His Resignation," *United Press International*, October 7, 1980.

57   Judy Mann, "Bauman's Constituency Right to Feel Betrayed,"
      Washington Post, October 8, 1980.
58   Lois Romano, "Bob Bauman, After the Fall," *Washington Post*, August 6,
      1986.
59   "Congress: Bad apples," *The Economist*, October 11, 1980.
60   "Hometown Paper Endorses Bauman," *Associated Press*, October 29,
      1980.
61   Joann Stevens, "The Boy-Whore World: Male Prostitutes Prowl DC
      Street Corners," *Washington Post*, October 7, 1980.
62   Lee Davidson, "Former Rep. Allan Howe dies at 73," *Deseret News*,
      December 16, 2000, accessed February 19, 2019, https://www.
      deseretnews.com/article/798966/Former-Rep-Allan-Howe-dies-at-73.
      html.
63   "Howe About It?" *Newsweek*, August 2, 1976.
64   Grace Lichtenstein, "Rep. Howe to Stay in Utah Campaign," *New York
      Times*, June 18, 1976, accessed February 19, 2019, https://www.nytimes.
      com/1976/06/19/archives/rephowe-to-stay-in-utah-campaign-says-he-
      is-innocent-on-sex-charge.html.
65   "Howe About It?" *Newsweek*, August 2, 1976.
66   *Associated Press*, March 11, 1977.
67   Lee Byrd, *Associated Press*, April 6, 1978.
68   Lawrence Martin, "Morals Issue in Brooklyn Primary Congressman
      Cheds 'Sick Man' Tag," *Globe and Mail*, September 11, 1978.
69   "Rule Congressman Faked Retirement for Big Pension," *Associated
      Press*, December 6, 1981.
70   Ibid.
71   "Report Newspaper Editor Got Financial Help from Congressman,"
      Associated Press, December 6, 1981.
72   Josh Barbanel, "Rep. Richmond is Contradicted on Political Aid," *New
      York Times*, December 11, 1981.
73   Josh Barbanel, "Court Depicts Rep. Richmond in Potential Conflicts,"
      New York Times, December 17, 1981.
74   Ralph Blumenthal, "Lawmaker's Funds Clouded by Flaws," *New York
      Times*, January 18, 1982.
75   Dan Collins, "Rep. Fred Richmond: 'A One-Man Crime Wave,'"
      Associated Press, August 18, 1982.
76   Michael Reese, Susan Agrest, and Elaine Shannon, "A Very Troubled
      Congressman," *Newsweek*, April 19, 1982.
77   Collins, "Rep. Fred Richmond...."
78   Judie Glave, *Associated Press*, August 25, 1982.
79   Maggie Haberman, "Bill's Plea for Crooked Pol—'82 Letter Begs Judge
      to Spare His Old Corrupt, Druggie Boss," *New York Post*, October 19,
      2009

80   "On Names in Rape Cases," *New York Times*, April 17, 1991.

81   Fox Butterfield and Mary B. W. Tabor, "Woman in Florida Rape Inquiry Fought Adversity and South Acceptance," *New York Times*, April 17, 1991.

82   Robin Toner, "For Kennedy, No Escaping a Dark Cloud," *New York Times*, April 17, 1991.

83   Ronald J. Ostrow, "Police to Seek Rape Charge Against Kennedy Nephew," *Los Angeles Times*, May 8, 1991.

84   Ronald J. Ostrow, "Rape, Battery Charge Filed Against Kennedy Nephew," *Los Angeles Times*, May 10, 1991.

85   Ronald J. Ostrow, "Smith Seeks AIDS Test on His Accuser," *Los Angeles Times*, May 31, 1991.

86   Val Ellicott, "TV Reporter: Smith Lawyer Hinted About the Woman's Past," *Palm Beach Post*, June 28, 1991.

87   David A. Kaplan, "Case No. 91-5482 Comes to Trial," *Newsweek*, December 8, 1991.

88   Ibid.

89   Val Ellicott, "Juror Becomes Part of Defense Victory Party," *Palm Beach Post*, December 12, 1991.

90   Jay Perkins, "Washington Dateline," *Associated Press*, July 1, 1982.

91   Frank Reynolds, "World News Tonight" (Transcript), ABC News, July 1, 1982.

92   Joseph Mianowany, "Rep. Studds Admits Homosexuality," *Associated Press*, July 14, 1983.

93   Jim Lehrer, "Congressional Page Scandal" (Transcript), *McNeil/Lehrer Report*, July 20, 1983.

94   Sandra Evans Teeley, "House Censures Crane and Studds," *Washington Post*, July 21, 1983.

95   Mianowany, "Rep. Studds Admits Homosexuality."

96   Steven V. Roberts, "House Censures Crane and Studds for Sexual Relations with Pages," *New York Times*, July 21, 1983.

97   Brent Kallestad, "Foley Denounces Reports That He Is Gay," *Associated Press*, May 23, 2003.

98   Buddy Nevins, "Anti-Gay Forces Could Derail Foley's Senate Bid," *Sun-Sentinel*, April 26, 2003.

99   Anthony Man and Buddy Nevins, "Foley Deflects Political Rumors: Senate Hopeful Blames Reports on Democrats," *Sun-Sentinel*, May 23, 2003.

100   Gregory L. Giroux, "Foley Cites Family Concerns for Ending Senate Bid: Will Seek House Re-Election," *Congressional Quarterly*, September 5, 2003.

101   H.R. Rep. 109-733, at 21 (2006).

102   Ibid, 17-18.

103 Ibid, 29-30.

104 James V. Grimaldi, Juliet Eilperin, and Jonathan Weisman, "Some Say They Felt Uneasy About Representative's Attention," *Washington Post*, October 4, 2006.

105 Walter F. Roche Jr., "Ex-Page Tells of Foley Liaison," *Los Angeles Times*, October 8, 2006.

106 Nevins, "Anti-Gay Forces Could Derail Foley's Senate Bid."

107 Lou Chibbaro, Jr., "LBJ's Gay Purge," *Washington Blade*, February 24, 2016, accessed January 13, 2019, https://www.washingtonblade.com/2016/02/24/lbjs-gay-purge/.

108 James Warren, "On the Brink of Scandal, LBJ Showed How to Act Very Fast," *Chicago Tribune*, March 28, 1999.

109 Bart Barnes, "LBJ Aide Walter Jenkins Dies," *Washington Post*, November 26, 1985.

110 Lisa McRee and Kevin Newman, "The Johnson White House Tapes" (Transcript), *Good Morning America*, September 21, 1998.

111 Laura Smith, "When LBJ's Closest Aide Was Caught in a Gay Sex Sting, the President Caved—the First Lady Stood Up," *Timeline.com*, September 28, 2017, accessed January 10, 2019, https://timeline.com/walter-jenkins-gay-lbj-21d71a731021.

112 William C. Sullivan and Bill Brown, "Hoover: Life With A Tyrant," *Washington Post*, September 23, 1979.

113 "Text of the Summary of Report by F.B.I. on the Security Aspects of the Jenkins Case," *New York Times*, October 23, 1964, accessed January 10, 2019, https://www.nytimes.com/1964/10/23/archives/text-of-the-summary-of-report-by-fbi-on-the-security-aspects-of-the.html?mtrref=www.google.com&gwh=B1162B8807D71F2852D5FAE733951BB8&gwt=payy

CHAPTER 12

1 Joan Walsh, "Unpardonable," *Salon.com*, February 23, 2001, accessed September 15, 2018, https://www.salon.com/2001/02/23/pardon_4/.

2 James Cannon, *Gerald R. Ford: An Honorable Life*, (Ann Arbor, MI: University of Michigan Press, 2013), 249.

3 Ibid, 248.

4 Ibid, 249–250.

5 Ibid, 254.

6 Ibid, 255.

7 Ibid, 255.

8 Ibid, 255.

9 Ibid, 444.

10   Aaron Tonken, *King of Cons*, (Nashville, TN: Nelson Current, 2004), 327.

11   R. Emmett Tyrrell Jr., *The Clinton Crack-Up: The Boy President's Life After the White House*, (Nashville, TN: Thomas Nelson, 2007), 84.

12   Tonken, *King of Cons*, 251.

13   July 15, 1998 check in the amount $250,000; August 7, 1999 check in the amount $100,000; and May 11, 2000 check in the amount $100,000.

14   Kenneth R. Bazinet, "Bill: Those I Pardoned 'Paid in Full,'" *Daily News*, January 22, 2001, 4.

15   Barbara Olson, *The Final Days: The Last, Desperate Abuses of Power by the Clinton White House*, (Washington, DC: Regnery, 2001), 138.

16   "The Story of Clinton's Marc Rich Pardon," *WorldNetDaily.com*, February 5, 2001, accessed September 15, 2018, https://www.wnd.com/2001/02/8051/.

17   Dick Morris, *Rewriting History*, (New York: Regan Books, 2004), 179.

18   Marc Rich, "Letter to Ruth H. Van Heuven, US Consul General, Zurich, Switzerland, Dated October 27, 1992."

19   Independent Inquiry Committee into the United Nations Oil-for-Food Programme, *Report on Programme Manipulation*, Chapter Two, October 27, 2005, page 63.

20   Nancy Luque, (ReedSmith, LLP), "Letter to House Committee on Government Reform," February 28, 2001.

21   Kurt Eichenwald, "Pardon for Subject of Inquiry Worries Prosecutors," *New York Times*, February 6, 2001.

22   *Larry King Live*, CNN, March 2, 2001.

23   Neil A. Lewis, "Swindle is Reported to Use the Name of Roger Clinton," *New York Times*, March 10, 2001.

24   Richard A. Serrano, "'Snookered' Out of a Pardon, Convict Says," *Los Angeles Times*, June 22, 2001.

25   Bruce A. Ragsdale, *The Sedition Act Trials*, (Washington, DC: Federal Judicial History Office, 2005), 32.

26   Ibid, 23.

27   Ibid, 32.

28   Ibid, 37.

29   Ibid, 24.

30   Thomas Hopson, "Honorable Disobedience: The Sedition Act and America's Partisan Martyrs," *The Creation of the American Politician, 1789-1820*, undated, 59.

31   Richard Peters, *The Public Statutes At Large of the United States of America*, (Boston, Charles C. Little and James Brown, 1846), 802.

32   S. Res. 202, 81st Cong. (1950), accessed January 3, 2019, https://www.senate.gov/artandhistory/history/common/investigations/Kefauver.htm.

33   "Guide to Senate Records: Chapter 18 1946-1969," National Archives, Sec. 18.136.

34   Gilbert King, "The Senator and the Gangsters," *Smithsonian Magazine*, April 18, 2012.

35   Ibid.

36   Kelo v. City of New London, 545 US 469 (2005).

37   Ilya Somin, "The Story Behind Kelo v. City of New London," *Washington Post*, May 29, 2015.

38   Kelo v. City of New London, 545 US 469 (2005).

39   Ibid.

40   Ibid.

41   Lynne Tuohy, "Battle Last, Eviction Starts: Defiance Persists in Fort Trumbull," *Hartford Courant*, September 14, 2005.

42   Department of Justice, Office of Professional Responsibility, *Ruby Ridge Task Force Report*, June 10, 1994, Executive Summary, B. Significant Findings.

43   Dan Eggen, "US Report Faulted Anthrax Prober," *Washington Post*, August 24, 2002.

44   Anonymous, "FBI's 'Perverse Culture,'" *The New American*, September 23, 2002.

45   Department of Justice, *Evaluation of the Handling of the Branch Davidian Stand-Off in Waco, Texas*, October 8, 1993.

46   Shelley Murphy, "Death, Deceit, Then Decades of Silence," *Boston Globe*, July 27, 2007.

47   Kevin Cullen, "A Lingering Question for the FBI's Director," *Boston Globe*, July 24, 2011

48   Nicholas D. Kristof, "Profile of a Killer," *New York Times*, January 4, 2002.

49   Nicholas D. Kristof, "The War on Terror Flounders," *New York Times*, May 10, 2002.

50   Nicholas D. Kristof, "Connecting Deadly Dots," *New York Times*, May 24, 2002.

51   Nicholas D. Kristof, "Anthrax? The F.B.I. Yawns," *New York Times*, July 2, 2002.

52   Nicholas D. Kristof, "The Anthrax Files," *New York Times*, July 12, 2002.

53   John P. Martin, "Scientist: I Never Set Foot in Princeton," *The Star-Ledger*, August 15, 2002.

54   "Another FBI Smear?" *New York Post*, August 13, 2002.

55   Kristof, "Anthrax? The F.B.I. Yawns."

56   Don Foster, "The Message in the Anthrax," *Vanity Fair*, October 2003, 180-200, accessed January 25, 2019, http://www.ph.ucla.edu/epi/bioter/messageanthrax.html.

57   Scott Shane, "FBI's Use of Bloodhounds in Anthrax Probe Disputed," *Baltimore Sun*, October 29, 2002.

58   Stephen Engleberg, "New Evidence Adds Doubt to FBI's Case Against Anthrax Suspect," *Pro Publica*, October 10, 2011, accessed January 27, 2019, https://www.propublica.org/article/new-evidence-disputes-case-against-bruce-e-ivins.

59   Stephen Kiehl, "Doubts About Anthrax Story," *Baltimore Sun*, August 5, 2008.

60   Bush, *Decision Points*, 171.

61   Jay S. Bybee, Memorandum for John Rizzo, Acting General Counsel of the Central Intelligence Agency, US Department of Justice Office of Legal Counsel, August 1, 2002.

62   Scott Shane and Mark Mazzetti, "In Adopting Harsh Tactics, No Look at Past Use," *New York Times*, April 21, 2009.

63   Caitlin Price, "CIA Chief Confirms Use of Waterboarding on 3 Terror Detainees," *The Jurist*, February 5, 2008.

64   Shane and Mazzetti, "In Adopting Harsh Tactics, No Look at Past Use."

65   "The Real Torturers," *Investor's Business Daily*, April 30, 2009.

66   Michah Zenko, "Obama's Final Drone Strike Data," *Council on Foreign Relations*, January 20, 2017.

67   Ben Rhodes, *The World As It Is: A Memoir of the Obama White House*, (New York: Random House, 2018), 274.

68   Peter Finn and Greg Miller, "Family Condemns Death of Awlaki's Son," *Washington Post*, October 18, 2011.

69   "Lawfulness of a Lethal Operation Directed Against a US Citizen Who is a Senior Operational Leader of Al-Qa'ida or an Associated Force," Department of Justice White Paper, undated.

70   "Prepared Remarks of Attorney-General Eric Holder before Northwestern School of Law," Chicago, March 5, 2012.

71   "Remarks of Mohamed ElBaradei, Director-General, International Atomic Energy Agency Before the United Nations Security Council," March 7, 2003.

72   "Notes—Niger/Iraq Uranium Meeting CIA (SECRET/NOFORN)," US Department of State, February, 9, 2002.

73   Robert Novak, "The Mission to Niger," *Chicago Sun-Times*, July 14, 2003.

74   Joseph C. Wilson IV, "What I Didn't Find in Africa," *New York Times*, July 6, 2003.

75   Novak, "The Mission to Niger."

76   "Armitage Admits Leaking Plame's Identity," CNN.com, September 8, 2006, accessed January 23, 2019, http://www.cnn.com/2006/POLITICS/09/08/leak.armitage/.

77   "The Ambassador's Wife," *Arizona Daily Star*, July 23, 2003.

78   Mike Allen and Dana Priest, "Bush Administration is Focus of Inquiry: CIA Agent's Identity was Leaked to Media," *Washington Post*, September 28, 2003.

79   Kenneth Bazinet, "Criminal Probe of CIA Leak," *New York Daily News*, October 1, 2003.

80   Allen and Priest, "Bush Administration is Focus of Inquiry."

81   Ibid.

82   Judith Miller, *The Story: A Reporter's Journey*, (New York: Simon & Schuster, 2015), 304-305.

83   Valerie Plame Wilson, *Fair Game*, (New York: Simon & Schuster, 2007), 320.

84   Miller, *The Story: A Reporter's Journey*, 310.

85   Miller, *The Story: A Reporter's Journey*, 316.

CHAPTER 13

1   Rachel Smolkin, "Justice Delayed," *American Journalism Review*, August/September 2007, accessed October 24, 2018, http://ajrarchive. org/Article.asp?id=4379.

2   Andy Edmonds, *Frame-up! The Untold Story of Roscoe "Fatty" Arbuckle*, (New York: William Morrow, 1991), 54-56.

3   Greg Merritt, *Room 1219: The Life of Fatty Arbuckle, the Mysterious Death of Virginia Rappe, and the Scandal that Changed Hollywood*, (Chicago: Chicago Review Press, 2013), 2.

4   Edmonds, *Frame-up!*,165.

5   Merritt, *Room 1219*, 43-44.

6   Ibid, 270.

7   Edmonds, *Frame-up!*, 254-256.

8   Elio Asinof, *Eight Men Out: The Black Sox and the 1919 World Series*, (New York: Henry Holt & Company, 1963), 8-9.

9   Ibid, 19.

10   Ibid, 43.

11   Ibid, 24.

12   Ibid, 64.

13   Ibid, 66.

14   Kat Eschner, "The 1919 Black Sox Baseball Scandal Was Just One of Many," Smithsonian.com, September 1, 2017, accessed November 30, 2018, https://www.smithsonianmag.com/ smart-news/1919-black-sox-baseball-scandal-wasnt-first-180964673/.

15   "Guide to the Black Sox Scandal," website of the National Baseball Hall of Fame, accessed November 30, 2018, https://baseballhall.org/ discover-more/digital-collection/ba-mss-16.

16   Asinof, *Eight Men Out*, 280.

17   David Bauder, "Super Bowl Ratings Up Slightly Over 2003," *Associated Press*, February 2, 2004.

18   Jennifer C. Kerr, "CBS Could Face $550,000 Fine for Janet Jackson's exposure," *Associated Press*, June 30, 2004.

19   Warren Richey, "Super Bowl Wardrobe Malfunction Saga Ends: Supreme Court Refuses Appeal," *Christian Science Monitor*, June 29, 2012.

20   Susannah Meadows, "Duke Lacrosse Accuser Crystal Mangum's Tragic Life," *Newsweek*, February 22, 2010.

21   Joseph Neff, Michael Biesecker, Samiha Khanna, "DA, Police to Be 'Tried,' Too," *The News & Observer*, April 30, 2006.

22   Gina Pace, "Second Duke Stripper Offers Account," CBS News, April 21, 2006.

23   Joseph Neff and Samiha Khanna, "Lacrosse Defense Witness Arrested," *The News & Observer*, May 11, 2006.

24   Joseph Neff, "New Details Emerge on Early Part of Duke Inquiry," *Charlotte Observer*, August 28, 2006.

25   Michael Biesecker, Samiha Khanna, and Matt Dees, "Detective Got Tough With Duke students," *The News & Observer*, September 9, 2006.

26   Joedy McCreary, "Two Durham Police Officers Charged with Simple Assault," *Associated Press*, July 27, 2006.

27   Samiha Khanna, "Jackson to Offer Scholarship to Accuser," *The News & Observer*, April 16, 2006.

28   Warren St. John and Joe Drape, "A Team's Troubles Shock Few at Duke," *New York Times*, April 1, 2006.

29   Ibid.

30   Ira Wojciechowska, "NY Times Coverage of Duke Lacrosse Scandal Scrutinized," *University Wire*, April 24, 2007.

31   Newsweek Staff, "What Happened at Duke?" *Newsweek*, April 30, 2006.

32   Polly Leider, "'Sex, Lies & Duke,'" CBS News, April 24, 2006.

33   Eugene Robinson, "Tough Questions in Durham," *Washington Post*, April 25, 2006.

34   Ibid.

35   Ruth Sheehan, "Team's Silence is Sickening," *News & Observer*, March 27, 2006.

36   "Ex-Lacrosse Player Sues Duke, Instructor Over Failing Grade," WRAL, January 4, 2007, accessed October 4, 2018, https://www.wral.com/news/local/story/1126808/.

37   Robert P. Mosteller, "The Duke Lacrosse Case, Innocence, and False Identifications: A Fundamental Failure to 'Do Justice,'" *Fordham Law Review*, Vol. 76, 1355.

38   William D. Cohan, "Remembering (and Misremembering) the Duke Lacrosse Case," *Vanity Fair*, March 10, 2016.

39   George J. Mitchell, "Report to the Commissioner of Baseball of an Independent Investigation into the Illegal Use of Steroids and Other Performance Enhancing Substances by Players in Major League Baseball," December 13, 2007.

40   Ibid, 168.

41   Ibid, 169.

42   Ibid, 171.

43   Jose Canseco, *Juiced: Wild Times, Rampant 'Roids, Smash Hits, and How Baseball Got Big*, (New York: Regan Books, 2005), 211-212.

44   Ronald Blum and Howard Fendrich, "Clemens Pressed by Congress," *Associated Press*, February 13, 2008.

45   Del Quentin Wilber and Ann E. Marimow, "Roger Clemens Acquitted of All Charges," *Washington Post*, June 18, 2012.

46   "Clemens Says Pettitte 'Misremembered' Him," ESPN.com, February 13, 2008, accessed September 11, 2018, http://www.espn.com/mlb/news/story?id=3243636.

47   Steven Zeitchik, "For Harassed Teens, It's a 'Bully' Pulpit," *Los Angeles Times*, March 6, 2012.

48   Patrick Goldstein, "The Big Picture: Private idealism, Public Cynicism," *Los Angeles Times*, August 14, 2012.

49   Hillary Busis, "Malia Obama's Next Move: An Internship with Harvey Weinstein," *Vanity Fair*, January 20, 2017, accessed March 21, 2019, https://www.vanityfair.com/hollywood/2017/01/malia-obama-harvey-weinstein-internship.

50   "A-List in Social Media Ban at $33,000 a Head Hillary Clinton Fundraiser," *WENN Entertainment News Wire Service*, June 21, 2016.

51   Ronan Farrow, "Abuses of Power," *New Yorker*, October 23, 2017.

52   Jodi Kantor and Megan Twohey, "Harvey Weinstein Paid Off Sexual Harassment Accusers for Decades," *New York Times*, October 5, 2017.

53   Ronan Farrow, "Abuses of Power," *New Yorker*, October 23, 2017.

54   Ibid.

55   Jodi Kantor and Megan Twohey, "Harvey Weinstein Paid Off Sexual Harassment Accusers for Decades," *New York Times*, October 5, 2017.

56   Ibid.

57   Farrow, "Abuses of Power."

58   Caroline Davies and Nadia Khomami, "Harvey Weinstein: The Women Who Have Accused Him," *The Guardian*, October 11, 2017.

59   Yohana Desta and Hillary Busis, "These Are the Women Who Have Accused Harvey Weinstein of Sexual Harassment and Assault," *Vanity Fair*, October 12, 2017, accessed March 11, 2019, https://www.vanityfair.com/hollywood/2017/10/harvey-weinstein-accusers-sexual-harassment-assault-rose-mcgowan-ashley-judd-gwyneth-paltrow.

60   Janice Williams, "Harvey Weinstein Accusers: Over 80 Women Now Claim Producer Sexually Assaulted or Harassed Them," *Newsweek*, October 30, 2017, accessed February 19, 2019, https://www.newsweek.com/harvey-weinstein-accusers-sexual-assault-harassment-696485.

61   Martha Ross, "Despite Warnings, Weinstein's Involvement Was 'Not a Problem' to Hillary Clinton Campaign Staff, Says Actress," *Mercury News*, December 6, 2017, accessed March 21, 2019, https://www.mercurynews.com/2017/12/06/hillary-clintons-harvey-weinstein-problem-detailed-in-new-report/.

62   John Koblin, "NBC News and Ronan Farrow Trade Jabs Over Weinstein Reporting," *New York Times*, September 3, 2018.

CHAPTER 14

1   Dan Barry et al, "Correcting the Record: Times Reporter Who Resigned Leaves Long Trail of Deception," *New York Times*, May 11, 2003.

2   Paula Cruickshank, "42 Seconds That Sullied Helen Thomas," Real Clear Politics, July 31, 2013, accessed January 14, 2019, https://www.realclearpolitics.com/articles/2013/07/31/42_seconds_that_sullied_helen_thomas_--_and_new_media_119431.html.

3   Jack Shafer, "Screw You, Mr. President," *Slate*, March 12, 2003.

4   Shafer, "Screw You, Mr. President."

5   Richard Adams, "Helen Thomas to Retire After 'Offensive and Reprehensible' Remarks," *The Guardian*, June 7, 2010.

6   Helen Thomas, "Washington Window UPI News Analysis," *United Press International*, July 27, 1994.

7   Dan Kennedy, "Helen Thomas: Good Riddance to a Garden Variety Antisemite," *The Guardian*, June 8, 2010, accessed 1/21/2019, https://www.theguardian.com/commentisfree/cifamerica/2010/jun/08/helen-thomas-antisemite-retirement.

8   Danny Schechter, "Helen Thomas: Thrown to the Wolves," *Al Jazeera*, December 29, 2010, accessed January 14, 2019, https://www.aljazeera.com/indepth/opinion/2010/12/20101229124751864918.html.

9   Helen Thomas, "Middle East an Ongoing Presidential Issue," *The Times Union*, December 1, 2000.

10   Helen Thomas, "Change US Image with Arab World—Or Else," *Houston Chronicle*, October 12, 2003.

11   Helen Thomas, "June 30 Could be a Deciding Day for Kerry," *Houston Chronicle*, May 23, 2004.

12   Helen Thomas, "Bush' Dramatic Shift in Mideast," *The Washington Report on Middle East Affairs*, June 2004.

13   Helen Thomas, "Will the Real Hillary Clinton Stand Up?" *Daily Gate City*, June 29, 2007.

14   Helen Thomas, "Laura Bush's New Calling," *The Times Union*, June 6, 2005.

15   Helen Thomas, "A First Step in Gaza," *The Times Union*, September 5, 2005.

16   Helen Thomas, "Bush Far From Neutral Player in Mideast," *Seattle Post-Intelligencer*, July 21, 2006.

17   Helen Thomas, "Bush Embarks on Personal Diplomacy," *Daily Gate City*, January 11, 2008.

18   Helen Thomas, "Israelis Celebrate Birthday while Palestinians Mourn Loss," *Salt Lake Tribune*, May 15, 2008.

19   "Helen Thomas Tells Jews to Go Back to Germany," YouTube, accessed 1/21/2019, https://www.youtube.com/watch?v=RQcQdWBqt14.

20   Cruickshank, "42 Seconds that Sullied Helen Thomas."

21   Schechter, "Helen Thomas: Thrown to the Wolves."

22   "Helen Thomas is Playboy's April Interview," Cision PR Newswire, March 17, 2011, accessed January 14, 2019, https://www.prnewswire.com/news-releases/helen-thomas-is-playboys-april-interview-118184139.html.

23   Janet Cooke, "Jimmy's Word: 8-Year-Old Heroin Addict Lives for a Fix," *Washington Post*, September 28, 1980.

24   Editorial, "An Addict at 8," *Washington Post*, September 8, 1980.

25   Bill Green, "The Only Promise That Was Kept," *Washington Post*, October 3, 1980.

26   Mike Sager, "The Fabulist Who Changed Journalism," *Columbia Journalism Review*, Spring 2016, accessed November 15, 2018, https://www.cjr.org/the_feature/the_fabulist_who_changed_journalism.php.

27   Lewis M. Simmons, "DC Authorities Seek Identity of Heroin Addict, 8," *Washington Post*, September 30, 1980.

28   Keith B. Richburg, "Mayor Says City Ending Its Search for 'Jimmy,'" *Washington Post*, October 16, 1980.

29   Bill Green, "The Players: It Wasn't a Game," *Washington Post*, April 19, 1981.

30   Barry et al, "Correcting the Record: Times Reporter Who Resigned...."

31   Kristina Nwazota, "Jayson Blair: A Case Study of What Went Wrong at The New York Times," *PBS NewsHour*, December 10, 2004.

32   Ibid.

33   Jayson Blair, *Burning Down My Masters' House: My Life at the New York Times*, (Beverly Hills, California: New Millennium Press, 2004), 84.

34   Ibid, 92.

35   David Folkenflik, "The Making of Jayson Blair," *Baltimore Sun*, February 29, 2004.

36   Ibid.
37   Ibid.
38   Ibid.
39   Barry et al, "Correcting the Record: Times Reporter Who Resigned...."
40   Blair, *Burning Down My Masters' House*, 253.
41   Howard Kurtz, "Rick Bragg Quits At New York Times," *Washington Post*, May 29, 2003.
42   Ibid.
43   Tara Burghart, "Reporter Resigns from New York Times Over Story Reported Largely by Freelancer," *Associated Press*, May 29, 2003.
44   Jack Shafer, "Rick Bragg's Lousy Alibi," *Slate*, May 27, 2003.
45   Barry et al, "Correcting the Record: Times Reporter Who Resigned...."
46   Blair, *Burning Down My Masters' House*, 57.
47   Dan Barry et al, "Correcting the Record: Times Reporter Who Resigned...."
48   Ibid.
49   Ibid.
50   Nwazota, "Jayson Blair: A Case Study...."
51   Jason Flanagan, "Former Blair Co-Workers Claim Warnings Ignored," *The Diamondback*, June 13, 2003.
52   Folkenflik, "The Making of Jayson Blair."
53   S. J. Taylor, *Stalin's Apologist: Walter Duranty The New York Time's Man in Moscow*, (Oxford University Press: New York, 1990), 212.
54   Ibid, 156-7.
55   Ibid, 153.
56   Ibid, 224
57   Richard Ingrams, "Seeing the Nightmare of Russia Changed His Politics Overnight," *Daily Mail*, September 20, 1995.
58   Taylor, *Stalin's Apologist*, 196.
59   Ibid, 160.
60   Ibid, 204-5.
61   Ibid, 207.
62   Charles Leroux, "Bearing Witness: In 1932, the Pulitzer Prize Went to a Foreign Correspondent Who Concealed a Famine and the Deaths of Millions," *Chicago Tribune*, June 25, 2003.
63   Taylor, *Stalin's Apologist*, 207-8.
64   Ibid, 220.
65   Ibid, 215.
66   Ibid, 222.
67   Sara Kugler, "Historian Hired by NY Times Says 1932 Pulitzer Prize Should Be Rescinded," *Associated Press*, October 22, 2003.
68   Michael Isikoff and John Barry, "Gitmo: SouthCom Showdown," *Newsweek*, May 9, 2005.

69   Ibid.

70   "Pakistan's Imran Khan Blasts Reported US Koran Desecration," *Agence France Presse*, May 10, 2005.

71   "Four Dead in Afghan Riot Over Reported US Koran Abuse," *Agence France Presse*, May 11, 2005.

72   "Worst Anti-US Protests Spread Across Afghanistan," *Agence France Presse*, May 12, 2005.

73   Carlotta Gall, "Protests Against US Spread Across Afghanistan," *New York Times*, May 23, 2005.

74   "High Alert in Afghanistan After Days of Anti-US Protests Leave 14 Dead," *Agence France Presse*, May 14, 2005.

75   Guy Taylor, "Koran Flushing Not Confirmed," *Washington Times*, May 13, 2005.

76   Dino Hazell, "Newsweek Apologizes for Quran Story Errors," *Associated Press*, May 15, 2005

77   "19 Killed in Anti-US Protests in Afghanistan," *Xinhua General News Service, May 14, 2005.*

78   Michael Dobbs and Thomas B. Edsall, "Records Say Bush Balked at Order: National Guard Commander Suspended Him From Flying, Papers Show," *Washington Post*, September 9, 2004.

79   Eric Boehlert, "Stung!" *Salon*, September 9, 2004.

80   Howard Kurtz, Michael Dobbs, and James V. Grimaldi, "In Rush to Air, CBS Quashed Memo Worries," *Washington Post*, September 19, 2004.

81   John Fund, "We'd Rather Be Blogging," *New York Sun*, September 14, 2004.

82   Peter Johnson and Kevin Johnson, "CBS Names Two to Investigate Documents Episode," *USA Today*, September 23, 2004.

83   "Political Grapevine: Ratings For 'CBS Evening News' Drops Considerably After Military Documents Debacle," *International Wire*, September 16, 2004.

84   Dave Moniz, Jim Drinkard, and Kevin Johnson, "Texan Has Made Allegations for Years," *USA Today*, September 21, 2004.

85   Ibid.

86   Dick Thornburgh and Louis D. Boccardi, *Report of the Independent Review Panel*, (Kirkpatrick & Lockhart Nicholson Graham LLP), January 5, 2005.

87   Michael Hiltzik, "Stephen Glass Is Still Retracting His Fabricated Stories—18 Years Later," *Los Angeles Times*, December 15, 2015.

88   Stephen Glass, "Prophets and Losses: The Futures Market for Phone Psychics," *Harper's*, February 1, 1998.

89   Buzz Bissinger, "Shattered Glass," *Vanity Fair*, September 5, 2007, accessed January 31, 2019, https://www.vanityfair.com/magazine/1998/09/bissinger199809.

90   Laura Sullivan, "Stephen Glass Returns to Reporting at 'Rolling Stone,'" *The Daily Pennsylvanian*, July 24, 2003, accessed February 9, 2019, https://www.thedp.com/article/2003/07/stephen_glass_returns_to_reporting_at_rolling_stone.

91   Stephen Glass and Jonathan Chait, "Amazon.con," *Slate*, January 5, 1997.

92   Ana Marie Cox, "Half Full of It: The Partial Truths of Stephen Glass," *Mother Jones*, July/August 1998.

93   Stephen Glass, "Job Training of the Future," *USA Today*, July 10, 1995.

94   Stephen Glass, "Incredible Yet Edible; How Rhode Island Beefed Up Its School Lunch Program," *Washington Post*, September 3, 1995.

95   Richard Horgan, "Stephen Glass Tells Journalism Students He Has Paid Back $200,000," *AdWeek*, March 28, 2016, accessed February 27, 2019, https://www.adweek.com/digital/stephen-glass-duke-university/.

96   Bissinger, "Shattered Glass."

97   Ibid.

98   Ibid.

99   Warren St. John, "How Journalism's New Golden Boy Got Thrown Out Of New Republic," *Observer*, Mary 25, 1998, accessed February 28, 2019, https://observer.com/1998/05/how-journalisms-new-golden-boy-got-thrown-out-of-new-republic/.

100   Bissinger, "Shattered Glass."

101   St. John, "How Journalism's New Golden Boy Got Thrown...."

102   Ibid.

103   Sabrina Rubin Erdely, "Reflections on a Shattered Glass," *Pennsylvania Gazette*, January-February 2004, accessed December 29, 2018, http://www.upenn.edu/gazette/0104/0104arts02.html.

104   Sean Davis, "Sabrina Erdely Was Once Disciplined by Stephen Glass for Fabrication," *The Federalist*, December 12, 2014, accessed February 25, 2019, http://thefederalist.com/2014/12/12/sabrina-erdely-was-once-disciplined-by-stephen-glass-for-fabrication/.

105   Hanna Rosin, "Hello, My Name Is Stephen Glass, and I'm Sorry," *The New Republic*, November 10, 2014.

106   Michael Noer, "Read the Original Forbes Takedown of Stephen Glass," *Forbes*, November 12, 2014, accessed January 31, 2019, https://www.forbes.com/sites/michaelnoer/2014/11/12/read-the-original-forbes-takedown-of-stephen-glass/#642d6a5d683a

107   Christine Haughney, "CNN and Time Suspend Journalist After Admission of Plagiarism," *New York Times Blogs*, August 10, 2012.

108   Jeffrey Goldberg, "The New Newsweek, Now With Less Reporting," *The Atlantic*, May 26, 2009, accessed February 1, 2009, https://www.theatlantic.com/international/archive/2009/05/the-new-newsweek-now-with-less-reporting/18260/#.

109   Jeffrey Goldberg, "Netanyahu to Obama: Stop Iran or I
       Will," *The Atlantic*, March 2009, accessed February 1, 2019,
       https://www.theatlantic.com/magazine/archive/2009/03/
       netanyahu-to-obama-stop-iran-or-i-will/307390/.

110   Jeffrey Goldberg, "Israel's Fears, Amalek's Arsenal," *New York Times*,
       May 17, 2009

111   Delia Lloyd, "Should Fareed Zakaria Be Forgiven for Plagiarizing?"
       Washington Post, August 13, 2012.

112   Paul Farhi, "Passage in Zakaria Book Is Challenged," *Washington Post*,
       August 14, 2012.

113   Ibid.

114   Michael Kinsley, "The Imitation Game," *Vanity Fair*, March 2015.

115   @blippoblappo & @crushingbort, "Did CNN, The Washington Post,
       and TIME Actually Check Fareed Zakaria's Work For Plagiarism?"
       Our Bad Media, August 19, 2014, accessed January 31, 2019, https://
       ourbadmedia.wordpress.com/2014/08/19/did-cnn-the-washington-
       post-and-time-actually-check-fareed-zakarias-work-for-plagiarism/.

116   Richard Leiby, "Columnist Fareed Zakaria Faces New Accusations of
       Plagiarism," *Washington Post*, August 20, 2014.

117   Paul Farhi, "Post Finds 'Problematic' Sourcing in Some Zakaria
       Columns," *Washington Post*, November 11, 2014.

118   Philip Bump, "No Haters vs. All Haters: The BuzzFeed/Gawker Battle
       for the Internet's Soul," *The Wire*, March 12, 2014.

119   Ben Smith, "Editor's Note: An Apology To Our Readers," *BuzzFeed*,
       July 25, 2014, accessed January 31, 2019, https://www.buzzfeed.com/
       bensmith/editors-note-an-apology-to-our-readers.

120   "Political Polarization and Media Habits," *Pew Research Center*, October
       21, 2014, accessed January 31, 2019, https://www.pewresearch.org/
       wp-content/uploads/sites/8/2014/10/Political-Polarization-and-Media-
       Habits-FINAL-REPORT-7-27-15.pdf.

121   Pamela Englel, "These Are the Most and Least Trusted
       News Outlets in America," *Business Insider*, March 27, 2017,
       accessed January 31, 2019, https://www.businessinsider.com/
       most-and-least-trusted-news-outlets-in-america-2017-3.

122   Chris Geidner, "A Short Section In Neil Gorsuch's 2006 Book Appears
       To Be Copied From A Law Review Article," *BuzzFeedNews*, April 4,
       2017, accessed January 31, 2019, https://www.buzzfeednews.com/
       article/chrisgeidner/a-short-section-in-neil-gorsuchs-2006-book-
       appears-to-be.

123   Asche Schow, "Gorsuch Likely to Join Supreme Court, Despite Last-
       Minute Attack From the Left," *The Observer*, April 6, 2017.

124   Samir Mezrahi and Rachel Zarrell, "An Investigation Into Whether
       Khloé Kardashian Is Stealing Her Tweets," *BuzzFeed*, March 22,

2016, accessed January 31, 2019, https://www.buzzfeed.com/samir/khloooooooeeeeeeeeeee.

125   Alex Rees, "BuzzFeed Just Accused Khloé Kardashian of Plagiarism," Cosmopolitan, March 23, 2016, accessed January 31, 2019, https://www.cosmopolitan.com/entertainment/celebs/news/a55674/buzzfeed-just-accused-khloe-kardashian-of-plagiarism/.

126   Cale Guthrie Weissman, "BuzzFeed Food Appears to Have Blatantly Plagiarized a Funny Tweet," Fast Company, February 14, 2018, accessed January 31, 2019, https://www.fastcompany.com/40531499/buzzfeed-food-appears-to-have-blatantly-plagiarized-a-tweet.

127   Smith, "Editor's Note: An Apology To Our Readers."

128   Adam Rowe, "6 Times Buzzfeed Was Accused of Stealing Content," Tech.Co, July 8, 2016, accessed January 31, 2019, https://tech.co/news/times-buzzfeed-accused-stealing-content-2016-07.

129   "Ask Advertisers to Stop Supporting BuzzFeed Video's Idea Theft," Change.org.

130   Caitlin Dewey, "Why Some YouTube Stars Accuse Buzzfeed of 'Stealing' Their Ideas," Washington Post, July 7, 2016.

131   Josh Katzowitz, "Australian YouTubers accuse BuzzFeed of stealing their jokes," The Daily Dot, October 24, 2018, accessed January 31, 2019, https://www.dailydot.com/upstream/rose-sisters-buzzfeed-ladylike-plagiarism-youtube/.

132   Sabrina Rubin Erdely, "A Rape on Campus: A Brutal Assault and Struggle for Justice at UVA," Rolling Stone, November 19, 2014.

133   Ibid.

134   Phi Kappa Psi, "Statement from Phi Kappa Psi," The Cavalier Daily, November 20, 2014.

135   Mike DeBonis and T. Rees Shapiro, "U-Va. President Suspends Fraternities until Jan. 9 in Wake of Rape Allegations," Washington Post, November 22, 2014.

136   Daniel W. Drezner, "Manners, Customs and the Rape Culture on College Campuses," Washington Post, November 21, 2014.

137   Richard Cohen, "Alleged Rape at U-Va. Reveals a Lack of Real Men," Washington Post, November 25, 2014.

138   Editorial Board, "U-Va. Response to Reports of Sexual Assault Is Too Little, Far Too Late," Washington Post, November 24, 2014.

139   Steve Sailer, "A Rape Hoax for Book Lovers," Taki's Magazine, December 3, 2014, accessed December 29, 2018, https://www.takimag.com/article/a_rape_hoax_for_book_lovers_steve_sailer/#axzz3L3KAsBFR

140   Allison Benedikt and Hanna Rosin, "Why Didn't a Rolling Stone Writer Talk to the Alleged Perpetrators of a Gang Rape at the University of Virginia?" Slate, December 3, 2014.

141   "VA Alpha Statement Regarding Rolling Stone Article," Phi Kappa
        Psi, December 5, 2014, accessed December 29, 2018, https://web.
        archive.org/web/20141230112018/http://www.phikappapsi.com/news/
        updateuvapressrelease.

142   Erick Wemple, "Updated Apology Digs Bigger Hole for Rolling Stone,"
        Washington Post, December 7, 2014.

143   T. Rees Shapiro, "Friends Recount Night with Alleged Rape Victim,"
        Washington Post, December 11, 2014.

144   Benedikt and Rosin, "Why Didn't a Rolling Stone Writer Talk…."

145   Paul Farhi, "Rolling Stone Never Asked U-Va. about Specific Gang
        Rape Allegations, According to Newly Released E-mails and Audio
        Recording," *Washington Post*, December 20, 2014.

146   "A Note to Our Readers," *Rolling Stone*, December 5, 2014, accessed
        December 29, 2018, https://www.rollingstone.com/culture/
        culture-news/a-note-to-our-readers-72612/.

147   T. Rees Shapiro, "Fraternity at U-Va. Cleared by Police," *Washington
        Post*, January 13, 2015.

148   *Sheila Coronel, Steve Coll, and Derek Kravitz,* "Rolling Stone and UVA:
        The Columbia University Graduate School of Journalism Report; An
        anatomy of a journalistic failure," *Rolling Stone*, April 5, 2015.

149   Sabrina Rubin Erdely, "Reflections on a Shattered Glass," *Pennsylvania
        Gazette*, January-February 2004, accessed December 29, 2018, http://
        www.upenn.edu/gazette/0104/0104arts02.html.

150   O'Reilly made statements about *Inside Edition* winning Peabody
        Awards on *The O'Reilly Factor* episodes of August 30, 1999, May 8, 2000,
        and May 19, 2000.

151   InsideEdition.com, accessed March 16, 2019, https://www.
        insideedition.com/awards.

152   Emily Steel and Michael S. Schmidt, "O'Reilly Thrives as Settlements
        Add Up," *New York Times*, April 2, 2017.

153   Emily Steel and Michael S. Schmidt, "Fox New Settled Sexual
        Harassment Allegations Against Bill O'Reilly, Documents Show," *New
        York Times*, January 10, 2017.

154   Steel and Schmidt, "O'Reilly Thrives as Settlements Add Up."

155   Ibid.

156   "Judge Dismisses Andreas Tantaros Wiretapping Suit Against Fox
        News," *Variety*, May 18, 2018.

157   Rachael Revesz, "Fox News Host Bill O'Reilly Loses Custody of His
        Children After Alleged Domestic Violence Incident," *The Independent*,
        February 29, 2016.

158   J.K. Trotter, "Court Transcripts: Bill O'Reilly's Daughter
        Saw Him 'Choking Her Mom,'" Gawker, May 20,

2015, accessed March 14, 2019, https://gawker.com/
court-transcripts-bill-o-reilly-s-daughter-saw-him-ch-1704717356

159   Emily Steel and Michael S. Schmidt, "New Harassment Claims at Fox Are Followed by Canceled Ads," *New York Times*, April 4, 2017.

160   "Advertiser Exodus," *New York Times*, April 6, 2017.

161   David Bauder, "O'Reilly says his ouster was hit job and business decision," *Associated Press*, September 19, 2017.

162   Emily Steel and Michael S. Schmidt, "O'Reilly Settled Claim, Then Got a New Fox Deal" *New York Times*, April 22, 2017.

163   Ibid.

164   Bill O'Reilly, "O'Reilly Addresses the Recent New York Times Hit Piece, the Trial for Kate Steinle's Murderer, & Bergdahl," Billoreilly.com, October 23, 2017, accessed March 16, 2019, https://www.billoreilly.com/b/OReilly-Addresses-the-Recent-New-York-Times-Hit-Piece-the-Trial-for-Kate-Steinles-Murderer--Bergdahl/-230454112543421248.html.

ACKNOWLEDGMENTS

I would like to thank my family for their love and understanding throughout the manuscript process when I missed family activities because I was squirreled away writing or was at some library doing research. I am especially grateful for Julie's support even when I missed church. I want Chris, Jenn, Kelly, and Kyle to know how proud I am of them. Not just for their accomplishments, but for treating everyone they meet with kindness, dignity, and respect. We could use a lot more people like them.

Thanks go out to the folks who have been encouraging me for several years to write a book. John Bilotta is one of my longest and dearest friends who not only suggested multiple times I write a book but also was the first person to suggest I should be an investigative reporter. That conversation took place in a London pub in 1989 when I worked for Uncle Sam and he was a reporter for *United Press International* and was planning a trip into Libya.

I thank Rich Miniter for his encouragement to write this book, and for his introduction to Anthony Ziccardi, the publisher at Post Hill Press. Thomas Lipscomb has been a long-time supporter and valuable friend. Our conversations are always enjoyable and always much too short. He has encouraged, dare I say lectured, me to write a book.

I am thankful to Anthony Ziccardi who offered to publish this book after only a thirty second verbal pitch. His offer was very much welcomed after countless other publishers turned down my 40-page proposal and marketing plan.

I sincerely appreciate the work of my managing editor Madeline "Maddie" Sturgeon who steered this process magnificently and had the right touch at all times. I would also like to thank editors Diana Carlyle and Travis Atria for making appropriate suggestions and challenging details when warranted.

Of course, I must thank R. Emmett "Bob" Tyrrell, Jr. whose friendship I value and who cut me off in mid-sentence and agreed to write the foreword before I could even tell him what this book was about. He never hesitated when I told him it was about thermodynamics.

I must give a shout-out to Ed Orgeron for having the greatest voice in all of sports.

Research is critical to a book like this one. I visited a few college and public libraries by stealing away for an hour or two when traveling, but must give special recognition to Nimitz Library at the U.S. Naval Academy and the Anne Arundel County Public Library system. Between the two, they had or were able to procure on loan nearly every single book I needed.

I cannot adequately express my gratitude to Jon Weingart who is one heck of a whisky connoisseur. Our conversations about the craft of how to distill, market, and drink a fine whisky are special moments. Jon is also my favorite neurosurgeon. Thank you for my life.

I would like to recognize the hundreds of colleagues I have worked with over the years at Sinclair television newsrooms across the country. The best part of traveling to cities around America is meeting and working with them.

Chris Manson was a dear friend who left us much too early. I will always value our friendship.

Each day I think of the Johns Hopkins three and I say a little prayer for them.

I will end these acknowledgements in the same manner in which I have ended hundreds of live TV news specials. I express my thanks and gratitude to our military, law enforcement, fire fighters, EMTs, and other emergency personnel for their service to our communities and our nation.